MEMORY

The third edition of *Memory* provides students with the most comprehensive introduction to the study of human memory and its applications in the field. Written by three leading experts, this bestselling textbook delivers an authoritative and accessible overview of key topic areas.

Each chapter combines breadth of content coverage with a wealth of relevant practical examples, whilst the engaging writing style invites the reader to share the authors' fascination with the exploration of memory through their individual areas of expertise. Across the text, the scientific theory is connected to a range of real-world questions and everyday human experiences. As a result, this edition of *Memory* is an essential resource for those interested in this important field and embarking on their studies in the subject.

Key features of this edition:

- it is fully revised and updated to address the latest research, theories, and findings;
- chapters on learning, organization, and autobiographical memory form a more integrated section on long-term memory and provide relevant links to neuroscience research;
- it has new material addressing current research into visual short-term and working memory, and links to research on visual attention;
- it includes content on the state-of-play on working memory training;
- the chapter on "memory across the lifespan" strengthens the applied emphasis, including the effects of malnutrition in developing nations on cognition and memory.

The third edition is supported by a Companion Website providing a range of core resources for students and lecturers.

Alan Baddeley is Professor of Psychology at the University of York, UK.

Michael W. Eysenck is Professor Emeritus in Psychology and Honorary Fellow at Royal Holloway, University of London, UK. He is also a Professorial Fellow at the University of Roehampton, UK.

Michael C. Anderson is Senior Scientist and Programme Leader at the MRC Cognition and Brain Sciences Unit, University of Cambridge, UK.

MEMORY

Companion Website

The Companion Website provides a range of essential supporting resources for students and instructors.

Please visit www.routledge.com/cw/baddeley to access the Companion Website.

STUDENT RESOURCES

- Interactive exercises and simulations of key experiments
- Multiple-choice questions
- "Fill in the blank" quizzes
- Glossary of key terms
- Research activities based on classic research studies
- Weblinks to further reading
- Biographies of key researchers in the field of memory

INSTRUCTOR RESOURCES

- Testbank of multiple-choice questions
- Figures from the book available in PowerPoint slides

Access to instructor resources is restricted to lecturers only by password protection. Instructor resources are free of charge to qualifying adopters.

MEMORY

THIRD EDITION

ALAN BADDELEY

MICHAEL W. EYSENCK

AND MICHAEL C. ANDERSON

Routledge
Taylor & Francis Group

LONDON AND NEW YORK

Third edition published 2020
by Routledge
2 Park Square, Milton Park, Abingdon, Oxon, OX14 4RN

and by Routledge
52 Vanderbilt Avenue, New York, NY 10017

Routledge is an imprint of the Taylor & Francis Group, an informa business

First edition published by Psychology Press 2009
Second edition published by Psychology Press 2015

British Library Cataloguing-in-Publication Data
A catalogue record for this book is available from the British Library

Library of Congress Cataloging-in-Publication Data
A catalog record has been requested for this book

ISBN: 978-1-138-32607-1 (hbk)
ISBN: 978-1-138-32609-5 (pbk)
ISBN: 978-0-429-44964-2 (ebk)

Typeset in Sabon and Gill Sans
by Wearset Ltd, Boldon, Tyne and Wear

Visit the companion website: www.routledge.com/cw/baddeley

"For Hilary"—Alan Baddeley

"To Christine with love"—Michael W. Eysenck

*"To Max, whose toddlerhood I hope always to remember"—
Michael C. Anderson*

CONTENTS

ABOUT THE AUTHORS

As described in his recent memoirs, *Working Memories: Postmen, Divers and the Cognitive Revolution*, Alan Baddeley graduated in Psychology from University College London. He spent the following year in Princeton, the first of five such stays in the US. He returned to a post at the Medical Research Council Applied Psychology Unit (APU) in Cambridge, completing a Ph.D. concerned with the design of postal codes. He continued to combine applied research, for example on deep-sea diving, with theoretical issues such as the distinction between long- and short-term memory. After moving to the University of Sussex, he and Graham Hitch proposed a multicomponent model of working memory.

He also began working with amnesic patients, continuing both these lines of research when he moved, first to a chair at the University of Stirling, then returning to the APU in Cambridge. After 20 years as its director, he moved first to the University of Bristol, then to his current position in York where he has resumed his collaboration with Graham Hitch. He was awarded a CBE for his contributions to the study of memory, is a Fellow of the Royal Society, the British Academy, the Academy of Medical Sciences, and the American Academy of Arts and Sciences.

Michael W. Eysenck graduated from University College London. He then moved immediately to Birkbeck University of London as a lecturer, where he completed his Ph.D. on the von Restorff and "release" memory effects. His research for several years focused on various topics within memory research (e.g., levels of processing; distinctiveness). However, for many years his research has focused mainly on anxiety and cognition (including memory). Most of this

research has involved healthy populations but some has dealt with cognitive biases (including memory ones) in anxious patients. This research has been carried out at Birkbeck University of London and at Royal Holloway University of London, where he has been Professor of Psychology since 1987 (Head of Department, 1987–2005). However, it was started during his time as Visiting Professor at the University of South Florida. He has published 40 books in psychology (many relating to human memory), including two research monographs on anxiety and cognition. He has been in *Who's Who* since 1989.

Michael C. Anderson received his Ph.D. in Cognitive Psychology from the University of California, Los Angeles in 1994. After completing a postdoctoral fellowship in cognitive neuroscience at the University of California, Berkeley, he joined the psychology faculty at the University of Oregon, where he was director of the Memory Control Laboratory through 2007. He is now Senior Scientist and Programme Leader at the MRC Cognition and Brain Sciences Unit in Cambridge, England. His research investigates the roles of inhibitory processes as a cause of forgetting in long-term memory. His recent work has focused on executive control as a model of motivated forgetting, and has established the existence of cognitive and neurobiological mechanisms by which we can willfully forget past experiences. This work begins to specify the mechanisms by which people adapt the functioning of their memories in the aftermath of traumatic experience.

PREFACE TO THE THIRD EDITION

The current edition uses the same broad structure as the two previous editions, but with a somewhat clearer delineation of the various sections. I continue to be responsible for the two introductory chapters involving relatively modest changes, followed by the chapter on short-term memory which now contains more on visual short-term memory. The working memory chapter is updated in the light of recent developments including current attempts to compare and contrast different theoretical approaches. The chapters covering the basic study of long-term memory are all now covered by Michael Anderson, who provides a more coherent overview from someone who was very actively involved in recent advances in the area and its links to neuroscience. The chapter on learning has been significantly updated to include exciting work on retrieval-based learning, cortical plasticity, spacing learning, the impact of motivation on the neural mechanisms of encoding, divided attention, an expanded treatment of implicit forms of memory, and the latest cutting-edge developments of the cellular basis of plasticity. The chapter on episodic memory has been expanded to include coverage of the neural mechanism of episodic encoding and consolidation, and innovative work identifying the neural basis of schemas and how they enhance retention by hastening consolidation. The chapter on autobiographical memory now includes expanded coverage of emotional effects, new reports of severely deficient autobiographical memory, updated coverage of psychogenic amnesia, and the latest findings in the neural basis of autobiographical memory. The retrieval and forgetting chapters have been updated with recent developments in these area at the cognitive, brain systems, and cellular levels. Michael Eysenck continues to cover theory and research on semantic memory, which has increasingly benefitted from the approach of cognitive neuroscience. He also continues to cover chapters on the application of the study of memory beyond the laboratory to eyewitness testimony, prospective memory, and memory improvement, areas that have seen impressive advances in the years since the previous edition. He has however passed on to me the chapter on memory in childhood, which I have adopted as part of a three-chapter block on memory development and decline. I take a slightly more applied approach reflecting my interest in the effect of disease and malnutrition on early development and the potential contribution of the study of memory to practical aspects of child development. The memory and aging chapter contains more on recent attempts to minimize the effects of age on cognition. The third chapter in this section focuses principally on applied issues of memory decline with particular reference to Alzheimer's disease and to traumatic brain injury concluding by discussing methods to help people deal with failing memory.

Once again I am heavily indebted to Lindsey Bowes for her contribution at levels ranging from typing my mumbled dictation through helping search for references to rescuing me from frustrations induced by my very limited IT skills. I again am also grateful to my wife Hilary who continues to tolerate my refusal to behave like a sensible retiree.

I (Michael Eysenck) am indebted to my wife Christine in every way for her support for my time-consuming book-writing efforts. The completion of this book has given me more time to spend with our delightful grandchildren Sebastian and Clementine.

Michael Anderson is grateful to his partner Nami for her considerable support in enabling work on this text, and to his son Max, who illustrates daily the power of learning, and who has provided inspiration for many examples in this book.

Finally, we are grateful to the staff at Taylor & Francis for their overall management of the project. In particular we would like to thank Ceri McLardy and Kirsten Shankland for keeping us on track with their customary efficiency and good humour and to the Production Editor Pip Clubbs for her friendly efficiency during the final stages of producing the book.

Alan Baddeley
York, 2020

Contents

CHAPTER 1

WHAT IS MEMORY?

Alan Baddeley

Memory is something we complain about. Why? Why are we quite happy to claim "I have a terrible memory!" but not to assert that "I am amazingly stupid"? Of course, we do forget; we do sometimes forget appointments and fail to recognize people we have met in the past, and rather more frequently we forget their names. We do not, however, often forget important events; if the bridegroom failed to turn up for his wedding he would not be believed if he claimed to have forgotten. Consequently, failing to recognize an old acquaintance suggests that the person was perhaps not of great importance to us. The obvious excuse is to blame one's terrible memory.

In the chapters that follow, we will try to convince you that your memory is in fact remarkably good, although fallible. We agree with Schacter (2001) who, having described what he refers to as the seven sins of memory, accepts that the sins are in fact the necessary consequences of the virtues that make our memories so rich and flexible. Our memories might be less reliable than those of the average computer but they are just as capacious, much more flexible, and a good deal more user friendly. We forget more than computers, but we are likely to retain what is important and useful and forget unimportant details. We are good at rapidly encoding the context in which an event happens, what happened, when and where, so as to access when appropriate. We are good at remembering patterns of repeating events, a skill that

helps us understand the world using this understanding to strip away redundant information and using the core meaning for future planning. Finally, we are very good at coping with forgetting by using knowledge to reconstruct partial memories. For these reasons, computer scientists are beginning to be interested in learning from human memory and importantly forgetting, with a view to potentially building some of these characteristics into computer memory (Mezaris, Niederee, & Logie, in press). Hence, despite their limitations our fallible memories play an absolutely crucial part in our ability to function independently in our complex world. Perhaps the most dramatic evidence for the usefulness of human memory comes from the plight of patients who have lost these capacities as in the case of Clive Wearing who has the misfortune to have had much of his memory capacity destroyed by disease (Wilson, Baddeley, & Kapur, 1995).

WHY DO WE NEED MEMORY?

Clive is an extremely talented musician, an expert on early music who was master of a major London choir. He himself sang and was asked to perform before the Pope during a papal visit to London. In 1985, he had the misfortune to suffer a brain infection from the herpes simplex virus, a virus that exists in a large proportion of the population, typically leading to nothing worse than cold sores but very occasionally breaking through the blood–brain barrier to cause encephalitis, an inflammation of the brain that can prove fatal. In recent years, treatment has improved, with the result that patients are more likely to survive, although often having suffered from extensive brain damage, typically in areas responsible for memory.

When he eventually recovered consciousness, Clive was densely amnesic and appeared to be unable to store information for periods longer than seconds. His interpretation of his plight was to assume that he had just recovered consciousness, something that he would announce to any visitor, and something that he repeatedly recorded in a notebook, each time crossing out the previous line and writing "I have now recovered consciousness" or "consciousness has now finally been recovered," an activity that continued for many, many years.

Clive knew who he was and could talk about the broad outlines of his early life, although the detail was very sparse. He knew he had spent four years at Cambridge University, but could not recognize a photograph of his college. He could remember, although somewhat vaguely, important events in his life such as directing and conducting the first modern performance of Handel's *Messiah* using original instruments in an appropriate period setting, and could talk intelligently about the historical development of the role of the musical conductor. However, even this selected knowledge was sketchy; he had written a book on the early composer Lassus, but could not recall any of the content. Asked who had written *Romeo and Juliet*, Clive did not know. He had remarried, but could not remember this. However, he did greet his new wife with enormous enthusiasm every time she appeared, even though she might only have been out of the room for a few minutes; every time declaring that he had just recovered consciousness.

Clive was totally incapacitated by his amnesia. He could not read a book or follow a television program because he immediately forgot what had gone before. If he left his hospital room, he was immediately lost. He was locked into a permanent present, something he described as "hell on earth." "It's like being dead—all the bloody time!"

However, there was one aspect of Clive's memory that appeared to be unimpaired, that part concerned with music. When his choir visited him, he found that he could conduct them just as before. He was able to read the score of a song and accompany himself on the keyboard while singing it. For a brief moment he appeared to return to his old self, only to feel wretched when he stopped playing. Over 20 years later, Clive is still just as densely amnesic but now appears to have come to terms with his terrible affliction and is calmer and less distressed.

ONE MEMORY OR MANY?

Although Clive's case makes the point that memory is crucial for daily life, it does not tell us much about the nature of memory. Clive was unfortunate in having damage to a range of brain areas, with the result that he has problems that extend beyond his amnesia. Furthermore, the fact that Clive's musical memory and skills are unimpaired suggests that memory is not a single simple system. Other studies have shown that densely amnesic patients can repeat back a telephone number, suggesting preserved immediate memory, and that they can learn motor skills at a normal rate. As we will see later, amnesic patients are capable of a number of types of learning, demonstrating this by improved performance, even though they do not remember the learning experience and typically deny having encountered the situation before. The evidence suggests, therefore, that rather than having a single global memory system, the picture is more complex. The first few chapters of this book will try to unpack some of this complexity, providing a basis for later chapters that are concerned with the way in which these systems influence our lives, how memory changes as we move through childhood to adulthood and old age, and what happens when our memory systems break down.

In giving our account of memory, we are of course presenting a range of psychological theories. Theories develop and change, and different people will hold different theories to explain the same data. As a glance at any current memory journal will indicate, this is certainly the case for the study of memory. Fortunately, there is a great deal of general agreement between different groups studying the psychology of memory, even though they tend to use somewhat different terminology. At this point, it might be useful to say a little bit about the concept of theory that underpins our own approach.

THEORIES, MAPS, AND MODELS

What should a psychological theory look like? In the 1950s, many people thought they should look like theories from physics. Clark Hull studied the learning behavior of white rats and attempted to use his results to build a rather grand general theory of learning in which the learning behavior of both rats and people was predicted using a series of postulates and equations that were explicitly modeled on the example set by Isaac Newton (Hull, 1943).

By contrast, Hull's great rival, Edward Tolman (1948), thought of rats as forming "cognitive maps," internal representations of their environment that were acquired as a result of active exploration. The controversy rumbled on from the 1930s to the 1950s, and then was abandoned quite suddenly. Both sides found that they had to assume some kind of representation that went beyond the simple association between stimuli impinging on the rat and its learned behavior, but neither seemed to have a solution to the problem of how these could be investigated.

The broad view of theory that we shall take is that theories are essentially like maps. They summarize our knowledge in a simple and structured way that helps us to understand what is known. A good theory will help us to ask new questions and that in turn will help us find out more about the topic we are

mapping. The nature of the theory will depend on the questions we want to answer, just as in the case of maps of a city. The map that will help you travel by underground around London or New York looks very different from the sort of map that you would need if you wanted to walk, with neither being a direct representation of what you would see if you stood at a given location. That does not of course mean that they are bad maps, quite the opposite, because each map is designed to serve a different purpose.

In the case of psychological theories, different theories will operate at different levels of explanation and focus on different issues. An argument between a shopkeeper and customer, for example, would be explained in very different ways by a sociologist, who might emphasize the economic and social pressures, a social psychologist interested in interpersonal relationships, a cognitive psychologist interested in language, and a physiological psychologist who might be interested in the emotional responses of the two disputants and how these are reflected in the brain. All of these explanations are relevant and in principle should be relatable to each other, but none is the single "correct" interpretation.

This is a view that contrasts with what is sometimes called reductionism. This assumes that the aim of science is to reduce each explanation to the level below: Social psychology to cognitive psychology, which in turn should be explained physiologically, with the physiology then being interpreted biochemically and ultimately in terms of physics. Although it is clearly valuable to be able to explain phenomena at different but related levels, this is ultimately no more sensible than for a physicist to demand that we should attempt to design bridges on the basis of

KEY TERM

Reductionism: The view that all scientific explanations should aim to be based on a lower level of analysis: Psychology in terms of physiology, physiology in terms of chemistry, and chemistry in terms of physics.

subatomic particle physics, rather than Newtonian mechanics.

The aim of the present book is to outline what we know of the *psychology* of memory. We believe that an account at the psychological level will prove valuable in throwing light on accounts of human behavior at the interpersonal and social level, and will play an important role in our capacity to understand the neurobiological factors that underpin the various types of memory. We suggest that the psychology of memory is sufficiently understood to begin to interface very fruitfully with questions at both the social and neurobiological levels, and hope to illustrate this over the subsequent chapters.

HOW CAN WE STUDY MEMORY?

The case of Clive Wearing demonstrates how important memory is, and how complex, but leaves open the question of how it can best be studied. The attempt to understand human memory extends at least as far back as Aristotle, and forms one of the classic questions within the philosophy of mind, although without reaching any firm conclusions. This was vividly illustrated by a lecture on memory by the eminent philosopher A. J. Ayer that I attended as a student. He began rather unpromisingly, by declaring that memory was not a very interesting philosophical question. He seems to have demonstrated this pretty effectively as I can remember none of the lecture, apart from his statement that his memory was totally devoid of imagery, prompting a skeptical questioner to ask "If I tell you that the band of the grenadier guards is marching past the end of the street, banners flying and trumpets sounding, do you not hear or see anything?" "No," replied the philosopher. "I don't believe you!" said the questioner and sat down crossly.

This point illustrates a limitation of a purely philosophical approach to the understanding of memory in particular, and to mind in general, namely its reliance on introspection, the capacity to reflect and report our ongoing thoughts. These are not unimportant, but are not a reliable indication of the way our minds work, for two principal reasons. The first of these, as our example shows, is that people differ in what they appear to experience in a given situation; does memory depend on visual imagery, and if not, why do some of us experience it? Second and even more importantly, we are only consciously aware of a relatively small proportion of the mechanisms underpinning our mental life, and as we will see, the tip of the mental iceberg that is available to conscious awareness is not necessarily a good guide to what lies beneath.

While there are still important issues addressed by the philosophy of mind, it is now generally acknowledged these can best be pursued in collaboration with a scientific approach based on empirical evidence. To return to the question of imagery, as I suspect Ayer knew, in the late 19th century, Sir Francis Galton had asked a number of "eminent men" to reflect on their breakfast table from that morning and describe the vividness of the resulting memory, finding a huge range of responses. What was not known by Galton is that these huge differences are not reflected in how accurate our memories are, suggesting that accuracy depends on some nonconscious process. Could it be that different people have the same experience but just describe it differently? Or do they have different memory systems? Or perhaps they have the same basic systems but have a different way of using them?

So how can we move beyond introspection?

An answer to this started to develop in Germany in the latter half of the 19th century. It was concerned initially with the discipline of *psychophysics*, an attempt to systematically map the relationship between physical stimuli such as brightness and loudness onto their perceived magnitude. Despite success in linking physical stimuli to the psychological experience of participants, capacities such as learning and memory were initially regarded as unsuitable for experimental study. This view was dramatically overturned by a German philosopher Herman Ebbinghaus who conducted an

Ebbinghaus (1850–1909) was the first person to demonstrate that it was possible to study memory experimentally.

basic principles of learning that will be discussed in Chapter 5 and the classic forgetting curve shown in Figure 1.1 that forms the basis of all subsequent work in this area (see Chapter 9).

The Ebbinghaus tradition was subsequently most strongly developed in the US, focusing particularly on the factors and conditions surrounding the important question of how new learning interacted with what was already known. Results were interpreted in terms of associations that were assumed to be formed between stimuli and responses, using a limited range of methods that typically involved remembering lists of nonsense syllables or words (McGeoch & Irion, 1952). This is often referred to as the verbal learning approach. It developed from the 1930s to the 1960s, particularly in US mid-Western laboratories, and emphasized the careful mapping of phenomena rather than the ambitious building of grand theories such as that proposed by Clark Hull's general theory of learning based largely on the behavior of rats

KEY TERM

Verbal learning: A term applied to an approach to memory that relies principally on the learning of lists of words and nonsense syllables.

intensive series of experiments on himself over a two-year period, showing that it was indeed possible to plot systematic relationships between the conditions of learning and the amount learned. Having published this, the first classic book on the science of memory (Ebbinghaus, 1885), he moved on to study color vision, intelligence, and a range of other questions in the newly developing field of experimental psychology.

So what did Ebbinghaus do? He began by simplifying the experimental situation, attempting to develop material that was devoid of meaning but was verbally learnable and reportable, inventing what has become known as the nonsense syllable, a consonant-vowel-consonant nonword such as *zug pij* and *tev*. He served as his own subject, always holding constant the room in which he learned, the time of day, and the rate of presentation which was rapid, so as to avoid any temptation to attempt to find meaning in the stimuli. Ebbinghaus established some of the

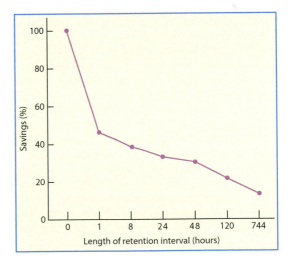

Figure 1.1 Forgetting over time as indexed by reduced savings during relearning. Data from Ebbinghaus (1885).

in mazes which was presented in an elaborate style based directly on that used by Isaac Newton in presenting his classic work, the *Principia*. However the various disputes between such theories appeared to reach deadlock in the late 1950s leading to their general abandonment. This allowed the more staid verbal learning approach, previously disparagingly discounted by its critics as "dust bowl empiricism," to attract a broader range of investigators interested in studying learning and memory. This in turn led to the founding of a new journal, *The Journal of Verbal Learning and Verbal Behavior*, which, when the term "verbal learning" later became unfashionable, became *The Journal of Memory and Language*.

A second development that occurred at this point had its roots in both Europe and North America. In the 1930s, a German approach known as Gestalt psychology began attempting to apply ideas developed in the study of perception to the understanding of human memory. Unlike the behaviorist approaches, *Gestalt* psychologists tended to emphasize the importance of internal representations rather than observable stimuli and responses, and to stress the active role of the rememberer. Gestalt psychology suffered badly from Nazi persecution, but enough Gestalt psychologists moved to North America to sow the seeds of an alternative approach to verbal learning; an approach that placed much more emphasis on the activity of the learner in organizing material. This approach was typified by two investigators who had grown up in Europe but had then emigrated and been trained in North America: George Mandler and Endel Tulving.

In Britain, a third approach to memory had developed, based on Frederic Bartlett's (1932) book *Remembering*. Bartlett explicitly rejected the learning of meaningless material as an appropriate way to study memory, using instead complex material such as folk tales from other cultures, reflecting his interest in social psychology and stressing the importance of the rememberer's "effort after meaning." This approach emphasized the study of the memory errors that people made, explaining them in terms of the participants' cultural assumptions about the world.

Bartlett proposed that these depended on internal representations that he referred to as schemas. His approach differed radically from the Ebbinghaus tradition that influenced the verbal learning approach, but left Bartlett with the problem of how to study these elusive inner representations of the world.

A possible answer to this problem evolved gradually during World War II with the development of computers. Mathematicians such as Weiner (1950) in the US, and physiologists such as Gray Walter (1953) in the UK described machines that were able to demonstrate a degree of control that resembled purposive behavior. During the 1940s, a Scottish psychologist, Kenneth Craik (1943), working with Bartlett in Cambridge produced a brief but influential book entitled *The Nature of Explanation*. Here he proposed the idea of representing theories as models, and using the computer to develop such models. He carried out what were probably the first psychological experiments based on this idea, using analog computers (digital computers were still being invented) and applying his computer-based theoretical model to the practical problem of gun-aiming in tanks. Tragically, in 1945 he was killed in a traffic accident while still a young man.

Fortunately, the new approach to psychology, based on the computer metaphor, was being taken up by a range of young investigators, and in the years following the war, this information-processing approach to psychology became increasingly influential. Two books were particularly important. Donald

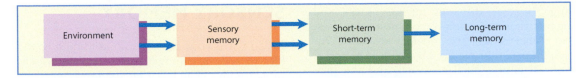

Figure 1.2 An information-processing approach to memory. Information flows from the environment through sensory storage and short-term storage to long-term memory.

Broadbent's *Perception and Communication* (1958) developed and applied Craik's seminal ideas to a range of work carried out at the Medical Research Council Applied Psychology Unit in Cambridge, England, much of it stimulated by practical problems originating during the war. Some nine years later, this growing field was then brilliantly synthesized and summarized by Ulric Neisser (1967) in a book whose title provided a name for this burgeoning field: *Cognitive Psychology*.

Using the digital computer as an analogy, human memory could be regarded as comprising one or more storage systems. Any memory system—whether physical, electronic, or human—requires three things, the capacity to *encode*, or enter information into the system, the capacity to *store* it, and—subsequently—the capacity to find and *retrieve* it. However, although these three stages serve different functions, they interact: The method of registering material or encoding determines what and how the information is stored, which in turn will limit what can subsequently be retrieved. Consider a simple physical memory device, a shopping list. If it is to work, you need to write legibly in a language the recipient shopper understands. If it were to get wet, the ink would blur (impaired storage) making it less distinct and harder to read (retrieval). Retrieval would be harder if your handwriting was poor (an encoding-retrieval interaction), and if the writing was smudged (a storage-retrieval interaction). The situation is further complicated by the discovery that our memories comprise not one, but several interrelated memory systems.

HOW MANY KINDS OF MEMORY?

As the influence of the cognitive approach to psychology grew, the balance of opinion moved from the assumption of a single memory system based on stimulus–response associations towards the idea that two, three, or perhaps more memory systems were involved. Figure 1.2 shows the broad view that came to be widely accepted during the 1960s. It assumed that information comes in from the environment and is first processed by a series of sensory memory systems, which could be best regarded as providing an interface between perception and memory. Information is then assumed to be passed on to a temporary short-term memory system, before being registered in long-term memory. A particularly influential version of this model was proposed by Atkinson and Shiffrin (1968). It was dubbed the modal model because it was representative of many similar models of the operation of human memory that were proposed at the time. As we shall see, a number of the assumptions underlying this model were subsequently questioned, causing it to be further elaborated.

The question of how many kinds of memory remains controversial; some theorists object to the very concept of a memory *store* as too static, arguing instead that we should be concerned with *processes* (e.g., Nairne, 1990, 2002; Neath & Surprenant, 2003). They point to similarities across a

KEY TERM

Modal model: A term applied to the model of memory developed by Atkinson and Shiffrin (1968).

range of very different memory tasks and suggest that these imply common processes, and hence a unitary memory system. Our own view is that we need to think in terms of both structures such as stores and the processes that operate on them, just as an analysis of the brain requires the contribution of both static anatomical features and a more dynamic concern with physiology. We should certainly look for similarities across domains in the way that these systems perform, but the presence of common features should not encourage us to ignore the differences.

Fortunately, regardless of the question of whether one emphasizes similarities or differences, the broad picture remains the same. In what follows, we ourselves use the distinctions between types of memory as a way of organizing and structuring our knowledge of human memory. As discussed below, we assume separate sensory, short-term, and long-term memory systems, each of which can be subdivided into separate components. We do not, however, assume the simple flow of information from the environment into long-term memory that is suggested in Figure 1.2, as there is abundant evidence that information flows in both directions. For example, our knowledge of the world, stored in long-term memory, can influence our focus of attention, which will then determine what is fed into the sensory memory systems, how it is processed, whether as familiar objects or as meaningless shapes, and hence how well it is subsequently remembered. This will become even more important with the perception of complex active scenes. Thus a keen football fan watching a game will see and remember particular plays that her less knowledgeable companion will miss.

We begin with a brief account of sensory memory. This was an area of considerable activity during the 1960s and provides a good illustration of the general principles of encoding, storage, and retrieval. However, given that it relates more to perception than memory, it will not be covered in the remainder of the book. Our outline continues with introductory accounts of short-term and working memory, before moving to a preliminary survey of long-term memory.

SENSORY MEMORY

If you wave your hand while holding a sparkler in a dark room, it leaves a trail, which rapidly fades. The fact that the image persists long enough to draw an apparent line suggests that it is being stored in some way, and the fact that the line rapidly fades implies some simple form of forgetting. This phenomenon forms the basis for movies; a sequence of static images is presented rapidly, with blank intervals in between, but is perceived as a continuous moving image. This occurs because the perceptual system stores the visual information long enough to bridge the gap between the static images, integrating each one with the next, very slightly different, image.

Neisser (1967) referred to this brief visual memory system as iconic memory, referring to its auditory counterpart as "echoic memory." In the early 1960s, a number of investigators at Bell Laboratories in the US used the new information-processing approach to analyze this fleeting visual memory system (Averbach & Sperling, 1961; Sperling, 1960, 1963). Sperling (1960) briefly presented a visual array of 12 letters in three rows of four, and then asked for recall (Figure 1.3). People could typically remember four or five items correctly. If you try this task, however, you will have the sensation that you have seen more than four or five, but that they have gone before you can report them. One way of avoiding the problem of forgetting during reporting is to present the same array but ask for only one row to be reported, but not telling the participant in advance which row will be tested, hence requiring the whole set to be encoded. The row to be recalled is then specified by presenting a tone; a high tone for the top line, a medium tone for line two, and a low tone for

B C X Y
N F R W
T Z K D

Figure 1.3 Stimulus array used by Sperling. Although 12 letters were presented, participants only had to recall one row, that cued by a high, medium, or low tone.

line three. As Sperling did not tell the participant in advance which line would be cued, the report could be treated as representative of the whole array; multiplying the score by three will thus give an estimate of the total number of letters stored. However, as shown in Figure 1.4, amount recalled depends on when the recall tone is presented. When recall is tested immediately, it should provide an estimate of the total capacity of the memory store, with the fall-off in performance as the tone is delayed representing the loss of information. Note that Figure 1.4 shows two curves, one with a bright field before and

after the letters, and the other with the letters preceded and followed by a dark visual field. A subsequent experiment (Sperling, 1963) found that the brighter the light during the interval, the poorer the performance, suggesting that the light is interfering with the memory trace in some way, a process known as masking.

Later work by Michael Turvey (1973) investigated two separate types of masking operating at different stages. The first of these involves *brightness masking*, with the degree of masking increasing when the mask becomes brighter, or is presented closer in time to the stimulus. This effect only occurs if the mask and the stimulus are presented to the same eye, suggesting that it is operating at a peripheral retinal level. If you were a subject in such an experiment, this type of masking would give rise to experiencing a composite of target and mask, with the brighter the mask the less distinct the target.

KEY TERM

Masking: A process by which the perception and/or storage of a stimulus is influenced by events occurring immediately before presentation (forward masking) or more commonly after (backward masking).

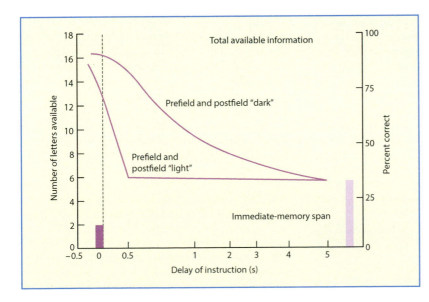

Figure 1.4 Estimated number of letters available using the partial report method, as a function of recall delay. From Sperling (1963). Copyright © 1963 by The Human Factors Society and Ergonomics Society Inc. Reprinted by permission of Sage Publications.

This is distinct from *pattern masking*, the second type studied which occurs when targets are followed by a mask comprising broadly similar features to the target, for example jumbled fragments of letters. This type of mask operates even when the target is presented to one eye and the mask to the other. This suggests that it influences a later stage of visual processing that occurs after information from the two eyes has been combined into a single percept. It is relatively insensitive to brightness and subjectively feels as if a clear image has been disrupted before the information could adequately be read off from it.

What function does iconic memory serve other than that of keeping psychologists busy, or as Haber concluded in desperation, reading at night in a thunderstorm? The answer is that its function is probably indirect, forming part of the process of perceiving the world. As we scan the visual world, stimuli of huge complexity will fall on our retina, comprising far more information than it is useful for us to process and store. It seems likely that iconic memory represents two early stages of a process whereby information is read off from the retina, and some of it then fed through to a more durable short-term visual store. It is this that allows us to build up a coherent representation of the visual world and that allows a movie to be perceived, not a series of static frames with gaps in between, but as a continuous and realistic visual experience. The early stages of iconic memory are probably best regarded as aspects of perception, while the subsequent more stable stage will be discussed in the chapter on short-term memory.

The auditory system also involves a brief sensory memory component that Neisser named echoic memory. If you are asked to remember a long telephone number, then your pattern of errors will differ depending on whether the number is heard or read. With visual presentation, the likelihood of an

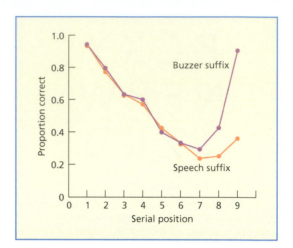

Figure 1.5 Serial recall of a nine-item list when an additional item, the suffix, is either the spoken word zero or a sound made by a buzzer. From Crowder (1972). © 1972 Massachusetts Institute of Technology, by permission of The MIT Press.

error increases systematically from the beginning to the end of the sequence, whereas, as shown in Figure 1.5, with auditory presentation the last one or two items are much more likely to be correct than are items in the middle of the list (Murdock, 1967). This recency advantage can be removed by interposing another spoken item between presentation and recall, even when this item itself does not need to be processed, and is always the same, for example, the instruction "recall." In an extensive series of experiments, Crowder and Morton (1969; Crowder, 1971) showed that the nature of this suffix is critical. A visual or nonspeech-like auditory suffix, such as a buzzer, does not disrupt performance, whereas a spoken suffix does, regardless of its meaning.

Crowder and Morton postulated what they term a precategorical acoustic store as the basis for the auditory recency effect. However, the question of whether the process responsible for the enhanced auditory recency effect is better regarded as a form of memory or an aspect of perception remains controversial (Jones, Hughes, & Macken, 2006; but see also Baddeley & Larsen, 2007). Regardless of its interpretation, the auditory recency component is sufficiently large and robust to play a potentially significant role in studies of

KEY TERM

Echoic memory: A term sometimes applied to auditory sensory memory.

verbal short-term memory, and has even been proposed as an alternative to more conventional views of performance on short-term verbal memory tasks (Jones et al., 2006). We will return to this issue when discussing short-term memory. In the meantime, it seems likely that an adequate explanation of echoic memory will need to be fully integrated with a broader theory of speech perception.

SHORT-TERM AND WORKING MEMORY

As this topic, and that of long-term memory, forms a major part of the book, for present purposes we will limit ourselves to a very brief outline. We use the term short-term memory (STM) in a theory-neutral way to refer to the temporary storage of small amounts of material over brief delays. This leaves open the question of how this storage is achieved. In most, if not all situations there is likely to be a contribution to performance from long-term memory that will need to be taken into account in evaluating the role of any more temporary storage systems. Much of the work in this area has used verbal material, and there is no doubt that even when the stimuli are not verbal, people will often use verbal rehearsal to help maintain their level of performance over a brief delay (see Chapter 4). It is important to bear in mind, however, that STM is not limited to verbal material, and has been studied extensively for visual and spatial information, though much less extensively for smell and touch.

The concept of working memory is based on the assumption that a system exists for the temporary maintenance and manipulation of information, and that this is helpful in performing many complex tasks. A number of different models of working memory have been proposed, with the nature and emphasis of each model tending to depend on the particular area of interest of the theorist, and their theoretical style. However, most assume that working memory acts as a form of mental workspace, providing a basis for

thought. It is usually assumed to be linked to attention, and to be able to draw on other resources within short-term and long-term memory (Miyake & Shah, 1999). By no means all approaches, however, emphasize the role of memory rather than attention. One approach that does so is the multicomponent model proposed originally by Baddeley and Hitch in 1974 as a means of linking research on the psychology and neuropsychology of STM to its functional role in performing important cognitive activities such as reasoning, comprehension, and learning. This approach has continued to prove productive for over 30 years (Baddeley, 2007) and is the principal focus of Chapter 4.

LONG-TERM MEMORY

We shall use the classification of long-term memory proposed by Squire (1992). As shown in Figure 1.6, this classification makes a broad distinction between explicit or declarative memory and implicit or nondeclarative memory. Explicit memory refers to situations that we would generally think of as involving memory, both for specific *events*, such as meeting a friend unexpectedly on

---

KEY TERM

Short-term memory (STM): A term applied to the retention of small amounts of material over periods of a few seconds.

Working memory: A memory system that underpins our capacity to "keep things in mind" when performing complex tasks.

Long-term memory: A system or systems assumed to underpin the capacity to store information over long periods of time.

Explicit/declarative memory: Memory that is open to intentional retrieval, whether based on recollecting personal events (episodic memory) or facts (semantic memory).

Implicit/nondeclarative memory: Retrieval of information from long-term memory through performance rather than explicit conscious recall or recognition.

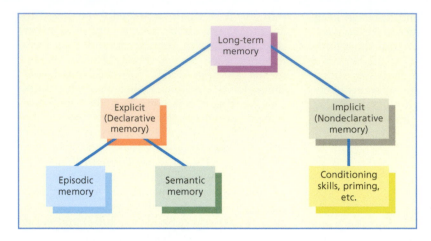

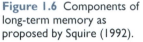

Figure 1.6 Components of long-term memory as proposed by Squire (1992).

holiday last year, and remembering *facts* or information about the world, for example the meaning of the word *testify* or the color of a ripe banana. Implicit memory refers to situations in which some form of learning has occurred, but which is reflected in *performance* rather than through overt remembering, riding a bicycle for example or reading a friend's handwriting more easily because we have encountered it frequently in the past. We will briefly discuss these in turn, leaving a full exploration to subsequent chapters.

Explicit memory

As Figure 1.6 shows, this can be divided into two categories, semantic and episodic memory. During the 1960s, computer scientists attempting to achieve automatic language processing discovered that their computer programs needed to have built into them some kind of knowledge of the world, which could represent the meaning of the words being processed. This led psychologists to attempt to study the way in which humans store such semantic information. At a conference convened to discuss these new

developments, a Canadian psychologist Endel Tulving (1972) proposed a distinction that was immediately adopted and has been used extensively ever since, that between *semantic* and *episodic* memory. Semantic memory refers to knowledge of the world. It goes beyond simply knowing the meaning of words and extends to sensory attributes such as the color of a lemon or the taste of an apple. It also includes general knowledge of how society works, what to do when you enter a restaurant, or how to book a theater seat. It is inherently general in nature, although it can in principle be acquired on a single occasion. If you heard that an old friend had died, this would be likely to

Semantic memory goes beyond the meaning of words, and extends to sensory attributes such as taste and color; and to general knowledge of how society works, such as how to behave in a supermarket.

KEY TERM

Semantic memory: A system that is assumed to store accumulative knowledge of the world.

Episodic memory: A system that is assumed to underpin the capacity to remember specific events.

become part of your general knowledge of that person, hence part of your semantic memory, although you might well forget where or when you had heard this.

If you subsequently recall the particular occasion when and where you had learned this sad news, then this would be an instance of *episodic memory*, which underpins the capacity to remember specific single episodes or events. Hence, a given event can be registered in both types of memory. Tulving himself (2002) now limits the use of the term "episodic memory" to situations in which you actually re-experience some aspect of the original episode, for example remembering how surprised you were that your informant knew your old friend. Tulving refers to this capacity as mental time travel and emphasizes its value, both in allowing us to recollect and "relive" individual events, and to use that information for planning a future action, for example sending a letter of condolence. It is this capacity to acquire and retrieve memories for particular events that tends to be most severely disrupted in amnesic patients, and it is this deficit that has made Clive Wearing's life so unbearably difficult.

How are semantic and episodic memory related? One possibility is that semantic memory is simply the residue of many episodes. For example, I know that Madrid is the capital of Spain, not only because I was told it at school but also because I have encountered this fact in countless news-reels and had it reinforced by visiting Madrid. Consistent with this assumed role of episodic memory in forming semantic memory is the fact that most amnesic patients have difficulty in building up new semantic knowledge. They typically would not know the name of the current President of the United States of America, or what year it is, or which teams were doing well in their favorite sport. Whether this means that semantic and episodic memory involve separate storage systems (Tulving, 2002), or whether they reflect separate retrieval routes to a common store as I have recently suggested (Baddeley, in press) remains to be decided.

Implicit memory

Amnesic patients thus tend to show not only grossly disturbed episodic memory, but also a greatly impaired capacity to add to their store of knowledge of the world. There are however a number of situations in which they do appear to learn at a normal rate, and the study of these preserved capacities has had an important influence on the development of the concept of implicit or nondeclarative memory.

One preserved form of learning is simple classical conditioning. If a tone is followed by a brief puff of air to the eye, amnesic patients will learn to blink in anticipation (Weiskrantz & Warrington, 1979). Despite learning at a normal rate, they do not remember the experience and cannot explain the function of the nozzle that delivers the air puff to their eye. Amnesic patients can also learn motor skills, such as improving with practice the capacity to keep a stylus in contact with a moving spot of light (Brooks & Baddeley, 1976). Warrington and Weiskrantz (1968) demonstrated that word learning was also preserved in densely amnesic patients under certain conditions. They presented their patients with a list of unrelated words and then tested for retention in a number of different ways. When asked to recall the words or recognize which of the subsequent sequence of words had already been presented, the patients performed very poorly. However, when the nature of the test was changed to one in which the task was to "guess" a word when given the first few letters, both patients and normal participants were likely to "guess" a word that had been seen earlier. For example, a patient who had

---

KEY TERM

Mental time travel: A term coined by Tulving to emphasize the way in which episodic memory allows us to relive the past and use this information to imagine the future.

Classical conditioning: A learning procedure whereby a neutral stimulus (e.g., a bell) that is paired repeatedly with a response-evoking stimulus (e.g., meat powder), will come to evoke that response (salivation).

been shown the word "bring" and was later given the letters "BR–" would be just as likely as control participants to guess "bring" rather than "bread," but would not remember having just seen that word. Patients could take full advantage of their prior experience, despite failing to remember that they had even been shown any words earlier, indicating that *something* had been stored. As we shall see, this phenomenon, known as priming, is found in a range of perceptual tasks, both visual and auditory, and can also be found in the progressive improvement in more complex activities such as reading mirror writing (Cohen & Squire, 1980) or assembling a jigsaw puzzle (Brooks & Baddeley, 1976).

Given that these are all examples of implicit learning and memory, do they all reflect a single memory system? While attempts have been made to account for them all in terms of a single system (see Neath & Surprenant, 2003), our own view is that although they have features in common, they represent a range of different learning systems using different parts of the brain that have evolved for different purposes. They seem to represent a tendency for evolution to develop similar ways of addressing problems across different systems.

MEMORY: BEYOND THE LABORATORY

We have so far discussed the question of how to develop a theoretical understanding of human memory: How it encodes, stores, and retrieves information. However, if our theory is to be useful as well as informative, then it needs to be applicable beyond the confines of the laboratory, to tell about how our memo-

ries will work in the world. It must aim to extend beyond the student population, on which much of the research is based, and tell us about how memory functions in children and the elderly, across different cultures, and in health and disease.

It is of course much more difficult to run tightly controlled experiments outside the laboratory, with the result that most of the theoretically focused studies that inform the initial chapters are laboratory based. Some investigators argue that we should confine our research to the laboratory, extending it only when we have a thorough understanding of memory. Others have followed Bartlett in suggesting that this is likely to lead to the neglect of important aspects of memory. In response to this rather conservative view, a group of psychologists in South Wales enthusiastically convened an international conference concerned with practical aspects of memory. It was a great success, with people coming from all over the world to talk about their research on topics ranging from memory for medical information to sex differences in facial memory, and from expert calculators to brain-damaged patients (Gruneberg, Morris, & Sykes, 1978).

Ulric Neisser was invited to give the opening address. In it, he lamented the laboratory-based tradition declaring that "If X is an interesting or socially significant aspect of memory, then psychologists have hardly ever studied X!" (Neisser, 1978, p. 4). He was in fact preaching to an enthusiastic audience of the converted, whose work presented over the next few days was already refuting his claim. However, his address was less well received in other quarters, resulting in a paper complaining of "the bankruptcy of everyday memory" (Banaji & Crowder, 1989). This led to a lively, although rather unfruitful, controversy, given that it was based on the false assumption that psychologists should limit their research to *either* the laboratory *or* the world beyond. Both approaches are valuable. It is certainly easier to develop and test our theories under controlled laboratory conditions, but if they tell us little or nothing about the way in which memory works in the world outside, they are of distinctly limited value.

In Medieval times, accurate and precise articulation of the words of the church liturgy was more important than the sound of the music, with errors taken very seriously. The demon Titivillus was believed to take time off from his other task of inducing errors in written manuscripts to collect such omissions and slips of the tongue. Each day a thousand bags of such lapses would be conveyed to his master Satan, written in a book of errors and used against the unfortunate cleric on the Day of Judgment. It appears that in due course the level of accuracy improved to a point at which Titivillus was driven to filling his sack with idle gossip from the congregation, a rather menial task for a respectable demon (Zieman, 2008).

elderly, and patients with memory problems. As we will see, these not only demonstrate the robustness and usefulness of cognitive theories, but have also provided ways of testing and enriching the theory. A good case in point is the study of patients with a very dense but pure amnesia, which has told us about the everyday importance of episodic memory, has helped develop tests and rehabilitation techniques for clinical neuropsychologists, and has, at the same time, had a major impact on our theories of memory.

A second major benefit from moving beyond the laboratory comes from a realization that certain very important aspects of memory were not being directly covered by existing theories. Some of these have led to important new theoretical developments. This is the case with the study of semantic memory which, as mentioned earlier, was initially prompted by the attempt of computer scientists to develop programs that could understand language (Collins & Quillian, 1969). Another area of very active research that was driven by a practical need is that of eyewitness testimony, where it became clear that the failures of the judiciary to understand the limitations of human memory were often leading to potentially very serious miscarriages of justice (Loftus, 1979). Other areas have developed as a result of identifying practical problems that have failed to be addressed by theory. A good example of this is prospective memory, remembering to do things. This use of memory is of great practical importance, but for many years was neglected because it reflects a complex interaction between attention and memory. These broader topics are covered in the latter part of the book, which will illustrate the now widely accepted view that theoretical and practical approaches to memory are allies and not rivals.

The contribution of neuroscience

Both the Ebbinghaus and Bartlett approaches to the study of memory were based on the psychological study of memory performance in normal individuals. In recent years, however, this approach has increasingly been enriched by data from neuroscience, looking

In general, attempts to generalize our theories have worked well, and have in turn enriched theory. One important application of theory is to the memory performance of particular groups such as children, the at the contribution of the brain to our capacity to learn and remember. Throughout this book, you will come across cases in which the study of memory disorders in patients has thrown light on the normal functioning of human memory. In particular, the problems faced by patients with memory problems can often tell us about the function that our memories serve, and how they can be further investigated. Recent years have seen a rapid development of methods that allow the neuroscientist to observe and record the operation of the brain in healthy people both at rest and while performing complex activities, including those involved in learning and remembering. These will be discussed in the next chapter.

SUMMARY

- Although we complain about our memories, they are remarkably efficient and flexible in storing the information we need and discarding what is less important.
- Many of our memory lapses result from this important need to forget nonessentials, if we are to remember efficiently.
- The study of memory began with Ebbinghaus, who greatly simplified the experimental situation, creating a carefully constrained approach that continued in North America into the 20th century.
- Alternative traditions developed in Germany, where the study of perception influenced the way in which Gestalt psychologists thought about memory, and in Britain, where Bartlett used a richer and more open approach to memory.
- During the 1950s and 1960s, these ideas, influenced further by the development of the computer, resulted in an approach that became known as cognitive psychology.
- In the case of memory, this emphasized the need to distinguish between encoding or input into memory, memory storage, and memory retrieval, and to the proposal to divide memory into three broad types, sensory memory, short-term memory, and long-term memory.
- The information-processing model is very well illustrated in Sperling's model of visual sensory memory, in which the various stages were ingeniously separated and analyzed.
- These were assumed to lead into a temporary *short-term* or *working memory*. This was initially thought to be largely verbal in nature but other modalities were subsequently shown to be capable of temporary storage.
- The short-term memory system was assumed to feed information into and out of long-term memory.
- Long-term memory was further subdivided into *explicit* or declarative memory, and *implicit* or nondeclarative memory.
- Explicit memory was further divided into two types: The capacity to recollect individual experiences, allowing "mental time travel," became known as *episodic memory*, whereas our stored knowledge of the world was termed *semantic memory*.
- A range of implicit or nondeclarative learning and memory systems were identified, including classical conditioning, the acquisition of motor skills, and various types of priming.
- An important development in recent years has been the increased interest in extending theory beyond the laboratory.
- However, this has led to controversy—it is clear that we need the laboratory to refine and develop our theories, but that we also need to move outside the laboratory to investigate their generality and practical importance.

POINTS FOR DISCUSSION

1 What are the strengths and weaknesses of the approach to memory taken by Ebbinghaus and Bartlett?
2 How did the cognitive approach to memory build on these foundations?
3 Do we need to assume more than one kind of memory? If so, why?

FURTHER READING

Banaji, M. R., & Crowder, R. G. (1989). The bankruptcy of everyday memory. *American Psychologist, 44*, 1185–1193. A reply to Niesser's challenge.

Craik, K. J. W. (1943). *The nature of explanation*. London: Cambridge University Press. A short but seminal book in cognitive psychology presenting the case for using models to embody theories, an approach that underpins the subsequent cognitive revolution.

Neisser, U. (1978). Memory: What are the important questions? In M. M. Gruneberg, P. E. Morris, & R. N. Sykes (Eds.), *Practical aspects of memory*. London: Academic Press. An influential paper in the movement to study everyday memory.

Rabbitt, P. (2008). *Inside psychology: A science over 50 years*. New York: Oxford University Press. A series of personal views of the recent history of psychology from individuals who have been involved in a wide range of areas, including memory.

Roediger, H. L., Dudai, Y., & Fitzpatrick, S. M. (2007). *Science of memory: Concepts*. Oxford: Oxford University Press. The proceedings of a conference at which leading figures in learning and memory were invited to summarize their interpretation of the basic concepts underlying the field, and to present their own views. Because available space was limited, this provides a very economical way of accessing current expert views concerning both the psychology and neuroscience of learning and memory.

Sperling, G. (1963). A model for visual memory tasks. *Human Factors, 5*, 19–31. A very good example of the application of the information-processing approach to the study of sensory memory.

REFERENCES

Atkinson, R. C., & Shiffrin, R. M. (1968). Human memory: A proposed system and its control processes. In K. W. Spence & J. T. Spence (Eds.), *The psychology of learning and motivation: Advances in research and theory* (Vol. 2, pp. 89–195). New York: Academic Press.

Averbach, E., & Sperling, G. (1961). Short-term storage of information in vision. In C. Cherry (Ed.), *Information theory* (pp. 196–211). London: Butterworth.

Baddeley, A. D. (2007). *Working memory, thought and action*. Oxford: Oxford University Press.

Baddeley, A. D. (in press). On trying to prove Endel Tulving wrong: A revised modal model of amnesia. *Neuropsychologia*.

Baddeley, A. D., & Larsen, J. D. (2007). The phonological loop unmasked? A comment on the evidence for a "perceptual-gestural" alternative. *Quarterly Journal of Experimental Psychology, 60*, 497–504.

Banaji, M. R., & Crowder, R. G. (1989). The bankruptcy of everyday memory. *American Psychologist, 44*, 1185–1193.

Bartlett, F. C. (1932). *Remembering*. Cambridge: Cambridge University Press.

Broadbent, D. E. (1958). *Perception and communication*. London: Pergamon Press.

Brooks, D. N., & Baddeley, A. D. (1976). What can amnesic patients learn? *Neuropsychologia, 14*, 111–122.

Cohen, N. J., & Squire, L. R. (1980). Preserved learning and retention of pattern-analyzing skill in amnesia: Dissociation of knowing how and knowing that. *Science, 210*, 207–210.

Collins, A. M., & Quillian, M. R. (1969). Retrieval time from semantic memory. *Journal of Verbal Learning and Verbal Behavior, 8*, 432–438.

Craik, K. J. W. (1943). *The nature of explanation*. London: Cambridge University Press.

Crowder, R. G. (1971). Waiting for the stimulus suffix: Decay, delay, rhythm, and readout in immediate memory. *Quarterly Journal of Experimental Psychology, 23*, 324–340.

Crowder, R. G. (1972). Visual and auditory memory. In J. F. Kavanagh & I. G. Mattingly (Eds.), *Language by ear and by eye: The relationship between speech and learning to read*. Cambridge, MA: MIT Press.

Crowder, R. G., & Morton, J. (1969). Precategorical acoustic storage (PAS). *Perception and Psychophysics, 5*, 365–373.

Ebbinghaus, H. (1885). *Über das Gedächtnis*. Leipzig: Dunker.

Gruneberg, M. M., Morris, P. E., & Sykes, R. N. (1978). *Practical aspects of memory*. London: Academic Press.

Hull, C. L. (1943). *The principles of behaviour*. New York: Appleton-Century.

Jones, D., Hughes, R. W., & Macken, W. J. (2006). Perceptual organization masquerading as phonological storage: Further support for a perceptual-gestural view of short-term memory. *Journal of Memory and Language, 54*, 265–281.

Loftus, E. F. (1979). *Eyewitness testimony*. Cambridge, MA: Harvard University Press.

McGeoch, J. A., & Irion, A. L. (1952). *The psychology of human learning*. New York: Longmans.

Mezaris, V., Niederee, C., & Logie, R. (Eds.). (in press). *Personal multimedia preservation: Remembering or forgetting images and video*. Springer.

Miyake, A., & Shah, P. (Eds.). (1999). *Models of working memory: Mechanisms of active maintenance and executive control*. New York: Cambridge University Press.

Murdock Jr., B. B. (1967). Auditory and visual stores in short-term memory. *Acta Psychologica, 27*, 316–324.

Nairne, J. S. (1990). A feature model of immediate memory. *Memory & Cognition, 18*, 251–269.

Nairne, J. S. (2002). Remembering over the short-term: The case against the standard model. *Annual Review of Psychology, 53*, 53–81.

Neath, I., & Surprenant, A. (2003). *Human memory: An introduction to research, data and theory* (2nd ed.). Belmont, CA: Wadsworth.

Neisser, U. (1967). *Cognitive psychology*. New York: Appleton-Century Crofts.

Neisser, U. (1978). Memory: What are the important questions? In M. M. Gruneberg, P. E. Morris, & R. N. Sykes (Eds.), *Practical aspects of memory*. London: Academic Press.

Schacter, D. L. (2001). *The seven sins of memory: How the mind forgets and remembers*. New York: Houghton-Mifflin.

Sperling, G. (1960). The information available in brief visual presentations. *Psychological Monographs: General and Applied, 74*, 1–29.

Sperling, G. (1963). A model for visual memory tasks. *Human Factors, 5*, 19–31.

Squire, L. R. (1992). Declarative and nondeclarative memory: Multiple brain systems supporting learning and memory. *Journal of Cognitive Neuroscience, 4*, 232–243.

Tolman, E. C. (1948). Cognitive maps in rats and men. *Psychological Review, 55*, 189–208.

Tulving, E. (1972). Episodic and semantic memory. In E. Tulving & W. Donaldson (Eds.), *Organization of memory* (pp. 381–403). New York: Academic Press.

Tulving, E. (2002). Episodic memory: From mind to brain. *Annual Review of Psychology, 53*, 1–25.

Turvey, M. T. (1973). On peripheral and central processes in vision: Inferences from an information processing analysis of masking with patterned stimuli. *Psychological Review, 80*, 1–52.

Walter, W. G. (1953). *The living brain*. London: Norton.

Warrington, E. K., & Weiskrantz, L. (1968). New method of testing long-term retention with special reference to amnesic patients. *Nature, 217*, 972–974.

Weiner, N. (1950). *The human use of human beings*. Boston: Houghton Mifflin.

Weiskrantz, L., & Warrington, E. K. (1979). Conditioning in amnesic patients. *Neuropsychologia, 8*, 281–288.

Wilson, B. A., Baddeley, A. D., & Kapur, N. (1995). Dense amnesia in a professional musician following Herpes Simplex Virus Encephalitis. *Journal of Clinical and Experimental Neuropsychology, 17*, 668–681.

Zieman, K. (2008). *Singing the new song: Literacy and liturgy in late medieval England*. Philadelphia, PA: University of Pennsylvania Press.

Contents

Alan Baddeley

While our main focus will be on the psychology of memory, as knowledge of the field develops, it becomes increasingly possible to link psychological concepts, methods, and findings to efforts towards understanding the biological basis of memory (see Box 2.1). Note that this is not a case of simple reductionism; knowing that a particular area of the brain is involved with a given memory function, for example, does not constitute an explanation, but does provide an additional source of evidence that may be useful in further developing a psychological explanation, in addition of course to the separate but related issue of understanding how the brain works. We will be referring to such evidence throughout the following chapters, and for that reason it is important to understand something of the methods that are currently used to study the relationship between memory and the brain. We will begin with one of the most established methods, neuropsychology, going on to discuss the rapidly developing field of brain imaging, concluding with a brief account of the more basic biological approaches that go beyond systems neuroscience to study the neurobiological basis of memory, and of its potential genetic control, areas that have so far had relatively little impact at the psychological level, but which may in the future prove to be of considerable importance.

NEUROPSYCHOLOGICAL APPROACHES

Patients who suffer brain damage often have memory problems, with the nature of the problem often being associated to a greater or lesser degree with the cause and anatomical location of the damage (see Chapter 16).

Group studies: This approach involves selecting patients whose damage is broadly associated with a specific disease or cause, for example the traumatic brain injury (TBI) that might result from a blow on the head in a traffic accident. This approach is clinically important in providing an overview of the condition necessary for treating patients and in prognosis for recovery, but may be difficult to interpret theoretically. Typically the more severe the accident, for example, the longer the period of unconsciousness or coma, the greater memory disturbance and the poorer the chance of good recovery. However, in addition to memory deficits such patients will typically have other problems, particularly

> **KEY TERM**
>
> **Traumatic brain injury (TBI):** Caused by a blow or jolt to the head, or by a penetrating head injury. Normal brain function is disrupted. Severity ranges from "mild" (brief change in mental status or consciousness) to "severe" (extended period of unconsciousness or amnesia after the injury).

Box 2.1 The biological basis of memory

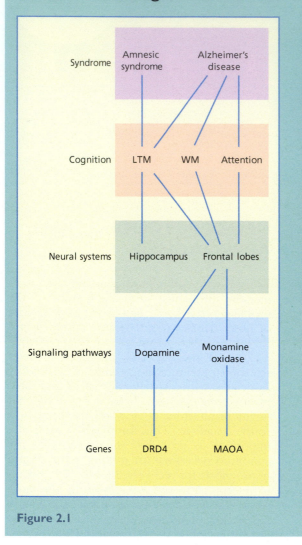

The psychology of memory and its dysfunction can be studied at a range of levels. These include its reflection in memory disorders which can then be mapped onto cognitive psychology. This in turn can be analyzed in terms of the neural systems underpinning cognition, together with their representation in different areas of the brain. Such systems themselves depend on neurochemically modulated signaling pathways that transmit information between the systems in ways that are themselves dependent on activity at the gene level. Adjacent levels of explanation tend to interact. Our own focus is at the cognitive level, but evidence from both syndromes and neural systems will be used in developing and evaluating both theory and practice.

Based on Poldrack et al. (2011).

Figure 2.1

attentional, making it difficult to separate the memory deficits from other factors. Hence, although TBI is an area of considerable practical importance, it does not lead to clear theoretical conclusions about the nature of memory.

More informative are diseases such as alcoholic Korsakoff syndrome, a result of drinking too much and eating too little, in which memory deficits are particularly prominent, while other cognitive functions can be relatively preserved. Even here, however,

most patients will show other deficits including subtle deficits of attentional control,

KEY TERM

Alcoholic Korsakoff syndrome: Patients have difficulty learning new information, although events from the past are recalled. There is a tendency to invent material to fill memory blanks. Most common cause is alcoholism, especially when this has resulted in a deficiency of vitamin B1.

again making clear theoretical interpretation difficult; does the patient have a problem of memory, or attention, or both? Most informative are the rare cases in which the brain damage appears to disrupt a single isolated function such as episodic memory, while intelligence, attention, perception, and language capacities are all preserved. The classic case of amnesia is that of Henry Molaison, known by his initials HM.

Box 2.2 HM

The most theoretically influential neuropsychological case ever was that of HM, a young man with temporal lobe epilepsy. In a successful attempt to reduce his seizures, areas of his brain associated with the left and right hippocampus were surgically removed. Unfortunately, HM then became densely amnesic. His capacity to acquire new information was severely limited, as was the case with Clive Wearing discussed earlier. Unlike Clive, however, HM's deficits were principally limited to episodic long-term memory. His digit span was normal, his intelligence was unimpaired, as was his language capacity but his LTM was grossly disrupted. He was unable to remember experiences for more than a few minutes, performed very badly on standard visual and verbal memory tests, failed to learn the names or faces of new people or indeed new presidents and to learn where things were kept when he moved to a new home. HM's case had a major influence on two aspects of memory. Neurosurgically he demonstrated the practical importance of anatomical location, stimulating extensive later work on brain–behavior relationship. Psychologically his case supported a separation of functions, between memory and intelligence and between long- and short-term memory.

When Henry died in 2008 at the age of 82, his importance was recognized worldwide by extensive obituaries, together with a book-length account of his life and its contributions to the science of memory (Corkin, 2013).

Henry Molaison, aged 60, at MIT in 1986. As a patient, Henry Molaison (HM) made a major contribution to our understanding of memory. Photograph and copyright: Jenni Ogden, author of *Trouble In Mind: Stories from a Neuropsychologist's Casebook.* New York: Oxford University Press, 2012.

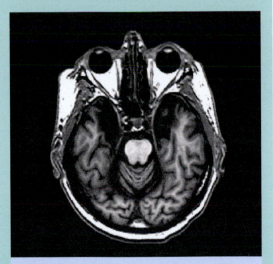

MRI images taken in 1992 of HM's brain. The light gray areas represent preserved brain structure and the dark areas an absence of brain tissue.

HM's case was important in demonstrating that episodic LTM is separable from other cognitive capacities, including STM (Corkin, 2013). Such separation is known as a *dissociation* since the specified deficit is separate or dissociated from deficits in other cognitive functions. As such it is considerably more theoretically powerful than a simple correlation whereby a deficit may just be a general consequence of degree of brain damage. Such rare single cases are informative, but need subsequently to be supported by other similar cases, and by coherence with what we already know of normal memory, before strong theoretical conclusions can be drawn. Such support rapidly accumulated in the case for HM (e.g., Baddeley & Warrington, 1970), but even so there is always a nagging fear that perhaps those tests that are impaired are simply harder or more open to disruption than those preserved. Perhaps preserved tasks such as digit span involving hearing and repeating back a sequence of numbers, are simply easier than learning word lists?

To guard against this it is valuable to have a second type of patient showing exactly the opposite pattern, providing what is known as a double dissociation. In the case of the amnesic syndrome, this was provided by the discovery of a class of patient who had apparently normal LTM together with grossly disrupted STM (Shallice & Warrington, 1970). Such patients did not appear to be amnesic and could learn lists of words, but had a memory span of two rather than six digits. This pattern could not easily be explained in terms of the greater difficulty or vulnerability of one of the types of task. Even a double dissociation is not a perfect design, however, since it is possible that more than two systems are involved.

As we shall see, such single cases have been extremely important in developing memory theory. They are however a very limited resource, for two reasons. First, because they are rare; most brain damage affects more than one system producing complex and variable deficits. The second problem concerns the increasing complexity of the models of memory that have emerged as study has advanced. While a double dissociation between two systems is desirable and possible, a three-component explanation would logically require a triple dissociation, and a four-component explanation a quadruple dissociation, becoming quite impracticable. At this point it is necessary to rely on a method known as *converging operations*. This involves carrying out a whole series of experiments using different methods and different participant groups, all focused on the same theoretical question. The hope is that although each single experiment is likely to be open to interpretation in more than one way, only one explanation will be able to explain all the results. This is the approach taken to a subsystem such as the phonological loop in working memory discussed in Chapter 4.

Neuropsychology has a further limitation. It requires access to patients, by no means easily achieved in the UK at least. It then needs the skills of a neuropsychologist with a keen eye for theoretically interesting patients, together with access to the experimental and conceptual tools necessary to bring out the significance of the findings. The substantial growth in the number of studies on memory and the brain in recent years has therefore not come principally from the study of such rare patients, but from the development of methods of studying the intact brains of healthy people.

KEY TERM

Double dissociation: A term particularly used in neuropsychology when two patient groups show opposite patterns of deficit, e.g., normal STM and impaired LTM, versus normal LTM and impaired STM.

OBSERVING THE BRAIN

Structural imaging

For many centuries, our knowledge of the structure of the brain was based on post-mortem evidence. It became possible to observe the structure of living patients with the development of the X-ray based technique known as *computerised tomography* (CT). This involves rotating an X-ray tube around the patient's head, providing multiple viewpoints of the brain which are then fed into a computer that creates a three-dimensional representation of the person's brain. This method is still used clinically, but for research purposes it has largely been replaced by mag-netic resonance imaging (MRI).

MRI involves placing the person's head in a strong magnetic field. The scanner emits radio waves in a series of brief pulses of different frequency. These are absorbed by the brain, which, when the field is turned off, release the absorbed energy. The absorption characteristics of the brain's gray matter (neuronal cell bodies), differ between white matter (axons linking different brain areas) and cerebro-spinal fluid which fills the ventri-cle. These comprise hollow chambers in the brain that carry away waste metabolites and also provide protective cushioning for the brain. MRI allows a three-dimensional image to be created that differentiates these aspects of brain structure. The spatial resolution of the resulting image depends upon the strength of the magnet. A typical clinical scanner would have a field strength of 3 Tesla, although scanners with field strengths of up to 7 Tesla are beginning to be available, allowing much finer spatial resolution.

MRI has the advantage over CT in that it does not involve radiation, and gives much more precise images. By varying the fre-quency of the radio pulse, MRI can be used to emphasise different aspects of brain struc-ture, for example gray matter versus white matter. An example from the brain of patient HM is shown in Box 2.2.

An increasingly important aspect of MRI is the technique known as *diffusion tensor imaging* (DTI). This takes advantage of the

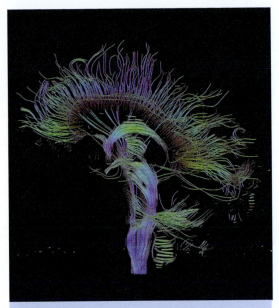

Visualization of a DTI measurement of a human brain. Depicted are reconstructed fiber tracts that run through the mid-sagittal plane.

fact that the myelin sheaths that surround the white matter fiber tracts connecting different areas of the brain are relatively fatty, causing the water within to flow along that fiber. This approach, sometimes known at *tractography*, allows the mapping of the important white matter bundles that transfer information from one area of the brain to another, allow-ing the different areas to coordinate functions across the brain.

Functional imaging: Observing the working brain

While imaging the structure of the brain is obviously important and helpful, from the viewpoint of a psychologist it is much more valuable to be able to observe the brain in action and to relate this to the ongoing mental activity of the participant. Some of the earlier developments here resulted from implanting electrodes in the brains of animals, a method that is clearly of limited application to humans. Exceptions do occur, however; for example, when patients are

KEY TERM

Magnetic resonance imaging (MRI): A method of brain imaging that relies on detecting changes induced by a powerful magnetic field.

undergoing brain surgery to treat intractable epilepsy. The brain itself does not contain pain receptors, and so the patient can remain conscious and report their experiences when different areas are stimulated. Of particular relevance to memory are studies involving the hippocampus. Early reports that this occasionally evoked specific and verifiable episodic memories have proved difficult to replicate; however, recent work suggests that such stimulation may evoke a feeling of déjà vu, a sense of familiarity when confronted with a quite novel complex stimulus event such as hearing someone playing a trumpet. Such an experience could have been interpreted by the patient as a genuine memory (Gloor, 1990; Vignal, Maillard, McGonigal, & Chauvel, 2007).

In addition to stimulation, implanted electrodes can be used to *record* from single cells, a procedure that is proving promising (Rutishauser, Schuman, & Mamelak, 2008). Although recording from implanted electrodes is giving exciting new data, its use is, of course, limited by the fact that it can only ethically be used in a very limited number of patients and is confined to brain areas that are directly relevant to treatment.

Transcranial magnetic stimulation (TMS)

A rather less invasive method of influencing the brain is offered by this method, in which a current is passed through a set of coils held close to the participant's head. This results in a magnetic field which can polarize or depolarize the underlying brain tissue, causing a temporary, hence reversible "lesion" that can then provide evidence for the importance of that area of the brain in the observed cognitive activities. Transcranial magnetic stimulation (TMS) can be delivered either as a single pulse at precise point in processing, for example before stimulus presentation, or used repeatedly, leading to a disruption of that brain area that can last for many minutes. It has the advantage that it allows the experimenter to control the situation, comparing performance with and without stimulation, in contrast to the brain observa-

tion studies we will discuss next. In such cases, unlike TMS, the investigator may observe that a particular area of the brain is activated during a specific task, but that does mean that it is *essential* for that task. TMS, like neuropsychological lesion studies, is able to go beyond this basic correlation between area and task and demonstrate that without this brain area, the task cannot be performed.

Limitations of TMS are that currently it tends to affect a relatively large area with its influence typically limited to areas near the surface of the brain. Furthermore, while in general safe, it can result in discomfort, and occasionally even seizure in susceptible patients. Nevertheless, as methods develop it is likely to continue to play an important role in cognitive neuroscience (see Widhalm & Rose, 2019 for a recent overview).

Transcranial direct current stimulation (tDCS)

Transcranial direct current stimulation (tDCS) is a procedure whereby a low direct current is delivered via electrodes on the skull to selected areas, resulting in a flow of current through the selected area of the brain which may increase or decrease the neuronal excitability of the area stimulated. Anodal stimulation with a positive voltage increases neuronal excitability, cathodal stimulation with a negative voltage reduces neuronal excitability, while sham stimulation which

---

KEY TERM

Transcranial magnetic stimulation (TMS): A technique in which magnetic pulses briefly disrupt the functioning of a given brain area; administration of several pulses in rapid succession is known as repetitive transcranial stimulation (rTMS).

Transcranial direct current stimulation (tDCS): A procedure whereby a low direct current is delivered via electrodes on the skull to selected areas, resulting in a flow of current through the selected area of the brain which may increase or decrease the neuronal excitability of the area stimulated.

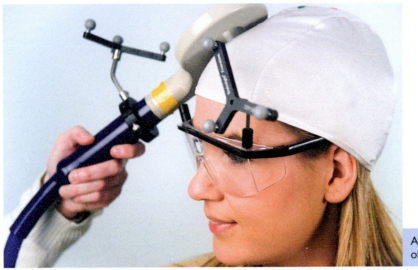

A woman undergoing TMS of the brain.

emits a brief initial current that remains off for the remainder of the stimulation time may be used as a control condition. There is some evidence that it may reduce depression (Mutz et al., 2019), and a number of studies have claimed that it may be used for cognitive enhancement (Chill, Fitzgerald, & Hoy, 2016), although the evidence from this has been questioned (Horvath, Forte, & Carter, 2015). This approach has not currently had a major effect on our understanding of human memory.

Electro-encephalography (EEG)

This much more widely applicable method involves recording the ongoing electrical activity of the human brain. It is noninvasive and involves picking up the electrical activity of the person's brain through an array of electrodes on the scalp. This process records fluctuating voltages across the brain, ranging in frequency from a few cycles to 70 cycles per second or more. Electro-encephalography (EEG) is used clinically to detect epileptic foci that may result in seizures; it also plays an important role in studying sleep, with the various stages of sleep being identified with different frequency bands. EEG has been widely used to study cognitive function, for example showing a different pattern of activation when particip-

ants in a memory experiment are actively remembering or recollecting an experience as opposed to merely finding it familiar (see Chapter 8). However, EEG reflects a complex pattern of activation across the whole brain, and it may be hard to identify the contribution to this overall pattern that is associated with the performance of particular processes or a specific area. It does however have one major advantage over many methods of imaging the brain, that of temporal specificity, providing a more precise way of evaluating the brain's response to specific cognitive activities through event-related potentials (ERPs). These are obtained by time-linking an event to a specific component of the EEG. This involves precise timing, allowing each stage of performance of a task to be linked to the EEG activation at that specific moment. This can allow the effects of cognitive processing to be monitored

KEY TERM

Electro-encephalography (EEG): A system for recording the electrical potentials of the brain through a series of electrodes placed on the scalp.

Event-related potentials (ERPs): The pattern of electroencephalograph (EEG) activity obtained by averaging the brain responses to the same stimulus (or similar stimuli) presented repeatedly.

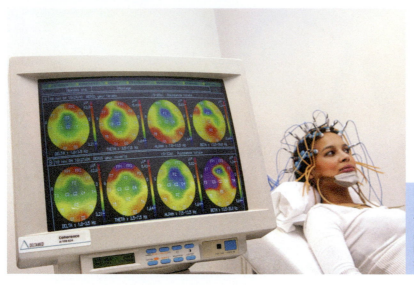

Electrophysiological recording of brain activity. The images on the screen show the distribution of brain activity across successive time periods.

over a period of milliseconds, hence providing a picture of the way in which the brain reacts to that specific event. Such ERP signals tend however to be weaker than the background EEG within which they are embedded, but nevertheless can be extracted by averaging over many repetitions of the same cognitive activity. While the location of evoked response signals is typically not precise, it is possible to identify broad regions of particular activity which may change over time, presumably reflecting the role of different brain areas in the successive processes involved in that particular task.

Magneto-encephalography (MEG)

While EEG and ERP signals reflect the variation in electrical voltage on the surface of the brain, such activity can also be detected by associated changes in *magnetic* activity using a technique known as magneto-encephalography (MEG). This also uses a

range of detectors around the head. It differs from ERP in being most sensitive to activity in the *sulci*, the valleys within the folds of the brain, whereas ERP is more sensitive to the peaks or *gyri*. MEG signals are less subject to distortion from passing through the skull and the electrodes than is the case with ERP. It gives a less complex pattern than ERP, and potentially offers a more precise localisation of its origin within the brain. Although substantially more expensive than ERP, these advantages are resulting in the increasingly wide use of MEG (see Figure 2.2).

BLOOD FLOW BASED MEASURES

Both ERP and MEG measures have good temporal resolution; they allow the tracking of brain activity over periods ranging from milliseconds to seconds, but have poor spatial resolution; it is unclear where the activity originates within the brain. Much more precise localization is possible by using methods that rely on the assumption that when a particular area of the brain is active, this is reflected in its metabolism, usually measured in terms of the amount of oxygen being used by that area.

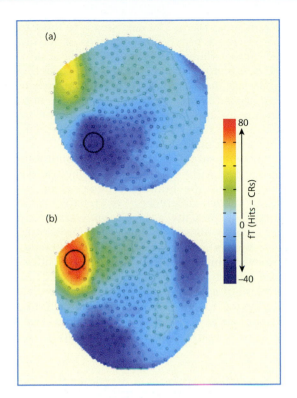

Figure 2.2 MEG reflects the rapidly changing activity of the brain across time. Level of activity is typically mapped by color, with brighter colors reflecting greater activity. The example shown is taken from a study by Horner et al. (2012). The brain activity linked to recognizing that a word had previously been presented is compared to that associated with the capacity to tell whether the given word had been presented together with that particular background. Activity peaked at two separate points. The early pattern shown in (a) peaks at 330 ms and is linked to recognizing words. The lower pattern (b), peaking about 60 ms, later reflects the capacity to link the word to its specific contextual scene. This second component was not found in patients with hippocampal damage. Reprinted from Horner et al. (2012), Copyright © 2012, with permission from Elsevier.

Positron emission tomography (PET)

The first of these methods to be developed was positron emission tomography (PET). This involves injecting a radioactive tracer substance into the blood stream; it is conveyed to the brain, with areas of greater activity demanding greater blood flow leading to more radiation. An array of detectors around the head is then able to pick up such radiation, hence localizing areas of maximum activity. PET was very important during the early years of functional imaging. It has much poorer temporal resolution than ERP and MEG, but is much more spatially specific. A major drawback however is the need for radioactive reagents, potentially dangerous if the same participant is to be scanned repeatedly, and costly, as preparation requires a cyclotron, preferably on-site.

Because of this, PET has largely been replaced as a research tool by *functional magnetic resonance imaging* (fMRI), which also depends on measuring the flow of oxygen within different areas of the brain, and on the assumption that an active area of the brain will utilize more oxygen. The oxygen is carried by haemoglobin. As the oxygen is depleted, the haemoglobin changes its magnetic resonance signal. This can then be picked up by a series of detectors arrayed around the brain, with the pattern of receptor activation being used to locate the various areas in which oxygen is being depleted. This method has the advantage that it is non-invasive since it relies on activities that are already happening within the brain being *externally* detected. Activation can be relatively precisely localized, providing better spatial resolution than PET, especially with more recent equipment containing more powerful magnets. It does however provide relatively poor temporal resolution. The typical response to a stimulus will start 1 or 2 seconds after stimulus presentation, peak at 5–6 seconds, and return to baseline 10–20 seconds later; very much slower than EEG or MEG.

As we shall see, fMRI has already begun to play an important part in the study of human memory, though like all methods it

KEY TERM

Positron emission tomography (PET): A method whereby radioactively labeled substances are introduced into the bloodstream and subsequently monitored to measure physiological activation.

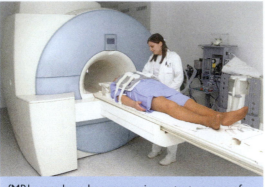

fMRI scans have become an important source of data in psychology. The patient is about to be slid into the machine that will create the magnetic field.

has its limitations. Although less expensive than PET, it is still sufficiently expensive and time-consuming in terms of analysis to make exact replication of studies relatively rare, with investigators tending to move on to the next question rather than checking the robustness of each study, resulting in problems of the reliability of observed results. The pattern of brain areas activated can be relatively large, resembling a mountain range of activation, although this is often simplified to show only the "peaks" (see Figure 2.3). Unfortunately, identifying such peaks will depend on a number of factors. First of all, on the comparison condition. A typical design will involve presenting a task, for example seeing and remembering a sequence of digits, together with a baseline control, for example seeing the digits but not attempting

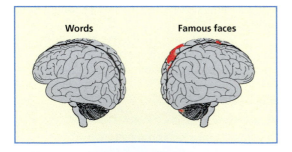

Figure 2.3 Brain regions associated with the remembering of words and famous faces by healthy controls. Reprinted from Simons et al. (2008), Copyright © 2008, with permission from Elsevier.

to remember them. The next step is to look at the difference between the patterns of activation across these two, typically using a *subtraction method* where what is shown is the *difference* in activation between trials when memory is required, and those when it is not. Finding an appropriate baseline condition to subtract is crucial and can be tricky, particularly with complex cognitive activities.

Having subtracted the baseline condition, we are left with a set of adjusted activation levels across the brain. Deciding which of these many differences is reliable and important presents a challenging statistical task whose outcome will depend on setting an appropriate significance level. Having achieved this statistically significant difference pattern, it must then be interpreted. In the case of a cognitive study, this will involve attempting to link the pattern to underlying psychological theory, not always an easy task, or one about which different investigators agree.

Multi-voxel pattern analysis (MVPA)

This and related problems has recently led to the development of a more automatic procedure known as *multi-voxel pattern analysis* (MVPA). A scan will result in a visual representation of the brain that can be divided into an array of tiny spatial areas known as voxels. In standard fMRI, each of these is treated as independent from the rest, hence losing information about any overall pattern resulting from the systematic co-occurrence of different areas of stimulation across the brain. MVPA uses powerful machine-learning techniques to look for cross-voxel regularities that occur in the brain, when the same event is presented repeatedly. Significance levels can be set in advance and the problem of possible experimenter bias reduced. Using this approach, the computer can be used as a pattern classifier, gradually building up a model of the brain's response to a particular type of stimulus, for example a human face or a house. Having acquired this statistical representation, the computer can then analyze new scans in which it can reliably detect whether houses or faces are presented (see Tong & Pratte, 2012 for a review).

Quite dramatic results have been obtained using the method which is sometimes referred to as "mind reading" since it appears to allow the scientist to know just what the participant is thinking. Commercial companies are already being set up claiming to use the method for lie detection (see Box 2.3). It is important to note, however, that it is not lying per se that is being detected, but the cognitive and emotional processes that are associated with lying. An attempt to use this method in an actual court case concluded that the method had not gained widespread acceptance among scientists, that its validity and accuracy had yet to be assessed in real-world settings and hence it should not be accepted as evidence (Shen & Jones, 2011).

THE CELLULAR BASIS OF MEMORY

This is a huge and highly active field, but one that has so far had relatively little impact on the analysis of memory at a cognitive level. Classic work by the Nobel Prize Laureate Eric Kandel used a very simple animal *Aplysia*, a sea slug, to analyze two basic types of learning, *habituation* and *sensitization*. Habituation was studied by repeatedly touching the animal's syphon; this resulted in withdrawal of its gill, a response that decreased systematically over repeated stimulation. The opposite effect, sensitization, occurred when touch was linked to the delivery of shock to the animal's tail, a basic form of classical conditioning as originally demonstrated by Pavlov with dogs. Repeated presentation of the touch-shock pairing can be shown to lead to gene expression, new protein synthesis, and the development of new synaptic connections, all of which are associated with the long-term retention of the enhanced response to touch.

Further research in this area has identified two potential mechanisms of learning, long-term potentiation (LTP) and *long-term depression* (LTD), and whose mechanisms

have been extensively studied at the molecular level, implicating neurotransmitter systems and genes. While this level of biological analysis is likely in the future to have clear implications for the understanding of memory at the cognitive level, and vice versa, it does not yet feature strongly in the chapters that follow.

GENETIC APPROACHES

Sir Francis Galton, a cousin of Charles Darwin, was probably the first to focus attention on the field that has become known as behavioral genetics. He noted that talent in particular areas tended to run in families, the Bach family in music for example, while in the UK a small number of academic families who included the Darwins, Wedgwoods, and Hodgkins appear to have produced a surprisingly large number of talented scientists. Galton was aware of course that the members of such families had much more in common than genes, notably including an environment and social position that was likely to foster their talent and facilitate its further development within society. He noted however that "twins have a special claim upon our attention; it is, that their history affords means of distinguishing between the effects of tendencies received at birth, and those that were imposed by the special circumstances of their after lives" (Galton, 1869).

The basis of twin studies is the comparison between identical twins, who share 100% of their genes, and fraternal twins who on average share only 50%, the same as is likely for any nonidentical sibling. Of course twins are typically brought up together, which means that their environment is also likely to be common. An exception, however, is when twins are separated at birth and

KEY TERM

Long-term potentiation (LTP): A process whereby synaptic transmission becomes more effective following a cell's recent activation.

Box 2.3 Neuroimaging and lie detection

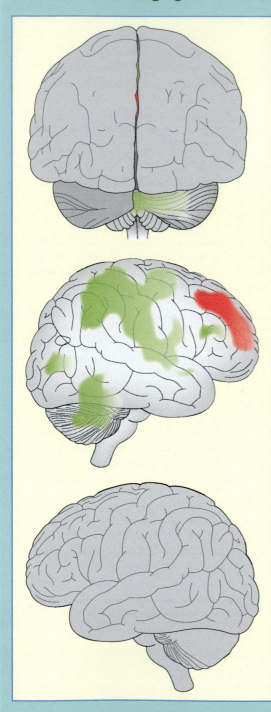

If "mind reading" is possible, could it not be used to tell whether a suspect is lying or not? A number of studies have explored this. In one study (Davatzikos et al., 2005), participants were given an envelope containing two cards, the five of clubs and the seven of spades, followed by a sequence of cards containing both other cards and examples of both. The task was to consistently tell the truth about possession of one of the cards and lie about the other. Brain activation was then recorded and a computer-based pattern analyzer used to identify those areas of the brain consistently accompanying truth and falsehood. The results are shown in Figure 2.4. Using the pattern analyzer, the experimenters were able to detect the instances of lying with over 80% accuracy.

It is important to bear in mind, however, that it is not lying per se that is being detected, but the activation of the certain areas of the brain which reflect a range of cognitive and emotional processes associated with lying. Such processes are likely to occur in other situations, particularly under stress, and in a legal situation may well be evoked in innocent people, emotionally disturbed by the threatening situation even when telling the truth. It is also not clear whether criminals, particularly those with psychopathy, will be equally emotionally aroused while lying. Furthermore, the guilty may be able to subvert the process by covertly engaging in other cognitive activities (Ganis, Rosenfeld, Meixner, Kievit, & Schendan, 2011).

Despite this, private companies are being set up claiming to detect lies using neuroimaging. In 2010, a hearing was held in Tennessee to decide whether fMRI lie detection could be

Figure 2.4 Different 3D views of regions showing relatively higher activity during truth telling (green) or lying (red). Reprinted from Davatzikos et al. (2005), Copyright © 2005, with permission from Elsevier.

(Continued)

(Continued)

accepted as valid scientific evidence. The CEO of one such private company presented evidence of scans which he claimed indicated the innocence of a defendant on a charge of fraud. A neuroscientist and a statistician were asked to comment on the technology, leading the judge to conclude that despite some support by peer-review publications the method was not widely accepted among scientists, had not yet been validated in real-world settings, and that a well-standardized protocol was not currently available, hence ruling out such evidence (Shen & Jones, 2011). A similar note of caution was reached in the UK by a recent committee of the Royal Society concerned with neuroscience and the law. They also noted that if reliable lie detection should become possible, there would be considerable ethical issues as to if and when such measures should be used (Mackintosh, 2011).

brought up within different families; the difference between the performance of fraternal and identical twins on any given function is then used to assess just how much is attributable to genetic and how much to environmental influences.

The whole area of genetic factors has been bedevilled by its association with the eugenics movement, originally driven by the fear in Victorian times that poorer and less intelligent people would have larger families, leading to a gradual degradation of the nation's intelligence. This has proved not to be the case; on the contrary, systematic measures of intelligence across a wide range of tests and countries shows a steady increase extending over many generations, called the Flynn effect after its discoverer (Flynn, 1987). A particular pernicious version of eugenics was developed by the Nazis in Germany who attempted to "purify" the population by encouraging the breeding of those who most resembled an invented racial type, the blond Aryans, coupled with the mass slaughter of those with "undesirable" genes such as Jews, gypsies, and the mentally handicapped. A milder echo of this issue arose in the US during the 20th century in connection with average differences in performance on standard intelligence tests between different races who do of course tend to grow up in radically different physical and social environments (see Neisser et al., 1996 for an extensive discussion).

Interest in genetics has grown substantially following the discovery some 50 years ago by Crick and Watson of the structure of the human genome, a structure that contains the genes that determine the way in which all organisms develop. This led to a huge effort focused on reading the genome, together with a growing interest in studies concerning the genetic basis of many aspects of life, including behavior. It had been known for many years that some diseases are genetically based. In some cases such as Huntington's Disease this was obvious because of the way in which it afflicted certain families, functioning as would be predicted by what was already known from earlier genetic studies. Other cases such as Down syndrome also proved to be *genetic* in the sense that they reflect chromosomal damage but *sporadic* in the sense that there is no evidence that it runs in families. Other diseases such as Alzheimer's are typically sporadic and probably not genetically determined, but can occasionally be found in a genetic form in which half the members of the family possess a gene leading them to succumb to the disease at an early age (see Chapter 16, p. 510).

However, although family and twin studies continue to provide valuable insights, much of the work on behavioral genetics comes from large population studies, typically measuring a range of psychological and behavioral measures and attempting to relate them to specific genes. This has tended to cause excitement in the press when a study appears to reveal "the gene for X," where X can be anything from intelligence to homosexuality. It is, however, proving increasingly clear that most complex behavior is dependent on many genes, each of which interacts with the environment, which may cause the relevant gene to be "switched on" only in specific circumstances. The study of gene–environment interaction, *epigenetics*, is clearly an area of great future importance, but one that is likely to require further methodological development before its full promise is realized.

SUMMARY

- A range of methods are increasingly able to link the psychological study of memory with the brain systems that underpin it (see Table 2.1).
- Among the earliest approaches are those based on the study of patients with memory deficits resulting from brain damage.
- Rare single cases with a very specific deficit are particularly informative theoretically, but group studies are of considerable practical importance.
- Patient-based approaches are supplemented by a range of methods of observing the structure of the healthy brain.
- Approaches began with *computerized tomography* (CT) relying on X-rays.
- This was followed by *magnetic resonance imaging* (MRI) which relies on the fact that different structures within the brain differ in their response to the energy produced by a surrounding magnetic field.
- In an extension of MRI, *diffusion tensor imaging* (DTI) is able to image the white matter tracts that connect different areas of the brain.
- A range of methods allow us to observe the working brain in real time. They include:
  - Stimulation by *implanted electrodes*, and *transcranial magnetic stimulation* (TMS). Both allow specific brain functions to be experimentally and temporarily disrupted.
  - *Electro-encephalography* (EEG) reflects the ongoing electrical activity of the brain and its response to specific stimuli, through *event-related potentials* (ERPs).
  - A more recent electrophysiological development is that of *magneto-encephalography* (MEG) which relies on the magnetic activity of the brain.
- A number of measures have developed for studying the activity of the brain through blood flow. These include:
  - *Positron emission tomography* (PET) which depends on injecting and then detecting a radioactive tracer within the blood. The need for radio activity is a problem, resulting in the development of noninvasive research methods.
  - *Functional magnetic resonance imaging* (fMRI) also depends on imaging blood flow in areas of the brain assumed to be activated by psychological processes, but is noninvasive, relying on picking up the tiny magnetic forces generated in the brain.
  - *Multi-voxel pattern analysis* (MVPA) uses a powerful statistical technique to identify patterns of activity associated with specific cognitive activities.
- Studies at the cellular level although of crucial basic importance have so far not connected strongly with the psychology of memory.
- Genetic studies are also promising but not yet influential in the memory field.

TABLE 2.1 Main sources of evidence regarding psychology of memory and the brain

Technique	Main advantages	Main disadvantages
Patient studies	Occur naturally. Can potentially strongly implicate a particular brain area.	Usually complex and varied in extent and location. Do not identify specific networks or temporal resolution. Patients may be rare and effects may change during recovery.
Transcranial magnetic stimulation (TMS)	Can implicate specific brain regions. Is reversible. Relatively inexpensive. Some temporal specificity.	Spatial resolution limited. Confined to surface of the cortex. Discomfort and some safety concerns.
Electroencephalography (EEG)	Rapid and inexpensive. Good temporal resolution. Noninvasive.	Poor spatial resolution. Not clearly specific to cognitive function.
Event-related potentials (ERPs)	Fast and inexpensive. High temporal resolution. Noninvasive.	Poor spatial resolution. May be hard to separate influence of different components. Correlational; may be present but not essential to a task.
Magneto-encephalography (MEG)	High temporal resolution. Noninvasive. Better localization than ERP.	Limited spatial localization. Relatively expensive. Susceptible to interfering noise. Correlational.
Positron emission tomography (PET)	Good spatial resolution. Can identify network of regions.	Very poor temporal resolution. Invasive, needs radioactive injection. Expensive, needs cyclotron. Indirect, relies on assumptions about blood flow. Correlational.
Functioning magnetic resonance imaging (fMRI)	Good spatial resolution. Reasonably good temporal resolution. Can identify networks. Noninvasive but relatively expensive.	Temporal resolution fairly low (seconds). Depends on indirect measure of blood flow. Correlational.

FURTHER READING

Gluck, M. A., Mercado, E., & Myers, C. E. (2014). *Learning and memory: From brain to behavior* (2nd edn.). New York: Worth. Complements our own approach to memory by providing a brain-based analysis.

Kolb, B., & Wishaw, I. Q. (2014). *An introduction to brain and behavior* (4th edn.). New York: Worth. Again takes a brain-based approach, with a somewhat greater emphasis on evidence from patients.

Ward, J. (2010). *The student's guide to cognitive neuroscience* (2nd edn.). Hove, UK: Psychology Press. Provides a broad and readable account of the ways in which cognition can be investigated using the rapidly developing methods of neuroscience.

Widhalm, M. L., & Rose, N. S. (2019). How can transcranial magnetic stimulation be used to causally manipulate memory representations in the human brain? *Wiley interdisciplinary reviews. Cognitive Psychology, 10,* e1469. doi:10.1002/wcs.1469. Provides an up-to-date overview of a range of methods using brain stimulation techniques.

REFERENCES

Baddeley, A. D., & Warrington, E. K. (1970). Amnesia and the distinction between long- and short-term memory. *Journal of Verbal Learning and Verbal Behavior, 9,* 176–189.

Chill, A. T., Fitzgerald, P. B., & Hoy, K. E. (2016). Effects of anodal transcranial direct current stimulation on working memory: A systematic review and meta-analysis of findings from healthy and neuropsychiatric patients. *Brain Stimulation, 9,* 197–208.

Corkin, S. (2013). *Permanent present tense: The man with no memory and what he taught the world.* New York: Basic Books.

Davatzikos, C., Ruparel, K., Fan, Y., Shen, D. G., Acharyya, M., Loughead, J. W. et al. (2005). Classifying spatial patterns of brain activity with machine learning methods: Application to lie detection. *NeuroImage, 28,* 663–668.

Flynn, J. R. (1987). Massive IQ gains in 14 nations: What IQ tests really measure. *Psychological Bulletin, 101,* 171–191.

Galton, F. (1869). *Hereditary genius.* London: Macmillan.

Ganis, G., Rosenfeld, J. P., Meixner, J., Kievit, R. A., & Schendan, H. E. (2011). Lying in the scanner: Covert countermeasures disrupt deception detection by functional magnetic resonance imaging. *NeuroImage, 55,* 312–319.

Gloor, P. (1990). Experiential phenomena of temporal lobe epilepsy: Facts and hypotheses. *Brain, 113*, 1673–1694.

Horner, A. J., Gadian, D. G., Fuentemilla, L., Jentschke, S., Vargha-Khadem, F., & Duzel, E. (2012). A rapid, hippocampus-dependent, item memory signal that initiates context memory in humans. *Current Biology, 22*, 2369–2374.

Horvath, J., Forte, J., & Carter, O. (2015). Evidence that transcranial direct current stimulation (tDCS) generates little-to-no reliable neurophysiologic effect beyond MEP amplitude modulation in healthy human subjects: A systematic review. *Neuropsychologia, 66*, 213–236.

Mackintosh, N. (2011). *Brain waves 4: Neuroscience and the law*. London: The Royal Society.

Mutz, A., Vigeinika, V., Carter, B., Hurlemann, R., Fu, C. H. Y., & Young, A. H. (2019). Comparative efficacy and acceptability of non-surgical brain stimulation for the acute treatment of major depressive episodes in adults: Systematic review and network meta-analysis. *British Medical Journal, 364*, 1079. doi:10.1136/bmj.l1079

Neisser, U., Boodoo, G., Bouchard, T. J., Boykin, A. W., Brody, N., Ceci, S. J., ... Urbina, S. (1996). Intelligence: Knowns and unknowns. *American Psychologist, 51*, 77. doi:10.1037/0003–066X.51.2.77

Poldrack, R. A., Kittur, A., Kalar, D., Miller, E., Seppa, C., Gil, Y., et al. (2011). The cognitive atlas: Toward a knowledge foundation for cognitive neuroscience. *Frontiers in Neuroinformatics, 5*, 17.

Rutishauser, U., Schuman, E. M., & Mamelak, A. N. (2008). Activity of human hippocampal and amygdala neurons during retrieval of declarative memories. *Proc Natl Acad Sci USA, 105*, 329–334.

Shallice, T., & Warrington, E. K. (1970). Independent functioning of verbal memory stores: A neuropsychological study. *Quarterly Journal of Experimental Psychology, 22*, 261–273.

Shen, F. X., & Jones, O. D. (2011). Brain scans as evidence: Truths, proofs, lies, and lessons. *Mercer Law Review, 62*, 861.

Tong, F., & Pratte, M. S. (2012). Decoding patterns of human brain activity. *Annual Review of Psychology, 63*, 483–509.

Vignal, J. P., Maillard, L., McGonigal, A., & Chauvel, P. (2007). The dreamy state: Hallucinations of autobiographic memory evoked by temporal lobe stimulations and seizures. *Brain, 130*, 88–99.

Widhalm, M. L., & Rose, N. S. (2019). How can transcranial magnetic stimulation be used to causally manipulate memory representations in the human brain? *Wiley interdisciplinary reviews. Cognitive Psychology, 10*, e1469. doi:10.1002/wcs.1469

Contents

CHAPTER 3

SHORT-TERM MEMORY

Alan Baddeley

You are a schoolteacher whose young pupils have been doing an arithmetic exercise. You tell them "Stop. Now put away your exercise books, hand in your pencils and then sit down as I am going to read you a story." Most readily obey but one or two look puzzled. Why? This is because even this apparently simple instruction requires the child to process and then remember the sequence of actions, and some forget. They have difficulty in holding information long enough because they have a particular problem with short-term memory, the system required for retaining small amounts of information over brief delays. In 1887, John Jacobs, a schoolmaster in London, wanted to assess the abilities of his students. He devised an apparently simple test in which the student heard a sequence of digits, like a telephone number, and repeated them back. The measure used was digit span, the longest sequence that could be repeated back without error (Jacobs, 1887). Digit span is still included in the most widely used intelligence test, the Wechsler Adult Intelligence Scale (WAIS). In this basic version, span does not correlate very highly with general intelligence but, as we will see, a somewhat more complex version, working memory span, does an excellent job of predicting a wide range of cognitive skills, including performance on the reasoning tasks often used to assess intelligence.

The digit span test is typically referred to as reflecting *short-term memory* (STM), and the more complex task as working memory span. The terms short-term memory (STM) and working memory (WM) seem often to be used interchangeably, so is there a difference?

SHORT-TERM AND WORKING MEMORY: WHAT'S THE DIFFERENCE?

The term "short-term memory" is a rather slippery one. To the general public, it refers to remembering things over a few hours or days, the sort of capacity that becomes poorer as we get older and is dramatically impaired in patients with Alzheimer's disease. To psychologists, however, these are long-term memory (LTM) problems. Remembering over a few minutes, hours, or a few years all seem to depend on the same long-term memory system.

KEY TERM

Digit span: Maximum number of sequentially presented digits that can reliably be recalled in the correct order.

Working memory span: Term applied to a range of complex memory span tasks in which simultaneous storage and processing is required.

We will use the term *short-term memory* (STM) to refer to performance on a particular type of task, one involving the simple retention of small amounts of information, tested either immediately or after a short delay. The memory system or systems responsible for STM do however form part of the *working memory* system. "Working memory" is the term we will use for a system that not only temporarily stores information but also manipulates it so as to allow people to perform such complex activities as reasoning, learning, and comprehension. Before going on to discuss working memory in the next chapter, we will examine the simpler concept of STM, the capacity to store small amounts of information over brief intervals, beginning with the digit-span task devised by Jacobs.

In contrast to our use of STM as a term to describe an experimental situation, the term *working memory* is based on a theoretical assumption, namely that tasks such as reasoning and learning depend on a system that is capable of temporarily holding and manipulating information, a system that has evolved as a mental work space. A number of different theoretical approaches to working memory have developed, some influenced strongly by the study of attention (e.g., Cowan, 2001), some strongly influenced by studies of individual differences in performance on complex tasks (e.g., Engle & Kane, 2004; Miyake et al., 2000), while others were driven principally by neurophysiological considerations (Goldman-Rakic, 1996). All, however, assume that WM provides a temporary workspace that is necessary for performing complex cognitive activities.

The approach used in the next two chapters reflects a multicomponent account of WM (Baddeley & Hitch, 1974) that was strongly influenced by the experimental and neuropsychological studies of human memory that form the core of the present book. It has proved durable and widely applicable, but should be seen as complementary to a range of other approaches rather than as *the* theory of working memory (Logie, Cowan, & Camos, in press).

Within the multicomponent WM framework, therefore, STM refers to tasks that involve the simple storage of information without a need to manipulate it. However, as we shall see, simple storage proves to be far from simple and certainly makes demands on other aspects of working memory, in particular attentional control. This is particularly the case in the highly active field of visual short-term and working memory as we shall see later in the chapter. The multicomponent model described in Chapter 4 provides a broader overall framework, linking a series of subareas such as visual and verbal STM with perception and LTM at a theoretical level that can readily be applied to a range of problems beyond the psychological laboratory. It offers a broad theoretical map that invites development of more detailed models of specific areas. The rest of this chapter, however, is concerned with the question of how we store limited amounts of verbal or visual information, using relatively simple STM tasks, tasks that will ultimately need to be explained within a broader WM framework.

MEMORY SPAN

Before proceeding, test yourself using Box 3.1.

If your digit span is rather lower than you might hope, don't worry; in this simple form, as we shall see later, it depends on a small but useful aspect of our memory system, not on general intelligence. It is limited to about six or seven digits for most people, although some people can manage up to ten or more, whereas others have difficulty recalling more than four or five. What sets this limit and why does it vary between one person and the next?

Memory span measures require two things: 1) remembering what the *items* are; and 2) remembering the *order* in which they were presented. In the case of the digits one to nine, we already know the items very well, so the test becomes principally one of memory for order. If, however, I were to present you with sequence of digits in an unfamiliar language, Finnish for example, your span would be very much less. You

Box 3.1 Digit span test

Read each sequence as if it were a telephone number, then close your eyes and try to repeat it back. Start with the four-digit numbers and continue until you fail on both sequences at a given length. Your span is one digit less than this.

9 7 5 4
3 8 2 5
6 5 1 4
9 4 3 1 8
6 8 2 5 9
3 8 1 4 7
9 1 3 8 2 5
6 4 8 3 7 1
5 9 6 3 8 2
7 9 5 8 4 2 3
5 3 1 6 8 4 2
7 9 1 8 5 4 6
8 6 9 5 1 3 7 2
5 1 7 3 9 8 2 6
5 1 3 9 8 2 4 7
7 1 9 3 8 4 2 6 1
1 6 3 8 7 4 9 5 2
6 2 5 9 4 3 8 2 6
9 1 5 2 4 3 8 1 6 2
7 1 5 4 8 5 6 1 9 3
1 5 2 8 4 6 7 3 1 8

would of course have much more to remember, as you would need to recall the order of the sounds comprising the Finnish digits, as well the order.

Suppose I were to use words, but not digits, would that matter? Provided I used the same words repeatedly, you would soon become familiar with the set, and would do reasonably well. However, if I were to use a different set of words on each trial it would become somewhat harder as you would again need to remember both what the items were and their order, although this would be easier than for unfamiliar Finnish words.

Suppose we move from numbers to letters; test yourself on the next sequence by reading each letter out loud, then close your eyes and try to repeat it.

C T A I I L T C S F R O

Very hard? Now try the next sequence.

F R A C T O L I S T I C

I assume you found the second sequence easier, even though it used exactly the same letters as the first. The reason is that the order of the letters in the second sequence allowed you to break it up into pronounceable word-like subgroups or *chunks*. In a classic paper, George Miller (1956) suggested that memory capacity is limited not by the number of *items* to be recalled, but by the number of *chunks*. The first sequence comprised 12 apparently unrelated letters, making it hard to reduce the number of chunks much below 12, whereas the second could be pronounced as a string of four pronounceable syllables that, together, made a sequence that, although meaningless, could plausibly be an English word.

Chunking in this case depends on letter sequences that are consistent with long-term language habits, making the important point that LTM can influence STM. Grouping can also be induced by the rhythm with which a sequence of items is presented. Suppose I were to read out nine digits. If I interposed a slightly longer pause between items three and four and items six and seven, recall would be significantly improved. Hence 791–684–352 is easier than 791684352. Pauses in other locations can also be helpful, but grouping in threes seems to be best (Ryan, 1969; Wickelgren, 1964). It seems likely that chunking is taking advantage of cues from prosody, the natural rhythms that occur in speech and that make its meaning clearer by separating into coherent phrases the continuous sequence of sounds that make up the normal speech stream.

KEY TERM

Chunking: The process of combining a number of items into a single chunk typically on the basis of long-term memory.

Although remembering strings of numbers was probably of little interest to Mr Jacobs' students, it has in recent years become much more critical because of the increasing use in our culture of digit and letter sequences, initially as telephone numbers, then as postal codes and subsequently as PINs and passwords. In the early 1960s, Dr R. Conrad was asked by the British Post and Telecommunications Service to investigate the relative advantages and disadvantages of codes based on letters and numbers. One of his experiments involved visually presenting strings of consonants for immediate recall. He noticed an interesting pattern in his results, namely that, despite being presented visually, errors were likely to be similar in *sound* to the item they replaced, hence *P* was more likely to be misremembered as *V* than the more visually similar letter *R* (Conrad, 1964). Conrad and Hull (1964) went on to investigate this effect further, demonstrating that memory for sequences of consonants is substantially poorer when they are similar in sound (e.g., *C P D V G T* versus *K R X L Y F)*. Conrad interpreted his results in terms of a short-term memory store that relies on an acoustic code, which fades rapidly, resulting in forgetting. This was assumed to be particularly disruptive of recall of the acoustically similar letters as they had fewer distinguishing features, making each item more likely to be confused with adjacent items, resulting in errors in order of recall (e.g., *P T C V B* recalled as *P T V C B*).

MODELS OF VERBAL SHORT-TERM MEMORY

By the late 1960s, the evidence seemed to be swinging firmly in the direction of abandoning the attempt to explain STM in terms of a unitary system, in favor of an explanation involving a number of interacting systems, one of which was closely identified with the extensive evidence accumulated from verbal STM. The most influential of these was Atkinson and Shiffrin's model,

sometimes referred to as the "modal model," as it combined much of the progress achieved during the 1960s into a coherent information processing theory. It involves the flow of information from the environment into a series of parallel sensory memory systems, the iconic and echoic systems described in Chapter 1. From here it enters a short-term memory store which also serves as a "working memory" capable of both storing and manipulating material which is then fed into a more durable long-term store. While subsequent development of the model tended to emphasize LTH (see Malmberg, Raaijmakers, & Shiffrin, 2019 for a recent review), for the purpose of the present chapter their concept of a short-term store is more relevant, forming as it did a basis for subsequent approaches to verbal STM, including our own model of verbal STM, and the concept of a *phonological loop* (Baddeley & Hitch, 2019; Baddeley, Hitch, & Allen, 2019) that I will use to tie together the rich body of research that continues to develop in this area, before going on to give a brief account of alternative theories.

The phonological loop

The concept of a phonological loop forms part of the multicomponent working memory model proposed by Baddeley and Hitch (1974). The phonological loop is assumed to have two subcomponents, a short-term store and an articulatory rehearsal process. The store is assumed to be limited in capacity, with items registered as memory traces that decay within a few seconds. However, the traces can be refreshed by subvocal rehearsal, saying the items to yourself, which depends on a vocal or a subvocal articulatory process.

Consider the case of digit span. Why is it limited to six or seven items? If there are few

---

KEY TERM

Phonological loop: Term applied by Baddeley and Hitch to the component of their model responsible for the temporary storage of speechlike information.

digits in the sequence, then you can say them all in less time than it takes for the first digit to fade away. As the number of items increases, total time to rehearse them all will be greater, and hence the chance of items fading before they are refreshed will increase, hence setting a limit to memory span. The loop model is able to account for the following prominent features of verbal STM:

The phonological similarity effect

A major signature of the store is the phonological similarity effect, Conrad's (1964) demonstration that letter span is reduced for similar sounding items.

Is Conrad's discovery based on letters also true for words or does meaning change the pattern of results? Try it for yourself: Read out this sequence of words at a rapid rate, close your eyes and try to recall it, then move on to the next sequence.

pit, day, cow, pen, top

Close your eyes and recall.

How well did you do? Try the next:

mad, can, man, mat, cap

Close your eyes and recall.

I assume you found this set somewhat harder. That suggests that similarity of sound creates problems and is consistent with Conrad's suggestion that STM uses an "acoustic" code. But perhaps any kind of similarity would cause similar confusion?

Try the next one. Ready?

big, wide, large, high, tall

Close your eyes and recall.

How did you do? Rather easier than the *mad can man* set I assume, since that is what we found with our subjects as shown in Figure 3.1.

One final point to this story is that the phonological similarity effect disappears if the lists are increased in length and participants are allowed several learning trials. Under these circumstances, similarity of meaning becomes much more important (Baddeley, 1966). This does not mean that phonological coding is limited to STM, as without phonological LTM we could never learn to pronounce new words. It is however the case that LTM typically gains more from relying on meaning than on sound. We return to this point in Chapter 4.

The phonological similarity effect is assumed to occur at retrieval, when information is read out from the short-term memory trace; similar items have fewer distinguishing features, and hence are likely to be confused. Auditory speech is assumed to feed directly into the phonological store. Visually presented items can also be fed into the store if they are nameable, such as digits, letters, or nameable objects, through a process of vocal or subvocal articulation, whereby you say the items to yourself.

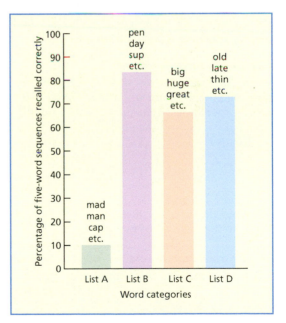

Figure 3.1 The effect of phonological and semantic similarity on immediate serial recall of five-word sequences. Phonological similarity leads to poor immediate recall whereas similarity of meaning has little effect. From Baddeley (1966a). Copyright © Psychology Press.

The subvocal rehearsal system can be blocked if you are required to repeatedly say something unrelated such as the word "the," an activity known as articulatory suppression. Saying "the" means that you are not able to refresh the memory trace by subvocally pronouncing the remembered material. It also prevents you from subvocally naming visually presented items, such as letters, which prevents them from being registered in the phonological store. For that reason, it does not matter whether items are phonologically similar or not, when they are presented visually and accompanied by articulatory suppression. Both similar and dissimilar items will be retained, but at a lower and equivalent level.

However, it is important to note that even when suppressing, while presenting the letters visually, people can still remember up to four or five items. This suggests that although the phonological loop typically plays an important role in digit span, it is not the only basis of span. We will return to this point later. With *auditory* presentation, the words gain direct access to the phonological store despite articulatory suppression, and hence a similarity effect still occurs.

The word length effect

Before moving on we should try just one more small experiment using exactly the same procedure. Remember, read rapidly, close your eyes, and then recall.

Ready?

> *pot, lark, stick, nut, flow*

Close eyes and recall.

How did you do? Pretty well, I suspect. Now try the next set of five words:

> *opportunity, refrigerator, tuberculosis,*
> *university, hippopotamus*

Close eyes and recall.

Did you find the long words harder? As Figure 3.2 shows, people can remember sequences of five dissimilar one-syllable words relatively easily. As word length increases, performance drops from around 90% for five monosyllables to about 50% for lists of five-syllable words. As word length is increased,

the time taken to speak the words also increases (Figure 3.2). This relation between recall and the rate of articulation can be summarized by the statement that people can remember about as many words as they can say in two seconds (Baddeley, Thomson, & Buchanan, 1975).

We explained our findings as follows: Rehearsal takes place in real time, as does trace decay, with the result that longer words, taking longer to say, allow more decay to occur. We thus attributed the word length effect to forgetting during both ongoing subvocal rehearsal and recall. If rehearsal is prevented, then the word length effect should be lost. This can be tested using *articulatory suppression*, requiring participants repeat an irrelevant sound such as the word "the" while performing the memory task. As predicted, this abolishes the word length effect (Baddeley et al., 1975) with people remembering fewer words, but with no difference between span for long and short words, presumably because suppression prevents the visually presented words reaching the articulatory rehearsal process.

The word length effect is extremely robust but its interpretation remains controversial. An alternative to the Baddeley et al. (1975) time-based trace decay interpretation, is the proposal that longer words are more complex and this leads to more interference (e.g., Caplan, Rochon, & Waters, 1992). A third interpretation suggests that long words, having more components to be remembered, are more vulnerable to fragmentation and forgetting (e.g., Neath & Nairne, 1995), although this interpretation has now been abandoned by its earlier proponents (Hulme et al., 2006), in favor of the SIMPLE model described in the section on free recall.

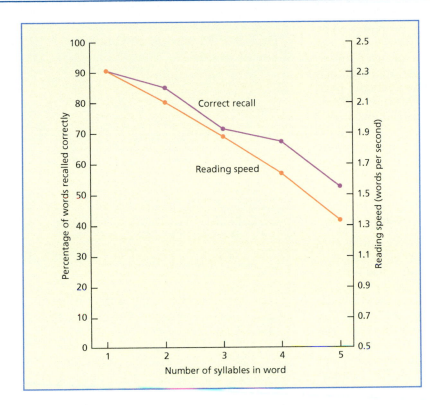

Correct recall

Reading speed

Figure 3.2 The relationship between word length, reading rate, and recall. Long words take longer to rehearse and also produce lower memory spans. From Baddeley, Thomson, and Buchanan (1975). Copyright © Psychology Press.

The precise nature of short-term forgetting remains controversial, in particular whether forgetting results from trace decay (e.g., Barrouillet & Camos, 2014) or some form of interference (e.g., Lewandowsky & Oberauer, 2009), but the basic phonological loop framework within which short-term forgetting occurs remains robust (Baddeley & Hitch, 2019).

Irrelevant sound effects

Students often claim that they work better to a background of their favorite music or radio program. Are they right? In 1976, Colle and Welsh showed that STM for sequences of visually presented digits was impaired when participants were required to ignore speech even though the speech was in an unfamiliar foreign language, and hence devoid of meaning. However, digit recall was not impaired when irrelevant foreign speech was replaced by unpatterned noise. Both Colle (1980) and Salame and Baddeley (1982) suggested that the irrelevant speech effect might be seen as the memory equivalent to the

masking of auditory speech perception by irrelevant sound. Perhaps the irrelevant spoken item gains access to the phonological store, and adds noise to the memory trace? However, unpatterned noise, like the sound of a waterfall, disrupts perception, but does not impair recall, whereas irrelevant speech does. Furthermore, in contrast to auditory masking, STM performance is not influenced by the intensity of the irrelevant sound (Colle, 1980). Even more problematic for the auditory masking analogy is the fact that the degree of disruption of STM is unrelated to the phonological similarity between the irrelevant sound and the items remembered. Irrelevant words that are similar in sound to the remembered items are no more disrupting than are dissimilar words (Jones & Macken, 1995; Le Compte & Shaibe, 1997).

But what about music? Salame and Baddeley (1989) found that music also interfered with digit recall, finding that vocal music was more disruptive than instrumental while Jones and Macken (1993) observed that even pure tones will disrupt verbal STM, provided they fluctuate in pitch. They proposed what they termed the *Changing State hypothesis*. This assumes that retention of serial order can be disrupted by irrelevant auditory stimuli provided that these fluctuate over time (Jones, Macken, & Murray, 1993). Jones (1993) relates the irrelevant sound effect to theories of auditory perception, emphasizing the evidence that the irrelevant sound effect is based on disruption of memory for serial order.

The problem of serial order

It was clear by this time that the purely verbally specified phonological loop model had two major shortcomings. First, it had no adequate explanation of how serial order is stored. Given that the classic digit-span task principally involves retaining serial order, this is clearly a major limitation. Second, the model had no clear specification of the crucial processes involved in *retrieval* from the phonological store. Both of these limitations demand a more detailed model, preferably computationally or mathematically simulated so that clear predictions can be made and tested. Fortunately, it has proved possible to convince several groups with the appropriate skills that this is a worthwhile enterprise.

A number of models based on the phonological loop have been developed, handling the question of serial order in somewhat different ways, agreeing on which issues are important but differing on how best to tackle them (see Box 3.2). The various models tend to agree in assuming both a phonological store, and a separate mechanism for serial order, with similarity influencing retrieval from the store. Most phonological-loop-related models reject a chaining interpretation of serial order, proposing instead that order information is carried either by some

KEY TERM

Irrelevant sound effect: A tendency for verbal STM to be disrupted by concurrent fluctuating sounds, including both speech and music.

Box 3.2 Methods of storing serial order

1 Chaining

A→B→C→D

Each item is associated with the next. Recall begins with the first item (A), which evokes the second (B).

2 Context

Each item is linked to a changing context, which may be time-based. The context then acts as recall cue.

3 Primacy

Each item presented receives activation. The first receives the most, the next a little less, and so forth. Items are recalled in order of strength. Once recalled, that item is suppressed and the next strongest chosen.

form of ongoing context (Burgess & Hitch, 1999, 2006), by links to the first item as in the *Primacy Model* of Page and Norris (1998), or links to both the first and last items (Henson, 1998). Rehearsal is assumed to involve the retrieval of items from the phonological store and their subsequent re-entry as rehearsed stimuli. These and other attempts to explain how order is maintained are reviewed by Hurlstone, Hitch, and Baddeley (2014) who note a range of points in which the various models agree, noting similarities between the retention of serial order between verbal and visual STM and raising the question of whether there is a general serial mechanism or whether maintaining order in visual and verbal STM involves separate processes that are based on similar principles.

COMPETING THEORIES OF VERBAL SHORT-TERM MEMORY

We have so far focused our discussion mainly on the explanation of short-term verbal memory offered by the phonological loop hypothesis. This approach has two advantages: it provides a coherent account of a range of very robust STM phenomena, and it does so in a way that explicitly links them to those other aspects of working memory that will be discussed in the next chapter. It is important to bear in mind, however, that other ways of explaining these data have been proposed. Some of these will be described briefly before moving on to a broader discussion of working memory, and the question of why we need a working memory.

One model that has been applied to verbal STM is James Nairne's *feature model* (Nairne, 1988, 1990), which replaces the proposed separation between LTM and STM with a single memory system in which each memory item is assumed to be represented by a set of features of two basic types: *modality dependent* and *modality independent*. If you read the word *HAT*, it will have both visually dependent features, such as the case in which it is printed, and visually independent features, such as its meaning. When you hear *HAT*, rather than read it, the independent features such as meaning will be the same but the dependent features will be acoustic rather than visual. Forgetting is assumed to depend on interference, with new items disrupting the features set up by earlier items, resulting in errors in recall.

The feature model is represented by a computer program that can be used to make predictions as to the outcome of different experimental manipulations. By making various assumptions, it is possible to use the model to account for many of the results that have been used to support the phonological loop hypothesis. The phonological similarity effect is explained on the grounds that similar items have more common features, leading to a greater likelihood that a similar but incorrect item will be retrieved. Irrelevant sound is assumed to add noise to the memory trace of each individual item. Articulatory suppression is also assumed to add noise, and in addition to be attention demanding (Nairne, 1990). By making detailed assumptions about the exact proportion of modality-dependent and modality-independent features and the relative effect on these of articulatory suppression and irrelevant sound, the feature model is able to simulate a wide range of results (Neath & Surprenant, 2003), although very little justification is given for the very specific assumptions required by the various simulations. At base, the feature model is a model of LTM applied to STM paradigms. Its aim is to account for memory over the first few seconds after presentation of the items. This will however typically reflect contributions from both temporary and long-term systems. This may result in apparently supportive evidence but encounters difficulty in explaining more detailed evidence.

The feature model for example predicts that irrelevant sound will impair recall only when it occurs as the same time as the memory items are encoded. However, it disrupts recall even when it occurs *after* presentation of the memory items, even when rehearsal is prevented by suppression (Norris, Baddeley, & Page, 2004). The feature model also has a problem explaining why the word-length effect disappears in mixed lists of long and short words. This has led to its abandonment by some of its proponents in favor of the next model to be described: the SIMPLE model (Brown, Neath, & Chater, 2007; Hulme et al., 2006).

Brown et al. (2007) propose a very broad-ranging memory model that they call the SIMPLE (Scale Invariant Memory, Perception, and Learning) model, which they apply to both STM and LTM. It is basically a model of forgetting based on retrieval, with more distinctive items being more readily retrievable. It places emphasis on temporal discriminability but goes beyond earlier attempts to use this mechanism to explain recency effects in free recall by developing a detailed mathematical model. SIMPLE handles free recall well but appears to be less well suited to explaining serial recall (Lewandowsky, Brown, Wright, & Nimmo, 2006; Nimmo & Lewandowsky, 2006). As in the case of the feature model, SIMPLE does not currently attempt to cover the executive aspects of working memory.

A further way of modeling serial order is to assume that order is maintained by a context signal. As mentioned earlier, one of these assumes a time-based context incorporating trace decay (Burgess & Hitch, 1999, 2006). This assumption is rejected by Farrell and Lewandowsky (2002, 2003), who propose in their SOB (Serial-Order-in-a-Box) model, that order is maintained using an event-based context signal, with forgetting based on interference between events.

It might seem strange that the apparently simple task of recalling a sequence of digits in the right order should prove so difficult to explain. However, as mentioned earlier, the problem of how a system like the brain that processes events in parallel can preserve serial order has challenged theorists since it was raised by Karl Lashley (1951), over 50 years ago. As Norris (2017) points out, it creates a problem for theories that try to explain working memory purely in terms of activated LTM. A particular problem arises when items are repeated as is the digit 1 in 71216 where it is necessary to create some form of temporary representation to distinguish the two examples of the digit 1. This issue that will be discussed further in Chapter 4 (p. 91).

FREE RECALL

Most of the work on verbal STM described so far has involved sequences of items drawn from limited sets of digits, letters, or words with the same items used repeatedly, and the emphasis on recalling serial order. The use of such constrained sets is of course intentional, so as to emphasize the demands of serial

order recall and minimize that of remembering the specific items. If, for example, new words are used on every trial, then aspects of verbal LTM would become more important, such as the meaningfulness of the words to be recalled (Walker & Hume, 1999). With short lists, people often begin by trying to recall in serial order, but then find this is not a good strategy with longer lists (Murdock, 1962).

Try it for yourself: Read out the following list of 16 words at a steady rate, then close your eyes and write down as many as you can remember in any order you like.

Ready? Read and remember:

barricade, children, diet, gourd, polio, meteor, journey, mohair, phoenix, crossbow, alligator, doorbell, muffler, menu, archer, carpet

Now close your eyes, look away, and write down what you can remember.

How well did you do? That would depend on how long you took and what you did with the words as you were reading them, but if you kept up a brisk pace you are likely to remember rather less than half of them. Now go back and check where your correct recalls came from within the list. Results from a single trial are inevitably rather unreliable, particularly in free recall where people are often still settling on a strategy, but the pattern of recall usually found is shown in Figure 3.3.

The most striking feature of recall is the influence of the order in which the words were presented, known as the serial position effect. The most marked feature, as shown in Figure 3.3, is the tendency for excellent recall on the last few items, the so-called recency effect. There is also a tendency for the first few items to be relatively well recalled, the

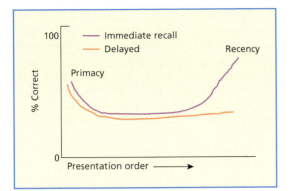

Figure 3.3 A typical serial position curve for free recall: when participants recall a list of unrelated words in any order they wish, there is a clear advantage to the last few items, the recency effect, which vanishes when recall is briefly delayed.

primacy effect, although this is usually much less pronounced than recency, unlike the case of serial recall, when primacy dominates. Note also the dotted line; this is the level of performance that can be expected if recall is delayed by the requirement to perform a brief attentionally demanding task such as counting backwards in threes for 10 seconds (Postman & Phillips, 1965).

How could we explain this pattern of results? A highly influential interpretation was offered by Glanzer and Cunitz (1966) who proposed that the earlier items were held in LTM, while recency reflected a separate component based on STM; a brief filled delay is sufficient to eliminate the STM contribution while leaving those items in LTM relatively unaffected. Evidence in favor of this interpretation came from a wide range of sources, finding that variables that are known to influence LTM impact upon the earlier items but not on the recency effect. LTM variables studied include:

1 presentation rate: slower is better;
2 word frequency: familiar words are easier;
3 imageability of the words: words that are visualizable are better;
4 age of the participant: young adults remember more than children or the elderly;
5 physiological state: drugs such as marijuana and alcohol impair performance.

While all of these were found to influence the earlier part of the serial position curve, none impacted on recency (Glanzer, 1972).

What of the primacy effect? This probably reflects a tendency to rehearse the first few items as they come in. People sometimes continue to rehearse these items throughout the list, particularly when they are encouraged to rehearse out loud (Rundus, 1971; Tam & Ward, 2000). This is however probably not a particularly good strategy; focusing on semantic coding is probably more fruitful. Attempts to base a general account of free recall on the results of overt rehearsal patterns (Rundus, 1971; Tam & Ward, 2000) are however of rather questionable generality in assuming that participants typically adopt this nonoptimal rehearsal strategy. Furthermore, standard recency effects also occur under conditions of incidental learning where participants have processed the words but do not expect to recall them (Baddeley & Hitch, 1977).

The assumption that recency simply reflects the output of a short-term store was subsequently challenged by the demonstration that recency effects can occur under conditions in which the short-term trace ought to have been disrupted. In one study, Bjork and Whitten (1974) required their subjects to recall sequences of words presented under three conditions. The baseline condition involved presenting a list of words for immediate free recall. As expected, this resulted in a clear recency effect. In a second condition, the gap between presentation and recall was filled by a 20-second backward counting task, which—as expected—removed the recency effect. In a third, crucial condition, 20 seconds of backward counting were interposed between each of the words presented, as well as between the end of the list and recall. Under these conditions, a recency effect re-emerged.

Recency effects have also been demonstrated over much longer intervals. In one study, for example, Baddeley and Hitch (1977) tested the capacity of rugby players to recall which teams they had played that season; their recall showed a clear recency effect. As not all the players had played in all the games, it proved possible to assess whether forgetting was more reflective of the amount of time elapsed, or of the number of intervening games. Number of games proved to be the better predictor, suggesting that a simple time-based decay hypothesis would not provide a good account of these findings. Similar long-term recency effects have been found in remembering a parking location (Pinto & Baddeley, 1991), although—sadly —I can report that as I get older, even recency does not always prevent the need for an embarrassed wander around the super-market parking lot!

The fact that recency effects are found across such a wide range of situations, with some cases being disrupted by a few seconds of unrelated activity such as counting whereas others persist over months, suggest that the recency effect is not limited to any single type of memory system but instead reflects a specific retrieval strategy that takes advantage of the fact that the most recent events are the most readily available to recall.

When was the last party you attended? Which was the party before that? And the one before? I suspect recalling your most recent party was the easiest, although it was perhaps not the best party.

The greater accessibility of the most recent experience of a given type could serve the highly important role of orienting yourself in space and time. When traveling and staying in a new place, how do you know where you are when you wake up? And if staying in a hotel, how do you remember your current room number and don't recall instead the number from the previous night or the night before that?

The most plausible interpretation of recency seems to be in terms of retrieval. Crowder (1976) likens the task of retrieving items from a free-recall list to that of discriminating telephone posts located at regular intervals. As illustrated by the picture below the nearest post will be readily distinguishable from the next, while as the posts recede into the distance, the problem of separating one from the other becomes increasingly hard. This process can be seen in terms of a discrimination ratio, based on the temporal distance between the item being retrieved and its principal competitor, the one immediately before it. On immediate recall, the most recent item has a consider-able advantage, but with increasing delay, discriminating an item from the one before becomes less and less easy (Baddeley &

Crowder's (1976) analogy likened the task of retrieval from a free-recall list to that of discriminating between a string of telephone posts; the further away the post is from the observer, the more difficult it becomes to distinguish it from its neighbor.

As distance in space or time increases, distinctiveness decreases.

Hitch, 1977; Glenberg et al., 1980). Brown et al. (2007) provide a detailed model of the discrimination ratio effect, demonstrating that it can be applied much more widely than its earlier application to free recall in STM experiments.

The telegraph pole analogy is particularly appropriate for the experimental situation typically used in measures of recency whereby a material comprises a sequence of easily separated words or events. The same principle operates more generally, however, as illustrated by the cover of our book:

VISUO-SPATIAL SHORT-TERM MEMORY

Imagine you are in a well-lighted room that is suddenly plunged into darkness. Would you be able to find the door? There was a box of matches on the desk in front of you, would you remember that it was there? These two questions concern two related but separable aspects of visual working memory, one concerned with spatial memory (*where*?) and the other with memory for objects (*what*?). The

evidence suggests that you would be able to maintain a general heading towards the door for about 30 seconds (Thomson, 1983). Your memory for precise location declines rather more rapidly (Elliot & Madelena, 1987).

But has nature endowed us with visual STM simply to prepare us for the occasional power cut? And even if this were the case, would LTM not suffice? We suffered a power cut last night and I fortunately remembered enough about the layout of our house to grope my way to the flashlight location. A brief consideration of the processes underlying visual perception suggest a rather more convincing interpretation of our need for visual STM. As we look around, we perceive objects within a complex environment. However, despite our experience of smoothly scanning a visual scene, the underlying process is not continuous, but rather is based on a series of discrete eye movements, to different parts of the scenes (see Box 3.3). These can be quite rapid. In reading for example they can occur at a rate of about two per second, with each fixation creating a separate image of the world. In the case of scanning a scene, where the eye may move from the foreground to the distance and from one object to another, these aspects may be very different. If the eye functioned like a camera, simply superimposing these images would lead to visual chaos. Nature's solution to this problem is to combine these successive brief glimpses into a coherent representation, namely visual STM.

If it is to work effectively in maintaining a representation of a world that is constantly changing as we move around, visual STM needs to hold its representation of the world over time, but to allow for a constant updating as we move around. The focus of attention may need to be switched, for example from where you are, to what you want to do, perhaps searching for and picking up a stone and aiming at a wolf that might be taking a little too much interest in you. To achieve this, the visual system needs to be able to bind together the perceptual features that constitute an object, the stone or the wolf, together with its spatial framework, and to hold these together long enough for action to be planned and the plan carried out. We will

Box 3.3 Eye movement

A scene used by Vogt and Magnussen (2007). The central picture shows a normal eye-movement scanning pattern and that on the right the scanning pattern of a typical artist.

When we look at scene such as that above, we experience it as continuous and static. This experience is, however, built up from a series of brief rapid eye movements; typically each will be focused on a separate aspect of the scene with the result that simply superimposing them would cause visual confusion. Instead, each is fed into a coherent framework based on visual STM. As the two examples show, the pattern of scanning is far from random, tending to focus on points likely to give most information, a factor that will reflect the aims and expertise of the perceiver. People typically focus on recognizable objects and on human figures, whereas trained artists tend to scan more widely. The central picture shows a normal scanning pattern and the right that of a typical artist.

consider these in turn, beginning with object-based STM, binding the features of the stimulus into a single perceived object before moving on to that of locating the objects within a spatial framework. We go on to discuss the more complex issue of the role of visual memory in thinking and planning in the next chapter.

Object memory

As is typical of many areas of experimental psychology, the study of visual STM has largely relied on simple easily specified stimuli such as colored shapes or letters rather than stones or wolves. The reason is that such stimuli are much easier to create, control, and specify and this means that others can repeat your findings; such replication is of course an essential and basic feature of all science. However carefully a study is designed and carried out, it may be subject to chance factors such as a nontypical participant group, or sample of stimulus material, as I myself can testify. Replication with different participants and a different sample of material avoids becoming misled by such problems.

Having developed principles and theories using simple and well-controlled material such as colored shapes, the next stage is to take such findings beyond the laboratory, demonstrating in due course what is termed its "ecological validity," its applicability to the "real world." A detailed analysis of visual STM has only developed relatively recently, hence most of the work to be described does use quite simple stimuli, although there is a growing interest in studying visual STM using more complex real-world scenes (see Henderson, 2008; Hollingworth, 2008).

Visual STM and LTM: How do they differ?

Using a method known as *change detection*, Phillips (1974) presented participants with a series of chequer board patterns varying in complexity from 4×4 to 8×8, with half the cells randomly black and half white in each case. After delays ranging from zero to nine seconds, a test stimulus followed, being either identical or having one cell changed. On immediate test, performance was virtually perfect, but declined over time with more complex patterns showing poorer performance (see Figure 3.4) suggesting that visual STM has a limited capacity.

In a later very influential paper Luck and Vogel (1997) developed a variant of this change detection task that has been extremely fruitful in probing the nature of visual STM. In a typical study, participants might view an array of squares differing in color, followed after varying delays by a pattern that is identical, or has the color of one square changed (see Figure 3.5). Unlike the complex matrix patterns used by Phillips, colored squares can be verbalized and hence remembered non-visually. To prevent this, participants are usually required to occupy the verbal rehearsal system by continually repeating a simple sequence such as *one two three* (see p. 46). Luck and Vogel varied the number of colored squares from 1 to 12, finding like Phillips that performance declined steeply as number of squares increased, but also showing that capacity was limited to three or four items (see Figure 3.5).

This differs dramatically from LTM, where capacity appears to be extremely large. In a classic study Standing, Conezio, and

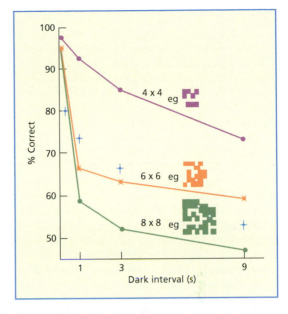

Figure 3.4 Recognition memory for random patterns as a function of complexity. Examples of the three types of pattern are shown. Each pattern was followed by a test item comprising either an identical pattern or one which had a single square changed. From Phillips (1974). Reprinted by permission of the Psychonomics Society, Inc.

Haber (1970) presented 2,560 color slides for 10 seconds each, subsequently testing memory several days later by presenting two items one of which had been shown before,

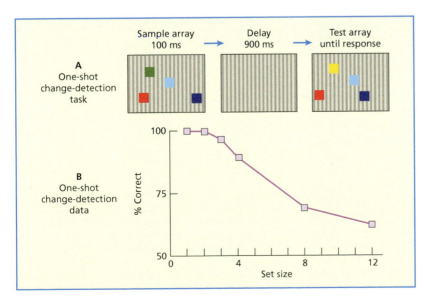

Figure 3.5 (A) The change detection task used by Luck and Vogel (1997). In this example, the green square has been changed to yellow. (B) The probability of detecting a change declines with the number of squares to be remembered. Adapted from Luck and Hollingworth (2008). Copyright © Oxford University Press. Reproduced with permission of the Licensor through PLSclear.

categorized as "old" and the others as "new." Despite the huge number of pictures and the delay, participants scored around 90% correct. This has been replicated and extended in recent years in a series of studies showing that people can detect often quite subtle changes such as left-right reversal or a full versus half-full glass of orange juice (see Brady, Konkle, & Alvarez, 2011 for a review). This does not necessarily mean that every detail of such pictures has been retained, and when pictures come from a single constrained category such as door scenes performance drops substantially (Evans & Baddeley, 2018) allowing sets of just 24 door scenes to provide a sensitive clinical test of visual LTM (Baddeley, Emslie, & Nimmo-Smith, 1994). However, while visual LTM may not be precise, it clearly does have the capacity to store enough of Standing et al.'s 2,560 scenes to distinguish most of them from new scenes, in contrast to the three to four item capacity of visual STM.

But why the huge difference in estimates of visual LTM capacity implied by the contrast between the massive capacity suggested by Standing et al. (1970) and Brady et al. (2011) and the evidence from Baddeley et al. (1994) that even a list of 24 doors challenges capacity? The answer lies in the nature of the test. Deciding which of two test stimuli in the Standing et al. study had been seen before, potentially requires only a single feature that seems more familiar among a rich and complex scene processed over many seconds. The doors used in the Baddeley et al. clinical test are carefully selected to vary in similarity between the target and three other nontargets, with some door scenes having targets and new distractor items being almost identical, resulting in performance only a little above the chance level of 25%. Subsequent work by Evans and Baddeley (2018) suggests a possible dual mechanism, one involving the rapid encoding of rich visual scenes and allowing a speedy indication of familiarity and a second more attention-demanding process that is involved when alternatives are very similar, a process that is principally reflected in a higher false alarm rate as new but similar items are wrongly categorized as old.

Regardless of the finer points as to just how much detail is contained in visual episodic LTM, there is no doubt that its capacity is substantially greater than visual STM. This is clearly also the same for visual semantic memory. Consider for example what you can recall of the contents of your own kitchen, the faces of your parents, or the colors of fruit and animals. Our visual LTM clearly holds a vast amount of information about the world around us.

Active rehearsal in visual STM

Visual STM appears to benefit from an active attempt to maintain an item in the focus of attention. McCollough, Machizawa, and Vogel (2007) have used event-related potentials (ERPs) to study this by measuring brain activity during the delay between presentation and test in a visual STM study. They asked participants to remember items presented on one side of the visual field, observing electrophysiological activity in the contralateral hemisphere which started some 200 ms later and persisted until the test item was presented (see Figure 3.6). They found that the amount of activation increased with number of items up to a maximum of around four. Furthermore, unsuccessful trials

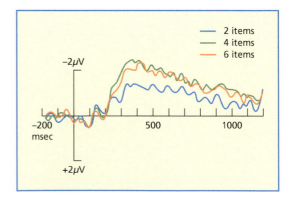

Figure 3.6 The effect of memory load on brain activity. Event-related potentials (ERPs) began some 200 ms following presentation of a visual stimulus array and persisted until the test item. Level of activation increased with stimulus load up to four items, assumed to be the limit of capacity. Data from McCollough et al. (2007). Copyright © 2007, with permission from Elsevier.

tended to be associated with a lower level of activation. A study by Vogel, McCollough, and Machizawa (2005) provided further evidence for their suggestion that such activity reflects the operation of short-term visual memory. They studied a range of participants who varied in their capacity to perform the visual STM task, showing a direct association between their neurophysiological measure and participants' memory performance.

What is stored in visual STM?

Most of the studies described so far involve relatively simple stimuli, typically colored squares. What happens when stimuli are allowed to vary on more than one dimension? This was studied by Vogel, Woodman, and Luck (2001) who used the stimuli that varied on a range of dimensions such as orientation, color, width, and texture.

Vogel et al. found that people were able to combine several features into a single object, with little apparent cost. This may not always apply, however, particularly for more complex stimuli such as objects made up from two or more components. If this were not the case, there would be no complexity effects and people would be able to remember 8 × 8 matrices as a single object as well as 4 × 4, which Phillips (1974) showed was not the case. But what constitutes an object?

As noted earlier, the visual system processes the world through a range of separate sensory channels, with shape, color, and movement for example all being detected by different neural systems. The fact that we experience an object such as a red square means that the *separate* features of color and shape that are present in the stimulus, must *then* have been recombined, allowing the separate channels encoding shape and color to be experienced as a single object, a colored square. The capacity to reunite the features of an object is known as "binding." The fact that binding has occurred can be shown as follows: suppose we have a range of different shapes (e.g., square, circle, triangle) and a range of different colors (e.g., red, green, blue) that are combined and presented as colored shapes. People can be asked to

remember only the colors in an array, or just the shapes, or both bound together as a single object such as a red triangle. Suppose we present a red triangle, a blue square, and a green circle and then test retention only of color, for example by presenting a red patch. Participants should say "yes" it has occurred, whereas a yellow patch should evoke a "no" response. Similarly, with a shape-only condition, a square should evoke "yes," a diamond "no." Participants might however be asked to remember the binding or combination of shape and color, in this case a red triangle should evoke "yes" but a red circle "no" since although red and circle have both been presented, they have not been bound together into a red circle. When participants perform these three tasks, the binding condition is often no worse than the harder of the two single feature conditions, suggesting that the additional process of binding shape and color may operate automatically. Allen, Baddeley, and Hitch (2006) took a different approach to the question of whether attentional resources are needed to form such bindings, proposing that if this were the case, then giving people an attentionally demanding task to perform at the same time should interfere more with the binding condition than with the conditions where only separate features needed to be maintained. Our results are shown in Figure 3.7. As is often the case,

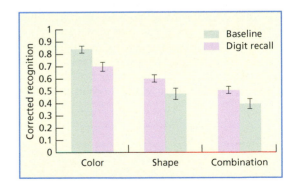

Figure 3.7 Effect of a demanding concurrent task on retention of colors, shapes, and colored shapes. The attentional disruption did not differ across conditions, suggesting that the process of binding shape and color is automatic. From Allen et al. (2006). Copyright © American Psychological Association. Reproduced with permission.

colors appear to be easiest to remember, shapes somewhat harder, and bound features nonsignificantly harder again. In each case, a concurrent attentional task interfered with performance, but crucially, the impairment was no greater in the binding condition than it was in the single feature cases. The act of binding appears to be relatively automatic, although remembering is clearly not, as overall performance in all conditions suffers from the additional task. We were somewhat surprised at this result, but were able to replicate it, and moved on to more demanding binding tasks, for example separating the color and shape spatially, a patch of color next to a shape, requiring participants to combine them into a bound shape in their "mind's eye," or presenting the shape visually and the color name auditorily. Despite this, we still found that the binding process did not depend on general executive resources (Karlson, Allen, Baddeley, & Hitch, 2010).

Does this mean that visual STM is totally divorced from attention? We think not. Chun and Johnson (2011) draw a distinction between two types of attention; one type is concerned with our capacity to direct and control the flow of *sensory* information from the world around us, perhaps best seen as an aspect of perception. A second type concerns the internally oriented executive aspects of attentional control. These are discussed in the next chapter through the concept of the *central executive* component of working memory. Our results suggest that this executive aspect of attention does play a role in overall memory performance, which is impaired when an executive load such as concurrent counting is required; the fact that the extra load does not disrupt binding in our studies, however, suggests that such perceptual binding does not depend on executive capacity but may instead reflect a separate perceptual attentional limitation (Hitch, Allen, & Baddeley, 2019).

Visuo-spatial STM

The visual–spatial distinction

We have made a distinction between spatial STM—remembering *where*—and object memory—remembering *what*. In practice, these two systems work together but tasks have been developed that particularly emphasize one or other of these two forms of visuo-spatial memory. A classic *spatial* task is the block tapping test in which the participant is faced with an array of nine blocks (Figure 3.8). The experimenter taps a number of blocks in sequence and the participant attempts to imitate this, with the length of sequence increasing until performance breaks down. This is known as the *Corsi span*, after the Canadian neuropsychologist who invented it, and is typically around five blocks, about two items below digit span.

Visual span can be measured using a series of matrix patterns of the type used by Phillips (1974) in which half the cells are filled and half left blank. The participant is shown a pattern and asked to reproduce it by marking the filled cells in an empty matrix. Testing starts with a simple 2×2 pattern, the number of cells in the matrix is gradually increased to a point at which performance breaks down, usually around the point at which the matrix reaches around 16 cells.

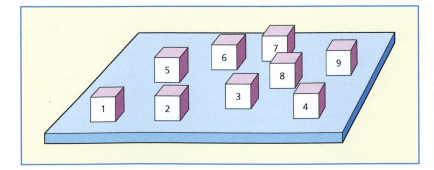

Figure 3.8 The Corsi test of visuo-spatial memory span. The experimenter taps a sequence of blocks and the participant seated opposite attempts to imitate. The numbers are there to help the experimenter.

Evidence for the distinction between these two measures of spatial and visual span comes from studies in which a potentially interfering activity is inserted between presentation and test. When this involves spatial processing, Corsi span involving sequentially tapping a series of keys is reduced, whereas pattern span based for example on remembering shapes is more disrupted by a visual task involving viewing visual rather than spatial stimuli (Della Sala, Gray, Baddeley, Allamano, & Wilson, 1999).

Visual STM is not of course limited to remembering patterns, but also involves shapes and colors. This is shown particularly clearly in a series of studies by Klauer and Zhao (2004) in which they contrast a spatial task that involves remembering the location of a white dot on a black background, with a visual task involving memory for Chinese ideographs, unfamiliar to participants. In each case, the stimulus is presented and followed by a 10-second retention interval, after which participants must choose which of eight test items has just been presented. During the 10-second delay, participants perform either a spatial or a visual task. In the spatial task, 12 asterisks are presented, with 11 moving randomly and the 12th stationary; the task is to identify the stationary item. The visual interfering task involves processing a series of colors, seven of which are variants of one color, perhaps red, whereas one, the target, is in the blue range. As shown in Figure 3.9, the spatial location of dots was disrupted by movement but not color, whereas ideographs showed the opposite effect.

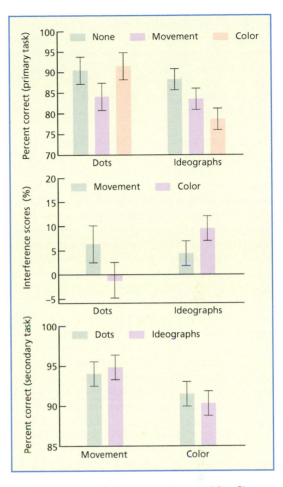

Figure 3.9 Memory for dot location and for Chinese ideographs. Spatial memory is disrupted by movement and pattern memory by color. Data from Klauer and Zhao (2004).

What limits the capacity of visual STM?

Attentional blindness

We do not remember everything we see. In one study a confederate stopped people on the Cornell University campus and asked for directions. While these were being given, two confederates carrying a door walked between them, during which the questioner was replaced by a second experimenter. When questioned afterwards, only 50% of

the people had noticed the change (Levin & Simons, 1997). Such "blindness" can extend over several seconds, as demonstrated in a video involving two basketball teams. The participant is instructed to perform a task such as counting the number of passes made by one of the teams, with the accuracy of their counting being checked. During this procedure someone in a gorilla suit walks through the scene. When questioned, around 50% of people failed to notice (Simons & Chabris, 1999). There are now many such demonstrations and they are important not only for illustrating that not everything that meets the eye is noticed, but also because of their practical importance for tasks such as driving while using a mobile phone, where the chance of "just not seeing" a motorcyclist, for example, is likely to increase with the attentional demand of the ongoing conversation.

Fixed slots versus flexible resources

In their original study, Luck and Vogel (1997) found that the number of objects that could be successfully retained in STM increased up to a maximum of three to four, then decreased as further items were presented. This and other studies agree on a typical limit of three or four items (Adam, Vogel, & Awh, 2017; Cowan, 2001). However, performance was apparently not affected by the complexity of the items, for example lines differing in both orientation and color. They explained their result in terms of a slot model in which memory comprised a limited number of slots which could hold integrated objects, regardless of their complexity. Later studies have however found evidence that number of objects held may reduce as they become more complex (Fougnie, Asplund, & Marois, 2010; Hardman & Cowan, 2015), leading to an alternative explanation in terms of limited memory resources that may be used flexibly, either to ensure the detailed retention of a small number of objects, or a less precise maintenance of a larger set (Bays & Husain, 2008; Wilken & Ma, 2004).

In order to test their proposal Wilken and Ma (2004) developed the continuous report method as a way of detecting the precision of the information retained. In this, participants were asked to retain a single feature such as color and were tested using a color wheel, a circular representation of the colors of the spectrum on which they were required to point to the color of the item being probed. Performance was then measured in terms of the angular difference between their response and the correct location of the target color. Wilken and Ma found that as set size increased the precision of response decreased, but still was centered on the true value of the item probed. When set size increased beyond four, however,

participants continued to show evidence across all items, although at a decreased level of accuracy, together with evidence of increased guessing as reflected in responses unrelated to the target hue. It could be argued however that memory for a single dimension is not typical of object retention in general. In particular, items for which there is already categorical knowledge such as a banana may indeed be stored categorically, rather than dimensionally, as is the case for simpler stimuli. Schurgin and Flombaum (2018) suggest that some combination of the slot and continuous resource models might be necessary.

Evidence in favor of a flexible version of the slot model came from a study by Alvarez and Cavanagh (2004) using a change detection task in which an array of stimuli ranging in size from one to 15 objects was presented for 500 ms followed by a 900 ms delay and re-presentation of the test array. This could be identical or with one object changed in identity. They used material ranging from simple colored squares to random polygons and Chinese characters. On the simple slot model, memory capacity should remain constant regardless of complexity. However, they found a maximum capacity of around four items but with substantial variation, ranging from 1.6 for shaded cubes to 4.4 for colored squares, indicating evidence of the slot model with a maximum maintenance of four objects, together with an important contribution from stimulus complexity. The controversy continues with growing evidence for an upper limit of around four but with clear evidence that the nature of the objects plays a further role (Schurgin, 2018). One problem may stem from the rather rigid implication of the term "slot." Miller's (1956) conception of the capacity limit in terms of "chunks," with visual stimuli varying in their "chunkability" has the advantage of less rigidity, together with clearer links to the extensive research on chunking in in verbal STM (Cowan, 2001).

NEUROPSYCHOLOGICAL APPROACHES TO THE STUDY OF SHORT-TERM MEMORY

Deficits in verbal short-term memory

The study of patients with a very pure deficit in STM has played a major role in theoretical development of the field. It began with a verbal STM study by Shallice and Warrington (1970) of patient KF who had a digit span of only two items, and showed little recency in free recall. Other patients were subsequently identified who showed an equivalent pattern (Vallar & Shallice, 1990). Shallice and Warrington's patient proved not to have a general deficit in STM, but rather a specific phonological STM deficit. Consequently, his performance was much better when his digit span was tested using visual presentation, consistent with his preserved visual memory as tested on the Corsi block tapping test. A similar pattern was shown by patient PV (Basso, Spinnler, Vallar, & Zanobia, 1982; Vallar & Baddeley, 1987), who developed a very pure and specific deficit in phonological STM following a stroke. Her intellect and language were otherwise unimpaired, but she had a digit span of two and failed to show either a phonological similarity or word length effect in verbal STM.

As is characteristic of such patients, PV showed a grossly reduced recency effect in immediate verbal free recall. She did however show normal long-term recency. This was tested using a task involving the solution of a series of anagram puzzles, followed by an unexpected request to recall the solution words (Vallar, Papagno, & Baddeley, 1991).

> **KEY TERM**
>
> **Corsi block tapping:** Visuo-spatial counterpart to digit span involving an array of blocks that the tester taps in a sequence and the patient attempts to copy.

Both PV and control patients showed a clear recency effect with better recall of later solutions, even though recall was unexpected. This pattern suggests that it is not PV's capacity to use a recency strategy that is impaired, but rather her capacity to use this to boost immediate verbal memory, which presumably relies on a phonological or verbal/lexical code.

Deficits in visuo-spatial short-term memory

Whereas some patients such as KF and PV have a deficit that is limited to verbal STM, other patients show the opposite pattern with normal verbal STM and impaired performance on either visual or spatial STM measures. One such patient, LH, had suffered a head injury in a traffic accident and was grossly impaired in his capacity to remember colors or shapes. However, he had excellent memory for spatial information such as locations and routes (Farah, Hammond, Levine, & Calvanio, 1988). Another patient, LE, suffered brain damage as a result of lupus erythematosus. She also had excellent spatial memory and was well able to drive an unfamiliar route between her home and the laboratory where her cognitive skills were tested. However, she did have impaired visual memory coupled with a grossly impaired capacity to draw from memory (Wilson, Baddeley, & Young, 1999). She was a talented sculptor, who found that she had lost her capacity to visualize. She could not remember what her earlier sculptures looked like and dramatically changed her style (Box 3.4).

Other cases occur whose visual STM is preserved, but who have impaired spatial memory. Carlesimo, Perri, Turriziani, Tomaiuolo, and Caltagirone (2001) describe patient MV, who suffered damage to the right frontal lobe following a stroke, whose visual memory performance was normal, but who was very impaired on the Corsi block tapping span and on a task requiring STM for imaging a path through a matrix. Luzzatti, Vecchi, Agazzi, Cesa-Bianchi, and Vergani (1998) report a similar case in which progressive deterioration of the right hemisphere led to spatial memory deficits on tasks such as

Box 3.4   Patient LE

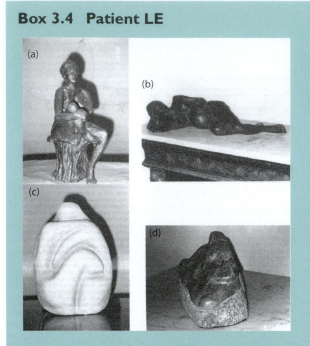

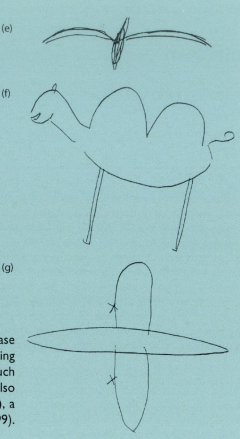

Patient LE was a talented sculptor before brain disease disrupted her ability to form visual images. Her sculpting style then changed from highly realistic (a and b) to much more abstract (c and d). Her capacity for drawing also suffered, as shown by her attempts to draw a bird (e), a camel (f), and an aeroplane (g). From Wilson et al. (1999). Copyright © Psychology Press.

describing the location of landmarks in her home town, while having a good memory for colors and shapes.

You might have noticed that the deficits shown by patients with visuo-spatial STM problems tend to go beyond the simple storage of visual and spatial stimuli, involving more complex tasks such as creating and manipulating mental images and using these in complex tasks, such as sculpting and spatial orientation. They have, in other words, led to deficits in both STM and working memory, the topic of the next chapter.

KEY TERM

Visuo-spatial STM: Retention of visual and/or spatial information over brief periods of time.

SUMMARY

- The term short-term memory (STM) refers to the temporary storage of relatively small amounts of information whereas working memory (WM) is a complex system that is capable of both storing and manipulating information.
- Early approaches to STM involved the digit span and related sequential verbal tasks.
- The concept of a phonological loop explains verbal STM by assuming a temporary store and an articulatory rehearsal process.
- It gives a simple account of the phonological similarity effect, the word length effect, and the effect on these of subvocal rehearsal.
- It is assumed to help in learning new words and also in controlling actions.
- Inherent in the memory span task is the problem of serial order and how it is maintained, a problem that has led to a number of detailed models.
- Free recall typically shows a marked recency effect which has resulted in a number of influential models applied to both STM and LTM.
- Most current studies of visual STM focus on simple stimuli such as colors and shapes and the question of how these are bound into unified colored shapes.
- Visual STM has a capacity limit of about four items and has been interpreted as depending on a storage system comprising four slots.
- However, it is also the case that the limited available attentional capacity can be used to store fewer items in more detail.
- Spatial STM is separable from its visual equivalent and depends on somewhat different neural systems.
- Laboratory studies of both verbal and visual STM have been extended and enriched by studies of patients with STM deficits.

POINTS FOR DISCUSSION

1 The concept of a phonological loop attempts to explain a range of major findings in verbal STM. What are they and what are the weaknesses of the basic model?
2 How can a parallel system like the brain remember serial order?
3 What is the evidence for separate storage of visual and spatial information?
4 What are the pros and cons of the slot versus general capacity interpretation of visual STM?
5 Some theorists argue that STM is best considered as an aspect of perception. Others see it as the activated portion of LTM. What might be the advantages and disadvantages of these viewpoints?

FURTHER READING

Baddeley, A. D., & Hitch, G. J. (2018). The phonological loop as a buffer store: An update. *Cortex*. doi:10.1016/j.cortex.2018.05.015. A recent account of the phonological loop and its development within the working memory model.

Brady, T. F., Konkle, T., & Alvarez, G. A. (2011). A review of visual memory capacity: Beyond individual items and toward structured representations. *Journal of Vision, 11*, 1–4. An account of studies suggesting a very large capacity to visual episodic LTM.

Evans, K., & Baddeley, A. D. (2018). Intention, attention and long-term memory for visual scenes: It all depends on the scenes. *Cognition, 180*, 24–37. doi:10.1016/j.cognition.2018.06.022. Considered factors that limit the apparently large capacity of visual LTM.

Klauer, K. C., & Zhao, Z. (2004). Double dissociations in visual and spatial short-term memory. *Journal of Experimental Psychology: General, 133*, 355–381. A good example of the careful use of the method converging operations to pin down the evidence for a distinction between visual and spatial STM.

Luck, S. J., & Hollingsworth, A. (Eds.). (2008). *Visual memory*. Oxford: Oxford University Press. A series of chapters by different authors covering various aspects of visual STM.

Luck, S. J., & Vogel, E. K. (1997). The capacity of visual working memory for features and conjunctions. *Nature, 390*, 279–281. An important paper that forms a link between the study of visual attention and visual STM.

Melton, A. W. (1963). Implications of short-term memory for a general theory of memory. *Journal of Verbal Learning and Verbal Behavior, 2*, 1–21. A classic paper presenting an interpretation of STM in terms of stimulus-response interference theory.

Repovs, G., & Baddeley, A. D. (2006). Multi-component model of working memory: Explorations in experimental cognitive psychology. *Neuroscience Special Issue, 139*, 5–21. A brief overview of visual short-term memory.

Vallar, G. (2006). Memory systems: The case of phonological short-term memory. A festschrift for *Cognitive Neuropsychology*. *Cognitive Neuropsychology, 23*, 135–155. An explanation in the account of the phonological loop from the viewpoint of neuropsychology.

REFERENCES

Adam, K. C. S., Vogel, E. K., & Awh, E. (2017). Clear evidence for item limits in visual working memory. *Cognitive Psychology, 97*, 79–97. doi:10.1016/j.cogpsych.2017.07.001

Allen, R., Baddeley, A. D., & Hitch, G. J. (2006). Is the binding of visual features in working memory resource-demanding? *Journal of Experimental Psychology: General, 135*, 298–313.

Alvarez, G. A., & Cavanagh, P. (2004). The capacity of visual short-term memory is set both by visual information load and by number of objects. *Psychological Science, 15*, 106–111.

Baddeley, A. D. (1966). The influence of acoustic and semantic similarity on long-term memory for word sequences. *Quarterly Journal of Experimental Psychology, 18*, 302–309.

Baddeley, A. D., Emslie, H., & Nimmo-Smith, I. (1994). *Doors and people: A test of visual and verbal recall and recognition.* Bury St Edmunds: Thames Valley Test Company.

Baddeley, A. D., & Hitch, G. J. (1974). Working memory. In G. A. Bower (Ed.), *The psychology of learning and motivation: Advances in research and theory* (Vol. 8, pp. 47–89). New York: Academic Press.

Baddeley, A. D., & Hitch, G. (1977). Recency re-examined. In S. Dornic (Ed.), *Attention and performance* (Vol. VI, pp. 647–667). Hillsdale, NJ: Lawrence Erlbaum Associates.

Baddeley, A. D. & Hitch, G. J. (2019). The phonological loop as a buffer store: An update. *Cortex, 112*, 91–106. doi:10.1016/j.cortex.2018.05.015

Baddeley, A. D., Hitch, G. J., & Allen, R. J. (2019). From short-term store to multicomponent working memory: The role of the modal model. *Memory & Cognition, 47*, 575–588.

Baddeley, A. D., Thomson, N., & Buchanan, M. (1975). Word length and the structure of short-term memory. *Journal of Verbal Learning and Verbal Behavior, 14*, 575–589.

Barrouillet, P., & Camos, V. (2014). *Working memory: Loss and reconstruction.* Hove, UK: Psychology Press.

Basso, A. H., Spinnler, G., Vallar, G., & Zanobia, E. (1982). Left hemisphere damage and selective impairment of auditory verbal short-term memory: A case study. *Neuropsychologica, 20*, 263–274.

Bays, P. M., & Husain, M. (2008). Dynamic shifts of limited working memory resources in human vision. *Science, 321*, 851–854. doi:10.1126/science.1158023

Bjork, R. A., & Whitten, W. B. (1974). Recency-sensitive retrieval processes. *Cognitive Psychology, 6*, 173–189.

Brady, T. F., Konkle, T., & Alvarez, G. A. (2011). A review of visual memory capacity: Beyond individual items and toward structured representations. *Journal of Vision, 11*, 1–4.

Brown, G. D. A., Neath, I., & Chater, N. (2007). A temporal ratio model of memory. *Psychological Review, 114*, 539–576.

Burgess, N., & Hitch, G. J. (1999). Memory for serial order: A network model of the phonological loop and its timing. *Psychological Review, 106*, 551–581.

Burgess, N., & Hitch, G. J. (2006). A revised model of short-term memory and long-term learning of verbal sequences. *Journal of Memory and Language, 55*, 627–652.

Caplan, D., Rochon, E., & Waters, G. S. (1992). Articulatory and phonological determinants of word-length effects in span tasks. *Quarterly Journal of Experimental Psychology, 45A*, 177–192.

Carlesimo, G. A., Perri, R., Turriziani, P., Tomaiuolo, F., & Caltagirone, C. (2001). Remembering what but not where: Independence of spatial and visual working memory in the human brain. *Cortex, 37*, 519–534.

Chun, M. M., & Johnson, M. K. (2011). Memory: Enduring traces of perceptual and reflective attention. *Neuron, 72*, 520–535.

Colle, H. A. (1980). Auditory encoding in visual short-term recall: Effects of noise intensity and spatial location. *Journal of Verbal Learning and Verbal Behaviour, 19*, 722–735.

Colle, H. A., & Welsh, A. (1976). Acoustic masking in primary memory. *Journal of Verbal Learning and Verbal Behavior, 15*, 17–32.

Conrad, R. (1964). Acoustic confusion in immediate memory. *British Journal of Psychology, 55*, 75–84.

Conrad, R., & Hull, A. J. (1964). Information, acoustic confusion and memory span. *British Journal of Psychology, 55*, 429–432.

Cowan, N. (2001). The magical number 4 in short-term memory: A reconsideration of mental storage capacity. *Behavorial and Brain Sciences, 24*, 87–114; discussion 114–185.

Crowder, R. G. (1976). *Principles of learning and memory.* Hillsdale, NJ: Lawrence Erlbaum Associates.

Della Sala, S., Gray, C., Baddeley, A., Allamano, N., & Wilson, L. (1999). Pattern span: A tool for unwelding visuo-spatial memory. *Neuropsychologia, 37*, 1189–1199.

Elliot, D., & Madalena, J. (1987). The influence of premovement visual information on manual aiming. *Quarterly Journal of Experimental Psychology, 39A*, 542–559.

Engle, R. W., & Kane, M. J. (2004). Executive attention, working memory capacity and two-factor theory of cognitive control. In B. Ross (Ed.), *The psychology of learning and motivation* (pp. 145–199). New York: Elsevier.

Evans, K., & Baddeley, A. D. (2018). Intention, attention and long-term memory for visual scenes: It all depends on the scenes. *Cognition, 180*, 24–37. doi:10.1016/j.cognition.2018.06.022

Farah, M. J., Hammond, K. M., Levine, D. N., & Calvanio, R. (1988). Visual and spatial mental imagery: Dissociable systems of representation. *Cognitive Psychology, 20*(4), 439–462.

Farrell, S., & Lewandowsky, S. (2002). An endogenous model of ordering in serial recall. *Psychonomic Bulletin & Review, 9*, 59–60.

Farrell, S., & Lewandowsky, S. (2003). Dissimilar items benefit from phonological similarity in serial recall. *Journal of Experimental Psychology: Learning, Memory and Cognition, 29*, 838–849.

Fougnie, D., Asplund, C. I., & Marois, R. (2010). What are the units of storage in visual working memory? *Journal of Vision, 10*, 27–27. doi:10.1167/10.12.27

Glanzer, M. (1972). Storage mechanisms in recall. In G. H. Bower (Ed.), *The psychology of learning and motivation: Advances in research and theory* (Vol. 5). New York: Academic Press.

Glanzer, M., & Cunitz, A. R. (1966). Two storage mechanisms in free recall. *Journal of Verbal Learning and Verbal Behavior, 5*, 351–360.

Glenberg, A. M., Bradley, M. M., Stevenson, J. A., Kraus, T. A., Tkachuk, M. J., Gretz, A. L., et al. (1980). A two-process account of long-term serial position effects. *Journal of Experimental Psychology: Human Learning and Memory, 6*, 355–369.

Goldman-Rakic, P. S. (1996). The prefrontal landscape: Implications of functional architecture for understanding human mentation and the central executive. *Philosophical Transactions of the Royal Society (Biological Sciences), 351*, 1445–1453.

Hardman, K. O., & Cowan, N. (2015). Remembering complex objects in visual working memory: Do capacity limits restrict objects or features. *Journal of Experimental Psychology: Learning, Memory, and Cognition, 41*, 930–931. doi:10.1037/xlm0000134

Henderson, J. M. (2008). Eye movements in scene memory. In S. J. Luck & A. Hollingworth (Eds.), *Visual memory* (pp. 87–123). Oxford: Oxford University Press.

Henson, R. N. A. (1998). Short-term memory for serial order. The Start-End Model. *Cognitive Psychology, 36*, 73–137.

Hitch, G. J., Allen, R. J., & Baddeley, A. D. (2019). Attention and binding in visual working memory: Two forms of attention and two kinds of buffer storage. *Attention, Perception & Psychophysics*. doi 10.3758/s13414–019–01837-x

Hollingworth, A. (2008). Visual memory for natural scenes. In S. J. Luck & A. Hollingworth (Eds.), *Visual memory* (pp. 123–163). Oxford: Oxford University Press.

Hulme, C., Neath, I., Stuart, G., Shostak, L., Suprenant, A. M., & Brown, G. D. A. (2006). The distinctiveness of the word-length. *Journal of Experimental Psychology: Learning, Memory and Cognition, 32*, 586–594.

Hurlstone, M. J., Hitch, G. J., & Baddeley, A. D. (2014). Memory for serial order across domains: An overview of the literature and directions for future research. *Psychological Bulletin, 14*, 339–373. doi:10.1037/a0034221

Jacobs, J. (1887). Experiments in "prehension." *Mind, 12*, 75–79.

Jones, D. M. (1993). Objects, streams and threads of auditory attention. In A. D. Baddeley & L. Weiskrantz (Eds.), *Attention: Selection, awareness and control* (pp. 87–104). Oxford: Clarendon Press.

Jones, D. M., & Macken, W. J. (1993). Irrelevant tones produce an irrelevant speech effect: Implications for phonological coding in working memory. *Journal of Experimental Psychology: Learning, Memory and Cognition, 19*, 369–381.

Jones, D. M., & Macken, W. J. (1995). Phonological similarity in the irrelevant sound effect: Within- or between- stream similarity. *Journal of Experimental Psychology: Learning, Memory, and Cognition, 21*, 103–115.

Jones, D. M., Macken, W. J., & Murray, A. C. (1993). Disruption of visual short-term memory by changing-state auditory stimuli: The role of segmentation. *Memory & Cognition, 21*(3), 318–366.

Karlson, P., Allen, R. J., Baddeley, A. D., & Hitch, G. J. (2010). Binding across space and time in visual working memory. *Memory and Cognition, 38*, 292–303.

Klauer, K. C., & Zhao, Z. (2004). Double dissociations in visual and spatial short-term memory. *Journal of Experimental Psychology: General, 133*, 355–381.

Lashley, K. S. (1951). The problem of serial order in behavior. In L. A. Jeffress (Ed.), *Cerebral mechanisms in behavior: The Hixon symposium*. New York: John Wiley.

Le Compte, D. C., & Shaibe, D. M. (1997). On the irrelevance of phonological similarity to the irrelevant speech effect. *Quarterly Journal of Experimental Psychology, 50A*, 100–118.

Levin, D. T., & Simons, D. J. (1997). Failure to detect changes to attended objects in motion pictures. *Psychonomic Bulletin & Review, 4,* 501–506.

Lewandowsky, S., Brown, G. D. A., Wright, T., & Nimmo, L. M. (2006). Timeless memory: Evidence against temporal distinctiveness models of short-term memory for serial order. *Journal of Memory and Language, 54,* 20–38.

Lewandowsky, S., & Oberauer, K. (2009). No evidence for temporal decay in working memory. *Journal of Experimental Psychology: Learning, Memory and Cognition, 35,* 1545–1551. doi:10.1037/a0017010

Logie, R. H., Cowan, N., & Camos, V. (Eds.). (in press). *Working memory: State of the science.*

Luck, S. J., & Vogel, E. K. (1997). The capacity of visual working memory for features and conjunctions. *Nature, 390,* 279–281.

Luzzatti, C., Vecchi, T., Agazzi, D., Cesa-Bianchi, M., & Vergani, C. (1998). A neurological dissociation between preserved visual and impaired spatial processing in mental imagery. *Cortex, 34,* 461–469.

Malmberg, K., Raaijmakers, J. G. W., & Shiffrin, R. M. (2019). 50 years of research sparked by Atkinson and Shiffrin (1968). *Memory & Cognition, 47,* 561–574. doi 10.3758/s13421–019–00896–7

McCollough, A. W., Machizawa, M. G., & Vogel, E. K. (2007). Electrophysiological measures of maintaining representations in visual working memory. *Cortex, 43,* 77–94.

Miller, G. A. (1956). The magical number seven, plus or minus two: Some limits on our capacity for processing information. *Psychological Review, 63,* 81–97.

Miyake, A., Friedman, N. P., Emerson, M. J., Witzki, A. H., Howerter, A., & Wager, T. D. (2000). The unity and diversity of executive functions and their contributions to complex "frontal lobe" tasks: A latent variable analysis. *Cognitive Psychology, 41,* 49–100.

Murdock, B. B., Jr. (1962). The serial position effect in serial recall. *Journal of Experimental Psychology, 64,* 482–488.

Nairne, J. S. (1988). A framework for interpreting recency effects in immediate serial recall. *Memory and Cognition, 16,* 343–352.

Nairne, J. S. (1990). A feature model of immediate memory. *Memory & Cognition, 18,* 251–269.

Neath, I., & Nairne, J. S. (1995). Word-length effects in immediate memory: Overwriting trace-decay theory. *Psychonomic Bulletin & Review, 2,* 429–441.

Neath, I., & Surprenant, A. (2003). *Human memory: An introduction to research, data and theory* (2nd ed.). Belmont, CA: Wadsworth.

Nimmo, L. M., & Lewandowsky, S. (2006). Distinctiveness revisited: Unpredictable temporal isolation does benefit short-term serial recall of heard or seen events. *Memory and Cognition, 34,* 1368–1375.

Norris, D. (2017). Short-term memory and long-term memory are still different. *Psychological Bulletin, 143,* 992–1009.

Norris, D., Baddeley, A. D., & Page, M. P. A. (2004). Retrospective effects of irrelevant speech on serial recall from short-term memory. *Journal of Experimental Psychology, 30,* 1093–1105.

Page, M. P. A., & Norris, D. (1998). The primacy model: A new model of immediate serial recall. *Psychological Review, 105,* 761–781.

Phillips, W. A. (1974). On the distinction between sensory storage and short-term visual memory. *Perception and Psychophysics, 16,* 283–290.

Pinto, A., da Costa, & Baddeley, A. D. (1991). Where did you park your car? Analysis of a naturalistic long-term recency effect. *European Journal of Cognitive Psychology, 3,* 297–313.

Postman, L., & Phillips, L. W. (1965). Short-term temporal changes in free recall. *Quarterly Journal of Experimental Psychology, 17,* 132–138.

Rundus, D. (1971). Analysis of rehearsal process in free recall. *Journal of Experimental Psychology, 89,* 63–77.

Ryan, J. (1969). Temporal grouping, rehearsal and short-term memory. *Quarterly Journal of Experimental Psychology, 21,* 148–155.

Salame, P., & Baddeley, A. D. (1982). Disruption of short-term memory by unattended speech: Implications for the structure of working memory. *Journal of Verbal Learning and Verbal Behaviour, 21,* 150–164.

Salame, P., & Baddeley, A. D. (1989). Effects of background music on phonological short-term memory. *Quarterly Journal of Experimental Psychology, 41A,* 107–122.

Schurgin, M. W. (2018). Visual memory, the long and the short of it: A review of visual working memory and long-term memory. *Attention Perception and Psychophysics, 80,* 1035–1056. doi:10.3758/s13414–018–1522-y

Schurgin, M. W., & Flombaum, J. I. (2018). Visual working memory is more tolerant than visual long-term memory. *Journal of Experimental Psychology: Human Perception and Performance, 44,* 1216–1227. doi:10.1037/xhp0000528

Shallice, T., & Warrington, E. K. (1970). Independent functioning of verbal memory stores: A neuropsychological study. *Quarterly Journal of Experimental Psychology, 22,* 261–273.

Simons, D. J., & Chabris, C. F. (1999). Gorillas in our midst: Sustained inattentional blindness for dynamic events. *Perception, 28,* 1059–1074. doi:10.1068/p2952.PIMD10694957

Standing, L., Conezio, J., & Haber, R. N. (1970). Perception and memory for pictures: Single-trial learning of 2500 visual stimuli. *Psychonomic Science, 19,* 73–74.

Tam, L., & Ward, G. (2000). A recency-based account of the primacy effect in free recall. *Journal of Experimental Psychology: Learning, Memory, and Cognition, 26,* 1589–1625.

Thomson, J. A. (1983). Is continuous visual monitoring necessary in visually-guided locomotion. *Journal of Experimental Psychology, 9,* 427–433.

Vallar, G., & Baddeley, A. D. (1987). Phonological short-term store and sentence processing. *Cognitive Neuropsychology, 4,* 417–438.

Vallar, G., Papagno, C., & Baddeley, A. D. (1991). Long-term recency effects and phonological short-term memory: A neuropsychological case study. *Cortex, 27,* 323–326.

Vallar, G., & Shallice, T. (1990). *Neuropsychological impairments of short-term memory.* Cambridge: Cambridge University Press.

Vogel, E. K., McCollough, A. W., & Machizawa, M. G. (2005). Neural measures reveal individual differences in controlling access to working memory. *Nature, 438,* 500–503.

Vogel, E. K., Woodman, G. F., & Luck, S. J. (2001). Storage of features, conjunctions, and objects in visual working memory. *Journal of Experimental Psychology: Human Perception and Performance, 27*(1), 92–114.

Vogt, S., & Magnussen, D. (2007). Expertise in pictorial perception: Eye-movement patterns and visual memory in artists and laymen. *Perception, 36,* 91–100.

Walker, I., & Hulme, C. (1999). Concrete words are easier to recall than abstract words: Evidence for a semantic contribution to short-term serial recall. *Journal of Experimental Psychology: Learning, Memory and Cognition, 25,* 1256–1271.

Wickelgren, W. A. (1964). Size of rehearsal group and short-term memory. *Journal of Experimental Psychology, 68,* 413–419.

Wilken, P., & Ma, W. J. (2004). A detection theory account of change detection. *Journal of Vision, 4,* 1120–1135.

Wilson, B. A., Baddeley, A. D., & Young, A. W. (1999). LE, a person who lost her "mind's eye." *Neurocase, 5,* 119–127.

Contents

CHAPTER 4

WORKING MEMORY

Alan Baddeley

How are you at mental arithmetic? Could you multiply 27 × 3? Try it. Different people use different methods; in my own case, I multiplied the 7 by 3 resulting in 21, then held the 1 in mind and carried the 2, before then going on to multiply 2 × 3, and so forth, interleaving the retrieval of numerical facts, with holding and manipulating the temporary totals. I had, in short, to use working memory (WM), simultaneously holding and processing information. This active use of memory is the focus of the present chapter.

The idea that short-term memory (STM) serves as a working memory was proposed by Atkinson and Shiffrin (1968), who devised the model briefly described in Chapter 3. Because it had a great deal in common with many similar models that were popular at the time, it became known as the *modal model*.

THE MODAL MODEL

As Figure 4.1 illustrates, the modal model assumes that information comes in from the environment and is processed first by a parallel series of brief temporary sensory memory systems, including the iconic and echoic memory processes discussed in Chapter 1. From here, information flows into the *short-term store*, which forms a crucial part of the system, not only feeding information into and out of the *long-term store*, but

also acting as a *working memory*, responsible for selecting and operating strategies for rehearsal and generally serving as a global workspace. Atkinson and Shiffrin (1968) created a mathematical simulation of their model, concentrating on the processes involved in the rote rehearsal of verbal items and on the role of rehearsal in the transfer of information from the short-term to the long-term store. For a while, the modal model seemed to offer a neat solution to the question of how information is manipulated and stored. Before long, however, problems began to appear.

One problem concerned the assumption that simply holding items in the short-term store for long enough would guarantee learning. This view was challenged by Craik and Lockhart (1972), who proposed instead the principle of levels of processing, which maintains that learning depends on the way in which material is processed, rather than time in short-term storage. This important theory is discussed in Chapter 6.

The Atkinson and Shiffrin model also had difficulty in accounting for some of the neuropsychological evidence. You may

KEY TERM

Levels of processing: The theory proposed by Craik and Lockhart that asserts that items that are more deeply processed will be better remembered.

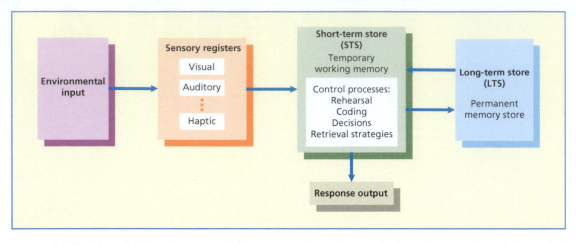

Figure 4.1 The flow of information through the memory systems as conceived by Atkinson and Shiffrin's modal model. Reproduced with permission. Copyright © 2020 Scientific American, a division of Nature America, Inc. All rights reserved.

recall that Shallice and Warrington (1970) described a patient who appeared to have a grossly defective short-term store, a digit span of two and no recency effect. According to the modal model, the short-term store plays a crucial role in transferring information into and out of long-term memory (LTM). This STM deficit should therefore lead to greatly impaired long-term learning in such patients. Furthermore, if the short-term store acts a general working memory, these patients should suffer severe disruption of such complex cognitive activities as reasoning and comprehension. This was not the case: one patient with grossly impaired STM was an efficient secretary, another ran a shop while raising a family, and a third was a taxi driver (Vallar & Shallice, 1990). In short, they showed no signs of suffering from a general working-memory deficit.

Within a very few years, the initial concept of STM had moved from simplicity to complexity. A wide range of new experimental techniques had been invented, but none of them mapped in a simple straightforward way onto any of the original theories proposed to account for the earlier studies of STM. At this point, many investigators abandoned the field in favor of the study of LTM, opting instead to work on the exciting new developments in the study of levels of processing and of semantic memory.

Just at the point that problems with the modal model were becoming evident, Graham Hitch and I were beginning our first research grant in which we had undertaken to look at the relationship between STM and LTM. Rather than attempt to find a way through the thicket of experimental techniques and theories that characterized both fields, we opted to ask a very simple question, namely, if the system or systems underpinning STM have a function, what might it be? If, as was generally assumed, it acted as a working memory, then blocking it should interfere with both long-term learning and complex cognitive activities such as reasoning and comprehending. Not having access to patients with this specific STM deficit, we attempted to simulate such patients using our undergraduate students, a process that happily did not require physical removal of the relevant part of their brain, but did involve keeping it busy while at the same time requiring participants to reason, comprehend, and learn (Baddeley & Hitch, 1974).

Virtually all theories agreed that if verbal STM was characterized by any single task, that task was digit span, with longer sequences of digits occupying more of the capacity of the underlying short-term storage system. We therefore combined digit span with the simultaneous performance of a range of other tasks such as reasoning, learning, and comprehension, which were assumed to depend on this limited-capacity system. Participants were given a sequence of digits that they were continually required to rehearse out loud at the same time as they were performing other cognitive tasks. By varying the number of digits being held, it should be possible to vary the demand on this limited-capacity system. If it did indeed reflect a working memory responsible for reasoning and other tasks, then the longer the sequence, the greater the digit load and the greater the interference should be.

One experiment involved presenting a simple reasoning task in which students had to verify a statement about the order of two letters, a test that correlates with verbal intelligence (Baddeley, 1968). The task is shown in Box 4.1. Try it yourself.

Somewhat to our surprise, people were able to do this, even when holding simultaneously and repeating sequences of up to eight digits, beyond memory span for many of those tested. As Figure 4.2 shows, average time to verify the sentences increased systematically with digit load, but not overwhelmingly so. The average time taken to verify a sentence while holding eight digits was about 50% more than that taken with no concurrent digit load. Perhaps more remarkably, the error rate remained constant at around 5%, regardless of concurrent digit load.

What are the implications of these results for the view that the short-term store serves as a working memory? The error rate sug-

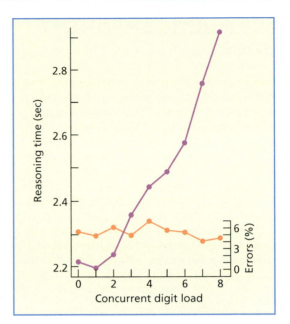

Figure 4.2 Speed and accuracy of grammatical reasoning as a function of concurrent digit load. From Baddeley (1986). Copyright © Oxford University Press. Reproduced with permission.

gests that performance can go ahead quite effectively regardless of concurrent digit load, whereas the processing time data suggest that there is *some* involvement, although not one of overwhelming magnitude. This suggests one system that is helpful, but disrupted by the concurrent digit task together with a second system that is able to perform the comprehension task efficiently though more slowly. Results from studies of learning and comprehension gave broadly equivalent results (Baddeley & Hitch, 1974), supporting some kind of working memory hypothesis, but not one that depended entirely on the memory system underpinning digit span.

We therefore proposed a somewhat more complex model which we called *working memory*, a term invented but not further developed by Miller, Galanter, and Pribram (1960). The emphasis on "working" aimed to dissociate it from earlier models of STM, which were primarily concerned with storage, and to emphasize its functional role as a system that underpins complex cognitive activities, a system that supports our capacity for mental work and coherent thought.

Box 4.1 Examples from the grammatical reasoning test used by Baddeley and Hitch (1974)

		True	False
A follows B	B → A		
B precedes A	A → B		
B is followed by A	B → A		
A is preceded by B	B → A		
A is not preceded by B	A → B		
B does not follow A	A → B		

Answers: T, F, T, T, T, F.

THE MULTICOMPONENT MODEL

The model we proposed had three components (Figure 4.3); one of these, the *phonological loop*, is assumed to be specialized for holding sequences of acoustic or speech-based items. A second subsystem, the visuo-spatial sketchpad, performs a similar function for visually and/or spatially encoded items and arrays. The whole system is controlled by the *central executive*, an attentionally limited system that selects and manipulates material in the subsystems, serving as a controller that runs the whole show. One way of gaining a feeling for the concept is to try the following: Think of your current house or apartment, and work out how many windows it has. Then move on to the next paragraph.

How many windows? How did you reach that number? You probably formed some sort of visual image of your house; this relies on the sketchpad. You presumably then counted the windows verbally using the phonological loop. Finally, throughout this process there was a need for your central executive to select and run the strategy. These three components of working memory will be considered in turn, beginning with the phonological loop, which—as mentioned previously—could be regarded as a model of verbal STM embedded within a more general theory of WM.

The phonological loop

As we saw in Chapter 3, the phonological loop is basically a model of verbal STM. It accounts for a wide and rich range of findings using a simple model that assumes a temporary store and a verbal rehearsal process. It is not free of critics, but has proved fruitful for over 40 years without—so far—being replaced by a widely accepted better model. But how does it fit into the broader context of working memory? What is it for?

What use is the phonological loop?

On the evidence presented in Chapter 3, blocking the phonological loop by articular suppression reduces span, suggesting that articulatory rehearsal is useful. However, it does so from about six or seven digits to four or five on immediate recall in the rather artificial task of simple repetition (Larsen & Baddeley, 2003; Murray, 1967). So what, if any, is the evolutionary significance of this small boost to immediate recall? Has evolution thoughtfully prepared us for the invention of the telephone? And if not, is the loop anything more than a pimple on the rear anatomy of cognitive psychology, as unkindly suggested by one critic?

In an attempt to answer this question, two Italian colleagues—Giuseppe Vallar and Costanza Papagno—and I began to study a patient—PV—who had a very pure phonological loop deficit. Her digit span was two items but her intelligence, LTM, and short-term visual memory were excellent. She spoke fluently and her general language skills seemed normal. PV ran a shop, successfully raised a family, and seemed to have few problems in her everyday life. Did she have

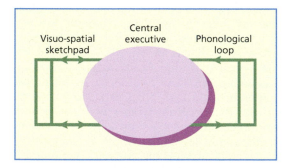

Figure 4.3 The initial Baddeley and Hitch working memory model. The double arrows are intended to represent parallel transfer of information to and from the sketchpad, and the single arrows the serial rehearsal process within the phonological loop.

KEY TERM

Visuo-spatial sketchpad: A component of the Baddeley and Hitch model that is assumed to be responsible for the temporary maintenance of visual and spatial information.

any areas of major difficulty? If she did, this would give us a clue as to what function was served by her defective phonological loop.

Functions of the phonological loop

We began with the hypothesis that the loop might have evolved to assist language comprehension (Vallar & Baddeley, 1987). PV did have some problems, but only with a particular type of long sentence, where it is necessary to hold on to the first few words until the end of the sentence in order to understand it. This was not enough to create problems for PV in everyday life, and it is hard to see evolution favoring the development of a special subsystem to support the use of long-winded sentences.

A second hypothesis was that the phonological loop system has evolved to help us learn language. People who have acquired a phonological loop deficit when adult, as is the case for PV, would experience few difficulties because they would already have mastered their native language. However, if they were required to learn a new language, they might have problems. We investigated this by requiring PV to learn to associate each of eight Russian words with their equivalent in Italian, PV's native language (Baddeley, Papagno, & Vallar, 1988). With spoken presentation, after ten trials, all of the control participants had learned all eight Russian words, whereas PV had not learned one (Figure 4.4). Could it simply be that she was amnesic? This was not the case, as when the task involved learning to associate two unrelated native language words such as *castle-bread*, a task that typically relies on semantic coding (Baddeley & Dale, 1966), she was quite unimpaired. Our results thus lent support to the possibility that the phonological loop is involved in language acquisition.

However, while a single case can be extremely informative, it is possible that the individual might be highly atypical, and

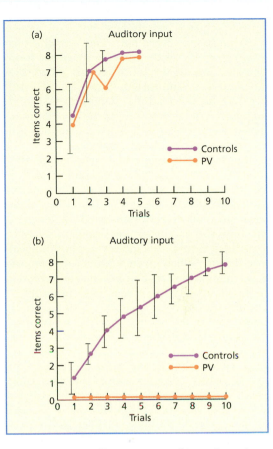

Figure 4.4 Rate of learning pairs of items by patient PV and controls. Her capacity to learn pairs of meaningful words was unimpaired (a), but she was not able to learn foreign language vocabulary (b). From Baddeley, Papagno, and Vallar (1988). Copyright © Elsevier. Reproduced with permission.

hence ultimately misleading. Given that STM-deficit patients are rare, we opted to test our hypothesis further by disrupting the phonological loop in normal participants who were attempting to learn foreign language vocabulary. In one study, articulatory suppression was used (Papagno, Valentine, & Baddeley, 1991). This proved to disrupt foreign language learning, assumed to rely on the phonological loop, but had little effect on learning pairs of native language words. In another study, Papagno and Vallar (1992) varied either the phonological similarity or the length of the foreign words to be learnt, two factors known to influence the phonological loop. Both manipulations impaired second-language vocabulary but not native language-based learning. The conclusions drawn from PV of the importance of the loop for learning new word forms therefore appeared to be supported. However, they still were confined to adults acquiring a second language. The system would clearly be more important if it also influenced the acquisition by children of their native tongue.

Susan Gathercole and I investigated this question by testing a group of children with a specific language impairment (Gathercole & Baddeley, 1990). These children were eight years old, had normal nonverbal intelligence, but had the language development of six-year-olds. Could this reflect a phonological loop deficit? When given a battery of memory tests, they proved to be particularly impaired in their capacity to repeat back unfamiliar pseudo words. Note that this task not only requires participants to hear the nonwords, but also to hold them in memory for long enough to repeat them. On the basis of this, we developed the nonword repetition test in which pseudo words of increasing length are heard and must be repeated (e.g., *ballop*, *woogalamic*, *versatrational*). We tested language-impaired children, other children of the same age with normal language development, and a group of six-year-olds who were matched for level of language development with the language-impaired group but who, being younger, had a lower level of nonverbal performance. The results are shown in Figure 4.5, from which it is clear that the language-disordered eight-year-old children performed more poorly even than the six-year-olds. In fact, they were equivalent to four-year-olds in their nonword repetition capacity. Could their poor nonword repetition performance be related to their delayed language development? Is level of vocabulary related to nonword repetition performance in normal children too?

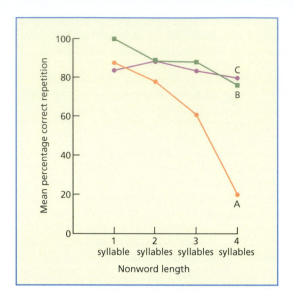

Figure 4.5 Percent correct repetition of nonwords by children with a specific language impairment (A), children of the same age (B), and children matched for language level (C). Adapted from Gathercole and Baddeley (1990).

In an attempt to investigate this, a cohort of children between the ages of four and five years who were just starting school in Cambridge, England, were tested using the nonword repetition test, together with a test of nonverbal intelligence and a measure of vocabulary. This involved presenting four pictures and pronouncing the name of one of them; the child's task was to point to the appropriate picture. As the test proceeded, the words became less and less common. Testing ended when performance broke down because the child no longer knew the words. Performance across these three tests was then correlated to see to what extent vocabulary was related to intelligence and to nonword repetition. The results are shown in Table 4.1, from which it is clear there was a substantial correlation between the capacity to hear and echo back a word and level of vocabulary development.

Of course, correlation does not mean causation. It is just as plausible to assume that having a good vocabulary will help you repeat back unfamiliar sounds, as it is to assume that capacity for repeating unfamiliar sounds will help you acquire new vocabulary.

TABLE 4.1 Relation between vocabulary scores at age four and other variables. There is a strong relationship with nonword repetition performance. From Gathercole and Baddeley (1989)

Measures	Correlation coefficient	Simple regression (% variance)	Stepwise regression (% variance)
Chronological age	0.218	5[a]	5[a]
Nonverbal intelligence	0.388	15[b]	13[b]
Nonword repetition	0.525	27[b]	15[b]
Sound mimicry	0.295	9[b]	0
Total	0.578	33[b]	—

[a] $P < 0.05$; [b] $P < 0.01$.

A study of the development of vocabulary in five- to six-year-old children (Gathercole & Baddeley, 1989) suggested that phonological memory was indeed the crucial factor at this stage. However, as children become older they are increasingly able to use existing vocabulary to help learn new words (Baddeley, Gathercole, & Papagno, 1998).

A related approach to exploring the role of the loop in language acquisition is to study children learning a second language at school. Service (1992) studied the learning of English by Finnish school children, finding that phonological STM was indeed a good predictor of success. A more recent attempt to tease apart the factors contributing to second-language vocabulary studied the acquisition of English vocabulary by French-speaking school children over a three-year immersion method class in which they were taught all subjects in English, rather than their native French (Nicolay & Poncelet, 2013). A range of measures correlated with English vocabulary acquisition, with phonological STM emerging as the best predictor, particularly over the initial phase. Broadly similar conclusions were reached by Engel de Abreu and Gathercole (2012) in a study of second-language learning in bi- and tri-lingual Luxemburgish children.

Whereas the link with vocabulary acquisition is probably the clearest evolutionary application of the phonological loop, it is likely that the loop also facilitates the acquisition of grammar, and probably also of reading (Baddeley et al., 1998; Ellis & Sinclair, 1996). Indeed, the nonword repetition test is used widely in the diagnosis of dyslexia, although reduced phonological loop capacity is likely to represent only one of a range of variables that can impact on the complex skill of the learning to read (Wagner & Torgersen, 1987).

The phonological loop and action control

The loop is, however, not only used as a limited capacity storage system but can also help to control action (Miyake & Shah, 1999). In one study, for example (Baddeley, Chincotta, & Adlam, 2001), we were interested in the capacity to switch attention between two tasks. We used the simple task of adding or subtracting one from a series of digits, thus, given 8, the response should be 9 in one case and 7 in the other. Participants were given a column of additions, a column of subtractions, or were required to alternate, adding to the first, subtracting from the second, adding to the third, etc. (e.g., $5 \rightarrow 6$: $8 \rightarrow 7$: $3 \rightarrow 4$, etc.). Go to Box 4.2 and try it yourself.

Alternation markedly slowed down performance, and there was a substantial further

---

KEY TERM

Immersion method: A strategy for foreign language teaching whereby the learner is placed in an environment where only the foreign language is used.

Box 4.2 Task switching

A simple task: For Column 1, add 1 to each of the ten digits. For Column 2, subtract 1. For Column 3, alternate adding for the first, subtracting for the second, etc. You'll probably find Column 3 slower.

1. Add 1 to each	2. Subtract 1 from each	3. Alternate + − + −
7	6	3
1	8	8
4	2	2
6	3	4
2	4	7
8	7	5
5	5	6
4	9	8
7	4	2
3	8	5

Now repeat the exercise below this time continuously saying the word "rabbit."

1. Add	2. Subtract	3. Alternate
4	2	7
8	9	4
1	6	2
6	8	9
8	3	6
5	9	3
2	4	7
7	2	5
4	5	8
7	3	2

Most people find that suppressing speech by saying an irrelevant word has little effect on Columns 1 and 2, but makes alternation harder. Why do you think this is the case?

slowing when participants had to suppress articulation by repeatedly uttering an irrelevant word while performing the switching condition. This did not however prevent accurate performance, suggesting that the loop was useful but not necessary for switching. We suspect that participants were relying on a subvocal set of self-instructions "add subtract-add-subtract-add …" to keep their place. Similar effects were observed and investigated further by Emerson and Miyake (2003) and by Saeki and Saito (2004) and more recently we have shown that subvocalized self-instruction appears to help in more long-term task switching where it seems to help people resist disruption from earlier habits (Saeki, Baddeley, Hitch, & Saito, 2013). The role of the loop in action control in these tasks at least, however, appears to be to provide a means of helping maintain a plan or strategy which itself is likely to depend on selection and control by the much more flexible central executive.

It is notable however that participants in psychological experiments do very frequently appear to rely on verbal coding to help them perform the task. This was investigated by two Russian psychologists—Alexander Luria (1959) and Lev Vygotsky (1962)—who emphasized the use of verbal *self-instruction* to control behavior, studying its application to the rehabilitation of brain-damaged patients and to its development in children (Box 4.3). Sadly, Luria and Vygotsky have so far had little direct influence on recent developments in mainstream cognitive psychology. One can only hope that further investigation of the role of speech in the control of action will remedy this.

We have described the development of the phonological loop model in some detail. This is not because it is the only, or indeed the most important, component of working memory; it certainly is not, but it is the component that has been investigated most extensively and, as such, provides an example of how relatively simple experimental tasks can be used to study complex cognitive processes and their practical implications.

We move on now to the visuo-spatial sketchpad, which has been rather less extensively investigated beyond the laboratory. The sketchpad involves visual and spatial STM as described in the previous chapter, but it goes beyond simple storage to include the manipulation of visual and spatial information, often relying heavily on executive resources. The most active area of investigation has been concerned with the topic of visuo-spatial imagery.

Box 4.3 Alexander Luria

The Russian psychologist Alexander Romanovitch Luria developed an ingenious method for studying the influence of language on the control of action. In one experiment, he asked children of different ages to squeeze a bulb when a red light came on, but not to squeeze for a blue light. Before the age of three, children typically press in response to both lights, even though they can report the instruction correctly, and can perform it correctly if given the instruction "press" when the red light comes on but no instruction with the blue light. A few months later, they are themselves able to make the appropriate verbal responses, but still do not perform the action. By age five, they are able both to speak and act appropriately, only later managing to act without giving themselves a verbal cue. Luria also demonstrated that patients with frontal lobe damage could have difficulty with this task, and could be helped through verbal self-cuing.

The influential Russian neuropsychologist Alexander Luria (1902–1977).

IMAGERY AND THE VISUO-SPATIAL SKETCHPAD

Suppose you were asked to describe a famous building such as the Taj Mahal or the White House. How would you do it? Close your eyes and try.

You probably based your description on some form of visuo-spatial representation, a visual image perhaps? An observer might also have seen you using your hands as a spatial supplement to your verbal account. People vary hugely in the extent to which they report having visual imagery. In the late 19th century, Sir Francis Galton, a Victorian gentleman, contacted his friends and asked them to remember their breakfast table from that morning, and then describe the experience. Some reported imagery that was almost as vivid as vision, whereas others denied having any visual imagery whatsoever. Such differences in reported vividness appear to have surprisingly little relationship to how well people perform on tasks that would be expected to make heavy demands on visual

imagery, such as visual recall (Di Vesta, Ingersoll, & Sunshine, 1971). Those studies that have found any difference tend, somewhat surprisingly, to observe *poorer* performance on visual memory tasks by participants reporting strong visual imagery (Heuer, Fischman, & Reisberg, 1986; Reisberg, Clayton, Heuer, & Fischman, 1986). The reason for this unexpected finding appears to be that people with vivid imagery do not have better *memories*, but use vividness as a sign of the accuracy of their recall and are more likely to misjudge a vivid but erroneous memory to be correct. This raises the question of whether different people have genuinely different subjective experiences, or simply describe their experience differently. Another possibility is that differences in retrieval strategy underpin the different reports. This could represent either differences in stored information, or alternative ways of accessing a common memory, a situation resembling that of a computer that can display the same information numerically, or graphically. We return to this issue in the section on the neurological basis of WM (p. **96**).

Image manipulation

Figure 4.6 shows a task studied by Shepard and Feng (1972). If the shapes depicted were made out of paper, both could be folded to create a solid, with the shaded area being the base. Your task is to imagine folding the shapes (shown on the left-hand side of Figure 4.6) and decide whether the arrows will meet head on. Try it.

Shepard and Feng found that the time it took participants to come to a solution was systematically related to the number of folds that would have been required.

Tasks like this are often used to select people for jobs, such as architect and engineer, that are likely to involve visual or spatial thinking. They also tend to be somewhat better performed by men than by women, who are likely to use a less spatial and more analytic and piecemeal approach (Linn & Petersen, 1985). A study by Hsi, Linn, and Bell (1997) found that female

How would you describe the Taj Mahal? Would vivid, visual imagery be the basis of your description?

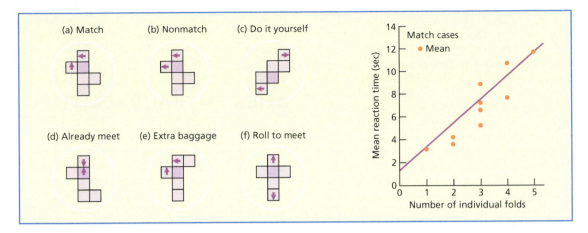

Figure 4.6 Left: Examples of six types of paper-folding problems used by Shepard and Feng (1972). Your task is to decide what would happen if the shapes were folded and made into a cube. Would the arrows meet? Right: Average time to decide whether the arrows on the cubes would match as a function of number of imaginary folds necessary to reach that decision. The circles represent each of 10 different types of problem. Data from Shepard and Feng (1972).

University of California Berkeley engineering students were less good at performing a spatial manipulation test and were also likely to do less well on a difficult graphics course for which 25% of female students obtained either a D or failed grade. Hsi et al. spoke to experienced engineers about the strategies of spatial manipulation they used and, on the basis of this, produced a one-day intensive course on spatial manipulation strategies. This was highly successful in improving performance to a point at which the gender differences disappeared and virtually no failures occurred.

A number of studies have tried to study spatial manipulation within the laboratory. Finke and Slayton (1988) developed the following task:

First, form an image of the capital letter J.

Then imagine capital D. Now rotate the D

through 90 degrees to the left and place it on

top of the J. What does it look like?

The answer is an umbrella. Pearson, Logie, and Gilhooly (1999) tried to analyze in more detail the processes involved. They gave their participants four, six, or eight symbols (e.g., square, triangle, circle, etc.), requiring them to use them to create an object that they should then name, and afterwards draw. If they had failed to produce an object after two minutes, participants were required simply to recall the memorized symbols. The roles of the visuo-spatial sketchpad and the phonological loop in the task were studied by means of concurrent tasks, using either articulatory suppression to disrupt the loop, or tapping a series of spatial locations to disrupt the sketchpad. Pearson et al. found that spatial tapping disrupted the capacity to create novel objects, suggesting that this aspect depends on the sketchpad, but had no effect on the capacity to remember what shapes were involved. However, the latter was disrupted by articulatory suppression, suggesting that the names of the shapes to be manipulated were held in the phonological loop.

The study by Pearson et al. is a good example of the way in which the visuo-spatial sketchpad and phonological loop can work together to enhance performance. A very striking example of this comes from a study using a group of Japanese experts in mental calculation who are very skilled at using the traditional calculating aid, the abacus, which involves manipulating beads within a framework. Hatano and Osawa (1983a, 1983b) studied calculators who were able to dispense with the actual abacus, relying instead on imagining the abacus. Experts can mentally add and subtract up to 15 numbers, each comprising from five to nine digits. They also have extremely high digit spans, around 16 for forward and 14 for backward recall. However, their enhanced span was limited to digits. Their span for other verbal material, such as consonants, for which the abacus imagery could not be used, was no better than that of a control group. As would be expected if the experts were relying on visuo-spatial imagery, their digit span was markedly disrupted by a concurrent spatial task, unlike control participants, whose performance was more disrupted by articulatory suppression.

Just as spatial activity can disrupt imagery, so imagery can interfere with spatial processing. A striking example of this occurred when I was visiting the US. I was listening to an American football game between UCLA and Stanford and forming a clear image of the game while driving along the San Diego freeway. I suddenly realized that the car was weaving from lane to lane. I switched to music and survived and on returning to Britain decided to study the effect under slightly less risky conditions. We did indeed find that a spatial task involving keeping a stylus in contact with a moving spot of light disrupted STM based on spatial imagery (Baddeley, Grant, Wight, & Thomson, 1973). The interference proved to be spatial in nature rather than visual, since performance was disrupted by the task of tracking the *location* of an *auditory* sound source while blindfolded, but not by making a *visual* but nonspatial brightness judgment (Baddeley & Lieberman, 1980).

Whereas this particular task appears to depend on spatial imagery, more purely visual imagery can also help in verbal recall. A powerful way of learning to associate pairs of words is to combine them into an inter-active image; for example, to associate *violin* and *banana*, one might imagine a concert violinist using a large banana as a bow. Such object-based imagery tends to be disrupted by presentation of irrelevant pictures or colors which participants are instructed to ignore (Logie, 1986, 1995). Indeed, under appro-priate conditions, even a flickering dot pattern can disrupt the use of visual imagery (Quinn & McConnell, 1996a, 1996b).

THE CENTRAL EXECUTIVE

Working memory is assumed to be directed by the central executive, an attentional controller rather than a memory system. Its main mode of operation is assumed to be that proposed by Norman and Shallice (1986), who assumed two modes of control, one of which is automatic and based on existing habits whereas the other depends on an attention-ally limited executive. Driving a car would be an example of the first type of semi-automatic control. The activities involved can be relatively complex, so that potential conflicts can occur, for example between continuing to drive and slowing down in response to a traffic signal, or another driver entering the road. There are assumed to be well-learned procedures for resolving such conflicts automatically. Because such behavior is based largely on well-learned habits, it requires little attention. Have you ever had the somewhat worrying experience of arriving at your driving destination with no recollection of how you got there? Were you conscious during the trip? You almost certainly were, but thinking about other matters and leaving the routine decisions to your conflict-resolution system.

However, when automatic conflict resolution is not possible, or when a novel situation arises, for example, a road is closed for repairs, then a second system is called into action, the supervisory attentional system (SAS). This is able to intervene, either in favor of one or other of the competing options or else to activate strategies for

> ### KEY TERM
>
> **Supervisory attentional system (SAS):**
> A component of the model proposed by Norman and Shallice to account for the attentional control of action.

seeking alternative solutions. It is the SAS component that is assumed to be linked to the central executive. Norman and Shallice (1986) did not specify just how the SAS operates and, as will become clear, this complex issue remains at the heart of subsequent theories of attentional control.

Norman and Shallice had somewhat different purposes in jointly producing their model. On the one hand, Norman was interested in slips of action, whereby a lapse of attention produces unforeseen consequences. These are sometimes trivial, as when you set off on a Saturday morning to drive to the supermarket and find yourself taking your regular route to work instead. On other occasions, such slips of attention can have tragic consequences, as when pilot error can lead to a plane crash. Both of these reflect situations in which the SAS *fails* to operate when it should.

Shallice, on the other hand, was principally interested in patients with frontal lobe damage, who appear to have problems of *attentional control*. This is sometimes reflected in perseveration, repetitively performing the same act or making the same mistake repeatedly. Patient RR, for example, suffered from bilateral damage to his frontal lobes following a car crash resulting in an attentional deficit which Baddeley and Wilson (1988) termed the dysexecutive syndrome. When he was asked during an occupational therapy session to measure and cut a series of lengths of tape, he persistently grasped the tape at the wrong point, leaving very short tape lengths. When this was pointed out, he crossly responded "I know I'm getting it wrong!" but was unable to break out of the incorrect action sequence.

On other occasions, the same patient might continually fail to *focus* attention, simply responding to whatever environmental cues are present. This sometimes leads to what is known as *utilization behavior*, in which the patient uninhibitedly makes use of whatever is around, drinking the tester's cup of tea, for example, or on one occasion picking up a hypodermic syringe and attempting to inject the examining doctor! In the absence of control from the SAS, the patient simply reverts to habit-based control,

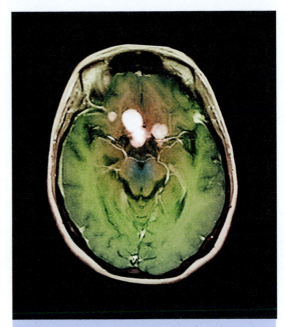

The central executive component of working memory is assumed to depend heavily on the frontal lobes. Much of the earlier evidence came from patients with frontal lobe damage such as the patient illustrated, whose MRI indicates a frontal lobe tumor.

responding automatically to any cues or opportunities afforded by the environment. The frontal lobes are assumed to be the part of the brain necessary for adequate operation of the SAS, with damage potentially leading to failures in the attentional control of action, particularly when the damage is extensive and extends to both the right and left frontal lobes.

Another function of the frontal lobes is to *monitor* behavior, checking that it is appropriate. Failure to do this can lead to bizarre behavior or confabulation. Patient RR, for example, woke up in bed on one occasion and demanded from his wife, "Why do you keep telling people we are married?" At that time, it was very unusual to live

KEY TERM

Confabulation: Recollection of something that did not happen.

together if not married. "But we are," she said, "we have three kids," going on to produce the wedding photographs. "That chap looks like me but it's not because I am not married," the patient replied. An hour or so later he appeared to have forgotten the incident and strongly denied it (Baddeley & Wilson, 1986).

A major function of the central executive is that of attentional focus, the capacity to direct attention to the task in hand. Consider a complex task like playing chess. What is the role of working memory? One approach is to use concurrent tasks to disrupt each of the subcomponents of working memory. Holding (1989) showed that counting backwards disrupted the capacity of players to remember a chess position, concluding that verbal coding was important. However, counting backwards also demands executive processing. We addressed this by comparing the effects on the recall of chess positions of articulatory suppression (to disrupt the loop), spatial tapping (to disrupt the sketchpad), and an attentionally demanding task known as random generation, in which participants try to produce a stream of numbers, making the sequence as random as possible. We tested both highly expert and relatively inexperienced players. The two groups differed greatly in overall performance, but all showed the same interference pattern. Articulatory suppression had no influence, suggesting that the phonological

According to Robbins et al. (1996), selecting good chess moves requires use of the central executive and the visuo-spatial sketchpad but not of the phonological loop.

loop was not involved, whereas the visuo-spatial task did impair performance but not as much as random generation. We found the same result when the task was changed from remembering the chess positions to choosing the best next move, indicating an important role for both the sketchpad and central executive in planning as well as remembering a chess position (Robbins et al.,1996).

Another attentional capacity that is attributed to the central executive is that of dividing attention between two or more tasks, for example chatting to a passenger while driving. On the whole, this seems to proceed reasonably safely. If the traffic situation becomes complex, the driver can cease speaking and the passenger is likely to see why, and postpone the conversation. This is not the case with a mobile phone conversation, however, during which there might also be a much more serious attempt to convey complex information or discuss an important business matter. As we saw in the section on the sketchpad, if spatial information is involved, this is likely to interfere with steering control. Even more important, however, is the effect of concurrent telephoning on the capacity to make sensible driving decisions. In an early study, Brown, Tickner, and Simmonds (1969) had their participants drive a route marked out on an airfield that involved going through gaps of varying width between polystyrene blocks. A concurrent verbal reasoning task did not impair the drivers' skill in steering through such gaps, but it seriously disrupted their judgment with the result that they tended to attempt gaps that were narrower than the car. The danger in telephoning while driving does not principally result from what the driver's hands are doing but from what the brain is neglecting to do (Box 4.4).

It has been suggested that the central executive is required if attention has to be switched between two or more tasks (Baddeley, 1996). However, the idea that switching might always be the function of a single attentional system appears to be an oversimplification, with some aspect of switching being relatively automatic whereas others are almost certainly attentionally demanding (Allport, Styles, & Hsieh, 1994; Monsell, 2005).

Box 4.4 Inattention when driving causes accidents

A naturalistic study that videoed drivers and the road ahead for a total of two million miles of driving time recorded 82 crashes, with 80% implicating driver inattention during the previous three seconds (National Highway Safety Administration, 2006). Cell (mobile) phone use is a potent source of such inattention, with accidents being four times more frequent when a cell phone is in use, regardless of whether or not it is hand held (Redelmeier & Tibshirani, 1997).

A laboratory study by Strayer and Johnston (2001) showed that drivers who were using cell phones were substantially more likely to miss a red light and were significantly slower at applying the brakes, regardless of whether or not the phone was hand held.

THE EPISODIC BUFFER

A major problem with the three-component model of working memory was that of explaining how it was linked to LTM. Memory span for words in a sentence is about 15 compared to a span of 5 or 6 for unrelated words (Brener, 1940). However, it is not clear how this can be accounted for within the three-component model. Fifteen words are substantially more than the capacity of the phonological loop, and enhanced recall of sentences is not limited to those that can readily be turned into visual imagery. At a broader level, it is of course unsurprising that this is the case. The order of words within a sentence is constrained by the rules of grammar and by the overall meaning of the sentence, both allowing the chunking process described in Chapter 3 to increase span, and in both cases depending on LTM. However, this then raises the question of exactly how working memory is able to take advantage of long-term knowledge: How do working memory and LTM interact?

This was by no means the only problem for the three-component model. Digit span itself presents a challenge. Given that we can typically remember seven or more digits, and two or three of these come from the loop, where are the other items stored? If in visual STM, how is this combined with phonological STM? Finally, a study of what determines the vividness of visual imagery by Baddeley and Andrade (2000) suggests that images such as that of a familiar market scene do not appear to depend at all heavily on the visuo-spatial and phonological subsystems. Instead they appear depend principally on the amount and type of information held in LTM. Hence, when shown a picture of a specific bird and asked later to recollect that picture, level of vividness reported depended on prior knowledge of birds rather than WM. So where is the information for complex visual images held while the judgment of vividness is made? In an attempt to provide an answer to these questions, I proposed a fourth component, the episodic buffer (Baddeley, 2000).

The episodic buffer is assumed to be a storage system that can hold about four chunks of information in a multidimensional code. It is assumed to be able to hold episodes or chunks based on a range of different dimensions, including visual, verbal, and semantic which may come from a range of sources in addition to working memory, notably including both perception and LTM. Each of these information sources uses a different code, but these can be combined within the multidimensional buffer (see Figure 4.7).

I also proposed that information was retrieved from the episodic buffer through conscious awareness. This linked the working memory model with an influential view as to the function of consciousness. Baars (1997, 2002) suggests that conscious awareness

KEY TERM

Episodic buffer: A component of the Baddeley and Hitch model of working memory model that assumes a multidimensional code, allowing the various subcomponents of working memory to interact with long-term memory.

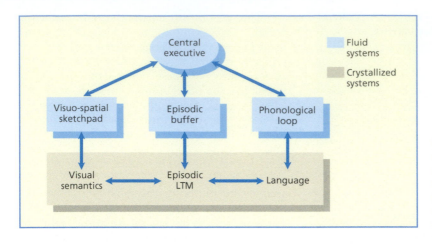

Figure 4.7 The Baddeley (2000) version of the multicomponent working memory. Links to long-term memory have been specified and a new component, the episodic buffer, added.

serves the function of pulling together separate streams of information from the various senses and binding them into perceived objects and scenes. He links this to the proposal that consciousness serves as a mental workspace that assists in performing complex cognitive activities, in short, a working memory. He uses the metaphor of a theater, in which consciousness is represented by the stage on which an ongoing play is played by actors, who are seen as analogous to the various interactive cognitive processes.

In its initial form (Baddeley, 2000), the episodic buffer was assumed to be an active system, entirely controlled by the central executive. It was assumed to be capable of binding together previously unrelated concepts to create new combinations, for example, the concepts of ice hockey and elephants to imagine an ice-hockey-playing elephant. This novel representation can be manipulated in working memory, allowing one to answer questions such as what position the elephant should play. It could, for instance, do some crunching tackles, but might it be even more useful in goal?

At a more routine level, it was suggested that executive processes were necessary to

bind the words in a sentence into meaningful chunks, or indeed to bind perceptual features such as shapes and colors into perceived objects. If this were the case, then you would expect that disrupting the executive with a demanding concurrent task would interfere with binding. In recent years, my colleagues and I have tested this hypothesis extensively. We found however that demanding concurrent tasks impair overall performance, but do not have the even greater impact on binding that we expected. Hence an executive load had no more impact on the binding of color and shape into colored objects than it had on storing the individual features (Allen, Baddeley, & Hitch, 2006). Similarly the process of binding of words into chunks when sentences are recalled, also appears automatic and resistant to the effect of an attentional load (Baddeley, Hitch, & Allen, 2009). In short, the episodic buffer seems to be less like Baars' stage, the center of the action, and to be more like a passive screen, with the action originating and being controlled from elsewhere. Furthermore, since binding still occurs regardless of disruption of the central executive, it seems likely that binding may depend on different systems for different materials; binding shape to color is probably based on visual-attentional systems, while binding in sentence processing seems to depend on long-term language processing (Baddeley, 2007, 2012).

The concept of an episodic buffer has proved useful in a number of ways. At a theoretical level, it bridges the gap between

KEY TERM

Binding: Term used to refer to the linking of features into objects (e.g., color red, shape square, into a red square), or of events into coherent episodes.

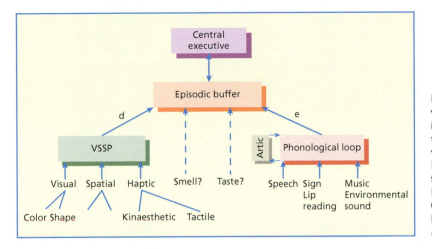

Figure 4.8 A speculative view of the flow of information from perception to working memory. VSSP, visuo-spatial sketchpad. Reproduced with permission from the Annual Review of Psychology, Volume 63 © 2012 Annual Reviews, http://www.annualreviews.org.

the multicomponent Baddeley and Hitch (1974) model with its emphasis on storage, and the more attentionally focused model of Cowan (1999, 2005). In doing so, it has emphasized the important question of how working memory and LTM interact, and more specifically has stimulated research on the issue of how different sources of information are bound together. This has led to further links between the multicomponent model and studies concerned with visual attention and memory (Luck & Vogel, 1997; Vogel, Woodman, & Luck, 2001), and with the classic issues of language comprehension (Daneman & Carpenter, 1980; Kintsch & van Dyck, 1977).

The current model of working memory is shown in Figure 4.8. This is essentially an elaboration of the original three-part model, with two major changes. One of these reflects the assumed link to LTM from the phonological and visuo-spatial subsystems, one allowing the acquisition of language, and the other performing a similar function for visual and spatial information. This is much less investigated than is the language link, but is assumed to be involved in acquiring visual and spatial knowledge of the world, for example learning the shape and color of a banana, or the layout of a city.

The second major change is the inclusion of the episodic buffer. In the original (Baddeley, 2000) version, the buffer was accessed only through the central executive. However, the evidence just described on binding visual

and verbal information into chunks suggests that information can access the buffer directly from the visuo-spatial and phonological subsystems and from LTM (arrows d and e). You will notice two additional arrows accessing the episodic buffer, dotted rather than solid, to emphasize their tentative status. They reflect the speculation that smell and taste may also gain access to the buffer when consciously experienced.

So how does WM relate to LTM? My own view is that the interface between WM, perception, and LTM is complex, flexible, and interactive. As shown in Figure 4.9, WM is assumed to provide a crucial link between cognition and action. It can take in information at a range of levels from sensory through perception to long-term memory. The precise way in which these links occur will depend

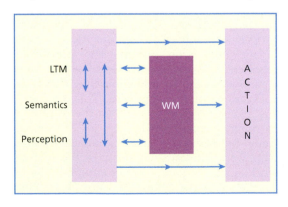

Figure 4.9 My current view of the complex and multiple links between WM and LTM.

on the information to be processed and the resultant action. Note also that not everything needs to go through working memory; threat stimuli can activate an avoidance response even before the stimulus is registered in conscious awareness. Öhman and Soares (1994) presented negative pictures such as spiders versus neutral pictures to spider-phobic and control participants. They found an emotional skin response in the spider-phobic group to the spiders even when the pictures were presented too briefly to be consciously detected. They interpret this in terms of a separate direct link between perception and action that is more rapid than the normal route via conscious awareness, hence providing a rapid early warning signal (see LeDoux, 1996, for an account of the neural basis of this effect). In conclusion, like Nelson Cowan (1999) and others, I am sure that working memory involves activated LTM. I do not however regard this as an explanation, but rather as a challenge to explore the ways in which the complex, multilevel interaction between WM and LTM is achieved.

INDIVIDUAL DIFFERENCES IN WORKING MEMORY

Virtually all the evidence described up to this point has been based on the experimental method of contrasting two or more groups or conditions. An alternative is the correlational approach that takes advantage of differences between individuals to explore the structure of the underlying system. The previously reported link between verbal span and second-language learning (Service, 1992) is an example of this approach. This approach has played a central role in the study of working memory, following an influential study by Daneman and Carpenter (1980), who were interested in the possible role of working memory in language comprehension. They took as the defining feature of working memory, the need for the simultaneous storage and processing of information, and then set out to develop a task that would

measure this. They were remarkably successful. The task they produced appears to be a very simple one. Participants are required to read a series of sentences out loud and subsequently recall the last word of each. Try it for yourself:

A sailor returned from a long voyage having acquired a parrot as a pet.

It was a terribly cold winter with many violent storms.

The play was an enormous success and ran for many years.

What were the three last words?

They were *pet*, *storms*, and *years*. Span is typically between two and four sentences.

Daneman and Carpenter (1980) showed that their working memory span task was able to predict the prose comprehension capacity of their student participants, a result that has been replicated many times. Daneman and Merikle (1996) review 74 studies showing broadly similar results. A total of 38 studies looked at working memory span and global comprehension. Correlations were consistently higher than those obtained for standard verbal STM tasks.

Working memory span has also proved able to predict a wide range of other capacities. High-span participants are better at prose composition (Benton, Kraft, Glover, & Plake, 1984), obeying complex instructions (Engle, Carullo, & Collins, 1991), and taking notes (Kiewra & Benton, 1988). The capacity to predict performance extends beyond language tests to performance on a course concerning logic gates (Kyllonen & Stephens, 1990), and on a 40-hour-long course on the PASCAL programming language (Shute, 1991). A study by Kyllonen and Christal (1990) compared performance on a series of working memory tasks with a battery of reasoning ability measures taken from standard IQ tests, finding a very high correlation. The principal difference was that the IQ tests appeared to depend somewhat more on prior experience, and the working memory

Children with low working memory scores are typically described by their teachers as "dreamy" or inattentive; however, ADHD may well be responsible as it is linked to working memory performance.

measures somewhat more on speed. Engle, Tuholski, Laughlin, and Conway (1999) obtained a similar result finding a high correlation between working memory and fluid intelligence.

Given the predictive power of complex span measures, there is great interest in understanding why they are successful in predicting such a wide range of cognitive activities. If we could identify the task component underpinning complex span, this might provide a deeper understanding of both working memory and intelligence. Attempts to develop a theory of working memory based on individual differences typically involve breaking working memory performance down into a number of more basic components, devising tasks that aim to tap these components, and then examining the extent to which each of these is able to predict performance on tests of reasoning, intelligence, or academic performance. Part of this process of analysis involves studying the extent to which particular tasks are related to each other, in ways that might suggest the nature of the underlying structure of the memory and processing systems involved.

Happily, there tends to be broad agreement, with most analyses stressing the importance of an attentionally based control system, analogous to the central executive within the multicomponent working memory

model. This tends to be strongly involved in complex tasks, with a smaller contribution from two or more components that appear to be responsible for the simple storage of verbal and visuo-spatial material, respectively (Engle et al., 1999; Gathercole, Pickering, Ambridge, & Wearing, 2004; Miyake, Friedman, Rettinger, Shah, & Hegarty, 2001). Again, this broadly resembles the structure proposed by the Baddeley and Hitch model. Most theories of working memory focus on the executive component, often simply attributing the STM functions to relatively unspecified "activation of LTM," although the use of active verbal rehearsal is typically accepted as a source of temporary storage.

Although most theories derived from the study of individual differences have proved to be broadly compatible with the multicomponent model, this resemblance is not always obvious. Nelson Cowan's influential approach to working memory is a good example of a conflict that, in my own view, is more apparent than real (Baddeley, 2007, 2012; Cowan, 2001, 2005).

ALTERNATIVE APPROACHES TO WORKING MEMORY

A major feature of the multicomponent model of working memory is that its approach is "bottom-up," beginning with the study of verbal span and only later addressing the difficult questions of attentional control. Most alternative approaches have, on the contrary, taken a "top-down" approach, starting with the hard questions and being less concerned with the links to STM. A good example of this is Nelson Cowan's influential model.

Cowan's embedded processes model

Cowan described working memory as "cognitive processes that retain information in an unusually accessible state" (Cowan, 1999,

p. 62). For Cowan, working memory depends on activation that takes place within LTM, and is controlled by attentional processes (Figure 4.10). Activation is temporary and decays unless maintained either through active verbal rehearsal or continued attention.

Activated LTM is multidimensional, as in my own concept of an episodic buffer, the main difference being that I assume that information is downloaded from LTM and represented within the episodic buffer, whereas Cowan suggests that a new representation is set up in LTM each time. We return to this issue later. Cowan's research has been particularly concerned with working memory capacity where he argues strongly for a capacity of about four chunks (Cowan, 2005), rather than the seven originally proposed by Miller (1956). His model reflects his interest in attention, and his research on the development of memory during childhood rather than in the more peripheral aspects of working memory and the neuropsychological evidence that influenced my own approach.

Both Cowan and I have principally used an approach based on the experimental method of research, and a recent attempt has been made to carry out an "Adversarial Collaboration" to design experiments that will distinguish between the predictions made by the models proposed by Cowan, by Barrouillet and Camos, and the multicomponent model as represented by Logie (e.g., Doherty et al., 2019; Rhodes et al., 2019). The outcome is that, after agreeing on a series of theoretically targeted experiments, all three proponents claim some success with no knockout blows. My own view is that the

models are not sufficiently different to allow a clear distinction to be made which I myself regard as appropriate given the complexity of the area covered and our stage of development.

This degree of broad agreement may seem strange given the apparent differences between the multicomponent model and Cowan's approach. Some of this comes from our different neuropsychological vantage points with much of my own approach being based on single-case neuropsychological patients while Cowan is more influenced by neuroimaging approaches. This has recently encouraged attempts by Morey and Cowan to deny the validity of some of the patient-based evidence (Morey, 2018a, 2018b; Morey, Rhodes, & Cowan, 2019). These claims have however been strongly criticized as based on an inadequate understanding and inaccurate reporting of the relevant studies (Hanley & Young, 2019; Logie, 2019, Shallice & Papagno, 2019). Cowan's model does not seem to be inherently inconsistent with the evidence for the neural basis for the phonological loop and sketchpad; it simply does not currently focus on these specific aspects of WM, while the papers criticizing the neuropsychological evidence offer little in the way of alternative accounts of the data. Furthermore, Cowan and I agree that the

KEY TERM

Working memory capacity: An assessment of how much information can be processed and stored at the same time.

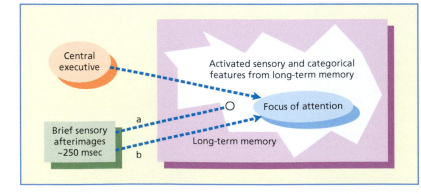

Figure 4.10 Cowan's embedded-processes model of working memory. A central executive controls focus of attention, which acts on recently activated features from LTM. The focus can hold approximately four objects in mind at the same time. Adapted from Cowan (1988).

concept of a central executive linked to an episodic buffer has much in common with his attentional control component focused on recently activated LTM. Where we differ is whether it is necessary to have a separate temporary storage system such as the episodic buffer or whether this can all occur in LTM.

A recent paper by Norris (2017) strongly attacks the idea that LTM can function as a temporary storage system. One major criticism of the activated LTM position that is raised by Norris stems from what is known in linguistics as "the problem of two" (Jackendoff, 1992) that occurs in the retention of sequences containing a repeat, for example 7 9 1 9 2. If the sequence is stored by encoding via the activation of existing long-term representations of the digits, the problem arises as to how to distinguish the two repeats, when recalling the sequence. Should 9 be followed by 1 or by 2? In a reply to Norris, Cowan (2019) proposes to solve this problem by assuming that each sequence will involve setting up a new representation in LTM. Such representations differ from old representations in their capacity to store sequences, comprising a separate and "special" kind of LTM, to which Norris (in press) responds that Cowan is simply relabeling STM by calling it a special kind of LTM. Could Cowan's "special LTM" perhaps be equivalent to the episodic buffer? Cowan and I informally agree that this merits further discussion.

Engle's inhibitory control model

One of the most active and innovative groups using the individual differences approach to working memory is that associated with Randy Engle and colleagues. Whereas much of the early work using the working memory span measure has been limited to observing correlations between span and various cognitive capacities, Engle has consistently focused on the theoretical issue of understanding what capacities and processes underpin such associations, and has used a fruitful combination of experimental and correlational methods.

Turner and Engle (1989), for example, demonstrated that the predictive capacity of complex span was not limited to measures based on sentence processing. They developed the *operation span* measure in which each to-be-remembered word is followed by an arithmetic operation; for example, *Apple*, $7 + 2 - 1 = ?$ *House*, $5 - 1 + 6 = ?$ and so on; after which the words must be recalled. This measure correlates highly with the initial sentence span task and is also a good predictor of a broad range of cognitive performance measures.

Engle (1996) proposes that performance on a complex span task is made difficult by the need to protect the memory of the presented items from *proactive interference (PI)*, the tendency for earlier items to compete at retrieval with the items to be recalled. Evidence for this comes from a range of sources and is typically based on a procedure whereby a complex span task is given to a large group of students, with those performing particularly well or particularly badly then being chosen for further investigation. Then, rather than looking for an overall correlation across participants, Engle uses an experimental design testing for differences between these two extreme high and low span groups in their capacity to perform various other tasks.

In one study (Kane & Engle, 2000), participants were required to remember three successive free recall lists, each based on words from a set of 10 semantic categories, for example one animal list, one color list, and one list of country names. If the same category is used for several successive lists, this leads to poorer recall of later lists, even though different words are used in each list, an example of proactive interference (see Chapter 9, p. 293). As predicted, this interference effect proved to be reliably greater in low working memory span participants. Performance on the first list did not differ, suggesting that resistance to interference from earlier lists rather than learning capacity was the crucial factor.

Engle suggests that the capacity to resist interference is not limited to memory. In one study Conway, Cowan, and Bunting (2001) required participants to repeat a stream of digits presented to one ear and ignore messages presented to other. Unexpectedly, the person's name was included in the unintended stream. When subsequently questioned, the low span participants were much more likely to have detected their names, even though instructed to ignore that source, presumably because they were less able to shut out the irrelevant material, as predicted by the inhibition theory (Conway et al., 2001).

These and other studies do indeed suggest that there is a genuine and important link between complex span and capacity to resist interference, although it is entirely plausible to assume that both reflect some kind of more general executive capacity that plays an equally important role in other cognitive functions (see Box 4.4). However, the nature of inhibition is itself open to question. A study by Friedman and Miyake (2004) found evidence for two types of inhibition, one reflecting a capacity to resist interference within memory, as previously described,

together with a separate ability to inhibit a powerful response tendency, such as moving your eyes to fixate on a visual target that has just popped up. Both were modestly related to the Daneman and Carpenter reading span measure. Further evidence for the importance of working memory in resistance to interference is shown in Box 4.5.

Unsworth and Engle (2007) have developed a model that interprets individual differences in working memory in terms of two components which they refer to as

Box 4.5 High WM capacity helps resistance to distractors in visual WM

Fukuda and Vogel (2009) used measures of evoked response potential to study resistance to distracting stimuli in participants varying in working memory capacity as measured by the number

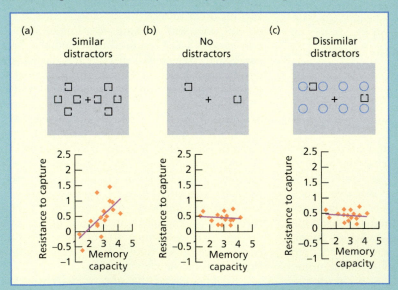

of visual targets they could successfully hold over a brief delay. When distractors are similar to targets, higher working memory capacity is needed to resist capture. When there are no distractors or dissimilar distractors, there is no effect of working memory capacity.

Figure 4.11 From Fukuda and Vogel (2009). Copyright © 2009 Society for Neuroscience.

primary and *secondary* memory. The primary component involves a dynamic attentional capacity for the temporary maintenance of items and is reflected in the recency effect in free recall of word lists. This secondary component involves the capacity for cue-dependent search in LTM. As the terminology suggests, this approach has much in common with views regarding working memory as a mode of operation of LTM. A more recent review of this approach (Shipstead, Lindsey, Marshall, and Engle (2014), however, accepts that multiple mechanisms may be needed to explain individual differences in WM capacity. These include the capacity for maintaining information in primary memory, as reflected in the recency effect together with retrieval from LTM and a more general attentional control capacity, with the degree of importance of each depending on the particular task involved. For example, they suggest that working memory span is particularly associated with attentional control while running memory span, memory for the last few items in a list, depends more on primary memory. It is currently unclear whether this approach can give an adequate account of other more detailed aspects of recency described in Chapter 3 (pp. 50–52).

An issue underpinning most models of WM concerns the source of forgetting. Engle and colleagues tend to focus on the importance of preventing interference with the remembered material, whereas an alternative possibility is that complex span reflects the capacity to prevent the decay of the memory trace through active rehearsal. This does not necessarily mean subvocal rehearsal, but also includes "refreshing" the act of keeping in mind the remembered items by focusing attention on the memory trace. Evidence for such rehearsal comes from the observation that the capacity to retain a small memory load such as three consonants is disrupted by a demanding backward counting task, but not when simple articulatory suppression is required (Baddeley, Lewis, & Vallar, 1984). This suggests that participants can maintain the items in some way without needing to continue to verbalize them, but that such activation is disrupted by a competing attentional activity.

The resource-sharing hypothesis has been strongly developed by a group led by Pierre Barrouillet and Valerie Camos, who replaced the arithmetic task used in Turner and Engle's (1989) operation span task with a simple letter-reading task that was, however, strictly paced. Thus, participants were required to remember words while concurrently processing letters coming rapidly one after the other. This apparently simple task correlated even more highly with measures of reading and arithmetic than did conventional complex span measures (Lépine, Barrouille, & Camos, 2005). Barrouillet, Bernardin, and Camos (2004) explained this, and other related findings, by arguing that most complex span tasks allow brief gaps in which attention-based refreshing might occur, whereas their more rigidly controlled simple task minimizes such rehearsal. A related theory is the task-switching hypothesis proposed by Towse and Hitch (1995; Towse, Hitch, & Hutton, 2000), who also assume a trace decay interpretation with participants switching attention between maintaining the trace and performing the secondary task. The concept of trace decay in STM is however strongly resisted by Lewandowsky and Oberauer (2008) who argue for an interference model resulting in a vigorous defense by Barrouillet and Camos (2014). The long-running saga of decay versus interference surges on!

A much more detailed approach to WM that resembles that of Cowan in assuming a limited attentional capacity is proposed in a very ambitious recent model by Oberauer and Hein (2012) who make the further assumption that only a single item can be held in focus at any one time. Oberauer and Hein provide a much more detailed model

KEY TERM

Resource sharing: Use of limited attentional capacity to maintain two or more simultaneous activities.

Task switching: A process whereby a limited capacity system maintains activity on two or more tasks by switching between them.

than those discussed previously including an interesting distinction between *declarative WM*, those aspects of which we are aware (the episodic buffer perhaps?), and *procedural WM*, the underlying processes that may or may not be accessible to conscious awareness (the processes underpinning the operation of the loop and sketchpad perhaps?). They are, however, much more specific in proposing detailed mechanisms that underpin their model than is the case more generally. It is currently too early to assess how successful this ambitious approach will be.

CAN WORKING MEMORY BE TRAINED?

While views differ on the theoretical interpretation of working memory, there is general agreement that it plays an important role in life, and that a working memory deficit can be a major handicap. Could it be remedied, perhaps by training? This question was addressed by Torkel Klingberg, a Swedish neurologist who developed a training program he named Cogmed which was presented in a format resembling a computer game, with participants encouraged to strive to improve their performance in regular sessions extending over many hours (Klingberg, 2002). Not only did performance improve,

but importantly, it appeared to generalize to tests other than those used for training. In one study, for example, Klingberg et al. (2005) administered their training program to groups of children with Attention Deficit Hyperactivity Disorder (ADHD) and matched controls, in each case, also testing control groups using a much less demanding regime that was not expected to be effective as a training routine. These were included to ensure that any advantage that might be gained was not simply the result of receiving more attention. Groups were then tested on a range of new and different working memory-related tests, together with Raven's Matrices, a widely used test of nonverbal intelligence. Klingberg et al. observed a clear improvement in performance in the Cogmed trained group over the control group that extended to both the novel working memory tests and to Raven's Matrices.

Klingberg's group went on to investigate the neurobiological bases of their training program. A study by McNab and Klingberg (2008) reported a correlation between WM performance and activity in the prefrontal cortex and basal ganglia. An fMRI study by Olesen, Westerberg, and Klingberg (2004) found that five weeks of practice on Cogmed led to increased activation in frontal and parietal cortex, areas that are generally accepted as being associated with WM.

Despite considerable skepticism, Klingberg's work evoked widespread interest. His

Cogmed is a memory training program presented in a format resembling a computer game.

program became commercially available but, given its complexity, was not cheap. Hence, people began to explore both the Klingberg and other possible training regimes, often with apparent success. The commercial potential of setting up such schemes rapidly became obvious, and a range of variants has become widely available. However, it is much easier to set up a training regime than to conduct adequate trials that demonstrate that it really achieves something of practical value, and many such products were often poorly supported by experimental evidence leading to an extensive range of further research.

So how good is the evidence for successfully training working memory? Melby-Lervåg and Hulme (2013) conducted a meta-analysis, combining the results of all the available studies that were at all adequately designed, and hence that at least included an appropriate control group. They found 30 such studies, concluding that there was good evidence for short-term gains that generalize to tasks other than those studied. However, those studies that had followed up and retested after a delay of weeks or months gave less encouraging results, with no evidence for improved verbal WM, some evidence for a continuing advantage to visual WM, but very little evidence for generalization to nonlaboratory tasks. Reviewing the data from a more theoretical perspective, Shipstead, Redick, and Engle (2012) identify methodological problems with many of the studies, and in the case of the studies that were adequately designed, they question the extent to which they generalize beyond the laboratory. Finally, Shipstead et al. comment that, where training appears to succeed, it is by no means clear that working memory is the crucial factor.

In a paper entitled "Let's be realistic about intervention research," Gathercole, Dunning, and Holmes (2012) suggest that such reviews might be unduly pessimistic, pointing out that it is in the nature of applied research, that the process of moving from a broad proof of concept to final application is likely to involve many stages. They initially decided to carry out a small study attempting to replicate the Cogmed findings on ADHD by Klingberg et al. (2005), attaching it to a larger already funded project. The results of this preliminary study were encouraging (Holmes et al., 2010), leading them to move on to study non-ADHD children with low WM performance. Their conclusions "after a gruelling three years" were broadly in line with the overall reviews, namely that there was good evidence for an effect of training, with generalization to other WM tasks, but little evidence that such improvement automatically generalized to general intelligence or to academic performance. Why should that be so, given that clear transfer did occur to tasks that are typically correlated with IQ?

Gathercole, Dunning, Holmes, and Norris (2019) attempt to tackle this question by moving beyond the empirical question of whether training helps, to the more theoretical issue of the conditions under which training on one task will enhance performance on another, and why. The link between the array of tasks used for WM training and academic performance or intelligence test scores is far from obvious. This might not matter if training were simply having a general effect on neural plasticity, or indeed enhancing some general pool of resources. However, the fact that training effects occur but often fail to generalize, casts doubt on this assumption. Gathercole et al. therefore suggest that more detailed analysis of those cases in which transfer does occur and those where it does not, might offer a way forward.

The approach they adopt is influenced by earlier work on the acquisition of skills by John Anderson (1993) which assumes a series of cognitive routines that need to be implemented in order to accomplish a given mental activity. These typically involve a hierarchical structure with overall control operating at an executive level which then utilizes lower level routines at both the input and response stages. Such routines will initially tend to be slow and error-prone but become increasingly automatic with practice. The capacity for training effects to generalize to other tasks is assumed to depend on features that are common to both the initial training and the new transfer tasks. If the cognitive routine hypothesis is to prove a useful way ahead, however, there is a clear need to specify the cognitive routines involved in

WM training and explain why transfer occurs in some cases but not in others.

Gathercole et al. then surveyed the literature, identifying some 117 WM training papers of which 94 were excluded for methodological reasons. This left 23 papers with data allowing detailed analysis of a limited range of common task types including verbal and visual versions of serial STM, complex span measures in which material must be manipulated, as well as stored and backward span. They found that when both trained and transfer tasks involved developing the same novel routine, training led to clear transfer to the new task. Tasks of this kind included visuo-spatial serial recall, serial recall, complex span when similar new manipulations had to be developed, and backward span which again involved developing new routines. As expected, they found little improvement when the two routines both involved an already well-practiced skill such as verbal rehearsal.

A limitation of this initial study was the range and potential variability among tasks from 23 different studies, making categorization tricky. Their next analysis avoided this by performing a similar process-based analysis on data collected from the tasks used consistently across their own earlier studies of children with a range of potential working memory deficits; these data had not been included in their initial analysis but yielded a broadly similar pattern of results. A third study concerned the question of individual differences in the extent to which training on one task enhances the performance of other related activities (Jaeggie, Buschkuehl, Jonides, & Shah, 2011). Do poor performers gain more, as might be suggested by an interpretation in terms of a general improvement in "learning to learn" (Bavelier, Green, Pouget, & Schrater, 2012) or do poor performers, having more to learn, perhaps benefit most? It proved to be the case that when transfer occurs, high performers gain more, perhaps because their greater executive capacity makes it easier for them to find ways of performing new tasks? Another case in which "the rich get richer," just the opposite to what one might have hoped for in developing a means of compensating for cognitive limitations.

The paper by Gathercole et al. (2019) provides a potentially important step forward in the controversy over whether working memory can be trained. It offers a new analysis and interpretation of earlier results that echoes but importantly extends earlier findings. It does however depend on the complex issue of task analysis and, as they point out, certainly needs replication and further extension. From a practical viewpoint, however, the Gathercole et al. (2019) study would seem to be disappointing in suggesting that rather than increasing the overall capacity of WM, training regimes simply improve performance on the routines underpinning the specific tasks that are practiced and that these are unlikely to map onto the complex array of processes underlying most important educational activities.

However, it remains possible that by identifying some of the crucial components of practically important tasks, it might be possible to select and train specific subroutines. The study by Hsi et al. (1997), for example, involving the training of specific visualization strategies in female engineers, is a case in point (see pp. 80–81). Meanwhile, from a theoretical viewpoint this study suggests an important potential bridge between theoretical approaches such as that reflected in the multicomponent model, and the practical analysis of skills reflected in John Anderson's production systems approach to cognition (Lee & Anderson, 2013).

THE NEUROSCIENCE OF WORKING MEMORY

This chapter has focused on the psychology of working memory based almost entirely on behavioral methods of study. However, a great deal of work has been concerned with investigating the anatomical and neurophysiological basis of working memory. Initially, this approach relied principally on patient-based neuropsychological evidence; more recently however the field has been dominated by neuroimaging studies based on healthy human participants.

Neuroimaging working memory

A closer and more extensive link between psychological and neurobiological approaches to memory is provided by work applying the various techniques of brain imaging described in Chapter 2 to the study of working memory. The initial studies used positron emission tomography (PET), which you might recall involves introducing a radioactive substance into the bloodstream and using this to monitor the amount of activity occurring in different brain regions (see Chapter 2, p. 31). Two research groups were initially particularly active in applying this method to the study of working memory. In London, Paulesu, Frith, and Frackowiak (1993) carried out a study that was based on the phonological loop hypothesis. They identified two separate regions, one in the area between the parietal and temporal lobes of the left hemisphere, which appeared to be responsible for phonological storage, and a second more frontally based region known as Broca's area, known to be involved in speech production, that appeared to be linked to subvocal rehearsal (Figure 4.12).

The second group, led by Jon Jonides and Edward Smith at the University of Michigan, was active in further extending the use of neuroimaging to investigate working memory, carrying out a sustained series of carefully designed and theoretically targeted experiments (Smith & Jonides, 1997). The first direct comparison of visual and verbal working memory was provided by Smith, Jonides, and Koeppe (1996). In their verbal memory task, participants were shown four letters, followed by a probe letter. Participants had to decide whether the probe letter had been contained in the previous set of four. A baseline control involved presenting both the stimulus and the probe simultaneously: everything was the same except for the need to remember. If the amount of brain activation in this baseline condition is subtracted from the activation involved when memory is also required, then the difference in blood flow should reflect the additional demand made by the need to remember, over and above that involved in perceiving and processing the experimental stimuli. Like Paulesu et al., Smith and colleagues found that verbal STM activated two separate areas in the left hemisphere.

In the case of visuo-spatial memory, participants were shown an array of three dots, followed after a delay by a circle (Figure 4.13). They had to decide whether

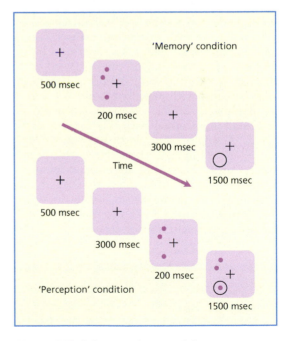

Figure 4.13 Schematic drawing of the events on each trial of the spatial memory and spatial perception tasks used by Smith et al. (1996). Copyright © Oxford University Press. Reproduced with permission.

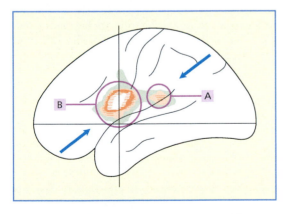

Figure 4.12 Neuroimaging the phonological loop. An early study using positron emission tomography identified area A with phonological storage and B with the articulatory rehearsal process. Redrawn from Paulesu et al. (1993).

this coincided with a location that had been occupied by one of the dots. Again, a baseline was established in which the dots and circle were presented at the same time. As indicated in Figure 4.14, visual memory resulted in activation in a series of areas mainly in the right hemisphere (Smith et al., 1996).

Further studies (reviewed by Smith & Jonides, 1997) observed a distinction between spatial working memory as described above, and memory for an *object or shape*. Spatial memory activates more dorsal or upper regions of the brain whereas object memory tends to be more concentrated on lower or ventral areas (Figure 4.15). It is notable that research on visual processing in nonhuman primates (Mishkin, Ungerleider, & Macko, 1983) has identified two separable visual processing streams, with the dorsal stream being concerned with spatial location (*where*), and the ventral processing stream with shape and object coding (*what*).

There is broad agreement that attentional control, as reflected in the central executive, is linked to the frontal lobes. The term attention is of course a rather broad one. An influential approach to the study of attention is that of Posner who distinguishes three types, each associated with a separate brain network. The first of these is concerned with alerting, the second with orienting attention, and the third with executive control (Posner & Rothbart, 2007). Working memory is principally concerned with this third system. Chun, Golomb, and Turk-Browne (2011) make a distinction between two broad aspects of the control of attention, one essentially perceptual in nature that takes in information from the world, while the other is internally focused and concerned with such factors as the selection of strategies and the

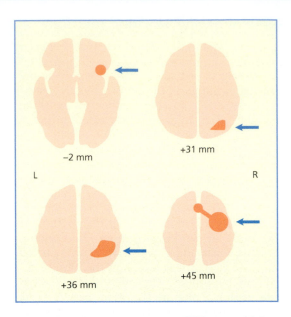

Figure 4.14 Illustration depicting PET images of the four areas activated in the visuo-spatial working memory study. Based on Smith et al. (1996).

control and manipulation of cognitive operations. Both of these draw on a common limited pool of attentional capacity; hence when we are "lost in thought" (or engaged in a mobile phone conversation?), we may not notice our neighbor who is wondering why we are being so standoffish. The neuromodulator dopamine appears to be associated with the executive control system and to involve the anterior cingulate area. Effortful attention and executive control tends to be associated with the anterior cingulate (Bush, Luu, & Posner, 2000), which also appears to be associated with difficulties in resolving conflicts in cognitive tasks and in children, with difficulty in controlling their emotions and behavior (Rothbart & Rueda, 2005).

However, although there is no doubt that the frontal lobes play a crucial role in executive processing, there is much less agreement on the extent to which specific executive capacities are located in particular frontal areas. Shallice (2002) suggests that a range of different areas each reflects a separable executive process, drawing evidence from studies ranging from single-case neuropsychology through group lesion studies to studies using neuroimaging, then attempting to account for

KEY TERM

Spatial working memory: System involved in temporarily retaining information regarding spatial location.

Object memory: System that temporarily retains information concerning visual features such as color and shape.

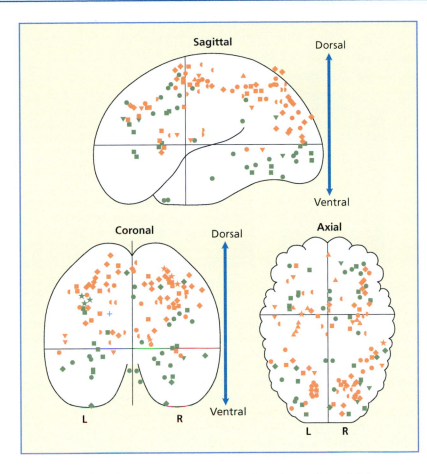

Figure 4.15 Combined data from studies involving short-term memory from visual objects (green) or spatial location (orange). The distinction is mainly between the ventral locations for object memory, and dorsal for locations. Based on Smith and Jonides (1999).

this array of evidence using a computer-based model (Shallice & Cooper, 2011).

A very different but crucial role of the central executive and of the frontal lobes is to energize and drive behavior. This capacity was studied by Alexander, Stuss, Shallice, Picton, and Gillingham (2005) in a large sample of patients with frontal lobe lesions, divided into groups on the basis of the localization of their lesions (Figure 4.16). The task was a simple one. A series of five lights were each associated with a key. The task was to press the relevant key when a light came on. After a brief 200 ms delay, the next light came on, continuing for a total of 500 responses. Despite this demanding schedule, most of the frontal lobe lesioned patients tended to maintain their speed throughout the session. Only one group was consistently slower than controls, those who had their damage in the superior medial area of the

frontal lobes, an area that contains the anterior cingulate gyrus, regarded by Posner and DiGirolamo (1998) as facilitating the supervisory aspect of attention and shown to be involved in the Stroop task which requires participants to override dominant habits.

In contrast to Shallice's attempt to identify specific processes within frontal regions, Duncan and Owen (2000) took a more general approach, pointing to the lack of consistency across a range of studies of the frontal lobes at anything other than the broadest level. They performed a meta-analysis of a wide range of functional imaging studies covering task novelty, working memory load, response competition, delay, and perceptual difficulty, finding that all of them appear to load on the anterior cingulate area, arguing for a common process which they link to Spearman's concept of general intelligence, *g*. A compromise position is suggested by Posner

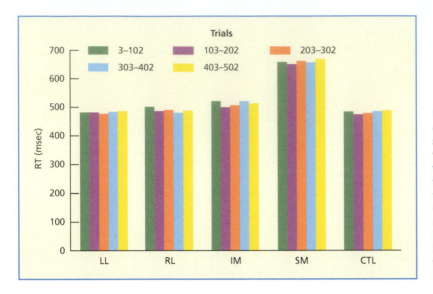

Figure 4.16 Performance of a control group (CTL) and four groups of patients with differing areas of frontal lobe damage on a five-choice serial reaction time task. Only patients with damage to the superior medial frontal lobes were impaired. Reproduced from Shallice and Cooper (2011) with permission from Oxford University Press.

(2013) who suggests that a good deal of neural computation operates within relatively localized networks, but accepts that "it is certainly possible and perhaps even likely that more complex reasoning and memory retrieval processes involve less specific localization" while cautioning that "these differences may be more due our weakness in correctly specifying the operations involved than they are to problems with localization" (Posner, 2013, p. 245).

A number of investigators using fMRI have detected activity in areas associated with both sensory processing and/or LTM (e.g., Ruchkin, Grafman, Cameron, & Berndt, 2003). Such findings are sometimes interpreted as supportive of a view that working memory is simply activated LTM, together with activation in the relevant sensory processing areas. As discussed earlier, LTM is certainly involved in several ways in most WM tasks; an adequate explanation however requires specifying just when and how.

This is an important question on which progress is being made, with some very interesting recent results based on multi-voxel pattern analysis (MVPA). As you may recall from Chapter 2 (p. 32) this is a method whereby the overall brain activation associated with a particular stimulus is averaged over many presentations, allowing a pattern categorizer to relate such neural regularities with the nature of the associated stimulus. The

categorizer is then directed at the participant's ongoing brain activity, and often proves capable of detecting which stimulus the participant is viewing. Harrison and Tong (2009) carried out a simple but ingenious STM experiment in which participants were presented with either red or green circles filled with lines of two different orientations. They were required to attend to color on some trials and orientation on others. The brain activation associated with each was recorded and fed into a pattern categorizer. The second, STM stage involved viewing stimuli which the participants were then required to retain for 15 seconds during which they were told whether color or orientation would be tested. As Figure 4.17 shows, this instruction evoked a pattern of activation similar to that produced by viewing the color or the orientation, suggesting that the participants may have been maintaining the relevant dimension at a quite peripheral level of the visual system.

This could be interpreted as a demonstration of the process of "refreshing" the stimulus representation, a term developed by Marcia Johnson (Chun & Johnson, 2011) to reflect the continued maintenance of a representation by focused attention, a method of rehearsal that appears to be common to many sensory systems which, unlike the phonological loop, lack a specialized rehearsal system. It could however be argued that such

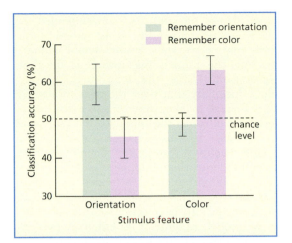

Figure 4.17 When participants are asked to view a figure and concentrate on either its color or the orientation of stripes within it, different brain areas are activated. A similar pattern is observed when they are required to hold each of the two types of feature in memory, prior to a test. As a result it is possible, in each case, to tell from the brain activation which of the two features the participant is "holding in mind." From Serences et al. (2009). Copyright © American Psychological Association. Reproduced with permission.

activation may reflect continuing attention, but this might not itself be necessary for continued storage of the memory trace. Two important studies by Lewis-Peacock and colleagues address this question, again using MPVA. Lewis-Peacock and Postle (2008) began their study by familiarizing their participants with a series of faces, locations, and common objects by asking them to make pleasantness judgments. During this phase, a pattern categorizer learned the pattern of activity associated with each of the stimulus types. Participants were then trained to remember pairs of such items and to recall the second item of each pair when presented with the first. In a final stage, each stimulus was presented for one second followed by an 11-second delay, after which either the appropriate or an inappropriate item was presented and the participant responded "yes" or "no" for a match or mismatch. If the correct response was, for example, a face, then the face pattern area was typically activated during the delay, as if the participant was holding the appropriate stimulus "in

mind" while waiting for the test item to be presented. The pattern recognizer seemed to tell us what the participant was "thinking about" during this delay. If so, what is this telling us about memory? It is not clear that the activation picked up by the analyser is causally linked to retention. It could be reflecting what was in attention while memory could depend on a separate source.

A later study by Lewis-Peacock, Drysdale, Oberauer, and Postle (2012) investigated this possibility. They studied STM for faces, pronounceable pseudo words, or line segments over a delay of 7.5 seconds. In each case they found ongoing activation of the appropriate brain areas for the relevant type of material that continued during the delay period. In a further condition, however, the delay was filled by a stimulus from one of the other two categories serving as a potential distractor. This resulted in a switch of activity during the delay, from the area concerned with the target item as previously observed, to the area of activation associated with the distractor. This did not however result in forgetting the memory item, suggesting that ongoing activation was *not* necessary for accurate recall.

As this study shows, the link between psychological models and neuroimaging evidence, while potentially important, is indirect, and may well be open to more than one interpretation. Such research has however been very extensive in recent years, as illustrated by two reviews of the field. Eriksson, Vogel, Lansner, Bergström, and Nyberg (2015) define WM as "The short-term maintenance of information in the absence of sensory input" (Eriksson et al., p. 33). They focus on processing rather than storage, describing a wide range of research concluding that there is little evidence for links between type of processing and specific brain regions, a conclusion also reached in a meta-analysis by Nee et al. (2013) of studies of executive control. WM is seen by Eriksson et al. (p. 33) as emerging from the dynamic interaction of a large number of brain regions concluding that general explanatory principles have not yet emerged. One reason for this is illustrated by a study by Owen, McMillan, Laird, and Bullmore (2005) of the N-back task, widely used in neuroimaging studies as a measure of

WM performance. They combined data from 668 sets of activation data from 24 different studies, finding activation in no fewer than eight different brain regions, reflecting the sheer complexity involved in just one WM paradigm.

A subsequent review of research that aims to link behavioral models of WM to neuroscience is presented by D'Esposito and Postle (2015) who note the size of such a task noting no fewer than 17,597 citations of papers on WM. They distinguish between more perceptually based "sensory recruitment" models as described above and those involving internal representations such as digits, letters, or words as typically used in developing the models of Cowan, Oberauer, and of the multicomponent model. D'Esposito and Postle cover an extensive range of studies, rejecting views that regard the activity of the prefrontal cortex as principally concerned with the storage buffers, as might be implied by some of the sensory recruitment models. They suggest a much broader mapping of WM onto brain regions concluding that "the prefrontal, basal ganglia, thalamic, and brain systems reviewed here can be construed as a neural substrate for this Central Executive" (D'Esposito & Postle, 2015, p. 133), while stressing the importance of neuroscience in continuing to update models of how working memory works.

CONCLUSION

The last two chapters have clearly been influenced by my own experience of developing the multicomponent model for over 40 years, during which time it has evolved considerably but retained the same overall framework. The field of WM has grown hugely over that period, with many much more detailed models being proposed most of which however could be seen as covering more detailed aspects of our basic framework. The multicomponent model was developed along the approach to theorization outlined in Chapter 1, namely that good theories serve as maps, summarizing what is known and enabling further productive questions to be asked. These questions are not intended as direct tests of the validity of the model in the sense that a negative result would require rejecting the model, but rather as lines of exploration. Using the map analogy, one might speculate that over the next mountain ridge there is a lake, only to find a river or a desert, requiring the map to be adjusted accordingly. In this sense, unexpected but reliable negative results are the lifeblood of development of the model, allowing it to continue to be productive, provided of course that the overall framework remains coherent and continues to develop. Given the breadth of the model, ranging from language perception and production through spatial and temporal orientation with crucial links to attentional control and long-term memory, our basic four-component model inevitably leaves very many unanswered questions concerning just how this complex system might work and how memory might be linked to the fields of attention, perception, action, and their neurobiological underpinning. Some questions will be most closely linked to perception, others to action, with the multicomponent model focusing on the nature of this complex interaction.

The multicomponent model was strongly influenced by the intention that it should be applicable beyond the psychological laboratory. It originated with a practical question concerning telephony (Baddeley, 2019) and was strongly influenced by single-case neuropsychology. This in turn was linked to an ongoing interest in developing tests that may be clinically useful. The limited basic framework, together with a small number of relatively simple techniques based on effects of similarity and the use of concurrent tasks have, over the years, led to a wide range of applications. Logie (2019) for example lists application of the multicomponent model to the following areas: child development, adult aging, education, developmental learning disorders, hyperbaric stress, acquisition of complex skills, mental arithmetic, and music, to which can be added a wide range of clinical applications from the study of cognitive effects of parasitic infection to Alzheimer's disease (see Logie, 2019 for more detailed references).

I would suggest therefore that the overall broad working memory framework continues to fulfil the criterion of a good theory proposed by Lakatos (1970) and described in Chapter 1, that it be productive, and not purely defensive. There are of course and will continue to be many more precise theories using more rigorously targeted methods that may in due course revise much of the detail of our current model. For the present at least, the multicomponent model still seems to be in good shape.

SUMMARY

- Working memory is a system that combines temporary storage and executive processing in order to help perform a range of complex cognitive activities.
- The multicomponent model of Baddeley and Hitch tries to combine storage and processing.
- It has four components: the phonological loop; the visuo-spatial sketchpad; the central executive; and the episodic buffer.
- The phonological loop provides temporary storage for verbal/acoustic material.
- The visuo-spatial sketchpad stores information from visual and spatial coding.
- The central executive is an attentionally limited system that provides overall control.
- The episodic buffer involves a passive multidimensional store that is accessible to conscious awareness.
- An alternative approach is that proposed by Cowan who sees working memory as reflecting a limited attentional capacity focused on activated representations in LTM.
- While this is often seen as incompatible with the multicomponent model, this depends on the assumptions regarding the nature of the role of activated LTM. Differences can potentially be seen as those of emphasis and focus, rather than fundamental.
- Much of the work on the executive control of working memory has used correlational measures based on individual differences, sometimes in combination with experimental methods.
- Influential in the area is the work of Engle and colleagues who emphasize the role of working memory in inhibiting potentially distracting material and facilitating retrieval from LTM.
- Other approaches such as that of Barrouillet and Camos emphasize the role of attentional maintenance in WM.
- Most agree with Cowan that the capacity of WM is about four chunks.
- Educational application of WM raises the question as to whether WM can be trained.
- Neuroscience approaches to WM extend from single-cell recording in monkeys to neuroimaging.
- Studies using fMRI suggest the joint activation of areas responsible for perception, LTM, and executive control when performing WM tasks.
- The question arises of whether such areas are essential to WM, or simply reflect a high degree of connectivity between these areas within the brain.
- Studies using MVPA show ongoing activation of brain areas specific to the material being retained.
- However, this appears to represent the focus of attention but is not necessary for successful retention.
- A major source of support for the multicomponent model stems from its wide applicability beyond the psychological laboratory.

POINTS FOR DISCUSSION

1 Why do we need models of working memory? Will models of attention and LTM not suffice?
2 Discuss the claims that working memory can be trained.
3 What are the major differences between the multicomponent model and Cowan's embedded processes approach?
4 What has neuroscience contributed to our knowledge of working memory?
5 What might be the practical applications of a good model of working memory?

FURTHER READING

Atkinson, R. C., & Shiffrin, R. M. (1971). The control of short-term memory. *Scientific American, 225*, 82–90. A good summary of the modal model for the general scientific reader.

Baddeley, A. D., Hitch, G. J., & Allen, R. J. (2019). From short-term store to multicomponent working memory: The role of the modal model. *Memory & Cognition, 47*, 575–588. doi:10.3758/s13421-018-0878-5. An overview of the development of the multicomponent model, relating it to its origins in the modal model. It forms part of a collection of papers marking the 50th anniversary of the modal model.

Cowan, N. (2005). *Working memory capacity*. Hove, UK: Psychology Press. An overview of Cowan's approach to working memory. It proposes that the capacity of working memory is four chunks, rather than Miller's magic number seven.

Cowan, N. (2017). The many faces of working memory and short-term storage. *Psychonomic Bulletin & Review, 24*, 1158–1170. An overview of the various approaches to short-term and working memory by one of the principal contributors to the field.

D'Esposito, M., & Postle, B. (2015). The cognitive neuroscience of working memory. *Annual Review of Psychology, 66*, 115–142. A review of the wide range of studies using neuroimaging to investigate working memory.

Engle, R. W. (2018). Working memory and executive attention: A revisit. *Perspectives on Psychological Science, 13*, 190–193. A recent account of Engle's current views on working memory and how it relates to the concept of fluid intelligence.

Engle, R. W., Cantor, J., & Carullo, J. J. (1992). Individual differences in working memory and comprehension: A test of four hypotheses. *Journal of Experimental Psychology: Learning, Memory, and Cognition, 18*, 972–992. Discusses a range of hypotheses about working memory and the methods for evaluating them.

Logie, R. H., Camos, V., & Cowan. N. (Eds.). (in press). *Working memory: State-of-the science*. Oxford: Oxford University Press. Attempts to bring together chapters by a range of working memory theorists who are each invited to summarize their approach via addressing the same series of questions. Including a brief overview of our own multicomponent model.

Logie, R. H., & Cowan, N. (2015). Perspectives on working memory: Introduction to the spatial issue. *Memory & Cognition, 43*, 315–324. A useful overview of two approaches to working memory, that of Logie within a broadly multicomponent framework and that of Nelson Cowan.

REFERENCES

Alexander, M. P., Stuss, D. T., Shallice, T., Picton, T. W., & Gillingham, S. (2005). Impaired concentration due to frontal lobe damage from two distinct lesion sites. *Neurology, 65*, 572–579.

Allen, R., Baddeley, A. D., & Hitch, G. J. (2006). Is the binding of visual features in working memory resource-demanding? *Journal of Experimental Psychology: General, 135*, 298–313.

Allport, A., Styles, E. A., & Hsieh, S. (1994). Shifting attentional set: Exploring the dynamic control of tasks. In C. Umilta & M. Moscovitch (Eds.), *Attention and performance XV* (pp. 421–462). Cambridge, MA: MIT Press.

Anderson, J. R. (1993). *Rules of the mind.* Hillsdale, NJ: Erlbaum.

Atkinson, R. C., & Shiffrin, R. M. (1968). Human memory: A proposed system and its control processes. In K. W. Spence & J. T. Spence (Eds.), *The psychology of learning and motivation: Advances in research and theory* (Vol. 2, pp. 89–195). New York: Academic Press.

Baars, B. J. (1997). *In the theater of consciousness.* New York: Oxford University Press.

Baars, B. J. (2002). The conscious access hypothesis: Origins and recent evidence. *Trends in Cognitive Sciences, 6*(1), 47–52.

Baddeley, A. D. (1968). A 3-min reasoning test based on grammatical transformation. *Psychonomic Science, 10*, 341–342.

Baddeley, A. D. (1986). *Working memory.* Oxford: Oxford University Press.

Baddeley, A. D. (1996). Exploring the central executive. *Quarterly Journal of Experimental Psychology, 49A*(1), 5–28.

Baddeley, A. D. (2000). The episodic buffer: A new component of working memory? *Trends in Cognitive Sciences, 4*(11), 417–423.

Baddeley, A. D. (2007). *Working memory, thought and action.* Oxford: Oxford University Press.

Baddeley, A. (2012). Working memory, theories models and controversy. *The Annual Review of Psychology, 63*, 12.11–12.29.

Baddeley, A. D. (2019). *Working memories: Postmen, divers and the cognitive revolution.* London: Routledge.

Baddeley, A. D., & Andrade, J. (2000). Working memory and the vividness of imagery. *Journal of Experimental Psychology: General, 129*(1), 126–145. doi:10.1037//0096-3445.129.1.126

Baddeley, A. D., Chincotta, D., & Adlam, A. (2001). Working memory and the control of action: Evidence from task switching. *Journal of Experimental Psychology: General, 130*, 641–657.

Baddeley, A. D., & Dale, H. C. A. (1966). The effect of semantic similarity on retroactive interference in long- and short-term memory. *Journal of Verbal Learning and Verbal Behavior, 5*, 417–420.

Baddeley, A., Gathercole, S., & Papagno, C. (1998). The phonological loop as a language learning device. *Psychological Review, 105*, 158–173.

Baddeley, A. D., Grant, S., Wight, E., & Thomson, N. (1973). Imagery and visual working memory. In P. M. A. Rabbitt & S. Dornic (Eds.), *Attention and performance V* (pp. 205–217). London: Academic Press.

Baddeley, A. D., & Hitch, G. J. (1974). Working memory. In G. A. Bower (Ed.), *The psychology of learning and motivation: Advances in research and theory* (Vol. 8, pp. 47–89). New York: Academic Press.

Baddeley, A. D., Hitch, G. J., & Allen, R. J. (2009). Working memory and binding in sentence recall. *Journal of Memory and Language, 61*, 438–456.

Baddeley, A. D., Lewis, V. J., & Vallar, G. (1984). Exploring the articulatory loop. *Quarterly Journal of Experimental Psychology, 36*, 233–252.

Baddeley, A. D., & Lieberman, K. (1980). Spatial working memory. In R. S. Nickerson (Ed.), *Attention and performance VIII* (pp. 521–539). Hillsdale, NJ: Erlbaum.

Baddeley, A. D., Papagno, C., & Vallar, G. (1988). When long-term learning depends on short-term storage. *Journal of Memory and Language, 27*, 586–595.

Baddeley, A. D., & Wilson, B. (1986). Amnesia, autobiographical memory and confabulation. In D. Rubin (Ed.), *Autobiographical memory* (pp. 225–252). Cambridge: Cambridge University Press.

Baddeley, A. D., & Wilson, B. (1988). Frontal amnesia and the dysexecutive syndrome. *Brain & Cognition, 7*(2), 212–230.

Barrouillet, P., Bernardin, S., & Camos, V. (2004). Time constraints and resource sharing in adults' working memory spans. *Journal of Experimental Psychology: General, 133*, 83–100.

Barrouillet, P., & Camos, V. (2014). *Working memory: Loss and reconstruction*. Hove, UK: Psychology Press.

Bavelier, D., Green, C. S., Pouget, A., & Schrater, P. (2012). Brain plasticity through the life span: Learning to learn and action video games. *Annual Review of Neuroscience, 35*, 391–416. doi:10.1146/annurev-neuro-060909-152832

Benton, S. L., Kraft, R. G., Glover, J. A., & Plake, B. S. (1984). Cognitive capacity differences among writers. *Journal of Educational Psychology, 76*(5), 820–834.

Brener, R. (1940). An experimental investigation of memory span. *Journal of Experimental Psychology, 26*, 467–483.

Brown, I. D., Tickner, A. H., & Simmonds, D. C. V. (1969). Interference between concurrent tasks of driving and telephoning. *Journal of Applied Psychology, 53*, 419–424. doi:http://dx.doi.org/10.1037/h0028103

Bush, G., Luu, P., & Posner, M. I. (2000). Cognitive and emotional influences in anterior cingulate cortex. *Trends in Cognitive Sciences, 4*, 215–222.

Chun, M. M., Golomb, J. D., & Turk-Browne, N. B. (2011). A taxonomy of external and internal attention. *Annual Review of Psychology, 62*, 73–101.

Chun, M. M., & Johnson, M. K. (2011). Memory: Enduring traces of perceptual and reflective attention. *Neuron, 72*, 520–535.

Conway, A. R. A., Cowan, N., & Bunting, M. F. (2001). The cocktail party phenomenon revisited: The importance of working memory capacity. *Psychonomic Bulletin and Review, 8*(2), 331–335.

Cowan, N. (1999). An embedded-processes model of working memory. In A. M. P. Shah (Ed.), *Models of working memory* (pp. 62–101). Cambridge: Cambridge University Press.

Cowan, N. (2001). The magical number 4 in short-term memory: A reconsideration of mental storage capacity. *Behavorial and Brain Sciences, 24*, 87–114; discussion 114–185.

Cowan, N. (2005). *Working memory capacity*. Hove, UK: Psychology Press.

Cowan, N. (2019). Short-term memory based on activated long-term memory: A review in response to Norris (2017). *Psychological Bulletin, 145*(8), 822–847.

Craik, F. I. M., & Lockhart, R. S. (1972). Levels of processing. A framework for memory research. *Journal of Verbal Learning and Verbal Behavior, 11*, 671–684.

Daneman, M., & Carpenter, P. A. (1980). Individual differences in working memory and reading. *Journal of Verbal Learning and Verbal Behaviour, 19*, 450–466.

Daneman, M., & Merikle, P. M. (1996). Working memory and language comprehension: A meta-analysis. *Psychonomic Bulletin & Review, 3*, 422–433.

D'Esposito, M., & Postle, B. (2015). The cognitive neuroscience of working memory. *Annual Review of Psychology, 66*, 115–142. doi:10.1146/annurev-psych-010814-015031

Di Vesta, F. J., Ingersoll, G., & Sunshine, P. (1971). A factor analysis of imagery tests. *Journal of Verbal Learning and Verbal Behavior, 10*, 471–479.

Doherty, J. M., Belletier, C., Rhodes, S., Jaroslawska, A., Barrouillet, P., Camos, V., ... Logie, R. H. (2019). Dual-task costs in working memory: An adversarial collaboration. *Journal of Experimental Psychology: Learning, Memory and Cognition, 45*, 1529–1551. doi:0.1037/xlm0000668

Duncan, J., & Owen, A. M. (2000). Common regions of the human frontal lobe recruited by diverse cognitive demands. *Trends in Neurosciences, 23*, 475–483.

Ellis, N. C., & Sinclair, S. G. (1996). Working memory in the acquisition of vocabulary and syntax: Putting language in good order. *Quarterly Journal of Experimental Psychology, 49A*, 234–250.

Emerson, M. J., & Miyake, A. (2003). The role of inner speech in task switching: A dual-task investigation. *Journal of Memory and Language, 48*, 148–168.

Engel de Abreu, P. M. J., & Gathercole, S. E. (2012). Executive and phonological processes in second language acquisition. *Journal of Educational Psychology, 104*, 976–986.

Engle, R. W. (1996). Working memory and retrieval: An inhibition-resource approach. In

J. T. E. Richardson, R. W. Engle, L. Hasher, R. H. Logie, E. R. Stoltfus, & R. T. Zacks (Eds.), *Working memory and human cognition* (pp. 89–119). New York: Oxford University Press.

Engle, R. W., Carullo, J. J., & Collins, K. W. (1991). Individual differences in working memory for comprehension and following directions. *Journal of Educational Research, 84*, 253–262.

Engle, R. W., Tuholski, S. W., Laughlin, J. E., & Conway, A. R. A. (1999). Working memory, short-term memory, and general fluid intelligence: A latent-variable approach. *Journal of Experimental Psychology: General, 128*, 309–331.

Eriksson, J., Vogel, E. K., Lansner, A., Bergström, F., & Nyberg, L. (2015). Neurocognitive architecture of working memory. *Neuron, 88*, 33–46. doi:10.1016/j.neuron.2015.09.020

Finke, R. A., & Slayton, K. (1988). Explorations of creative visual synthesis in mental imagery. *Memory and Cognition, 16*, 252–257.

Friedman, N. P., & Miyake, A. (2004). The relations among inhibition and interference control functions: A latent variable analysis. *Journal of Experimental Psychology: General, 133*, 101–135.

Fukuda, K., & Vogel, E. K. (2009). Human variation in overriding attentional capture. *The Journal of Neuroscience, 29*, 8726–8733.

Gathercole, S. E., & Baddeley, A. D. (1989). Evaluation of the role of phonological STM in the development of vocabulary in children: A longitudinal study. *Journal of Memory & Language, 28*, 200–213.

Gathercole, S., & Baddeley, A. (1990). Phonological memory deficits in language-disordered children: Is there a causal connection? *Journal of Memory & Language, 29*, 336–360.

Gathercole, S. E., Dunning, D. L. & Holmes, J. (2012). Cogmed training: Let's be realistic about intervention research. *Journal of Applied Research in Memory and Cognition, 1*, 201–203.

Gathercole, S., Dunning, D., Holmes, J., & Norris, D. (2019). Working memory training involves learning new skills. *Journal of Memory and Language, 105*, 19–42. https://doi.org/10.1016/j.jml.2018.10.003

Gathercole, S. E., Pickering, S. J., Ambridge, B., & Wearing, H. (2004). The structure of working memory from 4 to 15 years of age. *Developmental Psychology, 40*, 177–190.

Hanley, J. R., & Young, A. W. (2019). ELD revisited: A second look at a neuropsychological impairment of working memory affecting retention of visuo-spatial material. *Cortex, 112*, 172–179.

Harrison, S. A., & Tong, F. (2009). Decoding reveals the contents of visual working memory in early visual areas. *Nature.* doi:10.1038/nature07832

Hatano, G., & Osawa, K. (1983a). Digit memory of grand experts in abacus-derived mental calculation. *Cognition, 15*, 95–110.

Hatano, G., & Osawa, K. (1983b). Japanese abacus experts' memory for numbers is disrupted by mechanism of action. *Journal of Clinical Psychology, 58*(1), 61–75.

Heuer, F., Fischman, D., & Reisberg, D. (1986). Why does vivid imagery hurt colour memory? *Canadian Journal of Psychology, 40*, 161–175.

Holding, D. H. (1989). Counting backward during chess move choice. *Bulletin of Psychonomic Society, 27*, 421–424.

Holmes, J., Gathercole, S. E., Place, M., Dunning, D. L. Hilton, K. A., & Elliott, J. G. (2010). Working memory deficits can be overcome: Impacts of training and medication on working memory in children with ADHD. *Applied Cognitive Psychology, 24A*, 827–836. doi:10.1002/acp.1589

Hsi, S., Linn, M. C., & Bell, J. A. (1997). The role of spatial reasoning in engineering and the design of spatial instruction. *Journal of Engineering Education, 86*, 151–158.

Jackendoff, R. (1992). *Semantic structures.* Cambridge, MA: MIT Press.

Jaeggi, S. M., Buschkuehl, M., Jonides, J., & Shah, P. (2011). Short- and long-term benefits of cognitive training. *Proceedings of the National Academy of Sciences of the USA, 108*, 10081–10086. doi:https://doi.org/10.1073/pnas.1103228108

Kane, M. J., & Engle, R. W. (2000). Working-memory capacity, proactive interference, and divided attention: Limits on long-term memory retrieval. *Journal of Experimental Psychology: Learning, Memory & Cognition, 26*(2), 336–358.

Kiewra, K. A., & Benton, S. L. (1988). The relationship between information-processing ability and note taking. *Contemporary Educational Psychology, 13*, 33–44.

Kintsch, W., & van Dyck, T. (1977). Toward a model of text comprehension and production. *Psychological Review, 85*, 63–94.

Klingberg, T. (2002). Training of working memory in children with ADHD. *Journal of Clinical and Experimental Neuropsychology, 24*, 781–791.

Klingberg, T., Fernell, E., Olesen, P. J., Johnson, M., Gustafsson, P., Dahlström, K., et al. (2005). Computerized training of working memory in children with ADHD—A randomized, controlled trial. *Journal of the American Academy of Child and Adolescent Psychiatry, 44*, 177–186.

Kyllonen, P. C., & Christal, R. E. (1990). Reasoning ability is (little more than) working memory capacity. *Intelligence, 14*, 389–433.

Kyllonen, P. C., & Stephens, D. L. (1990). Cognitive abilities as the determinants of success in acquiring logic skills. *Learning and Individual Differences, 2*, 129–160.

Lakatos, I. (1970). Falsification and the methodology of scientific research programmes In I. Lakatos & A. Musgrave (Eds.), *Criticism and the growth of knowledge* (pp. 91–195). Cambridge: Cambridge University Press.

Larsen, J., & Baddeley, A. D. (2003). Disruption of verbal STM by irrelevant speech, articulatory suppression and manual tapping: Do they have a common source? *Quarterly Journal of Experimental Psychology, 56A*, 1249–1268.

LeDoux, J. E. (1996). *The emotional brain*. New York: Simon & Schuster.

Lee, H. S., & Anderson, J. R. (2013). Student learning: What has instruction got to do with it? *Annual Review of Psychology, 64*, 445–469. doi:10.1146/annurev-psych-113011-143833

Lépine, R., Barrouillet, P., & Camos, V. (2005). What makes working memory spans so predictive of high-level cognition? *Psychonomic Bulletin & Review, 12*, 165–170.

Lewandowsky, S., & Oberauer, K. (2008). The word length effect provides no evidence for decay in short-term memory. *Psychonomic Bulletin & Review, 15*, 875–888. doi:10.3758/PBR.15.5.875

Lewis-Peacock, J. A., Drysdale, A. T., Oberauer, K., & Postle, B. R. (2012). Neural evidence for a distinction between short-term memory and the focus of attention. *Journal of Cognitive Neuroscience, 24*, 61–79.

Lewis-Peacock, J., & Postle, B. R. (2008). Temporary activation of long-term memory supports working memory. *The Journal of Neuroscience, 28*, 8765–8771.

Linn, M. C., & Petersen, A. C. (1985). Emergence and characterization of sex differences in spatial ability: A meta-analysis. *Child Development, 56*, 1479–1498.

Logie, R. H. (1986). Visuo-spatial processing in working memory. *Quarterly Journal of Experiment Psychology, 38A*, 229–247.

Logie, R. H. (1995). *Visuo-spatial working memory*. Hove, UK: Erlbaum.

Logie, R. H. (2019). Converging sources of evidence and theory integration in working memory: A commentary on Morey, Rhodes, and Cowan (2019). *Cortex, 112*, 162–171. doi:10.1016/j.cortex.2019.01.030

Luck, S. J., & Vogel, E. K. (1997). The capacity of visual working memory for features and conjunctions. *Nature, 390*, 279–281.

Luria, A. R. (1959). The directive function of speech in development and dissolution, Part I. *Word, 15*, 341–352.

McNab, F., & Klingberg, T. (2008). Prefrontal cortex and basal ganglia control access to working memory. *Nature Neuroscience, 11*, 103–107. doi:10.1038/nn2024

Melby-Lervåg, M., & Hulme, C. (2013). Is working memory training effective? A meta-analytic review. *Developmental Psychology, 49*, 270–291.

Miller, G. A. (1956). The magical number seven, plus or minus two: Some limits on our capacity for processing information. *Psychological Review, 63*, 81–97.

Miller, G. A., Galanter, E., & Pribram, K. H. (1960). *Plans and the structure of behavior*. New York: Holt, Rinehart & Winston.

Mishkin, M., Ungerleider, L. G., & Macko, K. A. (1983). Object vision and spatial vision: Two cortical pathways. *Trends in Neurosciences, 6*, 414–417.

Miyake, A., Friedman, N. P., Rettinger, D. A., Shah, P., & Hegarty, P. (2001). How are visuospatial working memory, executive functioning, and spatial abilities related? A latent-variable analysis. *Journal of Experimental Psychology: General, 130*(4), 621–640.

Miyake, A., & Shah, P. (1999b). Toward unified theories of working memory: Emerging general consensus, unresolved theoretical issues and future directions. In A. Miyake & P. Shah (Eds.), *Models of working memory: Mechanisms of active maintenance and executive control* (pp. 28–61). Cambridge: Cambridge University Press.

Monsell, S. (2005). The chronometrics of task-set control. In J. Duncan, L. Phillips, & P. McLeod (Eds.), *Measuring the mind: Speed, control, and age* (pp. 161–190). Oxford: Oxford University Press.

Morey, C. (2018a). The case against specialized visual-spatial short-term memory. *Psychological Bulletin, 144*, 849–883.

Morey, C. (2018b). Correction to Morey. *Psychological Bulletin, 144*, 1246.

Morey, C., Rhodes, S., & Cowan, N. (2019). Sensory-motor integration and brain lesions: Progress toward explaining domain-specific phenomena within domain-general working memory. *Cortex, 112*, 149–161.

Murray, D. J. (1967). The role of speech responses in short-term memory. *Canadian Journal of Psychology, 21*, 263–276.

National Highway Safety Administration. (2006). *The impact of driver inattention on near crash/crash risk: An analysis using the 100-car naturalistic driving study data (DOTHS810–594)*.

Washington, DC: US Department of Transportation.

Nee, D. E., Brown, J. W., Askren, M. K., Berman, M. G., Demiralp, E., Krawitz, A., & Jonides, J. (2013). A meta-analysis of executive components of working memory. *Cerebral Cortex, 23*, 264–282. doi:10.1093/cercor/bhs007

Nicolay, A., & Poncelet, M. (2013). Cognitive abilities underlying second-language vocabulary acquisition in an early second-language immersion education context: A longitudinal study. *Journal of Experimental Child Psychology, 115*, 655–671.

Norman, D. A., & Shallice, T. (1986). Attention to action: Willed and automatic control of behaviour. In R. J. Davidson, G. E. Schwartz, & D. Shapiro (Eds.), *Consciousness and self-regulation: Advances in research and theory* (Vol. 4, pp. 1–18). New York: Plenum Press.

Norris, D. (2017). Short-term memory and long-term memory are still different. *Psychological Bulletin, 143*, 992–1009.

Norris, D. (in press). The need for separate short-term memory system won't go away just by calling it activated long-term memory: A reply to Cowan (2019). *Psychological Bulletin*. doi: 10.17863/CAM.42584

Oberauer, K., & Hein, L. (2012). Attention to information in working memory. *Current Directions in Psychological Science, 21*, 164–169.

Öhman, A., & Soares, J. J. F. (1994). "Unconscious anxiety": Phobic responses to masked stimuli. *Journal of Abnormal Psychology, 103*, 231–240.

Olesen, P. J., Westerberg, H., & Klingberg, T. (2004). Increased prefrontal and parietal brain activity after training of working memory. *Nature Neuroscience, 7*, 75–79.

Owen, A. M., McMillan, K. M., Laird, A. R., & Bullmore, E. (2005). N-back working memory paradigm: A meta-analysis of normative functional neuroimaging studies. *Human Brain Mapping, 25*, 46–59.

Papagno, C., Valentine, T., & Baddeley, A. D. (1991). Phonological short-term memory and foreign language vocabulary learning. *Journal of Memory and Language, 30*, 331–347.

Papagno, C., & Vallar, G. (1992). Phonological short-term memory and the learning of novel words: The effect of phonological similarity and item length. *Quarterly Journal of Experimental Psychology, 44A*, 47–67.

Paulesu, E., Frith, C. D., & Frackowiak, R. S. J. (1993). The neural correlates of the verbal component of working memory. *Nature, 362*, 342–345.

Pearson, D. G., Logie, R. H., & Gilhooly, K. J. (1999). Verbal representations and spatial manipulation during mental synthesis. *European Journal of Cognitive Psychology, 11*(3), 295–314.

Posner, M. I. (2013). The expert brain. Expertise and skill acquisition. In J. J. Staszewski (Ed.), *Expertise and skill acquisition: The impact of William G. Chase*. New York: Psychology Press.

Posner, M. I., & DiGirolamo, G. J. (1998). Executive attention: Conflict, target detection, and cognitive control. In R. Parasuraman (Ed.), *The attentive brain* (pp. 401–423). Cambridge, MA: MIT Press.

Posner, M. I., & Rothbart, M. K. (2007). Research on attention networks as a model for the integration of psychological science. *Annual Review of Psychology, 58*, 1–23.

Quinn, G., & McConnell, J. (1996a). Irrelevant pictures in visual working memory. *Quarterly Journal of Experimental Psychology, 49A*(1), 200–215.

Quinn, G., & McConnell, J. (1996b). Exploring the passive visual store. *Psychologische Beiträge, 38*(314), 355–367.

Redelmeier, D. A., & Tibshirani, R. J. (1997). Association between cellular-telephone calls and motor vehicular collisions. *New England Journal of Medicine, 336*, 453–458.

Reisberg, D., Clayton, C. L., Heuer, F., & Fischman, D. (1986). Visual memory: When imagery vividness makes a difference. *Journal of Mental Imagery, 10*, 51–74.

Rhodes, S., Jaroslawska, A. J., Doherty, J. M., Belletier, C., Naveh Benjamin, M., Cowan, N., … Logie, R. H. (2019). Storage and processing in working memory: Assessing dual-task performance and task prioritization across the adult lifespan. *Journal of Experimental Psychology: General, 148*, 1204–1227. doi:10.1037/xge0000539

Robbins, T., Anderson, E., Barker, D., Bradley, A., Fearneyhough, C., Henson, R., et al. (1996). Working memory in chess. *Memory and Cognition, 24*(1), 83–93.

Rothbart, M. K., & Rueda, M. R. (2005). The development of effortful control. In U. Mayr, E. Awh, & S. Keele (Eds.), *Developing individuality in the human brain: A tribute to Michael I. Posner* (pp. 167–188). Washington, DC: American Psychological Association.

Ruchkin, D. S., Grafman, J., Cameron, K., & Berndt, R. S. (2003). Working memory retention systems: A state of activated long-term memory. *Behavioral and Brain Sciences, 26*, 709–777.

Saeki, E., Baddeley, A. D., Hitch, G. J., & Saito, S. (2013). Breaking a habit: A further role of the phonological loop in action control. *Memory & Cognition, 41*, 1065–1078. doi:10.3758/s13421–013–0320-y

Saeki, E., & Saito, S. (2004). The role of the phonological loop in task switching performance: The effect of articulatory suppression in the alternating runs paradigm. *Psychologia, 47,* 35–43.

Service, E. (1992). Phonology, working memory and foreign-language learning. *Quarterly Journal of Experimental Psychology Section A—Human, 45*(1), 21–50.

Shallice, T. (2002). Fractionation of the supervisory system. In D. T. Stuss & R. T. Knight (Eds.), *Principles of frontal lobe function* (pp. 261–277). New York: Oxford University Press.

Shallice, T., & Cooper, R. P. (2011). *The organisation of mind.* Oxford: Oxford University Press.

Shallice, T., & Papagno, C. (2019). Impairments of auditory-verbal short-term memory: Do selective deficits of the input phonological buffer exist? *Cortex, 112,* 107–121. doi:10.1016/j.cortex.2018.10.004

Shallice, T., & Warrington, E. K. (1970). Independent functioning of verbal memory stores: A neuropsychological study. *Quarterly Journal of Experimental Psychology, 22,* 261–273.

Shepard, R. N., & Feng, C. (1972). A chronometric study of mental paper-folding. *Cognitive Psychology, 3,* 228–243.

Shipstead, Z., Lindsey, D., Marshall, R. L., & Engle, R. (2014). The mechanisms of working memory capacity: Primary memory, secondary memory, and attention control. *Journal of Memory and Language, 72,* 116–141. doi:10.1016/j.jml.2014.01.004

Shipstead, Z., Redick, T. S., & Engle, R. W. (2012). Is working memory training effective? *Psychological Bulletin.* doi:10.1037/a0027473

Shute, V. J. (1991). Who is likely to acquire programming skills? *Journal of Educational Computing Research, 7,* 1–24.

Smith, E. E., & Jonides, J. (1997). Working memory: A view from neuroimaging. *Cognitive Psychology, 33,* 5–42.

Smith, E., Jonides, J., & Koeppe, R. A. (1996). Dissociating verbal and spatial working memory using PET. *Cerebral Cortex, 6,* 11–20.

Strayer, D. L., & Johnston, W. A. (2001). Driving to distraction: Dual-task studies of simulated driving and conversing on a cellular telephone. *Psychological Science, 12,* 462–466.

Towse, J. N., & Hitch, G. J. (1995). Is there a relationship between task demand and storage space in tests of working memory capacity? *Quarterly Journal of Experimental Psychology, 48A*(1), 108–124.

Towse, J. N., Hitch, G. J., & Hutton, U. (2000). On the interpretation of working memory span in adults. *Memory & Cognition, 28*(3), 341–348.

Turner, M. L., & Engle, R. W. (1989). Is working memory capacity task-dependent? *Journal of Memory and Language, 28,* 127–154.

Unsworth, N., & Engle, R. W. (2007). The nature of individual differences in working memory capacity: Active maintenance in primary memory and controlled search from secondary memory. *Psychological Review, 114,* 104–132.

Vallar, G., & Baddeley, A. D. (1987). Phonological short-term store and sentence processing. *Cognitive Neuropsychology, 4,* 417–438.

Vallar, G., & Shallice, T. (1990). *Neuropsychological impairments of short-term memory.* Cambridge: Cambridge University Press.

Vogel, E. K., Woodman, G. F., & Luck, S. J. (2001). Storage of features, conjunctions, and objects in visual working memory. *Journal of Experimental Psychology: Human Perception and Performance, 27*(1), 92–114.

Vygotsky, L. S. (1962). *Thought and language* (E. Hanfmann & G. Vakar, Trans.). Cambridge, MA: MIT Press.

Wagner, R. K., & Torgesen, J. K. (1987). The nature of phonological processing and its causal role in the acquisition of reading skills. *Psychological Bulletin, 101,* 192–212.

Contents

CHAPTER 5

LEARNING

Michael C. Anderson

While brushing my teeth one morning at my brother's house, I wandered downstairs to the living room. There I found Kimberly, my six-month-old niece, bouncing energetically in her Jolly Jumper. The Jolly Jumper is a creation of pure genius. Composed of a cloth harness suspended by elastic straps clamped to the top of a door frame, it allows a baby to sit upright with her toes dangling to the floor. Quickly, babies discover that moving their feet makes them bounce. Before long, they realize how fun this is, and thrill in making themselves bounce up and down with a jumping motion (never was there a product more aptly named). Kimberley absolutely loved this. She bounced for long stretches with delight, and, as her uncle, I was captivated by her sheer joy in this activity.

Except on this occasion. When I entered the room, she abruptly stopped bouncing. Surprised at her reaction, I stopped brushing my teeth and after a little while, she resumed. When I resumed brushing, her bouncing halted again as she stared intently at me. Only then did it dawn on me what was happening. She was watching me brush my teeth. She had no clue whatsoever what I was doing. Everything was new to her: The sound I was making, the stick I was holding, and the odd noise it made filled her with curiosity. She didn't even know what teeth were or why they needed to be brushed. This realization filled me with wonder. She had *absolutely no idea what it meant to brush one's teeth*. Why would she? She knew so little.

Imagine what you might have been like at that age. Look around you now. Perhaps you are sitting on a chair at a desk, with a cup of coffee. Perhaps there is some music on, and various objects like pens, notebooks, and mobile phones lie on the desk. There was a point when you did not have any of these concepts. You didn't know what a pen or writing was; you couldn't read; you didn't even know what a chair was or even how to sit in one without falling; you had no clue what birds or socks were. Your views about cake versus pie: nonexistent. Every single object in your world that you understand, and every activity you can do, whether physical or mental, had to be learned. You climbed Mt. Everest to be where you are now. Your college education and this course are at the very top of an already Himalayan enterprise you and your parents and teachers have been working on for years. As a father, I remember the first moment when my son Max learned what a tooth was, and that he also had them, just like his dad (18 months old). Learning is miraculous. It transforms babies into college students and college students into Nobel-winning scientists, artists, and even, on occasion, professors. Learning is, after all, the reason why you are reading the very sentence that you are reading at this precise moment.

So, what do we know about this miraculous process? In this chapter, we consider what science has taught us about how learning works. In addressing this topic, we first discuss broad factors that govern the rate and success of learning, irrespective of the type of learning one is engaged in. We follow this with a consideration of different types of learning, each with different characteristics and neural substrates. For example, how my son Max will learn how to tie his own shoes differs from how he learns words, or his preferences for his stuffed Penguin (aka Pengu) over his stuffed bear. Appreciating these many different flavors of learning will illustrate the tremendous complexity of the process that made you the person you are today.

THE CONTRIBUTION OF HERMANN EBBINGHAUS

Believe it or not, you are sitting in your seat right now, studying this text, in part because of a heavily bearded, 19th-century German philosopher named Hermann. As implausible as it may seem to you, this is actually true. To see why, consider the surprising fact that as recently as 150 years ago, some philosophers argued with conviction that the mind could not be scientifically studied. How could it be? To be studied with science, it must be governed by rules and causality, and it must be observable. None of these things seemed like it could possibly be true. So, when in the 1880s, a young German philosopher, Hermann Ebbinghaus, proposed an experimental study of memory, he was being rather bold. Ebbinghaus devoted two or three years to this pioneering enterprise before moving on to scientifically study other topics such as intelligence and color vision. However, in that brief period he laid the foundations of a new science of learning and memory, a science that is particularly relevant to rapidly changing societies like our own, in which people need to learn far more than did earlier generations; a science that helps us to understand how we make the miraculous transition from our Jolly Jumpers to the people we are today. This science yielded the current textbook, your class, and ultimately, your decision to study this book today.

Ebbinghaus's contribution to the science of memory was as simple as it was profound (see Chapter 1 for a picture!). Ebbinghaus decided that the only way to tackle the complex subject of human memory was to simplify the problem. He tested only one person—himself—and as he wished to study the learning of new information and to minimize any effects of previous knowledge, he invented some entirely new material to be learned. This material consisted of nonsense syllables: word-like consonant–vowel–consonant sequences, such as *wux, caz, bij*, and *zol*, which could be pronounced but had no meaning. He taught himself sequences of such syllables by reciting them aloud at a rapid rate, and he carefully scored the number of recitations required to learn each list, or to relearn it after a delay had caused him to forget it. During his learning, he carefully avoided using any associations with real words, and he always tested himself at the same time of day under carefully controlled conditions, discontinuing tests whenever "too great changes in the outer or inner life occurred." Clearly, Hermann was a fun guy to be around.

Despite, or perhaps because of his use of this rather unpromising material, Ebbinghaus demonstrated to the world that memory can indeed be investigated scientifically, and in the short period of two years, documented fundamental characteristics of human memory. For example, to assess any system for storing information, three basic questions must be answered: How is information fed into the system? How much information can be stored? How rapidly is information lost? In the case of human memory, the storage capacity is clearly enormous, so Ebbinghaus concentrated on assessing the rate of input and, as we shall see in later chapters, the rate of forgetting. In this chapter, we illustrate

KEY TERM

Nonsense syllables: Pronounceable but meaningless consonant-vowel-consonant items designed to study learning without the complicating factor of meaning.

some of Ebbinghaus's fundamental contributions to studying the learning process, laying the groundwork for all the work that has come since then.

FACTORS DETERMINING LEARNING SUCCESS

Wherever you want to end up in life, chances are, learning mechanisms in your brain are going to be instrumental in transforming you into the person you wish to become. What determines how much people learn, and the rate at which they learn it? Do some ways of learning yield more lasting retention than other ways? Are there ways to get "more bang for your buck" when you are trying to learn? We consider several general factors that determine both the amount and rate of learning, and what experimental studies have taught us about them.

Total time spent learning

It may come as no surprise to you that people generally learn more, the more time they spend trying to learn. You might not, however, have given any thought to the precise relationship between time spent and the amount learned. If you spend twice as much time learning, do you remember twice as much information? Or is there perhaps a law of diminishing returns, with each additional learning episode for the same material putting a little less information into storage? Or perhaps the relationship is the other way around: The more information you have acquired, the easier and quicker it is to add new information, rather like a rolling snowball picking up more snow with each successive revolution?

The issue of how new material gets registered in memory was first investigated by our protagonist, Hermann Ebbinghaus. Ebbinghaus investigated the rate of learning very simply, by creating a number of lists each containing 16 meaningless syllables. On a given day, he would select a fresh list (one he

had not learned before) and he would recite it at a rate of 2.5 syllables per second for either 8, 16, 24, 32, 42, 53, or 64 repetitions. Twenty-four hours later, he would find out how much of the list he had remembered by seeing how many additional trials he needed to relearn the list by heart. To get some idea of what his experiment was like, try reading the following list of nonsense syllables as rapidly as you can for two successive trials:

jih, baz, fub, yox, suj, xir, dax, leq, vum,
paq, kel, wab, tuv, zof, gek, hiw

The results of this very tedious exercise are shown in Figure 5.1. The relationship between the number of learning trials on day 1 and the amount retained on day 2 proved to be a straight line, signifying that the process of learning shows neither diminishing returns nor the snowball effect, but obeys the simple rule that the amount learned depends on time spent learning: If you double the learning time, you double the amount of information stored. In short, as far as

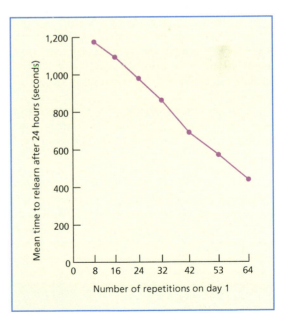

Figure 5.1 Influence of number of learning trials on retention after a 24-hour delay. From Ebbinghaus (1885).

learning is concerned, you get what you pay for. This simple relationship has been explored extensively in the 100 years since it was discovered by Ebbinghaus and is known as the total time hypothesis.

It would, of course, be unwise to base such a sweeping conclusion on a single study, even by someone as august as Herman Ebbinghaus, but there is ample further evidence. For example, do you want to become a more skilled writer? If so, the answer is to practice. A study by Astin (1993) found that the best predictor of self-reported skill in writing was number of writing skills classes taken, with amount of feedback provided by the instructor being the second-best predictor. One might reasonably argue that this result is based on self-assessment, which is likely to be an unreliable measure. However, a similar conclusion was obtained by Johnstone, Ashbaugh, and Warfield (2002), who observed a steady increase in writing skill over a sequence of courses as assessed by others. This is further illustrated in the case of professional writers such as Norman Mailer (2003), who reports that he learnt to write by writing, estimating that he must have written more than half a million words before he came to his famous novel *The Naked and the Dead*. The amount of time dedicated to practicing something important to us therefore plays a critical causal role in the level of expertise we can reasonably expect to exhibit.

The origins of exceptional expertise and how to build it through practice have received much attention in experimental psychology. Ericsson, Krampe, and Tesch-Römer (1993) emphasized the importance of practice across a number of skills, including chess, typing, and music. In relation to the last, they suggest that the very best violinists have accumulated more than 10,000 hours of solitary practice compared to 7,500 for lesser experts, 5,000 for the least accomplished

KEY TERM

Total time hypothesis: The proposal that amount learned is a simple function of the amount of time spent on the learning task.

experts, and around 1,500 hours for the committed amateur. This theme has been picked up by popular science writer Malcolm Gladwell who asserted that:

The emerging pictures from such studies is that 10,000 hours of practice is required to achieve the level of mastery associated with being a world-class expert—in anything. In study after study of composers, baseball players, fiction writers, ice skaters, concert pianists, chess players, common master criminals and what have you, this number comes up again and again.
(Gladwell, 2008, p. 44)

Ericsson (2013) objects, however, to the concept of a "10,000 hours rule." He points out that although the average for a violinist was 10,000 hours, half of them practiced for fewer than 5,000 hours, while winners of piano competitions continuing beyond their twenties can often clock up over 25,000 hours of practice, while in less heavily populated fields such as digit sequence memorizers, 500–1,000 hours are typical. Nevertheless, although the amount of practice necessary to master a skill may vary across domains, there is general agreement that one's level of mastery usually increases with the amount of practice devoted to it, consistent with the total time hypothesis.

Although the total time dedicated to an activity clearly improves a skill, more time is often not enough to ensure consistent learning. Indeed, Gladwell's "10,000 hours" rule misses a theoretical claim by Ericsson that simple repeated experience is not enough to develop true expertise. Ericsson argues that for many skill domains, performing a given skill repeatedly will, after very high levels of practice, lead to a performance plateau, after which further practice yields little improvement, even after many repetitions. Ericsson thus proposes that the total time hypothesis must be qualified in that, after extensive practice, further repetitions benefit a person little. By his view, to move beyond these plateaus and become a true expert, deliberate practice is required. According to Ericsson, deliberate practice is the "engagement with full concentration in a training activity designed to improve a particular aspect of performance with immediate feedback, opportunities for graduate refinement with repetition and problem solving" (Ericsson, 2013, p. 534). Deliberate practice involves identifying weaknesses in a skill and developing training exercises to overcome these and improve performance, with careful attention to feedback. Only through such deliberate practice can one break out of plateaus and continue to reap the benefits of further time. A study by Young and Salmela (2010) of national versus regional middle-distance runners, for example, found that the number of hours of training did not differ greatly, but the national runners devoted more time to weight and technical training (see Figure 5.2). In essence, if you want to be a professional novelist, an Olympic athlete, or an accomplished poet, mere repetition is not enough—you need to continue to strive to focus on your weaknesses and develop your strengths.

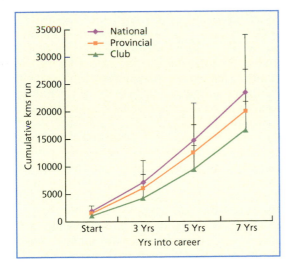

Figure 5.2 Young and Salmela (2010) found that the number of hours of training done by national and regional middle-distance runners was the same, but that national runners devoted more of their time to weight and technical training. From Young and Salmela (2010). Reprinted with permission of International Journal of Sport Psychology.

But can time and deliberate practice lead every person to the same heights of skill? Clearly, the time invested influences how well information will be stored. But is learning rate influenced by talent or ability? Might this vary depending on the content being learned? As described in Chapter 2, there are many instances of talents such as music (the Bach family) or an aptitude for science (Darwins and Huxleys) that run in families, although it is hard to separate out the genetic from the environmental influences. If you were born into a family with several generations of professional musicians like the Bach family, you would be expected to learn an instrument, and practice from an early age. Nevertheless, studies with twin samples have provided evidence for genetic heritability of many different skills, including, for example, musical achievement and aptitude, with estimates of heritability of 50% for rhythm discrimination and 59% for melody discrimination (Hambrick, Burgoyne, Macnamara, & Ullén, 2018; see also Ackerman, 2014 for a discussion of genetic influences on expertise). Estimates of genetic influences on musical achievement are sizable (20%) even when carefully controlling for variations in music practice. Intriguingly, the tendency to engage in practicing itself is genetically heritable! Mosing, Madison, Pedersen, Kuja-Halkola, and Ullén (2014) examined 10,500 Swedish twins and found that the tendency for people to practice playing music was genetically heritable, with heritability estimates ranging from 40% to 70%. So, remarkably, people are genetically inclined to gravitate towards certain kinds of activities and give them extra practice. This finding illustrates the complexity in deciding whether the skills a person has derive from practice and hard work (time learning) or instead from genetic potential: If genetics lead people to favor activities building on their talents, then people will learn more both because of practice and also because of superior learning ability for that skill. So, whereas deliberate practice may help, the rate of learning and propensity to invest in practice may ultimately be influenced by natural abilities. Consistent with this, estimates suggest that individual variations in the amount of deliberate practice only account for 30–43% of the variance between people in musical ability (Hambrick et al., 2018).

Naturally, when we think about what we get in return for our time learning something, our focus is on the new skill or knowledge itself, and what it enables us to do. This focus is of course perfectly reasonable. We don't necessarily think about the fact that learning changes us, literally making us physically different. Did you know, for example, that extensive practice changes your brain structure, and that these changes are visible with brain imaging? Over the last two decades, a very large number of studies indicate the intimate connection between practicing different perceptual, motor, or cognitive tasks and changes in cortical thickness and white matter connectivity in regions contributing to those tasks. The brain's capacity to alter its structure to adapt to environmental demands is known as structural plasticity. For example, Eleanor Maguire and colleagues (Maguire et al., 2000) found significantly larger hippocampi in a sample of London taxicab drivers, who had been continually engaged in complex navigational problems for years. Because the hippocampus is critical for spatial navigation, this extensive practice had presumably driven experience-related changes in that structure, enabling superior performance. Consistent with this, London bus drivers, who drive as much as taxicab drivers, but who follow fixed routes, show no such increase in hippocampal volume (Maguire, Woolett, & Spiers, 2006). Similar

effects have been observed in motor and auditory cortex with musical proficiency (see Draganski, Kherif, & Lutti, 2014 for reviews). Structural changes are not limited to gray matter, but also affect connectivity between brain regions: Pianists show enhanced white-matter pathways connecting regions necessary for playing the piano, with the amount of modification linked to the hours of practice at piano playing (Bengtsson et al., 2005; see also Steele & Zatorre, 2018 for a review). Amazingly, monkeys given extensive training on a motor task show, in motor cortical neurons, a decrease in the synaptic activity required to generate the same neural firing, showing that even neurons get better at what they do for a well-trained task (Picard, Matsuzaka, & Strick, 2013).

Most convincing of all, however, are *longitudinal studies* of the very same individuals before, during, and after practice. Such longitudinal studies have been done with training in juggling, spatial navigation, and foreign language acquisition (see Wenger, Brozzoli, Lindenberger, & Lövdén, 2017, for a review), and they all show robust increases in brain areas relevant to these tasks, and changes usually correlate with better performance. Of particular interest to students, Draganski and colleagues (Draganski et al., 2006) studied German medical students before, during, and after their three-month intensive preparation for their German preliminary medical exam (including content on biology, chemistry, psychology, anatomy, and physiology), with each brain imaging measurement separated by three months. The students showed robust increases in cortical volume in the parietal cortex and in the posterior hippocampus and these increases remained even three months after studying (see Figure 5.3). Importantly, however, large increases in volume do not always last. Indeed, given the limited space inside our skulls, perpetual expansion of cortex with learning would seem ill advised. It has been proposed that, over time, the brain renormalizes the volume in the regions enhanced by practice. According to the expansion-normalization hypothesis, this renormalization reflects a "Darwinian" pruning away of cells, astrocytes, and con-

---

KEY TERM

Structural plasticity: The ability of the brain to undergo structural changes in response to altered environmental demands.

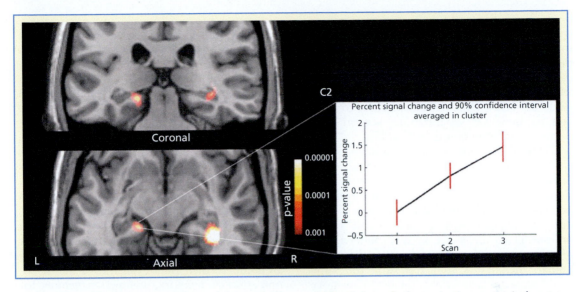

Figure 5.3 Draganski et al. (2006) found that studying material for their medical examinations extensively over three months led to a significant increase in the hippocampal volume for German medical students that remained even three months after the exam.

nections that, after forming initially, proved unnecessary during skill execution. Thus, just as in a "casting call" in Hollywood in which many actors show up for an audition, but few are chosen, some structural changes related to learning a task may be selected and others dropped (Wenger et al., 2017).

Clearly then, the amount of time you spend learning something is remodeling your brain in ways that allow you to do the things you wish to do in life, setting up machinery of excellence. The precise nature of this remodeling depends upon how we spend our time, and what brain areas we choose to exercise in pursuit of our goals. The performance benefits of learning time first documented by Ebbinghaus, surely are reflections in behavior of such structural plasticity in the brain (one wonders what areas increased during his nonsense syllable training). The idea that "you get what you pay for" through repeated learning effort thus applies to performance, but also the underlying transformation of your brain—something that is surely occurring to you at this very moment, as you read this material. But to move beyond competence in a domain to true excellence is likely to require much more than simple repetitive practice, as Ericsson rightly

points out. Furthermore, despite the general relationship between practice and the amount learned, there are ways in which one can get better value for the time spent. We discuss several powerful ways of beating the total time hypothesis next.

Distributed practice

Given the previous discussion, you are hopefully prepared to spend a great deal of time mastering the things you want to learn, inspired by visions of your expanding brain. But spending 10,000 hours practicing something is not something you can always do, except perhaps for the one or two things you are most passionate about. Given your limited time, you must consider how to allocate it wisely, to get the most out of it. This issue affects you right now, when you are deciding how to study. Imagine, for example, that you have an exam coming up in 10 days and you have 10 hours to study the chapter. Should you, (a) study everything in a single sitting, so that you can focus fully on it, reviewing and re-reviewing it until you feel that you have mastered it, or (b) divide your time into two separate sessions of five hours, reviewing and re-reviewing as often as you can in each segment? In each case, the total time studying is constant, and it's only the distribution of practice that varies. Does it make a difference? And if you take the latter approach, how should you schedule the study sessions? On consecutive days, to keep you focused? Or separated by several days during which you do other things?

Happily, there is an extremely clear answer that you can personally capitalise on: distribute your studying over multiple sessions. Restudying a piece of information immediately after you learn it is very clearly not an efficient way to learn and retain knowledge in an enduring way. Indeed, one of the most solid and widely studied laws of human memory is that repeating the same study material twice yields far better memory if repetitions are spaced in time (preferably with other intervening activities), rather than massed together, with no interval separating the repetitions. Improved learning that arises from separating repeated study attempts compared to massing repetitions is known as the spacing effect, or more broadly, the distributed practice effect. Spacing effects are ubiquitous. This effect is incredibly general across types of materials (see, e.g., Pashler, Rohrer, Cepeda, & Carpenter, 2007); it occurs with people of all ages, ranging from preschool children to the elderly. Indeed, the spacing effect even occurs in simple organisms like fruit flies, bees, and rodents, suggesting that it is an evolutionarily old property of memory (see Cepeda, Pashler, Vul, Wixted, & Roher, 2006; Gerbier & Toppino, 2015; Toppino & Gerbier, 2014, for reviews). As far as learning is concerned, "little and often" is an excellent precept.

One can get a feel for this effect from a simple study by one of the great early researchers on human memory, Arthur Melton. Melton showed people a list of words, one at a time,

with some presented once, and others twice (Melton, 1970). For the ones that appeared twice, he varied the number of other words that intervened between the repetitions from 0, all the way up to 40 words. He also varied the presentation rate, with words being presented for either 1.3, 2.3, or 4.3 seconds apiece. The data can be seen in Figure 5.4. For words presented only once (far left side of the figure), increasing study time from 1.3 to 4.3 seconds per word unsurprisingly improved memory, as expected based on the total time hypothesis. Again unsurprisingly, adding repetitions, in general, improved memory across the board, irrespective of presentation rate or the spacing between repetitions (compare points on the far left side, which were presented only once, with all points to their right), illustrating the *repetition effect* on memory, or superior memory for repeated stimuli, compared to nonrepeated stimuli. More striking, however, is the spacing

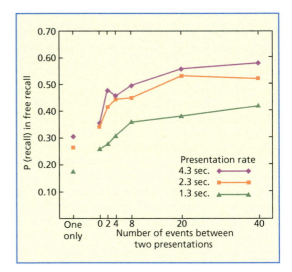

Figure 5.4 Melton (1970) found that increasing the number of other words in between two study attempts on the same word significantly increased final recall performance, more so, the more words intervened between repetitions. This occurred despite a constant total study time. In addition, the graph depicts data from three different rates of presentation, and also performance for items presented only once, for different amounts of time. Reprinted from the Journal of Verbal Learning and Verbal Behavior , Vol. 9, Issue 5, Arthur W. Melton , The Situation with Respect to the Spacing of Repetitions and Memory © 1970. With permission from Elsevier.

effect: Compared to words repeated twice with no intervening words (the 0 condition), adding intervening words between the repetitions leads memory to skyrocket, regardless of how many intervening words there were. Indeed, in the 4.3 second presentation rate (top line), performance goes from around 35% with a lag between repetitions of a word of 0 to nearly 60% when the lag was 40 intervening words, a near doubling of performance. In general, the benefit of repeated study attempts increases as the lag between the two study occasions increases, known as the *lag effect*. The lag effect can be seen here by the increasing performance from the zero condition to the 40 condition (as spacing increases). It is amazing to realize that this doubling of memory arose in Melton's study, despite total study time being held constant. For example, in the 4.3 second presentation rate, the 0-lag condition involved two presentations of the same word for a total of 8.6 seconds; the 40-lag condition also presented words twice for 4.3 seconds each, for 8.6 seconds. Yet recall went from 35% to 60%! Only the spacing differed. If this study is any indication, students would learn vastly more if they spaced their reviews of material widely, getting far more value from their precious time.

One might wonder, however, whether this type of experiment really applies to the kinds of things that students need to learn, which typically involves facts, concepts, and systems of knowledge. Moreover, the delays of main concern in real life are much larger than they are in this experiment, more on the order of months and years than a few minutes. Do we have any evidence that spaced repetitions really make a difference for factual knowledge? Is there an optimal spacing that helps maximize retention over the long term? Nicholas Cepeda, Edward Vul, Doug Rohrer, John Wixted, and Harold Pashler (2008) investigated this issue in a very thorough and convincing way. In an ideal experiment, one would, after learning something, study the effects of repetition over a wide range of very long lags, and then test people's memory after a range of delays, some of them very long. Such a study is difficult to do in the laboratory. To solve this problem, they turned to the Internet, con-ducting the study entirely online. They had people learn 32 obscure, but true, trivia facts until they could answer each of the trivia questions. For example, one question was "What European nation consumes the most spicy Mexican food?" Answer: Norway. After learning these facts, participants logged on again to restudy these facts at delays ranging from 0 to 105 days. After this opportunity for review, participants logged on for a final test on the facts either 5, 35, 70, or 350 days later, to see how spacing affected recall at realistically long delays. This study fits the kind of circumstances of direct concern to students, who are likely to review material a long time after they first study it, and who hope to learn something that lasts a long time.

As can be seen in Figure 5.5, Cepeda and colleagues found a sizable lag effect on final test scores that occurred regardless of how long they waited to test people. For example, when the participants were given the final test 70 days after the review, they recalled 30% of the facts if there was no delay (0) between initial study and the review; in contrast, participants recalled about 62% of the facts if a 20-day gap ensued between the initial learning and the review. In this example, recall literally doubled simply because the 20-day gap was inserted. Importantly, however, there appeared to be a maximum gap between the study and the review, beyond which further increases in the gap diminished the benefit of spacing somewhat. Cepeda and colleagues refer to this as the *non-monotonic lag effect*, or the tendency for the lag effect to first increase and to then decrease if it gets too long. Even in cases when the lag was too long to be ideal (e.g., right side of the graph), memory was always better than the 0-lag condition (far left), so spacing always helped. These findings illustrate the compelling benefits you can gain in your learning with a little patience and planning; after learning, wait a little while to review the materials, and you will reap tremendous rewards for your time. Similar real-world benefits of spacing have been found for learning calculus in a classroom setting (Lyle, Bego, Hopkins, Hieb, & Ralston, 2019), and in a study of 10,500 people taking part

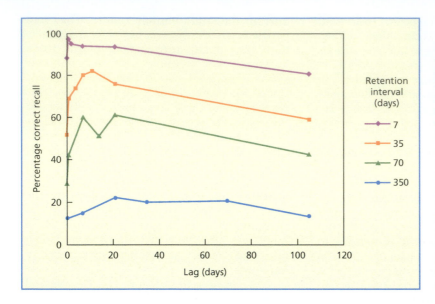

Figure 5.5 Cepeda at al. (2008) found compelling evidence for the benefits of distributed practice with factual materials and naturalistic delays, and found, moreover, that increases in lag do not always translate into increases in benefit. Reprinted by permission from Springer Nature. Psychonomic Bulletin & Review. Enhancing Learning and Retarding Forgetting: Choices and Consequences Harold Pashler, Doug Rohrer, Nicholas J. Cepeda et al © 2007

in workplace training courses on safety and store operations and product knowledge (Kim, Wong-Kee-You, Wiseheart, & Rosenbaum, 2019).

The distributed learning effect is not limited to learning arbitrary information or facts but can be seen in virtually every type of learning including, for example, the learning of motor skills. A good example of this arose a number of years ago when one of the authors of this text (A.B.) was asked to advise the British Post Office on a program that aimed to teach a very large number of postal workers to type. Postal coding was being introduced and this required the mail sorters to type the postal code using a keyboard resembling that of a typewriter. The Post Office had the option of either taking postal workers off their regular jobs and giving them intensive keyboard training, or of combining the training with their regular jobs by giving them a little practice each day. There were four feasible schedules: an intensive schedule of two two-hour sessions per day; intermediate schedules involving either one two-hour or two one-hour sessions per day; or a more gradual approach involving a single 1-hour session of typing per day. They therefore assigned postal workers at random to one of the four groups and began the training.

Figure 5.6 shows the rate at which the four groups acquired typing skill. The time it took to learn the keyboard (the point at

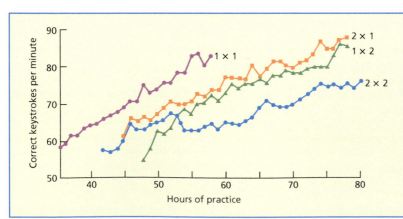

Figure 5.6 Rate of learning a typing skill for a range of training schedules: 1 × 1 equals one session of 1 hour per day, 2 × 1 equals two such sessions, 1 × 2 is one session of 2 hours and 2 × 2 two 2-hour sessions. From Baddeley and Longman (1978). Copyright © 1978 Taylor & Francis. Reproduced by permission (http://www.tandf.co.uk/journals).

which each learning curve starts) and the subsequent rate of improvement were both strongly affected by the particular training schedule used. The postal workers who trained for only one hour a day learned the keyboard in fewer hours of training and improved their performance more rapidly than those who trained for two hours a day; and they in turn learned more rapidly than those who trained for four hours per day. Indeed, the one-hour-per-day group learned as much in 55 hours as the four-hours-per-day group learned in 80. They also appeared to continue to improve at a faster rate and, when tested after several months without further practice, they proved to have retained their skill better than the four-hours-per-day group (Baddeley & Longman, 1978).

This result did not stem from fatigue or discontent on the part of the four-hours-per-day group. Indeed, when questioned afterwards, the one-hour-per-day postal workers were the least contented with their training schedule because, when measured in terms of the number of days required to acquire typing skill, they appeared to be progressing less rapidly than their four-hours-per-day colleagues. In drawing practical conclusions, of course, this should be borne in mind; four hours per day might be a relatively inefficient way of learning to type when measured on an hourly basis, but it did mean that the group reached in four weeks the standard it took the one-hour-a-day group 11 weeks to achieve. Distributed practice is more efficient in terms of the benefit for the time invested, but it might not always be practical or convenient for the learner.

Given this impressive evidence about the benefits of spacing on learning, you might wonder why this approach is not more widespread. One reason has to do with the inconvenience it poses to the learner and also to instructors. Using spacing to enhance your learning requires that you plan your study or practice efforts out well in advance, which is not always practical, given people's busy lives, or constraints in the classroom. It also requires patience from the learner and the instructors, as the previous study by Baddeley and Longman (1978) illustrates. Postal workers on the "slow and spaced" schedule

took 11 weeks to get to the point that it took the other group four weeks to achieve, which was surely frustrating to them, even if it was far more efficient, and the learning was proven to be more enduring. But another important obstacle to the using spacing to optimise learning and retention is people's beliefs about the learning process itself, which are sometimes dramatically wrong. People show a very strong tendency to prefer learning procedures that give them satisfaction and a good feeling of mastery *in the moment of training itself*, without attention to how it will affect retention in the longer term, which may not be as obvious to them. This occurs despite the fact that retention in the longer term is most people's ultimate goal.

Perhaps the most vivid illustration of this "disconnect" between how people prefer to learn and what is actually beneficial comes from an elegant study by Nate Kornell and Robert Bjork (2008). Kornell and Bjork were interested in the best way to teach people a general concept, a task that requires them to form a generalization from many particular examples—a process known as *induction*. For example, if you are interested in art history, you might want to learn the general style of famous artists in a way that would allow you to recognize a new painting you have never seen before, based on the other paintings by them that you have seen. Kornell and Bjork wanted to know whether people can learn the style of an artist better by viewing many paintings by that artist in a row, or instead, by interleaving paintings by the artist in question with paintings by other artists, much like you might encounter in a typical art museum. Participants viewed six paintings by each of 12 artists either in massed presentation (all six in a row) or distributed with other artists. On a later test, participants were presented with entirely new paintings by each of the artists and asked to pick the name of the artist that did each one, from a list in front of them. Examples of the kinds of paintings people saw are shown in Figure 5.7.

If you imagine which of these procedures you would prefer to follow if you had to learn about artists' style, you probably would

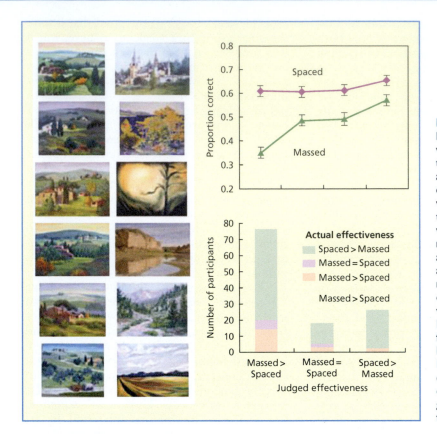

Figure 5.7 Kornell and Bjork (2008) found that when students tried to learn the artistic styles of 12 artists, they were far more effective when the artists were interleaved than when they were massed, even when they were tested on novel paintings by the artists. The students' beliefs about which learning method was better were diametrically opposite to what was truly effective. Reprinted by permission from Springer Nature. Psychonomic Bulletin & Review. Principles of cognitive science in education: The effects of generation, errors, and feedback. © 2007.

want to view many paintings by the same person in a row, probably because you could more easily cross-compare the paintings and figure out what they have in common. If this is your intuition, then you will be heartened to know that it is shared by the vast majority of the participants in Kornell and Bjork's experiment: overall, 78% of the people said that the massed presentation led them to learn the styles better. Unfortunately, you, like most of Kornell and Bjork's participants, would be desperately wrong. As you can see in Figure 5.7, spaced presentation of the paintings led to much better identification of new paintings by the artists than massed presentation. Indeed, 78% of the participants showed better performance in the spaced than the massed condition. The extent to which people were wrong is startling and sobering: The superiority of spacing was true, irrespective of what people's intuitions led them to say, with 75% of those people claiming the superiority of massed presentation

showing precisely the opposite pattern (see lower right figure). Clearly, if people believe that massing is better for learning, they will not adopt spacing as a method of learning, even if it is vastly superior. This type of belief about how your own memory works is known as metamemory (R. A. Bjork, 1994; Soderstrom, Yue, & E. L. Bjork, 2016; see also Dunlosky & Tauber, 2016), and such metamorial beliefs often guide people in their choices about how to learn.

Why would people believe that massed presentations are superior when this belief is so at odds with what is actually true? The most likely reason is that massed presentation is easier, and makes people feel like learning is going more smoothly. People may be quite

KEY TERM

Metamemory: Knowledge about one's own memory and an ability to regulate its functioning.

right that it is easier to think back to the last painting you saw to compare it to the current one if that painting was viewed a mere second ago, compared to minutes ago or longer. This momentary feeling of "fluency" in learning, however, may be a misleading indicator of what is good for the person's retention in the long run, leading people to form the erroneous metamemory belief that blocked learning is better. This pattern has been observed many times. To take another example, Hall, Domingues, and Cavazos (1994) compared the merits of training junior college baseball players to hit different kinds of pitches (e.g., either fastballs, curveballs, or changeups) either by giving them batting practice blocked by pitch type (e.g., a whole session of fastballs, or curveballs, etc.) or practice in which different pitch types came at random. During the practice sessions themselves, which took place over six weeks during a regular season, players receiving random practice performed much more poorly than the players receiving blocked practice, making fewer solid hits. In striking contrast, on a delayed test, players receiving random practice significantly outperformed the blocked group, getting many more solid hits. Undoubtedly, the random training group hated the random practice and felt that they were doing worse. Indeed, coaches often make the same mistake, insisting on blocked training of skills until people "get it right." The coaches, players, and learners in general would be far better off, however, with the more difficult and less satisfying training regimen. Robert Bjork has argued that, when it comes to improving learning, instructors should focus on introducing such *desirable difficulties* in training, and resist the easy path, going so far as to say that "forgetting is the friend of learning" (Bjork, 2014).

At this stage you may be very persuaded about the usefulness of spacing your learning, but also wondering "Why does it work?" As you might imagine, there has been a great deal of experimental work addressing this important finding, and several major theories have emerged, each with at least some evidence consistent with it. According to the *deficient processing hypothesis*, the spacing and lag effects both arise because people pay less attention to recently encountered things, and don't process them as well as something that they saw a longer time ago. This makes sense: If you just studied something for five seconds, and then you get another five seconds to study the same exact thing, you probably can imagine feeling like you already know it enough and may only give it cursory attention. Something you saw three days ago, on the other hand, may well capture your attention and lead you to spend more time encoding it. A second theory attributes the advantage of spacing and increasing lags to a factor known as *encoding variability*. According to this idea, you will tend to remember something better if you encode it in a variety of different ways, and have different thoughts about it, because if you do, you are creating a richer array of associations for accessing the memory. By this view, both spacing and longer lags produce better memory because at longer lags, you are more likely to encode the repetition in new ways that enrich your memory trace. A final proposal is known as the *study-phase retrieval hypothesis*. According to this idea, when you see something a second time, you tend to be reminded of the first time you saw it, which is what they mean by "study phase retrieval." By this idea, the very act of retrieving the prior occurrence is what strengthens your memory, more so, the more difficult the retrieval is (we discuss this further in our next section on retrieval-based learning). The spacing and lag effects both occur because as the spacing between repetitions increases, retrievals become a bit harder, and therefore, more beneficial. So, if something is repeated after three days, you may say to yourself "hey, wait, I saw that before, right ..." and you would check your memory in an effortful process, which would yield big benefits to you.

Which theory does the data most favor? Most researchers agree that the jury is still out on this question, and there is some data to support each idea. Having said that, neuroscience evidence has supported both the deficient processing and the study phase retrieval hypothesis more so than encoding variability (see Gerbier & Toppino, 2015, and Toppino & Gerbier, 2014, for reviews). One fascinating brain imaging study by Xue et al. (2010), for example, makes an elegant case for study phase retrieval and against encoding variability. Xue and colleagues had participants study either words or faces several times, while brain imaging data was collected. After brain imaging was complete and after a delay of several hours, they tested how well people remembered the stimuli. When analyzing the brain data, these authors focused not merely on which large brain areas were more active, but on the precise pattern of brain activity across thousands of small areas (see Figure 5.8). They then looked at the pattern of activity across these areas when the very same item repeated (i.e., the same word, or the same face) to see how similar the brain's response was to each repetition. They reasoned that if encoding variability improves memory, then items that people remembered successfully on

the test should show very different brain activity patterns across repetitions, reflecting the different processing the item received each time people saw it. Alternatively, if study-phase retrieval helps memory, then brain activation patterns should be highly similar from repetition to repetition, reflecting the fact that, on each occasion, people remembered studying it before, and reinstated the original brain pattern.

The data overwhelmingly favored the study-phase retrieval hypothesis: items that were remembered on the final test always showed more similar brain activation patterns across their repetitions in the study phase than did items that were forgotten. So, upon seeing a face or word, again and again, if people recollected the prior occasion and recreated the original brain activation pattern faithfully, then memory was always better on the later test. This suggests that actively retrieving information may play an especially important role in helping people to firmly learn something. Other data do indeed support this intriguing possibility. We turn to this idea next.

Retrieval-based learning

So far, we have discussed the benefits of "practice" and "learning" without attention to any particular activities that people might perform during repeated learning sessions. For example, when you try to learn the content in this chapter by reviewing it repeatedly, you could take different approaches. You could re-read the entire chapter again at various delays, which is—by far—the most commonly reported approach students take to studying. Alternatively, you could, after reading the chapter, try to recall everything you learned from memory, or, instead, ask a fellow student to drill you with questions. There would seem to be arguments for both approaches. On the one hand, re-reading the chapter multiple times would expose you to all of its content fully, whereas retrieval is likely to be incomplete and error prone. On the other hand, retrieval is much more demanding, and puts your knowledge to the test, whereas re-reading may be too easy. Is there a reason to prefer one approach or the other?

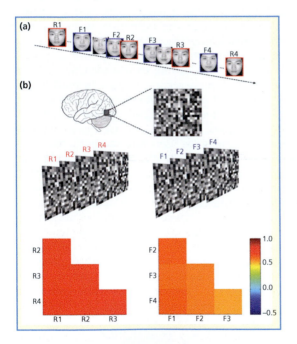

Figure 5.8 Xue et al. (2010) found that when either faces or words were repeated in spaced fashion, successful memory on a final test was associated with greater similarity in brain activity patterns across the repeated study attempts. This suggests that the ability to recreate the same brain activity patterns with retrieval processes is the mechanism driving spacing benefits, rather than encoding variability, which would have predicted the opposite.

Research on this question is spectacularly clear: testing yourself is vastly superior, in most cases, to simply restudying or reviewing what you are trying to learn. The reason is that recalling something from memory is, in itself, an extremely powerful learning event. We tend to think of "remembering" as simply reaching into memory and reporting on what we know, like pulling a book off of a shelf in your mental library. In fact, however, the very act of remembering modifies memory powerfully (Bjork, 1975). The improvement in later memory for material that is tested is known as a testing effect and is one example of the broader benefits of retrieval to learning known as *retrieval-based learning*.

Testing effects are not subtle. This fact is shown particularly clearly in an elegant study by Karpicke and Roediger (2008). They examined foreign language vocabulary learning across four conditions. In each condition, participants' mission was the same: to memorize 40 Swahili-English word pairs (e.g., *mashua–boat*) as well as they could. The first condition involved repeatedly presenting and testing the entire list of 40 pairs over four learning trials (called the ST condition, where S means study, and T means test). A second adopted the procedure of dropping a pair from further study (SnT, where "n" means only *nonrecalled* pairs were studied) once it had been learned but continuing to test the person on all 40 pairs each time, a procedure often recommended in study guides as it allows the learner to concentrate their study effort on only the unlearned items. A third condition presented all 40 pairs every time for study but dropped out items gotten right on earlier tests from later tests, to focus quizzing on only the nonrecalled items (STn). The final condition dropped learned items from both later study cycles and later tests (SnTn). Essentially, the first two conditions *always tested people* on all pairs, and simply varied in whether additional study was given to already recalled items; the second two conditions *always dropped recalled pairs from the tests* and varied as to whether those items also got further review. Recall was then tested a week later. Which conditions do you think led to best recall?

The results are shown in Figure 5.9. We should first note that the rate of learning in week 1 was identical across conditions (left side of figure). At this stage, students might well have felt perfectly happy with any of the learning procedures. Retention at the one-week delay was most certainly not equivalent (see right side of figure). The two conditions that had continued *testing* learned pairs (left columns) both recalled 80%; the two conditions in which testing was abandoned when pairs were learned were equally poor, at around 30% recall. Repeatedly presenting pairs for further study without testing had had no effect at all when it came to the test a week later. The participants who had practiced recalling the pairs recalled over twice as many of the pairs! This type of testing effect is not limited to memorising vocabulary pairs, but occurs for diverse materials, including facts, lengthy text passages, diagrams and maps, and scientific concepts; it occurs across age groups from elementary school children to older adults, and can be elicited by nearly any kind of test, including ones that require free recall of a large body of material, to more focused questions (e.g., short answer, fill in the gap), multiple choice questions, and even tests that simply ask a person to recognize whether they have seen something before. The benefits of retrieval practice over restudying become especially pronounced at longer delays, and studies have looked as far as several weeks or months (e.g., Carpenter, Pashler, & Cepeda, 2009). Retrieval is truly a powerful general learning process with significant implications for education (for reviews, see Bjork, 1975; Pan & Rickard, 2018; Rawson & Dunlosky, 2012; Roediger & Butler, 2011; Roediger, Putnam, & Smith, 2011; Rowland, 2014).

Not all retrieval tests are equally effective in enhancing later recall, however. In general, the more difficult the retrieval test is, the

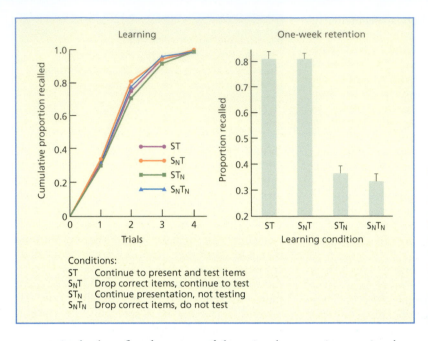

Conditions:

ST	Continue to present and test items
$S_N T$	Drop correct items, continue to test
ST_N	Continue presentation, not testing
$S_N T_N$	Drop correct items, do not test

Figure 5.9 The importance of testing for later remembering. The pattern of learning and test trials had no effect on rate of learning, but the presence of tests had a major effect on what was remembered one week later. From Karpicke and Roediger (2008). Copyright © 1980 AAAS. Reprinted with permission.

greater is the benefit of a successful retrieval (Bjork, 1975; Bjork & Bjork, 1992). Consider a nice study by Mary Pyc and Katherine Rawson (2009), who set out to test this retrieval difficulty hypothesis. Participants learned 70 Swahili-English word pairs by practicing the retrieval of the English word, given the Swahili cue. Pyc and Rawson manipulated both the time between successive retrievals (one minute or six minutes) and the number of retrievals (with feedback). Figure 5.10(a) shows how well participants could recall the vocabulary items either after 25 minutes or one week later. Several features of these data stand out. First, the more that participants did retrieval practice, the better their later recall (as seen by increasing recall from left to right) indicating that multiple retrievals help a lot. More importantly, however, is the striking effect of lag between the initial study and retrieval practice of the item: when separated by a mere minute, participants were nowhere near as good on the final test as when the tests were separated by six minutes. This effect is particularly impressive at the one-week delay, where it seems that repeated retrieval provided no benefit to performance when done after only one minute. This confirms the idea that harder retrievals are far more beneficial than

easier retrievals, a pattern that has been widely replicated (see, e.g., Rowland, 2014). This pattern is also reflected in the fact that free and cued recall tests, in general, benefit memory more than recognition tests, which are generally easier (Rowland, 2014).

One danger in encouraging learners to use retrieval practice is that retrieval is not always successful, or sometimes can generate wrong answers. Obviously, if you fail to recall something, little benefit will occur, and if you recall the wrong thing, you may strengthen incorrect answers. Although robust testing effects occur even when people aren't given feedback about their performance, feedback greatly improves retrieval-based learning. In fact, studying the right answer immediately after a retrieval test improves memory far more than exactly the same amount of study time when it's not conducted after a retrieval test. This is known as test-enhanced learning. Test-enhanced

KEY TERM

Test-enhanced learning: The tendency for a period of study to promote much greater learning when that study follows a retrieval test of the studied material.

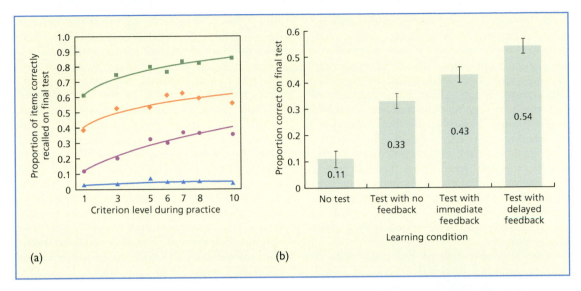

Figure 5.10 (a) Pyc and Rawson (2009) found that increasing the delay between successive retrievals of the same material dramatically enhanced later test performance at both 25 minutes and one week later. With permission from Elsevier. (b) Butler and Roediger (2008) found that providing tests with feedback about right answers were superior to tests without feedback, and that delaying the feedback produced even more learning.

learning effect means that testing with feedback should be an especially powerful way to magnify the benefits of testing. This effect is illustrated in a study by Andrew Butler and Henry Roediger (Butler & Roediger, 2008). Students read a text passage. Afterwards, one group was dismissed, and the other groups got retrieval practice with a multiple-choice test. One week later, all groups were tested on the passage. As can be seen in Figure 5.10(b), all groups receiving retrieval practice vastly outperformed the group that didn't get a test initially (more than a three-fold increase in recall). However, the participants who were given feedback about their multiple-choice responses did even better later on, with participants receiving delayed feedback (all answers given after the test was over) showing even bigger effects than students receiving immediate feedback after each question. Feedback also corrects mistakes and reinforces the right answer.

One might wonder whether retrieval tests are really helping people to learn new material in a meaningful way, or whether this method simply promotes rote memory of the retrieved material. Clearly, meaningful learning matters. For example, your objective in

reading this text is to deeply understand what you are learning in a meaningful way that will enable you to make future inferences and solve problems. It's not enough to simply be able to parrot back random facts. Interestingly it seems that retrieval practice not only induces a test-effect (better literal memory for what you have retrieved), but also more broadly encourages retrieval-based learning that transfers widely to a variety of inference and problem-solving contexts. In fact, retrieval tests (somewhat ironically) do this to a greater extent than methods that current educators use to promote meaningful learning. In an elegant example, Jeff Karpicke and Janell Blunt asked students to study a science text under one of four conditions (Karpicke & Blunt, 2011). One group simply studied the passage of text once, much like you would do if you only read this chapter a single time without further review. A second group got the chance to repeatedly study the text over four consecutive study periods within the same session. A third group read the text and created a concept map with the text readily available to them. *Concept maps* are graphical diagrams that one draws of the concepts in a text and their relationships, to clarify its meaning and organization, and are widely promoted in educational settings (see Chapter 17 on improving your memory for more on concept maps). The final group read the text, and then were asked to recall it, without any hints. Afterwards, they got to read the text again, followed by a second recall attempt. Notably, the total time spent on learning was carefully matched in the latter groups. After completing the learning process, students were asked how effectively they had learned the text by asking them to predict how much they would remember of the text in one week. Students returned one week later and were tested with a short answer test.

One key objective of this study was to examine whether retrieval practice not only benefitted later verbatim knowledge of the text, but also performance on inference questions which required students to connect multiple concepts in the text. If retrieval only facilitates rote learning, it should promote performance on the verbatim test, but fare poorly on the questions requiring meaningful inference. The results are illustrated in Figure 5.11. Impressively, retrieval practice not only promoted vastly superior rote memory for verbatim facts from the text, relative to both repeated study and concept mapping, it also was superior in promoting meaningful infer-

ences. This is despite the fact that the concept mapping process is widely touted as a way to promote and emphasize meaningful learning. Revealingly, despite the clear superiority of retrieval-based learning, the students themselves judged retrieval to be the least effective method of learning, again illustrating that people can have poor metamemorial judgment when it comes to allocating their study time effectively. Here again, this likely reflects the perceived difficulty of the retrieval tests during study, relative to the other conditions, which, while easier, created an inflated sense of competence and mastery. It is now very well established that retrieval tests not only enhance literal recall, but also promote learning that *transfers* to many situations in a generalizable way (Pan & Rickard, 2018), justifying the phrase retrieval-based learning.

Motivation to learn

Larry Walters wanted to be a pilot in the Air Force, but poor eyesight stopped him. Instead, on July 2, 1982, at age 33, he executed a careful plan to strap 42 helium-filled weather balloons to an aluminium lawnchair. Aided by his girlfriend Carol, he strapped on a parachute, packed sandwiches, a two-litre bottle of Coke, a CB radio, and a pellet gun, and set off

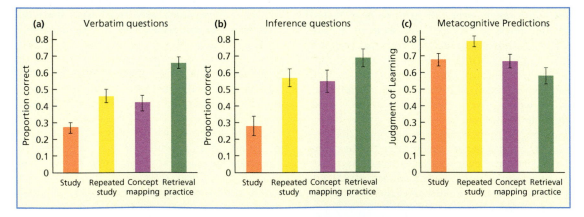

Figure 5.11 Karpicke and Blunt (2011) found that retrieval practice yielded far superior retention of science content after retrieval practice, than after either repeated study or concept mapping. Importantly, this superiority extended to the ability of students to answer inference questions on the final test, not just rote memory. Students believed retrieval practice to be the least effective method of study. From Science, Retrieval Practice Produces More Learning than Elaborative Studying with Concept Mapping. Vol. 331, Issue. 6018. Jeffrey D. Karpicke, Janell R. Blunt. Reprinted with permission from AAAS.

for a ride into the sky. He had hoped to fly up 30 feet above his backyard for a view of the Mojave desert, and, after hours of sightseeing, descend by gradually shooting the balloons with his pellet gun. Instead, due to miscalculations and wind conditions, Larry's balloon craft shot up higher and far faster than he expected, rising 1,000 feet per minute, to 16,000 feet. Flying through the airspace over Los Angeles airport, an airline pilot looked out the window and saw a guy wafting past him in a lawnchair, holding a pistol, and radioed the airport "Uh, you're not going to believe this but…."

At this stage, you are surely curious about Larry Walters. What happened to him? Indeed, when I first heard news about Larry, I was riveted, and I truly will never ever forget it. Nor will the airline pilots, I suspect. Who could not be curious about what happened? Well, let me put you out of your misery: After 45 minutes, Larry summoned the courage to shoot some balloons, and gently returned to earth, landing in power lines in Long Beach California, triggering a power outage. Upon landing, he was swarmed by admiring neighbors and children. Before being taken away by police, a journalist asked why he had done it, and he said "A man can't just sit around." Larry, naturally, became a minor celebrity in the US, known fondly as "Lawnchair Larry."

Chances are, you will never forget the saga of Lawnchair Larry. This superior memory on your part will require no spaced learning, no retrieval practice, and will not require massive time investment of studying. The learning occurred naturally, driven by a desire to know and an enjoyable and rewarding feeling of learning something interesting. The state that you were in while reading this story, or while you learn about things on your own, outside of coursework somehow seems qualitatively different than intentionally studying. Why is learning so easy when you are in this state? Is there something special about motivation?

Over the last decade, a growing body of work in neuroscience has begun to document how motivation affects memory storage (see Dickerson & Adcock, 2018; Miendlarzewska, Bavelier, & Schwartz, 2016;

Shohamy & Adcock, 2010 for reviews). One important form of *intrinsic motivation* is interest or curiosity, which requires no external incentives to encourage. In a fascinating study on this subject, Mathias Gruber, Bernard Gelman, and Charan Ranganath were curious about what curiosity does to the brain (Gruber, Gelman, & Ranganath, 2014). Sadly, they did not study people's reactions to Lawnchair Larry, but they did manage to come up with a crude approximation: trivia questions. In a first phase, participants reviewed a large body of trivia questions (without the answers) and were asked to rate (a) whether they knew the answer, and (b) how curious they were to know the answer. After eliminating questions that participants already knew the answers to, they selected high curiosity (e.g., "What does the term "dinosaur" actually mean?) and low curiosity questions, unique to each participant. Participants then entered the fMRI scanner and performed trials presenting one of the questions and had to wait about 10 seconds until they saw the answer (see Figure 5.12). While waiting patiently, they would see a face and make a simple incidental judgment on it (the face in the figure is Mathias Gruber himself!). Their memory was tested after about an hour, to see if people could remember the answers to the questions, and also whether they could recognize the faces.

As you can see in Figure 5.12, participants showed robustly superior recall of answers they were curious about (about 15–20%), even though the questions and answers were viewed for the same total time and were not repeated or given retrieval practice. Simply being curious was enough to make memory better. Intriguingly, however, not only did people remember the answers better, they also were more likely to recognize the face that they saw while waiting for the answer (see Figure 5.12), even though the face had nothing at all to do with the question. This finding suggests that curiosity creates a powerful state favorable to encoding new information, even incidental information not related to what you are curious about.

So, what is this magical state? Gruber and colleagues uncovered a very interesting answer. They found that when people felt very curious about a soon-to-be-received

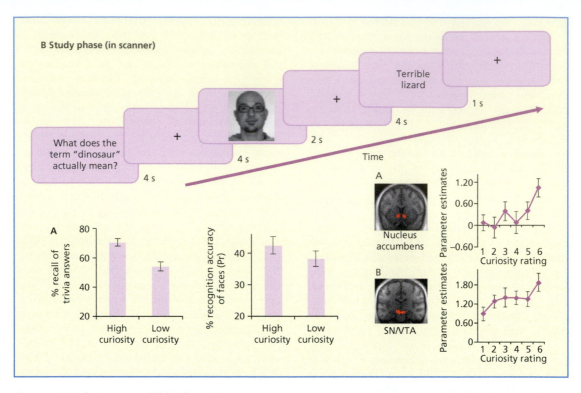

Figure 5.12 Gruber et al. (2014) found that when people were curious to know the answer to a question that they didn't know the answer to, they showed significantly better memory for the answer later on, compared to answers they weren't curious about (lower row, first set of columns). This benefit extended to incidental materials (faces) presented while they were waiting for the answer (for data, see lower row, second set of bars). Both of these effects were linked to curiosity-driven activity in the ventral tegmental area and nucleus accumbens, with the former linked to increased dopamine release in the hippocampus under conditions of reward. With permission from Elsevier.

answer, it increased activity in a midbrain area called the ventral tegmental area (the VTA), and a second region in the ventral striatum known as the nucleus accumbens (see Figure 5.12, lower right). Prior work had shown that these two areas work together with the hippocampus to facilitate learning (for reviews, see Düzel, Bunzeck, Guitart-Masip, & Düzel, 2010; Lisman & Grace, 2005). Indeed, work with rodents has found that the VTA promotes the release of a neurotransmitter called dopamine in the hippocampus when a reward is anticipated, and, in so doing, enhances learning at the neural level (later in this chapter, we will discuss the neural basis of learning). In fact, blocking dopamine release in the hippocampus with drugs seriously disrupts learning in rats. So, if

feeling curious about something genuinely triggers the VTA to release more dopamine into the hippocampus, this change in state would could greatly improve your memory. Consistent with this idea, Gruber and colleagues found that when participants were curious about an answer, there was stronger communication between the VTA and the hippocampus, and this interaction predicted improved memory for answers and the faces on the delayed test! In essence, a curious state bathes your hippocampus in dopamine, and makes the machinery of learning more effective. You may also be interested to know that other important situations drive greater dopamine release in the hippocampus (by the VTA), including when people encounter novel stimuli and especially when they actively explore novel environments, which leads to a persistent and superior encoding state (see Düzel et al., 2010; Shohamy & Adcock, 2010 for reviews). So, it seems that you will remember Lawnchair Larry later in life, in part, because he (rather unintentionally) led your VTA to enhance dopamine release in your hippocampus!

If curiosity is rewarding, then perhaps other forms of reward might also drive similar effects on memory. Might, for example, the promise of money for accurate memory for a stimulus produce a similar effect? What about chocolate cake? Juice? The chance to watch Conan O'Brien and Jordan Schlansky videos on YouTube? Or, if you are my son Max, a chance to run through mud puddles during the next rainstorm? In contrast to intrinsic motivation, such as curiosity and interest, these forms of external incentives in exchange for proper performance, are forms of extrinsic motivation. For example, although you may be naturally motivated to learn the content in this course, you also have powerful extrinsic motivators, such as your score on exams covering this material. Interestingly, many scientific studies have now shown evidence for this form of reward-based enhancement of memory encoding (for a review, see Dickerson & Adcock, 2018). Signaling people in advance that a picture or word that they are about to see will yield a large monetary reward (e.g., five dollars) if remembered in 24 hours yields superior memory compared to low reward (e.g., 25 cents), an effect that is sometimes more pronounced at longer delays. This effect occurs even if the picture is only presented for two seconds and is immediately followed by a distractor task that prevents people from devoting special strategies or additional time to memorizing the item. This automatic reward-enhanced encoding effect appears to be driven by the same VTA–hippocampus interaction produced by curiosity and is believed to also reflect an increase in dopamine (see Adcock, Thangavel, Whitfield-Gabrieli, Knutson, & Gabrieli, 2006; Dickerson & Adcock, 2018; Miendlarzewska et al., 2016 for reviews). Interestingly, just as with curiosity, the promise of a reward also enhances memory

for incidentally presented information while someone is awaiting the reward. Indeed, when the reward is finally delivered, it improves episodic memory for events that precede and follow it, even if the reward has nothing at all to do with those events (Mather & Schoeke, 2011; Murayama & Kitigami, 2014). It's as though basking in the glow of the reward makes the world more memorable.

So, it seems that motivation—whether intrinsic or extrinsic—has the potential to create a special brain state that makes you more likely to remember things later on. It would be a mistake, however, to chalk up the effects of motivation entirely to such automatic effects. Clearly when study time and strategy is not carefully controlled as it is in the preceding studies, motivation and rewards also will lead people to spend more time studying, or instead use different strategies for high priority information. How people strategically prioritize their study time given what they think is important and valuable to know has received some attention (Ariel, Dunlosky, & Bailey, 2009). One interesting approach uses a *value-directed remembering procedure*, in which people intentionally memorize items for a later memory test, with each item being assigned a point value when it is presented and the goal to maximize point value is explicitly stated (Castel, Benjamin, Craik, & Watkins, 2002). Evidence from this procedure illustrates that people often use deeper and more elaborate memorization strategies for high value items. Undoubtedly, you would do the same if your instructor told you that only certain parts of this chapter would appear on the examination. Thus, motivation affects learning in both automatic (driven by lower level factors like dopamine) and strategic ways. Indeed, according to Ericsson (see our earlier discussion of practice time), only highly

KEY TERM

Reward-based enhancement of memory encoding: The tendency for offering rewards for successful memory to improve long-term retention of studied material.

motivated people will achieve true excellence at something and the pathway to that excellence is *deliberate practice*. A person can't just sit around, after all.

Amount of attention available

As you read this chapter, other things may be calling your attention. You may have music on in the background; or your phone may chime every time someone posts on social media or directly messages you; or an email may come in, or a reminder message may pop up on your computer screen. One of the most glaring changes over the last few decades is the extent to which our devices, which are supposed to serve us, now routinely capture and demand our attention, whatever we may be doing. Recently, while working on something upstairs in my office, the helpful "I'm done" tone from my washing machine kept ringing intermittently, insisting that I come down two flights of stairs to appease it. Eventually, irritated and distracted, I made the journey to address my washing machine's urgent priorities.

Given these conditions, it is miraculous that you can learn anything at all. Research on the effects of divided attention uniformly decries the detrimental effect that this condition has on how effectively you learn. This effect is particularly dramatic when people do a second task while learning something (e.g., Baddeley, Lewis, Eldridge, & Thomson, 1984; Craik, Govoni, Naveh-Benjamin, & Anderson, 1996). Such experiments usually arrange it so that the second activity doesn't require the same sensory modality (e.g., if you are trying to learn things presented to you visually, the other task would be auditory or vice versa) to avoid the possibility that poor learning reflects a sensory limit (e.g., you can't look at two things at once). In real life, this would be like you listening to an e-book or a podcast while driving or monitoring a conversation in the background while reading something, or perhaps reading your text while you are on an exercise machine. For example, Moshe Naveh-Benjamin and Matthew Brubaker (2019) tested whether dividing attention mainly affected intentional learning strategies, which you might think would be hard to carry out if your mind is elsewhere. Participants viewed 12 words, one at a time, with each word presented twice in spaced format, for six seconds. The experimenters told participants that they were interested in their physiological responses to the words, collected by electrodes that they had attached to them. In the incidental learning group, participants were told nothing further. But in the intentional learning group, people were also asked to memorize the words for a later test. Presumably, the latter group would apply study strategies, more so than the group who did not expect a test.

Of key interest was whether people were permitted to view the words with full attention or were asked to do a second task at the same time. The second task simply involved listening to tones over headphones and classifying them as "high" "medium," or "low." Nothing about this task overlaps with the memorization task—the tones were auditory and had no meaning, and the words visual. Yet, people needed to attend to the tones and make decisions about them, which ought to be distracting on a more general level (not unlike my dreaded washing machine). Figure 5.13 illustrates the results. Participants' final recall plummeted from 50–60% down to 10–20% in the divided attention condition. It didn't matter whether people were intentionally memorizing the items—simply having another task tugging away at attention dramatically limited their ability to register the words in memory, even though they saw each word twice, for six seconds each time. Clearly, people who feel as though they can easily multitask between checking emails, replying to texts, and studying for a class are committing a grave error in limiting their encoding processes. This finding is fairly typical in illustrating the devastating effects of divided attention. Sizable disruptions occur not only on recall tests but also tests where people simply need to recognize what they studied. Distraction also makes you forget where objects are located (Naveh-Benjamin, 1987) and the order in which events occurred (Naveh-Benjamin, 1990). The next time you absent-mindedly put your keys someplace when you arrive home and

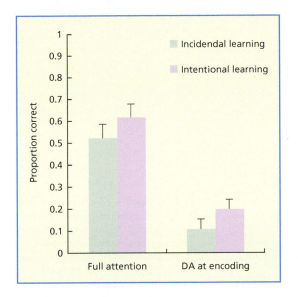

Figure 5.13 Naveh-Benjamin and Brubaker (2019) found that dividing attention at encoding disrupted later memory for a set of 12 words, regardless of whether participants intentionally memorized them or encoded them incidentally.

you can't find them later you now know why —inattention to the location of the keys, due to your activities upon arrival.

Why does dividing attention harm memory? Brain imaging studies have looked into this and have suggested some answers. In most studies, participants are given words that they either study intentionally or encode incidentally for a later test, either under full or divided attention. Many studies have found that doing a second task during encoding significantly reduces activation in the prefrontal cortex, especially in the left ventrolateral prefrontal cortex (Kensinger, Clark, & Corkin, 2003; Shallice et al., 1994; Uncapher & Rugg, 2008; see Long, Kuhl, & Chun, 2018, for a review). Although this region likely contributes to many functions, one important role that it is believed to play is to control memory encoding in part, by enhancing encoding activity in the hippocampus. The hippocampus, as we will discuss later, is critical for forming new memories of personal experiences, and when this structure is damaged it yields profound amnesia (see Chapter 16 on memory disorders). Thus, by facilitating activity in this region, the left

prefrontal cortex enhances encoding and makes memories more durable. The prefrontal cortex does this whether you are intending to memorize something or not, as long as you are paying attention to an event, especially to its meaning. In this sense, the left prefrontal cortex may contribute to attentional processes that guide memory formation (see Long et al., 2018). By dividing attention, this function is undermined, as reflected in its reduced activity. Perhaps partly as a result of this, these studies also find that when your attention is divided, hippocampal activity no longer predicts whether you remember something. This suggests that the hippocampus's role in forming memories is vastly reduced when attention doesn't help it along. Recent findings point to a reason why: Attention helps to create a stable memory trace in the hippocampus that faithfully reflects the precise type of content we seek to focus on (Aly & Turk-Browne, 2016). For example, if, while walking through the art museum, you are staring longingly at paintings (rather than the layout of the room), attention ensures that hippocampal encoding activity is more "painting-like" by encouraging its communication to other brain areas that help you to look at the paintings.

At this stage, you are surely switching off your smartphone, instant messaging, and email announcements, so you can devote your full attention to learning. If so, I'd just like to say Outstanding Move! But lest you come to believe that you have now eradicated the main source of attentional limits to what you remember, let me correct you, dear reader. It seems altogether likely that the very subject we are discussing right now is why you will remember so precious little of your life. To see what I mean, consider a rather disconcerting study conducted by Pranav Misra, Alyssa Marconi, Matthew Peterson, and Gabriel Krieman (2018). In this remarkable study, they attached the contraption depicted in Figure 5.14 to participants' heads and asked them to walk a particular route along the streets of Boston for an hour, with no particular goal. The contraption was a wearable video camera, fitted with an eye tracker that could precisely record where people were looking at every moment. So, the

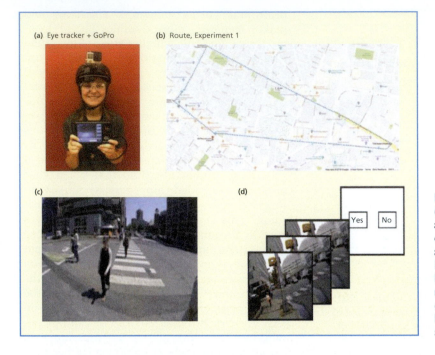

(a) Eye tracker + GoPro

(b) Route, Experiment 1

(c)

(d)

Yes   No

Figure 5.14 Misra et al. (2018) asked people to wear a head-mounted camera and eye tracker (a) and walk along a fixed route in Boston (b), and 24 hours later, tested them on their memory for 2-second video clips (c) which could have been from their walk or another subject's walk (d).

experimenters had an objective record of every tiny thing that participants saw during their journey, and where they were looking. After returning the equipment, participants came back 24 hours later and were given a test. They were shown a large number of brief two-second-long videos that were either taken from their own walk, or from the walk of another person who followed the same route. Participants simply had to decide whether the video was from their own trip, or someone else's. Naturally, although there were many similarities between people's videos, every person's had unique features, like people they passed on the sidewalk, things that they closely inspected and so forth. How well do you think you would do on this test? Well, on average, participants only correctly recognized 55.7% of their own videos! You should bear in mind here that if people had randomly guessed, they would have gotten 50% correct, on average. This pattern held even when they examined what people's eyes were focused on, which improved recognition only slightly. In essence, this study illustrates how shockingly little we retain of our daily experience.

Why is our memory for the details of our daily life so shockingly poor, even after just one day? Surely, this has to do with what we pay attention to, and the incredibly important role that attention plays in filtering out the irrelevancies of life. How many of us, while walking down the street, get lost in our thoughts about current concerns, with our mind wandering from one topic to the next? If you do this—allow your mind to wander as you walk—you are, in effect, in a divided attention situation, limiting the ability of your life to register in memory. Incredibly, when we don't pay attention to our world, it even seems to matter little how many times we encounter things, much like Naveh-Benjamin and Brubaker's (2019) participants. Indeed, unattended repetitions utterly defy the total time hypothesis and the repetition effect discussed at the outset of this chapter. To illustrate the point, think of a penny in your pocket. Can you remember exactly what is on each side? Try it! Figure 5.15 shows the results of a study by Rubin and Kontis (1983), who asked their participants to recall the features of four American coins. The coins are shown on the left of the figure, and

| (a) | (b) |
| Actual | Modal |

Figure 5.15 The results of a study by Rubin and Kontis (1983) recording the features that most US students thought appeared on each of four coins. Column (a) shows the actual features and column (b) the most frequent responses. From Rubin and Kontis (1983). Reprinted with permission from AAAS.

the most commonly recalled version of each coin is shown on the right.

Of course, one could argue that it's not particularly impressive to fail to remember the details of a penny, given that such fine details are of no real interest. You don't need to check your pennies to make sure they are genuine. Somewhat more surprising, perhaps, are instances of what has become known as change blindness, whereby some prominent feature of the visual environment is dramatically changed, without the perceiver noticing. Rosiell and Scaggs (2008), for example, asked students to identify what was wrong with a picture of a familiar location on college campus that students likely have visited hundreds of times. The changes they

made to the pictures were quite dramatic, for example removing the library from the scene (Figure 5.16). Although 97% of participants rated the scene as familiar, only 20% successfully detected the missing library. How could you not detect a missing library? Despite frequent repetitions our LTM for complex scenes can be less detailed than one might imagine, almost surely because of lack of attention. Attention clearly is an exceptionally powerful force determining what we come to remember of our worlds, and, indeed of our life histories.

Sleep and the consolidation of learning

If, by some chance, you happened to doze off while reading this chapter, let me offer you some consolation. While taking that nap, your brain was doing something very important. Of course, a nap is restorative, giving you energy and attention to go on, and we know from the last section that attention is indeed important to memory. But more surprisingly, the nap not only will help you to focus your attention on the new material, but also will very likely strengthen your memory of the content studied before the nap. There is now a tremendous body of research in both psychology and neuroscience that has examined the relationship between a night's sleep or naps and the enhancement of nearly every form of memory, including explicit memory of past events, and the many other varieties of memory to be detailed later in this chapter (Diekelman & Born, 2010; King, Hoedlmoser, Hirshauer, Dolfen, & Albouy, 2017; Pace-Schott, Germain, & Milad, 2015). These findings are not only observed in sleeping humans, but also in many other animals including, for example, mice, rats, and birds. So, by taking your wee nap, you were rather cleverly deploying one of the

> **KEY TERM**
>
> **Change blindness:** The failure to detect that a visual object has moved, changed, or been replaced by another object.

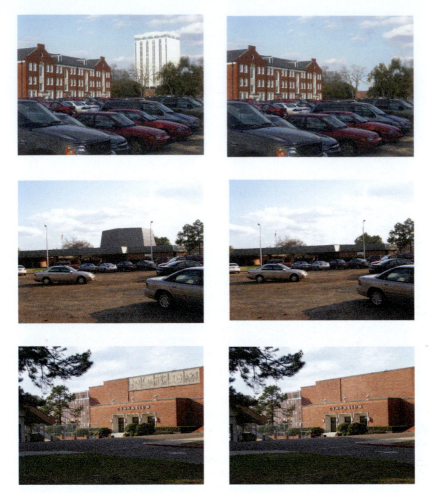

Figure 5.16 Change blindness: the original scenes are on the left; the images on the right are the altered versions that participants were required to judge. From Rosiell and Scaggs (2008). Copyright © Psychology Press.

more effective things you can do to facilitate the successful storage of your new memories in your brain.

The idea that sleep benefits memory is not new. The Roman teacher of rhetoric, Quintillian, noted, for example, that the interval of a single night would increase the strength of memory, a process he likened to ripening or maturing. In the very early history of psychology, the term consolidation

was proposed by two German psychologists, Müller and Pilzecker (1900), to describe a proposed process by which a memory was hardened or made more robust over time for an association just learned. The connection of this proposed consolidation process to sleep was experimentally examined nearly a century ago in a classic study by Jenkins and Dallenbach (1924) who found, just as Quintillian suggested, that participants who slept after learning remembered more than those who learned and then recalled after the same amount of time awake.

Being critical for a moment, there are of course other possible explanations for such a result. For example, it could be due to *retroactive interference*, the process whereby new learning disrupts old learning (see Chapter 9,

p. 291); thus, by this view, sleep protects you from further experiences that would otherwise interfere with the earlier learning. There are also problems of interpretation resulting from the 24-hour fluctuations that occur in alertness. People tested in the evening might be more fatigued than those tested next morning, and if both groups are tested at the same time of day, one is likely to have to sleep at an unaccustomed time. Such complexities discouraged research for many years, but more recently with surging interest in the neuroscience of consolidation, people have increasingly been willing to tackle these complexities, and a coherent and interesting pattern of evidence is beginning to emerge.

Evidence for the importance of sleep in word learning comes from a series of studies by Gaskell and Dumay (2003). They took advantage of the fact that the time to recognize a spoken word takes a little longer if it has a near neighbor, for example detecting the word *catalyst* would be slowed down by *catalogue*, presumably because you need to wait until the middle of the word to be sure which of the two has been spoken. They taught people new words that resembled old, e.g., *cathedruke*, then tested speed of responding to *cathedral*. Despite being able to recall *cathedruke*, it only interfered with *cathedral* after a night's sleep, suggesting that new words need sleep to be fully integrated into the language system.

If sleep is necessary for learning, then one might expect retention of learning to be poorer after sleep deprivation. This was indeed found by Stickgold, James, and Hobson (2000) who required people to learn a visual discrimination task. A group given normal sleep showed improvement increasing over several days following training, whereas those deprived of a night's sleep immediately after learning showed no such improvement. There is now growing evidence for the importance of sleep in memory consolidation that is detectable long after the initial learning (Gais et al., 2007).

There is increasing evidence that sleep-dependent memory processes are selective, with material that is salient in some way showing an advantage, as if the brain is sorting through memories from the previous day and favoring those that are most important. For example, Payne, Stickgold, Swanberg, and Kensinger (2008) presented a series of negatively valenced objects presented against neutral backgrounds, testing after delays ranging from 30 minutes to 12 hours while awake, and after a 12-hour delay that included sleep. During waking, memory declined for both negative objects and their background at the same rate, whereas during sleep, less forgetting occurred for the negative objects. They suggest that such a pattern might be valuable from an evolutionary viewpoint. Jessica Payne and Elizabeth Kensinger later suggested that the elevated stress near to the encoding of a new memory plays a pivotal role in the later sleep related consolidation benefit for emotional memories (Payne & Kensinger, 2018).

It is also the case that simply instructing participants that one set of items is more important than another, or more likely to be tested, enhances the positive effect of sleep. Fischer and Born (2009) trained participants on two different sequential finger tasks. When training was complete, a monetary reward was offered for one of the two. This was followed by 12 hours including sleep, after which a slightly different instruction was given, namely that the reward would be based on the *average* performance across the two conditions. Nonetheless, the sequence that had been emphasized *before* sleep showed enhanced performance, an effect that was not present in a second group who remained awake during the 12 hours. It appears therefore that sleep had favored the designated task, an effect that showed despite the changed instructions. Findings such as these and the ones by Payne et al. (2008) led Stickgold and Walker to propose that sleep plays a pivotal role in what they call sleep dependent triage, in which only the more

---

KEY TERM

Sleep dependent triage: The finding that sleep improves memory for content learned before sleep in a selective way, favoring salient material (due to emotion or perceived importance) and facilitating the forgetting of less important material.

salient and important memories are favored for consolidation and integration with existing knowledge (Stickgold & Walker, 2013), and less salient information is actively forgotten (see also Feld & Born, 2017).

Why does sleep enhance learning? Protection from interference may be one factor, but it is not enough to explain the rich range of studies that have recently implicated sleep in the learning process (see Stickgold & Walker, 2013 for a review). The generally accepted current view is that sleep helps the process of consolidation of the memory trace, whereby its representation within the brain becomes more robustly established. But how is this achieved? An early study by Wilson and McNaughton (1994) monitored individual cells within the hippocampus of rats that were becoming familiar with a novel environment. This process leads to the development of *place cells* which fire when the rat approaches a particular part of the learned environment. During the process of deep sleep, the place cells were reactivated as if facilitating some process of transfer or consolidation. Neural activity generated by daytime singing in birds also has been found also to occur during sleep (Dave & Margoliash, 2000). It is not of course feasible to carry out single-unit cell recordings in healthy human participants; however, neuroimaging studies have shown brain activations linked to motor skill learning and spatial navigation that appear to recapitulate those observed during the learning process, and to be associated with sleep spindles within the EEG (see

Oudiette & Paller, 2013 for a review). The notion that the day's events may, in part, be reactivated during sleep is known as sleep-dependent replay, which is thought to be a process critical to the consolidation and transfer of memories to the neocortex.

A recent elegant study illustrates this proposed transfer, and the importance of sleep in achieving it (Sawangjit et al., 2018). Rats explored a simple novel object in an arena, and then either allowed to nap for two hours or instead remained awake. Three weeks later, the rats' memory was tested for the novel object. On this delayed test, the rats who had previously remained awake showed no evidence of remembering the object, whereas the rats who had napped showed robust recognition. Critically, the investigators duplicated the study, but intervened with drugs that inactivated the hippocampus. If they inactivated the hippocampus just prior to the two-hour nap, it abolished rats' memory for the objects three weeks later, illustrating the critical role of the hippocampus during sleep in facilitating the delayed sleep benefit. In contrast, if they

KEY TERM

Sleep-dependent replay: The observation that during sleep, material learned prior to sleep is often reactivated or "replayed" in the hippocampus, which is thought to facilitate the consolidation of that content into long-term memory.

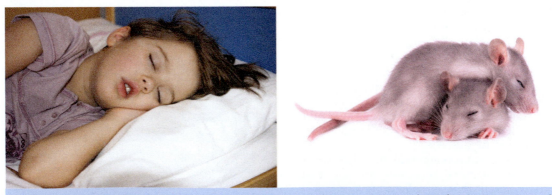

While there is little evidence that we can learn while sleeping, there is growing evidence for the importance of sleep in consolidating memory of what has been learned.

instead inactivated the hippocampus just before the test, three weeks after encoding (instead of doing it before the nap), the rats continued to show the napping advantage. The latter finding shows that, as long as the hippocampus is allowed to do its job replaying the memory during the nap right after encoding (and is not inactivated), its services are no longer needed three weeks later, suggesting that the memory had been transferred. This interpretation was favored by the factor that sleep-related electrical activity in the hippocampus during the nap predicted the memory advantage at the delay.

Where does this leave us? Clearly, to increase the chances that the hard work that you put into learning something new will be consolidated in your brain and be embedded into the fabric of memory, one needs to be sure to get a good night's sleep. Moreover, one shouldn't be shy about taking naps from time to time during the day, particularly if they can be arranged to occur right after you have learned something. These neuroscience-based recommendations are increasingly being recognized by the educational community and could ultimately lead to practical changes including (a) starting school at a later time to allow more sleep, and (b) encouraging naps at school (Sigman, Peña, Goldin, & Ribeiro, 2014).

VARIETIES OF LEARNING

So far, we have discussed general factors influencing the amount we learn and retain, irrespective of the type of learning that one considers. As we mentioned at the outset of this chapter and also in Chapter 1, however, there are different types of learning, each supported by distinct brain systems and with unique characteristics. How my son Max has come to prefer his stuffed penguin over his stuffed lamb differs quite a lot from how he will learn to tie his shoes, how he remembers where the playground is located in our local park.

You might recall that in Chapter 1 we distinguished broadly between *explicit memory*, in which we intentionally remember information or experiences, and *implicit memory*, in which the evidence of learning comes indirectly from a change in behavior. When riding a bicycle, for example, we do not need explicitly to remember the steps; we simply get on the bike and pedal away. The learning of motor skills is just one of a wide range of abilities that can be expressed implicitly. In this section, we will discuss several subcategories of implicit memory: classical conditioning; priming in which the act of processing a stimulus makes it easier for us to process it again; and procedural learning, of which motor skills are one example. Each of these types of learning will be described in turn. We reserve more in-depth discussion of explicit memory for our later chapters on episodic memory and amnesia.

Classical conditioning

In 1902, a young American psychologist, E. B. Twitmyer, reported work on the kneejerk reflex in which a bell sounded after which a lead hammer struck the subject's knee causing an involuntary twitch. He noted that on one occasion the bell rang but the hammer was not delivered; nevertheless the reflex occurred, something that the participant reported as involuntary. Twitmyer (1902) pursued this line of research and reported it at a meeting of the American Psychological Association some two years later. However, his enthusiasm for the topic was not shared by the session's chairman, Professor William James of Harvard, who cut short the discussion to avoid delaying lunch. Intensely disappointed by the disinterest, Twitmyer abandoned this line of research in favor of other aims.

At about the same time, an eminent Russian physiologist, Professor I. P. Pavlov, who was shortly to receive the Nobel Prize for his work on digestion, made a similar observation. He was working on the salivatory reflex using dogs and noted that the dogs began to salivate when they heard the experimenter arrive. He pursued this insight and became even more famous than he already was (Pavlov, 1927).

As every basic textbook describes, Pavlov found that when a bell was presented at the same time as meat powder, after a few presentations, the bell alone would evoke salivation, reflecting the basic feature of classical conditioning—that pairing a neutral stimulus, the bell, with a reflex response, salivation, leads to learning. Pavlov also noted that if he sounded the bell repeatedly without food powder, salivation would reduce and gradually cease, a process that he termed the *extinction* of the conditioned response.

What would one expect if the bell followed the meat powder? Would backward conditioning occur? Although some evidence of backward conditioning has been reported, the effect is very weak.

Given that sounding the bell alone leads to extinction of the conditioned response, what is the effect of sounding the bell alone for many times *before* introducing the association with food powder? This impairs the capacity to condition the salivating response; a phenomenon known as latent inhibition. Presenting the bell alone, whether before or after the food, breaks the clear link between bell and food.

One might wonder why so much attention has been paid to how much dogs salivate in response to food, which may seem of questionable relevance in daily life. The reason is that classical conditioning is not all about dog spit. As it turns out, this process is a profoundly general and important mechanism allowing us to associate stimuli in the world, and our own bodily responses, tuning exactly how our bodies work, based on experiences in the environment. This learning process is so ancient that virtually every species known shows classical conditioning, including the humble fruit fly (drosophila). For example, in one study, fruit flies were placed in a tube covered in a surface capable of delivering electric shocks. If a strong odor was pumped into the tube and then followed by electric shocks, the flies learned to associate the odor with the aversive outcome. This was discerned by testing the flies later on by putting them in a chamber with two exits, one leading to a chamber with the shock-associated odor, and another leading to a nonshocked odor. Can you guess which odor the flies flock to? Virtually all of the flies exit the chamber towards the nonshocked odor, exhibiting classically conditioned avoidance behavior (Tully & Quinn, 1985). This simple method has been used to understand the fundamental molecular mechanisms that drive learning at the cellular level (see, e.g., Davis, 2011, for a review).

In humans and other organisms, the diversity of biological processes that can be classically conditioned is astounding, including, for example, emotional responses such as conditioned fear (see, e.g., LeDoux, 2000; Maren, 2001; and Tovote, Fadok, & Lüthi, 2015 for reviews), eyeblinks, and other discrete behavioral responses to avoid aversive stimuli (e.g., Kim & Thompson, 1997; Thompson & Steinmetz, 2009), drug taking (Everitt & Robbins, 2016; Koob & Volkow, 2016) and even

Russian psychologist Ivan Pavlov, a dog, and his staff, photographed circa 1925–1926.

conditioned immune system and hormonal responses (Hadamitzky, Lückemann, Pacheco-López, & Schedlowski, 2019; Skvortsova et al., 2019). Put simply, your body has evolved to learn to feel cravings, release hormones, kick the immune system into higher gear, or make you very afraid, simply based on what stimuli you happen to be encountering in the world at the moment and your personal history with them. The precise neural circuits underlying these forms of learning have, in many cases, been very carefully mapped out, and are very different from one another.

How can we be sure that classical conditioning is a different "species" of learning that is not related to explicit memory? One reason is that classical conditioning does not generally require the same brain systems that support explicit memory. To convince you how different this process really is, consider how people learn to fear certain things. Studies based on animals suggested an important role for the amygdala, an almond-shaped structure within the brain that has repeatedly been found to be involved in emotion and fear conditioning (LeDoux, 1998). Evidence for the importance of the amygdala in human conditioning comes from a study by Bechara et al. (1995), who describe a conditioning study involving a healthy control group and three very different patients with brain lesions. One had bilateral damage to the amygdala; a second had bilateral damage to the hippocampus, which is known to be important for episodic memory for past events; and a third had bilateral damage to both structures. In one study, a series of different-colored slides was presented, with one color—blue—being followed by a blast from a loud horn. As you could imagine, this very loud stimulus is quite aversive to the participants, who likely jumped off their chairs. The aversiveness is reflected in an increase in skin conductance (measured with electrodes), a measure of anxiety that became conditioned as a response to the blue slide but not to slides of other colors in the healthy control participants. After the experiment, each of the three patients and the control group were asked what colored slides they had seen, and whether one was associated with the loud horn.

The results are shown in Figure 5.17. The patient with bilateral amygdala damage (SM) failed to show classical conditioning but was nevertheless able to remember the colors and identify the blue slide as associated with the horn. In short, he had explicit episodic memory but did not condition. The second patient, a classic amnesic case with hippocampal damage but intact amygdala (WC), showed clear evidence of conditioning but was unable to report any memory of having seen the slides, let alone which one was

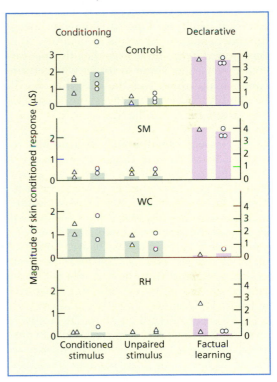

Figure 5.17 Control data and performance of three contrasted patients (SM, WC and RH) studied by Bechara et al. (1995). Copyright © 1995. Reprinted with permission from AAAS.

KEY TERM

Amygdala: An area of the brain close to the hippocampus that is involved in emotional processing.

Hippocampus: Brain structure in the medial temporal lobe that is important for long-term memory formation.

associated to a boat horn (Boat horn? What boat horn?). The third patient with damage to both the hippocampus and the amygdala (RH) showed no conditioning and no evidence of remembering the conditioning process. The control participants showed both conditioning and episodic memory for the slides. This study shows that the learning that enables you to correctly predict the arrival of frightening events (e.g., the blue slide in this example) can happen even if you have absolutely no ability to explicitly remember the experiences that led you to have that reaction. One can imagine, given the independence of explicit memory and conditioned fear, how even healthy people might, over time, come to forget why certain stimuli make them feel the way they do, if the conditioned emotional response survives long after the episodic memory has been forgotten.

If classical conditioning contributes to how we learn to fear things, might it have something to do with our feelings about stimuli in general, whether positive or negative? For example, might conditioning underlie why my son Max likes his stuffed penguin more than his stuffed lamb? Or why you develop certain tastes in art, films, or potential mates? This general idea has been proposed in research into a phenomenon known as evaluative conditioning, inspired by Pavlovian conditioning (Gast, Gawronski, & De Houwer, 2012; Hofmann, De Houwer, Perugini, Baeyens, & Crombez, 2010). Evaluative conditioning refers to one's tendency to like or dislike a particular stimulus to change as a result of its consistent association with a pleasant or unpleasant stimulus following it. This topic has been of interest in social psychology, consumer psychology, emotion research, nutrition research, and also in clinical psychology. In advertising, for example, it is common to attempt to improve the public's evaluation of a product by associating it with a pleasant and attractive surrounding experience. In a relevant study, Stewart, Shimp, and Engle (1987) presented participants with a slide picture of a "new" brand of toothpaste in a green and yellow tube, labeled "Brand L Toothpaste." The toothpaste was presented with three other fictitious

commodities, "Brand R Cola," "Brand M Laundry Detergent," and "Brand J Soap," which were paired with neutral pictures, whereas the toothpaste was always followed by one of four particularly pleasant slides, sunset over an island, for example, or sky and clouds seen through the masts of a yacht. Different groups experienced the items from 1 to 20 times and were then asked which products they would buy. As the graph in Figure 5.18 shows, the toothpaste was rated as more likely to be bought than the other three items, with likelihood of purchase increasing with the number of exposures.

The investigators went on to test two more detailed predictions from the conditioning laboratory. The first of these was that presenting the toothpaste for many trials under neutral conditions would reduce the effect of pairing it with the pleasant slides later, the latent inhibition effect. This is indeed what

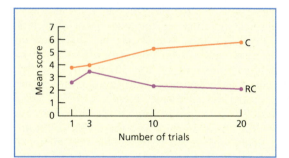

Figure 5.18 Conditioned attitude to a novel brand of toothpaste as a function of the number of conditioning trials. Participants rated the likelihood that they would choose the positively conditioned brand over the randomly associated control brand. C, conditioning; RC, random control. Data from Stewart et al. (1987).

KEY TERM

Evaluative conditioning: The tendency to one's liking of a stimulus to be influenced by how frequently it is followed by pleasant or unpleasant stimuli unrelated to it, with positive stimuli enhancing liking, and negative stimulus decreasing liking.

Latent inhibition: Classical conditioning phenomenon whereby multiple prior presentations of a neutral stimulus will interfere with its involvement in subsequent conditioning.

happened. A third study presented the pleasant slides immediately *before* the toothpaste, setting the scene for backward conditioning, which is known to be much weaker than forward conditioning. As predicted, the level of acquired pleasantness was much less, suggesting that conditioning might indeed provide a suitable model for this aspect of advertising. Might such a process contribute to decisions you have made that are affecting you right now (e.g., Which type of coffee you are drinking? Which mate to prefer?).

Perhaps poor old E. B. Twitmyer, the true discoverer of "Pavlovian conditioning" mentioned at the outset, fell victim to the very learning process that he had discovered: given that presenting his discovery in 1904 was followed by a very discouraging reception from his colleagues, perhaps the subject lost its allure. One can only ponder.

Repetition priming

Most English speakers are familiar with the idiom "Been there, done that." This is a pithy way of saying, "I have personal experience or knowledge of a particular place or topic." Well, it turns out that your brain behaves rather like it thinks this, each time you encounter a stimulus you have seen before. Specifically, if you process a stimulus once, you are better at processing it again if you come across it in the world, which is usually reflected in faster or more efficient processing. If you see an object once, you can see it better next time; if you hear a tune once, you can hear it better next time. This also happens for thoughts and ideas that you have. Simply engaging in the daily business of thinking, perceiving, and acting in the world leaves traces of the perceptual and conceptual work you have done, traces that make your life just a bit easier next time. When presenting a stimulus enhances its subsequent perception or processing without your awareness, you are showing repetition priming (Schacter, 1992), with the sensory version of it referred to as *perceptual priming*, and the conceptual version as *conceptual priming*.

Perceptual repetition priming can be remarkably durable and does not require conscious memory for the object. In a striking example, David Mitchell found that the benefits of looking at line drawings of common objects a few times in 1988 could be seen 17 years later (Mitchell, 2006; see also, Mitchell, Kelly, & Brown, 2018)! In 1988, participants viewed line drawings of objects and were asked to name them as quickly as possible. After a delay of 1–6 weeks, Mitchell found that participants were faster at naming the pictures they had viewed before compared to new pictures, exhibiting repetition priming. Participants then led their lives for 17 years and then Mitchell sent them an implicit memory task by mail. This task included pages of drawing fragments (like visual puzzles) and a request to identify the fragmented objects, some of which were seen in the original study, others of which were new. Impressively, participants were far better at identifying objects they had seen three times in 1988. This same result occurred for four participants who reported having *no memory whatsoever* of ever having participated in the experiment. Consciously remembering the stimuli has little to do with the enhanced perceptual processing. Consistent with this, amnesic patients with severely compromised episodic memory show intact repetition priming on such tasks (Roediger & McDermott, 1993; Tulving & Schacter, 1990; Warrington and Weiskrantz, 1970). This durability of priming appears limited, however, to perceptual priming and does not arise for conceptual priming (Mitchell et al., 2018).

What kind of learning does repetition priming reflect, and why does it not require conscious memory? It is widely believed that the repetition benefit derives in part from changes in areas of the brain devoted to perceptually processing the stimulus when you encountered it the first time. In the normal course of perception, perceptual regions form new representations of the stimulus that contribute to your ability to see and process it. These representations, it seems, stick around, making it easier for your brain to see the same thing again (Tulving & Schacter, 1990). This form of learning is incredibly useful. For example, if you are struggling to identify what a sound is amidst significant noise, or what an object is under degraded viewing conditions, you are far more effective at identifying the sound or the object if it is something you have experienced before, making sensing the world easier. This benefit to perception is readily observable in the brain. For example, in brain imaging studies, brain areas involved in perceiving a visual object show robustly reduced activity when processing a previously viewed stimulus compared to a novel stimulus, an effect known as repetition suppression (see Barron, Garvert, & Behrens, 2016 and Grill-Spector, Henson, & Martin, 2006 for reviews; see Chapter 8 on retrieval for further discussion). Repetition suppression reflects the fact that the brain is more efficient at processing things it has already encountered. These effects are ubiquitously observed in every type of sensory cortex and are widely taken to reflect the formation of perceptual memory traces. Because these memories are formed in sensory processing regions, it makes sense that amnesic participants would show normal levels of repetition priming, because sensory cortical regions are usually unaffected in these patients, who often have damage to the hippocampus.

Several characteristics of perceptual priming illustrate how different this type of learning is from explicit memory. Quite often, the kinds of activities that seem to improve conscious memory make very little difference to implicit memory priming tasks. For example, Graf and Mandler (1984) visually presented a list of words, such as *stamp*, instructing subjects to process them either semantically, or in terms of their visual appearance. Retention was then tested either by stem completion (i.e., an implicit memory task that gives participants the initial couple letters of the word and asking them to complete the stem with any valid word) or instead by asking them to consciously recall words, in response to an associated semantic cue (e.g., *letter*). On the explicit memory task, there

was a major advantage to semantic coding, as would be expected, as semantic coding is, in general, a good method of explicit learning, as we will see in Chapter 6. However, no semantic advantage was found when performance was tested implicitly using the word fragment completion test (Figure 5.19). Perceptual priming tasks, however, are sensitive to the perceptual match between encoding and test. For example, presenting the word *car* auditorily will not produce perceptual priming of a

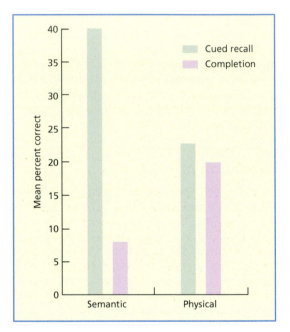

Figure 5.19 Influence of encoding semantically or physically on explicit cued recall versus implicit stem completion. Based on Graf and Mandler (1984) Experiment 3.

KEY TERM

Repetition suppression: Reduced activity in a brain area responsible for processing a stimulus when that stimulus is repeated, compared to when it is encountered for the first time.

Stem completion: A task whereby retention of a word is tested by presenting the first few letters.

Word fragment completion test: A technique whereby memory for a word is tested by deleting alternate letters and asking participants to produce the word.

picture of a car that has never been seen before, illustrating that perceptual priming owes mainly to the prior direct perceptual experience, not the underlying meaning of the picture. In another example, dividing attention during implicit memory tests often has little effect on the magnitude of priming, even when the same divided attention task harms explicit memory recall. This indicates that the benefits of priming to performance do not accrue from any deliberate, effortful retrieval process (Clarke & Butler, 2008; Lozito & Mulligan, 2010; Spataro, Cestari, & Rossi-Arnaud, 2011).

Finally, whereas many priming studies have examined perceptual priming, equivalent effects can be obtained at a deeper more conceptual level. Srinivas and Roediger (1990) required participants to process lists of words that included animal names such as *rat* and *hyena*. This was followed by an apparently unrelated task involving generating as many words as possible in 60 seconds from a series of semantic categories. Items that had been encountered earlier such as *rat* and *hyena* were more likely to be generated. Unlike perceptual repetition priming, conceptual priming is thought to depend to a greater extent on brain regions involved in higher level semantic processing rather than perceptual cortex. For example, the perirhinal cortex in the medial temporal lobes, is involved in representing object concepts and shows clear evidence for repetition suppression effects. Interestingly, repetition suppression in this region predicts the magnitude of conceptual priming participants show (Heusser, Awipi, & Davachi, 2013; Wang, Ranganath, & Yonelinas, 2014). When this area of the brain is damaged, conceptual priming is correspondingly reduced (Wang, Lazzara, Ranganath, Knight, & Yonelinas, 2010). These findings underscore that priming is not a uniquely perceptual phenomenon, but represents a general property of the brain, and the brain's tendency to "save its work" for its later benefit.

Procedural learning

Each morning, when I get my son ready for nursery, I help him put on his trousers, shirt, socks, and his jacket, and tie his shoes. I often try to show him how to do these things, and he usually gets part of the way. But then he understandably gets frustrated because he doesn't know what the steps are, or how his muscles and digits need to move to achieve them. Watching his struggle reveals how he has to learn something as simple as putting on a shirt in the morning as a sequence with discrete steps, movements in space of multiple muscles and body parts. And there is a very long road ahead: we haven't even gotten to bicycle riding, typing, driving, or reading. Nearly everything people do is supported by some procedural memory. Procedural learning is simply learning how to do things. Once learned, you hardly think about procedures, often doing them while talking to somebody else or some other task. Indeed, as William James said: "Ninety-nine hundredths or, possibly, nine hundred and ninety-nine thousandths of our activity is purely automatic and habitual, from our rising in the morning to our lying down each night" (James, 1899).

Procedural learning is a broad category of learning that encompasses several varieties. In general, skill learning refers to practice-induced changes on a task that allow a person to perform it better, faster, and more accurately than before, with tasks usually composed of steps done to achieve a goal. Skill learning can be divided into *motor skill learning*, which concerns the learning of physical skills, such as tying one's shoes, skiing, or typing, and *cognitive skill learning*, which concerns mental activities, such as reading and mental calculation. Moreover, procedural learning also includes habit learning, which refers to gradually learning a tendency to perform certain actions, given a particular

KEY TERM

Skill learning: A practiced induced change on a task that allows a person to perform it better faster and or accurately than before. Skill learning encompasses both cognitive and motor skills.

Habit learning: Gradually learning a tendency to perform certain actions, given a particular stimulus or context, based on a history of reward. Instrumental conditioning is a form of habit learning.

stimulus or context. Habits are different from the goal-directed actions embodied in skills in both how and when they are triggered and executed. Whereas skills are often initiated with an intentional goal (execution of the skill to achieve a desired end), habits instead are usually not explicitly guided by goals and are not carefully monitored; rather, they are triggered responses to stimuli emitted based on one's history of reward upon making the response, often done automatically, and somewhat inflexibly. Habits can usually be considered examples of *instrumental conditioning* in which a response to a stimulus becomes more frequent upon being reinforced. A hallmark of habits, however, is that they often persist when rewards for their outcomes are lessened or removed (referred to as *outcome devaluation*), driven mainly by the strength of association of the action to the triggering context.

Skill learning usually proceeds from an effortful stage, which requires careful attention and conscious remembering and monitoring of individual steps to more fluid, less effortful performance, exhibiting what is referred to as automaticity. When a skill gradually achieves automaticity, it can usually be done effectively with minimal attention, which is then freed up to be devoted to other endeavors. This automaticity reflects not only reduced need to consciously consider and select individual components of a skill and get them in the right order, but also improved synergy of engaging many different muscle actions in parallel to one another. For example, a tennis serve involves the sequence of throwing the ball, taking a back swing, and accelerating the arm forward. Each of these phases involves the parallel coordination of multiple body parts working in concert. On top of this, learning a skill requires learning about the amount of force needed, and about the

relative timing of actions, not to mention the coordination of actions with perception not only from vision or audition, but also from proprioception (our body sense). A skill representation would bind these disparate elements together into a single skilful sequence of multi-joint movements that implements the intended action, fully coordinated with feedback from our senses. Who knew that tying your shoes was so complicated?! (my son knows).

Given the unruly complexity of getting all of these parts right, we should be quite glad that optimizing a skill often proceeds without any verbalizable understanding of why one is getting better. The basis for skilled performance is hard to convey to other people. Once, while teaching somebody to ride a bike, I honestly said "just balance!" as the would-be rider flopped to the ground. Indeed, procedural knowledge is so different from conscious explicit knowledge that the latter often seems to interfere with the former. It is a truism amongst athletes that conscious thoughts about a skill make matters worse. For example, Marlin Mackenzie, a famous sports counsellor and author of *Golf: The Mind Game* trumpets this claim in advertising of his book:

> *Whether you're a world-class player or a weekend enthusiast, improving your golf game begins with your mind. You may be amazed to discover what happens when you free yourself from overthinking your shots and let your unconscious mind play the game. (Mackenzie, 1990)*

But is this really true? Curious, I conducted a study with Kristin Flegal to see whether consciously reflecting on a skill disrupted performance (Flegal & Anderson, 2008). We brought people into the lab to learn how to make a golf put on a putting green we built. This putting green was a straight-ahead put, but we inserted a moderate incline at the very end, near where the regulation-sized hole sat, so getting the put right involved learning a new skill. In what had to be one of the more fun experiments for our participants,

KEY TERM

Automaticity: When a skill is practiced to the extent that it no longer requires significant attentional monitoring to be performed and is less effortful.

we asked them to get "three sinks" of the ball in a row, taking as much time as they needed. Once this was achieved, one group sat down at a table for five minutes with a pen, and wrote down, in intricate detail, every single step involved in their put, specifying where they looked, how they held themselves, and anything else they considered relevant. A control group spent five minutes solving verbal puzzles. Afterwards, we asked them to once again get three sinks in a row. Our experiment was populated both by novice golfers, and a group with moderate skill, the latter solicited from local golf courses. Would thinking about their recently developed skill affect their ability to sink the puts in the second run?

As you can see from Figure 5.20, our manipulation did not affect novice golfers, presumably because they had little skill before the experiment. In contrast, the moderately skilled golfers were severely disrupted at relearning the put in the second run. Indeed, amongst moderately skilled golfers, those in the Experimental condition took *twice as many puts* to get three in a row, compared to the Control group that was

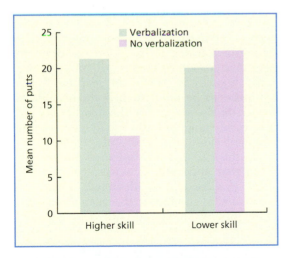

Figure 5.20 Flegal and Anderson (2008) found that for golfers higher in skill, attempts to describe their skilled behavior in detail after practicing it disrupt their later execution of the skill dramatically. Lower skill golfers are unaffected by this. This suggests that proceduralized knowledge can be disrupted by attempts to put it into words.

allowed to solve puzzles for five minutes. This disruption can't be attributed to divided attention, because the description was done offline, prior to the second putting session. Moreover, it could not be attributed to the length of the descriptions, which were identical for the novice and skilled golfers. Rather, the disruption reflects the fact that moderately skilled golfers had proceduralized knowledge of the new task that built on their prior skills, and the process of putting this ineffable knowledge into words disrupted their procedures, at least temporarily. This finding is an example of *verbal overshadowing*, a phenomenon in which verbalizing difficult to articulate knowledge disrupts it (Schooler & Engstler-Schooler, 1990). These findings illustrate vividly that knowing how to do something well involves a type of learning that is distinct from explicit knowledge. It also intriguingly suggests that teaching somebody a skill can be harmful to one's own skill.

How is it possible to develop procedural knowledge without a verbalizable understanding of what one is doing? One factor surely has to do with the very different brain systems involved. Whereas explicit memory relies primarily on medial temporal lobe structures, including the hippocampus, procedural knowledge (both skills and habits) relies on a distributed set of brain structures that includes the basal ganglia, but also the premotor cortex, supplementary motor cortex, motor cortex, parietal cortex, and cerebellum (e.g., Diedrichsen & Kornysheva, 2015; Hardwick, Rottschy, Miall, & Eickhoff, 2013). The *basal ganglia* are considered particularly important to both cognitive and motor skill learning, as well as in learning habitual behavior (Graybiel & Grafton, 2015; Seger, 2018). This distinct anatomy implies that it should be possible to lack the ability to form conscious memories and still be able to learn and retain cognitive and motor skills. This has been repeatedly confirmed. For example, Sara Cavaco and colleagues (Cavaco, Anderson, Allen, Castro-Caldas, & Damasio, 2004) gave a group of 10 amnesics an array of complex procedural tasks to learn and tested their retention 24 hours later. Across learning trials, the

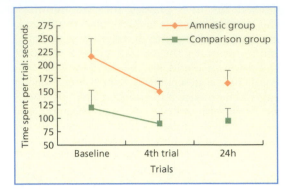

Figure 5.21 Cavaco et al. (2004) found that amnesic patients could learn a complex multi-step motor skill involving a weaver's loom at the same rate as control subjects and retain this skill 24 hours later, despite no memory of ever having done the task.

amnesics learned the tasks as quickly as controls and retained their skill 24 hours later, despite having no memory for ever having performed the tasks the day before. This even arose with a complex multilimb five-step "weaving task" in which they weaved a piece of fabric from wool strings using a weaver's loom (see Figure 5.21). Amnesics can also reassemble a jigsaw puzzle more quickly each time they do it, with retention perfectly normal after a week, despite no memory of solving the puzzle before (Brooks & Baddeley, 1979). Presumably, they must have thought that they were naturally gifted at jigsaw puzzles. Are you so different? Can you even remember when you learned to tie your shoes? Probably not, but I bet your parents can.

THE NEUROBIOLOGICAL BASIS OF LEARNING

Have you ever seen your own brain? Most likely not. In fact, the fraction of humanity throughout all of human history who has seen any human brain at all is preposterously tiny. Until neuroimaging was developed, to see a brain, you would have had to have been a neurosurgeon, a murderer, an anatomist, or involved in a terrible event. Now, however, not only can you see the brains of living people, but you can also see your own if you get a magnetic resonance imaging (MRI) scan. If you did, you would see highly detailed proof that you do indeed have a brain and it looks very much like other brains (though better of course). Having seen my own, I can tell you that it sets you down an existential path, wondering how in the world I could emerge from that gray rubbery thing. How could such a thing learn to do the amazing things we do? What are the ultimate physical changes in the brain that underlie learning?

In 1949, the great Canadian psychologist Donald Hebb produced a speculation about the biological basis of learning that continues to be influential. He proposed that long-term learning is based on cell assemblies. These occur when two or more nerve cells are excited at the same time. This involves the synapse—the gap between two separate neurons—being repeatedly activated, whereupon the chemistry of the synapse changes, leading to a strengthened connection. This is often summarized by the phrase "neurons that fire together wire together." Hebb (1949) contrasts the long-term development of cell assemblies with a short-term process based on temporary electrical activity within existing cell assemblies. Hebb's proposal that long-term learning is based on the development and growth of further synaptic connections, known as "Hebbian learning," has continued to be influential, both through its impact on the search for the neurobiological basis of learning and also for its influence on computer-based simulations of learning.

In the 1970s, a neurophysiological mechanism that appeared to perform in the way Hebb proposed was identified. Bliss and Lomo (1973) administered repeated electrical stimulation at an axonal pathway emanating

KEY TERM

Cell assemblies: A concept proposed by Hebb to account for the physiological basis of long-term learning, which is assumed to involve the establishment of links between the cells forming the assembly.

from a sending neuron. They expected that this high frequency stimulation naturally would excite the other neurons to which it was connected, but their real interest was to see whether it had longer-term effects on how the stimulated neuron communicated with its neighbors. To test this, after repeated stimulation, they found a persisting change in the ability of the stimulated neuron to influence activity in the receiving neuron, a process that has become known as *long-term potentiation (LTP)*. Specifically, thereafter, a mere single stimulation of the sending neuron led to larger, faster, and more long-lasting increases in the size of the electrical potentials created in the receiving neurons. Essentially, the earlier repeated stimulation had enhanced the ability of the sending neuron to communicate with the receiving neuron, manifesting Hebb's "neurons that fire together, wire together." They found that LTP was strongly represented in the hippocampus and in surrounding regions, an area that research on animals and on brain-damaged patients suggests is intimately concerned with long-term memory (see Chapter 16). Thousands of papers have since accumulated on the physical changes that underlie LTP and the extent to which it may be generated naturally during learning (see Nicoll, 2017, for an outstanding overview; see also Lømo, 2018 for reflections on this seminal discovery).

Evidence for the importance of long-term potentiation in learning first came from a series of studies using the Morris water maze. The water maze involves a circular tank filled with milky water that obscures the location of a platform located just below the water's surface. A rat placed in the tank will swim around until it finds the platform and then pull itself up onto it. As shown in Figures 5.22(a) and 5.22(b), in later trials the rat can locate the platform very rapidly, swimming right to it. This is not the case for rats with lesions to the hippocampus, which, as Figure 5.22(c) demonstrates, show little evidence of learning where the platform was located, swimming about randomly. Critically, in a second series of studies, instead of being lesioned, the rats were administered a substance known as AP5, which has been shown to block the induction of LTP in the hippocampus. Administering this drug impaired spatial learning in the water maze, with the degree of impairment increasing as the size of dose of AP5 increased (Morris, Davis, & Butcher, 1990; Morris, Garrud, Rawlings, & O'Keefe, 1982). This suggests that the capacity to induce LTP in the hippocampus is necessary for the rat to learn about and remember where things are in its world.

Further evidence for the possible role of LTP came from studies demonstrating that drugs that enhance synaptic transmission also tend to enhance learning (Staubli, Rogers, & Lynch, 1994). LTP is also found in many other parts of the brain, including the amygdala, a structure that is closely associated with fear-based learning (see previous section on Classical Conditioning). Drugs that block LTP have also been shown to reduce conditioned fear learning (LeDoux, 1998). Perhaps the first direct evidence for the role of LTP in learning came, however, in a study by Whitlock, Heynen, Shuler, and Bear (2006). These authors directly showed that rodents, given only a single trial of training in conditioned avoidance procedure, came to naturally induce observable LTP in their hippocampi just through their behavior, directly linking

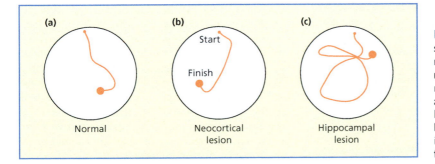

Figure 5.22 Typical swimming paths shown by rats within a Morris water maze. Normal rats (a) rapidly acquire a direct path, as do rats with cortical lesions (b), whereas hippocampal lesions result in a failure to learn (c). Data from Morris et al. (1982).

natural learning behavior to the induction of LTP in the hippocampus.

If LTP truly is the basis of experience-dependence changes in the brain, some process must ensure that the temporary changes in communication between neurons are rendered more lasting. In general, LTP is thought to undergo a shift over time, wherein a transient increase in the efficacy of transmission between two cells is transformed into something more lasting by changes in synaptic structure that "stamp in" the learning. As mentioned earlier, the idea that memories grow to be more firmly represented in the brain over time is known as consolidation of memory. The term consolidation is used in two ways in the neurobiology of memory. First, there is *synaptic consolidation*, which refers to changes at the synaptic level, as discussed here, wherein individual neurons involved in a memory undergo structural remodeling so that their interactions are altered in an enduring way by learning. The second sense of consolidation instead refers to *systems consolidation*, a process operating at a level of brain systems, whereby information initially represented by one part of the brain (e.g., the hippocampus) may be "transferred" to another part (e.g., neocortex), putatively ensuring its longer-term survival. These concepts are covered more in Chapter 6, as well as some recent challenges to these concepts.

For over four decades, the mechanisms underlying LTP and consolidation (especially synaptic consolidation) have been considered the best candidate for understanding how the experiences of our lives change our brains. These mechanisms have been traditionally thought to underlie all of the different types of learning discussed in this chapter, including both explicit and implicit memory and the various subtypes of the latter. It is worth noting, however, that a sea change is occurring in the neurobiology of memory whereby the primacy of the synapse is being questioned. Instead, inspired by rigorous critiques of the sufficiency of synaptic plasticity to account for learning phenomena (Gallistel & Balsam, 2014; Gallistel & Matzel, 2013; see also Tonegawa, Pignatelli, Roy, & Ryan, 2015), recent work has found that learning also is reflected by changes in *intrinsic plasticity* within a neuron, relating to its intrinsic excitability (Lisman, Cooper, Sehgal, & Silva, 2018; Titley, Brunel, & Hansel, 2017). Intrinsic excitability refers to the tendency for a neuron to send action potentials, given a certain amount of input, and it appears that this tendency is modifiable with experience. Indeed, changes in intrinsic excitability may be critical in governing which neurons ultimately come to be involved in contributing to cell assemblies that contribute to a memory trace (Josselyn & Frankland, 2018). Although LTP is surely important, it will be exciting to see how these new ideas contribute to our understanding of how we come to have the memories we do.

CONCLUDING REMARKS

Understanding learning is a fundamental aim in the science of memory. In this chapter, we have provided a broad overview of how the field of memory has blossomed from the time of our friend Hermann Ebbinghaus, the heavily bearded 19th-century German philosopher first memorizing his nonsense syllables to today's world in which we are able to conduct molecular studies of conditioned fear in the fruit fly. The pace of scientific discovery in memory—at all levels, whether cognitive, systems neuroscience, or cellular neuroscience—is truly breathtaking. It is arguably not long before we isolate cells involved in individual memories of personal experiences and see how the brain stores them. This topic—memory for personal experiences, or explicit memory—is the topic of our next chapter.

KEY TERM

Consolidation of memory: A process whereby the memory becomes more firmly established. It is commonly now divided into two processes: synaptic consolidation, a process that is assumed to involve the hippocampus and operate over a 24-hour timescale, and systems consolidation. This is assumed to operate over a much longer period, and to involve the transfer of information from the hippocampus to other parts of the neocortex (see Chapter 6, p. 189 for further discussion).

SUMMARY

- The study of human learning began with Ebbinghaus in 1885, who, using himself as a subject, demonstrated regular and measurable features of memory.
- The *total time hypothesis* refers to the proposal that the amount learned is a simple function of the amount of time spent on the learning task.
- True expertise in a domain requires a massive amount of practice, with some skills averaging as much as 10,000 hours of practice to achieve mastery, illustrating the effect of learning time on performance.
- Deliberate practice is a concept emphasized by Anders Ericsson, and refers to not mere repetition of a skill, but the engagement with full concentration in a training activity to improve a particular aspect of performance, with feedback, and opportunities for refinement and problem solving. Ericsson argues that this practice is needed to break out of performance plateaus at very high levels of skill.
- The maximum level of skill one is likely to achieve in a domain is not merely a function of time learning, but also of genetic influences on the skills involved, and even genetic influences on the propensity to practice.
- Increased training on a task improves performance, in part, by inducing structural plasticity in the brain regions involved, which may be reflected in increased cortical volume in task-related regions, increased white matter connectivity, and even increased efficiency of neural firing. These physical changes can be directly tied to performance.
- The structural changes due to practice may not always persist in the form of increased cortical volume, as the brain may prune away unnecessary physical changes induced initially as they prove less useful, an idea known as the expansion-normalization hypothesis.
- Distributing repeated study efforts of the same material over multiple sessions increases the rate of learning and yields more durable learning than spending the same amount of time repeating the materials in massed fashion. The benefit increases, the longer the lag is between repetitions.
- Distributed practice has been demonstrated to be vastly superior even in naturalistic conditions with very long delays until test, and complex materials. At extensive delays between repetitions, the benefits of spacing begin to decline somewhat, an effect known as the nonmonotonic lag effect.
- Distributed practice benefits have been observed in all types of learning, including motor skill acquisition and even induction of generalizations from particular examples. However, people often don't enjoy distributed practice because the learning process is harder and makes them feel less fluid in the moment, despite the far greater benefit. This can make it harder to implement these approaches.
- The feeling of fluency that arises in massed learning often leads people to have incorrect metamemory beliefs about what practices yield successful learning which can present an obstacle to acceptance of spaced learning. However, it is precisely the difficulties that people resist that lead to greater learning, leading to the term desirable difficulty.

(Continued)

(Continued}

- Different mechanisms may contribute to distributed practice effects, including deficient processing of repetitions, encoding variability, and study phase retrieval. All of these proposed mechanisms have evidence supporting them, but neuroscience methods have tended to favor deficient processing and study phase retrieval.

- Retrieving information from memory is a powerful learning event that strengthens memory for retrieved content. Retrieval is far more effective than restudying, even more so when the lag between study and retrieval is greater, making retrieval more difficult. Retrieval practice is even more effective when feedback is given about the correct answers, especially when feedback is delayed.

- The benefits of retrieval practice are not limited to rote memorization, but rather extend to answering meaningful interference questions about the studied material, outperforming other popular methods such as concept mapping which are thought to promote meaningful learning.

- Motivation can enhance later memory for study material in both automatic and strategic ways. On the automatic side, having either an intrinsic motive (e.g., curiosity) or an extrinsic motive (e.g., the promise of some reward, be it money, food, etc.) prior to being exposed to material significantly improves memory, especially at longer delays, even when the ability to use special memorization strategies is tightly controlled.

- Curiosity, the promise of reward, or high novelty environments create a special encoding state in the hippocampus in which the ventral tegmental area heightens the release of dopamine to facilitate learning. This general encoding state improves memory not only for the particular material people seek to learn, but also stimuli that both precede and follow the reward that have nothing to do with the reward.

- Motivation also leads people to take special strategic action to ensure that they learn material more effectively, including the use of deeper study strategies and the devotion of more study time to important materials. The value-directed remembering procedure is one method for studying both the automatic and strategic effects of motivation.

- The amount of attention available while you are learning something strongly influences learning success, irrespective of the type of learning. Divided attention dramatically reduces encoding.

- Dividing attention appears to reduce the involvement of the left ventrolateral prefrontal cortex in memory encoding, altering its ability to enhance hippocampal encoding activity. Attention appears to enhance hippocampal encoding by tuning activity patterns in the hippocampus to be more in accord with the precise content being stored, in part by enhancing its connectivity parts of the brain that represent the studied content.

- In real-life settings, we often remember very little of the details of our lives, most likely because we walk through the world with attention divided by the thoughts on our minds. One can be exposed to a particular scene or stimulus a very large number of times with no benefit to memory if attention is divided during repetitions. This may partially explain some instances of change blindness.

- Sleep, either in the form of naps or overnight sleep, improves memory for events of the day by a process known as consolidation. These benefits occur for nearly all types of learning.

- Sleep does not consolidate all memories equally but appears to prioritize salient events and to facilitate forgetting of irrelevant details of life. Salient events include things that are stressful or emotional, but also things that are considered important or rewarding.
- Sleep-related consolidation is thought to work, in part, by a process known as sleep-dependent replay, which may hasten the transfer of new content from the hippocampus to neocortical representations.
- Memory can be broadly divided into explicit and implicit memory, with the latter category encompassing classical conditioning, priming, and procedural learning.
- Classical conditioning is a basic form of learning in which a neutral stimulus can come to elicit a conditioned response by consistently pairing the stimulus with an unconditioned stimulus, which can be pleasant (e.g., food) or aversive (e.g., shock). Classical conditioning does not require explicit memory to occur, and many different aspects of our physiology can be classically conditioned, including conditioned emotional responses, immune system and hormonal responses, and motor reflexes.
- According to research on evaluative conditioning, our tendency to like or dislike certain things is driven, in part, by processes underlying emotional conditioning, in which a neutral stimulus is followed by a pleasant or unpleasant stimulus consistently.
- Repetition priming refers to enhanced processing of a stimulus arising from a previous exposure to it. This arises in all sensory modalities and occurs outside of awareness and without explicit memory. It is thought to be reflected in brain activity by repetition suppression, or the tendency for brain areas involved in processing a stimulus to show less activity when a stimulus is repeated.
- Repetition priming can be either perceptual or conceptual. Conceptual priming arises when a certain concept is easier to process and more readily available if it has been recently thought about. Conceptual priming appears to be related to repetition suppression in perirhinal cortex.
- Procedural learning is learning how to do things, whether physical or cognitive activities. Procedural learning can occur without explicit memory, and is supported by distinct brain systems, including the basal ganglia and a network of other regions.
- Procedural learning includes not only motor and cognitive skills, but also habits.
- As skills are practiced, they become progressively more automated, and nonreliant on attention to be performed. Proceduralized knowledge is very difficult to articulate, and often is disrupted by attempts to articulate it.
- Amnesic patients can learn new complex procedural skills at a normal rate despite a complete absence of memory for the training sessions themselves.
- Learning appears to occur at the neural level by enhancement in the ability of neurons to communicate with one another. This enhancement arises in an experience-dependent way by structurally remodeling the synapses involved in an event, which occurs through LTP.
- LTP arises when a sending neuron and a receiving neuron are coactivated together, and this occurs throughout the brain.
- Disrupting LTP disrupts new learning, indicating that this simple change may underlie our capacity to remember.
- Recent work suggests new horizons beyond LTP, such as intrinsic plasticity which may play an important role in learning.

POINTS FOR DISCUSSION

1 A student just starting college believes that learning time and repetition should be the basis of study. How would you advise him to improve on this?
2 What are the major differences between implicit and explicit memory?
3 What has the study of sleep told us about the nature of learning?
4 How does attention during study improve later memory for studied material?
5 What do we know about how memories are stored at the cellular level?

FURTHER READING

Brown, P. C., Roediger, H. L, & McDaniel, M. A. (2014). *Make it stick: The science of successful learning*. Cambridge, MA: Belknap Press/Harvard University Press.

Carey, B. (2015). *How we learn and why it happens*. New York: Random House.

Eichenbaum, H., & Cohen, N. J. (2001). *From conditioning to conscious recollection: Memory systems of the brain*. Oxford: Oxford University Press.

Kandel, E. R. (2006). *In search of memory: The emergence of a new science of mind*. New York: Norton. A scientific autobiography from the Nobel Prize laureate. It covers the neurobiological basis of memory in a very clear and accessible way.

REFERENCES

Ackerman, P. L. (2014). Nonsense, common sense, and science of expert performance: Talent and individual differences. *Intelligence, 45*, 6–17.

Adcock, R. A., Thangavel, A., Whitfield-Gabrieli, S., Knutson, B., & Gabrieli, J. D. (2006). Reward-motivated learning: Mesolimbic activation precedes memory formation. *Neuron, 50*(3), 507–517.

Aly, M., & Turk-Browne, N. B. (2016). Attention promotes episodic encoding by stabilizing hippocampal representations. *Proceedings of the National Academy of Sciences of the USA, 113*(4), E420–E429.

Ariel, R., Dunlosky, J., & Bailey, H. (2009). Agenda-based regulation of study-time allocation: When agendas override item-based monitoring. *Journal of Experimental Psychology: General, 138*(3), 432–447.

Astin, A. W. (1993). *What matters in college?: Four critical years revisited*. San Francisco, CA: Jossey-Bass.

Baddeley, A., Lewis, V., Eldridge, M., & Thomson, N. (1984). Attention and retrieval from long-term memory. *Journal of Experimental Psychology: General, 113*(4), 518–540.

Baddeley, A. D., & Longman, D. J. A. (1978). The influence of length and frequency of training sessions on the rate of learning to type. *Ergonomics, 21*, 627–635.

Barron, H. C., Garvert, M. M., & Behrens, T. E. J. (2016). Repetition suppression: A means to index neural representations using BOLD?. *Philosophical Transactions of the Royal Society B: Biological Sciences, 371*(1705), 20150355.

Bechara, A., Tranel, D., Damasio, H., Adolphs, R., Rockland, C., & Damasio, A. R. (1995). Double dissociation of conditioning and declarative knowledge relative to the amygdala and hippocampus in humans. *Science, 269*, 1115–1118.

Bengtsson, S. L., Nagy, Z., Skare, S., Forsman, L., Forssberg, H., and Ullén, F. (2005). Extensive piano practicing has regionally specific effects on white matter development. *Nature Neuroscience, 8*, 1148–1150. doi:10.1038/nn1516

Bjork, R. A. (1975). Retrieval as a memory modifier: An interpretation of negative recency and related phenomena. In R. L. Solso (Ed.), *Information processing and cognition: The Loyola Symposium* (pp. 123–144). Hillsdale, NJ: Lawrence Erlbaum.

Bjork, R. A. (1994). Memory and metamemory considerations in the training of human beings. In J. Metcalfe and A. Shimamura (Eds.), *Metacognition: Knowing about knowing* (pp. 185–285). Cambridge, MA: MIT Press.

Bjork, R. A. (2014). Forgetting as a friend of learning. In D. S. Lindsay (Ed.), *Remembering* (pp. 39–52). Hove, UK: Psychology Press.

Bjork, R. A., & Bjork, E. L. (1992). A new theory of disuse and an old theory of stimulus fluctuation. In A. F. Healy, S. M. Kosslyn, & R. M. Shiffrin (Eds.), *From learning processes to cognitive processes: Essays in honor of William K. Estes* (Vol. 2, pp. 35–67). Hillsdale, NJ: Erlbaum.

Bliss, T. V. P., & Lømo, T. (1973). Long-lasting potentiation of synaptic transmission in the dentate area of the unanaesthestized rabbit following stimulation of the perforant path. *Journal of Physiology, 232*, 331–356.

Brooks, D. N., & Baddeley, A. D. (1976). What can amnesic patients learn?. *Neuropsychologia, 14*(1), 111–122.

Butler, A. C., & Roediger, H. L. (2008). Feedback enhances the positive effects and reduces the negative effects of multiple-choice testing. *Memory & Cognition, 36*(3), 604–616.

Carpenter, S. K., Pashler, H., & Cepeda, N. J. (2009). Using tests to enhance 8th grade students' retention of US history facts. *Applied Cognitive Psychology: The Official Journal of the Society for Applied Research in Memory and Cognition, 23*(6), 760–771.

Castel, A. D., Benjamin, A. S., Craik, F. I., & Watkins, M. J. (2002). The effects of aging on selectivity and control in short-term recall. *Memory & Cognition, 30*(7), 1078–1085.

Cavaco, S., Anderson, S. W., Allen, J. S., Castro-Caldas, A., & Damasio, H. (2004). The scope of preserved procedural memory in amnesia. *Brain, 127*(8), 1853–1867.

Cepeda, N. J., Pashler, H., Vul, E., Wixted, J. T., & Rohrer, D. (2006). Distributed practice in verbal recall tasks: A review and quantitative synthesis. *Psychological Bulletin, 132*(3), 354–380.

Cepeda, N. J., Vul, E., Rohrer, D., Wixted, J. T., & Pashler, H. (2008). Spacing effects in learning: A temporal ridgeline of optimal retention. *Psychological Science, 19*(11), 1095–1102.

Clarke, B. A. J., & Butler, L. T. (2008). Dissociating word stem completion and cued recall as a function of divided attention at retrieval. *Memory, 16*(7), 763–772.

Craik, F. I., Govoni, R., Naveh-Benjamin, M., & Anderson, N. D. (1996). The effects of divided attention on encoding and retrieval processes in human memory. *Journal of Experimental Psychology: General, 125*(2), 159–180.

Dave, A. S., & Margoliash, D. (2000). Song replay during sleep and computational rules for sensorimotor vocal learning. *Science, 290*, 812–816.

Davis, R. L. (2011). Traces of drosophila memory. *Neuron, 70*(1), 8–19.

Dickerson, K. C., & Adcock, R. A. (2018). Motivation and memory. In J. T. Wixted, E. Phelps, & L. Davachi (Eds.), *Stevens' handbook of experimental psychology and cognitive neuroscience* (Vol. 1, pp. 1–36). New York: Wiley.

Diedrichsen, J., & Kornysheva, K. (2015). Motor skill learning between selection and execution. *Trends in Cognitive Sciences, 19*(4), 227–233.

Diekelmann, S., & Born, J. (2010). The memory function of sleep. *Nature Reviews Neuroscience, 11*(2), 114–126.

Draganski, B., Gaser, C., Kempermann, G., Kuhn, H. G., Winkler, J., Buchel, C., et al. (2006). Temporal and spatial dynamics of brain structure changes during extensive learning. *Journal of Neuroscience, 26*, 6314–6317. doi:10.1523/JNEUROSCI.4628-05.2006

Draganski, B., Kherif, F., & Lutti, A. (2014). Computational anatomy for studying use-dependant brain plasticity. *Frontiers in Human Neuroscience, 8*, 380.

Dunlosky, J., & Tauber, S. U. K. (Eds.). (2016). *The Oxford handbook of metamemory*. Oxford: Oxford University Press.

Düzel, E., Bunzeck, N., Guitart-Masip, M., & Düzel, S. (2010. Novelty-related motivation of anticipation and exploration by dopamine (NOMAD): Implications for healthy aging. *Neuroscience & Biobehavioral Reviews, 34*(5), 660–669.

Ebbinghaus, H. (1885). *Über das Gedächtnis*. Leipzig: Dunker.

Ericsson, K. A. (2013). Training history, deliberate practice and elite sports performance: An analysis in response to Tucker and Collins review—"What makes champions?" *British Journal of Sports Medicine, 47*, 533–535.

Ericsson, K. A., Krampe, R. T., & Tesch-Römer, C. (1993). The role of deliberate practice in the acquisition of expert performance. *Psychological Review, 100*, 363–406.

Everitt, B. J., & Robbins, T. W. (2016). Drug addiction: Updating actions to habits to compulsions ten years on. *Annual Review of Psychology, 67*, 23–50.

Feld, G. B., & Born, J. (2017). Sculpting memory during sleep: Concurrent consolidation and forgetting. *Current Opinion in Neurobiology, 44,* 20–27.

Fischer, S., & Born, J. (2009). Anticipated reward enhances offline learning during sleep. *Journal of Experimental Psychology: Learning, Memory, and Cognition, 35,* 1586–1593. doi:10.1037/a0017256

Flegal, K. E., & Anderson, M. C. (2008). Overthinking skilled motor performance: Or why those who teach can't do. *Psychonomic Bulletin & Review, 15*(5), 927–932.

Gais, S., Albouy, G., Boly, M., Dang-Vu, T. T., Darsaud, A., Desseilles, M. et al. (2007). Sleep transforms the cerebral trace of declarative memories. *Proceedings of the National Academy of Sciences of the USA, 104,* 18778–18783.

Gallistel, C. R., & Balsam, P. D. (2014). Time to rethink the neural mechanisms of learning and memory. *Neurobiology of Learning and Memory, 108,* 136–144.

Gallistel, C. R., & Matzel, L. D. (2013). The neuroscience of learning: Beyond the Hebbian synapse. *Annual Review of Psychology, 64,* 169–200.

Gaskell, M. G., & Dumay, N. (2003). Lexical competition and the acquisition of novel words. *Cognition, 89,* 105–132.

Gast, A., Gawronski, B., & De Houwer, J. (2012). Evaluative conditioning: Recent developments and future directions. *Learning and Motivation, 43*(3), 79–88.

Gerbier, E., & Toppino, T. C. (2015). The effect of distributed practice: Neuroscience, cognition, and education. *Trends in Neuroscience and Education, 4*(3), 49–59.

Gladwell, M. (2008). *Outliers: The story of success.* New York: Little, Brown & Co.

Graf, P., & Mandler, G. (1984). Activation makes words more accessible, but not necessarily more retrievable. *Journal of Verbal Learning and Verbal Behavior, 23,* 553–568.

Graybiel, A. M., & Grafton, S. T. (2015). The striatum: Where skills and habits meet. *Cold Spring Harbor Perspectives in Biology, 7*(8), a021691.

Grill-Spector, K., Henson, R., & Martin, A. (2006). Repetition and the brain: Neural models of stimulus-specific effects. *Trends in Cognitive Sciences, 10*(1), 14–23.

Gruber, M. J., Gelman, B. D., & Ranganath, C. (2014). States of curiosity modulate hippocampus-dependent learning via the dopaminergic circuit. *Neuron, 84*(2), 486–496.

Hadamitzky, M., Lückemann, L., Pacheco-López, G., & Schedlowski, M. (2019). Pavlovian conditioning of immunological and neuroendocrine functions. *Physiological Reviews.*

Hall, K. G., Domingues, D. A., & Cavazos, R. (1994). Contextual interference effects with skilled baseball players. *Perceptual and Motor Skills, 78*(3), 835–841.

Hambrick, D. Z., Burgoyne, A. P., Macnamara, B. N., & Ullén, F. (2018). Toward a multifactorial model of expertise: Beyond born versus made. *Annals of the New York Academy of Sciences.*

Hardwick, R. M., Rottschy, C., Miall, R. C., & Eickhoff, S. B. (2013). A quantitative meta-analysis and review of motor learning in the human brain. *Neuroimage, 67,* 283–297.

Hebb, D. O. (1949). *The organization of behavior.* New York: Wiley.

Heusser, A. C., Awipi, T., & Davachi, L. (2013). The ups and downs of repetition: Modulation of the perirhinal cortex by conceptual repetition predicts priming and long-term memory. *Neuropsychologia, 51*(12), 2333–2343.

Hofmann, W., De Houwer, J., Perugini, M., Baeyens, F., & Crombez, G. (2010). Evaluative conditioning in humans: A meta-analysis. *Psychological Bulletin, 136*(3), 390–421.

James, W. (1899). *Talks to teachers on psychology: And to students on some of life's ideals.* New York: Henry Holt and Company.

Jenkins, J. G., & Dallenbach, K. M. (1924). Oblivescence during sleep and waking. *American Journal of Psychology, 35,* 605–612.

Johnstone, K. M., Ashbaugh, H., & Warfield, T. D. (2002). Effects of repeated practice and contextual-writing experiences on college students' writing skills. *Journal of Educational Psychology, 94,* 305–315.

Josselyn, S. A., & Frankland, P. W. (2018). Memory allocation: Mechanisms and function. *Annual Review of Neuroscience, 41,* 389–413.

Karpicke, J. D., & Blunt, J. R. (2011). Retrieval practice produces more learning than elaborative studying with concept mapping. *Science, 331*(6018), 772–775.

Karpicke, J. D., & Roediger III, H. L. (2008). The critical importance of retrieval for learning. *Science, 319,* 966–968.

Kensinger, E. A., Clarke, R. J., & Corkin, S. (2003). What neural correlates underlie successful encoding and retrieval? A functional magnetic resonance imaging study using a divided attention paradigm. *Journal of Neuroscience, 23*(6), 2407–2415.

Kim, A. S. N., Wong-Kee-You, A. M. B., Wiseheart, M., & Rosenbaum, R. S. (2019). The spacing effect stands up to big data. *Behavior Research Methods,* 1–13.

Kim, J. J., & Thompson, R. E. (1997). Cerebellar circuits and synaptic mechanisms involved in classical eyeblink conditioning. *Trends in Neurosciences, 20*(4), 177–181.

King, B. R., Hoedlmoser, K., Hirschauer, F., Dolfen, N., & Albouy, G. (2017). Sleeping on the motor engram: The multifaceted nature of sleep-related motor memory consolidation. *Neuroscience & Biobehavioral Reviews, 80*, 1–22.

Koob, G. F., & Volkow, N. D. (2016). Neurobiology of addiction: A neurocircuitry analysis. *The Lancet Psychiatry, 3*(8), 760–773.

Kornell, N., & Bjork, R. A. (2008). Learning concepts and categories: Is spacing the "enemy of induction"?. *Psychological Science, 19*(6), 585–592.

LeDoux, J. (1998). *The emotional brain*. London: Weidenfeld & Nicolson.

LeDoux, J. E. (2000). Emotion circuits in the brain. *Annu. Rev. Neuroscience, 23*, 155–184.

Lisman, J., Cooper, K., Sehgal, M., & Silva, A. J. (2018). Memory formation depends on both synapse-specific modifications of synaptic strength and cell-specific increases in excitability. *Nature Neuroscience, 21*(3), 309–314.

Lisman, J. E., & Grace, A. A. (2005). The hippocampal-VTA loop: Controlling the entry of information into long-term memory. *Neuron, 46*(5), 703–713.

Lømo, T. (2018). Discovering long-term potentiation (LTP): Recollections and reflections on what came after. *Acta Physiologica, 222*(2), e12921.

Long, N. M., Kuhl, B. A., & Chun, M. M. (2018). Memory and attention. In J. T. Wixted, E. Phelps, & L. Davachi (Eds.), *Stevens' handbook of experimental psychology and cognitive neuroscience* (Vol. 1, pp. 1–37). New York: Wiley.

Lozito, J. P., & Mulligan, N. W. (2010). Exploring the role of attention during implicit memory retrieval. *Journal of Memory and Language, 63*(3), 387–399.

Lyle, K. B., Bego, C. R., Hopkins, R. F., Hieb, J. L., & Ralston, P. A. (2019). How the amount and spacing of retrieval practice affect the short- and long-term retention of mathematics knowledge. *Educational Psychology Review*, 1–19.

Mackenzie, M. (1990). *Golf: The mind game*. New York: Dell.

Maguire, E. A., Gadian, D. G., Johnsrude, I. S., Good, C. D., Ashburner, J., Frackowiak, R. S., & Frith, C. D. (2000). Navigation-related structural change in the hippocampi of taxi drivers. *Proceedings of the National Academy of Sciences of the USA, 97*, 4398–4403.

Maguire, E. A., Woollett, K., & Spiers, H. J. (2006). London taxi drivers and bus drivers: A structural MRI and neuropsychological analysis. *Hippocampus, 16*(12), 1091–1101.

Mailer, N. (2003). *The spooky art: Some thoughts on writing*. New York: Random House.

Maren, S. (2001). Neurobiology of Pavlovian fear conditioning. *Annu. Rev. Neurosci., 24*, 897–931.

Mather, M., & Schoeke, A. (2011). Positive outcomes enhance incidental learning for both younger and older adults. *Frontiers in Neuroscience, 5*, 1–10.

Melton, A. W. (1970). The situation with respect to the spacing of repetitions and memory. *Journal of Verbal Learning and Verbal Behavior, 9*(5), 596–606.

Miendlarzewska, E. A., Bavelier, D., & Schwartz, S. (2016). Influence of reward motivation on human declarative memory. *Neuroscience & Biobehavioral Reviews, 61*, 156–176.

Misra, P., Marconi, A., Peterson, M., & Kreiman, G. (2018). Minimal memory for details in real life events. *Scientific Reports, 8*(1), 16701.

Mitchell, D. B. (2006). Nonconscious priming after 17 years: Invulnerable implicit memory?. *Psychological Science, 17*(11), 925–929.

Mitchell, D. B., Kelly, C. L., & Brown, A. S. (2018). Replication and extension of long-term implicit memory: Perceptual priming but conceptual cessation. *Consciousness and Cognition, 58*, 1–9.

Morris, R. G. M., Davis, S., & Butcher, S. P. (1990). Hippocampal synaptic plasticity and NMDA receptors: A role in information storage?. *Philosophical Transactions of the Royal Society of London B, 329*, 187–204.

Morris, R. G. M., Garrud, P., Rawlings, J. M. P., & O'Keefe, J. (1982). Place navigation impaired in rats with hippocampal lesions. *Nature, 297*, 681–683.

Mosing, M. A., Madison, G., Pedersen, N. L., Kuja-Halkola, R., & Ullén, F. (2014). Practice does not make perfect: No causal effect of music practice on music ability. *Psychological Science, 25*(9), 1795–1803.

Müller, G. E., & Pilzecker, A. E. (1900). Experimentelle Beiträge zur Lehre vom Gedächtniss (Experimental contributions to the science of memory). *Zeitschrift für Psychologie. Ergänzungsband, 1*, 1–300.

Murayama, K., & Kitagami, S. (2014). Consolidation power of extrinsic rewards: Reward cues enhance long-term memory for irrelevant past events. *Journal of Experimental Psychology: General, 143*(1), 15–20.

Naveh-Benjamin, M. (1987). Coding of spatial location information: An automatic process?. *Journal of Experimental Psychology: Learning, Memory, and Cognition, 13*(4), 595–605.

Naveh-Benjamin, M. (1990). Coding of temporal order information: An automatic process?.

Journal of Experimental Psychology: Learning, Memory, and Cognition, 16(1), 117–126.

Naveh-Benjamin, M., & Brubaker, M. S. (2019). Are the effects of divided attention on memory encoding processes due to the disruption of deep-level elaborative processes? Evidence from cued- and free-recall tasks. *Journal of Memory and Language, 106,* 108–117.

Nicoll, R. A. (2017). A brief history of long-term potentiation. *Neuron, 93*(2), 281–290.

Oudiette, D., & Paller, K. A. (2013). Upgrading the sleeping brain with targeted memory reactivation. *Trends in Cognitive Sciences, 17,* 142–149. doi:0.1016/j.tics.2013.01.00

Pace-Schott, E. F., Germain, A., & Milad, M. R. (2015). Effects of sleep on memory for conditioned fear and fear extinction. *Psychological Bulletin, 141*(4), 835–857.

Pan, S. C., & Rickard, T. C. (2018). Transfer of test-enhanced learning: Meta-analytic review and synthesis. *Psychological Bulletin, 144*(7), 710–756.

Pashler, H., Rohrer, D., Cepeda, N. J., & Carpenter, S. K. (2007). Enhancing learning and retarding forgetting: Choices and consequences. *Psychonomic Bulletin and Review, 14,* 187–193.

Pavlov, I. P. (1927). *Conditioned reflexes: An investigation of the physiological activity of the cerebral cortex.* London: Oxford University Press.

Payne, J. D., & Kensinger, E. A. (2018). Stress, sleep, and the selective consolidation of emotional memories. *Current Opinion in Behavioral Sciences, 19,* 36–43.

Payne, J. D., Stickgold, R., Swanberg, K., & Kensinger, E. A. (2008). Sleep preferentially enhances memory for emotional components of scenes. *Psychological Science, 19,* 781–788.

Picard, N., Matsuzaka, Y., & Strick, P. L. (2013). Extended practice of a motor skill is associated with reduced metabolic activity in M1. *Nature Neuroscience, 16*(9), 1340–1347.

Pyc, M. A., & Rawson, K. A. (2009). Testing the retrieval effort hypothesis: Does greater difficulty correctly recalling information lead to higher levels of memory?. *Journal of Memory and Language, 60*(4), 437–447.

Rawson, K. A., & Dunlosky, J. (2012). When is practice testing most effective for improving the durability and efficiency of student learning?. *Educational Psychology Review, 24*(3), 419–435.

Roediger III, H. L., & Butler, A. C. (2011). The critical role of retrieval practice in long-term retention. *Trends in Cognitive Sciences, 15*(1), 20–27.

Roediger, H. L., & McDermott, K. B. (1993). Encoding specificity in perceptual priming. In A. Garriga-Trillo, P. R. Minon, C. Garcia-Gallego,

P. Lubin, J. M. Merino, & A. Villarino (Eds.), *Fechner Day' 93: Proceedings of the Ninth Annual Meeting of the International Society for Psychophysics* (pp. 227–232). Madrid, Spain.

Roediger III, H. L., Putnam, A. L., & Smith, M. A. (2011). Ten benefits of testing and their applications to educational practice. In J. P. Mestre and B. H. Ross (Eds.), *Psychology of learning and motivation* (Vol. 55, pp. 1–36). San Diego, CA: Academic Press.

Rosiell, L. J., & Scaggs, W. J. (2008). What if they knocked down the library and nobody noticed? The failure to detect large changes to familiar scenes. *Memory, 16,* 115–124.

Rowland, C. A. (2014). The effect of testing versus restudy on retention: A meta-analytic review of the testing effect. *Psychological Bulletin, 140*(6), 1432–1463.

Rubin, D. C., & Kontis, T. C. (1983). A schema for common cents. *Memory and Cognition, 11,* 335–341.

Sawangjit, A., Oyanedel, C. N., Niethard, N., Salazar, C., Born, J., & Inostroza, M. (2018). The hippocampus is crucial for forming non-hippocampal long-term memory during sleep. *Nature, 564*(7734), 109–113.

Schacter, D. L. (1992). Priming and multiple memory systems: Perceptual mechanisms of implicit memory. *Journal of Cognitive Neuroscience, 4,* 244–256.

Schooler, J. W., & Engstler-Schooler, T. Y. (1990). Verbal overshadowing of visual memories: Some things are better left unsaid. *Cognitive Psychology, 22*(1), 36–71.

Seger, C. A. (2018). Corticostriatal foundations of habits. *Current Opinion in Behavioral Sciences, 20,* 153–160.

Shallice, T., Fletcher, P., Frith, C. D., Grasby, P., Frackowiak, R. S. J., & Dolan, R. J. (1994). Brain regions associated with acquisition and retrieval of verbal episodic memory. *Nature, 368*(6472), 633–635.

Shohamy, D., & Adcock, R. A. (2010). Dopamine and adaptive memory. *Trends in Cognitive Sciences, 14*(10), 464–472.

Sigman, M., Peña, M., Goldin, A. P., & Ribeiro, S. (2014). Neuroscience and education: Prime time to build the bridge. *Nature Neuroscience, 17*(4), 497–502.

Skvortsova, A., Veldhuijzen, D. S., Kloosterman, I. E., Meijer, O. C., van Middendorp, H., Pacheco-Lopez, G., & Evers, A. W. (2019). Conditioned hormonal responses: A systematic review in animals and humans. *Frontiers in Neuroendocrinology, 52,* 206–218.

Spataro, P., Cestari, V., & Rossi-Arnaud, C. (2011). The relationship between divided attention and implicit memory: A meta-analysis. *Acta Psychologica, 136*(3), 329–339.

Soderstrom, N. C., Yue, C. L., & Bjork, E. L. (2016). Metamemory and education. In J. Dunlosky and S. K. Tauber (Eds.). *The Oxford handbook of metamemory* (p. 197). Oxford: Oxford University Press.

Srinivas, K., & Roediger, H. L. (1990). Classifying implicit memory tests: Category association and anagram solution. *Journal of Memory and Language, 29*, 389–412.

Staubli, U., Rogers, G., & Lynch, G. (1994). Facilitation of glutamate receptors enhances memory. *Proceedings of the National Academy of Sciences of the USA, 91*, 777–781.

Steele, C. J., & Zatorre, R. J. (2018). Practice makes plasticity. *Nature Neuroscience, 21*(12), 1645–1646.

Stewart, E. W., Shimp, T. A., & Engle, R. W. (1987). Classical conditioning of consumer attitudes: Four experiments in an advertising context. *Journal of Consumer Research, 14*, 334–349.

Stickgold, R., James, L., & Hobson, J. A. (2000). Visual discrimination learning requires sleep after training. *Nature Neuroscience, 3*, 1237–1238.

Stickgold, R., & Walker, M. P. (2013). Sleep-dependent memory triage: Evolving generalization through selective processing. *Nature Neuroscience, 16*, 139–145.

Thompson, R. F., & Steinmetz, J. E. (2009). The role of the cerebellum in classical conditioning of discrete behavioral responses. *Neuroscience, 162*(3), 732–755.

Titley, H. K., Brunel, N., & Hansel, C. (2017). Toward a neurocentric view of learning. *Neuron, 95*(1), 19–32.

Tonegawa, S., Pignatelli, M., Roy, D. S., & Ryan, T. J. (2015). Memory engram storage and retrieval. *Current Opinion in Neurobiology, 35*, 101–109.

Toppino, T. C., & Gerbier, E. (2014). About practice: Repetition, spacing, and abstraction. In B. H. Ross (Ed.), *Psychology of learning and motivation* (Vol. 60, pp. 113–189). San Diego, CA: Academic Press.

Tovote, P., Fadok, J. P., & Lüthi, A. (2015). Neuronal circuits for fear and anxiety. *Nature Reviews Neuroscience, 16*(6), 317–331.

Tully, T., & Quinn, W. G. (1985). Classical conditioning and retention in normal and mutant Drosophila melanogaster. *Journal of Comparative Physiology A, 157*(2), 263–277.

Tulving, E., & Schacter, D. L. (1990). Priming and human memory systems. *Science, 247*(4940), 301–306.

Twitmyer, E. B. (1902). *A study of the knee jerk.* Philadelphia, PA: Winston.

Uncapher, M. R., & Rugg, M. D. (2008). Fractionation of the component processes underlying successful episodic encoding: A combined fMRI and divided-attention study. *Journal of Cognitive Neuroscience, 20*(2), 240–254.

Wang, W. C., Lazzara, M. M., Ranganath, C., Knight, R. T., & Yonelinas, A. P. (2010). The medial temporal lobe supports conceptual implicit memory. *Neuron, 68*(5), 835–842.

Wang, W. C., Ranganath, C., & Yonelinas, A. P. (2014). Activity reductions in perirhinal cortex predict conceptual priming and familiarity-based recognition. *Neuropsychologia, 52*, 19–26.

Warrington, E. K., & Weiskrantz, L. (1970). Amnesic syndrome: Consolidation or retrieval? *Nature, 226*, 628–630.

Wenger, E., Brozzoli, C., Lindenberger, U., & Lövdén, M. (2017). Expansion and renormalization of human brain structure during skill acquisition. *Trends in Cognitive Sciences, 21*(12), 930–939.

Whitlock, J. R., Heynen, A. J., Shuler, M. G., & Bear, M. F. (2006). Learning induces long-term potentiation in the hippocampus. *Science, 313*(5790), 1093–1097.

Wilson, M. A., & McNaughton, B. L. (1994). Reactivation of hippocampal ensemble memories during sleep. *Science, 265*, 676–679.

Xue, G., Dong, Q., Chen, C., Lu, Z., Mumford, J. A., & Poldrack, R. A. (2010). Greater neural pattern similarity across repetitions is associated with better memory. *Science, 330*(6000), 97–101.

Young, B. W., & Salmela, J. H. (2010). Examination of practice activities related to the acquisition of elite performance in Canadian middle distance running. *International Journal of Sport Psychology, 41*, 73–90.

Contents

CHAPTER 6

EPISODIC MEMORY: ORGANIZING AND REMEMBERING

Michael C. Anderson

When I first met Henry Molaison, he put down his crossword puzzle, and reached out and shook my hand firmly. I introduced myself and my Ph.D. student, Geeta Shivde, the two of us keenly aware of the extraordinary moment we were experiencing. Geeta and I had flown thousands of miles to Boston just to meet Henry. We were intrigued and could talk of nothing else during the trip. What would it be like to meet him in the flesh? Would it be obvious from the moment we met him? Would he seem like he was in his early twenties? Would he be willing to do what we wanted him to do? When we met him, he was as pleasant and personable as we had heard he would be, with the air of a humble, well-meaning young man, wanting to make us feel at home. Genuinely glad to meet us, he made small talk about where we came from and why we were there. He was keen to help.

If the name Henry Molaison does not ring a bell, it may help to learn that he is more widely known by his initials: HM. HM is nothing short of an historical figure, whose circumstances in his early life changed the direction of science in a way that directly affects you. HM appears in every introductory psychology text and in nearly every text on memory or cognition. In his early twenties, Henry's family took him to a neurosurgeon, William Scoville, to see whether he could help Henry with his intractable epilepsy, which was so severe that he was having major seizures with alarming frequency. As

an experimental surgery, Scoville removed HM's hippocampus on both the left and right side of his brain, hoping that it would quell the seizures. Little did Scoville know that he was removing a critical part of Henry's brain necessary for memory. As a result of the surgery, Henry was rendered profoundly and permanently amnesic. Henry's life history, for him, stopped in his late teens or early twenties, several years before his surgery, and no personal experiences were stored after it. Henry was a permanent 20-year-old. The surgery happened in the 1950s, and so when we met Henry, he was in his seventies, with his parents long passed away, a fact that Henry did not consciously remember because it happened after his surgery.

I confess to wondering, despite what I knew about Henry and amnesia, whether it could really be true. What if I did something so extreme in Henry's presence that it would surely be memorable? Dancing on a table-top near him, perhaps? Would that "make it in"? I managed to restrain this impulse, but I did try subtle things. For example, after getting up and leaving the room, when I returned, I reintroduced myself once again, as though we had never met. I thought he would surely remember, as I had been with him all morning and I had only left for a few minutes. I was mistaken. Henry reintroduced himself and then asked me all the same pleasant small talk questions he had already asked me that morning. It was as though he had never laid eyes on me. This was truly odd to experience. It turns out, reintroduction was painfully necessary every time we left and returned for the whole week. I also was curious about how he saw himself. I first asked him who he thought was older, me, or Geeta. He correctly answered that I was (I was in my late thirties, and she, in her twenties). I then asked who was older, me or him. Seeming a bit taken aback and embarrassed to answer such an obvious question, and not wanting to cause offense, he politely said, "Well, you are." Clearly, the last 50 years of his life were nowhere to be found, a fact that profoundly influenced how he viewed himself. Henry's memory deficit was so basic, in fact, that he would lose track of what he was doing during our experiments and couldn't remember why he was doing what he was doing. Some early life memories were just fine though: he would tell us about his life history prior to his surgery, literally scores of times, not remembering he had already told us. It was like hearing the same story from your grandfather 40 times in one week.

No experience I've ever had as a scientist of memory has ever made me feel so deeply about the profound role of memories to our lives than did this 1-week encounter with Henry. Can you imagine what your life would be like if you were him? Nothing you ever did, today, tomorrow, or yesterday, would ever make it into memory. Moreover, you couldn't even remember the most basic facts and information long enough to do anything with it. Reading this book would be pointless, as you would forget what you learned on one page before getting to the next. Yet, as we discussed in Chapter 5, and as we will elaborate in more depth in our later chapter on disorders of memory, amnesics like Henry can learn new skills, show priming, show conditioning, and a host of other implicit forms of memory. This critical difference—between explicit and implicit memory, accounts for what was missing for Henry, after his hippocampus had been removed. The hippocampus and the medial temporal lobes more broadly are truly vital to explicit memory. This fact, which you may be learning for the first time in this text, owes its existence in your brain (ironically, your

hippocampus) to what happened to poor Henry. Henry made possible the many thousands of papers and discoveries that have happened since, both with humans and animals, that have gone on to characterize how the brain supports memory for specific events. Memory for specific events that occurred at a particular time and place is known as *episodic memory*.

In this chapter, we will discuss what is known about successful storage of information in episodic memory. You will recall from Chapter 1 that this term was devised by Endel Tulving to emphasize the difference between the recollection of specific events and *semantic memory*, generalized knowledge of the world. It is episodic memory that allows what Tulving calls "mental time travel," allowing us to travel back and "relive" earlier episodes, and to use this capacity to travel forward and anticipate future events. To remember specific events, you need some kind of mental filing system that will allow you to distinguish that event from similar events on other occasions. This in turn needs three things. The first is a system that allows you to encode a particular experience in a way that will distinguish it from others. Second, it requires a method of storing that event in a durable form, and finally it requires a method of searching the system and retrieving that particular memory. This chapter is concerned with the first of these processes, or the factors contributing to the encoding of experiences in a durable form; we reserve a discussion of retrieval processes for Chapter 8. Our focus here will be on basic cognitive and neuroscience research on the factors and mechanisms that contribute to good episodic memory in healthy participants, reserving in-depth elaboration of amnesic cases like Henry for our later chapter on memory disorders. In discussing episodic memory encoding, we emphasize the critical roles of meaning and organization in ensuring that our experiences remain accessible when we need to remember them later on. This emphasis showcases a rich body of work that demonstrates the power of these factors in promoting good episodic memory, and also foreshadows exciting new work in neuroscience that helps to understand the mechanisms underlying these findings. Given this emphasis, it's necessary to tell you about a fellow by the name of Sir Frederic Bartlett.

THE CONTRIBUTION OF SIR FREDERIC BARTLETT

In Chapter 5, we paid homage to Hermann Ebbinghaus and the fundamental contribution he made to the science of memory. Hermann Ebbinghaus made an experimental science of memory possible by showing how the scientific method could be applied to identify rules by which memory worked. Nevertheless, Ebbinghaus's approach, despite its virtues, also had shortcomings. Ebbinghaus focused on very clearly specified experiments with artificial materials and tightly constrained goals. The danger of this approach is that it could lead science to focus on very narrow problems that tell us little about how memory works in the world outside the laboratory.

Although the Ebbinghaus approach continues to influence the psychology of memory, a second approach also evolved in the early years of memory research that continues to influence research that is done today. This second tradition attempts to tackle memory in all its complexity, accepting that our capacity to control any single study will inevitably be limited, but trusting in the belief that multiple studies will allow clear conclusions to be drawn. This more naturalistic approach was pioneered by Frederic Bartlett, a British philosopher turned experimental psychologist who had wide interests in anthropology and social psychology.

Bartlett (1932) argued that, in attempting to control the experimental situation and use meaningless materials, Ebbinghaus had thrown out the most important and interesting aspects of human memory. Bartlett deliberately chose to study the recall of complex material, such as drawings and folk tales from unfamiliar cultures. Rather than study the gradual accumulation of information over successive learning trials, he preferred to use

the errors that his participants made as a clue to the way in which they were encoding and storing the material. His methods of study were much more informal than those used by Ebbinghaus, often including several recalls by the same participant over periods of days or even longer. In a typical study, Bartlett (1932) would present his Cambridge University students with North American Indian folk tales such as:

The War of the Ghosts

One night two young men from Egulac went down to the river to hunt seals, and while they were there it became foggy and calm. Then they heard war-cries, and they thought: "Maybe this is a war-party." They escaped to the shore, and hid behind a log. Now canoes came up, and they heard the noise of paddles, and saw one canoe coming up to them. There were five men in the canoe, and they said: "What do you think? We wish to take you along. We are going up the river to make war on the people."

One of the young men said: "I have no arrows."

"Arrows are in the canoe," they said.

"I will not go along. I might be killed. My relatives do not know where I have gone. But you," he said, turning to the other, "may go with them."

So one of the young men went, but the other returned home. And the warriors went up the river to a town on the other side of Kalama.

The people came down to the water, and they began to fight, and many were killed. But presently the young man heard one of the warriors say: "Quick, let us go home: that Indian has been hit."

Now he thought: "Oh, they are ghosts."

He did not feel sick, but they said he had been shot.

So the canoes went back to Egulac, and the young man went ashore to his house, and made a fire. And he told everybody and said: "Behold I accompanied the ghosts, and we went to fight. Many of our fellows were killed, and many of those who attacked us were killed. They said I was hit, and I did not feel sick."

He told it all, and then he came quiet. When the sun rose he fell down. Something black came out of his mouth. His face became contorted. The people jumped up and cried. He was dead.

Now close the book and try to recall the story as accurately as you can.

What Bartlett (1932) found was that the remembered story was always shorter, more coherent, and tended to fit in more closely with the participant's own viewpoint than the original story. A central feature of Bartlett's approach was to stress the participant's *effort after meaning*; exactly the opposite of Ebbinghaus's explicit attempt to *avoid meaning*. Rather than being a simple recipient of information, participants were actively striving to discern the meaning of stimuli, trying to capture the essence of the material presented. Indeed, one of Bartlett's students, Bronislav Gomulicki (1956), observed that the recall protocols provided by people attempting to remember one of Bartlett's stories were indistinguishable by independent judges from the attempts of others to produce summaries, with the story present.

A second feature of Bartlett's theory was his postulation of the concept of a *schema*, a long-term structured representation of knowledge that was used by the rememberer to make sense of new material and subsequently store and recall it. This concept of schema has subsequently proved to be highly influential and will be discussed further in Chapter 7, which is concerned with semantic memory. Bartlett emphasized the role of social and cultural influences on the development of schemas, which in turn determine the way in which material is encoded, stored, and subsequently recalled. These tendencies were especially great with a story like *The War of the Ghosts*, in which several features were incompatible with European expectations (or those of Americans unfamiliar with the North American Indian culture). Hence, the supernatural aspect of the story was often omitted. In addition, features of the story that were puzzling to the readers were rationalized by distorting them to fit their expectations. Hence "something black came out of his mouth" became "foamed at the mouth." Bartlett (1932) interpreted his findings by arguing that the systematic errors and distortions produced in the participants' recalls were due to the intrusion of their schematic knowledge. There is also an important methodological point here. In contrast to the Ebbinghaus tradition, which focuses more on the amount learned or retained, it can be quite profitable to focus on the memory errors people make. Indeed, much research in the psychology of memory has focused in recent years on errors, as is well illustrated in Schacter's (2001) excellent *The Seven Sins of Memory*, and further discussed in Chapter 12 on eyewitness memory.

Later research in the Bartlett tradition has provided convincing support for his major findings from more well-controlled studies. For example, consider a study by Sulin and Dooling (1974). They set out to test Bartlett's theory, including his assumption that systematic, schema-driven errors will be greater at a long retention interval than after a short delay because schematic information lasts longer in memory than more detailed information in the text. Sulin and Dooling presented some participants with a story about Gerald Martin: "Gerald Martin strove to undermine the existing government to satisfy his political ambitions ... He became a ruthless, uncontrollable dictator. The ultimate effect of his rule was the downfall of his country" (Sulin & Dooling, 1974, p. 256). Other participants were given the same story but the main actor was called Adolf Hitler. Those participants told the story was about Adolf Hitler were much

In Sulin and Dooling's (1974) study, participants used their schematic knowledge of Hitler to incorrectly organize the information about the story they had been told. The study revealed how schematic organization can lead to errors in long-term memory and recall.

interval (one week) but not at a short one (five minutes).

Instead of story recall, a more controlled way of studying the impact of prior knowledge on memory is by using ambiguous stimuli and providing disambiguating labels. The classic study here is again a very old one. Carmichael, Hogan, and Walter (1932) presented the visual stimuli shown at the center of Figure 6.1 for subsequent recall. Each item was sufficiently ambiguous as to fit two different verbal labels, for example a beehive or a hat. If participants were given a label at encoding, would the underlying concept of the label influence the way people remembered the picture later on? The answer is was very clearly yes. When participants were later asked to draw the stimuli from memory, their drawings were strongly influenced by the label they had been given. It is tempting to think of this again as a bias in the way in which the material was perceived and stored. However, a subsequent study by Prentice (1954) suggested otherwise. The encoding conditions were the same as for the Carmichael et al. study, but retrieval load was minimized by using recognition rather than recall. The label effect disappeared under these circumstances, suggesting that the bias occurred at retrieval rather than encoding; the appropriate information was stored but the difficult task of recalling by drawing led

more likely than the other participants to believe incorrectly they had read the sentence, "He hated the Jews particularly and so persecuted them." Their schematic knowledge about Hitler distorted their recollections of what they had read at a long retention

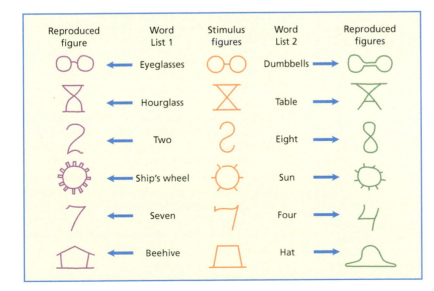

Figure 6.1 Examples of the ambiguous items used by Carmichael et al. (1932). Copyright © American Psychological Association. Reproduced with permission.

to an undue influence of the participants' background knowledge underlying the verbal labels. We shall return to the topic of schematic bias and memory in Chapter 12 on eyewitness testimony.

The impact of prior schematic knowledge is quite often very positive, however. One example of this was provided by Bower, Karlin, and Dueck (1975) in a study in which people were asked to recall apparently meaningless patterns or "droodles" such as shown in Figure 6.2. Free recall of these patterns was very poor. However, recall was greatly improved when each droodle was accompanied by an interpretative label. Bower et al. conclude that memory is aided whenever contextual cues during encoding arouse appropriate schemata. We will return to the powerful influence of schemata on encoding and consolidation later in this chapter.

As can be seen in these examples, Bartlett's approach to memory focuses on how episodic encoding, and learning in general,

occurs in the context of a person's existing knowledge. More broadly, Bartlett shifted the focus away from quantitative factors such as total study time or number of repetitions during learning to the meaning underlying a stimulus. We turn next to a discussion of the fundamental role of meaning in episodic encoding.

MEANING ENHANCES EPISODIC MEMORY ENCODING

Bartlett's principal criticism of Ebbinghaus was that his attempt to separate memory from meaning by using nonsense syllables meant that he was studying simple repetition habits that were not especially relevant to the way in which our memories work in everyday life. A basic premise is Bartlett's approach was that people seek to identify meaning in their experiences, which he described as an *effort after meaning*. The history of memory research since Ebbinghaus has very strongly supported Bartlett's perspective, providing repeated demonstrations of the benefits of meaning and knowledge to how well experiences are encoded.

Early evidence of a role of meaning

By the time Bartlett was making his criticism of Ebbinghaus's approach, it was clear that, whereas Ebbinghaus himself might have succeeded in excluding meaning from his learning strategy, this was not the case for the less determined students who subsequently participated in memory experiments using nonsense syllables. For example, in 1928, Glaze had his students rate the extent to which each possible consonant–vowel–consonant nonsense syllable suggested one or more real words; some suggested several words, for example, the nonsense syllable *CAS* might suggest to participants *castle*, *cast*, and *casino*, whereas a syllable such as *ZIJ* is far harder to link with meaningful existing

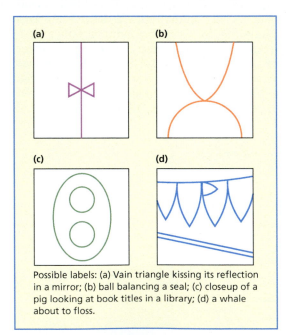

(a)

(b)

(c)

(d)

Possible labels: (a) Vain triangle kissing its reflection in a mirror; (b) ball balancing a seal; (c) closeup of a pig looking at book titles in a library; (d) a whale about to floss.

Figure 6.2 A set of droodles of the type used by Bower et al. (1975). Subsequent recall was greatly enhanced when the droodles were accompanied by their titles. What titles would you suggest? Possible answers are given below the figure.

words. Thus, despite Ebbinghaus's attempt to study pure learning that was devoid of any influence of prior experience, the typical participant, if prompted, could readily find a way to relate the supposed nonsense syllable to what they knew. There is clear evidence that syllables rated as more meaningful are easier to recall (Jung, 1968), suggesting that people do indeed benefit from having relevant background knowledge, even for these very simple materials.

So does that mean that participants in experiments with nonsense syllables are explicitly relying on words to remember the syllables? The rate at which Ebbinghaus recited these syllables made that unlikely, and even at the subsequent slower standard rate of two seconds per syllable, forming and using associations is very difficult for all except the most meaningful syllables. It seemed more likely that Bartlett's suggestion that this task involves developing "repetition habits" might be closer to the mark, with those syllables that follow most closely the structure of English being the easiest to acquire because they are consistent with well-learned language habits, an effect that we have already noted for immediate memory. This indeed also proved to be the case for long-term learning (Baddeley, 1964; Underwood & Schulz, 1960).

Because using nonsense syllables didn't really eliminate prior knowledge for many participants, as Ebbinghaus had believed, by the 1960s, memory researchers had abandoned that strategy in favor of using lists of words, for which meaning was quite important. The dominant tradition in verbal learning research in this period was still that of stimulus–response associationism, with interest focusing on the influence of pre-existing associations between words on ease of list learning. Underpinning this approach was the view that memory could be explained purely in terms of associations or links between words. When prior interword associations were strong, such as *bread–butter*, learning would be easier than when they were more remote, such as *castle–tower*, or absent, as in *lobster–symphony*. The fact that knowledge of associations that existed prior to the experiment significantly improved participants' ability to learn such pairs in laboratory tasks is a clear instance of the influence of prior meaning on encoding.

Up to this point, investigations into learning had relied largely on such standard tasks as serial recall, in which items are recalled in the order presented, and paired-associate learning, in which participants were required to learn word pairs (e.g., *dog–bishop*), so that when given the first item the stimulus (*dog*) they must produce the response (*bishop*). By the 1950s, however, experimenters were increasingly using the less constrained task of free recall, in which participants are asked to produce as many words from the list as they can remember, in any order (for a discussion of different memory tests, see Chapter 8 on retrieval). Using this method, Deese (1959) showed that lists of words that were highly associated with each other were easier to recall than lists with few interword associations. Similarly, Jenkins and Russell (1952) noted that when a number of associated words, such as *thread, needle*, and *mend*, were included in the list, even though they were presented separately, they tended to be recalled later on as a cluster. Here again, these findings indicate that participants, when encoding items in these experiments, were relating the words to one another, via their background knowledge prior to entering the experiment, demonstrating the influence of prior meaning on episodic encoding.

It is worth a brief interlude to address a question that might have occurred to you, amidst all of this discussion of nonsense syllables, paired associates, and word lists. One might reasonably wonder "How does the ability to remember words on a study list relate to memory for personal experiences?" How is this relevant to episodic memory? These studies are not testing participants' memories for real-life events and seem far off from the materials that Bartlett had encouraged people to study, and that indeed are of interest to most people. Indeed, any lessons learned with such simple materials would certainly need to be validated with more complex and naturalistic events before their relevance to everyday episodic memory could be established. Nevertheless, these studies really do concern episodic memory. The reason is that the experiment is asking participants to recall the particular words that they saw on the prior study list at a particular point in time—not just any words from any occasion. So, the presentation of each word is, in essence, a very small event that prompts the participant to have certain idiosyncratic thoughts unique to that moment in time, that later enable them to know that that word was seen on that particular list. Researchers using these methods make the assumption that these "mini episodic events" provide a simple and experimentally controllable way to study episodic memory. Validating this assumption, many key lessons learned about episodic memory from simple lists of words do indeed generalize to other materials and everyday events. Reinforcing this point, amnesics are just as prone to forget lists of words as they are the faces of well-meaning experimenters who fly across the country to meet them. As far as the hippocampus is concerned, those two very different stimuli are both unique events that fall within its job description.

So, what exactly are these idiosyncratic thoughts that people have while they are episodically encoding words in these experiments? Although such thoughts will include thoughts about the meanings of the words and their associations, research also points to mental imagery. Indeed, the importance of visual imagery to episodic encoding of words came surprisingly early in this research tradition (in the mid-1960s). During that era, the verbal learning tradition was firmly against the use of introspection and did not welcome the idea of participants indulging in anything as nonbehavioral as visual imagery. However, there was overwhelming evidence that ratings of the extent to which a word evoked an image powerfully predicted how well it would be remembered. The person who made this discovery was Allen Paivio, a muscular Canadian of Finnish descent, who had had the further distinction of being Mr. Canada (Paivio, 1965). Paivio placated traditionalist verbal learners by pointing out that he was merely predicting one form of behavior, remembering word lists, on the basis of another behavior, the rating responses of

participants. The fact that the rating relied on introspection, the extent to which a given word evoked a subjectively experienced image, could then be conveniently ignored.

Paivio's work suggests that imagery is yet another way in which people try to tie new experiences they are encoding to things they already know, namely pre-existing representations of things they have seen before, albeit in novel combinations unique to encoding each word. This connection to already known images can provide a powerful basis for forming a new and highly accessible episodic memory. To get a feel for this, I suggest you try a free recall experiment for yourself. Take a sheet of paper and a pen. Then read out the following list of words (List A), at a steady rate of about two seconds per word. Then close your eyes and recite the alphabet to get rid of the recency effect before writing down as many words as you can in any order.

List A:

virtue, history, silence, life, hope, value, mathematics, dissent, idea

How many did you remember? Now try the next list (List B) using exactly the same procedure.

List B:

church, beggar, carpet, arm, hat, teapot, dragon, cannon, apple

You probably found the second list easier. As you might have noticed, the second list comprises words that are more concrete and more imageable than the first. Paivio studied the effect of imageability extensively, explaining his findings in terms of the dual-coding hypothesis, whereby words that were imageable, such as the name of concrete objects (e.g.,

KEY TERM

Dual-coding hypothesis: Highly imageable words are easy to learn because they can be encoded both visually and verbally.

crocodile), could be encoded in terms of both their visual appearance and their verbal meaning. For example, a visual image of a crocodile could be generated and linked to one or more other imageable words from the list. If football had also occurred, you might image the crocodile biting a football. Creating interacting images tends to be much harder for abstract words such as *hope* and *theory*. There are therefore two routes to retrieval for imageable words or word pairs —visual and verbal—so if one route is lost the other might still survive and allow recall (Paivio, 1969, 1971).

Before we move on, try one more list, reading it out and then recalling in just the same way as lists A and B.

List C:

large, gray, elephants, terrified, by, roaring, flames, trampled, tiny, defenseless, rabbits

How many did you get that time? I suspect rather more than for lists A or B for an obvious reason. Unlike A and B, list C comprised a meaningful, if slightly odd sentence. Rather than being a random collection of distinct words, the set of words as a whole contribute to a coherent interpretation to which all the elements can be linked—an interpretation that likely also conjured an image of the unfortunate scene. In one simple example,

The dual-coding hypothesis assumes that concrete and imageable words can be encoding in terms of both their visual appearance and their verbal meaning, whereas abstract words are only encoded verbally. The visual representations can then be combined into a single composite image. For example, if one imagined a crocodile biting a football, then later, when one word of the pair is presented, for example *crocodile*, it automatically tends to evoke the football.

this encapsulates the importance of Bartlett's emphasis on the role of meaning construction in successful memory encoding, and also Paivio's emphasis on the power of imagery to enhance memory.

Meaning arrives in the spotlight: Levels of processing

At this stage, you may well be persuaded that processing new stimuli in a meaningful manner improves your episodic memory for those stimuli. Although there were many early advocates of this idea in the history of memory research, the importance of meaning in episodic encoding did not fully arrive in the spotlight until the highly influential work of Craik and Lockhart (1972), who sought to understand the puzzle of why meaning matters as much as it does.

As an answer to this puzzle, Craik and Lockhart (1972) proposed their *Levels of Processing* hypothesis. The starting premise of this hypothesis is that the way in which material is processed powerfully determines its durability in LTM. Specifically, the propose that information is taken in and processed to varying depths. In the case of a printed word, for example, they suggest that its visual characteristics would be processed first, followed by the spoken sound of the word, and then its meaning. They suggest that whereas each of these processes will leave a memory trace, deeper processes leave a more durable trace.

To test this hypothesis, Craik and colleagues carried out experiments in which words were presented visually and participants were asked to make one of three types of judgment on each word. One involved shallow visual processing (Is this word in upper or lower case? *TABLE*), one was phonological (Does this word rhyme with dog? *Log*), and the deepest required semantic processing (Does the word *field* fit into this sentence? The horse lived in a —). Having performed these various operations on the words, participants were unexpectedly confronted with a list of words and asked which ones they had just been shown. Half of the words were new and half had been processed in one of the three ways, involving case, rhyme, or semantic judgment. Craik and Tulving (1975) found that the greater the depth of processing had been on a word the better people were at correctly recognizing that they had seen it before on the list. As Figure 6.3 shows, this was a truly dramatic effect, with memory quintupling between the letter case and sentence encoding conditions. The effect was particularly marked for questions to which the answer was "yes." It is worth emphasizing that in all three conditions participants only saw the words a single time, demonstrating, in dramatic fashion, how much meaning really matters.

This demonstration of better recognition following deeper processing was, of course, exactly as predicted by the levels of processing hypothesis, but why were "yes" responses better recalled than "no"? Craik and Tulving suggest that this is because, for positive items, the word to be recalled was integrated more closely with the encoding question, particularly in the semantic condition. If a sentence made sense when linked with the target words, as in "The horse lived in a field," remembering the sentence would help remind you of the target, perhaps an image of a horse in a field. This source of help would not be so readily available for a negative item such as "Does the word *fork* fit into 'The horse lived in a —'?"

Could it be the case that semantic judgments lead to better recognition simply

because they take longer for people to decide, in line with the total time hypothesis? In their initial experiments, it was certainly the case that deeper processing took longer. In a later experiment, Craik and Tulving slowed down the two more superficial processing tasks by making them more difficult, for example by replacing the decision as to whether the word was in upper or lower case with the requirement to count the number of vowels in the target word. They found no evidence that slower processing led to enhanced recognition. Thus, even when the total amount of time devoted to encoding an event is held constant, dramatic gains in later episodic memory can be had by ensuring that one processes the stimulus in a meaningful way, consistent with the levels of processing idea.

The general principle that deeper and more elaborate processing leads to better memory has been supported by a large number of other studies. Hyde and Jenkins (1973), for example, carried out an extensive series of experiments studying no fewer than 22 different encoding tasks and finding general support for a major influence of processing level on episodic memory. This level of processing effect is found for both recall and recognition and occurs regardless of whether participants do or do not expect a later memory test to be given. During the 1970s, many similar studies provided substantial support for Craik and Lockhart's proposals. Indeed, as a basic generalization or rule of thumb, the principle that deeper and more elaborate processing leads to better retention is arguably one of the most useful generalizations about episodic memory. The effect is robust, reliable, and, as we will see, very useful for anyone wanting to maximize their learning capacity. It has not, however, escaped criticism, at both a theoretical and practical level.

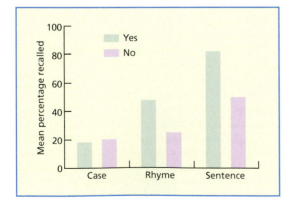

Figure 6.3 Effects of type of encoding task on subsequent word recognition. Based on Craik and Tulving (1975).

Conceptual and empirical challenges to levels of processing

As useful as the rule of thumb about "deeper" processing may be, the idea was challenged by several difficulties that were immediately raised. One problem acknowledged by Craik and Tulving (1975) is that of measuring the *depth of processing*. As we saw earlier, simply using processing time as a measure does not work, as a slow but superficial processing task such as counting the number of vowels in a word leads to longer processing but not to better recall. Indeed, the whole concept of processing depth has come under criticism, with evidence suggesting that many different features of a stimulus might be processed at the same time, rather than in the strict serial order that they had assumed, of vision-then-phonology-then-semantics. It is indeed unlikely that when a participant decides whether *dog* rhymes with *log*, he or she is totally unaware of the meanings of the words, although the attention paid to that aspect is likely to be much less than it is in the semantic processing case. Consequently, in the nearly 50 years following Craik and Lockhart's seminal paper, levels of processing has come to be seen as an extremely valuable rule of thumb, but has not itself generated great further theoretical development.

A second set of problems with the levels of processing hypothesis concerns situations in which deeper processing does not always lead to better performance. Students might do poorly on retrieving information during exams not because they fail to study but because they focus on the wrong type of knowledge. Consider this thought experiment. Suppose you don't know how to ride a bicycle. You approach an expert on bicycle riding, who has written a 200-page book detailing all the rules and facts that one needs to know, describing even the minutest adjustments in posture. Being an excellent student, you spend weeks memorizing everything. If you were given a test on the book, you would score 100%. Then you get on the bicycle and what happens? You crash within seconds, unable to keep balanced. You don't really know what is important about riding bicycles. You have excellent factual knowledge, but no skill.

This illustrates a broad principle known as transfer-appropriate processing. This principle states that for a test to reveal prior learning, the processing requirements of the test should match the processing conditions at encoding. This principle has been invoked to explain the powerful effect of depth of processing. As mentioned earlier, people are quite poor at later recalling words about which they have made visual or phonological judgments, but are very good at remembering words about which they made a meaning-based judgment. This might partially reflect a bias in the way items are tested. In particular, during recall tests, people might be used to remembering the meanings of words they just encountered, and so the test implicitly places emphasis on meaning. To illustrate this point, Morris, Bransford, and Franks (1977) examined whether retention was determined by what people do while encoding, or was instead determined by how well the processing requirements of the test matched encoding. Morris and colleagues asked participants to make either a phonological or semantic judgment about each item in a word list.

As is commonly the case in experiments on levels of processing, participants were not warned they would have to recall. This feature, known as incidental learning, has the advantage over intentional learning in that participants are not tempted to use other learning strategies over and above performing the task requested by the experimenter. The deep condition involved semantic processing, for example "Does the word that follows fit the gap in the sentence, 'The — ran into the lamppost': *car*"?; whereas the shallow

---

KEY TERM

Transfer-appropriate processing (TAP): Proposal that retention is best when the mode of encoding and mode of retrieval are the same.

Incidental learning: Learning situation in which the learner is unaware that a test will occur.

Intentional learning: Learning when the learner knows that there will be a test of retention.

condition involved a judgment of rhyme such as "Does it rhyme with fighter? *Writer*." Memory was then tested by one of two recognition tests; the first was a standard condition in which the words were presented (e.g., *car, writer*), mixed in with an equal number of nonpresented words (e.g., *fish, lawyer*). The second type of test involved presenting a series of words and asking if an item had been presented that rhymed with that word (e.g., *bar, lighter*).

Morris et al. found that deeper processing led to much better performance under the standard recognition conditions, just as Craik and Tulving (1975) had shown. However, the opposite occurred with rhyme recognition: The shallower rhyme-based encoding task led to better performance than did the deeper processing condition.

A subsequent study by Fisher and Craik (1977) broadly replicated this result. However, Fisher and Craik emphasized that there was, overall, a clear advantage to deeper processing. Support for both claims can be seen in Figure 6.4. As Morris and colleagues had claimed, rhyme processing at encoding is clearly better than meaning-based encoding (the sentence condition) when the final test was rhyme based; the opposite was true when the final test was meaning based, illustrating

the transfer-appropriate processing effect. On the other hand, it is clear that there is an overall advantage to semantic encoding: Even in the best of cases for rhyme-based encoding (when there is a rhyme-based test), performance only rose to 40%; in contrast, the best-case scenario for semantic encoding (i.e., a semantic test) yielded double the recall (80%). Similarly, the worst-case scenario (according to transfer appropriate processing), when encoding and test styles differed, though disadvantageous, was clearly more disadvantageous for rhyme-based encoding. So, it would seem that part of the effect from the original levels of processing arose from transfer appropriate processing effects, but part also arose from the superior nature of meaningful processing for episodic memory.

WHY IS DEEPER ENCODING BETTER?

Although the levels of processing work provided a compelling demonstration for how much meaningful processing matters, it is not clear in our discussion thus far why deeper processing should yield more enduring episodic memories. Why should this be? Craik and Tulving (1975) suggested that semantic encoding is advantageous because it allows a richer and more elaborate memory, which in turn becomes more readily retrievable. They describe an experiment that supports this view. Their participants are required to judge whether a given word will or will not fit into a sentence. The sentences can be either relatively simple, such as "She dropped her *pen*" or more complex, for example: "The little old man hobbled across the castle courtyard and dropped his *pen* in the well." Memory was then tested by giving the sentence frame, and requiring the target word to be recalled. There was a very clear advantage to words embedded in the semantically richer sentences. This advantage was also found with unprompted free recall, but was much weaker (Craik & Tulving, 1975). By this explanation, meaningful processing, in general, may produce more elaborate memory traces that link to many

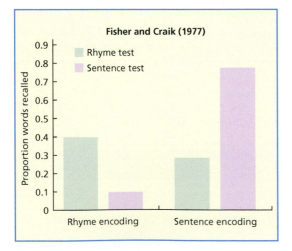

Figure 6.4 Findings from Fisher and Craik (1977) demonstrating both transfer appropriate processing and levels of processing effects. Only the "yes" responses at encoding are plotted here.

different concepts, yielding a memory that can be accessed in many different ways.

The idea that elaboration helps recall extends back at least to William James (1890), who suggested that of two people with equivalent mental capacity:

The one who THINKS over his experiences most, and weaves them into systematic relations with each other will be the one with the best memory…. All improvement of the memory lies in the line of elaborating the associates.
(James, 1890, p. 662)

The proposal that deeper processing involves elaboration aligns neatly with a distinction made by Craik and Lockhart (1972) between two different kinds of rehearsal. One of these, maintenance rehearsal, involves continuing to process an item at the *same* level; the rote rehearsal of a telephone number by saying it to oneself would be a good example of maintenance rehearsal. They contrast maintenance rehearsal with elaborative rehearsal, which involves linking the material being rehearsed to other knowledge in memory, both within the set of items being learned and beyond, just as James proposes. Craik and Lockhart suggest that only elaborative rehearsal enhances delayed episodic memory.

Evidence for this view comes from an ingenious study by Glenberg, Smith, and Green (1977), who presented their participants with numbers that were to be remembered over a delay. During the delay, participants were required to read aloud words presented to them, a task that they were led to believe was used simply to stop them from rehearsing the numbers. Some words occurred only once during this delay-filling activity, whereas others occurred many times. Having recalled the numbers, participants were then asked unexpectedly to recall as many of the words as they could. Fascinatingly, a nine-fold increase in number of repetitions led to only a 1.5% increase in recall performance, although it did have an effect on the ability to recognize the words, with

recognition probability increasing from 0.65 to 0.74. It seems likely that the slight increase in familiarity based on the recent repetition is enough to boost recognition, but that this does not provide a sufficiently powerful cue to allow the original words to be evoked. This finding echoes demonstrations of the inefficacy of unattended repetitions in promoting learning, discussed in Chapter 5 (e.g., Rubin & Kontis, 1983), and further suggests that even when attended, repetitions may do very little good if they are processed identically each time.

Although the elaborative rehearsal hypothesis provides a reasonable account for why deep processing matters, an alternative view is that deep processing may be advantageous for the very simple reason that new experiences undergo integration with things that are already successfully stored in memory. To give a concrete example, if you are introduced to someone at a party named Henry, you are more likely to remember Henry's name if you take a moment to think whether you know of anyone else named Henry and, if so, comparing the new to the old Henry. Doing this very often has the magical effect of making later memory for the person's name quite easy, particularly to the extent that you can find interesting ways of relating the two. Perhaps, for example, if the person seems forgetful, they could be related to our friend Henry Molaison. What makes this such a useful strategy is that you are using something that you already safely know well as a "hook" onto which to hang the new information. As such, the existing body of knowledge that you have acquired in life is

KEY TERM

Maintenance rehearsal: A process of rehearsal whereby items are "kept in mind" but not processed more deeply.

Elaborative rehearsal: Process whereby items are not simply kept in mind but are processed either more deeply or more elaborately.

Integration: The process of linking new information to pre-existing knowledge structures, such as prior schemas, concepts, and events.

rather like a "conceptual coatrack" onto which you can hang new information. Or, in a different analogy, you can describe the process of acquiring new memories as one of "scaffolding," in which your current knowledge and experience provides the very basis for further growth. The idea that meaningful processing is superior because it integrates newer to older knowledge structures would have been very popular with Sir Frederic Bartlett and his emphasis on schemas. Later in this chapter, we will discuss new evidence from neuroscience that suggests that this process of integrating new experiences with prior knowledge may be critical in accounting for the advantage of meaningful processing on memory.

ORGANIZATION ENHANCES ENCODING

Our focus up until now has been on how meaningful processing can improve the retention of individual stimuli, such as individual words. However, as Bartlett would have been the first to point out, in everyday memory we quite often have to remember many things at once. For example, to remember a story like the War of the Ghosts requires the recounting of sequences of events and pertinent facts in an organized way. Similarly, learning the material in this chapter is not merely a matter of remembering individual facts or findings, but how they all fit together as an organized topic. Even something as simple as remembering a photograph of even moderate complexity involves encoding many individual parts, and their relationships to comprehend the whole. Indeed, the very episodic memories of main interest in this chapter are usually dynamic sequences of events with many objects, people, and actions, each of which may benefit individually from meaningful processing; but to remember the whole episode requires a larger structure through which the event coheres. In this section, we discuss evidence showing the powerful effects of organization on encoding, and some reasons why it is so beneficial.

Evidence for spontaneous organization

A key element of Bartlett's approach to memory was his emphasis on how people actively and inevitably seek meaning in new experiences, and, in doing so, impose their own organization on the events they perceive in the world, often through schemas. If this view is correct, we should be able to see that when people are confronted with a new body of information to encode, they should spontaneously, without any guidance from experimenters, begin to organize the information in a way that makes sense to them, and that helps them to recall the information.

Very early evidence for this tendency was reported by Tulving (1962), who repeatedly presented people with the same set of words to remembering. The words were not designed to be related to one another, and each time that participants received the words, they were in a different random order. Participants' goal was to learn to recall as many words as they could, and to increase this amount over repetitions. Faced with this goal, one approach would be to focus one's attention intently on each individual word, perhaps by processing it meaningfully. Alternatively, if people try to identify meaning in these items and to identify organization, as Bartlett would claim they should do, then they very likely would find ways in which the words cohere. Tulving found evidence consistent with the latter tendency. Interestingly, despite the fact that the presentation order of the words was scrambled every time the list was presented, Tulving observed that as people gradually learned the list, they tended to produce words in clusters or chunks that were recalled in the same order trial after trial. Improvements in memory consisted of building bigger and bigger chunks, a process that Tulving referred to as subjective organization.

KEY TERM

Subjective organization: A strategy whereby a learner attempts to organize unstructured material so as to enhance learning.

What sort of factors encourage *chunking*? As you might expect, such organization tends to reflect semantic relatedness. Read through the list below three times and then see how many you can recall.

thread, pin, eye, sewing, sharp, point, prick, thimble, haystack, thorn, hurt, injection, syringe, cloth, knitting

You probably did rather well. Why?

The list was easy to recall because all the items were *associatively related*. They were, in fact, all *associates* of a single key word, *needle*. This effect was originally reported by James Deese (1959). Recall is also helped if the items can be chunked in terms of their semantic *categories*. Tulving and Pearlstone (1966) tested recall of lists containing groups of one, two, or four words per semantic category for example; try the following:

pink, green, blue, purple, apple, cherry, lemon, plum, lion, zebra, cow, rabbit

How may did you recall? Now try the next set:

cabbage, table, river, shirt, gun, square, iron, dentist, sparrow, mountain, hand, granite

How many that time?

Participants given sets of four items from the same category did better; they tended to recall items in category-based chunks, although sometimes omitting some categories completely. This was not because these items were entirely forgotten, as when participants in either group were then given the category names, new words from omitted categories were then recalled.

Organization as a memorization strategy

The examples above clearly illustrate that, when push comes to shove, people's natural instinct is to organize what they must learn rather than processing each individual stimulus in isolation. Presumably, people do this because they feel that it helps them to reproduce a large and otherwise unwieldy body of information that they must recall. The need to recall drives people to seek the deeper structure linking the disparate elements.

To get a feeling for how effective organization can be in remembering a large body of information, consider a classic experiment by Bower, Clark, Lesgold, and Winzenz (1969). Bower and colleagues set participants the task of remembering a list of 112 mineral names for a later recall test. You, no doubt, upon hearing this are thinking "112 mineral names!" That is a very large number of terms to commit to memory in one sitting but is a task not entirely unlike what many students confront when they try to learn complex material. This is particularly true for disciplines like medicine, for example, which requires students to acquire a massive body of anatomical and physiological terms and knowledge in a short amount of time. Can organization help with this? The key manipulation in their study concerned whether they presented this material either in the form of a logically structured hierarchy or with the same items in scrambled order (see Figure 6.5). The hierarchy thus provided the critical organization into which the 112 items could be placed. The participants studied and then were tested on the list four times, each time trying to improve the number of words they could recall. The results are illustrated in Figure 6.6.

As this figure illustrates, participants, right off the bat on the first learning trial, recalled 65% of the minerals when they were organized, compared to 18% in the random condition. So, organization led to three times the number of words being recalled, an astonishing benefit. With further learning trials, the benefit persisted, although the group who organized the terms were nearly perfect by the second run through the list. In contrast, the group that did not receive an organization, even after four trials, only mastered about two-thirds of the items. These findings illustrate the compelling benefits of finding structure in what you must learn, rather than focusing on each thing individually, no matter how meaningfully you do so. For example, rather than simply making a list

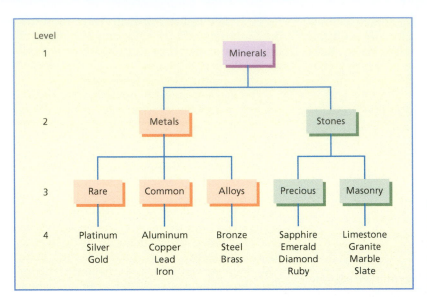
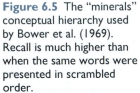

Figure 6.5 The "minerals" conceptual hierarchy used by Bower et al. (1969). Recall is much higher than when the same words were presented in scrambled order.

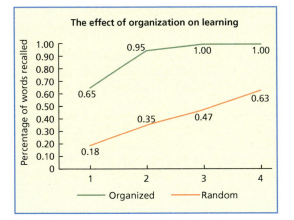

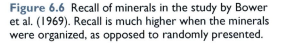

Figure 6.6 Recall of minerals in the study by Bower et al. (1969). Recall is much higher when the minerals were organized, as opposed to randomly presented.

of terms from this chapter that you try to understand and remember, you would be vastly better off if, in addition to doing that, you organized how all of those terms fit together (for an interesting approach, see the discussion of concept maps in Chapter 17 on improving your memory). Research on organization indicates that these effects grow even larger the longer one waits to test memory, indicating that organization does not merely enhance short-term performance, but long-term retention. Many strategies of organization can be effective. As Broadbent,

Cooper, and Broadbent (1978) demonstrated, considerable benefit can also be obtained by structuring material in a matrix such as that shown in Table 6.1.

The examples we have provided so far rely on material that is chosen to fit into generally accepted semantic categories. It is often the case, however, that the material we must remember is not formally organized in this way. Does that mean that organization is not relevant? Certainly not, as we saw from Tulving's (1962) subjective organization study; when asked to learn an apparently meaningless jumble of unrelated words, people will begin to make links that form them into meaningful chunks. Indeed, given the semantic richness of language and the ingenuity of learners, it is virtually impossible

TABLE 6.1 Data from Broadbent et al. (1978).

	Mammals	Birds
Farmyard	Cow	Chicken
	Sheep	Turkey
	Pig	Duck
	Goat	Goose
Pets	Dog	Budgerigar
	Cat	Canary
	Hamster	Parrot
	Guinea pig	Macaw

to produce a string of words that do not suggest at least some possible clusters. As Bartlett would say, people's effort after meaning is strong and persistent.

There are, however, some techniques that are more effective than others. One of these is to try to link the various words into a coherent story. This has the advantage that it not only creates chunks, but it also links the chunks together, making it less likely that any will be left out. For example, given a list such as:

church, beggar, carpet, arm, hat, hand,

teapot, dragon, cannon, apple

A participant might create a story such as the following: "He came out of the *church* and gave an *apple* to a *beggar* sitting on a *carpet*. With his withered *arm* he clutched a *hat* and held his *hand* out for money, which he put in a *teapot* decorated by a *dragon* being shot at by a *cannon*."

Although it might be very effective, creating such stories is quite demanding and it can prove very difficult to form semantic links, particularly with rapid presentation of unrelated words (Campoy & Baddeley, 2008). There is also a danger of recalling words that were included to make a good story but which were not in the original, as in the case of "money," included in the above example to help make a plausible story. A more flexible method is that based on visual imagery, in which items are linked by imagining them interacting in some way. The interaction need not be plausible, so one can, for example, imagine a *swan* riding a *motorbike* if one wished to link those two words. Imagery mnemonics have formed an important part of the craft of memory since classical times. They are discussed in more detail as part of Chapter 17, which is concerned with improving your memory.

The benefits of organization need not be intentional

Although the preceding examples focused on the intentional memorization of large bodies of knowledge, it is important to emphasize that the benefits of organization are not tied, in any necessary way, to someone's intention to learn something. The critical necessary ingredient is that a person perceives or discovers the organization that exists in whatever it is that they are seeing, reading, or hearing. Simply thinking about new events or facts when trying to understand how things all fit together is often enough to do the trick.

A good illustration comes from a study by Mandler (1967), which involved memory for a list of unrelated words. Participants were presented with a pack of cards, with a word on each. One group was told to commit the words to memory, a second group was asked to sort the words into categories comprising items that had something in common, while a third group was given this instruction together with a warning that recall would then be required. Finally, a fourth group was simply asked to arrange the words in columns. A later memory test showed that the group asked to organize the words based on their meaning, *with no mention of later recall*, did just as well as the participants instructed to learn, or indeed to organize *and* learn. The first three groups all remembered more than the fourth group, who had simply arranged the words in columns.

As we saw earlier, the levels of processing effect does not depend on whether participants *know* that recall will be required, performance depends only on what processing task is performed (Hyde & Jenkins, 1973). These results have clear implications for how you should study. The important thing is not the desire to remember, but the way in which you *process* the material. If you think about its meaning, relate it to what you already know, and consider its wider implications you have a much better chance of learning than if you simply read and note the major points. The importance of organization in memory does, of course, extend well beyond the standard laboratory experiment, a point that is well illustrated by the study of expertise.

Organization that develops from expertise

If people instinctively seek organization, meaning, and structure in their experiences, then one should find that as people acquire expertise in a task or profession, they should develop ever more systematic ways of organizing their knowledge. Their wealth of background knowledge and experience should influence how they spontaneously perceive and remember new experiences. The capacity at organizing could be an intentional strategy, or instead it could also simply emerge from a deepening understanding of their area of interest that provides a filter through which they perceive. In essence, the development of expertise provides a testbed for demonstrating how people develop and apply their background schemas in remembering new events and knowledge.

There have been a number of dramatic demonstrations confirming this hypothesis, starting from the 1970s. For example, in July 1977, Anders Ericsson (mentioned in Chapter 5 for his views on deliberate practice), a young Swedish psychologist, joined Carnegie-Mellon University in the US on a two-year fellowship. A major interest in the department was the way in which expertise developed, a topic that played an important role in the theorizing of Herbert Simon, a psychologist who had incidentally won a Nobel Prize for economics (as more recently did Daniel Kahneman). Looking for a project, Ericsson and William Chase decided to see if they could improve digit span by extensive practice. They employed a graduate student, SF, who dutifully came regularly and practiced hearing and repeating back sequences of digits for about an hour a day. Figure 6.7 shows his performance over 200 such sessions—even Ebbinghaus didn't show this devotion to duty!

As you can see, the results of this exercise were quite stunning. SF's performance steadily improved, and by the end of the experiment, he could recall, in their exact order of presentation, sequences of 80 digits, appearing at a rate of one per second. If you had this capacity and illustrated it in front of your friends, they would assume you were a

genius. But was SF a genius? No. He simply had developed an intricate and highly practiced organization scheme. It turned out that he was an enthusiastic runner. Based on his background knowledge of running, he worked out ways of encoding successive digits in terms of running times, for example recording the digits 4 3 8 as four minutes 38 seconds, a reasonable time for a mile. Other groups such as 7 9 2 which were not readily encodable in terms of running times were coding in terms of age, 79.2 years. These were then encoded within a hierarchical structure which also involved a degree of spatial coding. Initially, this process was relatively slow, but with practice it speeded up dramatically. It was, of course, specific to digits, and depended on a remarkably rich and detailed knowledge of times achieved in a range of races, but particularly mile running, for which Chase and Ericsson (1982) report no fewer than 15 subcategories, ranging from the broad "good collegiate time," to specific notable races, for example

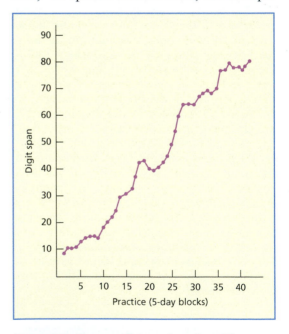

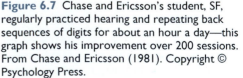

Figure 6.7 Chase and Ericsson's student, SF, regularly practiced hearing and repeating back sequences of digits for about an hour a day—this graph shows his improvement over 200 sessions. From Chase and Ericsson (1981). Copyright © Psychology Press.

"Coe versus Ovett." Note that "a good collegiate" time does not give a precise mapping. The model thus requires the further assumption that a more precise memory trace has been bound to the broad location in the organization during initial learning. Revealingly, when they tested SF on the same exact memory task, but using letters rather than numbers, he scored no better than the average participant, illustrating the critical reliance of his superior memory on the organized knowledge structure he developed for numbers. So, genius was not involved.

Of course, the job market for digit sequence memorizers is limited, and so it's not clear whether SF's organization is of any value. But do similar types of organization develop spontaneously in real-life professions, and are they related to expertise? Ericsson and many others have studied expert memory more widely, moving on to study many forms of naturalistic expertise. The general pattern is that as the level of expertise in a domain increases, the capacity to spontaneously remember new information relevant to the domain increases, sometimes dramatically. Here again, as with SF, the superiority of the expert's memory is entirely specific to their area of expertise, and reliant on the ability to apply their knowledge to understand the new material. In one classic demonstration, Chase and Simon (1973) showed that chess masters, when shown a chess board for a mere five seconds, could accurately reconstruct the positions of, on average, 16 out of the 28 pieces. In contrast, "A" rated players (not masters) could only remember seven, and novices only four. Revealingly, when Chase and Simon positioned the pieces in a way that did not "make sense" according to most chess players' expectations, all three groups could only reconstruct three or four positions. Clearly, chess masters are not recalling more simply because they are smarter but are instead benefitting from how well the positions match their knowledge. Norman, Brooks, and Allen (1989) found that expert medical diagnosticians, when shown a page of results from 20 different medical tests with precise values could, after trying to diagnose the patient, recall the exact value of 13 of the tests, compared to medical students, who could only recall five. Interestingly, when both groups were asked instead to intentionally memorize the test results, they both recalled the same amount, around nine results. So, when the diagnosticians simply engaged in their regular diagnostic thinking, and applied well-learned schemas, they remembered far more than when they tried to use an artificial strategy. Similar contrasting patterns have been observed between expert and novice ballet dancers who needed to reproduce sequences of dance movements (Starkes, Deacon, Lindley, & Crisp, 1987) and between expert and novice basketball players, shown photos of a mid-game position and asked to recall where the players were afterwards (Allard, Graham, & Paarsalu, 1980).

What these many examples illustrate is that as we, over time, learn more about the things we care about, this knowledge provides the scaffold for further learning. Acquired knowledge provides a lens through which we perceive and understand new information, and when that lens is applied in the act of comprehension, the information gets spontaneously integrated with the schematic knowledge structures, making successful episodic memory effortless. It is noteworthy that in many of the demonstrations of the impact of expertise on memory, the experts are not even trying to remember, but rather are trying to understand something; for example, the medical diagnosticians were simply trying to diagnose a patient, and the basketball players were likely trying to make sense of what was going on in the game shown in the picture, to anticipate what would happen next—something that they do as a matter of habit in the course of basketball playing. By simply trying to deepen the meaning of what they were perceiving by understanding what was going on, they were spontaneously organizing the many different items of information. But when the content made no sense—for example when chess pieces were randomly positioned—their pre-existing knowledge became irrelevant and their memory was perfectly ordinary. Collectively, this body of work illustrates the fundamental truth of Bartlett's insight that we learn and remember in the context of our schematic knowledge, which is fundamental to perception and memory.

Inspired by this sort of work, Ericsson and Kintsch (1995) developed the concept of *long-term working memory* as a way of characterizing the consequences of prior knowledge and expertise for online performance. This concept refers to the development of refined structures in long-term memory that are then actively used for temporary storage of new information during a task. An example might be expert calculators in Japan who initially performed their calculations on an abacus, a simple but potentially rapid and effective computational device comprising a frame with beads representing digits. Given sufficient practice, experts are able to discard the abacus and replace it with an imaginary mental representation. This allows them to add and subtract up to 15 numbers, each comprising from five to nine digits. They also have very high digit spans, around 16 for forward and 14 for backward recall. This is, however, limited to digits, with their letter span being normal. The fact that their skill is based on visual imagery was demonstrated by its disruption by a concurrent spatial task, a task that had no influence on control participants, whose coding was verbal and was disrupted by articulatory suppression (Hatano & Osawa, 1983a, 1983b).

How does Ericsson's *concept of long-term working memory* (LTWM) differ from the multicomponent working memory system described in Chapter 4? The most crucial difference is that LTWM is a term to describe a particular *function*, not a single unified cognitive system. It refers to any situation whereby a complex skill has been developed in order to deal with future accessibility to relevant knowledge within a particular domain of expertise. As such it can reflect many different mechanisms based on quite different processes occurring in different parts of the brain. In the examples discussed semantic knowledge of typical times for running a mile is of course very different from the sophisticated visual imagery used by abacus experts. In contrast, the multicomponent WM system referred to by Ericsson and Delaney (1999) as *short-term working memory* assumes that the *same* system is used

for many different tasks. The system is of course assumed to comprise more than one component, and not all of these would be used equally, but effectively working memory is regarded as an integral whole and can in principle be mapped onto underlying brain structures. An important characteristic of this latter system is that it has limited capacity, whereas LTWM has no fixed capacity. Ericsson and Delaney (1999) assume that LTWM is the set of knowledge structures that are currently active. These are based on long-term memory structures that are likely to be large in capacity. In short, the concept of LTWM tries to capture a class of situations in which *expert* long-term knowledge is used to help perform specific cognitive tasks. This can be applied either in the strategic act of memorization, as in the case of SF, or in the spontaneous learning that applies in the context of everyday expertise.

Organization and memory for personal experiences

Hopefully, the preceding examples have persuaded you about the power of organization to enhance memory, and perhaps have encouraged you to apply it to your benefit. You may be wondering, however, what all of this has to do with episodic memory for personal experiences. Most of the examples have concerned memory for new knowledge, which while interesting, does not seem related to how you remember the events of your life. In fact, however, organization plays a critical role in your memory for everyday events, though you may not realize that it does. The key point is that schemas and "expert knowledge structures" just described are not limited to idiosyncratic domains of expertise but apply to many of the sorts of activities we engage in daily life.

Many of the things you do are guided by well-worn routines that you have developed through experience and repetition, such as getting coffee at Starbucks, making breakfast in the morning, and getting ready for work and so forth. We have a massive number of highly routinized schemas for nearly every circumstance in modern life and we are adept at using these schemas to guide our perception, comprehension, and action effortlessly. When we apply our schemas to understand and act, we spontaneously associate events to these knowledge structures, enabling us to remember them. Indeed, when we recount experiences, our descriptions of the sequence of events often conform to the prototypical sequence, suggesting that episodic memory retrieval is guided by the organized knowledge structure. In this sense, the superior memory of experts for their content areas is a special case of an effect that we all show for everyday events (a theme that we will elaborate further on in our discussion of the neural mechanisms of episodic encoding). Our ability to remember details of any particular instance of our routines is limited over time, however, by interference from the many episodes of performing the routine, as discussed in Chapter 9 on forgetting.

Memory for sequential order

As the previous examples highlight, real events are composed of sequences of occurrences unfolding over time. So, rather than being organized strictly by intellectual content (like the study involving minerals discussed earlier, or medical experts' knowledge of disease conditions), they have a temporal order that is important for perception and comprehension of its meaning. If you witnessed a fight, for example, it matters whether Person A hit Person B first, or vice versa. It's not enough to remember that Person A and Person B hit each other as though they were two unrelated facts. While perceiving routine events, sequence knowledge helps to predict the next step we are likely to witness, as, for example, when seeing someone put toothpaste on a toothbrush leads us to expect them to start brushing their teeth; if they instead brush their hair with it, you would be quite surprised. Thus, memory for the order of events—whether in a unique episodic experience (as in the fight example above) or in highly repeated activities requires a representation of sequential organization that guides perception and comprehension in the moment, and that supports

the ability to relive events later on through episodic retrieval. Even for more general conceptual knowledge, order is a form of organization that can be important to capture. It supports our memory for the days of the week, months of the year, and, of course, counting.

In research on long-term learning, the development of sequence knowledge has often been studied with an emphasis on sequences acquired over a large number of repetitions, rather than sequences acquired in the context of a single episodic memory. Might those theoretical models of serial order in STM in Chapter 3 help us to understand how sequential organization is achieved in LTM? If you recall, chaining, whereby each item is associated with the next, did not fare very well in comparison to theories that assumed that individual items were attached to some form of marker involving either the initial item in the case of the primacy model (Page & Norris, 1998), or the temporal context in the case of the proposal by Burgess and Hitch (1999). But can those models work for LTM? Or might chaining play a greater role? Have you ever experienced playing a song on a playlist you have not listened to recently; when one song finishes, you "know" what is coming next. That would seem to suggest something like chaining—we have learned to associate the end of one song with the start of the next. What about the experience that I have of hearing the first few notes of a piece of music and immediately knowing what comes next? Is that a result of chaining, or can the primacy and positional marker models still explain these apparent effects?

Of course, intuitions may be quite wrong. A more evidence-based demonstration of chaining-like effects in serial LTM has been provided by Oliver and Ericsson (1986) who studied the memory of actors participating in a visiting Shakespeare festival. They chose expert actors who had mastered at least two substantial parts. They checked first that accurate verbatim recall was shown in the productions, as opposed to the recreation within a broad narrative framework constrained by rhyme and rhythm, the method shown by traditional bards in some cultures

(Rubin, 1995). The actors did indeed all know their lines; but how well? This was tested by selecting lengthy passages that contained words or phrases unique to that passage, and then asking the actors what followed. They used probes of one, two, or four words, observing virtually perfect recall for their four-word sequences while even a single word probe yielded 77% correct recall. Recall typically took a few seconds, so that the actors could not have been using a primacy cue based on the beginning of the play. Nor was it plausible to assume serial markers for every word in the play. This suggests that the actors' memory of words and sentences to some degree may have been supported by associations linking earlier words to later ones, consistent with the involvement of chaining as an organization, at least for highly repeated, well-learned sequential material.

These findings do not rule out the possibility that models of serial order based on STM could be extended to account for sequences in LTM, at least in some cases. This possibility is being actively pursued by STM theorists, including the advocates of both the primacy model (Page & Norris, 2009) and of a contextual marker model (Burgess & Hitch, 1999, 2006). In both cases the approach principally focuses on a phenomenon known as the Hebb effect.

In addition to his major contribution to theory, the Canadian psychologist Donald Hebb invented an ingenious experimental technique that has continued to generate productive theoretical challenges. The method captures the essence of the problem of acquiring sequences through repetition in an extremely simple way: participants are presented with a sequence of digits, just beyond their span, for immediate serial recall. What they do not know, however, is that every third sequence will be identical; will performance on this regularly repeated item gradually improve, suggesting a persisting long-term memory component, or will it function as just another short-term sequence? As Figure 6.8 shows, performance on the repeated sequence gradually improves. Perhaps people just spot the repetition and give it enhanced attention? This seems not to be the case, as people who become aware do

no better than those who do not notice. Furthermore, the Hebb effect occurs even with very long gaps in between repetitions, making detection unlikely. These findings indicate that through sheer repetition (perception and also production) of a sequence of numbers, people gradually develop a representation of their serial order.

Is the kind of sequential learning measured in the Hebb effect useful in understanding sequence learning in real-life situations? The Hebb effect has not featured prominently in memory theory until recently revived by groups interested in modeling serial order in verbal STM, mainly within a broadly phonological loop framework. As you may recall from Chapter 4, Baddeley, Gathercole, and Papagno (1998) suggested that the loop may have evolved to facilitate vocabulary acquisition. This of course involves the long-term learning of the sequential *order* of the sounds comprising a new word. We proposed that this could be helped by holding the sequence in the phonological loop, hence providing more time for long-term learning to occur. Understanding this process presented an important challenge that was taken up by groups who had already developed models of serial order in verbal STM. The scope of such models and indeed of the Hebb effect itself would increase

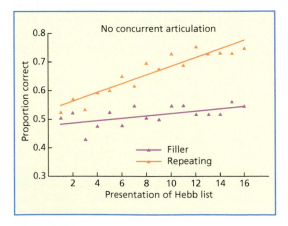

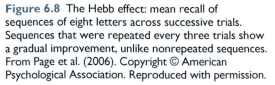

Figure 6.8 The Hebb effect: mean recall of sequences of eight letters across successive trials. Sequences that were repeated every three trials show a gradual improvement, unlike nonrepeated sequences. From Page et al. (2006). Copyright © American Psychological Association. Reproduced with permission.

substantially if they could be shown to be relevant to language learning, an issue of considerable evolutionary significance, for which sequential learning is paramount.

Steady progress has been made both in understanding the Hebb effect and in applying theories of serial order developed initially for the phonological loop. At an empirical level, Hitch, Flude, and Burgess (2009) showed that, unlike the verbal STM task on which it was based, the Hebb effect was *not* sensitive to either phonological similarity or articulatory suppression, reinforcing the case for separable long- and short-term components in the serial STM task. Hitch et al. also showed that participants can learn several Hebb sequences at the same time, an important feature if the results are to generalize to vocabulary learning in normal language acquisition. Direct evidence has now begun to accumulate for a positive link between Hebb performance and vocabulary learning. Mosse and Jarrold (2008) showed that Hebb performance correlates positively with a long-term verbal task involving learning pairs of nonwords. In a study involving nonwords, Szmalek, Page, and Duyck (2012) incorporated occasionally repeated sequences in a Hebb paradigm. The repeated nonwords subsequently behaved like words. Both results suggest that Hebb-based nonwords were registering in long-term memory. Evidence from neuroimaging supports a long-term memory contribution to the Hebb effect. Using multi-voxel pattern analysis (see Chapter 2, p. 32), Kalm, Davis, and Norris (2013) compared the pattern of brain activation found across trials in the Hebb effect to the pattern of activation found on nonrepeated sequences. They showed that Hebb-based learning was associated with areas previously known to be related to long-term learning, namely the hippocampus, the temporal lobes, and the insula, reinforcing the evidence for a separate long-term learning process underlying the effect.

At a theoretical level, two groups have been particularly active. Hitch, Flude, and Burgess (2009) have attempted to generalize their context-based model to results from the Hebb effect, while Page and Norris (2009) have applied their primacy model to Hebb

results. The two groups combined in an important recent study, specifically targeted at a series of questions concerning the plausibility of a link between STM and word learning (Page, Cumming, Norris, McNeil, & Hitch, 2013). They propose that repeated presentation leads to implicitly acquired chunks, each comprising a subsequence, with each chunk being based on the primacy process. In principle, this seems plausible for the acquisition of new words. But what about our Shakespearian actors? So long as the stimulus word or phrase was unique within that speech, it can presumably act as a cue to the relevant chunk; or can it? I suspect all would agree that it is too soon to rule out chaining in long-term serial recall.

The foregoing studies seems more well suited to understanding how we acquire sequences after a large number of repetitions, which help us to detect the temporal regularities in events. But does this apply to events that we have only experienced a single time? Some researchers have argued that such episodic sequence learning needs to be distinguished because there is no opportunity to identify temporal regularities because the sequence does not recur (Davachi & DuBrow, 2015). Alternative mechanisms must exist. One possibility mentioned at the outset is that generalized *schemas* play a critical role. Thus, your ability to remember that your friend Maria's remark came earlier in time than Fred's joke in a recent visit to a coffee shop could be derived from the fact that Maria's comment came whilst waiting in line for the coffee, whereas Fred's joke happened while seated at the table. Here, you would be relying on your schematic knowledge that ordering coffee generally comes before sitting down and drinking it. Because you likely perceived the events in the coffee shop visit through the lens of your coffee shop schema, later memory of the temporal order of these particular events would be derived from the

---

KEY TERM

Episodic sequence learning: The ability to represent the temporal sequence of occurrences within a larger event.

temporal organization encoded into the episodic memory from the schema.

Another possibility is that temporal order can be derived from where actions took place in a *spatial representation* of the environment. For example, if, while walking to work one morning, you take off your coat while passing the library, you know that this came before the bicyclist who almost hit you, which occurred farther along in your spatial trajectory. Here, order is inferred from knowledge of your spatial trajectory, a capacity strongly supported by the hippocampus. Indeed, one of the most exciting discoveries in the neuroscience of memory has been the discovery of place cells, which are neurons that fire selectively in response to a particular position in an animal's spatial environment (Moser, Kropff, & Moser, 2008; O'Keefe & Dostrovsky, 1971). A final possibility is suggested by intriguing evidence from nonhuman animals, which has identified the existence of time cells in the hippocampus that fire at successive moments in a temporally structured experience. These cells represent the flow of time in a manner that is not directly tied to spatial information, schemas, or external stimuli (Eichenbaum, 2014). As such, the sequence of events in an episodic memory may be inferred from information derived directly from time cells, providing a relatively direct representation of time in memory. The joint representation of both space and time in the hippocampus begins to reveal some reasons why this structure is so critical for episodic memory, and why Henry Molaison became amnesic. We turn to this topic next.

KEY TERM

Place cells: Neurons in the hippocampus that respond whenever an animal or person is in a particular location in a particular environment, the collective activity of which is believed to be a critical ingredient in representing particular spatial environments, either perceived or remembered.

Time cells: Neurons in the hippocampus that code for particular moments in time in a temporal sequence, independent of any particular external stimuli, the activity of which may contribute to representing time in episodic memories.

EPISODIC MEMORY AND THE BRAIN

Remembering events benefits from thinking about them meaningfully and relating them to what we know. Henry Molaison, however, did not benefit from these encoding activities. For example, surely when Henry was told about his parents' death, he not only understood what was said to him, but also thought about the consequences of this news in a meaningful way. All of these thoughts would have involved relating the event to his prior knowledge. Yet, as with everything else in Henry's life, this too, amazingly, was very quickly forgotten. On a more mundane level, Henry could make decisions about words based on semantics as accurately as age-matched controls, but nevertheless remembered none of them when later tested. Henry, it seems, was missing a critical mechanism that most people have that transforms meaningful processing into an enduring memory. Surgical removal of the hippocampus was critical to this deficit.

Since Henry first became known to the field, a great deal of work has examined the role of the hippocampus in episodic memory. In fact, as became clear much after his surgery, Henry's lesion included more than the hippocampus, affecting adjacent cortical regions including the *parahippocampus, entorhinal cortex*, and *perirhinal cortex*. A large body of work has focused on the contributions of these regions to memory, and on the broad question of what the hippocampus may be doing. This research has included studies of other amnesics, but also research with functional imaging, and with other species, including mice, rats, and primates, each of which also has a hippocampus, and capacities resembling episodic memory (see Box 6.1). In this section, we consider broad lessons that this work has taught us about the neural basis of episodic memory.

The hippocampus and episodic memory construction

Before describing how the hippocampus contributes to memory, it is worth reflecting on

Box 6.1 Is episodic memory uniquely human?

It all depends. Using Tulving's definition, in terms of the experience of mental time travel it would be very difficult to establish that an animal had this particular experience. Defined behaviorally, however, as the capacity to combine memory for *what, where*, and *when*, there is evidence for this ability in scrub jays, birds that hide food (*what*) and subsequently remember *where* it was hidden. An ingenious experiment by Clayton and Dickinson (1999) indicates that the birds also remember the *time* at which the food was hidden. Clayton and Dickinson allowed their birds to hide two types of food—mealworms, which were most preferred but that deteriorate over time, and less attractive but more durable peanuts. Depending on the delay between hiding and the opportunity to retrieve the food, birds prefer mealworms after a short delay, but peanuts when the delay is longer.

In this photo, a female Western scrub jay, Sweetie Pie, is caching mealworms, as part of an experiment showing a capacity to remember what, where, and when; which can be interpreted as a demonstration of episodic memory in birds.

how episodic memory differs from the other forms of learning discussed in Chapter 5. Memories of personal experiences have several distinctive features. First, they involve *diverse content*, including details from many sensory modalities, emotion, and also from thoughts during the event. Which sensory information gets stored depends on what we attend to, but many senses may be involved. For example, in 1994, I lived through the famous Northridge Earthquake, a quake of considerable power that struck Los Angeles in the middle of the night. I remember peering at the dim light coming through the windows across the living room, their rectangular frames bending and buckling as the house swayed like a ship on a stormy sea; and I remember the house moving under my feet as I braced myself under a door frame. Astonishingly, I have no recollection of any sounds, and even assumed afterwards that nothing must have broken (the room was dark), only to discover that virtually everything (including kitchen cabinets) had toppled over, and many items were destroyed. I remember sheer terror, and having the conscious thought, as the painfully long 30-second quake persisted, that my doom was imminent. So, my memory for this event binds together perceptions from many senses, from thoughts, and from emotions into a single package, a process known as *binding*.

Second, episodic memories concern events that occur in a particular location at a particular time. As such, episodic memories contain a representation of an event's spatial-temporal context. In my earthquake memory, I recall what room I was in, including the exact location, and how I was facing, and I know that it took place in the wee hours of the morning. Third, as discussed in the preceding section, memories are not static pictures, but rather concern a flow of actions or occurrences, which requires representations of serial order. I remember leaping out of bed, tripping across the room to lurch under the door frame (which is what you are supposed to do in an earthquake), and then waiting until the chaos ended. Afterwards, I found my roommate Bruce; I remember a cacophony of hundreds of car alarms set off by the quake and an eerie alien green glow of exploding power transformers throughout the city. My ability to tell you this order of events means that their sequence is represented in my brain. Finally, recalling an episodic memory often feels like traveling back in time. Remembering involves actively recapitulating its perceptual, emotional, and temporal facets, despite the absence of the original sensory input, partially re-creating a previous conscious experience, with the ghosts of brain states past.

How then, does the hippocampus achieve these wonderful outcomes? First, the hippocampus is well positioned, given the flow of information in the cortex, to build a multimodal representation of an episodic experience (i.e., a representation involving many senses). The hippocampus receives converging information from different sensory modalities and this input is highly processed. Specifically, the hippocampus sits on the top of a hierarchy of cortical systems, each stage of which puts together information from previous stages, in ever more complex representations of sensory input (see Moscovitch, Cabeza, Winocur, & Nadel, 2016 for a review). In turn, each level of the hierarchy (including the hippocampus) sends back-projections that influence earlier stages of perception. For example, the parahippocampal and perirhinal cortices feed input into the hippocampus via the entorhinal cortex (regions also removed in Henry's surgery). Whereas the parahippocampal cortex contains viewpoint-specific representations of visual scenes (and is sometimes called the *parahippocampal place area*), the perirhinal cortex contains high-level representations of objects (see also discussion in Chapter 5 of conceptual priming). Representations in each of these areas are built up from basic visual information at earlier stages in the hierarchy. The hippocampus, in turn, receives high-level input such as this from many senses and also from the amygdala and temporal cortical regions likely to contribute to an event's emotional and conceptual processing. Evidence strongly suggests that the hippocampus binds these contents together into a single representation indexing the diverse features necessary to recreate the event (see Figure 6.9). The hippocampus incorporates these features into a viewpoint independent representation of the particular spatial environment where the event happened, most likely supported by place cells and time cells that situate event details with respect to space and time (see Moscovitch et al., 2016 for a review of episodic memory processes).

Critically, encoding in the hippocampus is believed not only to create an integrated trace, but also the ability to reactivate (when later called upon) the component memory features in parts of the cortex involved in processing the experience. According to this idea, the totality of an episodic memory does

---

KEY TERM

Spatio-temporal context: The particular place and time of an event, with spatial information about an environment contributing to specifying where something happened, and temporal information contributing to encoding when it happened.

Multimodal representation: A representation that draws together inputs from many different sensory modalities, such as vision, hearing, touch, taste, and smell. A multimodal representation can also include conceptual and emotional features.

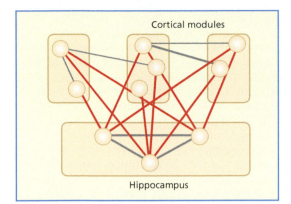

Cortical modules

Hippocampus

Figure 6.9 Schematic illustration of the hippocampus receiving inputs from diverse sensory regions in the neocortex and binding them together into a single episodic representation. After this representation is formed, retrieval happens when a cue related to the memory (e.g., a visual object that activates one of the cortical modules' representations) sends input to the hippocampus, which retrieves the whole trace; this in turn sends activation out of the hippocampus back to all related cortical modulates to recreate the episodic memory in the neocortex, reinstating the memory. Figure adapted from Squire et al. (2015)

not merely reside in the hippocampus; rather, it is the particular constellation or ensemble of neurons residing in the diverse parts of the brain that processed the event initially, bound together with those hippocampal neurons that package the whole thing together. The hippocampal representation provides a "road map" or "index" for reinstating the cortical elements. Later on, when a related cue occurs, the visual system processes it, and relays information into the hippocampus, wherein it makes contact with the hippocampal trace to which it is associated; this triggers the hippocampal trace to send signals, via back-projections to all of the neurons in cortical areas to which that hippocampal trace is linked. These signals activate those component parts of the memory in cortex. To draw an analogy, the hippocampus is like the conductor with the master plan for a beautiful symphony, and the cortical regions are the orchestra that responds to the conductor and plays the music. In unison, through their diverse specialties (oboes, flutes, violins), the different cortical areas, via output from the hippocampus, create a

flowing, integrated experience that mimics the original one, though necessarily less well. The effect of this process is an outcome referred to as cortical reinstatement of the original episode (see Figure 6.9). The coordinated activity of the hippocampal trace, with reinstated cortical neural ensembles, creates a conscious experience mimicking the perceptions, thoughts and feelings of the event.

How then did I build a memory of the Northridge Earthquake? When the earthquake hit, I woke and quickly remembered where I was, identified what was going on and I took action. Comprehending my situation in this manner activated a hippocampal representation of my spatial context (a mental map of my room and apartment that was well developed through living there) providing the spatial framework for encoding the event; it also probably activated schematic knowledge of what to do in case of earthquakes, which led me to jump under a doorway, and to encode my actions in relation to that schematic knowledge. As I struggled to stay under the doorway, my visual system provided information about the windows in the distance and their movements, and my somatosensory (sense of touch), kinesthetic (body sense), and balance senses provided an acute perception of my jerking movements in space; and my fears about death not only triggered amygdala activity, but also thoughts supported by concepts in my temporal cortex. The scene of the dim windows likely formed a representation in the parahippocampal place areas, whereas the concept of the door frame I was holding may well have relied on the perirhinal cortex. Information from these diverse sources fed into the hippocampus and were bound together into a single integrated memory trace, also including the strengthening of

KEY TERM

Cortical reinstatement: The reactivation of sensory memory traces stored by neurons within individual cortical modulates, by virtue of back-projections from the hippocampus that activate the constituent parts of a memory, reinstating the original experience.

back-projections coming out of the hippocampus back to the cortical regions responsible for generating those hippocampal inputs. Miraculously, later on, when I relive the event, thoughts about the quake reawaken the hippocampal trace which, by the previously mentioned back-projections from the hippocampus reawakens the elementary parts of the memory in visual, somatosensory, and temporal cortex, and, in all likelihood, the amygdala, conjuring a feeling of fear. So, as I travel back in time to 1994 into my Los Angeles apartment, my hippocampus kicks into gear.

Apart from the devastating effects of Henry's surgery, how do we know all of these things, in such detail? There is a vast amount of evidence one could mention (from humans or animals, with many different methods), so I will mention only a few items, to illustrate. Consider, for example, the remarkable cases reported by Farenah Vargha-Khadem and colleagues. Vargha-Khadem et al. (1997) reported the cases of three young people who became amnesic at a very early age and who show a very interesting pattern of amnesia. The clearest of these cases is a young man, Jon, who suffered from anoxia (lack of oxygen) at birth, which resulted in a severe deficit in memory for personal experiences as he entered childhood. He is now fully grown up and on standard memory tests is clearly amnesic, sufficiently so as to make it challenging, although not impossible, to live independently. Neuroimaging studies indicate that, unlike Henry, Jon has damage that is strictly limited to the hippocampus, which is abnormal in structure and only half the size expected. Despite this, Jon has developed above-average intelligence and has an excellent semantic memory. This seems to clash with the widely held assumption that semantic memory is built from episodic memories, which in turn rely on the hippocampus (Jon will be discussed in more detail in Chapter 16 on amnesia). Jon's case (and those of many others) illustrates something important: If damage only affects the hippocampus by itself and not also the surrounding tissue, the memory deficit is limited to episodic events and does not affect the ability to learn concepts and to feel a sense of episodic familiarity. Because the latter abilities (semantic learning and familiarity) are clearly impaired in Henry, it suggests that cortical regions surrounding the hippocampus contribute distinct memory functions that can be done without a representation of context (see Aggleton & Brown, 1999, for an early attempt to distinguish the functions of the hippocampus and surround cortex).

Neuroimaging evidence also strongly confirms the role of the hippocampus in episodic encoding. Most studies concerning this issue use event-related fMRI (see Chapter 2, p. 31). This involves separate scans for each designated event, allowing the experimenter to study the encoding of each individual item presented. It is then possible to separate out those items that were subsequently remembered from those forgotten and go back to study the brain activation associated with successful episodic encoding. A large number of studies have used this technique (for the original studies, see Brewer, Zhao, Desmond, Glover, & Gabrieli, 1998; Wagner et al., 1998), including studies done with words, photographs of scenes, and others requiring associations between words or between scenes, for example. The general pattern across all such studies can conveniently be summarized in a "meta-analysis" (a summary analysis conducted on other people's studies), of regions related to later successful episodic memory. The results of one such meta-analysis including 72 studies and over 1,000 participants is illustrated in Figure 6.10 (Kim, 2011).

As can be seen, during the encoding of words and pictures both the left and the right hippocampus showed robustly more activation for items that are later remembered on the final test, compared to items that are later forgotten (top panels). In addition, a collection of other brain regions was also more active, including the left inferior prefrontal cortex (see bottom panel, left side). You may recall from Chapter 5 that dividing attention during encoding reduces activation in this same left prefrontal cortex area, reducing its capacity to modulate encoding activity in the hippocampus—the consequences of which can be seen in severely impaired memory. Moreover, other studies have found more

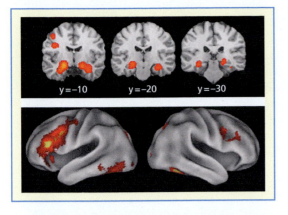

Figure 6.10 A meta-analysis by Kim (2011) of brain areas more active during encoding for items later remembered compared to items later forgotten (aka "subsequent memory effects"). The bilateral hippocampus can be seen in the coronal sections in the top half of the figure; the left inferior prefrontal cortex can be seen in the 3D rendering of the brain in the bottom panel, left image (the large swath of red and yellow on the left side). Copyright © Elsevier. Reproduced with permission.

activation in the hippocampus during encoding for those memories for which people can later correctly recollect details of the context, compared to recognized items for which they cannot do so (e.g., Davachi, Mitchell, & Wagner, 2003). In contrast, encoding processes that later lead people to merely judge that an item is familiar in the absence of context details often rely on the perirhinal cortex more so than the hippocampus (e.g., Davachi et al., 2003), as suggested ought to occur by Aggleton and Brown (1999). In other words, when healthy people show the pattern exhibit by Jon (feeling that things are familiar, but not remembering the event itself), their performance is less related to the hippocampus, and more to surrounding cortex.

According to the model described at the start of this section, the hippocampus also should be involved at a later stage after encoding when people try to remember a past event. Imaging studies have strongly confirmed this prediction (see, e.g., Spaniol et al., 2009). Perhaps most interestingly, a number of imaging studies have gone beyond using simple laboratory materials and looked at people's ability to remember real autobiographical events from their lives (memories like my earthquake example). These studies reveal strong hippocampal activity during retrieval of personal events, with more activity observed the more vivid and detailed people's memories are of their original experience (Sheldon & Levine, 2013; Winocur & Moscovitch, 2011; for a review, see Cabeza & St. Jacques, 2007). Moreover, when people retrieve episodic memories, one sees not only hippocampal activation, but also activation in regions in the neocortex involved in the original perception of the event. For example, when an auditory experience is being remembered, one sees auditory cortex activation; but if a face is being remembered, one would instead see activation in the fusiform face area of the brain (see Danker & Anderson, 2010, for a review). The mechanisms of episodic retrieval will be discussed in further detail in Chapter 8 on retrieval and Chapter 11 on autobiographical memory.

Given this evidence about the hippocampus, it is no wonder why Henry could not remember being told about his parents dying, let alone me leaving the room and returning. For Henry, he possessed normal intelligence and normal language, and experienced events in the present much like you or I would. So, when told about his parents, all the relevant parts of the brain involved in interpreting the meaning of the words and the feelings generated by the news, did what they were supposed to and generated a conscious experience. The key difference is that once that initial set of sensory impressions and thoughts faded for him, there was no enduring record created, because the inputs that were sent to the hippocampus were stopped in their tracks by the void where his hippocampus should have been. The result for poor Henry was a life in which the present moment washed over him and then disappeared forever. It makes you truly appreciate how your own sense of life relies on this tiny structure in your brain and how it creates memories that can last a lifetime.

Box 6.2 Mental time travel

Welcome time travelers! You may be pleased to know that you all have your personal time machine, courtesy of episodic memory, with a little help from working memory and of course semantic memory to make sense of what you see. David Ingvar (1985), a Swedish neuroscientist who was a pioneer of neuroimaging, pointed out that an important function of LTM was to use past experience to predict the future; we remember what has happened before and use this to imagine what is going to happen next, and plan accordingly. Endel Tulving (1985) labeled this process *mental time travel*, emphasizing the importance of episodic memory for this activity. Appropriately, given its originator, neuroimaging has featured prominently in exploring this idea (see Schacter, Addis, & Buckner, 2007 for a review).

In one study Schacter et al. asked their participants to recall a series of specific episodes, one might be *meeting Anna in Harvard Square*, another, *losing your keys at the cinema*. Testing took place under fMRI, and was followed by the request to combine two of these episodes into a future scenario, imagining, for example, losing your keys in Harvard Square. They found the same areas of the hippocampus activated in both the initial recollection and in the subsequent creation of a future scenario, a process which also involved frontal lobe activity, suggesting the need for executive processing, presumably involving working memory, to achieve this recombination. Further evidence for the importance of the hippocampus comes from the observation that amnesic patients have great difficulty in carrying out the future thinking task (Hassabis, Kumaran, Vann, & Maguire, 2007), although not all amnesic patients appear to show this deficit (Squire et al., 2010). This is currently a very active area of research where there is considerable evidence for an involvement of episodic memory and the hippocampus, although given the complexity of the task other memory systems and areas of the brain are almost certainly also involved (Berryhill, Phuong, Picasso, Cabeza, & Olson, 2007; Hassabis & Maguire, 2007).

The hippocampus and consolidation of episodic memories

You might have noticed that when I told you about my time with Henry, I mentioned that he had repeatedly told me stories from his childhood. How could he do that if he didn't have a hippocampus, you might wonder? What this observation reveals is that some memories of personal experiences seem to survive after the hippocampus is damaged. Generally, these are memories that occurred long before the damage and that appear to somehow have become independent of the hippocampus's involvement. This is a consistent pattern in both human and animal studies of episodic memory. Based on this pattern of spared memory for older events, many theorists maintain that the role of the hippocampus in episodic memory is time-limited, and that this structure must, therefore, be doing something additional to gradually strengthen memories over time. This hypothesized strengthening process that gradually renders an episodic memory independent of the hippocampus is known as systems consolidation (see Squire, Genzel, Wixted, & Morris, 2015 for a review).

How is systems consolidation believed to work? According to many theorists, the mechanism involves a process wherein the hippocampus "replays" memories periodically, which would involve the hippocampal trace reactivating the relevant ensembles on neurons in cortical areas that represent the memory (see Figure 6.11). This replaying need not be accompanied by conscious experience of the memory and in fact is thought to occur "offline" when you are sleeping, or even when you are awake, but not otherwise engaging your hippocampus, a concept known as offline processing or offline replay. The recurring replaying of the event generated by the hippocampus is believed to gradually strengthen

memories in the neocortex so that eventually they no longer require the hippocampus. This process traditionally was thought to take a very long time, with some researchers suggesting that it may continue for years (Squire, 1992). The idea that offline replay triggers systems consolidation underlies the large amount of research that has been done examining the benefits of sleep for improving memory, discussed in Chapter 5.

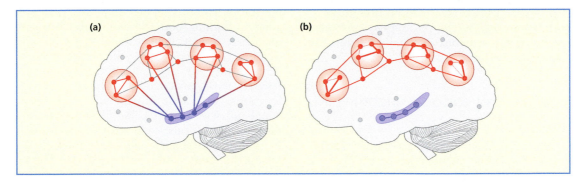

Figure 6.11 Initially, an episodic memory is believed to be formed when a bound representation (area in blue) is created in the hippocampus that links together the sensory, conceptual, and affective elements that were part of the original event, which are stored in cortical modules (red areas). According to the systems consolidation view, over time, the hippocampus replays the memories in your cortex (via back-projections from the hippocampus to cortical modules), fostering the creation of direct links between the cortical modules (when a new links forms between red modules). When this occurs, the memory is thought to be consolidated and hippocampally independent (denoted by absence of links from hippocampus). Figure adapted from Squire et al. (2015).

Although the idea that the hippocampus is involved in strengthening cortical memories over time is widely accepted, researchers disagree about whether or not memories ever truly become independent of the hippocampus (Moscovitch et al., 2016). A more recent view proposes that the hippocampus is always required to support a detailed recollection of a conscious experience, with a full reinstatement of spatio-temporal context, irrespective of the age of the memory. By this view, the memory never gets "transferred" out of the hippocampus. Rather, what consolidation does is to strengthen those aspects of a memory that do not require spatio-temporal context and that could better be described as the "semantics" of an episodic memory devoid of any perceptual re-experiencing. In essence, as memories are gradually repeated over time, they become coarse "gist" representations of what happened, more like stories than like real episodic memories. This is consistent with the idea that structures outside the hippocampus can represent general concepts and meanings, but the hippocampus is required for spatio-temporally bound episodic experiences. If this view is correct, when I think about my earthquake experience in all of its vividness, I am still using my hippocampus, 25 years later; but if I were to lose my hippocampi for some reason, I would no longer have that rich vivid re-experiencing. What I would have is a story of the event, absent any "mental time travel." Both views of the hippocampus, however, agree that this structure gradually strengthens memories over time.

Schemas and episodic encoding in the brain

So far, our discussion of the brain mechanisms of episodic memory has not addressed why meaningful processing enhances long-term episodic memory, the main theme of the first portion of this chapter. Recently, animal and human research has shed light on this question. Over the last decade, a surge of research in cognitive neuroscience has illustrated important new mechanisms by which episodic experiences can be transformed into durable memory traces by virtue of their integration with general schemas already held in long-term storage independent of the hippocampus. The key to how episodic memories get integrated with existing schematic knowledge concerns interactions between the hippocampus and the ventromedial prefrontal cortex, a structure whose importance to long-term memory had not until recently been appreciated.

This exciting body of research was triggered by important experiments reported by Richard Morris at the University of Edinburgh. Morris and colleagues wanted to see whether rats, like humans, would show better episodic memory for unique events if those events could be integrated with a pre-existing schema that they had learned. But how could one possibly train a schema in a rat? And even if one had a way, how could one really tell whether a schema had truly been formed, given that unlike humans, rats can't tell us very much about the knowledge they've acquired? Could we really create the rodent equivalent of master chess players with their superior memory for positions of chess pieces? And if so, what would that reveal about the brain?

Morris and colleagues used a clever approach (Tse et al., 2007). Rats, like most of us, enjoy food, and if given a wee taste of food will want more, much like giving somebody a taste of one's butterscotch ice cream inevitably leads to further requests. Rats are adept at finding food and will readily learn to dig for it if they believe food to be buried. Building on these facts, the experimenters trained rats to associate locations in an "arena" with particular foods buried in those locations, such that if they dug a bit, they could uncover a food pellet. The arena contained six locations, each with a "sand well" in which differently flavored food (e.g., bacon, banana) could be buried (see Figure 6.12). Given this apparatus, the rats were trained over many weeks to learn where all the foods were. On each trial, rats began in a start box at the side of the arena and received a brief taste of the food that was on offer for that trial. The "rules of the game" were that, on any trial, only one of the food wells was "baited" (i.e., contained food), and the brief

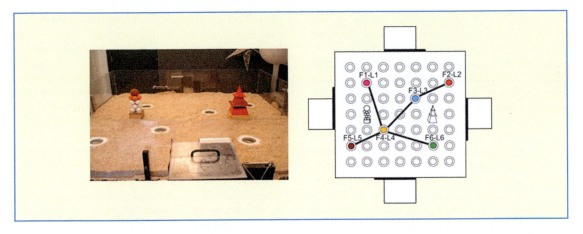

Figure 6.12 Illustration of the arena used in Morris's study of associative schemas in rats. Note the food wells in which food could be buried, and the appearance of local landmarks (e.g., the red pyramid) that help rats to navigate. Starting box can be seen in the foreground. Panel B illustrates the spatial schema and where different food wells were located and which food was associated with each (e.g., Foodwell 5, Flavor 5 indicated by F5-L5).

taste in the start box told the rat which one of the foods was available. If the rat was smart, it took the hint, and would go directly to the relevant food well when allowed into the arena and start digging immediately without wasting any time in the other unbaited food wells. Life continued like this for the rats for weeks and weeks on end, until by the end of the training, rats knew exactly where to go immediately for each of the taste cues. Morris and colleagues speculated that during this process, rats were gradually acquiring a generalized "associative schema" for the arena, including where food was buried, and what kind. They wondered whether this schema may support new episodic learning.

To test this prediction, Morris examined what would happen if his newly trained "rat experts" were given a single exposure to a brand new location-food association. To do this, he shut down two food wells and introduced two new ones nearby, as though two of your favorite restaurants in town shut down, only to be replaced by new places to eat. Each of the new wells could contain one of two new foods. On these trials, the rat was given a wee taste of one of the novel foods in the starting box and had to figure out where to go in the arena, given that it wasn't trained on this food before. Eventually, after digging

around, it found and ate the food. The process repeated for the second new food. After this, no further trials with these foods were given, making the experience of the taste and of hunting down and discovering its location entirely unique in space and time, a true episodic memory for the rat. Yet, this episodic memory was encoded in the context of a well-learned associative schema for where foods were located in this arena, potentially a source of benefit to episodic encoding. Would the rat now be like the chess master spontaneously remembering the locations of pieces for a novel chess game? Would they be like you remembering that particular morning at the coffee shop when you tried a mocha latte for the first time, a unique event associated to a well-worn schematic routine? If so, the rats should show superior episodic memory for this unique event, compared to control rats which did not have the relevant schema.

When tested 24 hours later, rats did indeed have superior episodic memory for this unique event. Superior relative to what, you might ask? To form a contrast, Morris and colleagues had trained rats in a different arena over the same prolonged period, but with a key difference. Whereas in the schema condition, the foods were always located in the same spot, in the control condition, they were trained the same number of times, but the food locations swapped up very often, so there was no consistency. Without consistency, the rat could not learn a consistent schema. Under these conditions, when rats were exposed to a novel taste–location pairing, their memory for where the taste was located on the next day was quite poor. This finding indicates that it was not merely the familiarity with the task or the amount of training trials that improved episodic memory, but rather it was the learning of a consistent spatial mapping of foods to locations. This schema enabled the rats in the experimental condition, upon encountering a new food, to integrate it rapidly into its prior knowledge and remember it the next day. Being a "rat expert" clearly had its benefits.

Even more striking, however, was the discovery that the rats' newly encoded episodic memory had been rapidly consolidated into long-term memory overnight, becoming independent of the hippocampus. When Morris and colleagues removed the rats' hippocampi a mere 24 hours after this unique experience, the rats nonetheless remembered the location of the new food the next time that they were tested on it in the arena. This is a striking finding because in most research using procedures like this in nonhuman animals, systems consolidation (in which an episodic memory becomes independent of the hippocampus) takes far longer to occur and is more gradual, taking many weeks or even months. Unlike our rat experts, rats trained in the inconsistent arena, in which a schema could not be developed, showed no such evidence of consolidation: removing the hippocampus abolished memory for the new location. This implies that when rats were able to relate their new episodic experience to an existing associative schema that they had gradually acquired over many weeks of practice, it led to unusually rapid transfer of the new event into a cortical memory. Morris and colleagues showed that this rapid consolidation of schema-linked knowledge relied on rats sleeping after the experience, reinforcing the notion that sleep helps to consolidate memories. Morris went on to demonstrate in later work that this rapid consolidation was due, to a large extent, to the involvement of the medial prefrontal cortex after the event was encoded (Tse et al., 2011). Indeed, pharmacologically blocking activity in this region disrupted new episodic learning and prevented the retrieval of consolidated knowledge. Thus, the ventromedial prefrontal cortex provides a schematic scaffold that links the cortical modules, rapidly eliminating the need for hippocampal involvement (see Figure 6.13).

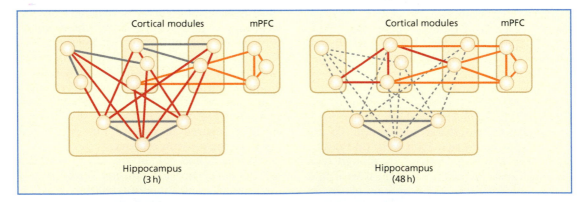

Figure 6.13 A modified version of Figure 6.9 in which the role of the medial prefrontal cortex (mPFC) can be seen providing a schematic scaffold that integrates cortical modules, rapidly consolidating them. Although the new memory is initially dependent on the hippocampus, it very rapidly (within a day or two) can undergo systems consolidation and become hippocampally independent (right side of figure). Note that the medial prefrontal cortex, when studied in humans, is often referred to as the ventromedial prefrontal cortex (vmPFC). Figure adapted from Squire et al., 2015.

Since these landmark studies, much work has examined whether in human participants schemas facilitate consolidation of new events, via the medial prefrontal cortex (for a review, see Gilboa & Marlatte, 2017). These studies generally echo Morris's work with rats and confirm that the ventromedial prefrontal cortex plays a pivotal role in integrating new information with pre-existing knowledge, and in rapidly consolidating it. In a simple illustration, Liu, Grady, and Moscovitch (2016) found that when people encoded associations between faces and houses, they remembered around 36% of the pairs when the faces were famous, compared to 18% when they were not. Thus, having background knowledge about the cue improved memory for the associated picture. Indeed, this effect grew even more strong when participants had greater knowledge of the faces (55%). This superior memory performance was related to activity in the ventromedial prefrontal cortex: pairs including famous faces elicited more activity in this structure than did those with nonfamous faces, even more so, the more participants knew about the faces. Moreover, when Liu and colleagues examined brain regions engaged for individual items that were later remembered (see earlier discussion of *subsequent memory effects*), pairs involving famous faces activated the ventromedial prefrontal cortex more so than nonfamous faces, pointing to a direct, and item-specific role of this structure in enhancing episodic memory. Other related studies have used simple manipulations such as varying whether participants studied schematically congruent picture pairs (such as a picture of a classroom and a second one of chalk) or incongruent pairs (a picture pair containing a tennis court and a soup ladle) and have observed similar evidence for the key role of the ventromedial prefrontal cortex (van Kesteren et al., 2013).

In a remarkable effort, Tobias Sommer even more directly mimicked the rodent study of Morris and colleagues. Participants learned to associate visual objects to locations in arrays of the sort seen in Figure 6.14, with each array presenting 12 objects in consistent locations dispersed throughout the array. Over an impressive 305 days, participants came in, week after week, to receive study and test trials on 10 such arrays (each with different objects and different arrangements of locations), trying to improve in their memory for where the objects were located in each one (Sommer, 2016). Though no food pellets were involved (that we know of), this study is otherwise remarkably similar to what rats in Morris's study were doing. On two critical days (days 91 and 301), participants were exposed, on just a single occasion, to a group of four new objects in four new locations. These new objects were presented either with other objects in one of the over-learned, schematized arrays, or, in the control condition, in an unfilled array that provided no schematic cues to which to attach the new items. During these encoding trials, which directly paralleled the novel food trials with rodents, Sommer observed activation in ventromedial prefrontal cortex (see Figure 6.14), together with evidence of enhanced communication between this structure and the hippocampus (see Figure 6.14, right lower panel). These findings suggest that the benefit of prior knowledge in integrating a new experience was related to the ventromedial prefrontal cortex. Importantly, Sommer found that after either 24 hours or two weeks, novel pairs encoded with the learned schema were recalled significantly better than those encoded without a schema, an enduring memory advantage. This effect was accompanied by reduced involvement of the hippocampus and an increased role of the ventromedial prefrontal cortex during the delayed retrieval of related pairs only. Thus,

KEY TERM

Ventromedial prefrontal cortex: A portion of the prefrontal cortex located along the midline of the brain (i.e., in the middle), lower in the prefrontal cortex (see Figure 6.14), thought to play an instrumental role in the integration of recent episodic experiences with well-consolidated background knowledge and schemas. The vmPFC (also referred to as medial prefrontal cortex in rodents) also plays a role in hastening the consolidation of schematically related episodic memories.

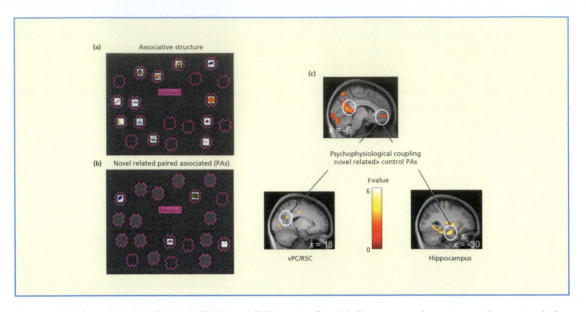

Figure 6.14 Stimuli used by Sommer (2016) and fMRI results. Panel A illustrates a schematic spatial array in which participants learned the locations of 12 visual objects; Panel B illustrates the control condition against which the schema condition in Panel A was compared, with the four novel objects presented without any schematic information. Panel C shows brain areas that were more active during the encoding of schema-relevant material than in the control condition (top), including the ventromedial prefrontal cortex (in white circle). Lower panels illustrate areas to which the vmPFC was communicating during encoding of novel schema-related items (more than control items), which includes the hippocampus (lower right). With permission from Oxford University Press.

the schema relatedness advantage did indeed reflect the rapid transformation of the new episodic memories into ones that were independent of the hippocampus and consolidated. These findings provide striking confirmation of the relevance of Morris's schema discoveries to human participants.

A great deal of work is now trying to understand what schemas are, and how they work to enhance the consolidation of experiences into long-term memory. It's clear, however, by the range of circumstances that have now related the benefits of prior knowledge to successful episodic encoding, that this process does indeed rely on interactions between the ventromedial prefrontal cortex and the hippocampus, and the amplified speed of systems consolidation that this interaction facilitates. These findings provide a new neuroscience perspective on the classical and richly supported body of evidence, discussed throughout this chapter, on how introducing both meaning and organization into the learning process can have profound effects on the encoding of personal experiences into episodic memory.

CONCLUDING REMARKS

The ability to remember our life defines who we are, what we've done, and ultimately a sense of meaning and purpose. As my story about Henry attests, his lack of memory even for the most basic occurrences prevented him from growing beyond the 20-year-old he was when the surgery occurred, leaving him permanently in the present and remote past. In this chapter, we have discussed what science has taught us about the cognitive and the brain mechanisms behind episodic encoding processes that Henry lacks, and the role that meaning and organization play in this remarkable form of mental time travel. We fittingly paid tribute to the seminal contributions of Sir Frederic Bartlett, who, contrary to Ebbinghaus, sought not to eliminate meaning in his studies of memory, but rather to embrace it as fundamental to human memory in everyday life. Bartlett's influence has reached through the decades, echoing in early work on levels of processing and its emphasis on deeper, meaningful processing, to modern work directly building on Bartlett's proposals about schemas. Bartlett never would have dreamt that even rats have schemas and that we would eventually use this fact to identify how the brain understands and remembers the present through the lens of the past. Doing so may allow us to understand how we transform memories from fleeting and frail reverberations of experience to the durable scaffolds of our autobiographies.

SUMMARY

- Episodic memory refers to our capacity to recollect specific experiences, and to use this for "mental time travel."
- It depends on the capacity to encode and then retrieve specific events, something that is greatly helped if material is meaningful and well organized.
- Bartlett, who was influential in breaking away from the Ebbinghaus rote learning tradition, studied memory for complex material such as folk tales from other cultures.
- He emphasized effort after meaning, and the role of schemas, mental structures that help us organize our world knowledge.
- Research on the role of meaning carried out within the traditional verbal learning tradition concentrated on associations between words.
- Evidence for schemas can be seen in the tendency for them to generate, especially at longer intervals, schema-consistent errors, wherein people claim to recall facts or information that was not present, simply because it is expected based on the schema.
- Schema-based errors on delayed tests are often caused by people's efforts to reconstruct the initial experience based on their schema, rather than by the schema distorting the original encoding.
- Paivio stressed the importance for the "imageability" of words, proposing the dual-coding hypothesis.
- Craik and Lockhart proposed the Levels of Processing hypothesis, whereby deeper processing leads to better memory.
- The need to specify the nature of both encoding and retrieval led to the concept of transfer-appropriate processing.
- One problem with the levels of processing framework is that it can be difficult to clearly define and independently establish what counts as "deeper processing."
- There are different accounts of why deeper processing is better. By one view, deeper processing promotes more elaborative processing than shallower processing, in which memories are connected to many other traces. Another view is that deeper processing is simply more likely to integrate new information with prior knowledge.
- Effective methods of organizing material include hierarchies, matrices, and the linking of concepts into coherent stories.
- Intention to learn is not essential but is helpful if it leads to persistence and to the use of good learning strategies.

(Continued)

(Continued)

- Accumulating a great deal of expertise in a skill or knowledge area leads to the development of stable long-term knowledge structures that make it far easier and faster to encode facts and episodic memories. Experts show superior memory for new content in their area, but not superior memory outside their area. Superior memory only occurs if the new content fits their knowledge and expectations.
- Long-term working memory refers to the idea that people skilled in using their expert memory can use well-developed long-term memory knowledge structures to functionally expand the capacity of working memory by the rapid storage and retrieval of information from organized structures in long-term memory.
- The benefits of organization also influence the perception, comprehension, storage, and retrieval of everyday events, for which we have many well-developed schemas that facilitate organized encoding.
- Memory for sequential order is a critical form of organization that affects both general knowledge and episodic memories.
- Solutions to storing and representing temporal sequences may vary from short-term memory to long-term memory, and from massively repeated experiences to unique episodic events.
- The Hebb effect is a useful way to study the encoding of temporal sequences that are learned as a result of extensive repetition, and research with this tool points to a role of the hippocampus in encoding temporal order.
- The Hebb effect may be related to learning of phonology for new vocabulary items.
- Episodic sequence learning may be achieved either by capitalizing on pre-existing schematic knowledge, organized spatial knowledge, or even with the direct representation of time in memories that might be achieved by time cells in the hippocampus.
- The hippocampus and its surrounding tissue (including the perirhinal, entorhinal, and parahippocampal cortices) plays a vital role in constructing, retrieving, and consolidating episodic memories.
- Most modern research points to the conclusion that whereas the hippocampus in particular is vital for encoding unique spatio-temporal events (episodes), surrounding regions like the perirhinal cortex and parahippocampus contribute different functions, including the representation of objects and scenes, respectively.
- The perirhinal cortex supports the acquisition of general semantic knowledge and also the feeling of familiarity arising from a recently encountered stimulus.
- Episodic memories involve the integration of information from multiple sensory modalities, from conceptual processing (thoughts) and emotion into a single bound trace in the hippocampus. A key function of the hippocampus is to bind multimodal inputs together, to a representation of the spatial temporal context.
- When the hippocampus encodes new events, it not only creates a new representation in the hippocampus that binds the inputs together, but also strengthens back-projections from that trace to ensembles of neurons in diverse cortical areas necessary to recreate the elements of an experience during later retrieval.
- The hippocampus contributes to retrieval from episodic memory by receiving cue inputs from outside the hippocampus, retrieving its associated hippocampal trace, and then

using that trace to reactivate cortical areas involved in the memory, a process known as reinstatement.

- The hippocampus also plays a role in systems consolidation, or the process by which an episodic memory that depends on the hippocampus gradually becomes independent of the hippocampus.
- Systems consolidation is thought to occur by the hippocampus replaying an event over time, gradually strengthening and interlinking cortical elements of the trace together, eventually transforming the memory to be independent of the hippocampus.
- Theorists disagree, however, about whether episodic memories can ever become independent of the hippocampus. Some authors, such as Moscovitch and Nadel, argue that the hippocampus always is required if one wishes to re-experience a memory as a unique event in space in time; by this view, consolidation only creates a "semantic" version of the memory stored in cortex, more akin to a story.
- Modern neuroscience has begun to identify the neural mechanisms by which episodic memory can benefit by encoding material meaningfully, in relation to well-established background knowledge and schemas.
- Richard Morris demonstrated in rodents that he could train new schemas in rats that enabled them to rapidly encode new episodic events in a single trial, and to consolidate them into the neocortex within a single day, greatly hastening the speed of systems consolidation.
- The medial prefrontal cortex (often referred to as the ventromedial prefrontal cortex in humans) plays a pivotal role in representing schemas, and in integrating new experiences with prior knowledge. It interacts with the hippocampus during encoding, but over time, plays a role in hastening the consolidation process by which memories become hippocampally independent.
- The profound influence of meaning and organization on long-term episodic memory may be mediated, in part, by the critical role of the vmPFC in linking new events to prior knowledge and in hastening their consolidation.
- Ebbinghaus's impact on memory continues to occur today and can be seen in modern work on the influence of meaning and schemas on consolidation.

POINTS FOR DISCUSSION

1 What are the relative strengths and weaknesses of the Ebbinghaus and Bartlett approaches to the study of memory?
2 To what extent does the impact of organization on memory reflect the concept of levels of processing?
3 What role do different parts of the brain play in episodic memory?
4 Describe how current theory explains the brain's ability to construct new episodic memory and then later on re-create the conscious experience of the event.

FURTHER READING

Hilts, P. J. (1996). *Memory's ghost: The nature of memory and the strange tale of Mr. M.* New York: Simon & Schuster.

Schacter, D. L. (2008). *Searching for memory: The brain, the mind, and the past.* New York: Basic Books.

REFERENCES

Aggleton, J. P., & Brown, M. W. (1999). Episodic memory, amnesia, and the hippocampal–anterior thalamic axis. *Behavioral and Brain Sciences, 22*, 425–489.

Allard, F., Graham, S., & Paarsalu, M. E. (1980). Perception in sport: Basketball. *Journal of Sport and Exercise Psychology, 2*(1), 14–21.

Baddeley, A. D. (1964). Language habits, S-R compatibility and verbal learning. *American Journal of Psychology, 77*, 463–468.

Baddeley, A. D., Gathercole, S., & Papagno, C. (1998). The phonological loop as a language learning device. *Psychological Review, 105*, 158–173.

Bartlett, F. C. (1932). *Remembering*. Cambridge: Cambridge University Press.

Berryhill, M. E., Phuong, L., Picasso, L., Cabeza, R., & Olson, I. R. (2007). Parietal lobe and episodic memory: Bilateral damage causes impaired free recall of autobiographical memory. *Journal of Neuroscience, 27*, 14415–14423.

Bower, G. H., Clark, M. C., Lesgold, A. M., & Winzenz, D. (1969). Hierarchical retrieval schemes in recall of categorised word lists. *Journal of Verbal Learning and Verbal Behavior, 8*, 323–343.

Bower, G. H., Karlin, M. B., & Dueck, A. (1975). Comprehension and memory for pictures. *Memory and Cognition, 3*, 216–220.

Brewer, J. B., Zhao, Z., Desmond, J. E., Glover, G. H., & Gabrieli, J. D. E. (1998). Making memories: Brain activity that predicts how well visual experience will be remembered. *Science, 281*, 1185–1187.

Broadbent, D. E., Cooper, P. J., & Broadbent, M. H. (1978). A comparison of hierarchical retrieval schemes in recall. *Journal of Experimental Psychology: Human Learning and Memory, 4*, 486–497.

Burgess, N., & Hitch, G. J. (1999). Memory for serial order: A network model of the phonological loop and its timing. *Psychological Review, 106*, 551–581.

Burgess, N., & Hitch, G. J. (2006). A revised model of short-term memory and long-term learning of verbal sequences. *Journal of Memory and Language, 55*, 627–652.

Cabeza, R., & St. Jacques, P. (2007). Functional neuroimaging of autobiographical memory. *Trends in Cognitive Sciences, 11*(5), 219–227.

Campoy, G., & Baddeley, A. D. (2008). Phonological and semantic strategies in immediate serial recall. *Memory, 16*, 329–340.

Carmichael, L., Hogan, H. P., & Walter, A. A. (1932). An experimental study of the effect of language on the reproduction of visually perceived form. *Journal of Experimental Psychology, 15*, 73–86.

Chase, W. G., & Ericsson, K. A. (1982). Skill in working memory. In G. H. Bower (Ed.), *The psychology of learning and motivation* (Vol. 16). New York: Academic Press.

Chase, W. G., & Simon, H. A. (1973). Perception in chess. *Cognitive Psychology, 4*(1), 55–81.

Clayton, N. S., & Dickinson, A. (1999). Scrub jays remember when as well as where and what food items they cached. *Journal of Comparative Psychology, 113*, 403–416.

Craik, F. I. M., & Lockhart, R. S. (1972). Levels of processing. A framework for memory research. *Journal of Verbal Learning and Verbal Behavior, 11*, 671–684.

Craik, F. I. M., & Tulving, E. (1975). Depth of processing and the retention of words in episodic memory. *Journal of Experimental Psychology: General, 104*(3), 268–294.

Danker, J. F., & Anderson, J. R. (2010). The ghosts of brain states past: Remembering reactivates the brain regions engaged during encoding. *Psychological Bulletin, 136*(1), 87–102.

Davachi, L., & DuBrow, S. (2015). How the hippocampus preserves order: The role of prediction and context. *Trends in Cognitive Sciences, 19*(2), 92–99.

Davachi, L., Mitchell, J. P., & Wagner, A. D. (2003). Multiple routes to memory: Distinct medial temporal lobe processes build item and source memories. *Proceedings of the National Academy of Sciences of the USA, 100*(4), 2157–2162.

Deese, J. (1959). Influence of inter-item associative strength upon immediate free recall. *Psychological Reports, 5,* 305–312.

Eichenbaum, H. (2014). Time cells in the hippocampus: A new dimension for mapping memories. *Nature Reviews Neuroscience, 15*(11), 732–744.

Ericsson, K. A., & Delaney, P. F. (1999). Long-term working memory as an alternative to capacity models of working memory in everyday skilled performance. In A. Miyake & P. Shah (Eds.), *Models of working memory: Mechanisms of active maintenance and executive control* (pp. 257–297). Cambridge: Cambridge University Press.

Ericsson, K. A., & Kintsch, W. (1995). Long-term working memory. *Psychological Review, 102*(2), 211–245.

Fisher, R. P., & Craik, F. I. M. (1977). Interaction between encoding and retrieval operations in cued recall. *Journal of Experimental Psychology: Learning, Memory and Cognition, 3,* 701–711.

Gilboa, A., & Marlatte, H. (2017). Neurobiology of schemas and schema-mediated memory. *Trends in Cognitive Sciences, 21*(8), 618–631.

Glaze, J. A. (1928). The association value of nonsense syllables. *Journal of Genetic Psychology, 35,* 255–269.

Glenberg, A. M., Smith, S. M., & Green, C. (1977). Type I rehearsal: Maintenance and more. *Journal of Verbal Learning and Verbal Behavior, 16,* 339–352.

Gomulicki, B. R. (1956). Recall as an abstractive process. *Acta Psychologica, 12,* 77–94.

Hassabis, D., Kumaran, D., Vann, S. D., & Maguire, E. A. (2007). Patients with hippocampal amnesia cannot imagine new experiences. *Proceedings of the National Academy of Sciences of the USA, 104,* 1726–1731.

Hassabis, D., & Maguire, E. A. (2007). Deconstructing episodic memory with construction. *Trends in Cognitive Sciences, 11,* 299–306.

Hatano, G., & Osawa, K. (1983a). Digit memory of grand experts in abacus-derived mental calculation. *Cognition, 15,* 95–110.

Hatano, G., & Osawa, K. (1983b). Japanese abacus experts' memory for numbers is disrupted by mechanism of action. *Journal of Clinical Psychology, 58*(1), 61–75.

Hitch, G. J., Flude, B., & Burgess, N. (2009). Slave to the rhythm: Experimental tests of a model for verbal short-term memory and long-term sequence learning. *Journal of Memory and Language, 61,* 97–111.

Hyde, T. S., & Jenkins, J. J. (1973). Recall for words as a function of semantic, graphic, and syntactic orienting tasks. *Journal of Verbal Learning and Verbal Behavior, 12,* 471–480.

Ingvar, D. H. (1985). Memory of the future: An essay on the temporal organization of conscious awareness. *Human Neurobiology, 4,* 127–136.

James, W. (1890). *The principles of psychology.* New York: Holt, Rinehart and Winston.

Jenkins, J. J., & Russell, W. A. (1952). Associative clustering as a function of verbal association strength. *Psychological Reports, 4,* 127–136.

Jung, J. (1968). *Verbal learning.* New York: Holt, Rinehart and Winston.

Kalm, K., Davis, M. H., & Norris, D. (2013). Individual sequence representations in the medial temporal lobe. *Journal of Cognitive Neuroscience, 25,* 1111–1121.

Kim, H. (2011). Neural activity that predicts subsequent memory and forgetting: A meta-analysis of 74 fMRI studies. *Neuroimage, 54*(3), 2446–2461.

Liu, Z. X., Grady, C., & Moscovitch, M. (2016). Effects of prior-knowledge on brain activation and connectivity during associative memory encoding. *Cerebral Cortex, 27*(3), 1991–2009.

Mandler, G. (1967). Organization and memory. In K. W. Spence & J. T. Spence (Eds.), *The psychology of learning and motivation: Advances in research and theory.* (Vol. 1, pp. 328–372). New York: Academic Press.

Morris, C. D., Bransford, J. D., & Franks, J. J. (1977). Levels of processing versus transfer appropriate processing. *Journal of Verbal Learning and Verbal Behavior, 16,* 519–533.

Moscovitch, M., Cabeza, R., Winocur, G., & Nadel, L. (2016). Episodic memory and beyond: The hippocampus and neocortex in transformation. *Annual Review of Psychology, 67,* 105–134.

Moser, E. I., Kropff, E., & Moser, M. B. (2008). Place cells, grid cells, and the brain's spatial representation system. *Annual Review of Neuroscience, 31,* 69–89.

Mosse, E. K., & Jarrold, C. (2008). Hebb learning, verbal short-term memory, and the acquisition of phonological forms in children. *Quarterly Journal of Experimental Psychology, 61,* 505–514.

Norman, G. R., Brooks, L. R., & Allen, S. W. (1989). Recall by expert medical practitioners and novices as a record of processing attention. *Journal of Experimental Psychology: Learning, Memory, and Cognition, 15*(6), 1166–1174.

O'Keefe, J., & Dostrovsky, J. (1971). The hippocampus as a spatial map: Preliminary evidence from unit activity in the freely-moving rat. *Brain Research, 34*(1), 171–175.

Oliver, W. L., & Ericsson, K. A. (1986). Repertory actors' memory for their parts. *Proceedings of the Eighth Annual Conference of the Cognitive Science Society, Amherst, MA* (pp. 399–406). Hillsdale, NJ: Lawrence Erlbaum.

Page, M. P. A., Cumming, N., Norris, D., McNeil, A. M., & Hitch, G. J. (2013). Repetition-spacing and item-overlap effects in the Hebb repetition task. *Journal of Memory and Language, 69,* 506–526.

Page, M. P. A., & Norris, D. (1998). The primacy model: A new model of immediate serial recall. *Psychological Review, 105,* 761–781.

Page, M. P. A., & Norris, E. (2009). A model linking immediate serial recall, the Hebb repetition effect and the learning of phonological word forms. *Philosophical Transactions of the Royal Society: B Biological Science, 364,* 3737–3753.

Paivio, A. (1965). Abstractness, imagery, and meaningfulness in paired-associate learning. *Journal of Verbal Learning and Verbal Behavior, 4*(1), 32–38.

Paivio, A. (1969). Mental imagery in associative learning and memory. *Psychological Review, 76,* 241–263.

Paivio, A. (1971). *Imagery and verbal processes.* London: Holt Rinehart and Winston.

Prentice, W. C. H. (1954). Visual recognition of verbally labelled figures. *American Journal of Psychology, 67,* 315–320.

Rubin, D. C. (1995). *Memory in oral traditions: The cognitive psychology of epic, ballads, and counting-out rhymes.* New York: Oxford University Press.

Schacter, D. L. (2001). *The seven sins of memory: How the mind forgets and remembers.* New York: Houghton-Mifflin.

Schacter, D. L., Addis, D. R., & Buckner, R. L. (2007). Remembering the past to imagine the future: The prospective brain. *Nature Reviews Neuroscience, 8,* 657–651.

Sheldon, S., & Levine, B. (2013). Same as it ever was: Vividness modulates the similarities and differences between the neural networks that support retrieving remote and recent autobiographical memories. *Neuroimage, 83,* 880–891.

Sommer, T. (2016). The emergence of knowledge and how it supports the memory for novel related information. *Cerebral Cortex, 27*(3), 1906–1921.

Spaniol, J., Davidson, P. S., Kim, A. S., Han, H., Moscovitch, M., & Grady, C. L. (2009). Event-related fMRI studies of episodic encoding and retrieval: Meta-analyses using activation likelihood estimation. *Neuropsychologia, 47*(8–9), 1765–1779.

Squire, L. R. (1992). Memory and the hippocampus: A synthesis from findings with rats, monkeys, and humans. *Psychological Review, 99*(2), 195–231.

Squire, L. R., Genzel, L., Wixted, J. T., & Morris, R. G. (2015). Memory consolidation. *Cold Spring Harbor Perspectives in Biology, 7*(8), a021766.

Squire, L. R., van der Horst, A. S., McDuff, S. T. R., Frascino, J. C., Hopkins, R. O., & Mauldin, K. N. (2010). The role of the hippocampus in remembering the past and imagining the future. *Proceedings of the National Academy of Sciences of the USA, 107,* 19044–19048.

Starkes, J. L., Deakin, J. M., Lindley, S., & Crisp, F. (1987). Motor versus verbal recall of ballet sequences by young expert dancers. *Journal of Sport and Exercise Psychology, 9*(3), 222–230.

Sulin, R. S., & Dooling, D. J. (1974). Intrusion of a thematic idea in retention of prose. *Journal of Experimental Psychology, 103,* 255–262.

Szmalec, A., Page, M. P. A., & Duyck, W. (2012). The development of long-term lexical representations through Hebb repetition learning. *Journal of Memory and Language, 67,* 342–354.

Tse, D., Langston, R. F., Kakeyama, M., Bethus, I., Spooner, P. A., Wood, E. R., ... & Morris, R. G. (2007). Schemas and memory consolidation. *Science, 316*(5821), 76–82.

Tse, D., Takeuchi, T., Kakeyama, M., Kajii, Y., Okuno, H., Tohyama, C., ... & Morris, R. G. (2011). Schema-dependent gene activation and memory encoding in neocortex. *Science, 333*(6044), 891–895.

Tulving, E. (1962). Subjective organisation in free recall of "unrelated" words. *Psychological Review, 69,* 344–354.

Tulving, E. (1985). Memory and consciousness. *Canadian Psychology, 26,* 1–12.

Tulving, E., & Pearlstone, Z. (1966). Availability versus accessibility of information in memory for words. *Journal of Verbal Learning and Verbal Behavior, 5,* 381–391.

Underwood, B. J., & Schulz, R. W. (1960). *Meaningfulness and verbal learning.* Chicago, IL: Lippincott Company.

van Kesteren, M. T., Beul, S. F., Takashima, A., Henson, R. N., Ruiter, D. J., & Fernández, G. (2013). Differential roles for medial prefrontal and medial temporal cortices in schema-dependent encoding: From congruent to incongruent. *Neuropsychologia, 51*(12), 2352–2359.

Vargha-Khadem, F., Gadian, D. G., Watkins, K. E., Connelly, A., Van Paesschen, W., & Mishkin, M. (1997). Differential effects of early hippocampal pathology on episodic and semantic memory. *Science, 277,* 376–380.

Wagner, A. D., Schacter, D. L., Rotte, M., Koutstaal, W., Maril, A., Dale, A. M., et al. (1998). Building memories: Remembering and forgetting of verbal experiences as predicted by brain activity. *Science, 281*, 1188–1191.

Winocur, G., & Moscovitch, M. (2011). Memory transformation and systems consolidation. *Journal of the International Neuropsychological Society, 17*(5), 766–780.

Contents

CHAPTER 7

SEMANTIC MEMORY AND STORED KNOWLEDGE

Michael W. Eysenck

INTRODUCTION

What is the capital of France? How many months are there in a year? Who is the current President of the United States? Do rats have wings? What is the chemical formula for water? Is *umplitude* an English word? What do seismologists do? Is New York south of Washington, D.C.? What is the typical sequence of events when having a meal in a restaurant?

I am sure you found all the above questions relatively (or very!) easy to answer and that you answered them rapidly. We could easily fill the whole of this book with such questions—we all possess an enormous store of general knowledge that we take for granted. All this information is stored in semantic memory. Binder and Desai (2011, p. 527) provided a detailed definition of *semantic memory*: "It is an individual's store of knowledge about the world. The content of semantic memory is abstracted from actual experience and is therefore said to be conceptual, that is, generalized and without reference to any specific experience."

If you stopped the first woman you saw and tested her vocabulary, you would probably discover she knew the meaning of between 20,000 and 100,000 words. She might also know a foreign language. She would certainly know a great deal (in geographical terms) about her own neighborhood and about the wider world. She functions well in her environment because

she has learned to drive a car, use a cell or mobile phone, use credit cards, and so on.

She also has a great deal of specialist knowledge acquired in connection with work, hobbies, and pastimes. In addition, she has the usual interesting but nonvital mental baggage (much of it media-related) that most of us carry around in our heads—facts and images to do with politics and sport, movies and music, TV programs and celebrities.

There is much overlap in the knowledge each of us has stored in semantic memory (e.g., basic vocabulary; general knowledge of the world). However, there are also large individual differences. For example, we have much more information than most people stored in semantic memory in those areas of special interest and importance to us (e.g., work-related knowledge). Consider expert chess players. Chassy and Gobet (2011) analyzed over 70,000 games played by chess players of varying skill levels. They estimated chess masters have memorized 100,000 opening moves! Overall, there was a very strong relationship between chess-playing skill and knowledge of opening moves.

How important is semantic memory? The devastating effects of lacking semantic memory were vividly described by the Colombian novelist Gabriel Garcia Márquez in his novel *One Hundred Years of Solitude*. In this novel, the inhabitants of Macondo are struck by the insomnia plague which leads them to lose information about the meanings and functions of the objects around them.

Here is how the central character (José Arcadio Buerdia) responds to this desperate situation:

The sign that he hung on the neck of the cow was an exemplary proof of the way in which the inhabitants of Macondo were prepared to fight against loss of memory: This is the cow. She must be milked every morning so that she will produce milk, and the milk must be boiled in order to be mixed with coffee to make coffee and milk.

SEMANTIC MEMORY VS. EPISODIC MEMORY

I have discussed briefly some key features of semantic memory. How does it differ from episodic memory (discussed in Chapter 6)? Episodic memories contain specific information about when and where they were formed, whereas semantic memories lack such contextual information (Moscovitch, Cabeza, Winocur, & Nadel, 2016).

Tulving (1972, 2002) identified other differences between semantic and episodic memory. For example, Tulving (2002, p. 5) argued,

Episodic memory ... shares many features with semantic memory, out of which it grew ... but also possesses features that semantic memory does not.... Episodic memory is a recently evolved, late-developing, and early-deteriorating past-oriented system, more vulnerable than other memory systems to neuronal dysfunction.

Tulving's views are discussed and evaluated by Eysenck and Groome (2015).

Tulving (1972, 2002) also argued that the subjective experiences associated with retrieval from episodic and semantic memory are different. Retrieval from episodic memory is typically accompanied by a sense of consciously recollecting the past lacking when we retrieve information from semantic memory.

In spite of the above differences, there are important similarities between episodic and semantic memory. Suppose you remember meeting a friend yesterday afternoon at a coffee shop. That clearly involves episodic memory because you are remembering an event at a given time in a given place. However, semantic memory is also involved —some of what you remember involves your general knowledge about coffee shops, what coffee tastes like, and so on.

Findings: Separate systems

One approach to testing the hypothesis that there are separate episodic and semantic memory systems is to focus on brain-damaged patients. We can predict there should be some patients whose episodic memory is much more impaired than their semantic memory whereas other patients (with damage to different brain areas) should exhibit the opposite pattern of impairment.

There is compelling evidence the hippocampus plays a central role in episodic memory (see Chapter 6). Accordingly, we would expect amnesic patients with damage to that brain area to have severely impaired episodic memory but not necessarily semantic memory (see Chapter 16). Spiers, Maguire, and Burgess (2001) reviewed 147 cases of amnesia. Episodic memory was impaired in all cases but many patients had only modest problems with semantic memory. Other research (reviewed by Clark & Maguire, 2016) confirms that patients with hippocampal amnesia have intact semantic memory for information acquired before the onset of the amnesia. However, the extent to which such patients can acquire semantic memories after amnesia onset is unclear.

We have seen that patients with hippocampal amnesia typically have greater problems with episodic than semantic memory. Are there patients exhibiting the opposite pattern? The short answer is, "Yes," based on research with patients suffering from

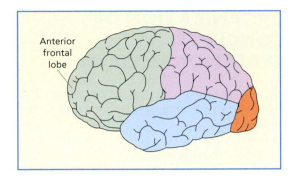

Figure 7.1 Semantic dementia is associated with damage to the anterior frontal temporal lobes.

semantic dementia, a condition that always involves degeneration of the anterior temporal lobes (see Figure 7.1). However, other areas are often also damaged.

Patients with semantic dementia have severe loss of concept knowledge from semantic memory (relevant evidence is discussed later in the chapter); indeed, their symptoms are remarkably similar to those of the fictional character José Arcadio Buerdia (described earlier; Rascovsky, Growdon, Pardo, Grossman, & Miller, 2009). However, their episodic memory and most cognitive functions (e.g., attention; non-verbal problem solving) are reasonably intact. For example, they often have an intact ability to reproduce complex visual designs (Irish et al., 2016). They also have an almost intact ability to recall recent autobiographical memories because they can use episodic information (e.g., sensory and perceptual features of events) to facilitate recall.

Landin-Romero, Tan, Hodges, and Kufor (2016) reviewed research on semantic dementia. The good episodic memory of patients with semantic dementia probably occurs because they make effective use of the frontal and parietal brain regions.

Findings: Interdependent systems

Episodic and semantic memory often combine in an interdependent fashion (see Greenberg & Verfaellie, 2010, for a review). Renoult et al. (2016) required participants to answer questions belonging to four categories: (1) unique events (e.g., "Did you drink coffee this morning?"); (2) general factual knowledge (e.g., "Do many people drink coffee?"); (3) autobiographical facts (e.g., "Do you drink coffee every day?"); and (4) repeated personal events (e.g., "Have you drunk coffee while shopping?").

Renoult et al. (2016) assumed that category 1 involves episodic memory and category 2 involves semantic memory. Categories 3 and 4 involve personal semantic memory (a combination of episodic and semantic memory). They tested their assumptions by using event-related potentials (ERPs) to assess the precise timing of brain responses during retrieval for all four question categories. There were clear-cut ERP differences between categories 1 and 2. Of most importance, ERP patterns for category 3 and 4 questions were *intermediate* between those for categories 1 and 2 suggesting they involved retrieval from both episodic and semantic memory.

Tanguay et al. (2018) reported similar findings. They interpreted the various findings with reference to personal semantics: "Like semantic memory [they] are factual and limited in spatial/temporal details, but (like episodic memory) [they] are idiosyncratically personal" (p. 65).

Finally, Robin and Moscovitch (2017) discussed another way in which episodic and semantic memory are related. They argued that initially episodic memories can be *transformed* into semantic memories over time: this is known as semanticization. For example, you undoubtedly formed episodic memories during your first seaside holiday. As an adult, you probably still remember that holiday but the personal and contextual information associated with it has mostly been forgotten. In essence, what has happened is that many memories exhibit a transformation from an initially detail-rich episodic representation to a gist-like representation involving semantic memory.

Conclusions

The distinction between episodic and semantic memory is important. Some of the strongest evidence for the distinction comes from brain-damaged patients. Amnesic patients typically have more severe problems with long-term episodic memory than patients with semantic dementia, whereas the opposite is the case so far as long-term memory is concerned.

In spite of the differences between episodic and semantic memory, many memories (perhaps especially autobiographical ones) combine episodic and semantic information. This is probably especially the case in everyday life where our behavior is often influenced by different types of memories at any given moment (Ferbinteanu, 2019). In contrast, researchers typically devise laboratory experiments to target a specific type of memory. In addition, there is evidence that many episodic memories are gradually transformed over time into semantic memories.

Some theorists (e.g., Cabeza, Stanley, & Moscovitch, 2018; Moscovitch et al., 2016) argue that the notion of separate memory systems (e.g., episodic and semantic) is an oversimplification. According to such theorists, we use numerous specific processes during learning and memory. In general terms, we use those processes most relevant for the task in hand rather than limiting ourselves only to episodic or semantic processes. This new theoretical approach has much potential. However, it is currently somewhat vague and considerable research is required to flesh out the details.

ORGANIZATION OF CONCEPTS: TRADITIONAL VIEWS

What information is stored in long-term memory? Much of it consists of concepts of various kinds and we will consider how these concepts are stored. Before you read this section, test yourself on the questions in Box 7.1.

Elizabeth Loftus and her colleagues carried out various experiments exploring the task of coming up with particular words given a category and a first letter as cues. Loftus and Suppes (1972) found participants responded faster when the category preceded the first letter (e.g., *fruit–p*) than when the first letter preceded the category (e.g., *p–fruit*). This suggests it is easier to activate the category *fruit* in preparation for searching for the appropriate first letter than all starting with, say, *p*. This is probably because the category *fruit* is reasonably coherent and manageable whereas words starting with *p* form too large and diffuse a category to be useful.

Evidence supporting the above viewpoint was obtained in a study where the category was *type of psychologist* and the first letter that of the psychologist's *surname*. Hence a typical question might be, "Give me a developmental psychologist whose name begins with P" (Piaget) versus "Initial letter P–a developmental psychologist." Students just starting to specialize in psychology showed no difference between the two orders of presentation, whereas those who had already specialized were faster when the category was provided first. Presumably they had already developed categories such as "developmental psychologist." In contrast, the novices simply searched all "psychologists" because they had not sufficiently developed their categories to operate otherwise.

Hierarchical network theory

The first systematic theory of semantic memory was put forward by Collins and Quillian (1969). Their key assumption was that semantic memory is organized into a

Box 7.1 Organization of concepts

Answer the following questions, noting how long it takes you to answer each one:

Set A   Set B

1 Fruit starting with p.   1 Fruit ending with h.
2 Animal starting with d.   2 Animal ending with w.
3 Metal starting with i.   3 Metal ending with r.
4 Bird starting with b.   4 Bird ending with n.
5 Country starting with F.   5 Country ending with y.
6 Boy's name starting with H.   6 Boy's name ending with d.
7 Girl's name starting with M.   7 Girl's name ending with n.
8 Flower starting with s.   8 Flower ending with t.

Total time taken =   Total time taken =

I imagine you took much less time to complete Set A than Set B. What does this mean? Of course, it indicates that the initial letter is a much more effective cue than the last letter when you are trying to retrieve words from a given category. This in turn tells us something about how the names of such categories are stored, as there is no logical reason why the above should be the case. For example, it would be entirely possible to devise a computer program where words could be retrieved equally rapidly regardless of whether the first, last, second, fourth, or any other letter were provided as a cue.

series of hierarchical networks. Part of one such network is shown in Figure 7.2. The major concepts (e.g., *animal*; *bird*; *canary*) are represented as nodes, and properties or features (e.g., *has wings*; *is yellow*) are associated with each concept.

Why is the property *can fly* stored with the *bird* concept rather than with the *canary* concept? After all, one property of canaries is that they can fly. Collins and Quillian (1969) argued it would waste space in semantic memory to have information about being

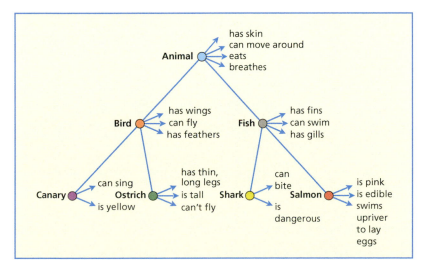

Figure 7.2 Collins and Quillian's (1969) hierarchical network.

able to fly stored with every bird name. If those properties possessed by nearly all birds (e.g., can fly; has wings) are stored only at the bird node or concept, this satisfies the notion of cognitive economy. The underlying principle is that property information is stored as high up the hierarchy as possible to minimize the amount of information needing to be stored in semantic memory.

According to the model, we can decide very rapidly that the sentence, "*A canary is yellow*," is true because the concept (i.e., *canary*) and the property (i.e., *is yellow*) are stored at the same level of the hierarchy. In contrast, the sentence "*A canary can fly*," should take longer because the concept and property are separated by one level in the hierarchy. The sentence, "*A canary has skin*," should take even longer because there are two levels separating the concept and property. Collins and Quillian's (1969) findings supported their predictions.

The model is on the right lines in assuming we often use *inference* to answer questions about semantic memory. For example, we know that Leonardo da Vinci had knees because we use an inferential process—we know he was a human being and that human beings have knees.

Limitations with the theory

The hierarchical network theory has several limitations. First, Conrad (1972) discovered people are slow to verify sentences such as, "*A canary has skin*," because it is very *unfamiliar* rather than because of the large hierarchical distance between the concept and its property. Thus, key findings do not actually provide much support for the model.

Second, consider the statements, "*A canary is a bird*," and "*A penguin is a bird*." According to the theory, both statements should take the same length of time to verify, because they both involve moving one level in the hierarchy. In fact, the latter statement takes longer because *canaries* are much more typical or representative of the bird category than *penguins*. Rips, Shoben, and Smith (1973) found verification times were faster for more typical or representative category members than atypical ones. This is the typicality effect.

Third, Collins and Quillian (1969) mistakenly assumed the concepts we use belong to rigidly defined categories. McCloskey and Glucksberg (1978) gave 30 people tricky questions such as, "*Is a stroke a disease?*" and "*Is a pumpkin a fruit?*" They found 16 said a *stroke* is a disease, but 14 said it was not. A *pumpkin* was regarded as a fruit by 16 participants but not as a fruit by the remainder. When McCloskey and Glucksberg tested the same participants a month later, 11 of them had changed their minds about "*stroke*" being a disease, and eight had altered their opinion about "*pumpkin*" being a fruit!

Verheyen and Storms (2013) identified two reasons for individual differences in deciding which items belong to a given category. First, there is *ambiguity*—individuals may use different criteria for categorization (e.g., is strenuous activity a necessary criterion for something to be regarded as a sport?). Second, there is *vagueness*—individuals may use different cut-offs to separate members from nonmembers. For example, two individuals may agree that being strenuous is a criterion for an activity being a sport but may disagree about *how* strenuous it must be.

Finally, have a look at the objects shown in Figure 7.3. Would you describe either or both of the objects as a *box*? White, Storms, Malt, and Verheyen (2018) found older people were more likely to assign an object to a category if it were made of traditional materials (e.g., a box made of cardboard) whereas younger ones were more influenced by the use of newer materials (e.g., a box made of plastic).

KEY TERM

Typicality effect: The finding that the time taken to decide a category member belongs to a category is less for typical than atypical members.

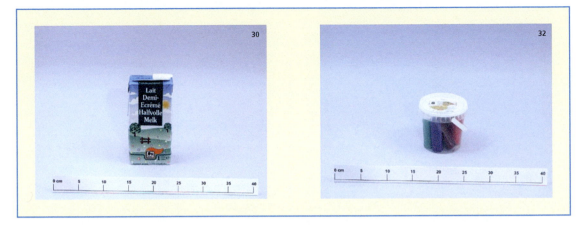

Figure 7.3 Two objects that could be described as a box (left object made of cardboard; right object made of plastic). From White et al., 2018

Spreading-activation theory and beyond

Collins and Loftus (1975) proposed a spreading-activation theory to resolve problems with Collins and Quillian's (1969) theory. They argued (correctly!) that the notion of logically organized hierarchies was too *inflexible*. They assumed semantic memory is organized on the basis of semantic relatedness or semantic distance. We can assess semantic relatedness by asking people to decide how closely related pairs of words are. Alternatively, people can list as many members as possible of a particular category. Those members produced most often are regarded as most closely related to the category.

You can see part of the organization of semantic memory assumed by Collins and Loftus (1975) in Figure 7.4. The length of the links between two concepts indicates the degree of semantic relatedness between them. Thus, for example, *red* is more closely related to *orange* than to *sunsets*.

According to spreading-activation theory, the appropriate node in semantic memory is activated when we see, hear, or think about a concept. Activation then spreads rapidly to other concepts, with greater activation for concepts closely related semantically than those weakly related.

Spreading-activation theory predicts the typicality effect (discussed earlier). Activation

passes strongly and rapidly from *robin* to *bird* in the sentence, "A robin is a bird"—*robin* is a typical *bird* and *robin* and *bird* are closely related semantically. Less activation passes from *penguin* to *bird* in the sentence, "A penguin is a bird"—*penguin* is an atypical *bird* and *penguin* and *bird* are only weakly related.

Findings

Numerous experimental studies provide general support for the major assumptions of spreading-activation theory. Much of this research has involved semantic priming, which is "the facilitation in the processing of a word when it is preceded by a related word" (Hoedemaker & Gordon, 2017, p. 881). The prediction from the theory is that semantic priming should be greater when the first word is strongly semantically related to the second word.

Semantic priming was first demonstrated by Meyer and Schvaneveldt (1971) using the lexical decision task (deciding rapidly whether a letter string forms a word). Consider, for example, what we would expect

KEY TERM

Semantic priming: The finding that word processing is facilitated by the prior presentation of a semantically related word.

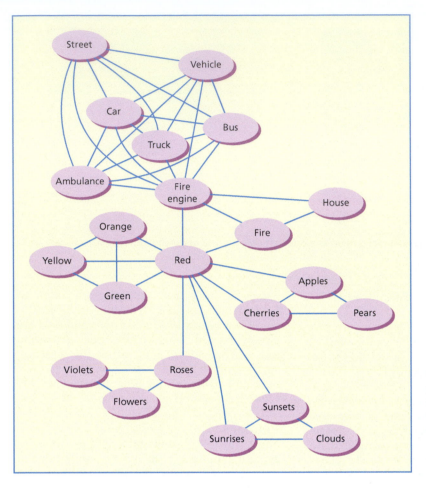

Figure 7.4 Example of a spreading activation semantic network. From Collins and Loftus (1975). Copyright © American Psychological Association. Reproduced with permission.

when a target word (e.g., *butter*) is immediately preceded by a semantically related word (e.g., *bread*) or an unrelated word (e.g., *nurse*). Theoretically, activation should have spread from the first word to the second only when they were semantically related and this activation should have facilitated recognizing the target as a word. This is what Meyer and Schvaneveldt found (Bauer & Just, 2017).

Subsequent research has confirmed the existence of semantic priming. However, such priming effects are sometimes rather small and unreliable (Heyman, Bruninx, Hutchison, & Storms, 2018).

More support for the theory was reported by Schacter et al. (1996). Participants were presented with word lists constructed as follows: an initial word (e.g., *doctor*) was selected and then several words closely associated with it

(e.g., *nurse*; *sick*; *hospital*; *patient*) were selected. All these words (*except* the initial word) were presented for learning, followed by a recognition-memory test. When the initial word (e.g., *doctor*) was presented on the recognition test, it was frequently falsely recognized. This occurred because it was highly activated due to its close semantic relationship with all the list words.

Semantic distance between words or concepts has been measured in various ways. Kenett, Levi, Anaki, and Faust (2017) used data from 60 individuals instructed to produce as many associations as possible in 60 seconds to 800 Hebrew cue words to assess semantic distance in terms of path distance: "the shortest number of steps connecting any two cue words" (p. 1473). Kenett et al. then asked different participants to judge whether word pairs were semantically related. These judgments were well predicted by path distance: 91% of directly linked words (one step) were judged to be semantically related, compared to 69% of two-step word pairs and 64% of three-step word pairs.

Of importance, Kenett et al. (2017) found semantic distance predicted performance on various tasks involving episodic memory rather than semantic memory. For example, *free recall* (recalling words presented in a list in any order) was greater when there were short semantic distances between the words than when the semantic distances were longer. In another experiment, participants were presented with word pairs. This was followed by presenting the first word of each pairs and instructing them to recall the associated word. Performance was much higher on directly linked word pairs (one step) than three-step word pairs: 30% versus 11%, respectively.

Semantic distance also predicts some aspects of language production. For example, Rose, Aristei, Melinger, and Abdel Rahman (2019) asked participants to name target pictures (e.g., *eagle*) in the presence of distractor pictures. These distractor pictures were semantically close (e.g., *owl*) or semantically distant (e.g., *gorilla*). There was an interference effect based on semantic distance: naming times were longer when distractors were semantically close than when they were distant.

Evaluation

The notion that activation spreads from a presented word or concept to semantically related words or concepts has been (and remains) extremely influential. The spreading activation theory has generally proved more successful than the hierarchical network theory at accounting for the various findings. One important reason is that it is much more flexible.

What are the limitations with the theory? First, the notion that each concept in semantic memory is represented by a *single* node is oversimplified. As we will see shortly, information about most concepts is distributed in various brain regions rather than all being represented in a node.

Second, the model implies that each concept has a *single*, fixed representation. In fact, however, our processing of any given concept is flexible (discussed further shortly). Consider the following two sentences:

1 Fred greatly enjoyed playing the piano.
2 Fred found it difficult to lift the piano.

I imagine your processing of the word *piano* in the second sentence focused on the heaviness of pianos but did not do so when processing the first sentence. Such findings cannot easily be explained by the spreading-activation model.

Third, several ways of measuring semantic distance have been proposed (see Kenett et al., 2017, for a review). There is, as yet, no consensus concerning the most appropriate measure of semantic distance.

Naming objects

Suppose you are shown a photograph of a *chair* and asked to identify it. You might provide various answers based on the relevant knowledge you have stored in semantic memory. For example, you might describe it as an *item of furniture*, a *chair*, or an *easy chair*. In fact, the great majority of people would describe it as a *chair*. Below we discuss *why* that is the case.

The above example suggests concepts are organized into hierarchies. Rosch, Mervis, Gray, Johnson, and Boyes-Braem (1976) identified *three* levels within such hierarchies. There are superordinate categories (e.g., *item of furniture*) at the top, basic-level categories (e.g., *chair*) at the intermediate level, and subordinate categories (e.g., *easy chair*) at the bottom.

We sometimes use superordinate categories (e.g., "*That furniture is expensive*") or subordinate categories (e.g., "*I love my new iPhone*"). However, we generally have a strong preference for using basic-level categories. Rosch et al. (1976) asked participants to name pictured objects. Basic-level categories were used 1,595 times during the course of the experiment, subordinate names 14 times, and superordinate names only once.

Why do we make such extensive use of basic-level categories? Most of the time, the basic level provides the best balance between informativeness and distinctiveness. Informativeness is lacking at the superordinate level (e.g., simply knowing an object is an item of furniture tells you little). Distinctiveness is lacking at the lowest level (e.g., most types of chairs possess very similar attributes or features).

Rigoli, Pezzulo, Dolan, and Friston (2017) developed the above ideas. They argued that, "Categorization requires computations that have benefits in terms of goal achievement [e.g., selecting an appropriate action] but also costs (e.g., metabolic, opportunity costs, etc.) that need to be balanced against the benefits" (p. 2). Categorizing objects at the basic level generally permits selecting the most appropriate action while incurring relatively modest costs.

Findings

Evidence consistent with the notion that basic-level concepts have advantages over subordinate ones was reported by Bauer and Just (2017). Many more brain regions were activated during the processing of basic-level concepts than subordinate ones. More specifically, brain areas associated with sensori-motor and language processing were activated with basic-level concepts whereas processing predominantly involved only perceptual areas with subordinate concepts.

In spite of what has been said so far, some individuals do *not* prefer to use basic-level categories. Consider a professional botanist describing the plants in their garden. We would expect them to distinguish among the various plants (i.e., to use subordinate categories) rather than simply describing them all as plants!

The prediction contained in the previous paragraph was confirmed by Tanaka and Taylor (1991) in a study of birdwatchers and dog experts naming birds and dogs. Both groups used subordinate names in their expert domain much more often than their novice domain. Bird experts used subordinate names 74% of the time with birds, dog experts used subordinate names 40% of the

time with dogs, and both groups used subordinate names only 24% of the time in their novice domain.

We sometimes use subordinate categories when they are familiar. Anaki and Bentin (2009) presented participants with photographs of familiar towers (e.g., *Eiffel Tower*; *Learning Tower of Pisa*). Categorization occurred faster at the subordinate level than at the basic level (i.e., *tower*). For example, most participants found it easier to decide the Eiffel tower was the Eiffel tower than that it was a tower. Thus, individual familiarity with objects at the subordinate level can produce very fast categorization.

Even though individuals generally *prefer* to use basic-level categories, that does not necessarily mean they categorize *fastest* at that level. Prass, Grimsen, König, and Fahle (2013) presented photographs of objects very briefly. Observers categorized these photographs at the superordinate level (*animal or vehicle?*), the basic level (e.g., *cat or dog?*), or the subordinate level (e.g., *Siamese or Persian cat?*). Performance was best in terms of both accuracy and speed at the superordinate level (see Figure 7.5).

Why does categorization often occur faster at the superordinate level than the basic level? One explanation is that less information needs to be processed at the superordinate level. For example, it seems probable that less information is required to detect human faces among animal faces (superordinate level) than to decide that a face is of a target person (basic level). As predicted, Besson et al. (2017) found categorization was faster in the former case.

More direct evidence that less information is required at the superordinate level than at the basic level was reported by Rogers and Patterson (2007). They studied patients with semantic dementia (a condition involving loss of concept knowledge; discussed earlier in the chapter). Patients with mild semantic dementia had comparably accurate categorization at the basic and superordinate levels. Of more theoretical importance, patients with severe semantic dementia performed better at the superordinate than the basic level because it required less information processing.

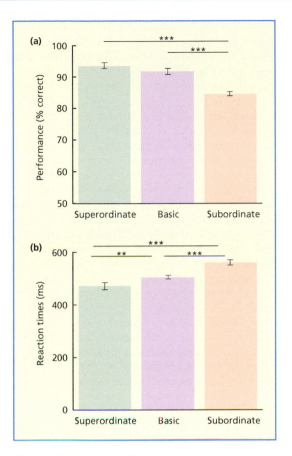

Figure 7.5 Accuracy of object categorization ([a] left-hand side) and speed of categorization ([b] right-hand side) at the superordinate, basic. and subordinate levels. From Prass et al. (2013).

USING CONCEPTS

As we have seen, numerous concepts are represented in semantic memory. What do these representations look like? This question is associated with considerable theoretical controversy (Mahon & Hickok, 2016). We start by considering the "traditional" viewpoint, according to which concept representations have the following characteristics:

1   They are *abstract* in nature and are thus detached from input (sensory) and output (motor) processes.
2   They are *stable* in that any given individual uses the same representation of a concept on different occasions.

3   Different people generally have fairly similar representations of any given concept.

At the risk of oversimplification, traditional theories assume that concept representations "have the flavor of detached encyclopedia descriptions in a database of categorical knowledge about the world" (Barsalou, 2012, p. 247). This approach forms part of what Barsalou (2016) described as the *sandwich model*: cognition (including concept processing) is "sandwiched" between perception and action but is regarded as being almost totally separate from them. This model seems problematical because it is unclear how we could use such concept representations to perceive the visual world or decide what actions are appropriate in a given situation.

Situated simulation theory

Barsalou (2012) argued in his situated simulation theory that *all* the theoretical assumptions of the traditional approach discussed above are incorrect. He argued we rarely process concepts in *isolation*. Instead, we process them in various settings with that processing being influenced by the current context or setting. More generally, our concept processing is influenced by our current goals and the major features of the situation.

Barsalou (2009) illustrated the limitations with many previous theories by considering the concept of a *bicycle*. Traditionally, it was assumed a fairly complete abstract representation of the concept would be activated in all situations. This representation would resemble the Chambers Dictionary definition: "vehicle with two wheels one directly in front of the other, driven by pedals."

According to Barsalou (2009), those aspects of the bicycle concept activated depend on your current *goals*. For example, information about the tires will be activated if you need to repair your bicycle, whereas the height of the saddle will be activated if you want to ride it.

In sum, Barsalou's situated simulation theory makes various predictions. Of particular importance, it predicts that conceptual processing involves extensive use of the perceptual system and the motor or action system.

Finally, Barsalou's theoretical approach differs substantially from the traditional approach with respect to the conduct of experimentation on concepts. Most concept research has involved presenting words referring to concepts in isolation (in the absence of relevant context). This is appropriate if concepts are detached from perception and action. In contrast, it follows from Barsalou's situated simulation theory that information acquired from studying concepts in isolation will often be limited and misleading (Barsalou, Dutriaux, & Scheepers, 2018, p. 1).

Findings

Evidence that conceptual processing can involve the perceptual system was reported by Wu and Barsalou (2009). Participants wrote down as many properties as possible for nouns or noun phrases. Those given the word *lawn* tended to focus on *external properties* (e.g., *plant*; *blades*) whereas those given *rolled-up lawn* focused more on *internal properties* (e.g., *dirt*; *soil*). The same pattern was found with other nouns. For example, *watermelon* generated external properties such as *rind* and *green* whereas *half watermelon* generated internal properties such as *pips* and *red*.

What do the above findings mean? Concept processing can have a perceptual or imaginal quality about it. Object qualities not visible if you were actually looking at the object itself are harder to think of than those that would be visible.

According to situated simulation theory, concept processing is influenced by the context or setting. Wu and Barsalou (2009) obtained support for that assumption. Participants in their study often wrote down properties referring to the background situation rather than the object itself. Indeed, between 25% and 50% of the total properties produced related to the background situation (e.g., properties of *lawn* can include *picnic* or *you play on it*).

So far we have focused on concrete concepts (objects we can see or hear). It is unsurprising such concepts should have perceptual properties. However, it is less clear that perceptual properties are relevant with abstract concepts (e.g., *truth*; *invention*). However, Barsalou et al. (2018) argued that situated simulation theory is equally applicable to abstract concepts because they are typically processed with respect to a relatively concrete context. Barsalou and Wiemer-Hastings (2005) asked participants to indicate the characteristic properties of abstract concepts. Many of these properties referred to concrete settings or events associated with the concept (e.g., scientists working in a laboratory for *invention*).

Neuroimaging has been used to identify the extent to which perceptual processing is involved in the processing of abstract concepts. Wang, Conder, Blitzer, and Shinkareva (2010) found in a meta-analytic review of numerous studies that brain areas associated with perceptual processing were much more likely to be activated when concrete (rather than abstract) concepts were processed. More recently, Borghi et al. (2017) also reviewed neuroimaging studies and concluded that abstract-concept processing sometimes involves perceptual processing.

There is an important limitation with most neuroimaging research on the processing of concrete and abstract concepts. Such research provides only correlational evidence (i.e., the brain areas associated with processing different kinds of concepts) and so fails to demonstrate that the brain areas activated are causally or necessarily involved in processing (Mkrtychian et al., 2019).

Hauk, Johnsrude, and Pulvermüller (2004) tested the notion that the motor system is often involved during access to concept information. When participants read words such as *lick*, *pick*, and *kick*, these verbs activated parts of the motor strip overlapping with areas activated when people make the relevant tongue, finger, and foot movements. Note that these findings do *not* show the motor system is *necessary* or *required* for concept processing—perhaps activation in areas within the motor strip occurs only *after* concept activation.

Miller, Brookie, Wales, Kaup, and Wallace (2018) obtained suggestive evidence that the motor system is often involved when we access concept information. Participants made hand or foot responses after reading hand-associated words (e.g., *knead*; *wipe*) or foot-associated words (e.g., *kick*; *sprint*). Responses were faster when the word was compatible with the limb making the response (e.g., hand response to a hand-associated word) than when word and limb were incompatible. These findings apparently support Barsalou's approach, according to which, "The understanding of action verbs requires activation of the motor areas used to carry out the named action" (Miller et al., 2018, p. 335).

Miller et al. (2018) tested the above prediction. They discovered that presentation of hand- and foot-associated words was *not* followed rapidly by limb-relevant brain activity. How can we explain the overall pattern of findings? In essence, the reaction-time findings discussed above were based on processing verb meanings and did *not* directly involve motor processing.

Why were the findings of Hauk et al. (2004) and Miller et al. (2018) so different? Miller et al. used a speeded task that did not allow sufficient time for motor imagery to occur within relevant brain areas. In contrast, the nonspeeded task used by Hauk et al. did allow such imagery to be generated.

According to situated simulation theory, patients with severe damage to sensori-motor brain systems should have impaired processing of action-related words (e.g., names of tools). In a review, Vannuscorps, Dricot, and Pillon (2016) found that patients with damage limited to sensori-motor areas generally had no deficit in conceptual processing of actions or objects that can be manipulated. For example, consider patient, JR, who had brain damage primarily affecting the action-production system. His naming performance with action-related concepts (e.g., *hammer*; *shovel*) was comparable to healthy controls.

Evaluation

There is much support for the theoretical assumption that conceptual processing in everyday life often involves the perceptual and motor systems. This assumption helps to explain why concept processing varies across situations depending on the individual's goals. In other words, the precise way we process a concept depends on the situation and the perceptual and motor processes engaged by the current task. In essence, Barsalou's approach explains much of the *flexibility* that characterizes conceptual processing.

What are the main limitations of Barsalou's theoretical approach? First, he exaggerates the extent to which concept processing *varies* across time and across situations or contexts. The traditional view that concepts possess a stable, abstract core has *not* been disproved by Barsalou (Borghesani & Piazza, 2017). As we will see below, both theoretical approaches are partially correct—concepts have a stable core *and* concept processing is context-dependent.

Second, much of our concept knowledge does not consist simply of perceptual and motor features. Borghesani and Piazza (2017, p. 8) give the following example: "*Tomatoes are native to South and Central America.*"

Third, we can recognize the similarities between concepts not sharing perceptual or motor features. For example, we categorize *watermelon* and *blackberry* as fruit even though they are very different visually and we do not eat them using the same (or similar) motor actions.

Fourth, the finding that concept processing often includes perceptual and/or motor features does *not* mean it is generally *necessary* to use perceptual and/or motor processes to understand concepts. Alternatively, perceptual and motor processes may not be necessary and may even occur *after* concept meaning has been accessed (Mahon & Hickok, 2016). The finding that some patients with damage to their motor system can nevertheless understand action-related words (Vannuscorps et al., 2016) is more consistent with the latter viewpoint as are the findings of Miller et al. (2018).

CONCEPTS AND THE BRAIN

Perhaps the most natural assumption is that everything we know about any given object or concept is stored at a *single* location within the brain. For example, I know several facts about my cat Lulu—she has gray fur, a small head, is very friendly, chases birds, has a hearty appetite, likes to play, purrs loudly, and so on. We might imagine all this

Different kinds of information about a given object are stored in different brain locations. For example, visual information about Lulu the cat may be stored in a different place from auditory information (e.g., her loud purr) and from information about what she does (e.g., likes to play).

information is stored very close together in the brain—perhaps in a "Lulu node"?

In fact, semantic memories are stored in more complex ways. As we will see, different kinds of information about an object are stored in different brain locations. For example, *visual* information about Lulu is probably stored in a different place from *auditory* information (e.g., her loud purr) and from information about what she does (e.g., likes to play). This is a feature-based approach and is consistent with Barsalou's emphasis on the role of perceptual and motor features in concept use.

Much research has involved studying brain-damaged patients. It is assumed that studying such patients will increase our understanding of the organization of semantic memory. Suppose we assume that different features of concepts are stored in different brain regions. It follows that we would expect to find category-specific deficits (problems with specific categories of objects). There is convincing evidence for the existence of various category-specific deficits (Chen, Lambon Ralph, & Rogers, 2017). For example, consider patients with herpes simplex encephalitis involving damage to the antero-medial temporal lobes. These patients have a category-specific deficit for biological entities (i.e., *animals*) (Gainotti, 2018).

Note that it is harder than you might imagine to interpret the findings from patients exhibiting category-specific deficits. For example, consider patients whose performance is much worse at identifying pictures of living than nonliving things. Living things have greater contour overlap than nonliving things, they are more complex structurally, and they activate less motor information (Marques, Raposo, & Almeida, 2013). It is difficult to disentangle the relative importance of these factors.

KEY TERM

Category-specific deficits: Disorders caused by brain damage in which semantic memory is disrupted for certain semantic categories (e.g., living things).

Hub-and-spoke model

We saw earlier that concept processing often (but not always) involves the perceptual and motor systems. However, there are several reasons for assuming there is more than that to concept processing. First, we would not have *coherent* concepts if our processing of any given concept varied considerably across situations. Second, we can detect similarities in concepts that are very different perceptually. For example we know *scallops* and *prawns* are both *shellfish* even though they differ in shape, color, and form of movement (Patterson, Nestor, & Rogers, 2007).

Patterson et al. (2007) put forward a hub-and-spoke model (developed by Lambon Ralph, Jefferies, Patterson, and Rogers, 2017) combining several ideas discussed earlier. You can see key features of this model in Figure 7.6. The spokes in the model consist of several modality-specific brain areas where sensory and motor processing occur. The six spokes shown in Figure 7.6 relate to visual features, verbal descriptors, olfaction (smell), sounds, praxis (motor information), and somatosensory information (sensations from the skin and internal organs).

Each concept also has a "hub"—a general, modality-independent unified conceptual representation that provides an efficient way of integrating our knowledge of any given concept. It is assumed within the theory that hubs are located within the anterior temporal lobes.

Findings

We saw earlier in the chapter that research on patients with semantic dementia indicates that the anterior lobes of the brain are of vital importance with respect to the hubs of the hub-and-spoke model. Supporting evidence was reported by Binder, Desai, Graves, and Conant (2009) in a meta-analysis (see Glossary) of 120 neuroimaging studies where participants performed tasks involving semantic memory. The anterior temporal lobes were consistently activated.

Murphy et al. (2017) found that the involvement of the anterior temporal lobes in concept processing was more complex than implied above. More specifically, ventral (bottom) regions of the anterior temporal lobes responded to meaning and acted as a hub. In contrast, anterior regions were responsive to differences in input modality (visual vs. auditory) and thus were *not* "hub-like."

Mayberry, Sage, and Lambon Ralph (2011) gave participants with semantic

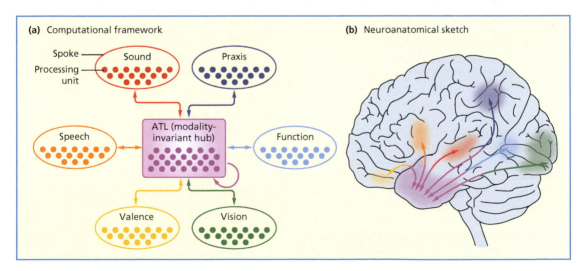

Figure 7.6 The hub-and-spoke model. (a) the hub within the anterior temporal lobe (ATL) has bi-directional connections to the spokes (praxis refers to object manipulability; it is action-related). (b) the locations of the hub and spokes are shown (same colour coding as in [a]). From Lambon Ralph, Jefferies, Patterson, K., & Rogers (2017). Copyright © 2016, Springer Nature.

dementia the task of deciding whether objects were (or were not) members of a given category. They argued that semantic dementia involves a progressive loss of core or "hub" information causing a blurring of the boundary separating category members (e.g., *birds*) from nonmembers (e.g., *non-birds*). Mayberry et al. predicted that patients with semantic dementia would have particular problems in making accurate predictions with two kinds of stimuli: (1) atypical category members (e.g., *emu* is an atypical bird); and (2) noncategory members resembling category members (e.g., *butterfly* is like a bird). Both predictions were supported.

We turn now to the "spokes" of the hub-and-spoke model. According to the model, we would expect some brain-damaged patients to have damage localized to a brain area involved in only one or two of the spokes. Such individuals should exhibit category-specific deficits (discussed above).

There is considerable evidence suggesting the existence of such deficits. Cree and McRae (2003) identified seven different patterns of category-specific deficits following brain damage. Patients exhibiting each pattern differed in the concept features or properties most impaired. Across the seven categories, the most impaired properties included the following: color; taste; smell; visual motion; and function (i.e., object uses). These findings indicate that concepts vary considerably in terms of those properties of most importance. Note that (as discussed earlier), it is often hard to interpret category-specific deficits.

As mentioned earlier, it is hard to interpret findings involving category-specific deficits. An alternative approach is to apply transcranial direct current stimulation (tDCS) (a weak electric current to various brain areas). Anodal tDCS is positive stimulation increasing neuronal excitability in the area stimulated. If a given brain area is involved in

concept processing, we would expect anodal tDCS to that area to enhance performance.

Consider a study by Ishibashi, Mima, Fukuyama, and Pobric (2018). They applied anodal tDCS to the inferior parietal lobule and the anterior temporal lobe while participants performed tasks requiring rapid access to semantic information concerning tool function (e.g., scissors are used for cutting) or tool manipulation (e.g., pliers are gripped by the handles). As predicted, anodal tDCS applied to the anterior temporal lobe facilitated performance on both tasks because this brain area contains much general object knowledge (see Figure 7.7). The effects of anodal tDCS applied to the inferior parietal lobule were limited to the manipulation task because this area processes action-related information.

Evaluation

The hub-and-spoke model provides a more comprehensive account of semantic memory than previous theoretical approaches. There is considerable support for the notion that concepts are represented in semantic memory by a combination of abstract core (hub) and modality-specific information (spokes). There has been good progress in identifying the brain areas associated with hubs and the various types of spokes.

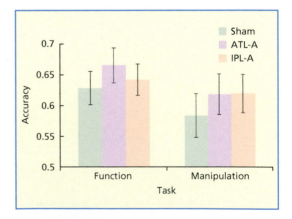

Figure 7.7 Performance accuracy on tool function and tool manipulation tasks with anodal transcranial direct current stimulation to the anterior temporal lobe (ATL-A) or to the inferior parietal lobule (IPL-A) and in a control condition (Sham). From Ishibashi et al., 2018.

What are the model's main limitations? First, the role of the anterior temporal lobes in concept processing is more complex than assumed theoretically (e.g., Murphy et al., 2017). Second, more remains to be discovered about the information contained within concept hubs. For example, is more information stored in the hubs of very familiar concepts than less familiar ones? Third, how is modality-specific "spoke" information *integrated* with modality-independent "hub" information? Fourth, there is still no consensus concerning the number and nature of concept "spokes."

Beyond the hub-and-spoke model

The original hub-and-spoke model focused on the semantic representations of concepts. However, if we are to use our semantic knowledge effectively, we need to *control* our processing to emphasize those aspects of our semantic knowledge of most current relevance in the present context. For example, consider the *piano* concept. As Hoffman, McClelland, and Lambon Ralph (2018) pointed out, if we want to play a piano, we need to focus on its keys and pedals. In contrast, if we want to move a piano, this information is irrelevant and our focus should be on features of a piano such as its weight and whether or not it has wheels.

The notion that current context strongly influences which aspects of any given concept are relevant has led theorists (Lambon Ralph et al., 2017) to develop the hub-and-spoke model. Hoffman et al. (2018) produced a detailed model combining a hub-and-spoke architecture with a mechanism to take account of the current context that accurately predicted concept processing in brain-damaged and healthy individuals.

SCHEMAS

Our discussion so far may have created the false impression that nearly all the information in semantic memory is in the form of simple concepts. In fact, however, much of the knowledge we have stored in semantic memory consists of larger structures of information.

What do these larger knowledge structures look like? Frederic Bartlett (1932) provided an extremely influential answer to that question. He argued for the importance of schemas, which are "superordinate knowledge structures that reflect abstracted commonalities across multiple experiences" (Gilboa & Marlatte, 2017, p. 618). Bartlett's key insight was that what we remember (including our errors when remembering) is strongly affected by our schematic knowledge.

Ghosh and Gilboa (2014) provided a more detailed definition of schemas. They argued schemas possess four necessary and sufficient features:

1 *Associative structure*: schemas consist of interconnected units.
2 *Basis in multiple episodes*: schemas consist of integrated information based on several similar events.
3 *Lack of unit detail*: this follows from the variability of events from which any given schema is formed.
4 *Adaptability*: schemas change and adapt as they are updated in the light of new information.

There are various kinds of schemas. Scripts contain information about sequences of events. For example, Bower, Black, and Turner (1979) asked people to list actions typically occurring during a restaurant meal. At least 73% mentioned the following: *being given a menu*; *ordering*; *eating*; and *paying the bill*. Frames are knowledge structures referring to some aspect of the world (e.g., *building*) containing fixed structural information (e.g., *has floors*; *has walls*) and slots for variable information (e.g., *materials from which the building is constructed*).

> ### KEY TERM
>
> **Scripts:** A form of schema containing information about a sequence of events (e.g., those occurring during a typical restaurant meal).
>
> **Frames:** A type of schema in which information about objects and their properties is stored.

Schemas vs. concepts

We have assumed there is an important distinction between two major types of information in semantic memory: (1) abstract concepts generally corresponding to individual words; and (2) broader and more flexible organizational structures based on schemas (e.g., scripts). What predictions can we make based on that assumption?

1   We would expect different brain areas to be activated during tasks involving concepts and schemas in healthy individuals.
2   We would expect to find some brain-damaged patients who have greater problems accessing concept-based information than schema-based information, and other patients exhibiting the opposite pattern. If we obtained these contrasting patterns, this would form what is known as a *double dissociation*; this would provide reasonable evidence that concept and schema processing involve somewhat different mechanisms.

Below we consider evidence relating to these predictions.

As we saw earlier, several areas including the anterior temporal lobes are activated during concept processing (Binder et al., 2009; Murphy et al., 2017). Several brain areas are also involved in schema processing. However, the ventromedial prefrontal cortex is of particular importance. Gilboa and Marlatte (2017) reviewed 12 neuroimaging studies where participants engaged in schema processing. Large areas within the ventromedial prefrontal cortex were consistently activated as well as other areas (see Figure 7.8). Overall, the findings indicate some separation of brain areas involved in concept and schema processing but there is some overlap of brain areas (e.g., anterior temporal lobe).

We turn now to research on brain-damaged patients. As we saw earlier, patients with semantic dementia (a condition involving damage to the anterior temporal lobe) have severe problems in accessing the meanings of words and concepts but have good executive functioning in the early stages of deterioration.

We would predict that patients in the early stages of semantic dementia should retain reasonable ability to use schema-relevant information. Supporting evidence was reported by Bier et al. (2013). They studied script memory in three such patients who were asked what they would do if they had unknowingly invited two guests to lunch. The required script actions included dressing to go outdoors, going to the grocery store, shopping for food, preparing the meal, having the meal, and clearing up afterwards. One patient described all these script actions

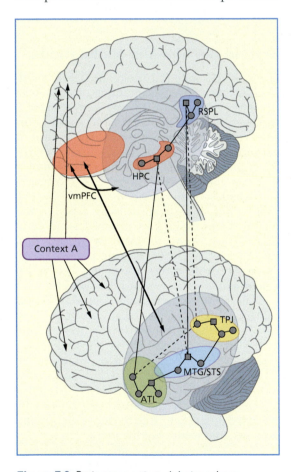

Figure 7.8 Brain areas activated during schema processing (RSPL = retrospenial cortex; HPC = hippocampal cortex; TPJ = temporo-parietal junction; MTG = middle temporal gyrus; STS = superior temporal sulcus; ATL = anterior temporal lobe; activation in these areas is coordinated by the vmPFC = ventromedial prefrontal cortex. From Gilboa & Marlatte, 2017. With permission from Elsevier.

accurately despite having severe problems with accessing concept information from semantic memory. The other patients needed assistance but remembered script actions relating to dressing and shopping.

Which brain-damaged patients have greater problems with accessing script-related information than concept meanings? Scripts typically have a goal-directed quality (e.g., using a script to achieve the goal of enjoying a restaurant meal). Since the prefrontal cortex is of major importance in goal-directed activity, we might expect patients with prefrontal damage to have particular problems with script memory. More specifically, as we saw earlier, the ventromedial prefrontal cortex is generally activated during schema processing and so damage to that area should impair such processing.

Cosentino, Chute, Libon, Moore, and Grossman (2006) studied patients with fronto-temporal dementia (involving damage to the prefrontal cortex as well as the temporal lobes). These patients had attentional deficits and poor executive functioning as well as impaired semantic memory. The fronto-temporal patients (as well as those with semantic dementia and healthy controls) were presented with various scripts. Some scripts contained sequencing or script errors (e.g., dropping fish in a bucket *before* casting the fishing line). Other scripts contained semantic or meaning errors (e.g., placing a flower on a hook in a story about fishing).

What did Cosentino et al. (2006) find? Patients with semantic dementia and healthy controls both detected as many sequencing errors as semantic ones. In contrast, the temporo-frontal patients with poor executive functioning failed to detect almost twice as many sequencing errors as semantic ones. Thus, these patients had relatively intact semantic knowledge of concepts combined with fairly severe impairment of script-based knowledge relating to sequencing.

Ghosh, Moscovitch, Colella, and Gilboa (2014) studied patients with damage to the ventromedial prefrontal cortex. They were given a schema (e.g., "*going to bed at night*") and instructed to decide rapidly whether each of a series of words was closely related to that schema. These patients performed more

slowly and less accurately than healthy controls indicating they had significant problems with schema-related processing.

Zahn et al. (2017) studied patients with fronto-temporal dementia with damage to parts of the ventromedial prefrontal cortex and the anterior temporal lobe. They assessed patients' knowledge of social concepts (e.g., *adventurous*) and script knowledge (e.g., the likely consequences of ignoring their employer's requests). Patients with greater damage to fronto-polar cortex than the anterior temporal lobe showed relatively poorer script knowledge than knowledge of social concepts. In contrast, patients with the opposite pattern of brain damage had relatively poorer knowledge of social concepts.

In sum, semantic memory for concepts centers on the anterior temporal lobe. Patients with semantic dementia have damage to this area causing severely impaired concept memory. In contrast, semantic memory for scripts or schemas involves the prefrontal cortex (especially ventromedial prefrontal cortex). However, when we use our script knowledge (e.g., preparing a meal), it is important to access relevant concept knowledge (e.g., knowledge about food ingredients). As a consequence, semantic dementia patients whose primary impairment is to concept knowledge also have great difficulties in accessing and using script knowledge.

How useful is schematic knowledge?

We have seen that schematic knowledge in the form of scripts is useful because it allows us to form realistic *expectations* about the immediate future. Schemas (including scripts) make the world more predictable than would otherwise be the case because our expectations are generally confirmed. If our script-based expectations are disconfirmed, we usually take action. For example, if no menu is produced in a restaurant, we try to catch the eye of the waiter or waitress.

There are other reasons why schematic knowledge is useful. First, schemas are important in reading and listening because they allow us to fill in the gaps in what we are reading or listening to and so enhance our understanding. More specifically, they enable us to draw *inferences* as we read or listen (see Box 7.2).

Second, schemas help to prevent cognitive overload. Consider **stereotypes** (schemas

Box 7.2 When it is difficult to understand a text (Bransford & Johnson, 1972)

Bransford and Johnson (1972) argued that people would not understand a passage properly if it were written so it was hard to work out the underlying schema or theme. They used a passage, the first part of which is given below. Put yourself in the position of participants in their study, and see whether you can understand it.

The procedure is quite simple. First, you arrange items into different groups. Of course one pile may be sufficient depending on how much there is to do. If you have to go somewhere else due to lack of facilities that is the next step; otherwise, you are pretty well set. It is important not to overdo things. That is, it is better to do too few things at once than too many. In the short run this may not seem important but complications can easily arise....
(Bransford & Johnson, 1972, p. 722)

Did you work out what the passage was all about? Participants reading the passage in the absence of a title rated it as incomprehensible and recalled an average of only 2.8 different ideas ("idea units") from it. In contrast, those supplied beforehand with the title "Washing clothes" found it easy to understand and recalled 5.8 idea units on average. Relevant schematic knowledge (i.e., the title providing the theme of the passage) had a beneficial effect on recall because it helped comprehension of the passage rather than because the title acted as a useful retrieval cue. We know this because participants receiving the title *after* hearing the passage but *before* recall recalled only 2.6 idea units on average.

involving simplified generalizations about various groups). When meeting someone for the first time, we often use stereotypical information (e.g., about their sex, age, and ethnicity) to help form an impression of that person. It is simpler and less demanding (but potentially very misleading) to use such information rather than engage in detailed cognitive processing of his/her behavior (Macrae & Bodenhausen, 2000).

Potential disadvantages of relying on stereotypical information were shown by Reynolds, Garnham, and Oakhill (2006). Read the following passage they used in their study and then answer the question:

A man and his son were away for a trip. They were driving along the highway when they had a terrible accident. The man was killed outright but his son was alive, although badly injured. The son was rushed to the hospital and was to have an emergency operation. On entering the operating theater, the surgeon looked at the boy, and said, "I can't do this operation. This is my son."

How can this be?

If you found the problem difficult, you are in good company. We tend to have a stereotypical view that surgeons are men. However, some surgeons are female and the surgeon in the passage above was the boy's mother. Thus, schemas in the form of stereotypical information can interfere with problem solving.

Third, schematic information can assist us when we are trying to recognize an object.

For example, Auckland, Cave, and Donnelly (2007) presented observers briefly with a target object (e.g., playing cards) surrounded by four context objects. Sometimes the context objects were semantically related to the target object (e.g., dice; chess pieces;

plastic chips; dominoes) and so provided information relevant to the game schema. The target was recognized more often in this condition than when the context objects were semantically unrelated. Lupyan (2017) reviewed research showing how top-down processes triggered by contextual or schematic information facilitate object recognition.

Fourth, as mentioned earlier, Ghosh and Gilboa (2014) identified adaptability as an important aspect of schemas. As Richter, Bays, Jeyarathnarajah, and Simons (2019) pointed out, adaptability is very useful. It means we can adapt to changing environmental conditions by flexibly making changes to incorporate additional information to a pre-existing schema structure or by modifying the existing structure itself. Richter et al. showed experimentally how schemas are modified and updated when the knowledge within them no longer reflects current environmental conditions.

Errors and distortions

So far we have emphasized the value of schematic knowledge—it makes the world a more predictable place, enhances our understanding of what we read and other people say, and it facilitates visual perception of the world around us. However, Bartlett (1932) argued that schematic knowledge can cause significant memory costs. He argued our memory for stories is affected not only by the presented story itself but also by the participant's store of relevant schematic knowledge.

Bartlett tested the above notions by presenting people with stories producing a *conflict* between what was presented and their prior knowledge. Suppose people read a story taken from a different culture. Their prior knowledge might produce distortions in the remembered version of the story, making it more conventional and acceptable from their own cultural background.

Bartlett (1932) carried out several studies in which English students read and recalled stories taken from the North American Indian culture. One such story was *The War of the Ghosts* (reproduced on p. 165). As predicted, participants' schematic knowledge

in the form of cultural expectations led to numerous recall errors conforming to that knowledge. Bartlett used the term rationalization for this type of error.

According to Bartlett (1932), memory for the precise information presented is forgotten over time whereas memory for the underlying schemas is not. Thus, there should be more rationalization errors (which depend on schematic knowledge) at longer retention intervals.

In the interests of historical accuracy, it should be noted that Bartlett's (1932) approach was less original than typically assumed (Davis, 2018). Henderson (1903) had previously used an experimental paradigm very similar to Bartlett's, and had anticipated many of Bartlett's theoretical ideas.

Findings

Numerous experimental studies have supported Bartlett's general approach (see Chapter 6 for a detailed account). However, it is arguable that most of these studies lack ecological validity (applicability to everyday life). For example, many studies involved participants reading artificially constructed texts knowing their memory for these texts would be assessed. In contrast, Brewer and Treyens (1981) argued that most information we remember during our everyday lives is acquired incidentally rather than deliberately.

In their own research, Brewer and Treyens (1981) used a naturalistic learning situation. Participants spent about 35 seconds in a room designed to look like a graduate student's office (see photograph). The room contained a mixture of schema-consistent objects you would expect to find in a graduate student's office (e.g., *desk, calendar,*

KEY TERM

Rationalization: A term introduced by Bartlett to refer to the tendency in story recall to produce errors conforming to the rememberer's cultural expectations.

Ecological validity: The extent to which research findings (especially laboratory ones) can be generalized to everyday life.

The "graduate student's" room used by Brewer and Treyens (1981) in their experiment.

eraser, *pencils*) and schema-inconsistent objects (e.g., *skull*; *toy top*). Some schema-consistent objects (e.g., books) were omitted. Finally, participants received unexpected recall and recognition tests.

What did Brewer and Treyens (1981) find? First, objects not present in the room but "recognized" with high confidence were nearly always schema consistent (e.g., *books*; *filing cabinet*). This is clear evidence of schemas leading to memory errors. Second, participants recalled more schema-consistent than schema-inconsistent objects for objects that were present *and* those that were not present. Thus, schematic knowledge had positive and negative effects on memory.

Webb, Turney, and Dennis (2016) presented participants with scenes (e.g., *bathroom*) containing schema-consistent objects (e.g., *shampoo bottles*; *shower head*) and schema-inconsistent objects (e.g., *spray bottle*; *mirror*). On the subsequent recognition-memory test, these objects were presented as well as schema-consistent objects not shown in the scene (e.g., *toilet paper*; *sink*). Webb et al. used neuroimaging to assess brain activation during retrieval of schematic and nonschematic objects as well

as false memories for schema-consistent objects.

What did Webb et al. (2016) find? First, successful retrieval of schema-inconsistent objects compared to schema-consistent objects involved greater use of brain areas (e.g., pre-frontal cortex) associated with effortful cognitive control. Thus, schematic knowledge can facilitate the retrieval of schema-consistent information, thus reducing the need for cognitive control.

Second, Webb et al. (2016) compared brain areas associated with false memory for nonpresented but schema-consistent objects with accurate memory for schema-consistent objects. Brain areas (e.g., lateral temporal regions) associated with retrieval of schematic gist were more activated during false memory than accurate memory. As Webb et al. concluded, "Retrieval of schematic information ... was a critical factor in mediating illusory memories" (p. 71).

The research discussed so far suggests our reliance on schematic information is costly in terms of memory errors and distortions. Steyvers and Hemmer (2012) argued that such research exaggerates the fallibility of human memory. Consider Brewer and Treyens' (1981) study. Guessing that a graduate student's office contains books is a very reasonable assumption in the real world but led to memory errors in their manipulated environment. According to Steyvers and Hemmer, people should be less likely to "recall" nonpresented objects in naturalistic environments.

Steyvers and Hemmer (2012) tested the above prediction in various experiments using five scene types (*kitchen*; *office*; *dining room*; *hotel room*; *urban scene*). Initially, participants named objects they would expect to see in each scene (e.g., a television set in a hotel scene) to assess the strength of each object's schema relevance. As predicted, the false recall rate was much lower for objects having high schema relevance than those having low schema relevance (9% vs. 18%, respectively). This happened in part because participants' guesses were more likely to be correct with high-schema-relevance objects.

In another experiment, Steyvers and Hemmer (2012) used five photographs representing each of the above five scene types. Objects' schema relevance was assessed by a consistency score based on the number of photographs of a given scene type in which they appeared. Participants saw photographs of the various scenes and then recalled the objects contained in them. Recall was easily the highest for objects in the most schema-consistent category (see Figure 7.9), showing the beneficial effects of schematic knowledge on long-term memory.

The other notable feature of Figure 7.9 is that recall was better for extremely schema-inconsistent objects (consistency score = 1) than those slightly less schema-inconsistent (consistency score = 2). This an example of the von Restorff effect (see Chapter 17), in which distinctive stimuli attract attention and are well remembered. Loftus and Mackworth (1978) found that schema-inconsistent objects (e.g., an *octopus* in a farm scene) were were fixated earlier, more often, and for longer durations than expected objects.

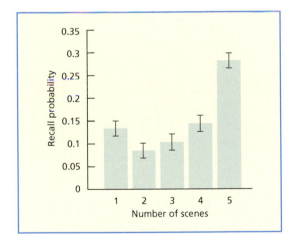

Figure 7.9 In Steyvers and Hemmer's (2012) experiment recall was highest for objects in the most schema-consistent category. Reprinted from Steyvers and Hemmer (2012), Copyright © 2012, with permission from Elsevier.

Evaluation

Schemas theories have proved generally successful. There is compelling evidence that learning and memory often involve top-down processes triggered by schematic knowledge. More generally, schemas allow us to form expectations that are often confirmed subsequently. Schemas are adaptable and can be altered in response to changing environmental conditions. Schemas often enhance long-term memory for both schema-consistent and schema-inconsistent information (Greve, Cooper, Tibon, & Henson, 2019; Steyvers & Hemmer, 2012) with the latter occurring because schema-inconsistent information conflicts with learners' expectations and leads to more thorough encoding. However, use of schematic knowledge can lead to various memory distortions and errors.

What are the limitations of schema theories? First, they are typically vague with their precise scope and nature remaining unclear. In addition, much remains to be discovered about how episodic and semantic memory processes interact.

Second, our memory representations are often more complex than implied by schema theories. For example, we do not just have a basic restaurant script. We also know you do not sit down before ordering your food at fast-food restaurants, expensive restaurants often have wine waiters, you need to book at some restaurants but not others, and so on. Most schema-based theories have not focused on these complexities.

Third, most schema theories exaggerate the number of schema-driven memory errors occurring in everyday life. As Steyvers and Hemmer (2012, p. 140) argued, "In a naturalistic environment, the prior knowledge of the occurrence of objects in a given scene type can lead to effective guesses ... Such guessing with prior [schematic] knowledge can result in high accuracy and a low number of intrusions."

SUMMARY

- There is an important distinction between semantic and episodic memory: the latter involves more conscious recollection of the past and is more "personal."
- The distinction between semantic and episodic memory is supported by research on brain-damaged patients: amnesic patients typically have greater problems with episodic than semantic memory whereas patients with semantic dementia show the opposite pattern.
- In spite of the differences between semantic and episodic memory, many long-term memories combine episodic and semantic information. In addition, memories that are initially episodic can become transformed into semantic memories over time: semanticization.
- According to Collins and Quillian's (1969) hierarchical network model, concepts are represented by nodes within hierarchical networks; concept properties or features are stored as far up the hierarchy as possible.
- The hierarchical network theory is based on the erroneous assumption that concepts are stored in semantic memory much more neatly than is actually the case. The theory also fails to acknowledge that many concepts are fuzzy or imprecise.
- According to Collins and Loftus's (1975) spreading-activation theory, semantic memory is organized by semantic distance. Activation of any given concept causes activation to spread to all other related concepts.
- The spreading-activation theory assumes all information about a given concept is stored at a single node, which is a substantial oversimplification.
- Many concepts within semantic memory are organized into hierarches consisting of superordinate, basic, and subordinate levels.
- Individuals generally prefer the basic level because it combines informativeness and distinctiveness. However, experts often prefer the subordinate level because it is more informative than the basic level.
- Categorization typically occurs faster at the superordinate level than the basic level because less information is required.
- Barsalou claimed in his situated simulation theory that concept processing (even with abstract concepts) involves the perceptual and motor systems and depends very much on the current context. It is the case that concept processing often includes perceptual and/or motor features, but this does *not* mean it is *necessary* to use perceptual and/or motor processes to understand concepts.
- Barsalou's theoretical approach de-emphasizes that evidence that most concepts have a stable, central core of meaning unaffected by context.
- According to the hub-and-spoke model, concepts consist of hubs (unified abstract representations) and spokes (modality-specific information). Evidence from patients with semantic dementia indicates that hubs are stored in the anterior temporal lobes. In contrast, spokes are stored in several different brain areas, as is indicated by the existence of category-specific deficits and brain-stimulation studies.
- It is not clear within the hub-and-spoke model how modality-specific "spoke" information *integrated* with modality-independent "hub" information.
- Schemas are well-integrated chunks of knowledge about the world, events, people, and actions. As such, they are broader in scope than concepts.

- Research on concepts and schemas has provided some evidence of a double dissociation: patients with semantic dementia generally have greater problems with accessing concepts than schematic information, whereas those with fronto-temporal dementia show the opposite pattern.
- Schemas are useful because they allow us to make predictions about the immediate future, to make inferences during reading, and they adapt to take account of changing environmental conditions. Schemas are also useful because they often enhance long-term memory for both schema-consistent and schema-inconsistent information.
- Schematic knowledge can cause distortions in long-term memory when what we read or hear is inconsistent with that knowledge. However, such distortions are relatively infrequent when we are exposed to natural scenes containing mostly objects that are highly probable in the particular context. In contrast, memory distortions are much more common when we are exposed to manipulated scenes in the laboratory where high-probability objects are often replaced by low-probability ones.

POINTS FOR DISCUSSION

1 Discuss the main similarities and differences between semantic and episodic memory.
2 Describe the semantic activation model and evaluate its contribution to our understanding of semantic memory.
3 What are basic-level categories? When is it advantageous (or disadvantageous) to make use of basic-level categories?
4 Discuss the involvement of the perceptual and motor systems in concept processing.
5 Describe the hub-and-spoke model. To what extent has this model been supported by neuroimaging research and research on brain-damaged patients?
6 Evaluate the contribution of schema theories to our understanding of memory performance and memory errors.

FURTHER READING

Barsalou, L. W., Dutriaux, L., & Scheepers, C. (2018). Moving beyond the distinction between concrete and abstract concepts. *Philosophical Transactions of the Royal Society B, 373* (Article 2017.0144). Larry Barsalou and his colleagues provide an up-to-date account of his situated simulation theoretical approach in light of the relevant research evidence.

Kenett, Y. N., Levi, E., Anaki, D., & Faust, M. (2017). The semantic distance task: Quantifying semantic distance with semantic network path length. *Journal of Experimental Psychology: Learning, Memory, and Cognition, 43*, 1470–1489. In this article by Yoed Kenett and colleagues, the value of semantic distance as a measure of the organization of concepts within semantic memory is demonstrated.

(Continued)

(Continued}

Lambon Ralph, M. A., Jefferies, E., Patterson, K., & Rogers, T. T. (2017). The neural and computational bases of semantic cognition. *Nature Reviews Neuroscience, 18,* 42–55. Matthew Lambon and his colleagues discuss their theory of semantic memory in light of the available evidence.

Robin, J., & Moscovitch, M. (2017). Details, gist and schema: Hippocampal-neocortical interactions underlying recent and remote episodic and spatial memory. *Current Opinion in Behavioral Sciences, 17,* 114–123. Jessica Robin and Morris Moscovitch discuss interactions between episodic and semantic memory (including schemas) and identify the underlying brain areas.

Yee, E., Jones, M. N., & McRae, K. (2018). Semantic memory. In S. L. Thompson-Schill (Ed.), *Stevens' handbook of experimental psychology and cognitive neuroscience, Vol. 3: Language and thought: Developmental and social psychology* (4th ed.) (pp. 319–356). New York: Wiley. This chapter provides a comprehensive account of our current understanding of semantic memory.

REFERENCES

Anaki, D., & Bentin, S. (2009). Familiarity effects on categorization levels of faces and objects. *Cognition, 111,* 144–149.

Auckland, M. E., Cave, K. R., & Donnelly, N. (2007). Non-target objects can influence perceptual processes during object recognition. *Psychonomic Bulletin & Review, 14,* 332–337.

Barsalou, L. W. (2009). Simulation, situated conceptualization, and prediction. *Philosophical Transactions of the Royal Society B: Biological Sciences, 364,* 1281–1289.

Barsalou, L. W. (2012). The human conceptual system. In M. J. Spivey, K. McRae, & M. F. Joanisse (Eds.), *The Cambridge handbook of psycholinguistics* (pp. 239–258). Cambridge: Cambridge University Press.

Barsalou, L. W. (2016). Situated conceptualisation: Theory and applications. In Y. Coello & M. H. Fischer (Eds.), *Foundations of embodied cognition* (Vol. 1): *Perceptual and emotional embodiment* (pp. 11–37). London: Routledge.

Barsalou, L. W., Dutriaux, L., & Scheepers, C. (2018). Moving beyond the distinction between concrete and abstract concepts. *Philosophical Transactions of the Royal Society B, 373* (Article 2017.0144).

Barsalou, L. W., & Wiemer-Hastings, K. (2005). Situating abstract concepts. In D. Pecher & R. Zwaan (Eds.), *Grounding cognition: The role of perception and action in memory, language, and thought.* New York: Cambridge University Press.

Bartlett, F. C. (1932). *Remembering.* Cambridge: Cambridge University Press.

Bauer, A. J., & Just, M. A. (2017). A brain-based account of "basic level" concepts. *NeuroImage, 161,* 196–205.

Besson, G., Barragan-Jason, G., Thorpe, S. J., Fabre-Thorpe, M., Puma, S., Ceccaldi, M., et al. (2017). From face processing to face recognition: Comparing three different processing levels. *Cognition, 158,* 33–43.

Bier, N., Bottari, C., Hudon, C., Jobert, S., Paquette, G., & Macoir, J. L. (2013). The impact of semantic dementia on everyday actions: Evidence from an ecological study. *Journal of the International Neuropsychological Society, 19,* 162–172.

Binder, J. R., & Desai, R. H. (2011). The neurobiology of semantic memory. *Trends in Cognitive Sciences, 15,* 527–536.

Binder, J. R., Desai, R. H., Graves, W. W., & Conant, L. L. (2009). Where is the semantic system? A critical review and meta-analysis of 120 functional neuroimaging studies. *Cerebral Cortex, 19,* 2767–2796.

Borghesani, V., & Piazza, M. (2017). The neuro-cognitive representations of symbols: The case of concrete words. *Neuropsychologia, 105*, 4–17.

Borghi, A. M., Binkofski, Castelfranchi, C., Cimatti, F., Scorolli, C., & Tummolini, L. (2017). The challenge of abstract concepts. *Psychological Bulletin, 143*, 263–292.

Bower, G. H., Black, J. B., & Turner, T. J. (1979). Scripts in memory for text. *Cognitive Psychology, 11*, 177–220.

Bransford, J. D., & Johnson, M. K. (1972). Contextual prerequisites for understanding. *Journal of Verbal Learning and Verbal Behavior, 11*, 717–726.

Brewer, W. F., & Treyens, J. C. (1981). Role of schemata in memory for places. *Cognitive Psychology, 13*, 207–230.

Cabeza, R., Stanley, M. L., & Moscovitch, M. (2018). Process-specific alliances (PSAs) in cognitive neuroscience. *Trends in Cognitive Sciences, 22*, 996–1010.

Chassy, P., & Gobet, F. (2011). Measuring chess experts' single-use sequence knowledge: An archival study of departure from "theoretical openings." *PLoS ONE, 6* (Issue 11), e26692.

Chen, L., Lambon Ralph, M. A., & Rogers, T. T. (2017). A unified model of human semantic knowledge and its disorders. *Nature Human Behavior, 1* (Article No. 0039).

Clark, I. A., & Maguire, E. A. (2016). Remembering preservation in hippocampal amnesia. *Annual Review of Psychology, 67*, 51–82.

Collins, A. M., & Loftus, E. F. (1975). A spreading-activation theory of semantic processing. *Psychological Review, 82*, 407–428.

Collins, A. M., & Quillian, M. R. (1969). Retrieval time from semantic memory. *Journal of Verbal Learning and Verbal Behavior, 9*, 432–438.

Conrad, C. (1972). Cognitive economy in semantic memory. *Journal of Experimental Psychology, 92*, 149–154.

Cosentino, S., Chute, D., Libon, D., Moore, T. P., & Grossman, M. (2006). How does the brain represent scripts? A study of executive processes and semantic knowledge in dementia. *Neuropsychology, 20*, 307–318.

Cree, G. S., & McRae, K. (2003). Analyzing the factors underlying the structure and computation of the meaning of chipmunk, cherry, chisel, cheese, and cello (and many other such concrete nouns). *Journal of Experimental Psychology: General, 132*, 163–201.

Davis, M. (2018). Frederic Bartlett: A question of priority. *Quarterly Journal of Experimental Psychology, 71*, 1030–1031.

Eysenck, M. W., & Groome, D. (2015). Memory systems: Beyond Tulving's (1972) episodic and semantic memory. In M. W. Eysenck & D. Groome (Eds.), *Cognitive psychology: Revisiting the classic studies* (pp. 105–116). London: Sage.

Ferbinteanu, J. (2019). Memory systems 2018—Towards a new paradigm. *Neurobiology of Learning and Memory, 157*, 61–78.

Gainotti, G. (2018). Why do herpes simplex encephalitis and semantic dementia show a different pattern of semantic impairment in spite of their main common involvement within the anterior temporal lobes? *Reviews in the Neurosciences, 29*, 303–320.

Ghosh, V. E., & Gilboa, A. (2014). What is a memory schema? A historical perspective on current neuroscience literature. *Neuropsychologia, 53*, 104–114.

Ghosh, V. E., Moscovitch, M., Colella, B. M., & Gilboa, A. (2014). Schema representation in patients with ventromedial PFC lesions. *Journal of Neuroscience, 34*, 12057–12070.

Gilboa, A., & Marlatte, H. (2017). Neurobiology of schemas and schema-mediated memory. *Trends in Cognitive Sciences, 21*, 618–631.

Greenberg, D. L., & Verfaellie, M. (2010). Interdependence of episodic and semantic memory: Evidence from neuropsychology. *Journal of the International Neuropsychological Society, 16*, 748–753.

Greve, A., Cooper, E., Tibon, R., & Henson, R. N. (2019). Knowledge is power: Prior knowledge aids memory for both congruent and incongruent events, but in different ways. *Journal of Experimental Psychology: General, 148*, 325–341.

Hauk, O., Johnsrude, I., & Pulvermüller, F. (2004). Somatotopic representation of action words in human motor and premotor cortex. *Neuron, 41*, 301–307.

Henderson, E. N. (1903). A study of memory for connected trains of thought. *Psychological Review, Series of Monograph Supplements, 5* (Whole No. 23). New York: Macmillan.

Heyman, T., Bruninx, A., Hutchison, K. A., & Storms, G. (2018). The (un)reliability of item-level semantic priming effects. *Behavior Research Methods, 50*, 2173–2183.

Hoedemaker, R. S., & Gordon, P. C. (2017). The onset and time course of semantic priming during rapid recognition of visual words. *Journal of Experimental Psychology: Human Perception and Performance, 43*, 881–902.

Hoffman, P., McClelland, J. L., & Lambon Ralph, M. A. (2018). Concepts, control, and context: A connectionist account of normal and disordered semantic cognition. *Psychological Review, 125*, 293–328.

Irish, M., Bunk, S., Tu, S. C., Kamminga, J., Hodges, J. R., Hornberger, M., et al. (2016). Preservation of episodic memory in semantic dementia: The importance of regions beyond the medial temporal lobes. *Neuropsychologia, 81*, 50–60.

Ishibashi, R., Mima, T., Fukuyama, & Pobric, G. (2018). Facilitation of function and manipulation knowledge of tools using transcranial direct current stimulation (tDCS). *Frontiers of Integrative Neuroscience, 11* (Article No. 37).

Kenett, Y. N., Levi, E., Anaki, D., & Faust, M. (2017). The semantic distance task: Quantifying semantic distance with semantic network path length. *Journal of Experimental Psychology: Learning, Memory, and Cognition, 43*, 1470–1489.

Lambon Ralph, M. A., Jefferies, E., Patterson, K., & Rogers, T. T. (2017). The neural and computational bases of semantic cognition. *Nature Reviews Neuroscience, 18*, 42–55.

Landin-Romero, R., Tan, R., Hodges, J. R., & Kufor, F. (2016). An update on semantic dementia: Genetics, imaging, and pathology. *Alzheimer's Research & Therapy, 8*.

Loftus, E. F., & Suppes, P. (1972). Structural variables that determine the speed of retrieving words from long-term memory. *Journal of Verbal Learning and Verbal Behavior, 11*, 770–777.

Loftus, G. R., & Mackworth, N. H. (1978). Cognitive determinants of fixation location during picture viewing. *Journal of Experimental Psychology: Human Perception and Performance, 4*, 365–372.

Lupyan, G. (2017). Changing what you see by changing what you know: The role of attention. *Frontiers in Psychology, 8* (Article 553).

Macrae, C. N., & Bodenhausen, G. V. (2000). Social cognition: Thinking categorically about others. *Annual Review of Psychology, 51*, 93–120.

Mahon, B. Z., & Hickok, G. (2016). Arguments about the nature of concepts: Symbols, embodiment, and beyond. *Psychonomic Bulletin & Review, 23*, 941–958.

Marques, J. F., Raposo, A., & Almeida, J. (2013). Structural processing and category-specific deficits. *Cortex, 49*, 266–275.

Mayberry, E. J., Sage, K., & Lambon Ralph, M. A. (2011). At the edge of semantic space: The breakdown of coherent concepts in semantic dementia is constrained by typicality and severity but not modality. *Journal of Cognitive Neuroscience, 23*, 2240–2251.

McCloskey, M. E., & Glucksberg, S. (1978). Natural categories: Well defined or fuzzy sets?. *Memory and Cognition, 6*, 462–472.

Meyer, D. E., & Schvaneveldt, R. W. (1971). Facilitation in recognizing pairs of words: Evidence of a dependence between retrieval operations. *Journal of Experimental Psychology, 90*, 227–234.

Miller, J., Brookie, K., Wales, S., Kaup, B., & Wallace, S. (2018). Embodied cognition: Is activation of the motor cortex essential for understanding action verbs?. *Journal of Experimental Psychology: Learning, Memory, and Cognition, 44*, 335–370.

Mkrtychian, N., Blagovechtchenski, E., Kurmakaeva, D., Gnedykh, D., Kostromina, S., & Shtyrov, Y. (2019). Concrete vs. abstract semantics: From mental representations to functional brain mapping. *Frontiers in Human Neuroscience, 13* (Article No. 267).

Moscovitch, M., Cabeza, R., Winocur, G., & Nadel, L. (2016). Episodic memory and beyond: The hippocampus and neocortex in transformation. *Annual Review of Psychology, 67*, 105–134.

Murphy, C., Rueschemeyer, S.-A., Watson, D., Karapanagiotidis, T., Smallwood, J., & Jefferies, E. (2017). Fractionating the anterior temporal lobe: MVPA reveals differential responses to input and conceptual modality. *NeuroImage, 147*, 19–31.

Patterson, K. E., Nestor, P. J., & Rogers, T. T. (2007). Where do you know what you know? The representation of semantic knowledge in the human brain. *Nature Reviews Neuroscience, 8*, 976–987.

Prass, M., Grimsen, C., König, M., & Fahle, M. (2013). Ultra-rapid object categorisation: Effect of level, animacy and context. *PLoS ONE, 8*(6), e68051.

Rascovsky, K., Growdon, M. E., Pardo, I. R., Grossman, S., & Miller, B. L. (2009). The quicksand of forgetfulness: Semantic dementia in *One Hundred Years of Solitude. Brain, 132*, 2609–2616.

Renoult, L., Tanguay, A., Beaudry, M., Tavakoli, P., Rabipour, S., Campbell, K., et al. (2016). Personal semantics: Is it distinct from episodic and semantic memory? An electrophysiological study of memory for autobiographical facts and repeated events in honor of Shlomo Bentin. *Neuropsychologia, 83*, 242–256.

Reynolds, D. J., Garnham, A., & Oakhill, J. (2006). Evidence of immediate activation of gender information from a social role name. *Quarterly Journal of Experimental Psychology, 59*, 886–903.

Richter, F. R., Bays, P. M., Jeyarathnarajah, P., & Simons, J. S. (2019). Flexible updating of dynamic knowledge structures. *Scientific Reports, 9* (Article No. 2272).

Rigoli, F., Pezzulo, G., Dolan, R., & Friston, K. (2017). A goal-directed Bayesian framework for categorization. *Frontiers in Psychology, 8* (Article 408).

Rips, L. J., Shoben, E. J., & Smith, E. E. (1973). Semantic distance and the verification of semantic relations. *Journal of Verbal Learning and Verbal Behavior, 12*, 1–20.

Robin, J., & Moscovitch, M. (2017). Details, gist and schema: Hippocampal-neocortical interactions underlying recent and remote episodic and spatial memory. *Current Opinion in Behavioral Sciences, 17*, 114–123.

Rogers, T. T., & Patterson, K. (2007). Object categorization: Reversals and explanations of the base-level advantage. *Journal of Experimental Psychology: General, 136*, 451–469.

Rosch, E., Mervis, C. B., Gray, W. D., Johnson, D. M., & Boyes-Braem, P. (1976). Basic objects in natural categories. *Cognitive Psychology, 8*, 382–439.

Rose, S. B., Aristei, S., Melinger, A., & Abdel Rahman, R. (2019). The closer they are, the more they interfere: Semantic similarity of word distractors increases competition in language production. *Journal of Experimental Psychology: Learning, Memory, and Cognition, 45*, 753–763.

Schacter, D. L., Reiman, E., Curran, T., Yun, L. S., Bandy, D., McDermott, K. B., et al. (1996). Neuroanatomical correlates of veridical and illusory recognition memory: Evidence from positron emission tomography. *Neuron, 17*, 267–274.

Spiers, H. J., Maguire, E. A., & Burgess, N. (2001). Hippocampal amnesia. *Neurocase, 7*, 357–382.

Steyvers, M., & Hemmer, P. (2012). Reconstruction from memory in naturalistic environments. In B. H. Ross (Ed.), *The psychology of learning and motivation* (Vol. 56, pp. 126–144). New York: Academic Press.

Tanaka, J. W., & Taylor, M. E. (1991). Object categories and expertise: Is the basic level in the eye of the beholder?. *Cognitive Psychology, 15*, 121–149.

Tanguay, A. N., Benton, L., Romio, L., Steens, C., Davidson, P. S. R., & Renoult, L. (2018). The ERP correlates of self-knowledge: Are assessments of one's past, present, and future traits closer to semantic or episodic memory?. *Neuropsychologia, 110*, 65–83.

Tulving, E. (1972). Episodic and semantic memory. In E. Tulving & W. Donaldson (Eds.), *Organization of memory* (pp. 381–403). London: Academic Press.

Tulving, E. (2002). Episodic memory: From mind to brain. *Annual Review of Psychology, 53*, 1–25.

Vannuscorps, G., Dricot, L., & Pillon, A. (2016). Persistent sparing of action conceptual processing in spite of increasing disorders of action production: A case against motor embodiment of action concepts. *Cognitive Neuropsychology, 33*, 191–209.

Verheyen, S., & Storms, G. (2013). A mixture approach to vagueness and ambiguity. *PLoS ONE, 8*(5), e63507.

Wang, J., Conder, J. A., Blitzer, D. N., & Shinkareva, S. V. (2010). Neural representation of abstract and concrete concepts: A meta-analysis of neuroimaging studies. *Human Brain Mapping, 31*, 1459–1468.

Webb, C. E., Turney, I. C., & Dennis, N. A. (2016). What's the gist? The influence of schemas on the neural correlates underlying true and false memories. *Neuropsychologia, 93*, 61–75.

White, A., Storms, G., Malt, B. C., & Verheyen, S. (2018). Mind the generation gap: Differences between young and old in everyday lexical categories. *Journal of Memory and Language, 98*, 12–25.

Wu, L. L., & Barsalou, L. W. (2009). Perceptual simulation in conceptual combination: Evidence from property generation. *Acta Psychologica, 132*, 173–189.

Zahn, R., Green, S., Beaumont, H., Burns, A., Moll, J., Caine, D., et al. (2017). Frontotemporal lobar degeneration and social behaviour: Dissociation between the knowledge of its consequences and its conceptual meaning. *Cortex, 93*, 107–118.

Contents

CHAPTER 8

RETRIEVAL

Michael C. Anderson

Imagine that it is 10:00 p.m. and you are packing for an international flight early the next morning. You need your passport, but it's nowhere to be found. Deep concern sets in.

It's midnight. Your flight is at 6:00 a.m. You drive to work, dig through drawers, and look on every shelf. *No passport*. Returning to your car, you peer under the floor-mats, rummage through the trunk, and grasp hopefully under the seats, as light rain soaks your back. You are now fully panicked.

Returning home, you march through every room, staring with the full laser beam of consciousness at every inch. You leaf through books, imagining that the passport will drop out gracefully on the floor. At 4:00 a.m., you begin dredging for memories. "When is the last time you had it? I remember putting it in this room that I'm sitting in, but I've already looked there." After concentrating intensely for 20 minutes, memory delivers nothing but fleeting images, and you're left with nothing but a powerful feeling that it's around somewhere. You decide to have one last look.

Then, in a box that you have already inspected numerous times, you lift a paper at the bottom. There it is! It all floods back— the when, how, and why. "OH YEAH … that's right, I put the passport in this box when I was cleaning my home office in preparation for guests arriving two months ago!" It's 5:00 a.m. You pack madly, race to the airport, and merciful flight attendants allow you on the plane, sleepless, and shoeless because you ran from airport security screening in your two differently colored socks.

This event actually occurred to me and was, to say the least, memorable. The story illustrates a crucial point about memory. Quite often, memories are stored perfectly well but, for whatever reason, we have difficulty retrieving them. Clearly the event of putting the passport into the box was alive and well in my memory; yet, even after 20 minutes of deliberate search, the trace remained vexingly inaccessible. But the instant I saw the passport, the memory returned, in full vividness. Why couldn't I retrieve this information?

Clearly, having good memory is not just about encoding material well. One also has to be able to retrieve information. As any student knows, it is possible to study material extensively, and then, on the exam, suddenly be unable to recall it. In this chapter, we consider the processes of retrieval, and what factors influence retrieval success.

THE EXPERIENCE OF RETRIEVAL FAILURE

Subjectively, perhaps the most convincing evidence that our memory contains information that we cannot access comes from the experience of being asked a question to

The tip-of-the-tongue state is an extreme form of pause, where the word takes a noticeable time to come out—although the speaker has a distinct feeling that he/she knows exactly what he/she wants to say.

which we are sure we know the answer, although we cannot produce it at that precise moment; we feel as though we have it "on the tip of the tongue."

Some years ago two Harvard psychologists, Roger Brown and David McNeill (1966), decided to see whether this feeling was based on genuine evidence or was simply an illusion. They set up a tip-of-the-tongue situation by reading out a series of definitions of relatively obscure words to their participants and asking them to name the object being defined. Take for example: A musical instrument comprising a frame holding a series of tubes struck by hammers. Participants were instructed to indicate if they were in the "*tip of the tongue*" state (convinced that they knew the word although they were unable to produce it). When this occurred they were asked to guess at the number of

---

Box 8.1 Tip-of-the-tongue experience

Try recalling the capital cities of each of the countries listed, first by covering up the letters to the right. When you feel you can't recall any more of them, then use the provided letter cues. Did you encounter a tip-of-the-tongue experience? Check your answers at the end of the chapter (Box 8.2).

	Country	First letter of capital city		Country	First letter of capital city
1	Norway	O	11	South Korea	S
2	Turkey	A	12	Syria	D
3	Kenya	N	13	Denmark	C
4	Uruguay	M	14	Sudan	K
5	Finland	H	15	Nicaragua	M
6	Australia	C	16	Ecuador	Q
7	Saudi Arabia	R	17	Colombia	B
8	Romania	B	18	Afghanistan	K
9	Portugal	L	19	Thailand	B
10	Bulgaria	S	20	Venezuela	C

syllables in the word and to provide any other information, such as the initial letter. They were consistently much better at providing such information than one would have expected by chance. Other studies have shown that giving the participant the initial letter, in this case x, frequently prompts the correct name, XYLOPHONE. The tip-of-the-tongue experience arises in a diversity of languages, and even occurs in sign language users, who report a similar a "tip of the finger" experience when recalling signs (Schwartz & Cleary, 2016).

The task of trying to remember the names of capital cities of countries is a good way of evoking this effect. Read rapidly through the list of countries in Box 8.1, covering up the initial letters of their capital cities. Eliminate those countries that you can immediately produce the answer for and also those for which you feel you do *not* know the answer. Concentrate on the rest. Any luck? If not, see if the letter cues jog your memory. Check your answers at the end of this chapter.

In general, the feeling that you know something is often a good indication that you do—given the right prompting. In a capital city recall test similar to that just described, recall was over 50% when letters were given for the cities people thought they knew, but only 16% for those they thought they didn't. Similarly, my powerful feeling that the passport was located in my home library was, in fact, correct.

Most people find it more than a little vexing to feel that they know something, but are unable to recollect it. In the tip-of-the-tongue state, many people struggle mightily to recall the delinquent knowledge. Imagine what your life would be like if you had this sort of experience on a regular basis. Like poor Tantalus, the tortured figure from Greek mythology, you would forever be reaching for your mnemonic fruit, never quite being able to grasp it. In fact, some people do have significant difficulties in retrieving their past, even when it can be shown that the sought-after experiences are clearly in memory. These individuals are not amnesic in the sense discussed in Chapter 16 on amnesia, wherein memories are not stored

and retained; rather, they suffer from disruptions in the retrieval processes necessary to intentionally access their memories. Such difficulties often accompany damage or dysfunction to the prefrontal cortex, a brain structure critically involved in cognitive control more generally (Szczepanski & Knight, 2014).

In one particularly clear example, Jennifer Mangels and her colleagues asked patients with damage to the prefrontal cortex to recall knowledge of events and facts that they learned long before suffering brain damage (Mangels, Gershberg, Shimamura, & Knight, 1996). Testing this type of older, remote memory was a clever approach, because it meant that the authors could be confident that the memories being tested were encoded and stored under normal conditions (i.e., without brain damage), allowing any memory deficits to be clearly attributed to retrieval problems. To assess patients' remote memory, Mangels and colleagues tested memory for salient public events and famous faces that most people alive during a certain era can be expected to know. For example, on the famous faces test, participants received photographs of once famous people (e.g., Telly Savalas, who was a famous actor in the 1970s), and were asked to recall their names. If, after viewing a photo for a generous amount of time, they clearly were having difficulty recalling the name, participants received additional hints (e.g., the person is an actor famous in the 1970s, whose name begins with T___). If even this information was not enough, participants were asked if they could recognize the correct name. Famous faces were selected from each of several decades prior to the experiment. As can be seen in Figure 8.1, patients remembered fewer of the names of famous people compared to age-matched control participants, regardless of the decade from which the face was drawn. This sizable retrieval disadvantage arose even when distinctive cues were given to aid recall, though overall performance clearly did improve. In contrast, patients could easily pick the correct famous names when asked to recognize them (right panel) and were no worse than control participants. Other studies have shown this

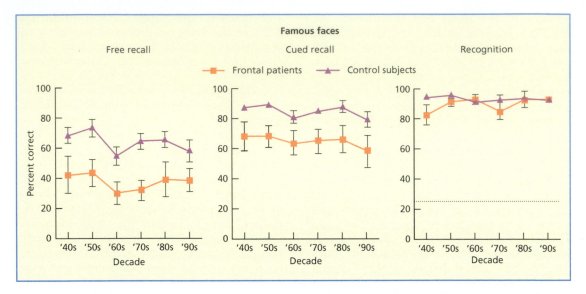

Figure 8.1 The effects of frontal lobe damage on free recall, cued recall, and recognition tests of remote memories. Participants were presented with the faces of people who were famous in each decade from 1940 through the 1990s, when the experiment was conducted. In the free recall test, frontal patients and age-matched control subjects were given the face and asked to recall the person's name. In the cued recall test, participants were given additional hints about the person's profession or other characteristics. In the recognition test, participants needed to select the correct name from a group of distractors. Frontal patients exhibit clear deficits in free and cued recall, even though recognition tests reveal that they have the right answers to the questions in memory. From Mangels et al. (1996). Copyright © American Psychological Association. Reproduced with permission.

pattern with events from patients' own lives, and that such autobiographical retrieval deficits were associated with performance on tests of cognitive control (Della Salla, Laiacona, Spinnler, & Trivelli, 1993). Thus, damage to the prefrontal cortex hinders recall even for very well-learned information from across our lifespans.

We have established, then, that our memory store contains more information than we can access at any given moment. Moreover, successful access often depends upon retrieval mechanisms that help to isolate traces in memory, a function that relies strongly on cognitive control processes supported by the prefrontal cortex, a finding supported by research with functional magnetic resonance imaging (Badre & Wagner, 2007). What therefore determines the accessibility of information in memory? To address this question, we need a basic idea of how the retrieval process works.

THE RETRIEVAL PROCESS: GENERAL PRINCIPLES

To describe how retrieval works, it's helpful to introduce some terminology. During retrieval, we are usually seeking a particular memory—either a particular fact, idea, or experience, often called the *target memory* or the *target trace*. Suppose, for example, I asked you to recall what you had for dinner last night. To answer, you would try to recollect the event. In this case, your memory for having dinner last night would be the target.

When we search for a target in memory, we usually have some idea of what we are looking for. In the dinner example, you knew you were searching for a dinner event that happened yesterday evening. This specification can be likened to the words one might type into the search window of an internet search engine, like Google™. Without such a specification, there is nothing for your memory to work with, and so it would return nothing, just as typing nothing into Google™ would not yield websites. These snippets of information that allow you to access a memory are known as *retrieval cues*, or simply *cues*. In general, retrieval is a progression from one or more cues to a target memory, with the aim of making that target available to influence ongoing cognition.

But how do cues help us to retrieve target memories? Traces in memory are believed to be linked up to one another by connections that are usually called *associations* or *links*. Suppose, for example, I ask you to say the first thing that comes to mind to each of the following words: DOG, HOT, UP, or COW. Chances are, you probably thought CAT or BONE for DOG, COLD for HOT, DOWN for UP, and MILK for COW. These ideas, like dog and cat, are strongly linked in most people's memories—that is, they are associated. Associations are structural linkages between traces and those linkages can vary in strength. For example, if I asked you to name a FRUIT, you might quickly say BANANA, but a GUAVA is also a fruit. The fact that guava does not come to mind so readily reflects its weaker association to FRUIT. Retrieval then, is a progression from one or more cues to a target memory, via associative connections.

Memories can be retrieved from a variety of cues. If instead of asking you, "What did you have for dinner last night," I had asked, "When was the last time you had peas?," you might say, "Oh, I had peas last night for dinner." You would have accessed the same memory but by means of different cues than in the former example. Many things can serve as cues; the smell of peas may remind you of last night; or the song on the radio may be the same one you played while dining on peas. Our memories are remarkably flexible; any aspect of the content of a memory can serve as a reminder that could access the experience, a property known as *content addressable* memory. We essentially have "mental Google™," but we can search with just about any type of information.

The preceding ideas give us basic language for talking about the structures involved in memory, but they do not say much about the process. How do we progress from cues to target memories, via associ-

ations? Although there are many theories, one useful and simple idea is that retrieval occurs by a process called spreading activation, examples of which are discussed in Chapter 7 on semantic memory. According to this idea, each memory has an internal state of its own, reflecting how "excited" or "active" it is, a state referred to as the memory's activation level. Activation has several important properties. The activation level varies, and determines how accessible a trace is in memory, with higher levels of activation reflecting greater accessibility. A trace's activation level increases when something related to it is perceived in the world (e.g., seeing a plate of peas will activate the idea PEAS and probably your dinner of peas), or when attention is focused directly on the trace (when I ask you to think of PEAS). This activation persists for some time, even after attention has been removed.

How does the concept of activation help us to think about retrieval? One idea is that memories automatically spread activation to other memories to which they are associated. This *spreading activation* is like "energy" flowing through connections linking traces. The amount of activation spread from the cue to an associate is larger the stronger the association, and activation is spread in parallel to all associates. If the target accumulates enough activation from the cue, it will be retrieved, even though other associates might be activated as well. So, if you saw the name BECKHAM, attention to this idea would increase its activation, which, in turn, would activate associates, like FOOTBALL. As a result, FOOTBALL. would be retrieved. The idea that traces have activation that spreads is central to many theories of memory, and provides a useful way of thinking about how cues access memories. To refine our definition of retrieval further then, retrieval is a progression from one or more cues to a target memory, via associative connections linking them together, through a process of spreading activation.

For simplicity, I have described retrieval as a progression from a single cue to a single "target" in memory, as though a memory of your past was a single entity, that simply varied in its activity level. Though this is a helpful simplification, memories are complex, being composed of many different features and details. Whilst eating dinner last night, you may have had peas, but you had overcooked peas, while seated at the dinner table with your roommate, with mashed potatoes, and told stories about your day, for example. So, in most instances, it is better to regard a memory as a collection of features that, if activated collectively by cues, would constitute retrieval. Considering this additional complexity then, retrieval involves the reinstatement, via spreading activation, of a *pattern of activation* over features that represent a memory. Several features of the original experience, provided as cues, will spread activation to other features, completing the missing components of the memory pattern. The process by which spreading activation from a set of cues leads to the reinstatement of a memory's features is often referred to as pattern completion.

Our description of the retrieval process so far is general, and fits cases when we are retrieving general semantic knowledge or particular experiences from long-term memory. The above concepts also apply whether we are spontaneously reminded of a past experience (incidental retrieval), or we are intentionally retrieving a memory. Additional concepts are useful, however, to describe intentional retrieval. During intentional retrieval, we are targeting a particular trace in memory. As such, cognitive control processes are thought necessary to focus the search process, including processes such as cue-specification (i.e., the careful specification of what we are trying to remember, which may also include a retrieval strategy), cue-maintenance in working memory, interference resolution processes which help to

overcome interference from competing memories brought to mind instead of the target (a process addressed in more detail in our next chapter), and post-retrieval monitoring of the products of search, which includes decision processes that evaluate whether what we have retrieved is what we are seeking. One can imagine how intentional recall would be impaired if any of these processes were to break down (Simons & Spiers, 2003). Indeed, damage to the prefrontal cortex disrupts many of these processes, accounting for the retrieval deficits described at the outset of this chapter.

Finally, it is useful to consider *what* is being retrieved, and how this happens in the brain. Although our understanding of the neural basis of memories and retrieval is still evolving, some broad principles are accepted. One central hypothesis with good support is

KEY TERM

Features: Elementary components from which a complex memory can be assembled, including perceptual aspects such as color and object shapes, as well as higher level conceptual elements.

Pattern completion: The process whereby presenting a subset of features that represent a memory spreads activation to the remaining feature units representing that memory, completing the pattern of activity necessary to retrieve it.

Cue-specification: When intentionally retrieving a target memory, the control processes by which one specifies the nature of the target and any contextual features that may constrain retrieval, and establishes these as cues to guide search.

Cue-maintenance: When intentionally retrieving a target memory, the process of sustaining cues in working memory to guide search.

Interference resolution processes: When trying to recall a particular target memory, control processes that help to resolve interference from competing memories coactivated by the cues guiding retrieval.

Post-retrieval monitoring: During intentional retrieval, the processes by which one evaluates the products of memory search, to determine whether the retrieved trace is what we seek.

the idea that retrieval involves *cortical reinstatement*, or the recreation of the pattern of neural activity present when an experience was encoded. For example, when I reminisce about going to see the first *Austin Powers, International Man of Mystery* movie in the cinema with my friends Chad and Scott in the 1990s, I immediately think of Austin Powers' (i.e., Mike Myers') and Dr. Evil's faces, the movie's ridiculous theme song, where we sat, and Chad's outrageous laugh. When remembering these aspects of the experience, I am likely reactivating the areas of neocortex that perceptually processed the original stimuli. Indeed, according to the reinstatement hypothesis, I should be reinstating the neural patterns associated with perceiving those faces (in the brain's face area, or the fusiform face area), the music (in temporal cortex), and the particular spatial environment (e.g., the parahippocampal place area in the brain). (Surely there must be a dedicated region of my brain for Chad's laugh!) I can recall these diverse features, represented in widely different areas of neocortex, because they are bound together into a memory for the event. Thus, the pattern completion process begins with some of these features as input, and recreates a brain state in which the remaining cortical perceptual processes are recapitulated. As Danker and Anderson put it, we are, in essence experiencing "ghosts of brain states past" (Danker & Anderson, 2010). So, many parts of the brain contribute to re-experiencing our memories with their activities orchestrated to reinstate something resembling the original event.

But how does retrieval reinstate the unique pattern of cortical activity representing a personal experience? Given that diverse content can be stored in each of our memories (that is likely widely distributed in the brain), something must bind these features into a single event and index the brain areas involved in recreating the event. As discussed in Chapter 6 on episodic memory, the hippocampus supports this binding function, integrating features into new episodic memories when an experience is stored. As it turns out, the retrieval process takes advantage of this hippocampal representation to achieve cortical reinstatement. When people see reminder cues to a past event, the brain areas involved in perceiving these cues send input to the hippocampus, where they activate the integrated representation to which they are associated. This triggers pattern completion, which, in turn, leads the hippocampus to send output signals to the relevant cortical regions necessary to remember the event. In one elegant example of this process, Staresina, Cooper, and Henson (2013) asked people to memorize picture pairs, with each pair containing a nature scene (like a mountain lake) and an object (e.g., a tire). Later on, they performed brain imaging while people retrieved the pairs. Sometimes people received the object as cue and had to recall the scene and other times the reverse. Unsurprisingly, when people saw the objects as cues, the parts of the brain involved in seeing objects quickly became active. This initial sensory activity led to activation in the hippocampus, followed next by activation in the parahippocampal place area, as the paired scene was retrieved. Interestingly, when people instead got the scenes as cues, the pattern reversed! Seeing the cue quickly activated the parahippocampal place area, followed by the hippocampus, and then object-related areas, as people retrieved the paired object. In a related study, Staresina recorded from individual neurons in the human hippocampus and in cortex and found a similar pattern using neural firing rates, with hippocampal activity preceding cortical reinstatement (Staresina et al., 2019). The hippocampus is clearly instrumental in progressing from cues in our perceptual worlds to target traces, contributing vital pattern completion and cortical reinstatement functions, at least for episodic memory. Retrieval of general semantic knowledge, however, does not require the hippocampus, as we discuss in Chapter 16 on amnesia.

FACTORS DETERMINING RETRIEVAL SUCCESS

Knowing that retrieval is the progression from cues to a target memory did not help when I needed to find my passport. Why does retrieval succeed sometimes, but not others? We consider several factors here, each demonstrating something important about retrieval (Figure 8.2).

Attention to cues

Retrieval is less effective if cues are present, but not attended, or not attended enough. Suppose, for example, that while searching for my passport, I didn't gaze upon the box that contained it. If so, there is no way that the box could have cued memory. In reality, I searched the box many times, and so was clearly looking at it. Even so, I might not have fully attended to the box, distracted by my worries. Many theories assume that the activation given to a concept increases with attention. If so, diminishing attention might make a cue less useful and lead retrieval to fail. This may partially contribute to retrieval deficits observed in patients with damage to the prefrontal cortex.

One way of reducing attention to cues is by giving people a secondary task to perform during retrieval. When distracted in this way, people's retrieval usually grows worse, especially if the secondary task requires them to pay attention to related materials. This point is made well in several studies by Myra Fernandes and Morris Moscovitch (2000, 2003). They asked people to recall out loud lists of words that had been presented auditorally. At the same time, participants made judgments about entirely different items appearing on a computer screen. Compared to a control condition in which people did not do a secondary task, distracting people reduced recall performance by as much as 30–50%, especially when the judgment items were words as well. In contrast, making judgments about numbers or pictures reduced recall much less. The latter finding illustrates that the mere need to do two things at once doesn't disrupt recall as much if the second task doesn't require people to process similar content. Such effects of dividing attention are largest when the retrieval task requires you to generate items from memory (recall), but are also found when you simply have to recognize you have seen something (Fernandes and Guild, 2009).

Nevertheless, dividing attention can also reduce retrieval even when the secondary task is totally unrelated, although the disruption is much smaller. For example, when Craik, Govoni, Naveh-Benjamin, and Anderson (1996) asked people to perform a simple visuo-motor secondary task, it reduced their recall of words presented earlier. The interfering effects of unrelated tasks grow when the task is more demanding (Rohrer & Pashler, 2003). It is worth highlighting, however, that dividing attention at retrieval is less disruptive to how much is recalled than dividing attention at encoding. This asymmetry has been taken to indicate that, under such circumstances, retrieval quite often can proceed with less attention, compared

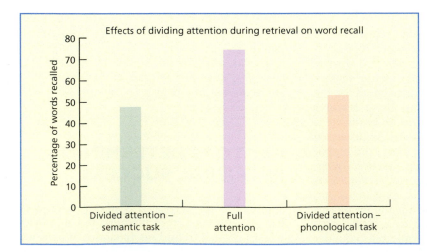

Figure 8.2 Retrieving words under divided attention conditions negatively affects retrieval success, especially with distractor tasks (e.g., semantic or phonological) that are similar to the task of interest (in this case, recalling words). Data from Fernandes and Moscovitch (2000).

to encoding (Baddeley, Lewis, Eldridge & Thomson, 1984; Craik et al., 1996), especially when the cues guiding search are more specific and complete. For instance, the disruptive effects of dividing attention are larger on recall than on recognition tests, presumably because the latter provide very specific cues for accessing a trace. This pattern resembles the retrieval difficulties observed for patients with prefrontal cortex damage. Thus, though retrieval can in many cases proceed with less attention, full attention is required if accurate and complete recall is necessary. In Chapter 9 on incidental forgetting, we discuss further a specific attentional control process—inhibition—that appears to be disrupted by dividing attention.

Relevance of cues

Having retrieval cues does little good if they are unrelated to the target. This might seem too obvious to mention, but we often search memory with inappropriate cues. Consider the time that I left the grocery store, and stood, trying to remember where I had parked my car. After several minutes of not

It's tough enough finding your car in a sea of vehicles, but it's even harder to find if you're using the wrong cues. For instance, trying to remember where your sports car is wouldn't be very useful if, in fact, you drove the family sedan.

recollecting anything, I realized that I had driven my neighbor's car. The moment I realized this, up popped the memory. I had essentially asked my memory the wrong question with the wrong cue (MY CAR). This type of mistake happens often. Have you ever tried to remember the location of your keys, presuming you must have placed them in one of their usual spots (e.g., a basket on the counter)? If you put your keys in an unusual spot, these retrieval cues will be fruitless.

Sometimes, cues that seem like they ought to be effective turn out not to be effective at all. Consider the time that I intended to pick up my dry cleaning. In the morning, standing by the breakfast table, I put the dry cleaning ticket in my backpack. On the way home later that day, while passing the dry cleaning shop, I looked right at it, but failed to remember to pull in and pick up the dry cleaning. When I got home, however, and saw the kitchen table, I remembered, "Ahhh, I forget to pick up the dry cleaning!" So, why did seeing the dry cleaning shop not remind me to pick up my clothes? It ought to have been an outstanding cue! And why was the kitchen table such an effective reminder, when kitchen tables have nothing to do with dry cleaning? Actually, this pattern makes sense, if you consider what was encoded. The thing to be remembered was the intention to pick up the dry cleaning, which was encoded in the morning in the kitchen, with the table present. Indeed, the ticket was lying on the table, and so was associated to it. By contrast, the dry cleaning shop was absent during encoding, and so was not associated with the ticket. Thus, when the dry cleaning shop became available later as a cue, there was no association that could spread activation to the intention to pick up my clothes.

The foregoing example illustrates a well-established idea known as the encoding specificity principle. This principle states that for a cue to be useful, it needs to be present at encoding, and encoded with the desired trace. In fact, cues that are specifically encoded with a target are more powerful even if, on the face of it, they might seem less good than other cues that have a pre-existing relationship with the target. In one experiment demonstrating this principle, Tulving and Osler (1968) presented participants with target words for later recall; each target was accompanied by a cue that had a weak association with the word to be retained. An example might be the word CHAIR accompanied by the cue word GLUE (e.g., participants might see GLUE-CHAIR). After encoding, participants were asked to recall the targets, either unaided or prompted by the cue with which each was paired. Cue words substantially increased recall of the targets, illustrating the power of cues to facilitate recall. But not all cues should be equally good, according to Tulving. For instance, although TABLE is a valid associate of CHAIR, it will not be as effective a cue as GLUE will be, if TABLE is not presented during encoding. Tulving and Thomson (1973) went on to show that this encoding specificity effect is powerful. There are other ways of showing the same effect. For example, if I give you a sentence such as "The man tuned the piano," but give another person the sentence "The man lifted the piano," then the cue SOMETHING HEAVY is likely to be a very poor retrieval cue for you, but a good one for your colleague (Barclay, Bransford, Franks, McCarrell, & Nitsch, 1974).

Thus we remember what we experience, and we access our memory by using a fragment of that experience as a key to the whole. So, even though a dry cleaning shop store front really seems like it *ought* to be a great cue for remembering to pick up my dry cleaning, it is far less effective than the kitchen table because only the latter was encoded with the intention to pick up my clothes.

Cue-target associative strength

Retrieval can fail if cues are relevant, but are weak. As discussed previously, associations vary in strength, and it is this strength that determines the rate at which activation spreads between a cue and a target. Hence, if an association between a cue and a target is poor, retrieval failure may occur. Anyone who has ever memorized vocabulary words in a foreign language knows that associating new words to their native language equivalents can be difficult; it is possible to have stored the foreign word (e.g., be able to recognize it as one that you have seen) and nevertheless be unable to retrieve the right meaning. Similarly, associating a new person's face to their name frequently fails, even when we recognize the person's face, and the name, if it is given to us. Thus, retrieval success depends on how associated the cues are to the target, which depends on the time and attention we spend encoding the association. Perhaps one reason why the box did not remind me of storing the passport is that in hurrying to neaten my home for guests, I did not devote enough attention to the passport's new location in the box.

When cue-target associative strength is low, people often can compensate by engaging cognitive control processes to facilitate retrieval. David Badre and Anthony Wagner, for example, have argued that when retrieval cues are too weak to automatically activate a desired memory, a *controlled retrieval process* mediated by the anterior part of the left inferior prefrontal cortex is engaged. In one illustration, Badre and Wagner asked participants to pick which of two words was more associated to cue words like *candle*. Participants showed significantly more activation in the left inferior prefrontal cortex when the correct option was weakly associated to candle (halo) than when it was strongly related (e.g., flame). This pattern is generally observed whenever people have to retrieve weakly associated items from semantic memory, and a similar principle is thought to apply to episodic memory retrieval. Badre and Wagner suggest that the prefrontal cortex acts to sustain attention to cues to bias neural activity in parts of the neocortex that represent the content that needs to be retrieved. In this way, the prefrontal cortex may enhance the pattern completion process and increase the chances of successful retrieval (Badre & Wagner, 2007). Given findings like this, the memory difficulties experienced by people with prefrontal cortex damage are easy to understand.

Number of cues

Retrieval often improves when more relevant cues are added. Consider the exercise you did on the "tip of the tongue." If you had initially tried to recall the meanings of the words and failed, but felt that you knew the right answer, getting the letter as an additional hint probably brought the meaning to mind. Similarly, the cardboard box by itself was insufficient to cue my memory of the passport, but when I saw the passport lying at the bottom of it, I recalled this event instantly. Importantly, the passport, by itself, would not have cued this memory. Suppose that I had been assisted by someone who found the passport while I was in another room. If the other person showed me the passport, I would not have suddenly remembered storing it in the box. I would have said, "Where did you find it?" It was the *combination* of the passport and the box that elicited the memory. It makes sense that adding cues helps. Assuming that the person attends to both cues, both will become activated. This activation will spread to the target; because there are two sources of activation, the target should grow active quickly, and be more easily retrieved.

There is evidence that adding cues does not simply cause additive improvements, however, but may sometimes be superadditive. Research on *dual cuing* suggests that having two cues is sometimes far more beneficial than you would expect than if you simply added the probability of retrieving the target from each cue separately. Consider an example based on research by Rubin and Wallace (1989), who examined how providing both semantic and rhyme cues affected the likelihood of generating particular responses from memory. If we asked you to name a MYTHICAL BEING, you might mention UNICORN or BOOGIE MONSTER or any number of other such creatures. If we asked you to name a word that rhymes with POST, you might say HOST or MOST, or

any of the numerous words that rhyme. But if we instead asked you to name a mythical being that rhymes with POST, you would be quite likely to say GHOST. Rubin and Wallace showed that the probability of generating a particular item like ghost in response to either cue alone could be quite low (e.g., 14% for a semantic category, 19% for a rhyme cue by itself), but was dramatically higher with the two in combination (97% for both semantic and rhyme cues together). This may be one reason why it is so useful to encode information elaboratively, as discussed in the chapter on encoding. Elaboration associates the material to many cues that might be used during later retrieval.

Strength of the target memory

If a memory is weakly encoded, even a good cue may be insufficient to trigger retrieval. In the framework described earlier, if the target has low activation, the lower starting point should make it more difficult for a cue to activate that item, even given a relevant cue. For example, words vary greatly in their frequency of usage in a language, with some words being very high frequency, such as DOG and others being known, but rarely used, such as KIOSK. Higher frequency words are better recalled. One interpretation is that higher frequency words are more strongly represented, owing to their repeated exposure. Similarly, how well people will recall a set of singly presented words or pictures varies with the amount of time or elaborative processing given to encode those items, reflecting greater success at encoding.

The strength of a memory depends, in part, on how effectively people engage the hippocampus and other structures within the medial temporal lobes when a memory is encoded. For instance, Anthony Wagner and colleagues (Wagner et al., 1998) scanned people with functional magnetic resonance imaging as they encoded a long list of words. Afterwards, they tested people's ability to recognize words, and then, for each person, divided the words into ones that they recognized, and ones that they didn't. Wagner and colleagues reasoned that the words that people correctly recognized were likely to have been encoded more effectively than were words that people failed to recognize. If so, then comparing neural activity at encoding for items that were remembered to those that were forgotten, should reveal brain areas whose activity is particularly important to good subsequent memory for those items. Wagner and colleagues found significantly greater activity near the hippocampus for successfully remembered than for subsequently forgotten items. When brain areas show greater activity for items that are remembered subsequently, it is called a *subsequent memory effect*. Such effects are often observed in the medial temporal lobes, but also are found in other brain areas, depending on the content that is being encoded (see Paller & Wagner, 2002; Spaniol et al., 2009, for reviews). These effects allow one to measure the neural activity that contributes to the formation of stronger, retrievable traces.

Retrieval strategy

Retrieval can be influenced by the strategy one adopts. For example, after studying a word list, I might (if I were naive) try to recall the words by working through the alphabet and retrieving items associated with each letter. If materials are organized at encoding, going through that organization at retrieval would be an ideal strategy, as discussed in Chapter 6 on organization. In addition, which order to recall a group of items is also a strategy choice; should I start at the beginning, or go in reverse order? In the case of retrieving my passport location, I tried many strategies for retrieving, such as remembering the last time I had the passport, and recalling all my recent trips.

One nice illustration of the impact of retrieval strategy comes from a clever study by Richard Anderson and James Pichert (1978). Their participants read a story about boys skipping school, hiding out in the home of one of the boys. The story described objects contained in the home, and participants were told, during reading, to adopt the perspective of either a burglar or a home-

buyer. On a later test both groups recalled a similar amount, though the items recalled were biased towards things relevant to their respective perspectives. Interestingly, however, participants were given a second recall opportunity, either adopting the same perspective, or an alternative one. Unsurprisingly, participants adopting same perspective recalled the same items again; intriguingly, however, those adopting a different perspective (e.g., the perspective of a burglar, after having initially encoded and retrieved as a homebuyer), recalled significantly more items relevant to that new perspective. Thus, retrieval improved because of a mere change in retrieval strategy. This study highlights how we may often—unbeknownst to us—adopt a viewpoint when recalling the past. This perspective provides a schematic structure that guides retrieval, constraining our recall to things relevant to the schema. Some have argued that to maximize recall, one should try to recall from different perspectives. We return to this idea in our discussion of the *cognitive interview method* in Chapter 14. Adopting alternative retrieval perspectives for the same event can have surprising unintended consequences, and modify one's experience of the memory itself. For example, in describing a personal experience to someone else, shifting visual perspective from an *own eyes perspective* (i.e., the event as visually perceived by you) to an *observer perspective* (the event as seen from a separate point of view) can induce enduring reductions in vividness and emotional intensity of the memory (Sekiguchi & Nonaka, 2014), and also can introduce distortions to the event (Marcotti & St. Jacques, 2018).

Using a retrieval strategy to increase one's recall relies on cognitive control processes that are believed to demand proper functioning of the prefrontal cortex. In fact, the development and use of a retrieval strategy is simply a more elaborated case of the process of cue-specification, described in our overview of the retrieval process earlier in this chapter. The ability to use retrieval strategies suffers a lot with prefrontal damage. For example, Felicia Gershberg and Art Shimamura found that patients with damage to the prefrontal cortex were significantly less likely to use retrieval strategies when asked to recall lists of words, compared to age-matched controls. Thus, whereas control participants would tend to retrieve items in meaningful clusters or categories, showing an orderly retrieval strategy, patients did so much less. Patients benefitted greatly, however, when a strategy was provided for them (Gershberg & Shimamura, 1995). Similar deficits in retrieval strategy use also arise in older adults without brain damage, likely owing to the well-established age-related decline in frontal lobe volume (see Chapter 15 on memory and aging).

Retrieval mode

During my passport mishap, I looked at the box containing the passport many times. I even searched the box, but it never reminded me of storing the passport. Although the box might have been weakly associated to the passport, another possibility exists: perhaps I was in the wrong frame of mind when looking at the box. It's true that I focused attention on the box while searching it. But perhaps I was so fixated on searching it that this got in the way of memory. If I had tried to remember that event while looking at the box, it may have proven to be an effective cue.

It is worth considering that many of the stimuli in our daily lives have associations to the past, but we aren't bombarded by memories every waking second. You put on your shoes this morning, but you probably didn't spontaneously remember, while tying your shoes, when you bought them, even though your shoes are a perfectly good cue for that event, and even though you could probably remember that event if you wanted to. Given the abundance of such cues in our everyday worlds, it is surprising that we are not always being reminded of something. It seems then, that in some cases, we have to be in the right frame of mind or retrieval mode to recollect our past (Tulving, 1983).

According to research on retrieval mode, for retrieval to be effective, it is necessary to adopt a cognitive set that ensures that stimuli will be processed as probes of episodic memory. A nice illustration was reported by Herron and Wilding (2006), who measured brain electrical activity during retrieval. Participants encoded lists of words that appeared on either the left or right side of a screen. Later, they were presented with these words mixed in with new ones, and were asked to do one of two tasks on each. On episodic trials, they had to judge whether the word was one they had seen earlier, and if so, what side of the screen it had appeared on; on semantic trials, they had to judge whether the word referred to an object capable of moving on its own (e.g., BUZZARD)—a judgment that did not require recalling what they had just seen. Importantly, each word was preceded for four seconds by a cue telling people which judgment they had to perform on the upcoming word. By recording brain activity over the four seconds when participants were getting ready to make their judgment, they could see whether there was a distinctive neural pattern linked to getting ready for retrieval. Herron and Wilding found relatively greater positive electrical brain activity over the right frontal cortex—an area involved in attentional control—when people were preparing to retrieve than when they were preparing to make a semantic judgment. Moreover, they found that when people did several episodic judgments consecutively, their judgment accuracy and speed improved with each trial, consistent with the idea that it takes time to "get into the swing" of retrieval. Thus, retrieval benefits from getting into the right mental configuration to access our past, a task accomplished by the right prefrontal cortex. This "mental preparation" for retrieval also involves getting the brain ready to search for a particular type of content. For example, given that one is in retrieval mode, one's mindset is likely highly different depending on whether one is trying to remember the location of something or its

KEY TERM

Retrieval mode: The cognitive set, or frame of mind, that orients a person towards the act of retrieval, ensuring that stimuli are interpreted as retrieval cues.

sound. The particular specification of the category of content (e.g., locations or sounds) one is looking for is known as a *retrieval orientation*, and having the right retrieval orientation contributes greatly to retrieval success (Herron & Evans, 2018).

Although retrieval mode certainly helps bring relevant information to mind, it is not required for all forms of retrieval. Often, events or ideas seem to "spring to mind" unbidden, with little effort or intention on our part. This phenomenon has come to be known as *involuntary retrieval*, and it has attracted much attention in recent years (see Berntsen, 2010; Mace, 2007, for reviews). Consider the following example, taken from a diary study described by Dorthe Berntsen (Berntsen, Staugaard, & Sorensen, 2013).

"I was running in the Botanical Garden, while thinking of something I had just read for my psychology class. It was a beautiful spring day with singing of birds, and not many other people out. I ran per routine— and suddenly got a side stitch (which is unusual for me). I then suddenly remembered a day in Hungary, where I was running with my friend from England. I got a severe side stitch, and, through his years in the military, he had learnt some breathing techniques against side stitches, which he then taught me."

Clearly, the participant reporting this reminding was not in retrieval mode at all, and the memory came back suddenly, in response to a distinctive cue. Berntsen argues that this form of unbidden, involuntary retrieval is a fundamental and basic mode of remembering. Based on numerous diary studies, she has argued that involuntary memories are equally frequent, in daily life to voluntarily retrieved memories (Berntsen, 2010), are universal across people, and are supported by the same underlying memory system as supports voluntary memory. Involuntary retrievals also occur for semantic content, such as facts and ideas (Kvavilashvili & Mandler, 2004). Indeed, the tendency for

both ideas and memories to be retrieved involuntarily, inserting themselves into awareness, is a key factor underlying the widely studied phenomenon of *mind wandering* (Smallwood & Schooler, 2015) in which, despite efforts to focus on a desired task (like reading this book), you nonetheless find yourself lost in thoughts.

Although evidence suggests that in healthy individuals, involuntary episodic memories are predominantly of positive events, unpleasant intrusive memories constitute a major symptom of numerous psychological disorders, including post-traumatic stress disorder, anxiety, and depression (see, e.g., Brewin, Gregory, Lipton, & Burgess, 2010). Understanding their causes and characteristics is an important problem for clinicians. Indeed, it is precisely these sorts of involuntary retrievals that trigger intentional forgetting that will be addressed in Chapter 10 on motivated forgetting. Clearly then, retrieval success is not always what people want!

CONTEXT CUES

Although we have been discussing cues generically, it is worth highlighting one variety of cue that is quite important: context cues. Context refers to the circumstances under which a stimulus has been encoded. For example, you would probably agree that general knowledge of the word POMEGRANATE differs from the particular memory of seeing a pomegranate at the local market, or from having seen the word POMEGRANATE on this page. The latter cases concern particular occasions or episodic memories, which are distinguishable by the place and time they took place (see Chapter 6 on episodic memory). The spatio-temporal or *environmental context* of the supermarket

KEY TERM

Context cues: Retrieval cues that specify aspects of the conditions under which a desired target was encoded, including (for example) the location and time of the event.

event includes the setting of your local market on Tuesday, for example.

Memory retrieval is often influenced by context, sometimes intentionally, other times not. When we intentionally retrieve the past, part of the cue-specification process involves isolating the part of the past we wish to recollect. If your roommate asks whether you took out the trash, they are not asking you to recollect any event from your past in which you took out the trash. If you did not constrain retrieval to the context of the last day, you might recollect some previous occasion and falsely say you took it out. The result: one annoyed roommate. Thus, one of the cues you must include during retrieval is the spatio-temporal context of the event you are hoping to recollect.

The concept of context is not limited to spatio-temporal context, but also includes other aspects of the circumstances. The *mood context* of an event refers to the emotional state that a person was in when the event took place, whereas the *physiological context* refers to the pharmacological/physical state that one was in (e.g., under the influence of a certain drug, or alcohol). One can also distinguish *cognitive context*, which can mean particular collection of concepts and ideas that one has thought about in the temporal vicinity of the event. In our later section on context-dependent memory, we will discuss how all of these types of context can constrain what we retrieve of our past, even when we are not aware of it. Context cues also play a role in defining the types of retrieval tasks often used to study memory.

RETRIEVAL TASKS

Each day, life leaves its bootprints in our mental clay, and these imprints influence us in many ways. Sometimes, we are deliberate users of memory, trying to consciously recollect what happened in times past. Other times, we may not intend to be influenced by memory, but are, without being aware of it. Psychologists have devised numerous methods for testing retrieval that get at these circumstances. These tests reflect various circumstances in daily life, and differences in memory across test types have taught us important lessons about the structures and processes of memory.

Direct memory tests

Tests that ask people to retrieve their past are known as direct/explicit memory tests (Richardson-Klavehn & Bjork, 1988; Schacter, 1987). Because they ask people to intentionally recall particular experiences, these tests require a representation of temporal context as a cue and also the adoption of an explicit retrieval mode (i.e., a mental set in which people intend to treat stimuli as cues to search memory). Direct tests vary in the amount of cues given, the amount to be retrieved, and in the involvement of retrieval strategies. *Free recall* relies on context the most heavily because people must retrieve an entire set of studied items without overt cues, freely—that is, any order. For example, if you studied 25 words and then tried to recall them in any order, you would be performing free recall. Free recall mimics situations in daily life in which we must produce a lot of information in no particular order. Recalling who was at a party last night, recalling the items on a grocery list that you left at home, and even answering the question, "What did you do today?" are all cases of free recall. Free recall also necessitates the use of strategies for generating the answers in some order. Thus, this test is sensitive to one's skills at organizing information at encoding, and selecting strategies at retrieval. As noted earlier, frontal patients have significant difficulties with free recall.

In contrast, *cued recall* provides additional cues, and very often focuses on particular items in memory. In laboratory studies, this might include providing an associate of a previously studied word or an initial letter as a cue. Cued recall tests are intended to mimic situations when we are recalling a particular item or experience in response to a cue. Recalling who drove you to the party last night, or which grocery store you went to today are examples of cued recall. Cued recall requires context as a cue, but context is supplemented with specific information that focuses search. Cued recall is often easier than free recall, and doesn't rely as heavily on retrieval strategies to recall items.

Recognition tests are usually the easiest type of direct test, because they simply require a decision: Did you encounter this stimulus on this occasion? If, after asking you to study a set of 25 pictures or words, I presented you with those 25 items, intermixed with 25 new ones, and asked you to indicate for each whether you had seen it in the original list, I would be giving you a recognition test. Recognition tests pop up all the time. One especially critical example that we discuss in Chapter 12 on eyewitness memory is when an eyewitness is asked if anyone in a lineup was the person they saw committing a crime. Recognition tests can be accomplished in two ways, one that relies heavily on context, another that relies on it less. We will return to this in depth in a later section on recognition.

Indirect memory tests

In a famous legal case, Bright Tunes Music v. Harrisongs Music, George Harrison of the Beatles was sued for borrowing substantial portions of the song *He's So Fine* by the Chiffons and using them in his song *My Sweet Lord*. Harrison lost his case, even though he insisted that he did not consciously copy the song. As a child, Helen Keller was accused of plagiarism due to her story *The Frost King*, which bore remarkable resemblance to Martin Canby's *The Frost Fairies*, a fairy tale that had been read to her when she was very young. Here again, Keller did not have any awareness of what she was doing, and the experience was traumatic for her. There are many apparent cases of such *cryptomnesia*, in which a person believes they are creating something new such as a piece of artwork, but is recalling a similar

work they have encountered. Can memories influence us unconsciously?

In fact, we are frequently influenced by our experiences, without being aware of it. Suppose, for example, you find an anagram puzzle in your newspaper. As you are trying to solve the anagram for "pomegranate," you might well find that the solution comes very easily if you had just read about pomegranates earlier in the day. Your performance on a task (anagram solving) has benefitted from the experience even though you were not trying to recall the past. Many demonstrations show that such influences are possible. The foregoing examples illustrate what is known as an *indirect memory* test, which is taken as a measure of *implicit memory* (Richardson-Klavehn & Bjork, 1988; Schacter, 1987).

Indirect tests measure the influence of experience without asking the person to recall the past. These measures have a "sneaky" quality to them, in that they try to eliminate, from the participants' viewpoint, any scent that they are memorizing, or, on the test, retrieving things. In a typical implicit memory experiment, participants might first encode a list of words. For each word, people might make a simple judgment, such as whether the object denoted by the word refers to a living thing—a task chosen to not arouse suspicions that memory might be tested. Afterwards, the participants would perform a task involving some of the old words, mixed with new words. The test usually asks the person to perform some task that can be done without recalling any particular experience. Many indirect tests are possible, and there is usually a "cover story" about why the experimenter is interested in the task. In a *lexical decision task*, participants would receive words and nonwords (e.g., GLORK) and for each would decide as quickly as possible whether the letter string presented was a real English word. In a *perceptual identification task*, participants receive briefly presented words (e.g., 30 milliseconds), covered by a visual mask (e.g., a row of Xs) to make it difficult to see. Participants' task is to simply say the word they saw. On *word fragment completion tests* (e.g., P_M_ GR_N_T_) or *word stem completion tests* (PO____), people would list the first word that comes to mind that fits the letters.

TABLE 8.1 Typical types of direct and indirect retrieval tasks used in the laboratory to study explicit and implicit memory

Test category	Test type	Example retrieval instructions
Free recall	Direct/explicit	"Recall studied items in any order."
Cued recall	Direct/explicit	"What word did you study together with leap?"
Forced-choice recognition	Direct/explicit	"Which did you study: ballet or monk?"
Yes/No recognition	Direct/explicit	"Did you study ballet?"
Lexical decision	Indirect/implicit	"Is ballet a word? Is mokn a word?"
Word fragment completion	Indirect/implicit	"Fill in the missing letters to form a word: b–l–e–."
Word stem completion	Indirect/implicit	"Fill in the missing letters with anything that fits: bal – – –
Conceptual fluency	Indirect/implicit	"Name all the dance types you can."

In each of the foregoing tests, people are better at doing the task for previously viewed words, compared to new words even when they are unaware of the connection to the prior phase: they make lexical decisions faster, identify difficult-to-see words more accurately, or generate word fragment completions more frequently. Similar tests exist for other stimuli classes, such as for pictures and sounds. Performance consistently shows characteristics that differ from those observed on explicit tests. For example, the benefit is often sensitive to the perceptual match between encoding and test stimuli. For instance changing perceptual modalities between study and test (from hearing words at encoding, to a visual test) can reduce the benefits observed. Although many of these tests focus on perceptual qualities of the stimulus (i.e., are *perceptually driven*), some indirect tests measure the influence of experience on conceptual tasks, and are known as *conceptually driven indirect tests*. For example, if I gave you semantic categories and asked you to generate as many members of each as possible—a measure known as *conceptual fluency*—you would be more likely to list BUZZARD in the BIRDS category than you would be if you had not read this chapter today.

How do indirect and direct tests differ? They do not necessarily differ in the core mechanisms described in the beginning of this chapter. For example, indirect tests provide cues that initiate a retrieval process that accesses a remnant of experience, perhaps through spreading activation. They do differ, however, in that indirect tests do not require recall of the past, and so context is not used intentionally as a cue. Rather, only the directly presented cues such as the letters of the word, or the fragments of the picture, are used consciously. Despite the absence of contextual cuing, recent experience with the stimulus improves performance, a phenomenon known as *repetition priming* (see Ochsner, Chiu, & Schacter, 1998 for a review). Repetition priming is widely thought of as a case in which past experience influences us unconsciously. This implicit influence does not mean that the memory traces accessed by indirect tests are identical to those that underlie episodic memory. In fact, research on the neural correlates of repetition priming indicates that it is mainly a neocortical (as opposed to hippocampal) phenomenon. For instance, stimulus repetitions are typically associated with reduced neural activity in the brain region that responds to the stimulus, a phenomenon known as repetition suppression (Barron, Garvert, & Behrens, 2016; Grill-Spector, Henson, &

KEY TERM

Repetition suppression: Reduced neural activity in brain regions that respond to a particular stimulus arising upon repetitions of that stimulus, often taken to reflect increased processing efficiency arising due to a stored memory trace.

Martin, 2006). Repetition suppression is a robust and general phenomenon thought to reflect increased efficiency of neural processing arising from persisting perceptual traces in sensory cortex. Stimulus repetition-related reductions in neural activity have also been observed at the level of single neurons in the temporal cortex of nonhuman primates (Miller & Desimone, 1994). In contrast, explicit memory is supported by additional contextual representations in the hippocampus and parahippocampus (Diana, Yonelinas, & Ranganath, 2013). Thus indirect tests differ both in the absence of contextual cuing, and likely in the content and neural locus of the traces which they access.

Of course, it is natural to wonder whether behavioral priming effects on indirect tests is truly unconscious. Perhaps people realize they are being tested on the earlier material, and just recall things intentionally. Indeed, not everyone is fooled. Nevertheless, even when people profess no awareness of the connection, benefits occur. Importantly, amnesic patients, who are unable to recollect much about an experience after just a few moments, show normal performance on indirect tests. This fact—that explicit memory is impaired in amnesia, but implicit memory is intact—led scientists to the view that memory is composed of multiple distinct systems (Squire, 1992; see Gabrieli, 1998 for a review). Indirect tests illustrate how the bootprints of experience can influence us without our knowing it. All of this ought to leave us more sympathetic to George Harrison and Helen Keller.

THE IMPORTANCE OF INCIDENTAL CONTEXT IN EPISODIC MEMORY RETRIEVAL

When people retrieve the past, they use context to focus retrieval on the desired place and time. But can we be influenced by context unintentionally? Suppose that you experienced an event in one environment or mood, and later wish to retrieve that experience whilst in a different environment or mood. How will memory compare to a situation in which one is in the same location or mood at retrieval that was present at encoding? As it turns out, the match of the current context to the one we are retrieving matters, a phenomenon known as context-dependent memory. Several types of context-dependent memory exist, including environmental-, mood-, and state-dependent memory.

Environmental context-dependent memory

One evening, I was sitting in my home office, when I decided that I could really go for a cup of tea. After walking downstairs I found myself in the kitchen wondering why I was there. I knew that I had come downstairs for something, and that that something was in the kitchen, but I couldn't remember what it was. So I went upstairs to my home office and it popped into my head: I wanted tea. Why did retrieval fail and then succeed? It seems likely that returning to the original environment reinstated the spatial context in which the event was originally encoded, aiding retrieval.

Context-dependent memory effects do in fact occur. Some decades ago Duncan Godden and the first author explored this phenomenon in connection with an applied problem, namely that of training deep sea divers (Godden & Baddeley, 1975). Earlier experiments of Baddeley's on the effect of cold on divers had suggested quite incidentally that the underwater environment might induce strong context dependency. This suggestion was supported by the observations of a friend who was in charge of a team of divers attempting to watch the behavior of fish about to enter, or escape from, trawl nets. Initially he relied on debriefing his

> **KEY TERM**
>
> **Context-dependent memory:** The finding that memory benefits when the spatio-temporal, mood, physiological, or cognitive context at retrieval matches that present at encoding.

divers when they surfaced, only to find that they had apparently forgotten most of the fishy behavior they had seen. Eventually he had to send his divers down with underwater tape recorders so that they could give a running commentary on the fishes' activities. Intrigued by this, Godden and Baddeley set up an experiment in which divers listened to 40 unrelated words either on the beach or under about 10 feet of water. After the 40 words had been heard, the divers were tested either in the same environment or in the alternative one. The results, shown in Figure 8.3, were very clear: material learned underwater was best recalled underwater, and material learned on land was best recalled on land. Similar findings have been observed with a variety of other changes in physical context, including changes in room, and with many types of stimuli, including pictures, words, and faces.

Smith and Vela (2001) reviewed research on context-dependent memory and drew several important conclusions. One broad principle that characterizes when people show sensitivity to environmental context is that people need to pay some attention to the physical environment during encoding. If people have a more inward focus of attention during encoding, it reduces or eliminates incidental context effects. Context-dependent memory effects also grow in size as the delay between encoding and retrieval increases, which may account for why returning to a childhood home one has not visited in a long time creates the feeling of being "flooded" with memories one has not thought about in years. Finally, and, quite usefully, the mere mental reinstatement of context greatly reduces context-dependent memory effects. Hence, if one is trying to retrieve an experience or fact encoded in a vastly different context, it can be highly beneficial to imagine the elements of the physical environment such as the objects that were present, layout, and other details.

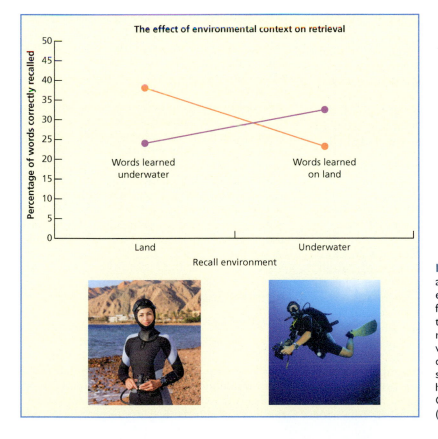

Figure 8.3 Words learned and tested in the same environment (i.e. data points falling within the top half of the graph) are better recalled than those items for which the environmental context varied between study and test (i.e. bottom half of the graph). Data from Godden and Baddeley (1975).

One area in which understanding context-dependent memory has proven useful is the treatment of individuals with debilitating phobias. One of the main therapeutic techniques for treating phobias involves graded exposure therapy in which patients are gradually exposed to the fearful stimulus in increasingly direct fashion, until the patient learns not to be afraid of the stimulus. Although this therapy can with time be very successful in reducing fear, one major problem with it is that patients' fears often return when the patient encounters the feared stimulus in some place other than the treatment location, a phenomenon known as a *renewal effect* (Bouton & Moody, 2004). Renewal happens because the treatment leads to learning that helps to reduce a person's fear, but that learning is strongly associated to the treatment context and not to the new location outside of therapy. Building on this insight, Jayson Mystkowski, Michelle Craske and colleagues (Mystkowski, Craske, Echiverri, & Labus, 2006) reasoned that if they asked spider phobics to mentally reinstate the location in which their prior exposure therapy took place, this should help them retrieve what they experienced in therapy and significantly reduce the renewal of fear they experience in a new context. Participants who did this successfully eliminated the renewal of fear, hopefully enabling them to experience the benefits of therapy in daily life.

State-dependent memory

Context-dependent memory effects also occur when the learner's *internal* environment is changed by means of a drug such as alcohol, an effect known as *state dependency*. Goodwin and colleagues (Goodwin, Powell, Bremer, Hoine, & Stern, 1969) cite clinical evidence of this. Heavy drinkers who hide alcohol or money when drunk are unable to remember where it is hidden once they are sober; when they become drunk again, they remember. Goodwin studied this effect using a whole range of tests and found, in general, that what is learned when drunk is best recalled when drunk. Similar results have been shown with a range of other drugs, for

example with nitrous oxide, sometimes used to anesthetise patients, marijuana (Eich, 1980), and even caffeine. In a review, Eich (1980) convincingly showed that state dependency is only observed when memory is tested by recall; it disappears when recognition testing is used. It appears that the participant's internal state helps to access the memory, but that when access is made easy by presenting an item for recognition, search is unnecessary.

State-dependent memory effects also occur from a variety of changes in physiological state that occur naturally. One interesting example comes from a study by Christopher Miles and Elinor Hardman (1998), who examined whether aerobic exercise might produce state-dependent memory. They had participants learn a list of auditorally presented words either while they were resting comfortably on an exercise bicycle, or while they were pedaling the bike quickly enough to raise their heart rate to 120–150 beats per minute. Then, after rest, they asked their participants to free recall the words while at rest, or while bicycling, as before. Strikingly, people who got to recall the words in the same cardiovascular state—whether at rest both times or exercising both times—recalled the words 20% better than did people who shifted their state between encoding and recall (see also Schramke & Bauer, 1997). Thus, aspects of our physiological state get encoded incidentally with the episodic experience, and recreation of that state at retrieval helps memory. Students who read course material while on their stairmaster or exercise bicycle should take note of this, as should athletes who need to remember the lessons about performance learned off the field, while on the field.

Mood-congruent and mood-dependent memory

When depressed people are asked to recall autobiographical memories, they tend to recall unhappy incidents; the more depressed the individual, the more rapidly the unpleasant experience is recalled. Of course, this may simply be because depressed people indeed lead less pleasant lives, explaining why they are depressed. One study avoided this problem by selecting patients whose level of depression fluctuated systematically throughout the day, as sometimes occurs in depression (Clark & Teasdale, 1982). During sad times of the day they were consistently less likely to produce happy memories than at other times. Similar results have also been obtained with healthy participants, using a procedure known as the Velten technique. A happy or sad mood is induced by encouraging participants to ponder sets of sad or happy statements (Velten, 1968). While sad, participants were slower at evoking positive memories (Teasdale & Fogarty, 1979).

The preceding findings provide evidence of mood-congruent memory (Blaney, 1986). This term refers to the greater ease in recalling events that have an emotional tone that matches the current mood of the person. Thus, it is easier to recall happy memories in a happy mood, and sad memories whilst in a sad mood. Indeed, the fact that people in a depressed mood have difficulty retrieving pleasant memories, may be part of the problem of depression. If a person is depressed, he or she will be likely to recall unpleasant incidents from the past, further deepening the depression. Cognitive approaches to the treatment of depression involve helping the person to access less depressing memories and revalue the more positive aspects of their lives. Moreover, given the biases in retrieval evident in mood-congruent memory, one would do well not to make hasty decisions in a powerful mood state. If you are upset with someone, chances are that all you will remember about them are unpleasant experiences, even if many positive memories might otherwise be available for retrieval.

Although mood-congruent memory is an interesting phenomenon, it is not a demonstration of incidental context-dependent memory because the main thing determining recall probability is the match of the mood context being retrieved to the current mood. As such, it is not that mood state at encoding is being incidentally attached to otherwise neutral events, and acting as incidental context. To establish such mood-dependent memory, one needs to show that the ease with which a memory is recalled depends on the match in mood states between encoding and retrieval, not merely on the congruency of what is recalled with the retrieval mood state. In one demonstration of this, Eric Eich, Dawn Macaulay, and Lee Ryan (1994) found evidence of mood-dependent memory when they asked people to generate events from their past in response to cues (e.g., SHIP, STREET). They induced participants to be in either a pleasant (P) or unpleasant (U) mood at encoding, and then again at retrieval, which took place two days later. Mood was induced by having participants listen to either merry or melancholy music, while entertaining elating or depressing thoughts. Once the relevant mood was established (as rated by the participant), encoding or, two days later, retrieval commenced. They found that free recall of the events generated two days earlier was better when the mood state at test matched that at encoding, irrespective of whether the event recalled was itself positive, neutral, or negative in tone. Mood-dependent memory also occurs with manipulations of stress and fear versus relaxation (Lang, Craske, Brown, & Ghaneian, 2001; Robinson & Rollings, 2010). For example, Sarita Robinson and Lucy Rollings asked participants to watch eight-minute clips of stressful Hollywood film clips (e.g., *Silence of the Lambs*) or neutral clips. They found that people recognized faces they had studied better when the mood state matched at both study and test. It seems that regardless of the emotional qualities of the content being retrieved, the match in mood between encoding and later retrieval influences whether memories will be retrieved.

> **KEY TERM**
>
> **Mood-congruent memory:** Bias in the recall of memories such that negative mood makes negative memories more readily available than positive, and vice versa. Unlike mood dependency, it does not affect the recall of neutral memories.
>
> **Mood-dependent memory:** A form of context-dependent effect whereby what is learnt in a given mood, whether positive, negative or neutral, is best recalled in that mood.

Cognitive context-dependent memory

One's internal context also includes the particular ideas, thoughts, and concepts that have occupied our attention around the time of encoding, and retrieval. It seems safe to speculate, for example, that during Picasso's Blue Period, that blue was very much on Picasso's mind. Can the general cognitive context in which one encodes an experience influence our ability to retrieve that information later?

One example of the influence of cognitive context is the tendency for language context to influence what memories one retrieves most easily. In a nice illustration by Viorica Marian and Ulric Neisser (2000), a group of Russian-English bilinguals were asked to tell stories about their lives in response to word prompts. The participants were told that half of the session would be conducted in English, and the other half in Russian. Within each segment only one of the languages was spoken, and participants received cue words in that same language in response to which they were to generate a memory from any time in their lives. Interestingly, when the interview was conducted in Russian, participants generated Russian memories (i.e., memories they had experienced in a Russian-speaking context) to 64% of those cues, whereas when the interview was conducted in English, they only generated Russian memories to 35% of the cues. The opposite pattern occurred for English memories.

Marian and Neisser argue that linguistic context acts like other forms of incidental context. They suggest that bilinguals may have two language modes, in which memories take place and are stored. When that mode is recreated by conversing in a given language, their incidental cognitive context favors retrieval of memories acquired in that mode. Other studies have replicated this pattern, and have extended it to memory for academic material, and even general semantic knowledge. For example, Marian and Fausey (2006) found that bilinguals were better at remembering information (e.g., about chemistry, history, etc.) when tested in the same language in which the material was studied.

It is fascinating to think that whole segments of your life—both personal memories and general knowledge—may be rendered less accessible by the language you currently speak—a fact that, if true, must affect the sizable portion of the planet that is bilingual. Given this, students who pursue studies in foreign countries have challenges not faced by their native language colleagues—challenges that extend beyond mastering a new language. The challenges they face provide an illustration of the influence of incidental context on the experiences that lie within our mental grasp.

RECONSTRUCTIVE MEMORY

So far, we have characterized retrieval as bringing to mind an intact memory. Retrieval is sometimes more involved when we are retrieving something on the fringe of accessibility, however. We may be able to recall aspects of the experience, but may be forced to "figure out" other aspects. The term reconstructive memory refers to this active and inferential aspect of retrieval. Some of the flavour of reconstructive memory is given by the following account, which AB, the first author, produced a few days after the experience had taken place.

November, 1978

On the train platform I notice a familiar face and I decide to see if I can remember who he is. Two associations occur, the name Sebastian and something to do with children. Sebastian seems to me to be a useful cue, but all it calls up is an association with teddy bears through Evelyn Waugh's Brideshead

> **KEY TERM**
>
> **Reconstructive memory:** An active and inferential process of retrieval whereby gaps in memory are filled-in based on prior experience, logic, and goals.

Revisited. *I also sense there are some associations with a darkish room with books, but nothing clear enough to suggest any useful further search.*

A little later, for no apparent reason, BABYSITTING pops up and I recall that we were both members of a mutual babysitting group, that his name is indeed Sebastian, although I cannot remember his second name, and that he lives in a road whose location I am quite clear about and in a house which I could visualize easily. A clear image of his sitting-room appears, together with the fact that it contains finely printed books, and that he is by profession a printer. I remember noticing that he has a printing press in one room. I have no doubt that I have identified him.

Two days later, it occurs to me that I still have not remembered his surname or the name of the street in which he lives. I have no clues about his name, but know that he lives in either Oxford Road or Windsor Road. I have a colleague who lives in the one that Sebastian does not live in. If I have to guess, I would say that he lives in Oxford Road, and that my colleague lives in Windsor Road. I try again to remember his surname. Sebastian.... Nothing. And then for no obvious reason CARTER appears. It feels right, although not overwhelmingly so. Then the association PENNY CARTER appears as his wife's name. I am sure that this is correct, reinforcing my belief that his name is Sebastian Carter.

I go to the telephone directory. After this effort I had better be right. CARTER is indeed in Oxford Road. I ring and ask him, "Was he on the 14.36 train to Liverpool Street on Tuesday?" He was.

This experience illustrates several important points. First, there certainly is an automatic retrieval process whereby information "pops up" for no obvious reason. The name SEBASTIAN and the association with babysitting were examples. Second, when the appropriate information does not spring to mind, we seem to take the fragments and use them like a detective might use a clue. In the case of the clue SEBASTIAN, the first author followed up associations, each of which could be rejected. In contrast, the vague association with children produced babysitting and then a clear image of the Carters' house. This in turn produced other information, including the fact that Sebastian Carter is a printer and a visual image of a printing press in his house. The whole episode also vividly illustrates the operation of the retrieval control processes mentioned at the outset of this chapter, including *cue-specification*, *cue-maintenance*, and *post-retrieval monitoring*, all of which were essential to this effortful retrieval.

Reconstruction is often driven by background knowledge that suggests plausible inferences. Such inferences may even lead us to believe we are remembering something when we are not. In one nice study, Dooling and Christiaansen (1977) gave participants the following passage to read and study:

Carol Harris's need for professional help

Carol Harris was a problem child from birth. She was wild, stubborn, and violent. By the time Carol turned eight, she was still unmanageable. Her parents were very concerned about her mental health. There was no good institution for her problem in her state. Her parents finally decided to take some action. They hired a private teacher for Carol.

The participants were tested one week later. Just before the test, half of the participants were told that the story about Carol Harris was really about Helen Keller, whereas the other half was told nothing. Interestingly, the participants told that the story was about Helen Keller were far more likely to claim that they recognized seeing sentences like, "She was deaf, dumb, and blind," when they had not seen them. Presumably, hearing about Helen Keller just before the test activated knowledge they had about her, leading them to believe they remembered something that they did not experience. Here we have a clear example of reconstructive inference influencing what people think they remember. Such errors grow more likely as time goes by, because the original memory grows less accessible (Spiro, 1977).

Helen Keller c. 1904. In Dooling and Christiaansen's (1977) study participants claimed that they had seen sentences describing Helen Keller as "deaf, dumb, and blind," when in reality they had not. This is an example of reconstructive inference influencing what people think they remember.

Although reconstructive processes often lead to errors in recollection, they are in fact quite useful, and often lead us to recall correct information and make plausible inferences about what must have happened. Nevertheless, when veridical recall is essential (e.g., eyewitness memory), reconstructive errors can have grave consequences. A person who witnesses a fight and later unintentionally misrecollects who started the fight based on stereotype-based reconstructive memory is a serious danger to the accused.

RECOGNITION MEMORY

Thus far, we have focused on free and cued recall as models of retrieval. Very often, however, we use our memories not to generate things, but to make a decision about whether we have encountered a stimulus. We may scan a list of phone numbers in hopes of picking out the one we wish to dial; we may see a person on the street and wonder whether we have met them before; or we may be called upon to identify the perpetrator of a crime in a police lineup. This situation, known as recognition memory, warrants a special discussion because different processes are engaged. Unlike recall, recognition presents the intact stimulus, and hence requires a judgment: Did you see this stimulus in a certain context? A number of consequences follow from this that pertain to the measurement of recognition, and to the way that people solve the task.

First, recognition tests fundamentally require a discrimination between stimuli that a person experienced in a particular context, and things that they didn't. Because the person must discriminate "Old" from "New," a test is only meaningful if it includes both old *and* new items, forcing the rememberer to show their skill at making good discriminations. These nonstudied items are called distractors, *lures*, or sometimes *foils*, and are akin to the other members of the lineup that the police think are innocent. In laboratory research, distractors are sometimes presented together with the old item, and the person must choose one of the items, which is known as a *forced-choice recognition test*. Other tests present one item at a time, and ask people to make a yes or no decision to each, with old and new items intermixed. This is known as a *yes/no recognition test*. Distractors on such tests provide valuable information about how much a person's recognition judgment can be trusted.

How do we take people's responses to distractors into account? In measuring recognition for a set of material, a single error does not make someone's retention bad. People with good memory sometimes make mistakes. If so, how do we take the number of mistaken identifications into account? Should somebody with 10% mistaken recognitions be judged as having deficient retention? If so, then is the memory of a person with 10% mistaken recognitions necessarily less good than a person with 5%? What about someone who correctly identifies 85% of the old items, but has 10% mistaken identifications? Is that person's memory worse than someone who recognizes 40% of the old items, but only has 5% mistaken identifications?

To make matters worse, we need to consider people's tendencies for guessing when making a recognition judgment. Sometimes an incorrect judgment of "Yes" to a new item does not reflect a sincere belief in having seen the item (unlike our hypothetical eyewitness), but rather the person's uncertainty together with a need to make a decision. For the same reason, some of the "Yes" responses to old items will reflect guessing. Indeed, in police lineups, the social situation puts pressure on witnesses to identify somebody, leading some people to guess, based on who seems familiar. To see how much influence guessing can have, imagine two participants given a recognition task. Person A is told that there will be both old and new items on the test, but that there will be no penalty for incorrectly circling new items; Person B is told that incorrect responses to new items will be harshly penalized. The latter person will surely be more conservative than the former, greatly reducing their tendency to respond "yes" to new items, and also their "yes" responses to old items about which they are somewhat unsure. Clearly, guessing is an issue, and the rate of guessing can vary, depending on people's biases.

This discussion raises a general issue in measuring recognition memory: distinguishing memory from decision making. Some means of estimating the amount of information in memory is essential, and this method must separate out judgment biases. To devise such a method, however, requires a theory of the memory processes that enter in a recognition judgment. We discuss such an approach next.

Signal detection theory as a model of recognition memory

One approach to understanding recognition builds on the concepts developed in signal detection theory. Signal detection theory evolved in research on auditory perception (Green & Swets, 1966). In a typical auditory detection experiment, people listen for a faint tone presented in a background of white noise, and are instructed to press a button if they detect a tone. Depending on how faint the tone is, people will not be perfect, and so four types of event can occur. A tone might be presented, and the person might correctly claim that they heard it, which is known as a *hit*. Sometimes tones are presented that people do not detect, however, which is called a *miss*. When a tone is not presented, people sometimes mistakenly claim that they heard a tone, which is called a *false alarm*. Finally, people quite often claim not to have heard a tone when the tone was not presented, which is called a *correct rejection*.

A similar situation exists on a yes/no recognition test. On a recognition test, a person must decide whether they sense "familiarity" in the stimulus. Deciding if a stimulus seems familiar enough to classify as "Old" is like deciding whether there is enough auditory evidence to claim you heard a tone. As with auditory detection, four outcomes are possible. If the item was studied, and the person correctly classifies it as "Old,"

KEY TERM

Signal detection theory: A model of recognition memory that posits that memory targets (signals) and lures (noise) on a recognition test possess an attribute known as strength or familiarity, which occurs in a graded fashion, with previously encountered items generally possessing more strength than novel items. The process of recognition involves ascertaining a given test item's strength and then deciding whether it exceeds a criterion level of strength, above which items are considered to be previously encountered. Signal detection theory provides analytic tools that separate true memory from judgment biases in recognition.

it's a hit; if it is old, but misclassified as "New" it is a miss. If the item is new, and the person misclassifies it as "Old," it is a false alarm, and if they correctly judge it as "New," it is a correct rejection.

Signal detection theory provides a useful way of thinking about recognition that comes with tools necessary to distinguish true memory and guessing. Signal detection theory proposes that memory traces have *strength* values (see foregoing discussion of *activation level*) that reflect their activation in memory, which dictate how familiar they seem. Traces are thought to vary in their familiarity, depending on how much attention the item received at encoding, or how many times it was repeated. Importantly, the theory assumes that new items will have familiarity as well, though usually less than items that

have been studied. Their familiarity might arise if the new items have been seen frequently outside the experiment, or, instead, if they are similar to studied items. In terms of the police lineup example, a person may seem powerfully familiar to a witness because the witness saw them before (just not at the crime), or because they look a lot like the actual perpetrator.

But how do these ideas help? One key idea is that the familiarity of a set of items is normally distributed, and that the studied and new items each have their own distributions. These distributions are likely to vary in the average level of familiarity. In most cases, the average familiarity for studied (old) items will be higher than the average for new items due to the recent exposure of old items, though, as illustrated in Figure 8.4, these distributions

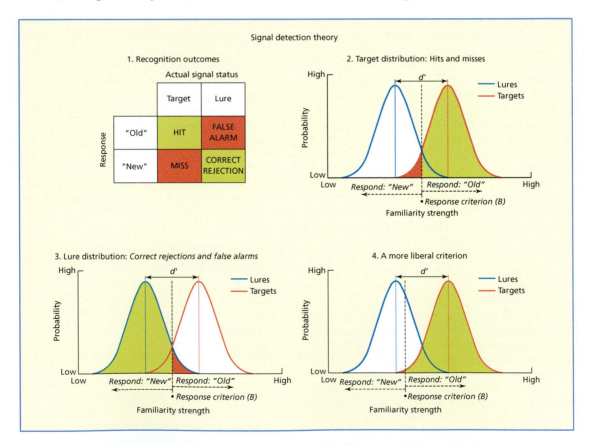

Figure 8.4 (1) Recognition outcomes, jointly based on item (signal) status and the participant's response. (2) Familiarity distributions for targets and lures. Hits are in green; misses in red. (3) Correct rejections (green) and false alarms (red). (4) Shifting the response criterion leftward increases hits and false alarms.

may overlap. This overlap arises because some old items may have been encoded poorly, and so will not have received much of a boost in memory strength, whereas some new items may seem especially familiar. For some participants, these distributions may be very close, with only a minimal difference in average familiarity across the old and new distributions. For others, these distributions might be very far apart, and even nonoverlapping, if they studied the list quite well. Increasing study time, or the number of repetitions of each studied item would also push the old distribution farther away from new items, increasing overall familiarity.

Importantly, how well a person can discriminate studied from new items depends on the difference in the average familiarity between their old and new distributions. In other words, a participant's ability to discriminate two sets of items can be measured by the distance between the averages of the old and new distributions, as shown in Figure 8.4. In the language of signal detection theory, this distance is known as *d' ("d prime").*

But how does a recognition judgment take place? To address this issue, the theory proposes that people choose a *criterion* level of familiarity, above which they will judge a test item as old, and below which they will judge an item as new. The bottom-right panel of Figure 8.4 illustrates one positioning of the criterion on the familiarity continuum. Notice that by placing the criterion in this location, some old items will fall below the criterion for "oldness," and so will be classified as misses. Old items that fall above the criterion, however, will be "hits." Similarly, some new items will have familiarity that exceeds the criterion, leading people to classify them incorrectly as old; these are false alarms. New items falling below the criterion will be classified as correct rejections. Thus, our four outcomes (hit, miss, false alarm, correct rejection) can be understood, given their familiarity, relative to the criterion and status (old or new).

The idea that people set a criterion for judging "oldness" helps to define what a judgment bias is. To see this, notice what would happen if the criterion is "loosened" by shifting it farther to the left on the familiarity continuum, allowing less familiar items to be classified as "old." This would ensure that the vast majority of old items will be hits, and there will be very few misses. Unfortunately, this would also increase the proportion of new items judged as old, and so will increase the false alarm rate. When the criterion is made strict (shifted to the right), a complementary thing happens: people will be unlikely to commit a false alarm, but will suffer increased misses. These two ways of shifting the criterion describe what happens when a person adopts either a liberal or conservative guessing strategy, respectively. By placing the criterion between the means of the two distributions, the person would be unbiased. The familiarity value at which a person places their criterion is referred to as *B (beta)*, and estimates the tendency to guess.

Given this analysis, signal detection theory provides mathematical tools for estimating a person's ability to discriminate old from new items and their guessing strategies. By computing a person's hit rate (proportion of old items judged old) and their false alarm rate (proportion of new items judged old), one can compute d' and beta and so disentangle these factors. More importantly, signal detection theory provides a conceptualization of how recognition judgments take place. The idea that memories lie on a continuum of strength, and that people use this internal "sense" of familiarity, to judge their experience with an item has proven to be an extremely useful theory.

Certain phenomena appear challenging, however, for signal detection theory to explain. For example, on free recall tests, words used frequently in a language are better recalled than are words used infrequently. This advantage makes sense considering that high frequency words, by virtue of repetition, are likely to be represented more strongly in memory than are low frequency words and therefore should be easier to encode (Hall, 1954; Sumby, 1963). If item strength underlies this effect, high frequency words should also be better recognized according to signal detection theory. In fact, the opposite occurs: low frequency words are better recognized than high frequency words, a phenomenon known as the *word frequency effect* in recognition memory (e.g., Glanzer & Bowles, 1976; Gorman, 1961; Kinsbourne & George, 1974). The word frequency effect thus suggests that some factor other than item strength must contribute to recognition memory. For these and other reasons, many theorists believe that another process contributes to recognition—a process that is much more akin to recall. We discuss this view next.

Dual-process accounts of recognition memory

Seeking technical advice one afternoon, I made my way to the Media Services Office where a pleasant woman greeted me, all smiles. Responding in kind, I extended my hand, introducing myself saying, "Hi, I'm Mike Anderson from the Psychology department, and I was wondering if there was someone here who might help me with my website." She looked at me blankly, paused, and said, "I know who you are." She did look exceedingly familiar, but I wasn't sure where from. She said, "You really don't remember, do you?" I had to admit that I couldn't place her. She explained that we had gone on a date several years earlier—a date lasting *six hours*. The date took place in an entirely different city (where she used to live) several hours from where we currently were. The moment she revealed this, I remembered the whole context, and recognized her completely, offering embarrassed apologies. Good friends now, she will never, ever, let me forget this event.

This story illustrates something that has happened to most of us—the experience of *knowing* somebody (or something), without having the ability to *remember* where from. The experience illustrates an important point: One can have a very high degree of familiarity for a stimulus, but still feel as though their recognition is incomplete. It seems as though recognition judgments can be made in one of two ways; you can make a judgment based on how familiar a stimulus seems, a process known as familiarity-based recognition. Alternatively, you can recognize something by recalling the particulars of the experience, a process known as recollection. According to dual-process theories of recognition, both

of these processes contribute to recognition (e.g., Aggleton & Brown, 1999; Atkinson & Juola, 1974; Jacoby & Dallas, 1981; Mandler, 1980; Yonelinas, 1999). The familiarity process is characterized as fast and automatic, yielding, as output, a perception of the memory's strength, without the recall of particulars. It is well characterized by signal detection theory. The recollection process, by contrast, is proposed to be slow, and more attention demanding, much more like the recall processes emphasized in the earlier part of this chapter—cued recall, to be precise. It involves generating information about the context of experiencing the stimulus. Dual-process models of recognition are therefore compatible with signal detection theory, but posit an additional process that contributes to recognition memory.

A number of methods have been developed to isolate the contributions of recollection and familiarity. One method, known as the remember/know procedure

KEY TERM

Familiarity-based recognition: A fast, automatic recognition process based on the perception of a memory's strength. Proponents of dual-process models consider familiarity to be independent of the contextual information characteristic of recollection.

Recollection: The slower, more attention-demanding component of recognition memory in dual-process models, which involves retrieval of contextual information about the memory.

Dual-process theories of recognition: A class of recognition models that assumes that recognition memory judgments can be based on two independent forms of retrieval process: recollection and familiarity.

Remember/know procedure: A procedure used on recognition memory tests to separate the influences of familiarity and recollection on recognition performance. For each test item, participants report whether it is recognized because the person can recollect contextual details of seeing the item (classified as a "remember" response) or because the item seems familiar, in the absence of specific recollections (classified as "know" response).

(Tulving, 1985), asks people to make judgments on the test about why they feel they recognize the item. In particular, people are asked to report whether they recognize each item on the basis of *remembering* (i.e., consciously recollecting the particulars of the study event), or *knowing* (i.e., judging that the item seems very familiar, in the absence of memory for the details of the event). "Remember" responses are taken to measure recollection, whereas "Know" responses are taken to measure familiarity-based recognition (Yonelinas, 2002; see also, Gardiner, Ramponi, & Richardson-Klavehn, 2000). Not all researchers agree that findings with this method imply two processes, however, arguing that the results may be explained by a single signal detection process based on familiarity (e.g., Rotello & Zheng, 2008; Wixted & Stretch, 2004). Nevertheless, other converging sources of evidence exist. For example, other methods relying instead on people's ability to prove that they can recollect the details of the conditions under which they encountered an item. For instance, in the process dissociation procedure (PDP) (Jacoby, 1991), participants might study a visually presented list of words, followed by a second list of auditorally presented items. On the later recognition test, one group of participants is told to say "Yes" for each test item they remember encountering in *either* the seen or the heard list (the *inclusion condition*). A different group is asked to say "Yes" *only* to items from the list they heard (i.e., the *exclusion condition*). In the inclusion condition, people's correct recognition of visually presented items (from the first list) should mix items they recognize based on familiarity, and items they recognize based on recollection. To measure how much of a person's performance is due to the recollection process, we need a way to "subtract out" familiarity. Thus, we need an estimate of familiarity, in the absence of recollection. Cleverly, this can be estimated from people's errors in the exclusion condition. That is, when people are specifically asked to only say "Yes" to an item if they heard it in the second list, then if they accidentally say "Yes" to an item that had been visually presented, it must imply that the item is familiar,

but that people can't remember for sure where the item is from, and so could not be recollecting it. So, recollection can be estimated by simply subtracting these erroneous errors from the overall recognition rate of items from List One in the inclusion condition. These methods can thus be used to isolate the contributions of recollection and familiarity.

In a review of research using these and other methods to measure familiarity and recollection, Andrew Yonelinas (Yonelinas, 2002) identified several generalizations that support the distinction between these processes. First, whether someone can recollect a stimulus appears to be far more sensitive to disruption by distraction. If your attention is divided during an experience, you are less likely to later have the ability to recollect it, but the stimuli involved in the experience may remain familiar. Similarly, distraction during the recognition process itself is consistently more disruptive to recollection than it is to the sense of familiarity. These findings support the claim that recollection is a controlled, attention-demanding process. Consistent with this view, groups with diminished attentional control such as older adults and patients with damage to the prefrontal cortex, often show deficits in recollection, but an intact sense of familiarity for recently seen stimuli. Information about how familiar a stimulus seems is also retrieved much more quickly than information necessary for recollection, consistent with the view that familiarity judgments reflect an automatic process. These findings strongly support the view that two qualitatively distinct retrieval processes underlie recognition.

Familiarity and recollection are supported by distinct structures within the medial temporal lobes. Recollecting past experiences, along with their spatial-temporal context relies critically on the hippocampus,

KEY TERM

Process dissociation procedure (PDP):
A technique for parceling out the contributions of recollection and familiarity within a recognition task.

especially posterior hippocampus (Moscovitch, Cabeza, Winocur, & Nadel, 2016). The feeling of familiarity, on the other hand, relies on traces in the perirhinal cortex, a brain region adjacent to the hippocampus. You may remember, from Chapter on episodic memory, the case of Jon, a developmental amnesic patient. At birth, Jon had breathing problems and was deprived of oxygen, and, as a result, he suffered remarkably selective damage to his hippocampus. Over two decades later, Jon is now an adult with profound deficits in episodic recollection, showing severely impaired ability to remember particular events. Nevertheless, Jon exhibits above average intelligence, a normal vocabulary, and he possesses a surprisingly intact sense of familiarity for stimuli to which he has been exposed (we will discuss Jon at greater length in Chapter 16 on amnesia). Interestingly, Jon's perirhinal cortex was largely spared from damage, perhaps accounting for his intact sense of familiarity. A large body of neuroimaging research in neurologically healthy participants indicate that familiarity and recollection are dependent on the perirhinal cortex and hippocampus respectively (Brown & Banks, 2015; Eichenbaum, Yonelinas, & Ranganath, 2007). For example, using the remember know procedure, Laura Eldridge and colleagues showed that when people claimed to consciously recollect seeing a word in an earlier study phase (i.e., they gave a "remember" response), they showed significantly greater hippocampal activation than when they claimed to simply "know" that they saw it, without conscious recollection (Eldridge, Knowlton, Furmanski, Bookheimer, & Engel, 2000), a finding well supported in subsequent work (for a review, see Spaniol et al., 2009). Indeed, the amount of hippocampal activity increases with the amount of detail that is retrieved (Rugg & Vilberg, 2013). Activity in perirhinal cortex during retrieval, however, is related to the degree of familiarity that one experiences (Montaldi, Spencer, Roberts, & Mayes, 2006).

I have, of course, explained all of the foregoing research to my (now) friend, who I forgot that I dated. I told her that I simply had a momentary lapse of recollection, perhaps due to failure to engage the hippocampal retrieval processes that support recollection, upon sensing the rhinal cortex activity indicating that she was familiar. This of course only led to more sophisticated jokes at my expense. There can be an upside to not being able to consciously recollect some things, however. Indeed, Faraneh Vargha-Kadem, who studied Jon and other developmental amnesics, has remarked that they consistently exude a pleasant demeanor, never seeming too upset for too long, and never holding grudges (unlike my friend). The capacity to forget may indeed be quite useful, which is a topic we will take up again in Chapter 10 on motivated forgetting.

Source monitoring

We have talked about retrieval as reactivating a trace based on cues. We often have need, however, to identify the source of what we retrieve. We have already discussed the need to recall the context of an event. Did we take our pills today or yesterday, and did I park here today, or last week? But this is only one case of the broader need to distinguish the sources of one's recollections. Did I hear this story from Susan or Maria? Did I learn this fact from the *National Enquirer* or *Consumer Reports*? Did I *see* the person perform this action, or did somebody *tell* me about it? The processes of examining the origins of what we retrieve and deciding whether it is from a particular source is known as source monitoring (Johnson, Hashtroudi, & Lindsay, 1993). Source monitoring is an example of the post-retrieval monitoring process discussed in our initial characterization of the retrieval process, and requires controlled processes mediated by the prefrontal cortex (see Mitchell & Johnson, 2009; Spaniol et al., 2009 for reviews).

KEY TERM

Source monitoring: The process of examining the contextual origins of a memory in order to determine whether it was encoded from a particular source.

Unfortunately, people are not always careful in monitoring where their recollections come from, and so make mistakes. Such mistakes sometimes occur when people let their guard down, as in casual conversations, in which it may not seem important to be sure of the source. For example, you may recall that Maria told you something, when Susan did, and get Maria into trouble. Grandparents may misremember which grandchild is interested in which hobby, or whether they have told you their most recent favorite joke, or someone else. When you misattribute the source of your recollections, it is referred to as a source misattribution error.

How do people monitor the sources of their memories? To evaluate source, contextual details need to be recollected so that people can ascertain a memory's origins. According to Marcia Johnson and colleagues, this occurs by exploiting regularities in the information we receive from different sources. For example, if we need to decide whether we learned a fact by hearing it or reading it, we would evaluate the auditory detail and visual detail in the trace. An abundance of auditory detail would allow us to conclude that we heard it, whereas the converse would be true for visual detail. In deciding whether something we have recalled was a real experience or was imagined, the relative prevalence of perceptual detail as opposed to memory for cognitive operations (e.g., as would be involved in generating an image) would guide our decision about the memory's "realness." Using source monitoring processes to make decisions about whether the contents of memory refer to a real event or something imagined is known as reality monitoring (Johnson & Raye, 1981; Simons, Garrison, &

Johnson, 2017). Of course, people make mistakes at reality monitoring. When someone is induced to form a mental image of a word, they are more likely to later mistakenly claim they saw a picture of the object (Henkel, Franklin, & Johnson, 2000). This reflects an unintended consequence of relying upon the above strategies, with people mistaking imagined details for perceptual experience. Breakdowns in reality monitoring appear to be partially responsible for hallucinations in which people cannot distinguish their imaginings from true occurrences, as are prevalent in schizophrenia. Even psychologically healthy people vary in how well they can distinguish whether a remembered event is real or imagined, an ability which relies on activity in and structural integrity of the anterior prefrontal cortex (Simons et al., 2017). We return to a discussion of source misattribution errors in Chapter 10 in our discussion of motivated forgetting, and in Chapter 12, on eyewitness memory.

CONCLUDING REMARKS

As we all know, retrieval sometimes fails even given effective encoding. Retrieval failures of the sort experienced by the author at the outset of this chapter clearly can arise from a variety of sources. It is important to understand the circumstances under which retrieval fails so that we can understand how retrieval works. When retrieval fails, it raises the question of whether information is truly there or has been forgotten. In our next chapter, we turn to the subject of forgetting.

KEY TERM

Source misattribution error: When deciding the source of information in memory, sometimes people make errors and misattribute their recollection from one source to another.

KEY TERM

Reality monitoring: Using source monitoring processes to decide whether a piece of information in memory referred to a real event or instead to something imagined.

SUMMARY

- Memory can fail us because retrieval processes fail, even when a memory trace has been successfully stored.
- The "tip of the tongue" state arises when we cannot think of a proper name or a word for a concept, even though we feel we know it.
- Patients with damage to the prefrontal cortex show substantial difficulties in recall, due to the disruption of control processes that support retrieval.
- Retrieval can be conceptualized as the effort to activate a target trace, given one or more cues, via a process of spreading activation. Activation spreads via associations in proportion to their strength.
- Memories are likely to be complex constellations of features, the majority of which need to be activated by spreading activation processes for a memory to be retrieved. The retrieval of the remainder of a memory, given a portion of it as cues, is known as pattern completion.
- Intentional retrieval (as opposed to incidental reminding) requires other controlled processes such as cue-specification, cue-maintenance, interference resolution, and post-retrieval monitoring, most of which depend upon the integrity of the prefrontal cortex.
- Retrieving a prior experience is thought to be accomplished, in part, by the reinstatement of the cortical pattern of activity present when an event was first perceived, including the particular sensory cortices that represent the sights, sounds, and spatial locations of the event.
- For episodic retrieval, the ability to cortically reinstate the pattern of activity present during the original experience depends on pattern completion processes in the hippocampus, which drive cortical reinstatement.
- Retrieval processes can break down when the cues are inappropriate or are only weakly associated to the target, when the target is poorly learned, when we cannot devote adequate attention to retrieval, when we do not have enough cues, or even when we are in the wrong "frame of mind" when retrieving (i.e., not being in retrieval mode or having the wrong retrieval orientation).
- Memories are often involuntarily retrieved, without any intention to search memory, and this involuntary retrieval may be the basis of mind wandering. Involuntary retrievals of upsetting events or thoughts are a major issue in several psychological disorders including post-traumatic stress disorder, anxiety, and depression.
- Retrieval success is also influenced, often without our realizing it, by elements of the incidental context at retrieval, and their match to those present at encoding, including environmental, state, mood, and cognitive context.
- Retrieval strategy can influence performance, especially when large amounts of information need to be recalled.
- There are different ways of testing memory retrieval, some of which rely on intentional conscious recall of the past (direct tests), others of which test memory indirectly by measuring its influence on some incidental task (indirect tests).
- Free recall, cued recall, and recognition are direct tests, all of which require the use of a context cue to direct search, although reliance on context cues is thought to be greatest on recall tests, especially free recall. Direct tests generally measure explicit memory.

- Indirect tests do not make reference to memory and thus do not specify contextual cues in the retrieval process, providing a measure of implicit memory.
- Implicit memory phenomena such as repetition priming provide evidence of the unconscious influence of memory on behavior and perception, and are largely intact in amnesic patients.
- Repetition priming is thought to rely more on neocortical representations rather than hippocampal representations.
- Repetition suppression is thought to be a neural manifestation of repetition priming, reflecting decreased neural demand to process the same stimulus more than once.
- Explicit memory reflects the contribution of additional brain structures, including the hippocampus, to recall contextual aspects of an experience.
- Memory can also be tested with a recognition test, which requires a judgment about when a stimulus has been encountered before. Recognition is thought to be accomplished by not one, but two psychological processes: familiarity and recollection.
- Signal detection theory has been used to characterize the retrieval processes underlying recognition memory. There is debate about whether signal detection theory can provide an account of all recognition memory, or simply the familiarity component.
- Recollection is thought to be a slower, more attention-demanding process that requires recall of greater contextual detail.
- Many modern theories of the role of the medial temporal lobes in memory distinguish between a contextual recollection process mediated by the hippocampus, and a familiarity process mediated by the rhinal cortex.
- Retrieval is quite often reconstructive in nature, involving not merely the reactivation of traces by spreading activation, but also a process of inference and problem solving. Reconstruction can sometimes lead to memory distortions when general knowledge is used to fill in the gaps of incomplete memories, or to interpret fragmentary recollections.
- People routinely infer the source of what they remember, for example, to ascertain whether a recalled trace is the one they sought, is trustworthy, and, is in fact, a memory or something imagined.
- Attributing a source to a memory involves considering the attributes of the trace recalled, in relation to what would be expected to be stored in memory, given a source.
- Source misattribution errors reflect one way in which retrieval can break down through an error of commission, rather than omission.
- The process of distinguishing real experience from imagination as the source of information stored in memories is known as reality monitoring, and ability that breaks down in certain psychiatric conditions, such as schizophrenia.

POINTS FOR DISCUSSION

1 Pick three real examples of something that you recently recalled from memory. Drawing on what you learned about the retrieval process, analyze your examples. What were the cues? What type of retrieval situation was it? What type of context cue was present? Try to be thorough in describing the steps and processes involved, using concepts learned throughout the chapter.

2 Describe what context is, including its different types. Describe when it does and does not come into play in retrieving information from memory.

3 While walking across campus, you see your Memory professor and approach her to say hello. She nervously admits knowing that you are familiar, but cannot place you. Seeing your golden opportunity, you explain to the professor what type of test they just did, what aspects of memory they just failed at, and what parts of the brain were involved. What would you say to them to ensure that they were impressed?

4 How is human memory retrieval similar to and different from doing a search in Google™? What parallels can you find?

FURTHER READING

Danker, J. F., & Anderson, J. R. (2010). The ghosts of brain states past: Remembering reactivates the brain regions engaged during encoding. *Psychological Bulletin, 136*(1), 87–102.

Eichenbaum, H., Yonelinas, A. R., & Ranganath, C. (2007). The medial temporal lobe and recognition memory. *Annual Review of Neuroscience, 30*, 123–152.

Mitchell, K. J., & Johnson, M. K. (2009). Source monitoring 15 years later: What have we learned from fMRI about the neural mechanisms of source memory? *Psychological Bulletin, 135*(4), 638–677.

Roediger, H. L., & Guynn, M. J. (1996). Retrieval processes. In E. L. Bjork & R. A. Bjork (Eds.), *Handbook of perception and cognition: Memory* (Vol. 10, pp. 197–236). San Diego: Academic Press.

Rugg, M. D., & Vilberg, K. L. (2012). Brain networks underlying episodic memory retrieval. *Current Opinion in Neurobiology*.

Yonelinas, A. P. (2002). The nature of recollection and familiarity: A review of 30 years of research. *Journal of Memory and Language, 46*, 441–517.

Box 8.2 Answers to Box 8.1

	Country	First letter of capital city			Country	First letter of capital city
1	Norway	Oslo		11	South Korea	Seoul
2	Turkey	Ankara		12	Syria	Damascus
3	Kenya	Nairobi		13	Denmark	Copenhagen
4	Uruguay	Montevideo		14	Sudan	Khartoum
5	Finland	Helsinki		15	Nicaragua	Managua
6	Australia	Canberra		16	Ecuador	Quito
7	Saudi Arabia	Riyadh		17	Colombia	Bogota
8	Romania	Bucharest		18	Afghanistan	Kabul
9	Portugal	Lisbon		19	Thailand	Bangkok
10	Bulgaria	Sofia		20	Venezuela	Caracas

REFERENCES

Aggleton, J. P., & Brown, M. W. (1999). Episodic memory, amnesia, and the hippocampal-anterior thalamic axis. *Behavioral and Brain Sciences, 22*(3), 425–489.

Anderson, R. C., & Pichert, J. W. (1978). Recall of previously unrecallable information following a shift in perspective. *Journal of Verbal Learning and Verbal Behavior, 17*(1), 1–12.

Atkinson, R. C., & Juola, J. F. (1974). Search and decision processes in recognition memory. In D. H. Krantz, R. C. Atkinson, R. D. Luce, & P. Suppes (Eds.), *Contemporary developments in mathematical psychology: Vol. 1: Learning, memory & thinking* (pp. 243–293). San Francisco: W. H. Freeman.

Baddeley, A., Lewis, V., Eldridge, M., & Thomson, N. (1984). Attention and retrieval from long-term memory. *Journal of Experimental Psychology: General, 113*(4), 518–540.

Badre, D., & Wagner, A. D. (2007). Left ventrolateral prefrontal cortex and the cognitive control of memory. *Neuropsychologia, 45*(13), 2883–2901.

Barclay, J. R., Bransford, J. D., Franks, J. J., McCarrell, N., & Nitsch, K. (1974). Comprehension and semantic flexibility. *Journal of Verbal Learning and Verbal Behavior, 13,* 471–481.

Barron, H. C., Garvert, M. M., & Behrens, T. E. (2016). Repetition suppression: A means to index neural representations using BOLD?. *Philosophical Transactions of the Royal Society B: Biological Sciences, 371*(1705), 20150355.

Berntsen, D. (2010). The unbidden past: Involuntary autobiographical memories as a basic mode of remembering. *Current Directions in Psychological Science, 19,* 138–142.

Berntsen, D., Staugaard, S., & Sørensen, L. (2012). Why am I remembering this now? Predicting the occurrence of involuntary (spontaneous) episodic memories. *Journal of Experimental Psychology: General, 142*(2), 426–424.

Blaney, P. H. (1986). Affect and memory: A review. *Psychological Bulletin, 99*(2), 229–246.

Bouton, M. E., & Moody, E. W. (2004). Memory processes in classical conditioning. *Neuroscience & Biobehavioral Reviews, 28*(7), 663–674.

Brewin, C. R., Gregory, J. D., Lipton, M., & Burgess, N. (2010). Intrusive images and memories in psychological disorders: Characteristics, neural basis, and treatment implications. *Psychological Review, 117,* 210–232.

Brown, R., & McNeill, D. (1966). The "tip of the tongue" phenomenon. *Journal of Verbal Learning and Verbal Behavior, 5*(4), 325–337.

Brown, M. W., & Banks, P. J. (2015). In search of a recognition memory engram. *Neuroscience & Biobehavioral Reviews, 50,* 12–28.

Clark, D. M., & Teasdale, J. D. (1982). Diurnal variation in clinical depression and accessibility of memories of positive and negative experiences. *Journal of Abnormal Psychology, 91*(2), 87–95.

Craik, F. I., Govoni, R., Naveh-Benjamin, M., & Anderson, N. D. (1996). The effects of divided attention on encoding and retrieval processes in human memory. *Journal of Experimental Psychology: General, 125*(2), 159–180.

Danker, J. F., & Anderson, J. R. (2010). The ghosts of brain states past: Remembering reactivates the brain regions engaged during encoding. *Psychological Bulletin, 136*(1), 87–102.

Della Salla, S., Laiacona, M., Spinnler, H., & Trivelli, C. (1993). Autobiographical recollection and frontal damage. *Neuropsychologia, 31,* 823–839.

Diana, R. A., Yonelinas, A. P., & Ranganath, C. (2013). Parahippocampal cortex activation during context reinstatement predicts item recollection. *Journal of Experimental Psychology: General, 142*(4), 1287–1297.

Dooling, D. J., & Christiaansen, R. E. (1977). Episodic and semantic aspects of memory for prose. *Journal of Experimental Psychology: Human Learning and Memory, 3,* 428–436.

Eich, E., Macaulay, D., & Ryan, L. (1994). Mood dependent memory for events of the personal past. *Journal of Experimental Psychology: General, 123*(2), 201–215.

Eich, J. E. (1980). The cue-dependent nature of state-dependent retrieval. *Memory & Cognition, 8*(2), 157–173.

Eichenbaum, H., Yonelinas, A. R., & Ranganath, C. (2007). The medial temporal lobe and recognition memory. *Annual Review of Neuroscience, 30,* 123–152.

Eldridge, L. L., Knowlton, B. J., Furmanski, C. S., Bookheimer, S. Y., & Engel, S. A. (2000). Remembering episodes: A selective role for the hippocampus during retrieval. *Nature Neuroscience, 3*(11), 1149–1152.

Fernandes, M., & Guild, E. (2009). Process-specific interference effects during recognition of spatial patterns and words. *Canadian Journal of Experimental Psychology/Revue canadienne de psychologie expérimentale, 63*(1), 24–32.

Fernandes, M. A., & Moscovitch, M. (2000). Divided attention and memory: Evidence of substantial interference effects at retrieval and encoding. *Journal of Experimental Psychology: General, 129*(2), 155–176.

Fernandes, M. A., & Moscovitch, M. (2003). Interference effects from divided attention during retrieval in younger and older adults. *Psychology of Aging, 18*(2), 219–230.

Gabrieli, J. D. (1998). Cognitive neuroscience of human memory. *Annual Reviews in Psychology, 49,* 87–115.

Gardiner, J. M., Ramponi, C., & Richardson-Klavehn, A. (2000). Response deadline and subjective awareness in recognition memory. *Consciousness and Cognition, 8*(4), 484–496.

Gershberg, F. B., & Shimamura, A. P. (1995). Impaired use of organizational strategies in free recall following frontal lobe damage. *Neuropsychologia, 33*(10), 1305–1333.

Glanzer, M., & Bowles, N. (1976). Analysis of the word-frequency effect in recognition memory. *Journal of Experimental Psychology: Human Learning and Memory, 2*(1), 21–31.

Godden, D. R., & Baddeley, A. (1975). Context-dependent memory in two natural environments: On land and underwater. *British Journal of Psychology, 66*(3), 325–331.

Goodwin, D. W., Powell, B., Bremer, D., Hoine, H., & Stern, J. (1969). Alcohol and recall: State-dependent effects in man. *Science, 163*(3873), 1358–1360.

Gorman, A. M. (1961). Recognition memory for nouns as a function of abstractness and frequency. *Journal of Experimental Psychology, 61,* 23–29.

Green, D. M., & Swets, J. A. (1966). *Signal detection theory and psychophysics.* New York: Wiley.

Grill-Spector, K., Henson, R., & Martin, A. (2006). Repetition and the brain: Neural models of stimulus-specific effects. *Trends in Cognitive Sciences, 10*(1), 14–23.

Hall, J. F. (1954). Learning as a function of word-frequency. *The American Journal of Psychology, 67*(1), 138–140.

Henkel, L. A., Franklin, N., & Johnson, M. K. (2000). Cross-modal source monitoring confusions between perceived and imagined events. *Journal of Experimental Psychology: Learning, Memory, & Cognition, 26,* 321–335.

Herron, J. E., & Evans, L. H. (2018). Preparation breeds success: Brain activity predicts remembering. *Cortex, 106,* 1–11.

Herron, J. E., & Wilding, E. L. (2006). Neural correlates of control processes engaged before and during recovery of information from episodic memory. *Neuroimage, 30,* 634–644.

Jacoby, L. L. (1991). A process dissociation framework: Separating automatic from intentional uses of memory. *Journal of Memory and Language, 30*(5), 513–541.

Jacoby, L. L., & Dallas, M. (1981). On the relationship between autobiographical memory and perceptual learning. *Journal of Experimental Psychology: General, 110*(3), 306–340.

Johnson, M. K., Hashtroudi, S., & Lindsay, D. S. (1993). Source monitoring. *Psychological Bulletin, 114*(1), 3–28.

Johnson, M. K., & Raye, C. L. (1981). Reality monitoring. *Psychological Review, 88*(1), 67–85.

Kinsbourne, M., & George, J. (1974). The mechanism of the word-frequency effect on recognition memory. *Journal of Verbal Learning and Verbal Behavior, 13*(1), 63–69.

Kvavilashvili, L., & Mandler, G. (2004). Out of one's mind: A study of involuntary semantic memories. *Cognitive Psychology, 48*(1), 47–94.

Lang, A. J., Craske, M. G., Brown, M., & Ghaneian, A. (2001). Fear-related state dependent memory. *Cognition and Emotion, 15*(5), 695–703.

Mace, J. H. (Ed.). (2007). *Involuntary memory.* Malden, MA: Blackwell.

Mandler, G. (1980). Recognizing—the judgment of previous occurrence. *Psychological Review, 87*, 252–271.

Mangels, J. A., Gershberg, F. B., Shimamura, A. P., & Knight, R. T. (1996). Impaired retrieval from remote memory in patients with frontal lobe damage. *Neuropsychology, 10*(1), 32–41.

Marcotti, P., & St. Jacques, P. L. (2018). Shifting visual perspective during memory retrieval reduces the accuracy of subsequent memories. *Memory, 26*(3), 330–341.

Marian, V., & Fausey, C. M. (2006). Language-dependent memory in bilingual learning. *Applied Cognitive Psychology, 20*(8), 1025–1047.

Marian, V., & Neisser, U. (2000). Language-dependent recall of autobiographical memories. *Journal of Experimental Psychology: General, 129*(3), 361–368.

Miles, C., & Hardman, E. (1998). State-dependent memory produced by aerobic exercise. *Ergonomics, 41*(1), 20–28.

Miller, E. K., & Desimone, R. (1994). Parallel neuronal mechanisms for short-term memory. *Science, 263*(5146), 520–522.

Mitchell, K. J., & Johnson, M. K. (2009). Source monitoring 15 years later: What have we learned from fMRI about the neural mechanisms of source memory?. *Psychological Bulletin, 135*(4), 638–677.

Montaldi, D., Spencer, T. J., Roberts, N., & Mayes, A. R. (2006). The neural system that mediates familiarity memory. *Hippocampus, 16*(5), 504–520.

Moscovitch, M., Cabeza, R., Winocur, G., & Nadel, L. (2016). Episodic memory and beyond: The hippocampus and neocortex in transformation. *Annual Review of Psychology, 67*, 105–134.

Mystkowski, J. L., Craske, M. G., Echiverri, A. M., & Labus, J. S. (2006). Mental reinstatement of context and return of fear in spider-fearful participants. *Behavior Therapy, 37*(1), 49–60.

Ochsner, K. N., Chiu, C. Y. P., & Schacter, D. L. (1998). Varieties of priming. *Current Opinion in Neurobiology, 4*, 189–194.

Paller, K. A., & Wagner, A. D. (2002). Observing the transformation of experience into memory. *Trends in Cognitive Sciences, 6*(2), 93–102.

Richardson-Klavehn, A., & Bjork, R. A. (1988). Measures of memory. *Annual Reviews in Psychology, 39*, 475–543.

Robinson, S. J., & Rollings, L. J. (2010). The effect of mood-context on visual recognition and recall memory. *The Journal of General Psychology, 138*(1), 66–79.

Rohrer, D., & Pashler, H. E. (2003). Concurrent task effects on memory retrieval. *Psychonomic Bulletin & Review, 10*(1), 96–103.

Rotello, C. M., & Zeng, M. (2008). Analysis of RT distributions in the remember–know paradigm. *Psychonomic Bulletin & Review, 15*(4), 825–832.

Rubin, D. C., & Wallace, W. T. (1989). Rhyme and reason: Analyses of dual retrieval cues. *Journal of Experimental Psychology: Learning, 15*(4), 698–709.

Rugg, M. D., & Vilberg, K. L. (2013). Brain networks underlying episodic memory retrieval. *Current Opinion in Neurobiology, 23*, 255–260.

Schacter, D. L. (1987). Implicit memory: History and current status. *Journal of Experimental Psychology: Learning, Memory, & Cognition, 13*(3), 501–518.

Schramke, C. J., & Bauer, R. M. (1997). State-dependent learning in older and younger adults. *Psychology and Aging, 12*(2), 255–262.

Schwartz, B. L., & Cleary, A. M. (2016). Tip-of-the-tongue states, déjà vu experiences, and other odd metamemory experiences. In J. Dunlosky & S. K. Tauber (Eds.), *The Oxford handbook of metamemory* (pp. 95–108). Oxford: Oxford University Press.

Szczepanski, S. M., & Knight, R. T. (2014). Insights into human behavior from lesions to the prefrontal cortex. *Neuron, 83*(5), 1002–1018.

Sekiguchi, T., & Nonaka, S. (2014). The long-term effect of perspective change on the emotional intensity of autobiographical memories. *Cognition and Emotion, 28*(2), 375–383. doi:10.1080/02699 931.2013.825233

Simons, J. S., & Spiers, H. J. (2003). Prefrontal and medial temporal lobe interactions in long-term memory. *Nature Reviews Neuroscience, 4*(8), 637–648.

Simons, J. S., Garrison, J. R., & Johnson, M. K. (2017). Brain mechanisms of reality monitoring. *Trends in Cognitive Sciences, 21*(6), 462–473.

Smallwood, J., & Schooler, J. W. (2015). The science of mind wandering: Empirically navigating the stream of consciousness. *Annual Review of Psychology, 66*, 487–518.

Smith, S. M., & Vela, E. (2001). Environmental context-dependent memory: A review and meta-analysis. *Psychonomic Bulletin and Review, 8*(2), 203–220.

Spaniol, J., Davidson, P. S., Kim, A. S., Han, H., Moscovitch, M., & Grady, C. L. (2009). Event-related fMRI studies of episodic encoding and retrieval: Meta-analyses using activation likelihood estimation. *Neuropsychologia, 47*(8), 1765–1779.

Spiro, R. J. (1977). Remembering information from text: Theoretical and empirical issues concerning the "state of schema" reconstruction hypothesis. In R. C. Anderson, R. J. Spiro, & W. E. Montague (Eds.), *Schooling and the acquisition of knowledge* (pp. 137–165). Hillsdale, NJ: Erlbaum.

Squire, L. R. (1992). "Memory and the hippocampus: A synthesis from findings with rats, monkeys, and humans": Correction. *Psychological Review, 99*(3), 582.

Staresina, B. P., Cooper, E., & Henson, R. N. (2013). Reversible information flow across the medial temporal lobe: The hippocampus links cortical modules during memory retrieval. *Journal of Neuroscience, 33*(35), 14184–14192.

Staresina, B. P., Reber, T. P., Niediek, J., Boström, J., Elger, C. E., & Mormann, F. (2019). Recollection in the human hippocampal-entorhinal cell circuitry. *Nature Communications, 10*(1), 1503.

Sumby, W. H. (1963). Word frequency and serial position effects. *Journal of Verbal Learning and Verbal Behavior, 1*(6), 443–450.

Teasdale, J. D., & Fogarty, S. J. (1979). Differential effects of induced mood on retrieval of pleasant and unpleasant events from episodic memory. *Journal of Abnormal Psychology, 88*(3), 248–257.

Tulving, E. (1983). *Elements of episodic memory.* Oxford: Oxford University Press.

Tulving, E. (1985). How many memory systems are there? *The American Psychologist, 40*, 385–398.

Tulving, E., & Osler, S. (1968). Effectiveness of retrieval cues in memory for words. *Journal of Experimental Psychology, 77*(4), 593–601.

Tulving, E., & Thomson, D. M. (1973). Encoding specificity and retrieval processes in episodic memory. *Psychological Review, 80*(5), 352–373.

Velten, E. (1968). A laboratory task for induction of mood states. *Behavior Research and Therapy, 6*(4), 473–482.

Wagner, A. D., Schacter, D. L., Rotte, M., Koutstaal, W., Maril, A., Dale, A. M., … & Buckner, R. L. (1998). Building memories: Remembering and forgetting of verbal experiences as predicted by brain activity. *Science, 281*(5380), 1188–1191.

Wixted, J. T., & Stretch, V. (2004). In defense of the signal detection interpretation of remember/know judgments. *Psychonomic Bulletin & Review, 11*(4), 616–641.

Yonelinas, A. P. (1999). The contribution of recollection and familiarity to recognition and source-memory judgments: A formal dual-process model and an analysis of receiver operating characteristics. *Journal of Experimental Psychology: Learning, Memory, and Cognition, 25*(6), 1415–1434.

Yonelinas, A. P. (2002). The nature of recollection and familiarity: A review of 30 years of research. *Journal of Memory and Language, 46*, 441–517.

Contents

CHAPTER 9

INCIDENTAL FORGETTING

Michael C. Anderson

Over the Christmas holiday, my sister asked, "Do you remember when you knocked over the Christmas tree?" I said, "What are you talking about? I never did that!" Puzzled, my sister said, "Yes you did, don't you remember?" My brother added, "Yes, you were hurrying to squeeze behind the tree so you could take a picture of Aunt Dotty and Uncle Jim as they came up the driveway when you knocked the tree over." Indignant, I said, "What ... what are you talking about ... you must be mixing me up with someone else." My father insisted, "No, you definitely knocked the tree over. It was a big mess, and we made fun of you for it." He added that he remembered me feeling bad about ruining the tree, even though everyone said it was okay. They simply couldn't believe that I had forgotten this.

Reluctantly, I accepted that this event must have happened. I struggled to recall details and couldn't come up with anything. I said, "When did this happen? When I was a kid?" My sister replied, "No, it was about 3–4 years ago when we were in New York." I was shocked. I called my other brother and he confirmed every detail and was able to recall the year it had occurred. In fact, I remembered that Christmas in New York and the new camera that my mother had gotten (which I was using), but I simply could not remember this event. After many months and repeated searching, I still could not bring any trace of the experience to mind.

From life's embarrassing mishaps, to the mundane details of our daily life, many of our memories are forgotten. How and why are certain memories lost while others remain vivid for a lifetime?

Before you start wondering whether I'm amnesic, consider how much of *your* life *you* remember. Take a break from reading and try an exercise. Get out a sheet of paper and list everything that you did from the time you got up until the time you went to bed yesterday, including details about who you saw, and any conversations or thoughts. Chances are, you did pretty well and came up with a lot of detail. Perhaps you left out one or two minor things that you would recall if reminded. Next, do the same thing for the day that occurred *one week* earlier. You can probably still recall a lot, but with much more effort, and you most likely feel like you are forgetting more. Finally, try the same thing, but for a day that occurred exactly *one year* prior to yesterday. Try very hard. Most likely, after significant effort, you probably didn't recall much except perhaps some broad outlines that you are probably only guessing at, and only then after much reconstruction. The same uncomfortable fact is true for the majority of the days in your life, except for truly special events and the recent past.

In fact, consider this: *this very moment* that you are consciously experiencing, will, if your history serves as any guide, join the rest of those lost experiences. One cannot help but wonder how it is possible for something that is the full focus of your consciousness right now can ultimately be so completely lost. Is this the fate of all experience? When you are 80, will you only remember 1% of your life in any detail? Are all of your memories there, and just inaccessible?

The function of memory is never more conspicuous and astonishing than when it fails us. In this chapter, we consider the mechanisms that underlie forgetting. One might wonder why forgetting should be treated in a separate chapter from retrieval, in which we discussed why retrieval fails us. Indeed, retrieval failure *is* a form of forgetting. Forgetting is worthy of being distinguished, however, because of the potential for distinct forgetting processes that contribute to retrieval failure. Moreover, an emphasis on forgetting leads one to focus on changes in retrievability over time. What factors produce those changes? What would life be like if we never forgot?

In addressing these questions, research on memory has focused on both incidental forgetting and motivated forgetting. Incidental forgetting occurs without the intention to forget. Motivated forgetting, on the other hand, occurs when people engage processes or behaviors that intentionally diminish accessibility for some purpose. It is likely that to explain the full range of experiences that people have with forgetting, theories of types of both forgetting are needed. We discuss incidental forgetting here, and motivated forgetting in the next chapter.

A REMARKABLE MEMORY

What would it be like to remember everything that ever occurred to you? Although no such person has yet been found, there are people with astounding memory. For example, Elizabeth Parker, Larry Cahill, and James McGaugh (2006) reported the fascinating case of AJ, a 41-year-old woman, who had a breathtaking capacity to remember her past. AJ remembers every single day of her life since her teens, in extraordinary detail. Mention any date over several decades, and she finds herself back on that day, reliving events and feelings as though they happened yesterday. She can tell you what day of the week it was, events that took place on all surrounding days, and intricate details about her thoughts, feelings, and public events, all of which can be verified by personal diaries she has kept over 30 years. AJ reports that these memories are vivid, like a running movie, and full of emotion. Her remembering feels involuntary, and not under conscious control, a claim supported by the fact that her recollections occur immediately, with no struggle.

One might think that having such a remarkable memory would be wonderful. But it's not all good. When unpleasant things happen, AJ wishes she could forget, and

KEY TERM

Incidental forgetting: Memory failures occurring without the intention to forget.

Motivated forgetting: A broad term encompassing intentional forgetting as well as forgetting triggered by motivations, but lacking conscious intention.

the constant bombardment by remindings is distracting and sometimes troubling. In AJ's words:

My memory has ruled my life…. It is like my sixth sense…. There is no effort to it … I want to know why I remember everything. I think about the past all the time…. It's like a running movie that never stops. It's like a split screen. I'll be talking to someone and seeing something else…. Like we're sitting here talking and I'm talking to you and in my head I'm thinking about something that happened to me in December 1982, December 17th, 1982, it was a Friday, I started to work at Gs [a store] … I only have to experience something one time and I can be totally scarred by it … I can't let go of things because of my memory…. Happy memories hold my head together … I treasure these memories, good and bad … I can't let go of things because of my memory, it's part of me…. When I think of these things, it is kind of soothing … I knew a long time ago, I had an exceptional memory … I don't think I would never want to have this but it's a burden.

Parker et al. (2006) have termed AJ's condition hyperthymestic syndrome, from the Greek word *thymesis*, meaning "remembering." In short, AJ has uncontrollable remembering. This groundbreaking study of AJ has prompted a new body of cognitive and brain imaging work on people with highly superior autobiographical memory (HSAM), suggesting that the phenomenon may be based, in part, on superior functional communication between the prefrontal cortex and the hippocampus (see, e.g., Santangelo et al., 2018). Clearly, AJ's experience of life is very different from ours and illustrates a cost she pays for her perfect memory: she can remember the good times but suffers from the persistence of bad times. Would you choose AJ's memory over your own? Perhaps forget-

ting is not all bad. Later in this chapter, we will discuss the possibility that forgetting serves a useful function.

THE FUNDAMENTAL FACT OF FORGETTING

Clearly AJ's experience is atypical, as most of us forget. How are we to understand forgetting? A good place to begin is to acknowledge a fundamental fact: for most people (and organisms), *forgetting increases as time progresses*. Although this surely comes as no surprise, you may not have considered the nature of the relationship between memory and time. If you had to guess, would you say that people forget at a constant rate? To address this question, one simply needs to measure how likely forgetting is as a memory grows older. Once again, Hermann Ebbinghaus (1913) conducted the classic study, using himself as the participant and nonsense syllables as the material to be learned. Ebbinghaus learned 169 separate lists of 13 nonsense syllables and then relearned each list after an interval ranging from 21 minutes to 31 days. He always found that some forgetting had occurred and used the time required to learn the list again as a measure of how much he had forgotten. He found a clear relationship between time and retention.

You will recall from Chapter 3 that the relationship between learning and remembering was more or less linear, with the long-term memory store behaving rather like a bath being filled by a tap running at a constant rate. But how about forgetting? Is it simply like pulling the plug out of the bath, causing information to be lost at a constant rate, or is the relationship less straight-forward? Figure 9.1 illustrates the results obtained by Ebbinghaus. This graph depicts a quantitative relationship between memory and time, referred to as a forgetting curve, or sometimes a retention function. As you can see, Ebbinghaus forgot very rapidly at first, but forgetting gradually slowed down over time; the rate of forgetting he exhibited was more logarithmic than linear. As with Ebbinghaus's other work, this result has stood the test of time (Murre & Dros, 2015) and applies across a wide range of learning and testing conditions, including both explicit and implicit memory (Averell & Heathcote, 2011).

Most studies on the rate of forgetting have, like Ebbinghaus's, concerned themselves with highly constrained materials such as lists of nonsense syllables or unrelated words. Is this representative of what happens to personal memories? What happens when more realistic material is recalled over longer intervals? Answering this presents a major problem. Consider the question posed earlier about what you were doing one year ago. If you were to give an answer, how would I know whether you were correct? It is extremely unlikely that the necessary information remains available. One solution is to question respondents about events that were sufficiently noteworthy to attract the

attention of most people at the time they happened. This strategy was followed by Meeter, Murre, and Janssen (2005), who selected headlines in both newspapers and television broadcasts for each day over a four-year period. They amassed over 1,000 questions about distinct and dateable events, of which each participant would answer a randomly chosen 40. These investigators used the Internet to attract participants, allowing them to test the memory for over 14,000 people from widely different age groups from countries across the world. They tested their respondents' memory for these events by both recall and recognition.

The results obtained by Meeter et al. (2005) show that substantial forgetting of public events does occur, with participants' recall for the events dropping from 60% to 30% in just a single year. The forgetting curves showed a steep initial decline, followed by a slowed rate of forgetting at longer delays, especially when recall was tested, much like that observed with nonsense syllables by Ebbinghaus over a century ago.

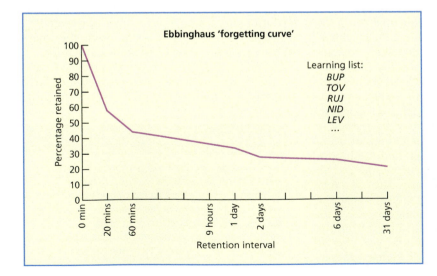

Figure 9.1 The forgetting curve that Ebbinghaus obtained when he plotted the results of one of his forgetting experiments. His finding, that information loss is very rapid at first and then levels off, holds true for many types of learned materials. Data from Ebbinghaus (1913).

They also found that people performed much more poorly when their recall was tested, recalling only 31% of the answers correctly over the years, compared to 52% correct when they simply had to recognize the answer from among options. These findings lend confidence to conclusions about forgetting from laboratory studies.

The forgetting curves discussed so far have been concerned mainly with memory for distinct events, which are relatively poorly learned. What of information that has been more thoroughly and deliberately learned? An intriguing study by Bahrick, Bahrick, and Wittlinger (1975) threw light on this question. These investigators traced 392 American high-school graduates and tested their memory for the names and portraits of classmates. Their study showed that the ability to both *recognize* a face or a name from among a set of unfamiliar faces or names and to match up names with faces, remained remarkably high for over 30 years. In contrast, the ability to *recall* a name given a person's picture showed more extensive forgetting, just like was found in the previously discussed study of memory for major news events.

Harry Bahrick is a professor at Ohio Wesleyan University, which in common with many American colleges has an annual reunion for alumni. Bahrick has made ingenious use of this tradition to study the retention by alumni of a range of material: from the geography of the town where the university is located to the vocabulary of foreign languages learned at college. Figure 9.2 shows the effect of delay on memory for a foreign language (Spanish, in this case). The most striking feature of the graph is the way in which forgetting levels out after about two years, with little further loss up to the longest delay, virtually 50 years later. It is as if forgetting occurs only up to a certain point, beyond which memory traces appear frozen. By analogy to the permanently frozen ground in Polar Regions, known as permafrost, Bahrick (1984) has suggested the term *permastore* for this stable language learning performance. The second point to note is that the overall retention is determined by the level of initial learning, at least as far as learning a foreign language is concerned. Thus, for well-learned materials, it seems, the forgetting curve may flatten out after an initial period of forgetting and show little additional forgetting over long periods. Together with Linda Hall and Melinda Baker, Bahrick has thoughtfully examined the conditions under which people can acquire complex knowledge in a way that resists forgetting throughout their entire lives (Bahrick, Hall, & Baker, 2013)—lessons every student would wisely covet.

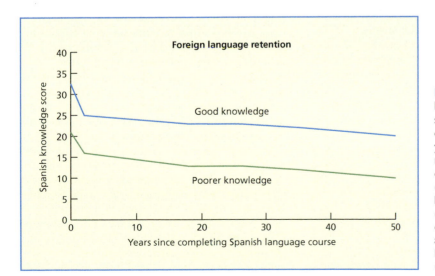

Figure 9.2 People who learned Spanish in college showed rapid forgetting over the first three or four years, followed by remarkably little forgetting over the next 30 years (Bahrick, 1984). Those who had a good knowledge (upper line, in blue) continued to have a clear advantage, even 50 years later. Data from Bahrick (1984).

ON THE NATURE OF FORGETTING

The discussion of forgetting functions raises an issue concerning what counts as "forgetting." Meeter et al.'s and Bahrick's studies found much greater forgetting when recall was tested, compared to recognition. This is a robust pattern that we touched on in our retrieval chapter: *recognition is generally easier than recall*. A reasonable conclusion to draw from this fact is that recognition tests reveal that more knowledge often resides in memory than is measured by recall. If so, is it truly fair to characterize failures to recall information evident in these forgetting functions as actual forgetting, when many of those unrecalled traces reside in memory? Shouldn't we reserve the term *forgetting* to refer to the permanent loss of traces? This issue highlights a distinction aptly named by Endel Tulving—the distinction between a memory's availability in the cognitive system (whether it is in storage or not), and its accessibility (whether one can access a memory, given that it is stored): the accessibility/availability distinction. Should we count inaccessibility as forgetting, or only unavailability?

Unfortunately, reserving *forgetting* to refer only to memories made unavailable renders it impossible to ever measure forgetting. The reason is that determining whether a memory has been permanently lost is quite a bit trickier than one might suspect. What will be our evidence of unavailability? Failed recall? Clearly not, as the foregoing results establish. Failed recognition? Again, recognition can fail, even when it can be proven that a trace is in memory, given the proper reinstatement of context. Although an experience

may seem lost forever, perhaps the right cue has just not come along. As discussed in the last chapter, it took the sight of the passport in the box to pry loose my memory for storing it there. It is thus quite difficult to distinguish inaccessibility from unavailability. Moreover, when memories transition from being recallable to only being recognizable, this may, in principle, be due to weakening of the trace. Permanent loss may not be all or none, but may happen in graded fashion. For these reasons, and because reduced accessibility is a memory failure, inaccessibility is considered forgetting.

FACTORS THAT DISCOURAGE FORGETTING

The studies by Harry Bahrick illustrate how forgetting, though perhaps inevitable for many memories, may be slowed for some types of knowledge. Which factors discourage forgetting? One obvious point is that if you learn something well to begin with, forgetting is less likely, or at least it takes much longer. But are there some ways of strengthening a memory that increase resistance to forgetting more than others? What memories will you have when you are 80?

The apparent flattening out of the forgetting curve over time demonstrates that memories are not equally vulnerable to forgetting at all points in their history. Another way of describing the relationship of time and memory is in terms of *Jost's Law*, named after a 19th-century psychologist, which states that if two memories are equally strong at a given time, then the older of the two will be more durable and forgotten less rapidly. It is as if two opposing forces may be at work to determine retention over time; the mechanisms of forgetting, but also some process that makes surviving memories grow tougher with age. Indeed, it is widely believed that new traces are initially vulnerable to disruption until they are gradually stamped into memory. The time-dependent process by which a new trace is gradually woven into

---

KEY TERM

Accessibility/availability distinction:
Accessibility refers to the ease with which a stored memory can be retrieved at a given point in time. Availability refers to the binary distinction indicating whether a trace is or is not stored in memory.

the fabric of memory and by which its components and their interconnections are cemented together is known as *consolidation*. At least two types of consolidation have been proposed. According to research on *synaptic consolidation*, the imprint of experience takes time to solidify, because it requires structural changes in the synaptic connections between neurons. These modifications rely on biological processes that may take hours to days to complete (Dudai, 2004). Until those structural changes occur, the memory is vulnerable. Research also implicates a process known as *systemic consolidation*, which holds that the hippocampus is initially required for memory storage and retrieval but that its contribution diminishes over time until the cortex is capable of retrieving the memory on its own (Dudai, 2004; Squire, 1992). As will be discussed further in Chapter 11, the hippocampus is thought to accomplish this by recurrently reactivating the brain areas involved in the initial experience (e.g., the areas involved in hearing the sounds, seeing the sights, essentially "replaying" the memory) until these areas are interlinked in a way that could recreate the original memory. Until the memory becomes independent of the hippocampus, it is vulnerable to disruption. Estimates of the duration of systemic consolidation vary, with some evidence suggesting that it may take years in humans. So, it seems that a process may exist that strengthens memories over time, retarding their forgetting, and that this process involves recurring retrieval of some sort.

Over the last decade, neurobiological research has questioned whether memories undergo a single, fixed period of synaptic consolidation. Instead, evidence suggests that under some conditions, when a trace is reactivated in memory (e.g., by exposing people to a partial reminder to the event), it may undergo restabilization once again. A key aspect of this idea is that reactivated memories enter a state of increased vulnerability to disruption. Thus, even consolidated memories, once reactivated, may be disruptable by interventions known to disrupt the normal synaptic consolidation process, such as the administration of consolidation-blocking drugs and electrical stimulation. In a particularly striking example of this heightened vulnerability of reactivated memories, Marijn Kroes and colleagues presented two separate emotionally aversive slide-show stories (with accompanying narrative) to depressed participants one week before they were scheduled to undergo *electroconvulsive therapy (ECT)* to mitigate symptoms of depression (Kroes et al., 2013). ECT involves administration of anesthesia followed by electrical stimulation of the skull (evoking generalized seizure activity) and is known to induce permanent amnesia for very recent, unconsolidated memories. Because patients watched the slide shows one week earlier, they should have undergone full synaptic consolidation (Dudai, 2004). However, just before ECT, Kroes and colleagues "reactivated" one of the two slide shows by testing participants' memory for a partially covered version of the first slide, a procedure hypothesized to trigger the reconsolidation process. Strikingly, one day after ECT, participants performed far worse on multiple-choice test about the reactivated slide show, compared to their performance on the non-reactivated slide show. This finding illustrates how after a retrieval or reactivation, a memory sometimes becomes vulnerable again and must restabilize or undergo reconsolidation (Nader, Schafe, & LeDoux, 2000; see Nader & Hardt, 2009 for a review). This reconsolidation process, though similar to synaptic consolidation, may be neurobiologically distinct. Some have speculated that reconsolidation may allow the memory system flexibility to update representations with new information (Hardt, Einarsson, & Nader, 2010). More generally, reconsolidation illustrates the key role retrieval plays in the fate of memories.

Interestingly, behavioral research indicates that intentionally retrieving an experience also has an especially potent effect on

---

KEY TERM

Reconsolidation: The process by which a consolidated memory restabilizes again after being reactivated by reminders. During the reconsolidation window, a memory is vulnerable to disruption.

the rate at which a memory is forgotten. This fact was illustrated compellingly by Marigold Linton (1975), using herself as a participant. Every day for five years, she noted in her diary two events that had occurred. At predetermined intervals she would randomly select events from her diary and judge whether she could recall them. Given the fact that she was sampling in this way any given event could crop up many times. She was therefore able to analyze her results to find out what effect earlier recalls had on the later memorability of the event. Her results are shown in Figure 9.3; the items that were not retested showed dramatic forgetting over a four-year period (65% forgotten). Even a single test was enough to reduce forgetting, whereas items tested on four other occasions showed an impressively low probability of forgetting after four years (only 12% forgotten). So, it seems that personal memories, if retrieved periodically, grow quite resistant to forgetting, in much the same way as did the cases of permastore for well-learned material reported by Bahrick and colleagues. Indeed, some researchers have suggested that intentional retrieval may be uniquely beneficial in establishing durability because it drives the previously discussed processes of systemic consolidation (Antony, Ferreira, Norman, & Wimber, 2017). Research on the beneficial

effects of retrieval on learning has expanded greatly in recent years (Karpicke & Roediger, 2008), and the educational implications of this finding are significant. For example, in a survey of study strategies conducted amongst college students, Karpicke found that 84% of students reported rereading chapters as a way to study for exams, with 55% reporting it as their number one strategy (Karpicke, Butler, & Roediger, 2009). Only 11% of students gave themselves self-tests! Yet, in a comprehensive evaluation of research on the benefits of testing in student learning (encompassing 118 studies with over 15,000 students), Olusola Adesope and colleagues found compelling evidence for the benefits of self-tests over all other methods reviewed (Adesope, Trevisan, & Sundararajan, 2017). Other examples of the memory-enhancing power of retrieval are discussed in Chapter 17 on improving your memory.

Although retrieval enhances retention, we must be cautious about what is being retrieved. People are tempted to assume that if they are recalling something that happened 20 years ago, that they are recalling a 20-year-old memory. This may be true if we have not recalled the memory in the interim. However, if we have retrieved the memory at all, perhaps we are retrieving a memory of what we have retrieved previously. The event of retrieving something is itself a memory, with its own context, and particulars. The more often that we retrieve an experience, the more of these retrieval events will exist in memory. As long as the information retrieved each time is accurate and complete, this process will enhance recall. If recollections are incomplete or inaccurate due to reconstructive inferences, what we remember may not be what originally happened. This is especially true if, during reconsolidation, incorrectly recalled details get integrated with the original memory traces (Hardt et al., 2010). We return to this concern in Chapter 10, in discussing recovered memories of abuse.

It appears then that retrieval may play a very special role in determining which elements of experience will be preserved throughout our lives. Each time that we get together and reminisce with friends or family,

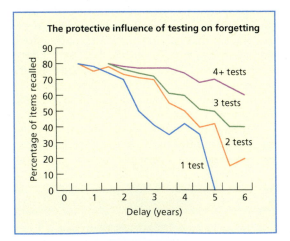

Figure 9.3 The probability of remembering something depends on the number of times it has been retrieved or called to mind. Recalling an event reduces the rate of forgetting. Data from Linton (1975).

we are implicitly selecting which memories to more firmly establish. And for those of us who keep a diary, reviewing the day's events and retrieving them not only provides an objective record of their occurrence, but also may increase the longevity of those memories, especially if they are reviewed from time to time. Retrieval clearly has a special effect on retention. Later on, I will discuss research demonstrating that, ironically, retrieval also plays a powerful and complementary role in determining what we forget.

FACTORS THAT ENCOURAGE INCIDENTAL FORGETTING

Knowing that retrieval retards forgetting is useful, but why does forgetting occur in the first place? What factors contribute to retention loss? Experimental psychologists have traditionally emphasized incidental forgetting, stressing the involvement of passive processes that occur as a bi-product of changes in the world or the person. For example, forgetting has been attributed to decay, contextual shifts, and to interference. This passive view fits the general feeling most of us have that we are the unwilling victims of memory loss. This perspective often fits reality: we do forget things unintentionally, even when they are important. Here, we consider several of the most important factors.

Passage of time as a cause of forgetting

The most obvious way of describing the forgetting curve is that memory gets worse as time goes by. Perhaps the cause is that simple: memory traces grow weaker with time. Memories may simply fade, rather like a notice that is exposed to sun and rain gradually fades until it becomes illegible. The idea that memories get weaker over time is known as trace decay. Many investigators favor the view that trace decay partially determines the loss of information from verbal and visual working memory (e.g., Baddeley, 1986; Broadbent, 1958; Cowan, 1988; Gold, Murray, Sekuler, Bennett, & Sekuler, 2005; Page & Norris, 1998; Towse, Hitch, & Hutton, 2000), although this approach has its critics (Nairne, 2002) and the existence of decay in verbal working memory is actively debated (Altmann & Schunn, 2012; Berman, Jonides, & Lewis, 2009; Oberauer & Lewandowsky, 2013). Decay also plays a role in how theorists think about repetition priming and familiarity, with some proposing that these effects decay quickly (e.g., Eichenbaum, 1994; McKone, 1998; Yonelinas & Levy, 2002). Many proposals about trace decay have in common the idea that activation decays gradually, even if the item remains stored. For example, recent exposure to the word *HELMET* may activate a pre-existing concept. Although activation may fade, the concept remains.

There is another sense of decay, however, in which a memory's structural elements degrade, not just activation levels. Thus, associations between features or the features themselves may deteriorate. Does this happen? This issue is related to the age-old question of whether memories are permanently stored, but merely grow inaccessible. On one level, the answer seems obvious: memories are not permanent and decay must exist. We cannot disregard that we are biological beings. Our memories survive in tissue that continually changes, with neurons dying and connections weakening or being modified. We know, for instance, that a time-dependent process degrades the synaptic connections between neurons that support a recently learned behavior in *Aplysia* (a sea slug), with a corresponding degradation in the learned behavior (Bailey & Chen, 1989).

KEY TERM

Interference: The phenomenon in which the retrieval of a memory can be disrupted by the presence of related traces in memory.

Trace decay: The gradual weakening of memories resulting from the mere passage of time.

More recently, evidence has rapidly accumulated for biologically regulated mechanisms of memory decay in multiple species, including insects and mammals. For example, fruit flies are known to actively forget odor fear conditioning via dopaminergic neurons that undo learning (Berry, Cervantes-Sandoval, Nicholas, & Davis, 2012; Davis & Zhong, 2017). Moreover, rodents possess mechanisms that actively forget object locations represented in their hippocampus via weakening of hippocampal synapses (Hardt, Nader, & Nadel, 2013; Migues et al., 2016). It is not far-fetched to believe that similar biologically regulated degradation occurs in humans, perhaps underlying time-dependent decay. If neurons die, and connections degrade, the survival of memories over long stretches of time in fact seems the greater mystery (Davis & Zhong, 2017).

Another potent cause of forgetting has been identified in the counter-intuitive proposal offered by Paul Frankland, Stephan Kohler, and Sheena Josselyn (Frankland, Köhler, & Josselyn, 2013). Rather than conceptualizing forgetting as deterioration of existing tissue supporting a memory, Frankland and colleagues have presented a strong case that memory loss also arises from the growth of new neurons (i.e., *neurogenesis*). Advances in neurobiology suggest that new neurons are generated regularly in the adult brain, especially in the hippocampus (see Kemperman et al., 2018 for a thorough consideration of the evidence for this). As newborn neurons become integrated into existing hippocampal circuitry (a process that can take several weeks), the hippocampus is, bit by bit, structurally remodeled, with its pattern of synaptic connections gradually modified with each generation of interloping neurons. Frankland and colleagues have shown that whereas this new tissue is good for helping us to learn new things (after the neurons are incorporated), it is bad for the retention of existing memories already stored in the hippocampus. In effect, new neurons change the pattern of communication between hippocampal neurons making the original pattern of firing present during encoding hard to recreate at retrieval, thus impairing retention. These authors present a

compelling case that this *neurogenesis-induced forgetting* may explain the striking phenomenon of infantile amnesia, to be discussed further in Chapter 12 (Akers et al., 2014; Josselyn & Frankland, 2012). Infantile amnesia refers to the difficulty most people have in remembering the first several years of their lives, a period that coincides with high levels of new neurogenesis. A key difference between this mechanism and memory decay processes described previously, however, is that adding new neural connections doesn't remove ones already established. Thus, although difficult to retrieve, the original memory remains, but lies beyond our grasp. Indeed, using advanced optogenetic techniques, Frankland and colleagues have compellingly established in mice that memories lost due to infantile amnesia remain stored in their brain, but, due to neurogenesis-induced forgetting, have been rendered inaccessible (Guskjolen et al., 2018).

Though trace decay clearly occurs, experimental psychologists are rightly skeptical about *behavioral* evidence for it. The reason is that demonstrating decay behaviorally is exceptionally difficult. Proving that decay exists requires a demonstration that forgetting grows over time, in the absence of other activities such as the storage of new experiences or rehearsal. Rehearsal of the memory in question must be controlled because, as discussed earlier, retrieval strengthens memories, which would undercut efforts to see decay. As we will later discuss, storing new experiences after a trace has been encoded must be controlled because new memories introduce interference that may disrupt recall. When these constraints are considered, the person would essentially need to be kept in a mental vacuum, devoid of rehearsal, thoughts, or experiences that might contaminate the state of memory and complicate the interpretation of forgetting. To make matters worse, even if forgetting occurred in

KEY TERM

Infantile amnesia: Tendency for people to have few autobiographical memories from below the age of 5.

the absence of interference, it remains unclear whether the trace has become unavailable, or is merely inaccessible. Indeed, the foregoing discussion of neurogenesis-induced forgetting proves this point compellingly: even when a memory has been rendered utterly inaccessible due to interference from new neurons, Frankland and colleagues were able to show, with modern optogenetic techniques, that the memory could be reactivated, given the right neural input (Guskjolen et al., 2018). Thus, with behavioral methods alone, it is impossible to establish evidence for decay, even though it clearly occurs (Awasthi et al., 2019; Hardt et al., 2013; Migues et al., 2016).

Correlates of time that cause forgetting

For the foregoing reasons, experimental psychologists have favored the view time is merely correlated with some other factor that causes forgetting. Two possibilities have been examined. First, as time goes by, the incidental context within which we operate gradually shifts, perhaps impairing retrieval of older memories. Second, over time, people store many new similar experiences that may interfere with retrieving a particular trace. Although these factors do not disprove decay, they provide alternative explanations for the forgetting curve that do not rely upon this process.

Contextual fluctuation

As discussed in Chapter 8, retrieval hinges on the number and quality of cues available during recall. When irrelevant cues are used, retrieval can fail. Retrieval can fail when a cue that was previously relevant changes over time. For instance, family members change in appearance, making them match less well the original cue associated to a memory. Moreover, when incidental context at retrieval does not match the one present at encoding, forgetting is more likely. One explanation of the forgetting curve then, is that as time progresses, changes in context become greater, on average because the world changes and we change. With time, we encounter new stimuli, people, and situations, and we have new

thoughts and emotions. As such, one's incidental context will be most similar to the one that we were in a short while ago, and grow less similar over time. The idea that contextual fluctuation contributes to memory has been advocated in numerous models of memory (e.g., Polyn, Norman, & Kahana, 2009).

An interesting example of how contextual change causes forgetting comes from research on mental context. Most of us have, from time to time, found ourselves lost in daydreams, imagining some future or past event. This happens to me whenever I'm on the train or a bus riding some place, and it can be a rather pleasant way to pass the time. When you do this, however, be careful, because you might just make yourself forget something you need to remember. This is particularly true if your imagination takes you to far-off places or times that are very different than the present moment. Peter Delaney and his colleagues reported a clever demonstration of this idea (Delaney, Sahakyan, Kelly, & Zimmerman, 2010). Participants studied two lists of 15 unrelated words for a later memory test. Immediately after studying the first list, participants received 90 seconds to perform a simple diverting activity. One group was asked to daydream about a vacation in the last three years within the United States. A second group was asked to daydream about an international vacation (participants were screened in advance to ensure that they had gone on US or international vacations). A rather less fortunate control group was given 90 seconds to read a passage aloud from a psychology textbook to pass the time. After daydreaming, the participants studied the second list of words, which was followed shortly thereafter by a test of the first list. Participants who

> ### KEY TERM
>
> **Contextual fluctuation:** The gradual and persistent drift in incidental context over time, such that distant memories deviate from the current context more so than newer memories, thereby diminishing the former's potency as a retrieval cue for older memories.

daydreamed after studying the first list remembered fewer words from that list, compared to control participants. This effect was especially pronounced for participants who daydreamed about their international holiday, presumably because such daydreams involve large changes to one's mental context, relative to those that might arise from imagining a more ordinary US holiday. Indeed, there was a correlation between the remoteness of the vacation destination (in miles) and how much participants forget the first list! Clearly, changes in mental context can lead to forgetting. We will revisit the context shift process in Chapter 10 on motivated forgetting.

Interference

Over time, experiences accumulate. Like the clutter of papers on your desk, adding new memories affects how easily we find things already stored. When memories are similar, this problem should be even worse, like having many similarly labeled papers on a desk. The idea that storing similar traces impedes retrieval is known as *interference*. Interference is likely to be a serious issue when you consider how people are, by nature, creatures of habit. People enjoy their routines, be they reading the newspaper in the morning, parking in the same spot each day, and getting their morning coffee. Sticking to routines, however, makes life less memorable. We remember what we had for dinner last night, but not two weeks ago. Such forgetting doesn't simply reflect the passage of time. We can easily remember experiences for a long time if they are unique: having dinner at the neighbors' house a year ago is far more memorable than having dinner at our own house three months ago. It is the presence of other traces in memory that compromises retrieval. Because the number of similar traces will increase over time, interference provides a straightforward account of the forgetting curve. The emphasis on interference as a source of forgetting has a long history (Müller & Pilzecker, 1900) and was a preoccupation of research on memory for nearly three-quarters of a century (see Anderson & Neely, 1996; Crowder, 1976; Postman, 1971, for reviews).

How does adding similar experiences into memory hurt us? To understand this, it is helpful to step back and discuss a fundamental discovery about what likely underlies interference. Early in the history of memory research, investigators identified a central feature in common to most situations associated with interference: interference arises whenever the cue used to access a target (Figure 9.4, top left) becomes associated to additional memories. The canonical interference situation is illustrated in the top right panel of Figure 9.4 in its most general form, with a single cue, linked to many associates. By this view, progressing from a cue to a target depends not only on how strongly that cue is associated to the target, but also on whether the cue is related to other items. Why does attaching more memories to a cue make retrieving a particular target difficult? Although theories vary about the particulars, most agree that when a cue is linked to multiple items, those items compete with the target for access to awareness, an idea known as the competition assumption (Anderson, Bjork, & Bjork, 1994). Essentially, a cue activates all of its associates to some degree, and they "fight" one another. As such, any associates other than the target memory are called *competitors*. In general, any negative effect on memory arising from having competitors is called interference. Interference increases with the number of competitors a target has. This idea is supported by the tendency for recall to decrease with the number of to-be-remembered items paired with the same cue, a generalization known as the cue-overload principle (see, e.g., Watkins, 1978). In essence, as a cue becomes attached to too many things, its capacity to access any one trace is compromised.

KEY TERM

Competition assumption: The theoretical proposition that the memories associated to a shared retrieval cue automatically impede one another's retrieval when the cue is presented.

Cue-overload principle: The observed tendency for recall success to decrease as the number of to-be-remembered items associated to a cue increases.

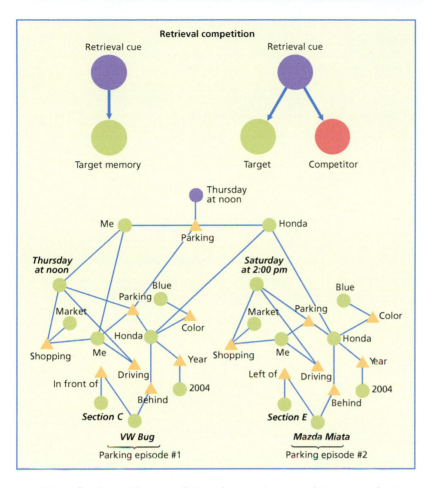

Figure 9.4 Top left: A retrieval cue associated to a single target item. Top right: A retrieval cue becomes associated to a competitor interfering with recall of the target. Bottom: A more complex example of interference, with multiple, shared retrieval cues and complex memories with many features. From Anderson and Neely (1996). Copyright © Elsevier. Reproduced with permission.

How do these ideas explain why storing similar memories causes interference? Consider an example in which you are recalling where you parked your car in a shopping center you visit frequently. While parking, you will have encoded aspects of your parking experience into a memory. Other parking memories similar to this one will also contain characteristics of the target, including the fact that you drove a car, the type of car you drove (e.g., a 2004 blue Honda) and, perhaps, your goal of shopping. If important elements of the target (e.g., the concepts of yourself, of parking, and of your Honda) serve as the cues to your car's location, other memories sharing those features will be evoked as well. Figure 9.4, bottom, illustrates this by showing how the situation illustrated with one cue may be scaled up to the many cues available in this example (e.g., "Me," "Parking," and "Honda"). Thus, competition for a shared cue is a useful way of viewing interference between similar traces.

The notion of competition among items that share retrieval cues is very general. For instance, items in memory need not be episodes to compete. Indeed, even retrieving the meaning of a word can involve retrieval interference. To convince yourself of this, try the following demonstration, illustrated in Box 9.1. Each of the words listed in this box has entirely distinct verb and noun meanings, with the verb meaning being the less common. For each word, try to generate an associate of its verb meaning. For instance, for the word *DUCK*, you would generate a word like *CROUCH*, signifying that you thought of the verb meaning. Do this for each word as quickly as possible.

Box 9.1   Interference effects

Each of the words listed in this table has entirely distinct verb and noun meanings, with the verb meaning being the less common. For each word, try to generate an associate of its verb meaning. For instance, for the word duck, you would generate a word like crouch, signifying that you thought of the verb meaning. Do this for each word as quickly as possible.

	Cue	Related verb
E.g.	Duck	Crouch
1	Loaf	
2	Post	
3	Court	
4	Root	
5	Sock	
6	Shed	
7	Fence	
8	Lobby	
9	Stump	
10	Fawn	
11	Lodge	
12	Sign	
13	Bark	
14	Pine	
15	Bowl	
16	Prune	
17	Duck	
18	Rail	
19	Sink	
20	Ring	

Adapted from Johnson and Anderson (2004).

For native speakers of English, this task is perplexingly difficult because they instantly retrieve the noun meaning of the word, and must work to get past that dominant association. If this happened to you, you experienced competition from the noun meaning during the retrieval of the verb.

Interference phenomena

A number of qualitatively distinct situations produce interference. For instance, the storage of new experiences can interfere with retrieving older ones, but older memories can also impede retrieval of newer ones. In this section, we review some of the most important interference phenomena and key results that have been discovered. It is important to bear in mind that although the particulars of these situations vary, the underlying mechanisms that produce forgetting may in fact be similar. In the section to follow, we consider candidate mechanisms.

Retroactive interference

At the beginning of this chapter, we asked you to list all of the things you did yesterday, the same day last week, and the same day last year. If you did this exercise, you undoubtedly confronted the uncomfortable fact that you remember little of what has happened in your life. Why? As we have discussed, the difficulty may be due to several sources, including decay and contextual fluctuation. But there is an excellent chance that a lot of that forgetting comes about due to retroactive interference. Retroactive interference refers to forgetting caused by encoding new traces into memory in between the initial encoding of the target and when it is tested. Essentially, some process associated with storing newer experiences impairs the ability to recall ones farther back in time. With every new trip to McDonald's, every morning ride on the bus, and every day you spend seated in front of a computer screen at work, previous McDonald's trips, morning rides, and days at work grow farther from your mental grasp.

The methods used to study retroactive interference have tended to focus on simple materials that conform closely to the canonical interference situation described earlier. This phenomenon is often studied using the classic retroactive interference design illustrated in the left half of Figure 9.5. In the *experimental condition*, people study a first list of pairs (upper box), and then a second list. Very often the pairs in the first list (e.g., *DOG-SKY*) have their cue words repeated in the second list, but are paired with a new response word (e.g., *DOG-ROCK*) that people have to learn in place of the older one. After the second list is learned, people are usually tested by giving them the first word of each pair and asking them to recall the response from the first list (e.g., *DOG-?*). In the control condition, people also study a first list, but engage in irrelevant filler activity in the interval during which people in the experimental condition study List Two. Thus, these two conditions allows us to ask the crucial question: What is the effect of learning new information (i.e., List Two) on the ability to remember information that was previously studied (i.e., List One), relative to a situation in which no additional information was learned at all (i.e., Control condition)?

The general findings are that (a) introducing a highly related second list impairs the ability to recall items from the first list, compared to the control, and (b) increased training on second-list items continues to harm retention of first-list items further, as training progresses. This is especially true when the Lists One and Two share a common cue word (e.g., *DOG*, as in the previous example); in fact, there is often little retroactive interference when the pairs on the two lists are unrelated. Thus, not every type of intervening experience impairs memory—the experience needs to share cues. A typical example of retroactive interference is illustrated in the right half of Figure 9.5, which is taken from a classic study by Barnes and Underwood (1959). Notice that as people were given increasing amounts of training on the second list of pairs, their memory for

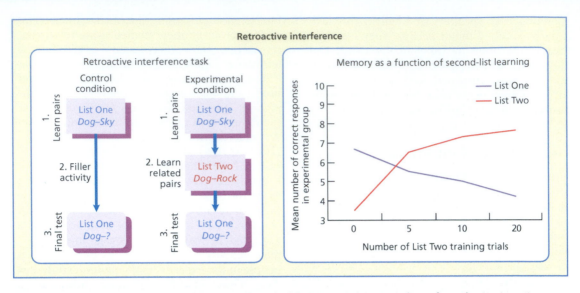

Figure 9.5 Left: A retroactive interference task in which participants learn two lists of word pairs, in series. A control group skips second-list learning. Right: Final cued-recall results (for both lists) by List-Two training trials. Memory for List Two increases with practice, while List One declines with List-Two practice. Data from Barnes and Underwood (1959).

those pairs gets better, whereas their retention of first-list pairs grows quite a bit worse. We know that this increased forgetting is not due to the mere passage of time, because in the control condition the same amount of time has gone by in between learning the pairs and the final test. Thus, learning something new can impair memory substantially.

But are the lessons from artificial laboratory materials applicable to memory for personal experiences? It would be helpful if it could be shown that something like retroactive interference occurs with realistic memories. Such studies exist and generally confirm the importance of retroactive interference. In one study by Hitch and Baddeley, rugby players were asked to recall the names of the teams they had played earlier in the season (Baddeley & Hitch, 1977). The graph in Figure 9.6 shows the probability of their recalling the name of the last team played, the team before that, and so forth. It proved to be the case that most players had missed some games either due to injury or other commitments, so that for one player the game before last might have taken place a week ago and for another it might have been two weeks or even a month before. It was therefore possible to ascertain whether

forgetting depended on elapsed time or on the number of intervening games. The result was clear. Time was relatively unimportant, whereas the number of intervening games was critical, indicating that forgetting was due to interference rather than trace decay. Apparently, their memory of having played a whole rugby game could be made less

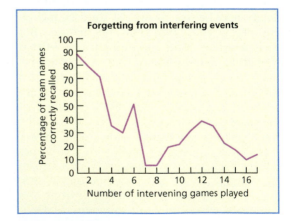

Figure 9.6 This graph, showing rugby players' memory for the names of teams recently played, demonstrates the tendency for recent events to interfere with memory of similar events from the past. Data from Baddeley and Hitch (1977).

accessible simply because they have played many rugby games since then.

Proactive interference

One afternoon, when visiting Berkeley, I walked up to the top of an exceptionally steep street outside the psychology department to discover, to my horror, that my car had been stolen. After a moment's reflection, I realized that I had not parked my car there this *afternoon*, but rather this *morning*. This afternoon, I had parked my car on an entirely different, preposterously steep hill one street over. I was the unhappy victim of proactive interference, or the tendency for older memories to interfere with the retrieval of more recent experiences and knowledge. Most of us are acquainted with the irritation of proactive interference. It occurs, for example, when we fail to recall our new password because our old one intrudes during recall, refusing to be ignored or abandoned simply because it is out of date. Or, if we are seriously unlucky, we may call our current partner by our previous partner's name in an absent-minded moment. In each case, well-encoded events or facts rear their ugly head and disrupt retrieval of something more recent.

Although we have emphasized how retroactive interference affects long-term retention, proactive interference plays a powerful role in determining the rate of forgetting. This was demonstrated dramatically by Benton Underwood. Underwood (1957) was interested in explaining why participants who had learned a list of nonsense syllables should show so much forgetting after 24 hours. It occurred to Underwood that proactive interference was a real possibility. The reason was that almost all work on human learning at the time was done in a few laboratories, all of which studied undergraduate participants. If you happened to be a student in one of these departments, you were likely to be required to participate for many hours in

> ### KEY TERM
>
> **Proactive interference:** The tendency for earlier memories to disrupt the retrievability of more recent memories.

verbal learning studies. Underwood thought that it might be interference from the many *previous* lists of nonsense syllables that caused forgetting. Fortunately it was possible to find out how many previous lists each participant had learned in other experiments and to plot the amount of forgetting in a 24-hour period as a function of this prior experience. In fact, naïve students, who had no previous experience, remembered 80% of the list items after 24 hours, whereas students with 20 or more prior learning trials on different lists remembered fewer than 20% 24 hours later. Proactive interference had a giant effect on retention, largely determining the rate at which students forgot the material after an extended delay.

Experiments examining proactive interference have often used an experimental design that is highly related to the retroactive interference design described earlier. The proactive interference paradigm (Figure 9.7) resembles the retroactive interference design, except that (a) it tests people's memory for the List Two responses rather than the List One responses, and (b) in the control condition, the rest period (or performance of irrelevant activity) replaces List One learning rather than List Two learning. Thus, this design allows us to explore how previously acquired knowledge (i.e., List One) might impair our ability to recollect new information (i.e., List Two), relative to a situation in which the previous knowledge had not been learned (Control, List Two). Studies using the proactive interference procedure have demonstrated that people are more likely to forget items from a list when a prior list has been studied. The amount of proactive interference is greatest when the two lists share a common cue. Proactive interference effects are most severe when recall is tested rather than recognition.

Part-set cuing impairment

Recent exposure to one or more competitors exacerbates the problems we have in retrieving a target memory. For example, most of us have forgotten the name of someone and have been offered assistance by a well-meaning friend who supplies guesses about the name we are seeking. Unless the friend is lucky and

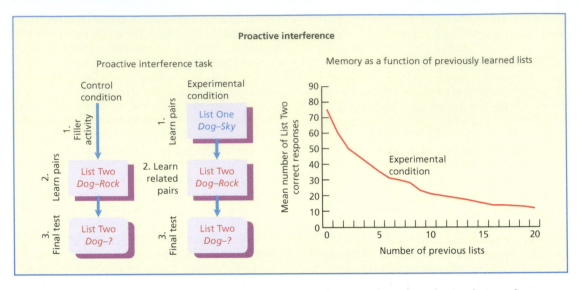

Figure 9.7 A proactive interference task, in which participants learn two lists of word pairs. A control group skips first-list learning. Right: A meta-analysis of final test cued-recall data following a 24-hour delay, given varying numbers of preceding lists. List-Two memory decreases as the number of prior lists increases. Adapted from Underwood (1957).

guesses correctly, it often feels as though his or her suggestions make matters worse. Sometimes recall fails until a much later point when, unencumbered by the clutter of incorrect guesses, your mind yields the delinquent name. If you have had this happen, you have had firsthand experience with the phenomenon of part-set cuing impairment.

Part-set cuing impairment refers to the tendency for target recall to be impaired by providing retrieval cues drawn from the same set (e.g., category) of items in memory (Mueller & Brown, 1977). The basic finding was discovered by Slamecka (1968). Slamecka had people study lists composed of words from several semantic categories (e.g., TREES, BIRDS). On the final test, some people received some of the members from each category as cues to help them recall the remainder; others were given no such cues. Of concern was people's recall of the remaining non-cue items in the experimental condition relative to recall for those items when no cues were given. Slamecka expected that the cues would help recall for the non-cue items. To his surprise, when recall was scored for the non-cue items, people receiving cues performed worse than those who received no cues! This has become known as part-set

cuing impairment because providing part of the set (in this case, part of the category) as cues impaired recall of the remaining items. Part-set cuing may be one reason why every musical album that we make a "mental note" to purchase the next time we are shopping for music seems to disappear from our minds the moment we peruse other music on sale.

The idea that supplying hints might impair memory is both surprising and ironic. In retrospect, however, it makes good sense, given the situation of interference described at the outset. Presumably a set of items is defined by some common cue (for example, FRUIT or BIRDS), to which many items are associated. If presenting some items from the set strengthens their associations to the cue, perhaps stronger items provide greater competition during the retrieval of non-cue items, impairing their recall. The idea that cues

KEY TERM

Part-set cuing impairment: When presenting part of a set of items (e.g., a category, a mental list of movies you want to rent) hinders your ability to recall the remaining items in the set.

increase competition is consistent with the finding that as more members of the set are provided as cues, the worse memory becomes for the remainder (see Nickerson, 1984, for a review).

The idea that simply re-presenting cue items strengthens them, causing part-set cuing, though appealing, has been questioned by a clever study reported by Karl-Heinz Bauml and Alp Aslan (Bauml & Aslan, 2004). Bauml and Aslan wondered whether merely presenting cues, by itself, was what made people forget the noncue items, or whether forgetting may instead be caused by how people use the cues during memory search. To look into this, they asked participants to study categories (e.g., fruit), each with 12 examples. Afterwards, one group was presented with four of the examples and told that the items should be used as cues for retrieving the remaining noncue items. After viewing these cues, the cues disappeared and participants recalled the remaining items from the list, cued with the initial letter for each. In contrast to this *part-set cuing* group, a second *part-set re-study* group saw the same four items, but were asked to study them again before being given the test on noncues. No mention was made of using these items as cues. A final *part-set retrieval* group was instead given a test on the same

Have you ever walked into a store, only to forget about your intended purchase? Blame part-set cuing, the tendency for the presence of some items as retrieval cues (like the CDs on display in the storefront) to impair one's ability to retrieve other items within the same set (the desired CD).

four items before proceeding to the key test of the noncues; each item's first letter appeared, and participants had to recall it. Interestingly, Bauml and Aslan found that whereas the part-set cuing and part-set retrieval groups showed forgetting of the noncue items, the part-set restudy group did not. A final post-test on the re-exposed items confirmed that re-exposure strengthened the recall of the four items similarly across the conditions. Bauml and Aslan argued that this finding shows that being re-exposed to items and strengthening them does not induce forgetting of the noncue items. Rather forgetting relied upon whether participants retrieved the cues. We will return to the critical role of retrieval in causing memory impairment in our later section on *retrieval-induced forgetting*.

If people's instinct to be helpful and provide cues sometimes harms memory, what would happen if a group of people got together and tried to collaboratively remember things that they had all experienced or learned? Would one person's recounting prompt others to remember more than they would have, or might it cause part-set cuing impairment? A large body of work indicates that when people get together to remember material that they each learned, they remember less when recalling the information as a group than they do when each person recalls information separately and their results combined into a common score. This phenomenon, known as collaborative inhibition, is extremely robust (see Marion & Thorley, 2016 and Rajaram & Pereira-Pasarin, 2010 for reviews). One interesting possibility is that these effects arise in part from the mechanisms that produce part-set cuing inhibition (Weldon & Bellinger, 1997). If group members are generating lots of items while you are listening, the interference this causes may disrupt your retrieval.

KEY TERM

Collaborative inhibition: A phenomenon in which a group of individuals remembers significantly less material collectively than does the combined performance of each group member individually when recalling alone.

Thus, research on part-set cuing may help to understand the effects of group effort on generating a diversity of new ideas and recollections.

Retrieval-induced forgetting

An ironic feature of human memory is that the very act of remembering can cause forgetting. Of course, it's not that remembering harms memory for the retrieved experience itself. Rather, retrieval can harm recall of other memories or facts related to the retrieved item. Anderson et al. (1994) have referred to this phenomenon as retrieval-induced forgetting (RIF).

Retrieval-induced forgetting is usually studied with the retrieval practice paradigm (Anderson et al., 1994), illustrated in Figure 9.8. In this procedure, people first study verbal categories, like *FRUITS, DRINKS*, and *TREES* for a later memory test. People would then be asked to repeatedly recall some of the examples that they just studied, from some of the categories. For example, participants might receive the cues *FRUIT-OR__* to help them retrieve the item *ORANGE*. Following this "retrieval practice," a test is given in which people are asked to recall all examples that they remember seeing from every category. On this final test, people clearly will recall the examples that they practiced quite well. More interesting, however, is how well they recall the remaining unpracticed examples (e.g., *FRUIT-BANANA*), compared to unpracticed items from baseline categories that are also studied, but none of whose examples receive retrieval practice (e.g., *DRINKS-SCOTCH*).

KEY TERM

Retrieval-induced forgetting (RIF): The tendency for the retrieval of some target items from long-term memory to impair the later ability to recall other items related to those targets.

Retrieval practice paradigm: A procedure used to study retrieval-induced forgetting.

Strikingly, as can be seen in Figure 9.8, retrieval practice improves recall of practiced items (e.g., *FRUIT-ORANGE*), but it leads people to forget the related items (e.g., *FRUIT-BANANA*). So, it seems, ironically, that the very act of remembering can cause forgetting. This observation fits well with our earlier discussion of Bauml and Aslan's (2004) finding that retrieval was an important factor in causing part-set cuing impairment.

If retrieval causes forgetting, students might have reason to be concerned about how they study for exams. Consider the plight of students who have limited time to prepare. You must prioritize your time, and the issue arises as to what to pass over. Research on retrieval-induced forgetting suggests that selectively reviewing facts impairs nonreviewed material, particularly related material. Neil Macrae and Malcolm MacLeod (1999) tested this idea by giving students facts like they might learn in a classroom. Participants studied 10 geography facts about each of two fictitious islands (*TOK* and *BILU*; e.g., *The official language of TOK is French* or *BILU'S only major export is copper*). Students then performed

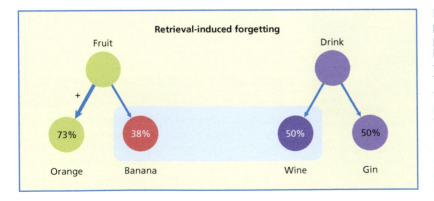

Figure 9.8 In this example, participants perform retrieval practice on orange but not banana or any members from the drink category (baseline). The final test scores indicate that, relative to baseline, practice facilitates recall of the practiced items, whereas unpracticed items from practiced categories suffer retrieval-induced forgetting. Adapted from Anderson (2003).

retrieval practice. For one island, they practiced retrieving five of its 10 facts. A final test followed, cued by the name of each island. Macrae and MacLeod found that practice facilitated the later recall of practiced facts (70%) over baseline facts about the unpracticed island (38%), but harmed memory for related but unpracticed facts (23%). Similar effects have been consistently demonstrated with complex textual materials, although there are conditions under which self-tests don't harm memory (see Storm et al., 2015 for a review). For example, tests that involve either short answer or essays often induce forgetting of untested material, but multiple-choice exams often do not (Carroll, Campbell-Ratcliffe, Murnane, & Perfect, 2007; Little, Bjork, Bjork, & Angello, 2012). So, students must be careful about leaving out material whilst studying, because omitted material may be more quickly forgotten. Indeed, this phenomenon may account for the vexing inability to recall knowledge during an exam for material that one has assumed was mastered (and therefore skipped in studying).

Selective retrieval occurs often in daily life. One situation arises when members of law enforcement, detectives, and lawyers interview a witness after a crime. Answering interrogators, of course, requires retrieval. John Shaw, a psychologist who had once been a Los Angeles public defender, thought that such questioning might harm witnesses' memories for nonquestioned material, an intuition based on experiences with some of his own clients. To examine this, Shaw, Bjork, and Handal (1995) told participants to imagine that they had attended a party and that, upon leaving, they noticed that their wallet was missing. Participants then watched slides of a student's apartment and paid attention to the details so that they might assist the police. The slides contained household items plus two categories of critical items (i.e., college sweatshirts and schoolbooks). Participants were then questioned about some of the objects (e.g., sweatshirts) during the *interrogation phase*. Consistent with Shaw's experience, interrogating people about some stolen items harmed their memory for related items. Malen Migueles

and Elvira García-Bajos also found retrieval-induced forgetting using a naturalistic bank robbery video, showing that questioning disrupted memory for offender characteristics (Migueles & García-Bajos, 2007), and such forgetting effects can last as least as long as a week (García-Bajos, Migueles, & Anderson, 2009). Interestingly, simply asking a witness about the haircut of one perpetrator makes them more likely to forget what color trousers they wore, or even the haircut of a second perpetrator (Camp, Wesstein, & De Bruin, 2012). When interrogation omits material, witnesses also become more vulnerable to misinformation about the omitted material, compounding the damage to their credibility (Saunders & MacLeod, 2002). So, retrieval-induced forgetting may have significant implications for how witnesses should be questioned (see Storm et al., 2015 for a review).

If retrieval causes forgetting, then simply discussing an experience with someone might alter whether people will remember what was omitted. Conroy and Salmon examined this idea by having young children participate in a staged event at school called *Visiting the Pirate*, during which the children did activities across a variety of scenes. For example, in the *Becoming a Pirate* scene, the children were asked to hoist a sail, bang a drum, put on pirate clothes, greet a pirate, and put their name in the pirate's book, whereas in the *Winning the Key* scene, they might have fed a bird, looked through a telescope, steered the pirate ship, and done a dance. On the next three days, the children discussed the event with another experimenter, who asked them questions about only some parts, such as, "Tell me about the animal that you fed." On the final day, the children recalled the nondiscussed elements less well than did a control group of children, who engaged in no discussion. Salmon speculated that children's memory of their growing-up years will be shaped by how parents and family members reminisce, with nondiscussed aspects growing appreciably less accessible over time (Conroy & Salmon, 2006; Salmon & Reese, 2015). Building on this work, Tammy Marche and colleagues have even found that children's memory for the unpleasant aspects of physically painful events can be forgotten by selective retrieval of the pleasant aspects, and the capacity to forget in this manner is related to how successfully young children cope with physical pain (Marche, Brier, and von Baeyer, 2016).

If discussions with other people about a shared past can lead one to forget what is not discussed, then forgetting can, in a sense, be contagious. If a friend has forgotten some parts of an experience, then they will leave the forgotten parts out while reminiscing about it. Might selective remembering in one person cause forgetting of the nondiscussed material in others? Alexandru Cuc, Jonathan Koppel, and William Hirst (2007) looked at this possibility in work on *socially shared retrieval-induced forgetting*. One study replicated the experiment of Anderson et al. (1994), discussed earlier, with a twist: they had two people, seated side by side, studying the same pairs. In the retrieval practice phase, however, one participant performed retrieval practice, whereas the other sat silently and observed, monitoring their partner's recollections for accuracy. Both then took the final test. As expected, the participant who performed retrieval practice showed retrieval-induced forgetting. Surprisingly, however, the silent observer did as well. Cuc and colleagues observed the same effect when they used stories as materials; they even observed it when people were allowed to discuss the stories freely with one another: the nondiscussed elements of the story for one person were more likely to be forgotten by the other. It seems that when we are amongst others discussing past events, we spontaneously recall those events along with the person doing the recounting, and, in doing so, subject ourselves to retrieval-induced forgetting for whatever the speaker remains silent about. If so, then retrieval-induced forgetting may be one mechanism by which a society's *collective memory* of an event comes to be more uniform over time (Stone, Coman, Brown, Koppel, & Hirst, 2012). Alin Coman, for example, found that after being exposed to a common set of facts, groups show increasingly similar memory for the material as they discuss it in individual pairs (Coman, Momennejad, Drach, & Geana, 2016). In essence, discussion aligns people's memories by encouraging remembering, but also retrieval-induced forgetting of the same things, a process they call *mnemonic convergence*. Such processes may provide a means of political manipulation, when silences about certain facts or events are deliberate, and mass media is used to trumpet certain elements of the past. As Cuc and colleagues remark, "Silence is not always golden."

It's not just selective discussions that may be shaping our memories. The technologies we have learned to love may also have a role: our mobile phones, tablets, and computers. We now, more than any time in human history, are a world able to photograph events around us in an instant, with little practical limit on the number we take. Moreover, the ease in reviewing those images and sharing them enables photo-driven reminiscing on a scale our grandparents never could dream of. Is all of this photo-reviewing altering our memories? Catarina Cinel, Cathleen Cortis Mack, and Geoff Ward suggest that it might be (Cinel, Cortis Mack, & Ward, 2018). Cinel and colleagues asked students to visit eight locations at the University of Essex to take pictures of six particular objects at each location with a mobile phone, recording a brief memorable comment about each one. Through this procedure, Cinel and colleagues hoped to mimic the situation studied in laboratory retrieval-induced forgetting work (which often uses semantic categories like fruits, drinks) except that campus locations served as the "categories' to which objects were linked. Later in the day, students returned to the lab, and reviewed their photographs for half (three) of the objects from half of the locations (four). On a later test, Cinel found that whereas students could recall the objects they reviewed very well, they suffered retrieval-induced forgetting for unreviewed objects from the reviewed locations, compared to memory for objects from unreviewed locations. This suggests that our digital devices are shaping memory by encouraging selective retrieval and retrieval-induced forgetting! Thanks to Cinel and colleagues, I now can offer my family an explanation for why I forgot knocking over the Christmas tree! Because I knocked the

Christmas tree over, it was the only thing that didn't get photographed and so in reminiscing through my slide shows, I became the victim of retrieval-induced forgetting. Are you also creating selective portraits of your past with your mobile phone?

Retrieval thus appears to be a powerful force that shapes memory, for the better and for the worse. As discussed, Marigold Linton's observations indicate that retrieval greatly enhances the longevity of a memory, but when retrieval is incomplete the benefits may be offset by forgetting of other things. If retrieval causes forgetting, then accessing what we already know might contribute to forgetting, independent of the encoding of new experience. The role of retrieval in causing forgetting has led to a new perspective on why interference is associated with forgetting. We discuss this perspective shortly.

Interference mechanisms

As the preceding discussion illustrates, many "interference" situations impair retention. Although these phenomena describe *when* forgetting will arise, they do not say *how* forgetting occurs. Why does presenting cues impair recall? Why does retrieval-induced forgetting occur? Why does introducing new learning impair retention of previously acquired material? First we consider classical mechanisms proposed to explain interference, and show how they can be extended to explain phenomena like part-set cuing and retrieval-induced forgetting. Then we consider a more recent view in which inhibitory processes associated with cognitive control underlie retrieval cause forgetting.

Associative blocking

Once, while recalling the British term for what Americans call a "Christmas ornament," I persistently recalled "Christmas balls" (what Belgians call Christmas ornaments), instead of "Christmas baubles." "Christmas balls" kept intruding until I gave up. In essence, "Christmas balls" blocked "Christmas baubles." After drifting off to other activities, the right answer "popped" to

mind. An elegant demonstration of this type of effect was reported by Steven Smith and Debora Tindell (1997), who had people encode a large set of words by making ratings on them (e.g., pleasantness ratings). Afterwards, they gave participants an apparently unrelated puzzle-solving task requiring them to complete word fragments. Unbeknownst to the subjects, some of these puzzles were orthographically similar to one of the words that they rated earlier, and others were not. For example, if they had initially encoded ANALOGY, they might later receive a highly similar puzzle, like A_L_ _ GY. Participants solved the puzzles related to earlier words more poorly (33%) compared to ones without related words (50%). Subsequent work has shown that these "memory blocks" are indeed accompanied by reminders of the original word, which the participant experiences as "getting in the way" of the right answer (Leynes, Brown, & Landua, 2011), confirming the blocking phenomenon.

Perhaps something like this experience might generalize to episodic memory more broadly explaining interference phenomenon. For instance, in retroactive interference, people may forget first-list responses because the cues used to access them now elicit the second-list responses. In part-set cuing, presenting exemplar cues may strengthen their association to the category, leading them to intrude when people try to retrieve noncue exemplars. In each case, a cue elicits a stronger competitor, leading us to helplessly perseverate on something that we know to be incorrect. The idea that such a process explains interference was proposed by McGeoch in his (1942) *response competition theory*, modern versions of which are known as associative blocking (see Anderson et al., 1994).

> **KEY TERM**
>
> **Associative blocking:** A theoretical process hypothesized to explain interference effects during retrieval, according to which a cue fails to elicit a target trace because it repeatedly elicits a stronger competitor, leading people to abandon efforts to retrieve the target.

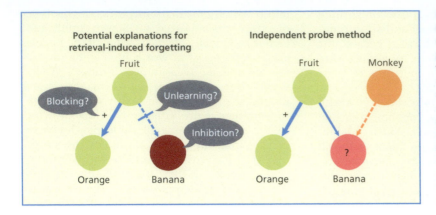

Figure 9.9 Left: Practiced items could block target recall during the final test, producing retrieval-induced forgetting. Alternatively, the connection between cue and target could have been unlearned during retrieval practice. Inhibition involves a reduction in the target memory's activation, itself. Right: Only inhibition correctly predicts that forgetting generalizes to independent cues.

The core assumption of the blocking hypothesis is the idea that memories compete for access to awareness when their shared cue is provided. The degree of interference should increase as the cue grows more strongly associated to the competitor, exhibiting what Anderson et al. (1994) refer to as *strength-dependent competition*. But how does a stronger competitor impair recall? Consider an example from retrieval-induced forgetting, in which you are trying to recall *BANANA* after having practiced *FRUIT-ORANGE*. According to the blocking theory, the cues on the final test (e.g., *FRUIT*) to recall *BANANA* lead the person to accidentally retrieve the stronger practiced item, *ORANGE*. Once accidentally retrieved, *ORANGE* will achieve greater prominence, having been practiced again, making it even more likely to be accidentally retrieved. And so the cycle would continue, because, with each accidental retrieval, the wrong answer grows stronger. Eventually, people may simply give up. So, according to the blocking theory, people forget unpracticed exemplars of practiced categories because associations to the practiced memories dominate retrieval. Blocking can also explain the cue-overload principle: the more memories associated to a cue, the more likely it should be to accidentally retrieve a wrong answer, setting the blocking process in motion. If so, the reason you can't remember your dinner four months ago is because retrieval calls to mind recent dinners to such an extent that you give up.

Associative unlearning

Associative unlearning is another theoretical account of interference effects, which can be illustrated intuitively with a real-life example. Suppose that your acquaintance describes a conversation at a party several years ago. You may recall, in good detail, elements of the party, including your friend's attendance, various conversations, as well as several amusing events. However, you may forget discussing a topic with your friend, despite your friend's most confident confirmations—even when you clearly recollect discussing the topic. Subjectively, it seems as though your memory has become fragmented, impairing your judgment about how elements of the experience go together. This apparent fragmentation may reflect damage to the associations between elements of that event caused by storing subsequent experiences. Perhaps such damage underlies my inability to recollect knocking over the Christmas tree.

Research on the unlearning hypothesis of retroactive interference (Melton & Irwin, 1940) is relevant to these ideas. According to the hypothesis, the association between a stimulus and a trace will be weakened whenever that trace is retrieved inappropriately. In effect, the bond between the cue and the

KEY TERM

Unlearning: The proposition that the associative bond linking a stimulus to a memory trace will be weakened when the trace is retrieved in error when a different trace is sought.

target gets "punished." For example, suppose that you try to retrieve the new password to your email account. According to the unlearning view, if you recall your old password and realize the mistake, the association between the cue "password" and the original password details will get weakened, decreasing the chances that it will pop up again in the future. If the old password is punished often enough, the association may grow so weak that the cue "password" will no longer activate that target. The cue will be decoupled from the target. This view can explain retrieval-induced forgetting, if we assume that during retrieval practice, competing items intrude and are punished. It explains retroactive interference in the same way. So whereas blocking attributes forgetting to very strong practiced competitors, unlearning says that associations into the target are too weak.

The unlearning and blocking hypotheses are not incompatible. In fact, according to the classical *two-factor model of retroactive interference* (Melton & Irwin, 1940), both mechanisms are needed. It is worth emphasizing, however, that proof of unlearning is difficult to establish, for the same reasons that it is difficult to prove that memories are permanently forgotten, as discussed earlier in this chapter. And although blocking explains why forgetting appears to grow as competitors are strengthened, there are reasons to doubt whether strengthening a competitor, by itself, produces forgetting, as will be illustrated shortly. For these reasons, an alternative view has emerged which attributes the forgetting arising from interference to inhibitory processes.

Inhibition as a cause of forgetting

The preceding discussion raises an important point: sometimes it is distracting for a trace to be accessible. The goal of retrieving a target memory can be disrupted by highly accessible competitors, and people need a way to limit this distraction. Although unlearning the link between the cue and the target memory is one way to achieve this, another is to inhibit the target itself. Consider an analogy. Suppose that you normally wear a watch, but one day the wristband breaks, and you can't wear it. If someone then asks you what time it is, you may look at your wrist reflexively, even when you know the watch is absent. This may happen several times before you learn to look at the clock instead. Clearly, what is normally a useful and over-learned habit has, for the time being, become an inappropriate response that must be shut down. Fortunately, humans and other organisms can stop responses in this way, a process thought to be achieved by inhibiting the to-be-stopped response. This inhibition reduces the activity level of the response, ceasing its production in a manner analogous to how inhibiting a neuron would reduce its influence on other neurons.

The same demands confronted in shutting down interfering responses occur for internal actions, such as retrieval. As discussed in the section on proactive interference, if somebody asks for our telephone number, we may automatically remember our old number even though we have switched phones. Recalling the new number requires that we stop retrieval of the old one, which may be accomplished by inhibition. If the old number is inhibited, however, it will grow harder to recall, even if it remains available. In the context of retrieval-induced forgetting, *BANANA* may become activated and intrude during the retrieval of *FRUIT-OR____*. To facilitate the retrieval of *ORANGE*, perhaps *BANANA* is inhibited, with persisting inhibition making it harder to retrieve that item. *BANANA*, like the habit of looking at one's wrist, may be inhibited to support the current goals. This inhibition proposal differs from the unlearning hypothesis in two key respects. First, unlike unlearning, the inhibition theory doesn't propose that the link between the cue and the response is unlearned; rather, it is the response itself that is inhibited, with the association left intact. Second, inhibition is thought to be produced by an attentional control process that suppresses the response, unlike unlearning, which is produced by an associative learning mechanism. Thus, by the inhibition view, the link between Fruit and Banana should be fine, but Banana itself is inhibited.

Are retrieval employ inhibitory processes? This question has often been studied with retrieval-induced forgetting (Levy &

Anderson, 2002). Inhibition makes several predictions about retrieval-induced forgetting that are not made by either the blocking or unlearning theories. According to inhibition, performing retrieval practice on *FRUIT-ORANGE* reduces memory for *BANANA* because *BANANA*, as the competing memory (like looking at the wristwatch), is inhibited by activation-reducing mechanisms. If *BANANA* is truly inhibited, one *BANANA* should be harder to recall generally, whether one tests it with *FRUIT* as a cue, or, say, another unrelated associate, such as *MONKEY-B___*. In other words, inhibition predicts that retrieval-induced forgetting should generalize to new cues, exhibiting *cue independence*. In contrast, both blocking and unlearning attribute forgetting to problems with the associations linking *FRUIT* to either *BANANA* or *ORANGE*. Hence, according to these theories, retrieval-induced forgetting should depend on the cue. That is, as long as you switch to another cue, like *MONKEY*, that circumvents the stronger association from *FRUIT* to *ORANGE* and the potentially weaker association from *FRUIT* to *BANANA*, no difficulty should arise in recalling *BANANA*. Cue-independent forgetting has been observed many times (Anderson & Spellman, 1995; see Anderson, 2003; Murayama, Miyatsu, Buchli, & Storm, 2014; Weller, Anderson, Gomez-Ariza, & Bajo, 2013, for reviews), indicating that inhibition does play a role in causing retrieval-induced forgetting.

According to the inhibition hypothesis, the need to overcome interference during retrieval triggers inhibition. If so, then active retrieval on practiced items should be necessary to induce forgetting of competitors. For example, simply replacing retrieval practice trials (e.g., *FRUIT-OR___*) with a chance to restudy *FRUIT-ORANGE* multiple times should eliminate later forgetting of competitors like *BANANA*. Forgetting should disappear because giving people *FRUIT-ORANGE* to study eliminates any struggle to retrieve *ORANGE*, and thus, any need to resolve interference from *BANANA*. This *retrieval-specificity* property is a consistent feature of retrieval-induced forgetting (see Anderson, 2003; Storm & Levy, 2012). Thus,

even though both retrieval practice and extra study exposures strengthen memory for the practiced items to the same degree, only retrieval practice impairs retention of the unpracticed competitors. There appears to be something special about the need to reach into memory and retrieve something that induces forgetting, consistent with the idea that inhibition is involved. This finding doesn't favor the blocking hypothesis, however, which predicts that strengthening practiced shapes should impair recall of competitors, regardless of whether strengthening is accomplished by retrieval or study. Inhibitory processes engaged during retrieval can also explain the part-set cuing findings of Bauml and Aslan (2004) discussed earlier.

One feature that speaks against blocking theories is that retrieval-induced forgetting is unrelated to how strong the practiced associations become as a result of practice. Research on retrieval-specificity, for example, shows that strengthening practiced items through repeated study doesn't induce forgetting of competitors. Indeed, strengthening a competitor appears unnecessary to trigger retrieval-induced forgetting. In one study, Benjamin Storm, Elizabeth Bjork, Robert Bjork, and John Nestojko (2006) had the clever idea to see whether it was merely the retrieval attempt that created retrieval-induced forgetting. Participants in this retrieval practice paradigm were, for some categories, given retrieval practice cues that were impossible to complete. So, for example, they might have received the cue *FRUIT-LU___* to complete, even though no fruit begins with *LU*. Strikingly, even though people could not complete any of these retrieval practice tests, they showed as much retrieval-induced forgetting for the remaining exemplars as they did for categories in which retrieval practice trials could be completed. So the struggle to extract a trace from memory, in the face of interference, is the important trigger for retrieval-induced forgetting, not the strengthening of the practiced items. This property is referred to as *strength independence*.

If inhibition overcomes distraction from competitors, how much retrieval-induced forgetting a person suffers should depend on interference during retrieval practice. If the other associates of a cue don't interfere, inhibition should be unnecessary. In an early example of this, Anderson et al. (1994) varied whether competing items were high-frequency examples of their respective categories (for example, *FRUIT-BANANA*) or were low-frequency examples (for example, *FRUIT-GUAVA*). Intuitively, one might imagine that a high-frequency example like *BANANA* would be resistant to forgetting, whereas a low-frequency item might be vulnerable. The analogy to the wristwatch example, however, suggests the opposite. It's precisely because one reflexively checks one's wrist when the watch is not there that one must inhibit that response. If so, then high-frequency examples, like *FRUIT-BANANA*, might be prime targets for inhibition because they come to mind readily, whereas low-frequency exemplars might not need to be inhibited. This is exactly what Anderson and colleagues found. This property is known as *interference dependence*, or the tendency for retrieval-induced forgetting to be triggered by interference from a competing memory (see Anderson & Levy, 2011; Storm, 2011; Storm & Levy, 2012 for reviews).

Research on retrieval-induced forgetting suggests that selectively retrieving facts or events places demands on attentional control processes like inhibition, to overcome interference from distracting memories. In our wristwatch example, it takes attention to suppress looking at your wrist reflexively when someone asks you what time it is. If inhibition truly requires attention, then retrieval-induced forgetting might be reduced if people are distracted during retrieval practice. Patricia Román, Felipa Soriano, Carlos Gomez-Ariza, and Teresa Bajo (2009) confirmed this prediction by studying what happens when attention is divided during retrieval practice. After studying a list of categories like fruits and drinks, participants performed retrieval practice according to the typical retrieval-induced forgetting procedure. Crucially, whereas some participants performed retrieval practice with full attention, others had to do a concurrent attention-demanding task: they listened to an audio recording of a speaker reading a series of digits and had to press a

button each time they heard three odd digits in a row. Remarkably, participants in the two groups were equally successful in performing retrieval practice, despite the differing attention demands. However, when it came to the final memory test, participants in the divided attention condition showed less retrieval-induced forgetting than full attention participants. Indeed, they showed no retrieval-induced forgetting at all. Relatedly, Koessler, Engler, Riether, and Kissler (2009) found that giving people a highly stressful task (having to give a presentation unexpectedly to a group of strangers) just before they performed retrieval practice abolished retrieval-induced forgetting. Storm and White (2010) further found that participants with attention deficit disorder showed reduced retrieval-induced forgetting. Taken together, these findings suggest that retrieval-induced forgetting is *attention dependent*. This feature is consistent with the role of inhibitory processes in suppressing distracting memories.

It makes sense that suppressing distraction from competing memories might require focused attention and effort. Does suppressing particular competing memories grow easier with each time that we retrieve the memory we want? In our wristwatch analogy, one is less likely to look at one's watch-less wrist with each successive occasion of being asked for the time. The increasing ease with repetitions may indicate that the habit that was once distracting has been inhibited, and so no longer demands effort to control. Research using brain imaging suggests that this process may also happen with inhibiting memories. Brice Kuhl and his colleagues used functional magnetic resonance imaging to scan people during retrieval practice. As in most retrieval-induced forgetting experiments, they asked participants to retrieve the same to-be-practiced items on several occasions, and they wondered what brain areas would be more engaged during the first retrieval practice compared to the third. On the first practice trial, competing memories are yet to be inhibited, and so produce substantial interference that needs to be resolved by engaging inhibition mechanisms. By the third trial, any interference caused by competitors should be much

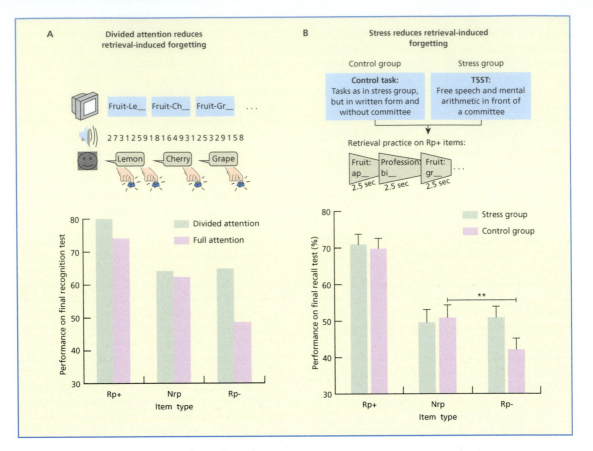

Figure 9.10 The effects of divided attention and stress on retrieval-induced forgetting. Panel A illustrates findings from Roman et al. (2009), who manipulated whether participants performed retrieval practice on category exemplars under full attention, or while simultaneously performing a digit monitoring task (described in the text). Participants in the full attention condition showed facilitation of practiced (Rp+) items and impaired retention of competitors (Rp-items) on a final recognition test; in contrast, participants who had their attention divided showed facilitation of practiced items, but no impairment for Rp-items. A similar pattern was shown by Koessler et al. (2009) (Panel B), though the stress manipulation was introduced before retrieval practice. In the experimental group, participants were asked to give an unannounced presentation in front of a committee. Thus, in both cases, inhibition effects could be selectively abolished without affecting practice benefits, by manipulations likely to compromise attention. Panel A from Román et al. (2009), copyright © Association for Psychological Science. Panel B from Koessler et al. (2009). Copyright © Association for Psychological Science.

reduced, eliminating the need for control. Intriguingly, Kuhl and colleagues observed more activation in the left and right ventrolateral prefrontal cortex and anterior cingulate cortex on early trials compared to later trials. These brain regions previously have been associated to cognitive control and the resolution of response conflict, suggesting that the attentional demands of retrieval practice indeed declined over repetitions, consistent with a diminished need to overcome

distraction. Importantly, the steeper the decline in activation in these areas from the first to the third retrieval practice trial, the greater was the retrieval-induced forgetting observed on the final test. Kuhl and colleagues argued that this finding revealed the adaptive advantage of forgetting: by reducing distraction from competing memories, people expended less neural effort during retrieval practice to retrieve the things they wanted to recall (Kuhl, Dudukovic, Kahn, & Wagner,

2007; see Levy, Kuhl, & Wagner, 2010 for a review). Other research has since built on this fascinating finding to reveal that as people repeatedly retrieve a particular memory, patterns of brain activity that are unique to other memories that compete with it are gradually suppressed, as might be expected if distracting memories were being actively inhibited. This phenomenon is known as *cortical pattern suppression* (Wimber, Alink, Charest, Kriegeskorte, & Anderson, 2015).

Needing to overcome distraction from competing memories during retrieval is not unique to human beings. After all, animals, like people, have many similar memories that may cause interference when they need to retrieve one of them. Do other mammals resolve interference in the same way as people? Does retrieval-induced forgetting occur across species? Together with Pedro Bekinschtein, Noelia Weisstaub, Francisco Gallo, and Maria Renner, I explored this issue with rats (Bekinschtein, Weisstaub, Gallo, Renner, & Anderson, 2018). We took an approach that was rather like the one taken by Cinel and colleagues (described earlier in this chapter) to study whether reviewing mobile-phone pictures causes retrieval-induced forgetting (Cinel et al., 2018). Instead of training rats on mobile phones, we simply let them explore two objects in a distinctive arena, and, afterwards, selectively exposed them to one of those objects on several occasions. So, like Cinel's participants, rats got to selectively "review" some objects from a particular location. Strikingly, simply reviewing one of the objects induced forgetting of the unreviewed object from that same location, compared to memory for objects encoded and tested in a different location, just as in Cinel's study (for an analogous finding with odors, see Wu, Peters, Rittner, Cleland, & Smith, 2014). Indeed, in additional experiments, this forgetting proved to be retrieval-specific, interference-dependent, and cue-independent, just like in humans. Critically, temporarily inactivating the rodents' prefrontal cortex right before retrieval practice abolished retrieval-induced forgetting entirely, even though the very same rats showed robust forgetting when the prefrontal cortex was intact! We even found that rats, like human

participants in Kuhl's study just discussed, showed decreasing prefrontal activation over repeated retrieval practice trials, revealing how forgetting competing memories made their lives a little easier with each passing retrieval. These findings show active forgetting mechanisms underlying retrieval-induced forgetting are both *species-general* and *prefrontal cortex-dependent*. So, the next time you review photos taken with your mobile device, you may well be engaging your prefrontal cortex to forget unreviewed aspects of your past.

Taken together, the properties of cue-independence, retrieval-specificity, strength-independence, interference-dependence, and attention-dependence converge with neuroscience evidence of prefrontal-dependence to support a role of active inhibition as a source of forgetting. If so, it suggests that many of our experiences with forgetting may arise from the need to control interference. It's precisely because we are distracted by momentarily irrelevant information in our memories—those unintended looks at our "mental wristwatch"—that we engage inhibition to refocus on what we hope to retrieve from memory. On the one hand, it may seem ironic that the mechanisms we use to direct retrieval are the ones that ultimately contribute to forgetting. On the other hand, as Robert Bjork suggests, such forgetting may be adaptive because it helps to reduce interference from information that may no longer be as relevant as it once was (Bjork, 1989). If information remains in memory and can be revived (e.g., by re-exposure), forgetting may be very functional.

A FUNCTIONAL VIEW OF INCIDENTAL FORGETTING

For over a century, experimental psychologists have focused on passive mechanisms of forgetting, including contextual fluctuation, the use of inappropriate retrieval cues, and interference processes such as blocking. The presumption has been that people are passive victims of forgetting, with memory loss

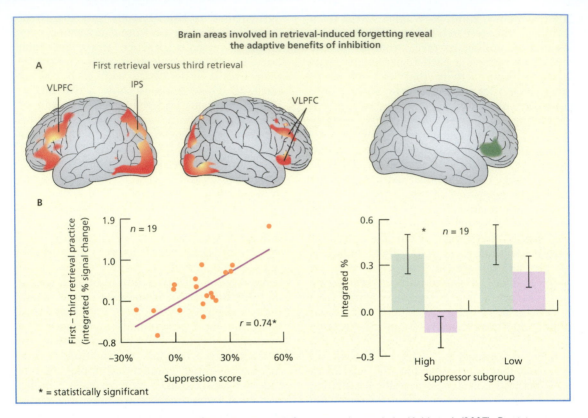

Figure 9.11 Brain areas involved in retrieval-induced forgetting in the study by Kuhl et al. (2007). Participants were scanned with fMRI as they performed retrieval practice trials on studied items. Panel A illustrates brain areas that were more active during the first retrieval practice compared to the third, which includes both left and right ventrolateral prefrontal cortex (VLPFC). This finding is consistent with a role for VLPFC in overcoming competition, which subsides over repetitions, as memories are inhibited. Consistent with this view, activation in a subregion of right VLPFC (Panel A, right side) predicted the amount of retrieval-induced forgetting (Panel B). Panel C illustrates how high suppressors (people who show a lot of retrieval-induced forgetting) show a steeper decline in VLPFC activation from the first to the third practice trial than do low suppressors (people who show little retrieval-induced forgetting). Thus, people who are good at forgetting via inhibition, exert less neural effort over time, as interfering memories are suppressed. From Kuhl et al. (2007). Copyright © Nature Publishing.

arising from factors that simply happen to us, such as random changes in the environment, and the addition of traces into memory. Although such processes contribute to forgetting, there is a powerful trend to view forgetting as a more active and functional process.

Increasingly, scientists studying memory at all levels—whether at the level of molecules, brain systems, or behavior—have recognized that forgetting is more than simply a failure of retention. There is now clear evidence that species have evolved mechanisms that specifically facilitate memory loss for a functional purpose (e.g., Bekinschtein et al., 2018; Davis

& Zhong, 2017; Hardt et al., 2013; Richards & Frankland, 2017) including biologically regulated mechanisms that undo synaptic plasticity (e.g., Davis & Zhong, 2017; Migues et al., 2016). Interesting hypotheses are being developed about the adaptive functions that forgetting may serve and several authors have emphasized the utility of forgetting for facilitating behavioral flexibility in organisms (e.g., Bekinschtein et al., 2018; Richards & Frankland, 2017).

A clear example of this functional view of forgetting can be seen in our discussion of the role of inhibition in forgetting in the current

TABLE 9.1 Properties of retrieval-induced forgetting

Property of retrieval-induced forgetting	Description
Cue independence	The tendency for forgetting caused by inhibition to generalize to novel test cues on the independent probe test (e.g. monkey–b— for banana, which was originally studied with the cue fruit).
Retrieval specificity	Active retrieval from long-term memory is necessary to induce forgetting of related information. For example, having to retrieve orange, given fruit—or—generates retrieval-induced forgetting of unpracticed competitors (e.g., banana), whereas simply studying the intact pairing (fruitorange) does not.
Strength independence	The degree to which competitors are strengthened by retrieval practice is unrelated to the size of the retrieval-induced forgetting deficit. Thus, strengthening an item by presenting the intact pairing (fruitorange) does not induce retrieval-induced forgetting, whereas engaging in an impossible retrieval attempt (e.g. fruit–lu—) still results in forgetting of unpracticed competitors.
Interference dependence	Interference by competitors during retrieval of targets is necessary for retrieval-induced forgetting of those competitors to occur. Therefore, high-frequency competitors (e.g., fruit–banana), which pose greater competition than low-frequency competitors (e.g., fruit–guava) are more likely to be inhibited than vice versa.
Attention dependence	During retrieval of a target, competitors are only inhibited if attentional control is available to suppress those distracting memories. Reduced attention during retrieval reduces inhibition aftereffects.

chapter. By this view, forgetting arises from the need to control the retrieval process in the face of competition. It is the process by which we combat interference—inhibition of competing traces—that precipitates forgetting, not the mere presence of other traces in memory. Reducing the accessibility of competing traces is adaptive because it facilitates retrieval, but also because it makes subsequent retrievals of the same information easier, reducing future competition. This functional view conceptualizes forgetting as a positive outcome and highlights how a properly functioning memory system must be as good at forgetting as it is at remembering (Anderson, 2003; Anderson & Spellman, 1995; Bjork, 1988; Bjork, Bjork, & Macleod, 2006). Thus, rather than being victims of forces beyond our control, forgetting may often be tied to mechanisms enabling the effective control of cognition.

SUMMARY

- Forgetting increases over time, though not at a constant rate. The function relating forgetting to time is known as a forgetting curve, and it follows a logarithmic function.
- At the same time, synaptic and systemic consolidation processes make memories more resilient over time, though consolidated memories sometimes need to undergo reconsolidation when reactivated.
- Repeated retrieval of memories slows their forgetting.

(Continued)

(Continued)

- The availability of a memory in the system (i.e., whether it remains in storage) must be distinguished from its accessibility (i.e., whether one can retrieve it).
- Permanent memory loss is very difficult to establish through behavior, as lack of availability and inaccessibility both predict memory failure.
- Neurobiological mechanisms actively degrade consolidated synaptic connections reducing the availability of a memory over time and confirming the existence of a decay process, even if this may be hard to establish behaviorally.
- The generation and integration of new neurons in the hippocampus throughout life structurally remodels hippocampal networks in a way that induces forgetting, a phenomenon known as neurogenesis-induced forgetting. This form of forgetting doesn't erase older memories, but may render them inaccessible, and likely forms the basis of infantile amnesia.
- Other factors correlated with time (apart from decay) make potent contributions to the forgetting function, including interference, inhibition, and fluctuations in physical and mental context.
- Interference arises when the retrieval cues used to access a memory becomes associated to other experiences that compete for access to conscious awareness. The more competitors that are attached to a cue, the worse recall of any one item becomes, a generalization known as the cue overload principle.
- When previously learned experiences (or knowledge) disrupt retention of more recently acquired experiences, it is known as proactive interference.
- When more recently acquired experiences (or knowledge) disrupt retention of previously acquired experiences, it is known as retroactive interference.
- When one has learned a set of material, presenting part of the set as cues for the recall of the remainder typically impairs the ability to recall the remainder, a phenomenon known as part-set cuing impairment.
- The very act of remembering can cause forgetting, a phenomenon known as retrieval-induced forgetting. Retrieval-induced forgetting happens when one tries to selectively retrieve some memories associated to a cue, a process which generally impairs the remaining associates.
- Blocking theories attribute interference to the tendency for stronger traces to persistently intrude during retrieval of weaker ones, leading the person to abandon search.
- Unlearning theories propose that interference causes destructive changes to the associations that underlie a trace, as a result of learning mechanisms that punish inappropriate retrievals.
- Inhibition theories propose that forgetting arises from the suppression of interfering traces by inhibitory mechanisms that resolve competition.
- Research using the retrieval-induced forgetting paradigm has provided specific evidence supporting the existence of inhibition.
- Retrieval-induced forgetting exhibits key functional properties that favor the involvement of inhibition, including interference-dependence, cue-independence, strength-independence, retrieval-specificity, and attention-dependence.
- Retrieval engages cognitive control processes mediated by the ventrolateral prefrontal cortex that have been linked to the suppression of interfering memories and the induction of retrieval-induced forgetting.

- Retrieval-induced forgetting is a species-general phenomenon and can be abolished by selective lesions to the rodent prefrontal cortex.
- Forgetting may often be adaptive, if it reduces demands on cognitive control processes that would otherwise be needed to suppress interference from competing memories. Thus, adaptive forgetting may increase cognitive efficiency.
- Research on memory at all levels of analysis (molecular, brain systems, cognitive) is increasingly revealing the active and functional nature of forgetting, with evidence accumulating that nature has evolved dedicated mechanisms to undo memories.

POINTS FOR DISCUSSION

1 Sometimes one's forgetting can be very costly in terms of time, money, embarrassment, or inconvenience to others. Pick the top three most significant examples of forgetting that you have experienced. Use the concepts described in this chapter to explain, in detail, why the forgetting happened to you.

2 You are trying to remember someone's name, and a well-meaning friend tries to help by supplying guesses, all of them wrong. Using your knowledge of interference mechanisms, describe how you would explain to your friend why they should stop doing this.

3 Cuc and colleagues colorfully noted that "Silence is not always golden" in their article on socially shared retrieval-induced forgetting. Explain what this means, and why socially shared retrieval-induced forgetting is important.

4 What are the key findings that suggest that inhibition mechanisms contribute to retrieval-induced forgetting?

FURTHER READING

Anderson, M. C., & Neely, J. H. (1996). Interference and inhibition in memory retrieval. In E. L. Bjork & R. A. Bjork (Eds.), *Memory: Handbook of perception and cognition* (2nd ed., pp. 237–313). San Diego: Academic Press.

Davis, R. L., & Zhong, Y. (2017). The biology of forgetting—a perspective. *Neuron, 95*(3), 490–503.

Levy, B. J., & Anderson, M. C. (2002). Inhibitory processes and the control of memory retrieval. *Trends in Cognitive Sciences, 6,* 299–305.

Levy, B. J., Kuhl, B. A., & Wagner, A. D. (2010). The functional neuroimaging of forgetting. In S. Della Sala (Ed.), *Forgetting* (pp. 135–163). New York: Psychology Press.

Richards, B. A., & Frankland, P. W. (2017). The persistence and transience of memory. *Neuron, 94*(6), 1071–1084.

Storm, B. C., Angello, G., Buchli, D. R., Koppel, R. H., Little, J. L., & Nestojko, J. F. (2015). A review of retrieval-induced forgetting in the contexts of learning, eyewitness memory, social cognition, autobiographical memory, and creative cognition. In B. Ross (Ed.), *Psychology of learning and motivation* (Vol. 62, pp. 141–194). New York: Academic Press.

REFERENCES

Adesope, O. O., Trevisan, D. A., & Sundararajan, N. (2017). Rethinking the use of tests: A meta-analysis of practice testing. *Review of Educational Research, 87*(3), 659–701.

Akers, K. G., Martinez-Canabal, A., Restivo, L., Yiu, A. P., De Cristofaro, A., Hsiang, H. L. L., ... & Ohira, K. (2014). Hippocampal neurogenesis regulates forgetting during adulthood and infancy. *Science, 344*(6184), 598–602.

Altmann, E. M., & Schunn, C. D. (2012). Decay versus interference: A new look at an old interaction. *Psychological Science, 23*(11), 1435–1437.

Anderson, M. C. (2003). Rethinking interference theory: Executive control and the mechanisms of forgetting. *Journal of Memory and Language, 49*(4), 415–445.

Anderson, M. C., Bjork, R. A., & Bjork, E. L. (1994). Remembering can cause forgetting: Retrieval dynamics in long-term memory. *Journal of Experimental Psychology: Learning, Memory, and Cognition, 20*, 1063–1087.

Anderson, M. C., & Levy, B. J. (2011). On the relationship between interference and inhibition in cognition. In A. S. Benjamin (Ed.), *Successful remembering and successful forgetting: A festschrift in honor of Robert A. Bjork* (pp. 107–132). Hoboken, NJ: Taylor & Francis.

Anderson, M. C., & Neely, J. H. (1996). Interference and inhibition in memory retrieval. In E. L. Bjork & R. A. Bjork (Eds.), *Memory: Handbook of perception and cognition* (pp. 237–313). San Diego: Academic Press.

Anderson, M. C., & Spellman, B. A. (1995). On the status of inhibitory mechanisms in cognition: Memory retrieval as a model case. *Psychological Review, 102*, 68–100.

Antony, J. W., Ferreira, C. S., Norman, K. A., & Wimber, M. (2017). Retrieval as a fast route to memory consolidation. *Trends in Cognitive Sciences, 21*(8), 573–576.

Averell, L., & Heathcote, A. (2011). The form of the forgetting curve and the fate of memories. *Journal of Mathematical Psychology, 55*(1), 25–35.

Awasthi, A., Ramachandran, B., Ahmed, S., Benito, E., Shinoda, Y., Nitzan, N., ... & Burk, K. (2019). Synaptotagmin-3 drives AMPA receptor endocytosis, depression of synapse strength, and forgetting. *Science, 363*(6422), eaav1483.

Baddeley, A. D. (1986). *Working memory*. New York: Oxford University Press.

Baddeley, A. D., & Hitch, G. (1977). Recency re-examined. In S. Dornic (Ed.), *Attention and performance* (pp. 647–667). Hillsdale, NJ: Erlbaum.

Bahrick, H. P. (1984). Semantic memory content in permastore: Fifty years of memory for Spanish learning in school. *Journal of Experimental Psychology: General, 113*, 1–29.

Bahrick, H. P., Bahrick, P. O., & Wittlinger, R. P. (1975). Fifty years of memory for names and faces: A cross-sectional approach. *Journal of Experimental Psychology: General, 104*(1), 54–75.

Bahrick, H. P., Hall, L. K., & Baker, M. K. (2013). *Life-span maintenance of knowledge*. New York: Psychology Press.

Bailey, C. H., & Chen, M. (1989). Structural plasticity at identified synapses during long-term memory in Aplysia. *Journal of Neurobiology, 20*(5), 356–372.

Barnes, J. M., & Underwood, B. J. (1959). Fate of first-list association in transfer theory. *Journal of Experimental Psychology, 58*(2), 97–105.

Bäuml, K.-H., & Aslan, S. (2004). Part-list cuing as instructed retrieval inhibition. *Memory & Cognition, 32*(4), 610–617.

Bekinschtein, P., Weisstaub, N. V., Gallo, F., Renner, M., & Anderson, M. C. (2018). A retrieval-specific mechanism of adaptive forgetting in the mammalian brain. *Nature Communications, 9*(1), 4660.

Berman, M. G., Jonides, J., & Lewis, R. L. (2009). In search of decay in verbal short-term memory. *Journal of Experimental Psychology: Learning, Memory, and Cognition, 35*(2), 317–333.

Berry, J. A., Cervantes-Sandoval, I., Nicholas, E. P., & Davis, R. L. (2012). Dopamine is required for learning and forgetting in Drosophila. *Neuron, 74*, 530–542.

Bjork, E. L., Bjork, R. A., & Macleod, M. D. (2006). Types and consequences of forgetting: Intended and unintended. In L. Nilsson & O. Nobuo (Eds.), *Memory and society: Psychological perspectives* (pp. 141–165). New York: Psychology Press.

Bjork, R. A. (1988). *Retrieval practice and the maintenance of knowledge*. Oxford: John Wiley & Sons.

Bjork, R. A. (1989). Retrieval inhibition as an adaptive mechanism in human memory. In H. L. Roediger & F. I. Craik (Eds.), *Varieties of memory and consciousness: Essays in honour of Endel Tulving* (pp. 309–330). Hillsdale, NJ: Lawrence Erlbaum Associates.

Broadbent, D. E. (1958). *Perception and communication*. New York: Pergamon Press.

Camp, G., Wesstein, H., & De Bruin, A. B. H. (2012). Can questioning induce forgetting? Retrieval-induced forgetting of eyewitness information. *Applied Cognitive Psychology, 26*, 431–435.

Carroll, M., Campbell-Ratcliffe, J., Murnane, H., & Perfect, T. J. (2007). Retrieval-induced forgetting in educational contexts: Monitoring, expertise, text integration and test format. *European Journal of Cognitive Psychology, 19*, 580–606.

Cinel, C., Cortis Mack, C., & Ward, G. (2018). Towards augmented human memory: Retrieval-induced forgetting and retrieval practice in an interactive, end-of-day review. *Journal of Experimental Psychology: General, 147*(5), 632–661.

Coman, A., Momennejad, I., Drach, R. D., & Geana, A. (2016). Mnemonic convergence in social networks: The emergent properties of cognition at a collective level. *Proceedings of the National Academy of Sciences of the USA, 113*(29), 8171–8176.

Conroy, R., & Salmon, K. (2006). Talking about parts of a past experience: The influence of elaborative discussion and event structure on children's recall of nondiscussed information. *Journal of Experimental Child Psychology, 95*, 278–297.

Cowan, N. (1988). Evolving conceptions of memory storage, selective attention, and their mutual constraints within the human information-processing system. *Psychological Bulletin, 104*(2), 163–191.

Crowder, R. G. (1976). *Principles of learning and memory*. Oxford: Lawrence Erlbaum.

Cuc, A., Koppel, J., & Hirst, W. (2007). Silence is not golden: A case for socially shared retrieval-induced forgetting. *Psychological Science, 18*(8), 727–733.

Davis, R. L., & Zhong, Y. (2017). The biology of forgetting—a perspective. *Neuron, 95*(3), 490–503.

Delaney, P. F., Sahakyan, L., Kelley, C. M., & Zimmerman, C. A. (2010). Remembering to forget: The amnesic effect of daydreaming. *Psychological Science, 21*, 1036–1042.

Dudai, Y. (2004). The neurobiology of consolidations, or, how stable is the engram. *Annual Review of Psychology, 55*, 51–86.

Ebbinghaus, H. (1913). *Memory: A contribution to experimental psychology* (H. A. Ruger & C. E. Bussenius, Trans.). New York: Teachers College, Columbia University.

Eichenbaum, H. (1994). The hippocampal system and declarative memory in humans and animals: Experimental analysis and historical origins. In D. L. Schacter & E. Tulving (Eds.), *Memory systems* (pp. 143–199). Cambridge, MA: MIT Press.

Frankland, P. W., Köhler, S., & Josselyn, S. A. (2013). Hippocampal neurogenesis and forgetting. *Trends in Neurosciences, 36*(9), 497–503.

García-Bajos, E., Migueles, M., & Anderson, M. C. (2009). Script knowledge modulates retrieval-induced forgetting for eyewitness events. *Memory, 17*(1), 92–103.

Gold, J. M., Murray, R. F., Sekuler, A. B., Bennett, P. J., & Sekuler, R. (2005). Visual memory decay is deterministic. *Psychological Science, 16*(10), 769–774.

Guskjolen, A., Kenney, J. W., de la Parra, J., Yeung, B. R. A., Josselyn, S. A., & Frankland, P. W. (2018). Recovery of "lost" infant memories in mice. *Current Biology, 28*(14), 2283–2290.

Hardt, O., Einarsson, E. Ö., & Nader, K. (2010). A bridge over troubled water: Reconsolidation as a link between cognitive and neuroscientific memory research traditions. *Annual Review of Psychology, 61*, 141–167.

Hardt, O., Nader, K., & Nadel, L. (2013). Decay happens: The role of active forgetting in memory. *Trends in Cognitive Sciences, 17*(3), 111–120.

Josselyn, S. A., & Frankland, P. W. (2012). Infantile amnesia: A neurogenic hypothesis. *Learning & Memory, 19*(9), 423–433.

Karpicke, J. D., Butler, A. C., & Roediger III, H. L. (2009). Metacognitive strategies in student learning: Do students practise retrieval when they study on their own?. *Memory, 17*(4), 471–479.

Karpicke, J. D., & Roediger, H. L. (2008). The critical importance of retrieval for learning. *Science, 319*(5865), 966–968.

Kempermann, G., Gage, F. H., Aigner, L., Song, H., Curtis, M. A., Thuret, S., … & Gould, E. (2018). Human adult neurogenesis: Evidence and remaining questions. *Cell Stem Cell, 23*(1), 25–30.

Koessler, S., Engler, H., Riether, C., & Kissler, J. (2009). No retrieval-induced forgetting under stress. *Psychological Science, 20*(11), 1356–1363.

Kroes, M. C., Tendolkar, I., Van Wingen, G. A., Van Waarde, J. A., Strange, B. A., & Fernández, G. (2014). An electroconvulsive therapy procedure impairs reconsolidation of episodic memories in humans. *Nature Neuroscience, 17*(2), 204–206.

Kuhl, B. A., Dudukovic, N. M., Kahn, I., & Wagner, A. D. (2007). Decreased demands on cognitive control reveal the neural processing benefits of forgetting. *Nature Neuroscience, 10*, 908–914.

Levy, B. J., & Anderson, M. C. (2002). Inhibitory processes and the control of memory retrieval. *Trends in Cognitive Sciences, 6*, 299–305.

Levy, B. J., Kuhl, B. A., & Wagner, A. D. (2010). The functional neuroimaging of forgetting. *Forgetting*, 135–163.

Leynes, P. A., Brown, J., & Landau, J. D. (2011). Objective and subjective measures indicate that orthographically similar words produce a blocking experience. *Memory, 19*(1), 17–35.

Linton, M. (1975). Memory for real-world events. In D. A. Norman & D. E. Rumelhart (Eds.), *Explorations in cognition* (pp. 376–404). San Francisco: Freeman.

Little, J. L., Bjork, E. L., Bjork, R. A., & Angello, G. (2012). Multiple-choice tests exonerated, at least of some charges: Fostering test-induced learning and avoiding test-induced forgetting. *Psychological Science, 23*, 1337–1344.

Macrae, C. N., & MacLeod, M. D. (1999). On recollections lost: When practice makes imperfect. *Journal of Personality and Social Psychology, 77*(3), 463–473.

Marche, T. A., Briere, J. L., & von Baeyer, C. L. (2015). Children's forgetting of pain-related memories. *Journal of Pediatric Psychology, 41*(2), 220–231.

Marion, S. B., & Thorley, C. (2016). A meta-analytic review of collaborative inhibition and postcollaborative memory: Testing the predictions of the retrieval strategy disruption hypothesis. *Psychological Bulletin, 142*(11), 1141–1164.

McGeoch, J. A. (1942). *The psychology of human learning: An introduction*. New York: Longmans.

McKone, E. (1998). The decay of short-term implicit memory: Unpacking lag. *Memory & Cognition, 26*(6), 1173–1186.

Meeter, M., Murre, J. M., & Janssen, S. M. (2005). Remembering the news: Modeling retention data from a study with 14,000 participants. *Memory & Cognition, 33*(5), 793–810.

Melton, A., & Irwin, J. (1940). The influence of degree of interpolated learning on retroactive inhibition and the overt transfer of specific responses. *American Journal of Psychology, 53*, 173–203.

Migueles, M., and García-Bajos, E. (2007). Selective retrieval and induced forgetting in eyewitness memory. *Applied Cognitive Psychology, 21*(9), 1157–1172.

Migues, P. V., Liu, L., Archbold, G. E., Einarsson, E. Ö., Wong, J., Bonasia, K., … & Hardt, O. (2016). Blocking synaptic removal of GluA2-containing AMPA receptors prevents the natural forgetting of long-term memories. *Journal of Neuroscience, 36*(12), 3481–3494.

Mueller, J. H., & Brown, S. C. (1977). Output interference and intralist repetition in free recall. *American Journal of Psychology, 90*(1), 157–164.

Müller, G. E., & Pilzecker, A. (1900). Experimentalle beitrage zur lehre com gedachtnis. *Zeitschrift fur Psychologie, 1*, 1–288.

Murayama, K., Miyatsu, T., Buchli, D., & Storm, B. C. (2014). Forgetting as a consequence of retrieval: A meta-analytic review of retrieval-induced forgetting. *Psychological Bulletin, 140*(5), 1383–1409.

Murre, J. M., & Dros, J. (2015). Replication and analysis of Ebbinghaus' forgetting curve. *PLoS ONE, 10*(7), e0120644.

Nader, K., & Hardt, O. (2009). A single standard for memory: The case for reconsolidation. *Nat. Rev. Neurosci., 10*, 224–234.

Nader, K., Schafe, G. E., & LeDoux, J. E. (2000). Fear memories require protein synthesis in the amygdala for reconsolidation after retrieval. *Nature, 406*(6797), 722–726.

Nairne, J. S. (2002). Remembering over the short-term: The case against the standard model. *Annual Review of Psychology, 53*, 53–81.

Nickerson, R. S. (1984). Retrieval inhibition from part-set cuing: A persisting enigma in memory research. *Memory & Cognition, 12*(6), 531–552.

Oberauer, K., & Lewandowsky, S. (2013). Evidence against decay in verbal working memory. *Journal of Experimental Psychology: General, 142*(2), 380–411.

Page, M. P., & Norris, D. (1998). The primacy model: A new model of immediate serial recall. *Psychological Review, 105*(4), 761–781.

Parker, E. S., Cahill, L., & McGaugh, J. L. (2006). A case of unusual autobiographical remembering. *Neurocase, 12*(1), 35–49.

Polyn, S. M., Norman, K. A., & Kahana, M. J. (2009). A context maintenance and retrieval model of organizational processes in free recall. *Psychological Review, 116*(1), 129–156.

Postman, L. (1971). Transfer, interference and forgetting. In J. W. Kling & L. A. Riggs (Eds.), *Woodworth and Schlosberg's experimental psychology* (pp. 1019–1132). New York: Holt, Rinehart and Winston.

Rajaram, S., & Pereira-Pasarin, L. P. (2010). Collaborative memory: Cognitive research and theory. *Perspectives on Psychological Science, 5*(6), 649–663.

Richards, B. A., & Frankland, P. W. (2017). The persistence and transience of memory. *Neuron, 94*(6), 1071–1084.

Román, P., Soriano, M. F., Gómez-Ariza, C. J., & Bajo, M. T. (2009). Retrieval-induced forgetting and executive control. *Psychological Science, 20*, 1053–1058.

Salmon, K., & Reese, E. (2015). Talking (or not talking) about the past: The influence of parent–child conversation about negative experiences on children's memories. *Applied Cognitive Psychology, 29*(6), 791–801.

Santangelo, V., Cavallina, C., Colucci, P., Santori, A., Macrì, S., McGaugh, J. L., & Campolongo, P. (2018). Enhanced brain activity associated with memory access in highly superior autobiographical memory. *Proceedings of the National Academy of Sciences of the USA, 115*(30), 7795–7800.

Saunders, J., & MacLeod, M. D. (2002). New evidence on the suggestibility of memory: The role of retrieval-induced forgetting in misinformation effects. *Journal of Experimental Psychology: Applied*, 8, 127–142.

Shaw, J. S., Bjork, R. A., & Handal, A. (1995). Retrieval-induced forgetting in an eyewitness-memory paradigm. *Psychonomic Bulletin & Review*, 2(2), 249–253.

Slamecka, N. J. (1968). A methodological analysis of shift paradigms in human discrimination learning. *Psychological Bulletin*, 69(6), 423–438.

Smith, S. M., & Tindell, D. R. (1997). Memory blocks in word fragment completion caused by involuntary retrieval of orthographically related primes. *Journal of Experimental Psychology: Learning, Memory, and Cognition*, 23(2), 355–370.

Squire, L. R. (1992). Memory and the hippocampus: A synthesis from findings with rats, monkeys, and humans. *Psychological Review*, 99(2), 195–231.

Stone, C. B., Coman, A., Brown, A. D., Koppel, J., & Hirst, W. (2012). Toward a science of silence: The consequences of leaving a memory unsaid. *Perspectives on Psychological Science*, 7(1), 39–53.

Storm, B. C. (2011). Retrieval-induced forgetting and the resolution of competition. In A. S. Benjamin (Ed.), *Successful remembering and successful forgetting: A festschrift in honor of Robert A. Bjork* (pp. 89–105). Hoboken, NJ: Taylor & Francis.

Storm, B. C., Angello, G., Buchli, D. R., Koppel, R. H., Little, J. L., & Nestojko, J. F. (2015). A review of retrieval-induced forgetting in the contexts of learning, eyewitness memory, social cognition, autobiographical memory, and creative cognition. In B. Ross (Ed.), *Psychology of learning and motivation* (Vol. 62, pp. 141–194). New York: Academic Press.

Storm, B. C., Bjork, E. L., Bjork, R. A., & Nestojko, J. F. (2006). Is retrieval success a necessary condition for retrieval-induced forgetting?. *Psychonomic Bulletin & Review*, 13, 1023–1027.

Storm, B. C., & Levy, B. J. (2012). A progress report on the inhibitory account of retrieval-induced forgetting. *Memory and Cognition, 40*, 827–843.

Storm, B. C., & White, H. (2010). ADHD and retrieval-induced forgetting: Evidence for a deficit in the inhibitory control of memory. *Memory*, 18(3), 265–271.

Towse, J. N., Hitch, G. J., & Hutton, U. (2000). On the interpretation of working memory span in adults. *Memory & Cognition*, 28(3), 341–348.

Underwood, B. J. (1957). Interference and forgetting. *Interference and Forgetting*, 64, 49–60.

Watkins, M. J. (1978). Engrams as cuegrams and forgetting as cue-overload: A cueing approach to the structure of memory. In C. R. Puff (Ed.), *The structure of memory* (pp. 347–372). New York: Academic Press.

Weldon, M. S., & Bellinger, K. D. (1997). Collective memory: Collaborative and individual processes in remembering. *Journal of Experimental Psychology: Learning, Memory, & Cognition*, 23(5), 1160–1175.

Weller, P. D., Anderson, M. C., Gomez-Ariza, C., & Bajo, M. T. (2013). On the status of cue independence as a criterion for memory inhibition: Evidence against the covert blocking hypothesis. *Journal of Experimental Psychology: Learning, Memory, and Cognition*, 39, 1232–1245.

Wimber, M., Alink, A., Charest, I., Kriegeskorte, N., & Anderson, M. C. (2015). Retrieval induces adaptive forgetting of competing memories via cortical pattern suppression. *Nature Neuroscience*, 18(4), 582–589.

Wu, J. Q., Peters, G. J., Rittner, P., Cleland, T. A., & Smith, D. M. (2014). The hippocampus, medial prefrontal cortex, and selective memory retrieval: Evidence from a rodent model of the retrieval-induced forgetting effect. *Hippocampus*, 24(9), 1070–1080.

Yonelinas, A. P., & Levy, B. J. (2002). Dissociating familiarity from recollection in human recognition memory: Different rates of forgetting over short retention intervals. *Psychonomic Bulletin & Review*, 9(3), 575–582.

Contents

CHAPTER 10

MOTIVATED FORGETTING

Michael C. Anderson

People usually think of forgetting as something bad. It is to lose our cherished past, to forget people's names, and to neglect our responsibilities. But as AJ's remarkable memory (discussed in Chapter 9) illustrates, forgetting may be more desirable than we think. AJ often yearns to forget, so that she can avoid continually reliving the events and emotions of terrible times. She has difficulty "letting go" and "getting past" things that most of us get over quickly. These observations reveal that more often than we realize, forgetting is exactly what we need to do. Sometimes we confront reminders of experiences that sadden us, as when after the death of a loved one, or after a broken relationship, objects and places evoke memories of the lost person. Other times, reminders trigger memories that make us angry, anxious, guilty, ashamed, or embarrassed; a face may remind us of an argument that we hope to get past; an envelope may bring to mind a very unpleasant task we are avoiding; or an image of the World Trade Center in a movie may elicit upsetting memories of September 11th. In the popular film, *Eternal Sunshine of the Spotless Mind*, the main character, Joel, suffers so badly from memories of his lost love, Clementine, he seeks out a memory deletion clinic, to remove all memories of her from his brain. Unfortunately, although we might at times yearn for them, no such clinics exist, and we cannot avoid life's tendency to insert memories we wish were not there.

Jim Carrey's character, Joel, in Michel Gondry's film, *Eternal Sunshine of the Spotless Mind*, hires a service to permanently erase painful memories of his ex-girlfriend from his mind. While such technology is science fiction, our desire and ability to control our memory is very much a reality.

People do not take this situation lying down, however. They do something about it. When we confront reminders to unwanted memories, a familiar reaction often occurs—a flash of experience and feeling followed rapidly by an attempt to exclude the memory from awareness. Unlike in most other situations, retrieval is unwanted, and must be shut down. Suppressing retrieval shuts out the intrusive memories, restoring control over the direction of thought and our emotional well-being. Indeed, for veterans, witnesses of terrorism, and countless people experiencing personal traumas, the day-to-day reality of the need to control intrusive memories is all too clear. Any general treatment of forgetting therefore needs to consider the motivated involvement of individuals as conspirators in their own memory failures. Is my failure to remember knocking over the Christmas tree (see Chapter 9) simply an accident of normal forgetting? Is the fact that you "forgot" to do that unpleasant task, *yet again*, truly an innocent mistake? In this chapter, we consider what is known about how people forget things that they would prefer not to remember.

LIFE IS GOOD, OR MEMORY MAKES IT SO

With surprising consistency, people across the world, of all ages, ethnicities, and income levels report being generally happy with their lives. This feeling of well-being is widespread, and often defies people's objective circumstances. It is found in people with physical or mental disabilities, people with low incomes, and in members of minority groups (Diener & Diener, 1996; Lykken & Tellegen, 1996). Research suggests that memory may contribute to this perceived well-being. Our assessment of how we are doing in life relies on what we remember. For example, people show a strong positivity bias in what they remember over the long term. In an early illustration of this bias, Waldfogel (Waldfogel, 1948) gave participants 85 minutes to generate as many memories as they could recall from the first eight years of their lives. Of these memories, people rated 50% as pleasant, 30% as unpleasant, and 20% as neutral, suggesting that, for whatever reason, positive memories were simply more accessible. A similar finding occurs when, instead of asking people to generate memories intentionally, you ask them to note memories that "spontaneously" pop into mind over a longer time period. Of the involuntary remindings reported in a study by Bernsten (Bernsten, 1996), 49% were pleasant, 32% neutral, and 19% unpleasant. This positivity bias increases as we get older, and grow to focus more on emotional goals, and on maintaining a sense of well-being. Why do such effects occur? Are memories of positive events more frequent because those types of events are more common, or might people's motivations have something to do with it?

Susan Charles, Mara Mather, and Laura Carstensen (2003) conducted a simple and compelling study suggesting that our memory biases are no accident. They asked younger and older adults to view 32 scenes. The scenes included a mixture of pleasant, neutral, and rather unpleasant images. After a 15-minute delay, participants recalled as many of the pictures as they could. As illustrated in Figure 10.1, pictures with emotional content were recalled better, in general, than were neutral pictures, and older adults recalled fewer pictures than did younger adults. Importantly, however, as participants got older, their memories became progressively more biased in favor of positive scenes over negative ones, even though all scenes were viewed for the same amount of time: whereas young participants recalled positive and negative scenes with equal frequency, older adults recalled nearly twice as many positive as negative scenes. A subsequent test revealed that older adults could recognize the positive and negative scenes equally well, indicating that they both made it into memory. For some reason, however, negative events were not recalled as well. Similar age-related emotional biases have been observed with words and faces (Leigland, Schulz, & Janowsky, 2004). In a review of research on aging and positivity effects, Mather and Carstensen (2005) build a compelling case that as we get older and life grows short, people focus more on maintaining a sense of well-being, and less on goals concerning knowledge and the future. As a result, people grow skilled in emotion regulation,

> ### KEY TERM
>
> **Positivity bias:** The tendency, increasing over the lifespan, to recall more pleasant memories than either neutral or unpleasant ones.
>
> **Emotion regulation:** Goal-driven monitoring, evaluating, altering, and gating one's emotional reactions and memories about emotional experiences.

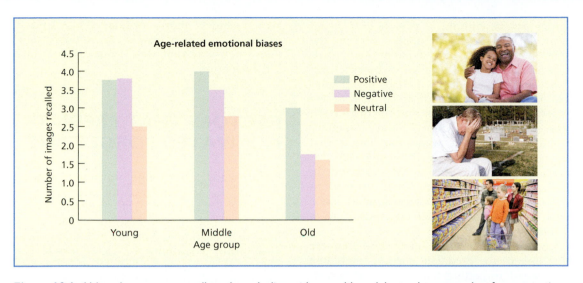

Figure 10.1 Although memory overall tends to decline with age, older adults tend to remember fewer negative memories relative to positive ones, demonstrating an age-related positivity bias. From Charles, Mather, and Carstensen (2003). Copyright © American Psychological Association. Reproduced with permission. Right: Examples of positive, negative, and neutral images used in the study.

which includes, in part, controlling what we remember (Engen & Anderson, 2018). How could this possibly happen? What processes contribute to motivated forgetting?

TERMINOLOGY IN RESEARCH ON MOTIVATED FORGETTING

It is important to clarify certain terms and distinctions that will arise in our discussion of how motives alter our memories. Perhaps the most well-known term relating to motivated forgetting is repression, popularized by Sigmund Freud through his psychoanalytic theory. In Freud's framework, repression refers to a psychological defense mechanism that banishes unwanted memories, ideas, and feelings into the unconscious to reduce conflict and psychic pain. It is one in an arsenal of defensive processes, including rationalization, projection, and many others. Although Freud used repression in a number of ways, he offered the following simple definition: "The essence of repression lies simply in the function of rejecting and keeping something out of consciousness" (Freud, 1917, p. 147).

Within this framework, repressed contents were not eliminated from the mind, but were excluded from conscious awareness. They could still influence behavior unconsciously, manifesting themselves in our dreams, preferences, choice of topics we discuss, and even our emotional reactions. Moreover, repressed contents were not guaranteed to remain unconscious, but were thought to pop up again on later occasions, a phenomenon Freud referred to as the *return of the repressed* (e.g., Freud, 1900, 1917).

A distinction is sometimes drawn between repression and *suppression*, with the former being an unconscious process, and the latter being conscious and intentional. By this view, repression is an automatic, defensive process by which a memory is excluded from

KEY TERM

Repression: In psychoanalytic theory, a psychological defense mechanism that banishes unwanted memories, ideas, and feelings into the unconscious in an effort to reduce conflict and psychic pain. Theoretically, repression can either be conscious or nonconscious. Often, the term *suppression* is used to refer to the conscious variety.

consciousness without a person ever being aware of its presence. Suppression, on the other hand, refers to the intentional, goal-directed exclusion of ideas or memories from awareness. Although the modern psychoanalytic field maintains this distinction, Mathew Erdelyi (2006) has shown that the distinction was introduced by Anna Freud, Sigmund Freud's daughter. He argues that Freud used the terms interchangeably, and that the distinction distorts his theoretical viewpoint. In this chapter, the term repression can refer to either sense, but when the term suppression is used, we intend to refer specifically to a voluntary process.

Several other terms often arise that are not linked to Freudian theory, including intentional forgetting and motivated forgetting. *Intentional forgetting* refers to forgetting arising from processes initiated by a conscious goal to forget. It includes conscious strategies to forget, such as suppression and intentional context shifts. Although we discuss intentional forgetting, this term omits cases when forgetting is nonaccidental, but not consciously intended. The broader term *motivated forgetting* encompasses these potential cases. For example, if every time you see someone associated to an unpleasant event, your mind steers towards topics unrelated to that event, this motivated bias may induce forgetting without being generated by an intention to forget. Nevertheless, this type of forgetting would clearly be motivated.

Motivated forgetting encompasses the term psychogenic amnesia, which means any forgetting that is psychological in origin, and not attributed to neurological damage or dysfunction—forgetting that is psychological in genesis. Although psychogenic amnesia and motivated forgetting might be treated synonymously, the term psychogenic amnesia is generally used for cases of profound and surprising forgetting of major chunks of one's life, or to profound forgetting of a particular event that ought to be remembered. The term is theoretically and mechanistically neutral in that it does not presume Freud's theoretical framework, nor does it say how forgetting is accomplished—merely that the source is psychological rather than biological. Motivated forgetting includes these cases, but it also includes more ordinary, day-to-day examples in which people forget unpleasant things in a way that would not call for clinical evaluation.

FACTORS THAT PREDICT MOTIVATED FORGETTING

Theoretically, controlling unwanted memories may be accomplished by intervening at any stage of memory. The simplest way to avoid remembering unpleasant events is to limit their encoding. You might literally look away from a stimulus or focus instead on only its pleasant aspects; or, if you are unfortunate enough to have looked at something unpleasant, you might cease elaborative thoughts. If an unwanted experience gets encoded, you might avoid reminders to prevent its retrieval. Or, if reminders are inescapable, you might endeavor to stop retrieval. In these examples, you are engaging mechanisms involved in "normal forgetting" in service of emotional goals. Research on motivated forgetting has addressed all of these factors, which we discuss next.

Instructions to forget

Have you ever told someone to "Forget about it?" Does saying that make a difference? When you recommend this, you presumably have reason to believe that the person can do it. We often have good reason to put things out of mind, even when they are not emotionally significant. Consider R. A. Bjork's (1970) example of a short-order cook, who during a typical morning breakfast shift, must process dozens of similar orders. Having completed an order such as, "Scramble two eggs, crisp bacon, and an

> **KEY TERM**
>
> **Psychogenic amnesia:** Profound and surprising episodes of forgetting the events of one's life, arising from psychological factors, rather than biological damage or dysfunction.

English muffin," the cook's performance can only suffer if prior orders have not been forgotten. Similarly, we have all experienced times when, after completing a demanding activity such as an examination we must "let go" of the information so that our minds may shift to new endeavors. When we return to the "dropped" material, we are often surprised that the knowledge once readily available now eludes us. These examples suggest that forgetting may sometimes be initiated to reduce proactive interference from impeding our concentration. This idea is often studied with the directed forgetting procedure (Bjork, 1970, 1989; see Anderson & Hanslmayr, 2014; Sahakyan, Delaney, Foster, & Abushana, 2013, for reviews), in which participants are instructed to forget recently encoded materials. There are two variants of this procedure, each involving different forgetting processes: the item method, and the list method.

Item-method directed forgetting

In *item-method directed forgetting*, a participant receives a series of items to remember. After each item, an instruction appears indicating whether they should either continue to remember it or to forget it, because they will no longer be held responsible for it. After the list ends, participants are tested on *all* of the to-be-remembered and to-be forgotten words. Interestingly, recall for to-be-forgotten words is substantially impaired, relative to to-be-remembered items. For example, Basden and Basden (1996) observed worse recall for to-be-forgotten than for to-be-remembered items regardless of whether the items presented were pictures (78% versus 36% for remember and forget items, respectively), words (72% versus 46%), or words for which participants were asked to construct imagery (85% versus 42%). Informatively, directed forgetting effects observed with the item method also occur on recognition tests (Basden, Basden, & Gargano, 1993). For these reasons, some theorists believe that item-method directed forgetting effects reflect differential episodic encoding. If you were a participant in such a procedure, you would likely refrain from elaborate rehearsal on an item, for example, until you knew whether it

was to be remembered or to be forgotten. The *remember instruction* would trigger elaborate semantic encoding, whereas the *forget instruction* would give you permission to simply release attention from the word. This finding illustrates one way in which people exercise control over what they permit into memory—by regulating whether a stimulus is granted elaborative processing. Mather and Carstensen's (2005) participants might have employed some version of this strategy, though their encoding was apparently deep enough to support subsequent recognition.

Although most researchers agree that item-method directed forgetting leads to differences in encoding quality across remember and forget items, researchers differ in their views about what mechanisms cause those differences. Naturally, when you ask someone to remember something, they will rehearse and elaborate the item more than something that you tell them to forget. This *selective rehearsal hypothesis* predicts better memory for remember items. But is it also possible that the *forget* instruction harms memory? A growing body of work suggests that a forget instruction engages an active process that disrupts encoding. According to the selective rehearsal account, people exert more cognitive effort after a remember instruction than after a forget instruction. If so, people should have less of their attention to spare when they are trying to implement a remember instruction compared to when they are trying to forget, because in the latter case they don't have to rehearse or elaborate the item. Interestingly, however, the opposite appears to be true. In one example, Jonathan Fawcett and Tracey Taylor (2008) gave participants a secondary task to perform right after the remember/forget instruction. After the memory instruction, an asterisk briefly appeared on the screen, and participants simply were asked to press a button as quickly as possible when they saw it.

Contrary to the selective rehearsal account, people pressed the button more slowly when it appeared after the forget instruction, indicating that implementing the forget instruction required more attention. This surprising pattern—greater effort associated with forgetting—has been found a number of times, raising the possibility of an active forgetting process. The existence of this additional *encoding suppression* process is supported by evidence about the brain processes engaged during item-method directed forgetting. For example, using brain imaging, Avery Rizio and Nancy Dennis found evidence that an inhibitory control process disrupts episodic encoding by interactions between the prefrontal cortex and the hippocampus during successful forgetting (e.g., Rizzio & Dennis, 2013; see also Wierzba et al., 2018; see Anderson & Hanslmayr, 2014 for discussion). Indeed, these top-down fronto-hippocampal interactions now have been observed with intracranial recordings in the human prefrontal cortex and hippocampus, and are greater during successful forgetting (Oehrn et al., 2018). This encoding suppression process may involve similar neural processes as are involved in retrieval suppression, discussed shortly.

Research on item-method directed forgetting illustrates how people often can regulate which experiences they allow into memory by intentionally disrupting encoding. One can imagine that people might use such processes to reduce the footprints in memory of life's less pleasant moments. For example, it may not come as much surprise to you to learn that people generally don't like to hear negative feedback about themselves, and greatly prefer to hear positive things. People's memory, it turns out, reflects this bias well. In one nice example, Constantine Sedikides and Jeffrey Green gave participants a mock personality inventory that asked them to provide ratings on various personality questions. Afterwards, the supposedly sophisticated program provided its analysis, and listed 32 behaviors that the participant was likely to exhibit. Each behavior pertained to key personality dimensions such as trustworthiness, kindness, modesty, and tendency to complain. Critically, some behaviors reflected

well upon the participant, whereas others were rather more negative. After carefully reviewing their report, participants were tested on their memory for these behaviors following a short delay. As one might guess, people recalled significantly more of the positive than the negative behaviors. This bias does not arise simply because the negative behaviors are intrinsically less memorable: when people were instead told that the behaviors in the report were from another participant's analysis, people showed no such bias, remembering the positive and negative behaviors comparably. This *mnemic neglect effect* (Sedikides & Green, 2000) suggests that people's desire to view themselves favorably leads them to limit the encoding of negative feedback. People seem to regulate their memory to protect their self-image, especially when feedback poses high levels of threat to that image (Sedikides & Green, 2009; see Sedikides, Green, Saunders, Skowronski, & Zengel, 2016 for a review and synthesis).

The list-method of directed forgetting

The *list-method directed forgetting* procedure presents the instruction to forget only after half of the list (often 10–20 items) has been studied, and usually as a surprise. Typically, deception is employed, in which the experimenter tells the participant that the list they just studied was for "practice," and that the real list is about to be presented. Other times, the experimenter may pretend that the participant had received the wrong list, which they should "forget about." Following this instruction, participants receive a second list. A final test is then given, quite often for both lists, but sometimes only for the first list. Participants are asked to disregard the earlier instruction to forget, and to remember as much as they can. Performance in this *forget group* is contrasted with a *remember group* who follows the same procedure, except that the instruction after the first list simply reminds people that they should continue remembering the first list. Two findings are consistently observed. First, when participants believe that they can forget the first list, they often do much better at recalling the second list on the final test, compared to the remember group. In other words, the proactive interference one finds from the first list often disappears when people believe that they can forget that list, providing a clear *benefit* of an instruction to forget. Second, forget instructions impair people's recall of items from the first list, compared to performance in the remember condition, reflecting a *cost* of a forget instruction. An illustration of the different varieties of directed forgetting is provided in Figure 10.2, along with a classic example of directed forgetting taken from a study by Geiselman, Bjork, and Fishman (1983) in Figure 10.2.

List-method directed forgetting exhibits interesting features that distinguish it from forgetting observed with the item method. First, in the list-method, it is unlikely that participants use shallow encoding to forget first-list items. Participants do not receive any hint that they will have to forget anything until the entire first list has been studied, and so have no motive to not encode effectively. Thus, list-method directed forgetting more likely does something to disrupt later retrieval. Consistent with this idea, list-method directed forgetting effects usually disappear when recognition is tested. Second, unlike in the item-method (Basden et al.,

1993), items in the list-method reveal their presence on implicit memory tests. Indeed, to-be-forgotten items can sometimes exert a greater influence on behavior when memory is tested implicitly. For example, Bjork and Bjork (2003) found that when some to-be-forgotten names were included on a later (apparently unrelated) *fame judgment test* presenting a set of famous and nonfamous names, to-be-forgotten (nonfamous) names were judged as more famous than were to-be-remembered (nonfamous) names in the remember condition. Presumably, participants had forgotten where they knew the name from, due to directed forgetting, and misattributed its familiarity to fame. This finding illustrates one circumstance in which intentionally forgotten materials influence behavior outside of people's awareness.

List-method directed forgetting illustrates how when people no longer wish to remember events, they can intentionally reduce their accessibility. Can such processes be engaged to forget more realistic personal experiences with emotional content? Susan Joslyn and Mark Oakes took a novel approach to this issue. They asked students to record in a diary two unique events that happened to them each day over a five-day period (Joslyn & Oakes, 2005). Participants wrote a brief narrative and a title summarizing each experience, and they also rated the events for emotional valence and intensity. For example, one student recorded this event, entitled *Crow Chase*.

> *A few friends and I were walking through campus when we suddenly saw a crow running around on the ground following a squirrel. It was so funny! We stood and watched them for a few minutes, exchanging funny squirrel stories and other animal stories.*
>
> (p. 4)

After the first week of recording, students turned in their diaries. The forget group was told that the events recorded on the first five days would be used for a different study and that they should forget them, so that they

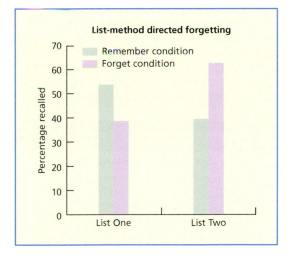

Figure 10.2 A classic example of results from a list-method directed forgetting experiment. Note that, relative to the remember condition, recall of List One is decremented in the forget condition, while List-Two recall is superior, thereby illustrating the cost and benefit of the instruction to forget. Data from Geiselman, Bjork, and Fishman (1983).

could focus on events from the second week, which they would have to remember. The remember group was told that they would have to remember the events from the first week, as well as the ones from the upcoming week. Over the next five-day period, the students then recorded a new set of events. After the second week ended, participants turned in their diaries and were then asked to remember all of the events they had recorded during both weeks. Joslyn and Oaks found that participants instructed to forget had poorer memory for events from the first week than did participants instructed to remember. This pattern was even observed for a group of "practice memories" that participants recorded in their first week that neither group believed they would have to recall. Interestingly, impairment was even found with negative and positive mood events. Related findings were observed by Amanda Barnier and colleagues (Barnier, Conway, Mayoh, & Speyer, 2007) for personal memories learned outside of the experiment.

There are two leading theories of list-method directed forgetting. According to the retrieval inhibition hypothesis, an instruction to forget the first list inhibits list-1 items, impairing recall. This inhibition does not, however, do permanent damage, and memories remain available. Inhibition merely limits retrieval by reducing activation of unwanted items. This view explains why intentionally forgotten items are difficult to recall, but can be recognized, if we assume that re-presentation of forgotten items restores their activation levels. In contrast, according to the context shift hypothesis (Sahakyan & Kelley, 2002), instructions to forget mentally separate the to-be-forgotten items from the second list. If a person's mental context changes between the first and the second lists and if the second list context remains active during the final test, to-be-forgotten items should be recalled more poorly because the new context is a poor retrieval cue for them, similar to the notion of cognitive context discussed in Chapter 8.

To test the context shift hypothesis, Sahakyan and Kelley varied people's mental context in between two lists of words. Might such a context shift produce the pattern observed in directed forgetting? In their context shift condition, participants studied a first list of words, and then performed a simple task designed to shift their "frame of mind." Participants were asked to imagine, for one minute, what their life would be like if they were invisible. The reasoning was that by performing such a bizarre task, participants would enter into studying the second list in a different mental context than was present while they were studying the first list (perhaps one in which they thought the experimenters were crazy). If the context shift hypothesis is correct, this simple manipulation should make people more likely to forget the first list, even in the absence of any instruction to forget it. This in fact occurred: participants given this context shift task showed poorer memory of the first list on a later test. These findings suggest that part of the directed forgetting effect may arise from a shift in mental context induced by the intention to forget. Consistent with this possibility, Jeremy Manning and colleagues used functional magnetic resonance imaging to show that instructing people to forget a first list of words actively reduces the availability of contextual information in the medial-temporal lobes, and that this reduction predicts later forgetting (Manning et al., 2016). This context-change hypothesis is not inconsistent with the retrieval inhibition hypothesis, if one assumes that an active inhibitory control mechanism purges the current mental context (Anderson, 2003).

KEY TERM

Retrieval inhibition hypothesis: A proposed mechanism underlying list-method directed forgetting suggesting that first-list items are temporarily inhibited in response to the instruction to forget and can be reactivated by subsequent presentations of the to-be-forgotten items.

Context shift hypothesis: An alternative explanation for list-method directed forgetting, positing that forget instructions separate first-list items into a distinct context, which unless reinstated during the final test will make the later context a relatively ineffectual retrieval cue.

Consistent with this possibility, list-method directed forgetting engages the prefrontal cortex and stimulating the activated region magnetically can significantly increase how well people can intentionally forget (Hanslmayr et al., 2012).

Research on directed forgetting establishes that people have some ability to intentionally forget recently experienced events. One method is to deprive experiences of rehearsal and elaboration, and to suppress the encoding process (item-method directed forgetting) increasing the chances that those memories will be forgotten quickly. The consequence of this method is a generalized deficit in recall or recognition, including diminished influence of the experience on indirect tests. Alternatively, unwanted memories can be rendered less accessible by a process that impairs access to the context to which to-be-forgotten memories are associated. The to-be-forgotten items can continue to influence people on indirect tests, suggesting that even in the absence of awareness, intentionally forgotten items might make their presence known. Both item and list-method directed forgetting can impair neutral as well as emotionally negative materials (e.g., Barnier et al., 2007; Josslyn & Oakes, 2005; Wierzba et al., 2018).

Motivated context shifts and changes in stimulus environment

The preceding discussion illustrates how changing one's mental context (e.g., intentionally shifting to a new line of thought) can diminish access to past events. If changing mental context can induce forgetting, perhaps changing other elements of incidental context might work as well. People know this intuitively. For example, when something traumatic happens in one context, people avoid returning to that context to prevent from being reminded. If the location is a home or a town of residence, people will often change homes or towns to get over the unpleasant incident. When the unwanted memory concerns a person, people often avoid exposure to that person. If people cannot remove themselves from an environment, they will

Sometimes people are so motivated to control their memories that they alter the physical environment to remove retrieval cues. Such was the case at Columbine High School in Colorado. Following the shootings, families of the victims lobbied to demolish and rebuild the library where the incident took place.

sometimes seek to change the environment itself. For example, in the aftermath of the fatal shootings at Columbine High School in Colorado, families of the victims lobbied to have the school library at which the shootings took place torn down and replaced with an entirely different structure, removing reminders to the horrible events.

Motivated context shifts are likely to occur when it is too late to minimize encoding. To limit awareness of the memory, people avoid reminders. The avoidance of cues, especially shifts in environmental context, might facilitate normal forgetting processes in several ways. First, by avoiding reminders, the person deprives a memory of retrievals that ordinarily strengthen and preserve it (Erdelyi, 2006). Essentially, retrieval practice is prevented. Preventing reactivation of the trace should encourage decay processes. Second, by changing the physical environment, the mental context within which one operates will come to mismatch the one in which the event took place, hindering retrieval. If the new context allows a person to recover, mood context will change, making spontaneous retrieval of the event less likely.

Intentional retrieval suppression

Sometimes we cannot avoid reminders to unpleasant events. When this happens, we have two choices: to be reminded, or stop retrieval. To see how people might stop retrieval, consider the following example. Suppose that you have an argument with a significant other. The next time you see them, chances are you will be reminded of the argument, recreating the upset feelings. If you are motivated to "get past" the argument, and sustain a good feeling about the person, you might put the memory out of mind, especially if the argument was not of great consequence. You may find this difficult at first, with the process requiring concentration to stop and redirect your thoughts and emotions. With repeated encounters to the reminder, however, the remindings often grow less frequent. After much time, you may be unable to recollect the argument. Such forgetting is not a bad thing. Healthy relationships require at least some "forgive and forget." Without this, people dwell on small transgressions, never forgetting any upset or wrongdoing. AJ wishes that she could forget, because unpleasant memories trouble her long past when others would have succeeded in banishing them from their minds. People often confront reminders to difficult memories that can make them sad, angry, anxious, or ashamed, and they quickly adjust their thoughts.

How do people suppress retrieval? To shed light on these issues, Collin Green and I considered an analogy between how people control unwanted memories and how they control action. We noted that unwanted memories have an "intrusive" quality, seeming to "leap" to awareness in response to reminders, despite our intention to avoid them. This reflexive quality seems similar to reflexive actions. Importantly, we clearly have the ability to stop physical actions. Consider the time that I knocked a potted plant off of my kitchen windowsill. As my hand darted to catch the falling object, I realized that the plant was a cactus. Mere centimeters from it, I stopped myself from catching the cactus. The plant dropped and was ruined, but I was relieved to have avoided being

People reflexively try to catch a falling object. But in certain situations (if the object is a cactus, for example), this prepotent motor response would be painfully inappropriate. We are fortunate to have the ability to stop ourselves in mid-action. Can we also stop ourselves from retrieving memories?

pierced with little needles. This illustrates the need to override a reflexive response to a stimulus. Without the capacity to override reflexive responses, we could not adapt behavior to changes in our goals or circumstances. If we can stop reflexive actions, perhaps we have the neural machinery to stop retrieval. Indeed, controlling retrieval may build upon these mechanisms of behavioral control to achieve cognitive control.

Retrieval suppression: Basic findings

How do we stop reflexive actions? As discussed in Chapter 9, stopping actions may be achieved by an inhibition process. Might suppressing retrieval work in the same way? To study this, Collin Green and I (Anderson &

> **KEY TERM**
>
> **Cognitive control:** The ability to flexibly control thoughts in accordance with our goals, including our ability to stop unwanted thoughts from rising to consciousness.

Green, 2001) developed a procedure that we modeled after the go/no-go task, a task sometimes used to measure how well people can stop motor responses. If you were participating in a go/no-go task, you might be asked to press a button as quickly as possible whenever you see a letter appear on a computer screen, *except* when the letter is an X, for which you are to withhold your response. Your cruel experimenters would arrange the task so that the overwhelming majority of letters that you see are not Xs, which would encourage you to get into a rhythm of automatically responding. When the rare X does appear, you might well have to catch yourself in order to stop the response, much like one stops oneself at the last minute from catching a pointy cactus in mid-air. How often you withhold your response successfully measures your capacity for inhibitory control over action (e.g., how well you can avoid catching the cactus). To see whether people's attempts to stop retrieval might engage inhibitory control, we adapted this procedure to create the think/no-think paradigm.

The think/no-think procedure mimics those times in life when we stumble on a reminder to an experience that we would prefer not to think about, prompting the desire to put the unwelcome memory out of mind. In the simplest version of this task, people memorize a set of cue-target pairs (e.g., ORDEAL–ROACH) until they can recall the second word (e.g., ROACH) whenever they encounter the first word as a reminder (e.g., ORDEAL). By training people to recall pairs in this way, we hoped that the cue word would thereafter serve as a powerful reminder. In the next step, participants enter the think/no-think phase, which requires them to exert control over memory retrieval. Most of the trials require the person to recall the paired word whenever they see the reminder, but for certain reminders (i.e., those colored in red), participants are admonished to avoid retrieval at all costs. So, for example, upon seeing the word Ordeal, participants are asked to stare directly at this reminder, but nevertheless willfully prevent the paired memory item from entering consciousness. We emphasize that it is not enough to avoid *saying* the response out

loud, and that preventing the memory from entering awareness is crucial. Can people recruit inhibitory control to prevent an unwanted memory from intruding into consciousness? If so, this procedure captures the essence of repression, which, as Freud said, "Lies simply in the function of rejecting and keeping something out of consciousness" (1917, p. 147).

Of course, we cannot observe people's conscious awareness, so it is hard to know whether someone has prevented a memory from entering consciousness. Instead, the think/no-think procedure measures the aftereffects of people's efforts to stop retrieval. If stopping retrieval repeatedly inhibits the unwanted memory, perhaps this process would make it harder for people to recall the memory later on, much like the memory of the argument seems to grow less accessible with each repeated encounter with your friend. To measure this predicted behavioral footprint of suppression, participants receive the studied cues (ORDEAL) once again on a final test and are asked to recall the target memory (ROACH) for every one of the cues, regardless of prior instructions.

As Figure 10.3 reveals, there is a large difference in how well people remember "think" and "no-think" items on the final test. This difference, known as the *total memory control effect* (Anderson & Levy, 2009; Levy & Anderson, 2008), vividly illustrates that how someone chooses to respond to a reminder of a past experience dramatically alters the fate of that experience in memory. Exactly how the intention to retrieve a memory influences performance cannot be discerned from this effect alone, however. Including a third set of pairs that people study initially, but that do not appear during the think/no-think phase (i.e., baseline items), allows us to separately measure the

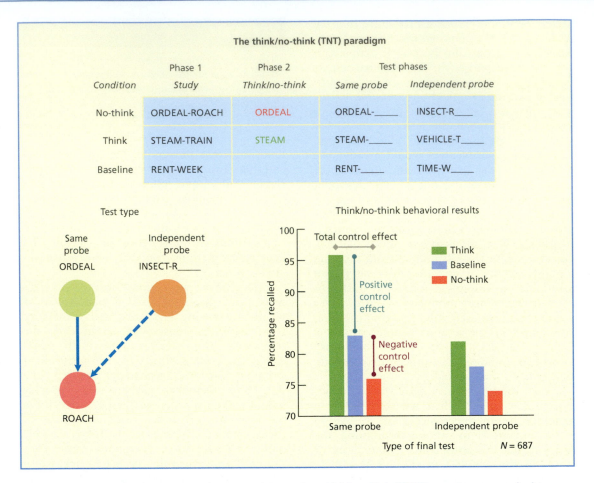

Figure 10.3 Top: After learning word pairs, participants in a think/no-think (TNT) experiment are asked to either think or not think about an item's associate. Participants' memory for all items is then assessed. Lower left: A depiction of the two types of final tests. Lower right: Results of a TNT meta-analysis by test type.

effects of retrieval and retrieval suppression on later memory. Figure 10.4 illustrates the *positive control effect*, which is enhanced memory for "think" items above baseline recall, arising from intentionally facilitating retrieval (positive control). The positive control effect confirms that when people are inclined to be reminded, cues improve memory for an experience, as one might intuitively expect. The negative control effect can be seen in the memory deficit for "no-think" items below baseline recall, an effect that arises when participants intentionally stop retrieval. Thus, when people suppress remindings, presenting cues triggers processes that impair memory, precisely the opposite to

what happens with intentional retrieval. This *negative control effect* is also often referred to simply as suppression-induced forgetting. Clearly the impact of recurring reminders depends on people's disposition as to whether they wish to be reminded. As can be seen in Figure 10.4, forgetting also arises when

KEY TERM

Suppression-induced forgetting: The impaired memory for a target item that often results when a person intentionally stops or suppresses the episodic retrieval of that target item triggered by a reminder cue.

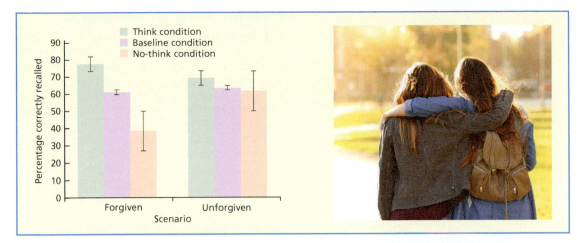

Figure 10.4 Mean percentage of forgiven and unforgiven scenarios correctly recalled in the think, baseline, and no-think conditions, in the study by Noreen et al. (2015). Right: forgiveness is an important part of maintaining social relationships. *Psychological Science* Forgiving You Is Hard, but Forgetting Seems Easy: Can Forgiveness Facilitate Forgetting? Vol 25, Issue 7, 2014. © SAGE

people try to recall the suppressed memory from a novel test cue, showing that forgetting is cue-independent. As discussed in Chapter 9, this suggests that the item was inhibited.

Much is now known about suppression-induced forgetting (Anderson & Hanslmayr, 2014; Anderson & Huddleston, 2012). Forgetting generally increases the more times people suppress a given memory and it arises with many stimulus types including word pairs, face-scene pairs, and other kinds of stimuli. Forgetting effects occur whether the memory is a neutral or an unpleasant word or scene, though is unclear whether emotional memories are more or less suppressible compared to neutral memories. Importantly, suppression-induced forgetting has even been observed with autobiographical experiences. For example, Saima Noreen and Malcolm MacLeod (2012) found suppression induced forgetting for both negative and neutral personal experiences from participants' own lives, though suppression mainly affected participants' memory for details of these events. Although few studies have examined how long forgetting lasts, one study found that a single suppression session produces forgetting that lasts at least 24 hours (Hotta & Kawaguchi, 2009). Interestingly, people with less effective cognitive control processes appear to be less able to suppress the retrieval

of unwanted memories. For instance, adults with attention deficit disorder show less suppression induced forgetting compared to control participants (Depue, Burgess, Willcutt, Ruzic, & Banich, 2010). This suggests that there may be something important in common between the processes underlying suppression-induced forgetting and broader control mechanisms.

Is this type of retrieval suppression something that you may have done before? Has it played a role in your life somehow? Naturally, it's hard to know for sure, but if you have ever been upset at somebody and have then forgiven them, you may well have engaged this process in the course of "getting past" the transgression. Saima Noreen, Raynette Bierman, and Malcolm MacLeod suspected that there was a relationship between forgiveness and forgetting and explored it in a very creative way (Noreen, Bierman, & MacLeod, 2014). They asked participants to rate 40 hypothetical scenarios in which some person (e.g., your boss, your friend, your partner) committed some hurtful act against you. The description not only included the action they took, but also the consequences for you, and what the person did to make it up to you when they found out they were wrong. For example, one scenario might have been *"The offence is that your professor does not believe you when you tell [him or her] you have not plagiarized your work. The consequence is that you are expelled from the university. Later your professor realizes you were telling the truth and tries to make amends by attempting to get you reinstated.*" Noreen and colleagues asked participants to rate whether they could forgive the person in each scenario. Several days later, participants returned to the laboratory, and were asked to associate each scenario to its own cue, so that they could recall all the details of the scenario given the cue. Following this, participants underwent the think/no-think task in which they received reminders and were asked to either think of the associated scenario or, for other reminders, to suppress retrieval of the scenario. Afterwards, they were given the cue for each scenario and asked to recall all details as well as they could. Amazingly, whereas participants showed robust suppression-induced forgetting for the offenses they could forgive, they showed none at all for offenses they found unforgivable (see Figure 10.4). These findings raise the intriguing possibility that forgiveness opens the door for somebody to "let the past go" and forget it, a process that may be facilitated by a willingness to exclude the unpleasant event from mind when later encountering the transgressor. Quite simply, your capacity to *forgive and forget* may rely on retrieval suppression to succeed. If you have ever been puzzled why details of a prior unpleasant incident are more hazy than they should be, this may well be why. Similar processes are at work not only for the past, but also for forgetting fears of the future. When you are reminded of a potential future event that makes you fearful and you try to push the feared images and thoughts from your mind, the same retrieval suppression process is recruited to help you forget your fears and remain focused (Benoit, Davies, & Anderson, 2016). These cases of forgetting may not be failures of your memory as much as your brain helping you adjust your responses to a person or situation in a constructive way. But how does your brain accomplish this?

Brain mechanisms underlying retrieval suppression

Do people really stop intrusive memories in the same way they stop overt actions? One way to look into this is to see whether common brain regions are involved in stopping retrieval and stopping action. In one example, with John Gabrieli, Kevin Ochsner, Brice Kuhl, and colleagues (Anderson et al., 2004), I conducted a functional magnetic resonance imaging study contrasting brain activity during no-think and think trials. If suppressing retrieval is similar to action stopping, then motor stopping regions should show increased activation during no-think trials, in which retrieval stopping is required than during think trials. Consistent with this hypothesis, we found that suppressing retrieval recruited a network of brain regions including right lateral prefrontal cortex, and anterior cingulate cortex. This network overlaps with that involved motor inhibition, even though people doing the no-think task never have to stop physical actions. The right lateral prefrontal cortex plays an especially critical role in stopping reflexive motor action (e.g., Aron, Robbins, & Poldrack, 2014). In fact, stimulating this brain region during a "go" motor response induces monkeys to stop their movement (Sasaki, Gemba, & Tsujimoto, 1989). This overlap is consistent with the possibility that stopping unwanted actions and memories engages a common inhibition process.

One can compare those moments when we want to avoid retrieving unwanted memories to how we might avoid crashing into a car that has had an accident on the road just ahead of us. When you initially spot the danger on the road ahead, you have a short time window to react quickly, and slam on the brakes and bring your car to a halt. If stopping retrieval is similar, how do people "slam on the brakes" to prevent retrieval from moving forward? Interestingly, the answer lies in a brain region that is targeted by control processes: the hippocampus. As discussed in Chapter 16 on amnesia, the hippocampus is essential for forming new episodic memories (Squire, 1992). Importantly, however, neuroimaging studies have linked increased hippocampal activation to retrieving one's past. We thought that if hippocampal activity is important to consciously retrieving a memory, then perhaps suppressing awareness of a memory involves decreasing hippocampal activity. This appears to be true: Anderson et al. (Anderson et al., 2004) found reduced hippocampal activity when participants suppressed retrieval (Figure 10.5) compared to when they engaged in retrieval. Later studies have shown that this reduction arises because right lateral prefrontal cortex actively reduces hippocampal activity during no-think trials (Benoit & Anderson, 2012). Thus, slamming on the "mental brakes" to prevent retrieval from unfolding involves an active termination of hippocampal processes that would otherwise carry the retrieval process forward. This ability to shut down hippocampal retrieval processes has been shown to rely upon inhibitory interneurons within the hippocampus that disengage retrieval, driven by inputs from the prefrontal cortex (Schmitz, Correia, Ferreira, Prescot, & Anderson, 2017). A similar modulation of hippocampal activity by the right lateral prefrontal cortex may contribute to encoding suppression in the item-method directed forgetting procedure, as discussed earlier (see Anderson & Hanslmayr, 2014, for a review).

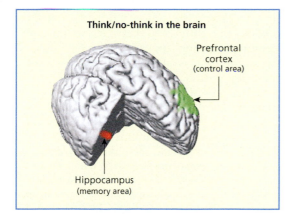

Figure 10.5 A rendering of the neuroimaging results of Anderson et al. (2004). The lateral prefrontal cortex (depicted in green) is recruited during no-think trials to suppress neural activity in the hippocampus (in red), thereby preventing unwanted memories from coming to mind.

People are very motivated to stop retrieval when memories are particularly unpleasant, and unpleasant experiences have a tendency to intrude often, especially right after they happen. Are retrieval stopping mechanisms effective for more complex emotional memories? It appears that they are. For example, Brendan Depue, Marie Banich, and Tim Curran (Depue, Banich, & Curran, 2006; Depue, Curran, & Banich, 2007) had participants learn to pair certain unfamiliar faces with unpleasant scenes. One face might have served as the reminder for a bad car accident, and another might have been paired with a badly deformed infant. Depue and colleagues found that presenting the face reminders and asking people to suppress retrieval impaired later recall of the aversive pictures, replicating suppression-induced forgetting effects observed with word pairs. Depue et al. (2007) also found activation of the right lateral prefrontal cortex and reduced hippocampal activity during "no-think" trials. More recent work has found that retrieval suppression doesn't simply reduce the memorability of the upsetting scene, but also reduces the intensity of one's emotional response to it, when it is seen yet again later on (Gagnepain, Hulbert, & Anderson, 2017). The reduced negative emotion accompanied by suppression appears to occur because retrieval suppression reduces amygdala activity during memory intrusions, possibly altering emotional associations to the suppressed imagery (Gagnepain et al., 2017). Thus, retrieval suppression can "tune down" unpleasant images and emotional responses to them, suggesting it may be a fruitful model for how people regulate emotions after upsetting events. However, when these brain mechanisms are not functioning efficiently, people are highly vulnerable to psychiatric conditions accompanied by persistent unpleasant intrusive memories and thoughts, such as post-traumatic stress disorder (Catarino, Küpper, Werner-Seidler, Dalgleish, & Anderson, 2015; Waldhauser et al., 2018), anxiety, and depression (see Engen & Anderson, 2018 for a review). If you have ever experienced difficulties with persisting intrusive memories or images, you can appreciate firsthand how incredibly important successful forgetting can be for maintaining our emotional balance. Forgetting is often our goal, not a human frailty.

Stopping the retrieval process is not the only way people try to stop unwanted memories, however. Following on our driving analogy, one can avoid crashing into the car ahead of us either by slamming on the brakes, or by steering quickly out of harm's way, into a different lane. Interestingly, it turns out that when reminders start to trigger an unpleasant memory, we have similar options: to either slam on the mental "brakes" and stop the retrieval process from bringing the memory to mind, or, instead, to rapidly redirect retrieval processes towards other thoughts. Several authors have shown that both approaches to preventing unwelcome awareness of a memory cause forgetting (Benoit & Anderson, 2012; Bergström, de Fockert, & Richardson-Klavehn, 2009; Hertel & McDaniel, 2010). For example, Roland Benoit and I wanted to see whether these *direct suppression* and *thought substitution* approaches truly engaged different processes, and whether we might be able to identify the brain systems underlying them. Using the think/no-think procedure, we gave two groups different instructions on how to prevent retrieval of a memory on no-think trials. We asked the direct suppression group to look right at the reminder and to prevent the memory from coming to mind, without distracting themselves using substitute thoughts. We told them that if the memory started to push its way into the mind, they should stop this retrieval process as soon as they could (i.e., slam on the brakes). In contrast, we told the thought substitution group to avoid retrieval on no-think trials by instead retrieving an alternative association to the reminder as a way to redirect their minds away from the memory, much like the quick steering of the car into another lane.

The results of this simple change in instructions were striking. On the one hand, we observed very similar amounts of forgetting for the no-think items in both groups, regardless of approach, as has been found before (Bergström et al., 2009). Despite this highly similar memory recall pattern, the two groups differed in how the brain accomp-

lished forgetting. The direct suppression participants recruited the right lateral prefrontal cortex area typically linked with stopping retrieval and this caused reduced hippocampal activity, as found in previous retrieval suppression studies. In stark contrast, the participants using thought substitution engaged areas in the left prefrontal cortex, and the more they engaged these areas, the higher was hippocampal activity. Thus, thought substitution had the opposite effect on the hippocampus (increased activity) to what we found for direct suppression. This pattern makes sense, given that activation in the hippocampus increases in general when one is remembering the past: suppressing retrieval (slamming on the brakes) reduces hippocampal activity that might have led a person to remember the unwanted memory, whereas retrieving an alternate thought (redirecting the car) actively engages retrieval processes that help to recollect the substitute memory and keep it in awareness, distracting oneself. These findings illustrate how the same goal (avoiding retrieval of an unwanted memory) can be achieved in two fundamentally different (in fact opposite) ways.

It thus appears that when people want to not "catch their mental cacti" and avoid an unwelcome reminding, they can engage at least two systems. One, which performs retrieval stopping, engages systems that are also necessary for action stopping. For this system, the difference between action and memory stopping appears to be the area of the brain that is stopped by control; with action inhibition, motor areas are suppressed by right lateral prefrontal cortex, but with memory inhibition, people instead "close down memory lane" by suppressing activation in the hippocampus (Anderson & Weaver, 2009). The second is involved in retrieving a substitute memory itself, to keep oneself distracted from the unwanted memory. This process not only does not suppress the retrieval process in general, it engages retrieval actively, but steers it in another direction. It is likely that in real-life settings, people use some combination of these mechanisms to suppress memories, rather than just one or the other: When an unwelcome memory pops to mind, direct suppression may purge the memory from mind (Levy & Anderson, 2012), but thought substitution processes may ensure that one's mind is quickly refocused.

Extreme emotional distress

Perhaps amongst the most striking form of motivated forgetting arises in psychogenic amnesia. Consider the dramatic case of AMN, a 23-year-old insurance worker (Markowitsch et al., 1998). AMN discovered a small fire in his basement and left the house to call for help. He did not inhale smoke, and he smashed the cellar door and immediately ran out of the house. That evening, he appeared dazed and frightened, and the next morning, when he awoke, he no longer knew what his profession was, or where he lived. After three weeks, he entered the hospital. Upon examination, it became clear that his memories only extended until the age of 17. He barely recognized his partner, whom he had known for three years, and did not recognize his friends or co-workers. After three weeks of therapy, he reported one of his earliest memories as a child: at the age of four, he saw a car crash which set another car in flames; he was then witness to the driver's screams and his death in the flames, with his head pressed against the window. Since that time, fire had been AMN's worst fear. Despite this, AMN showed normal psychological and physical development, and, throughout his life, showed no evidence of psychological illness. A full examination revealed no obvious evidence of brain damage, though greatly reduced metabolism was discovered in memory-related areas. Eight months later, at the time of the report, AMN's deficits in personal memory remained.

Cases like this illustrate several characteristics of psychogenic amnesia. First, psychogenic amnesia is triggered by severe psychological stressors. For AMN, a particular event made contact with a trauma, and triggered a massive reaction. The stressful event can cause a profound loss of personal memories, often despite a lack of observable neurobiological causes. In striking contrast, memory for public events and general knowledge is often intact. Unlike in

Members of the military, like many nonuniformed individuals, suffer unimaginable traumas all too often. Such events have the potential to spark psychogenic amnesia, in which memories for the trauma become inaccessible.

AMN's case, amnesia can be global, in that it affects the entirety of a person's history. Indeed, in a form of psychogenic amnesia known as a psychogenic fugue state (Hunter, 1968), the person forgets their entire history, including who they are. In such cases, people are often found wandering, not knowing where to go or what to do. Triggering events include such things as severe marital discord, bereavement, financial problems, or criminal offense. A history of depression and also head injury make a person more vulnerable to fugue states, when coupled with acute stress and trauma. Fugue typically lasts a few hours or a few days, and when the person recovers, they remember their identity and history once again. However, they often have persisting amnesia for what took place during the fugue.

Functional amnesia can also be situation specific, with the person experiencing severe memory loss for a particular trauma. Committing homicide, experiencing or committing a violent crime such as rape, or torture,

KEY TERM

Psychogenic fugue: A form of psychogenic amnesia typically lasting a few hours or days following a severe trauma, in which afflicted individuals forget their entire life history, including who they are.

experiencing combat violence, attempting suicide, and being in automobile accidents, and natural disasters have all induced cases of situation-specific amnesia (Arrigo & Pezdek, 1997; Kopelman, 2002). As Kopelman (2002) notes, however, care must be exercised in interpreting cases of psychogenic amnesia, when there are compelling motives to feign memory deficits for legal or financial reasons. Although some fraction of psychogenic amnesia cases can be explained in this fashion, it is generally acknowledged that true cases are not uncommon. Both global and situation-specific amnesia are often distinguished from the organic amnesic syndrome (discussed in Chapter 11) in that the capacity to store new memories and experiences remains intact.

Although the mechanisms of psychogenic amnesia remain poorly understood, one recent study suggests an intriguing connection between at least some cases of this condition and the mechanisms studied in research on retrieval suppression. Hirokazu Kikuchi and colleagues studied two psychogenic amnesia patients, with amnesia extending years prior to scanning (Kikuchi et al., 2009). Both patients were well educated, and neurologically normal, and of normal intelligence, but both had undergone a recent stressful event or period of time that led to extensive retrograde amnesia. For instance, Patient 1, a 27-year-old businessman exhibited focal retrograde amnesia for all events, people, and activities that took place in the 4.5-year period prior to the onset of his amnesia, even though he could recall experiences and people from before that period. Patient 2 presented a similar, but more extensive retrograde amnesia. No neurological abnormalities could be detected, and they appeared to remember all new experiences that happened to them after the onset of the amnesia, showing normal new learning.

Both of these patients were scanned with functional magnetic resonance imaging as they identified faces. Some faces were of strangers (novel faces). Others were of people the patients knew, with half of them drawn from people they met prior to their window of amnesia (identifiable faces), and the other half from during the window of time affected by amnesia (unidentifiable faces). Unsurprisingly, patients did not recognize the novel faces, and could recognize all of the identifiable faces. Intriguingly, although neither patient remembered any of the unidentifiable faces, these faces elicited increased activation in right lateral prefrontal cortex, together with reduced activity in the hippocampus, as observed in laboratory studies of retrieval suppression. After treatment, one patient recovered his memories, and upon rescanning, no longer exhibited the suppression pattern. These findings suggest that extreme psychological distress may lead retrieval suppression to be engaged involuntarily in reaction to certain stimuli. Much more work remains to be done to understand this phenomenon, however.

Given the dramatic nature of memory loss in such cases, there is usually a concerted effort to help the person recover their identity and history, as in the study by Kikuchi and colleagues. Deliberate attempts to remind the person of their past and identity rarely work, however. Memories can sometimes be recovered spontaneously when particular cues are encountered (Abeles & Schilder, 1935; Schacter, Wang, Tulving, & Freedman, 1982). For example, Kopelman (1995) reported a patient who spontaneously recalled, upon seeing the name of an author on the spine of a book, that he had a friend who was dying of cancer who shared that name. Although some patients appear to recover spontaneously or with supportive therapy, Kritchevsky, Chang, and Squire (2004) found that only two of the 10 patients they studied recovered fully, even 14 months after onset. Clearly, the conditions under which memories may be recovered need to be more fully understood.

FACTORS THAT PREDICT MEMORY RECOVERY

As the preceding discussion highlights, people may be motivated to forget at one time, but then wish to recall forgotten memories later. Although the need for recovery is dire in psychogenic amnesia, it is also an important goal in less dramatic instances of forgetting. At some point, you need to face that unpleasant task that you keep suppressing, and to do so, you need to extract it from memory when making your to-do list. Or you may encounter people who remember some embarrassing event that occurred to you that you simply cannot recall (like knocking over a Christmas tree), and, in your astonishment, may seek to release it from the dungeons to which it has been banished. Perhaps you are undergoing therapy and need to discuss past experiences. In this section, we consider factors that predict when motivated recovery can occur.

Passage of time

The passage of time is, of course, associated with forgetting. In some cases, however, memory paradoxically improves with delay even when no effort to retrieve is made. The classic demonstration comes from Ivan Pavlov, in his studies of classical conditioning. Pavlov found that when a classically conditioned salivary response was extinguished, the response gained in strength again after 20 minutes (Pavlov, 1927). Pavlov referred to this finding as spontaneous recovery. Spontaneous recovery is a robust phenomenon (Rescorla, 2004), including in research on conditioned emotional responding. After a conditioned response has been extinguished, spontaneous recovery increases with time, though conditioned responses do not generally return to full strength. Moreover, with repeated recovery/extinction cycles, the conditioned response recovers less each time. Spontaneous recovery illustrates that some types of memory, when seemingly forgotten, can once again return unbidden.

KEY TERM

Spontaneous recovery: The term arising from the classical conditioning literature given to the re-emergence of a previously extinguished conditioned response after a delay; similarly; forgotten declarative memories have been observed to recover over time.

Similar findings have been observed for declarative memory. The idea that memory might improve over time originated in research on retroactive interference and was premised on an analogy between retroactive interference and extinction in conditioning (Underwood, 1948). In particular, according to the unlearning hypothesis discussed in Chapter 9, whenever a "response" is retrieved by accident, the association between the cue and the mistaken response is punished via a process akin to extinction. If so, retroactive interference should dissipate. Consistent with this hypothesis, Underwood (1948) found significant retroactive interference at short delays, but performance on the first list improved at longer delays. Spontaneous recovery has been observed in a large number of retroactive interference studies since that time (see Brown, 1976; Wheeler, 1995, for reviews).

Mark Wheeler (Wheeler, 1995) reported several nice illustrations of spontaneous recovery in episodic memory. In one study, Wheeler presented students with 12 pictures, giving them three opportunities to study the items. The students were then told that the list had been for practice, and that the real lists would begin. They then received two additional lists of 12 pictures, with a free recall test occurring after each. After the third list was presented, students were given a free recall test for the pictures studied on the first list either immediately, or after about 30 minutes. As can be seen in Figure 10.6, recall from the first list suffered significant retroactive interference from learning two intervening lists, compared to a control group who performed irrelevant distractor activities instead of learning second and third lists. Notice, however, that after about 30 minutes, free recall of the first-list pictures actually gets better. Wheeler demonstrated the same effect with lists of categorized words, and also with word pairs, showing that recovery is general. Although most studies of spontaneous recovery have examined intervals up to 30 minutes, some have found recovery after several days. The stronger memories are, the more likely they will be to exhibit recovery (Postman, Stark, & Henschel, 1969).

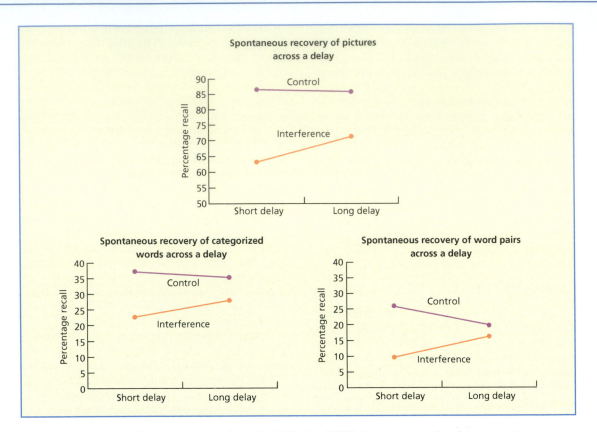

Figure 10.6 A series of experiments conducted by Wheeler (1995) demonstrating that the retroactive interference produced by intervening lists of pictures, words, or word pairs observed at short delays is diminished after a longer delay. Note that memory for items in the interference condition improves with delay in each case. From Wheeler (1995). Copyright © American Psychological Association. Reproduced with permission.

Why does episodic memory improve over time, when the overwhelming majority of research indicates the opposite relationship? One feature shared by spontaneous recovery in both classical conditioning and episodic memory is the explicit rejection of particular responses that had previously been relevant. As discussed earlier, the need to stop unwanted responses is one of the main conditions thought to engage inhibition. If retroactive interference reflects the persisting effects of inhibition, perhaps forgotten items recover because inhibition is gradually released. Thus, the factor that differentiates when memory will improve and when it will decline may be the involvement of inhibition. Consistent with this, Malcolm MacLeod and Neil Macrae (2001), found that retrieval induced forgetting was reduced after a 24-hour delay, suggesting

that in some cases inhibition may dissipate over time. Given the tendency for emotionally unpleasant experiences to come back and haunt us, even after frequent suppression, spontaneous recovery seems likely to be a force behind the reappearance of forgotten traces.

Repeated retrieval attempts

After a long struggle trying to recall an experience, is it worth continuing to search even when your intuition tells you that there is nothing to be recalled? Doesn't that feeling mean that the event has been lost forever? Perhaps not. Consider my experience trying to remember the location of my passport. After strenuous effort, I had no recollection whatsoever of storing this item, and felt that I would never remember. Yet, the moment I found it, I instantly recalled placing it in that location, showing that the memory was there. On the other hand, my efforts to remember knocking over the Christmas tree discussed in the last chapter have proven fruitless, despite prolonged recall attempts, stretching over months. When you fail to recall numerous times, doesn't it mean that the memory will not be recovered?

Interestingly, the answer this question often is "no." Repeated retrieval attempts typically increase the amount recalled, even when the person feels that they cannot recall more. This phenomenon was first discovered by Ballard (Ballard, 1913), who asked young school children to memorize poetry. Over successive recalls, Ballard found that the children would often recall new lines of poetry that they had failed to recall previously. Ballard referred to this phenomenon as reminiscence, which he defined as, "the remembering again of the forgotten without relearning," or "a gradual process of improvement in the capacity to revive past experiences" (Ballard, 1913). Ballard noted that even when the overall number of lines of poetry did not increase across retrievals, students often included newly recalled lines in later attempts not present in earlier ones. Overall recall sometimes didn't improve, however, because the benefits of recalling new lines were countered by students' failures to recall lines previously recalled. Nevertheless, often the amount of reminiscence exceeded this inter-test forgetting, yielding improvement overall. When overall recall improves through repeated testing (when reminiscence exceeds inter-test forgetting), a person has exhibited hypermnesia, a term

introduced by Mathew Erdelyi to contrast this with the amnesia normally arising from the passage of time.

Although neglected for decades, Mathew Erdelyi and colleagues revived interest in this phenomenon through striking demonstrations. In an amusing example, Erdelyi tricked a psychology Ph.D. student, Jeff Kleinbard, into becoming a participant in a weeklong study of hypermnesia. The student was interested in pursuing research on hypermnesia. To help him get a feel for the phenomenon, Erdelyi had Kleinbard join participants in a testing session. Participants studied 40 line drawings of objects. Participants then spent five minutes recalling as many of the pictures as possible (by writing the name of the object) on a blank sheet with 40 lines. If they could not recall all 40 items, the students were required to make educated guesses about what the remaining unrecalled pictures might be. This testing procedure continued for five recall attempts. When Kleinbard went to Erdelyi's office to score his recall, Erdelyi challenged him to continue his recall efforts over an entire week—a challenge that Kleinbard accepted. Each day, Kleinbard filled out recall sheets as many times as he cared to. When done, he inserted each sheet into an envelope and did not review them again. As can be seen in Figure 10.7, Kleinbard's total recall improved dramatically over the testing

KEY TERM

Reminiscence: The remembering again of the forgotten, without learning or a gradual process of improvement in the capacity to revive past experiences.

Hypermnesia: The improvement in recall performance arising from repeated testing sessions on the same material.

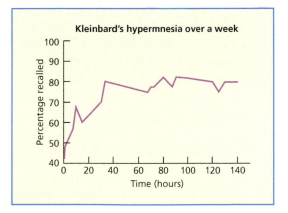

Kleinbard's hypermnesia over a week

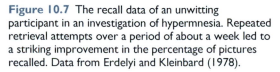

Figure 10.7 The recall data of an unwitting participant in an investigation of hypermnesia. Repeated retrieval attempts over a period of about a week led to a striking improvement in the percentage of pictures recalled. Data from Erdelyi and Kleinbard (1978).

days, starting at 48% on the first day and rising to 80% by the final day. Indeed, when one considers his cumulative recall (i.e., giving him credit for each item recalled at any point up until and including a given test), Kleinbard's recall went from 48% to 90%. This occurred despite the fact that on the first day, Kleinbard had tried his hardest to recall as many items as possible. Thus, Erdelyi and Kleinbard had essentially reversed Ebbinghaus's forgetting curve, by which memory gets progressively worse over time.

How might hypermnesia come about? Kleinbard stated that one of the most important factors was by visualization and reconstruction. In his own words:

> *By far, the most interesting subjective experience was getting a general "visual feeling" in my mind for a particular shape such as a length or roundness. I remember seeing a vague, oblong shape in my mind from which I was able to extract such items as gun, broom, and baseball bat; from an oval shape—football and pineapple; from an inverted cup form—bell, funnel, and bottle (the bottle in the stimulus resembled a bell-jar); from a rectangular box—table and book. Just before many of these recoveries, I often experienced what might best be described as a "tip-of-the-eye" phenomenon, in which I was certain a particular item was on the verge of recovery but which would take its time before suddenly coalescing into an image in consciousness.*
> *(Erdelyi & Kleinbard, 1978, p. 280)*

Erdelyi and Kleinbard (1978) found the same pattern with a group of six additional participants, three of whom studied pictures, and three of whom studied words. Participants who studied words, however, showed modest hypermnesia compared to those who studied pictures, suggesting that imagery plays an important role in determining whether traces can be unearthed with repeated recall. Indeed, several participants noted "tip of the eye" experiences much like that of Kleinbard.

Hypermnesia is a robust phenomenon and can be observed in simple laboratory sessions lasting less than an hour (Payne, 1987). Hypermnesia is largest on free recall tests but has been found on cued recall and recognition tests. The effect has been found with both verbal and visual materials, though effects are consistently larger with imageable materials. Of course, hypermnesia increases with increasing numbers of recall tests, and several investigations indicate that this effect does not simply reflect increases in time per se, as giving a single long test often does not yield as much benefit as many repeated tests. Nor does hypermnesia seem to reflect participants more loosely guessing as time goes on, because the frequency of false recalls often does not go up with repeated testing.

But can hypermnesia be found with complex, realistic memories? In one interesting illustration, Susan Bluck, Linda Levine, and Tracy Laulhere (1999) studied memory for a public event that many people had witnessed, and for which objective verification of details was possible: the televised reading of the verdict in the OJ Simpson murder trial. The reading of the verdict took place at 10:04 a.m. on October, 2, 1995 in Los Angeles, and the 14.5-minute proceedings was televised by a single courtroom camera shared by all television networks. Eight months after the verdict had been televised, Bluck et al. recruited people who viewed the coverage, and asked them to remember as much as they could, including details that occurred before, during, and after the reading of the verdict. Participants were interviewed three times in a row to obtain their complete recollection of every detail. Within each interview, participants were prompted several times with requests for further details, making sure that they had recalled everything they could. Significant hypermensia occurred, with the number of verifiable details remembered increasing from 27% to 52% across the three attempts.

But can hypermnesia occur for memories that people have deliberately tried to forget? On the one hand, the motivation to not remember may engage processes that have a special impact, making memories difficult to recall. Moreover, the same motivational factors that led the memories to be forgotten may also come into play during retrieval, undermining recovery. On the other hand, if someone decides to remember something they had previously tried to forget, might the change in disposition undo avoidant tendencies, and render forgotten material subject to hypermnesia? I may initially have been motivated to not think about knocking over the Christmas tree, but my motivations certainly changed years later. Although research examining hypermnesia for intentionally forgotten memories is rare, several studies using the directed forgetting procedure indicate that hypermnesia does occur for intentionally forgotten items (Goernert, 2005; Goernert & Wolfe, 1997).

It is natural to worry whether repeated retrievals may introduce persisting errors that come to be attributed to actual experience. In a nice illustration, Linda Henkel (Henkel, 2004) showed participants slides that contained either line drawings with their names (e.g., an image of a lollipop, plus the word LOLLIPOP), or simply the names with no picture. For each slide, participants were asked to think of functions of the object, and when a drawing was absent, to try to visualize a typical example. Participants then received three recall tests. Participants exhibited robust hypermnesia, but also showed an increase in source misattribution errors. With each test, participants grew more likely to falsely claim that they had *seen* an image of an object that they had only imagined. This tendency was especially likely when participants had seen physically or conceptually similar objects on the list. However, the overall rate of erroneous recalls is often surprisingly low, compared to accurate recall, in studies examining repeated recall of emotional eyewitness events (Bornstein, Liebel, & Scarberry, 1998) or autobiographical memory (Bluck et al., 1999).

Cue reinstatement

After putting unwanted memories out of mind, we sometimes stumble upon reminders. Walking around a corner, you may see a car matching the model your former partner used to drive. Rummaging through a box, you may find a gift from a loved one who has died. Veterans of Iraq may see someone make a sudden movement alongside the road while driving, transporting them back to the roadside bomb attack they experienced. Unintended remindings illustrate the power of cues to reinstate unwanted memories. Cues have the same power, of course, when one reverses course, and intends to remember something that one previously wished to forget.

Steve Smith and Sarah Moynan (2008) compellingly demonstrated how people may come to forget, and then later recover experiences, given the right cues. Very often one may need to confront reminders of unpleasant experiences on a recurring basis. One way of handling this may be to think about or discuss only some aspects of the experience while avoiding the unpleasant parts, perhaps rendering the nondiscussed elements less accessible. To simulate this, Smith and Moynan presented people with a categorized word list. The 21 categories included things such as FURNITURE, FRUIT, DRINKS, but also emotional categories like DISEASE, DEATH, and GROSS. Following encoding, the experimental group made judgments about the examples from 18 of the 21 categories, three times each, encouraging selective reprocessing of parts of the list. In the control group, the same time was spent on irrelevant tasks. Participants were then asked to recall all of the category names, including ones that were left out of the intervening phase. As can be seen in the top portion of Figure 10.8, participants exhibited truly remarkable forgetting of the three category names omitted from the intervening phase. Importantly, this occurred even when categories involved emotional items such as curse words or words concerning death. In some cases, recall of the avoided categories was 70% lower than the control group, despite comparable delays and demands on attention in the intervening phase. Clearly, biasing attention to certain elements of an experience can induce dramatic rates of forgetting.

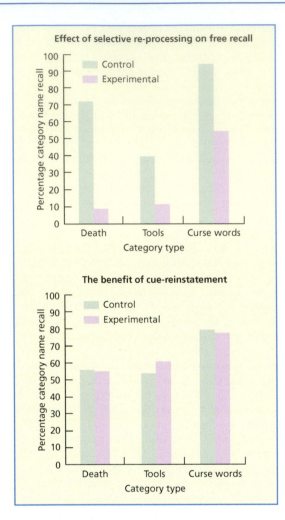

Effect of selective re-processing on free recall

The benefit of cue-reinstatement

Figure 10.8 Smith and Moynan (2008) asked participants to selectively review a subset of categorized word lists. Top: The free-recall test revealed forgetting for nonreviewed categories. Bottom: Exemplars from categories participants failed to generate during free recall could often still be retrieved using category cues. From Smith and Moynan (2008). Copyright © Blackwell Publishing. Reproduced with permission.

What happened to the forgotten items? Participants in the experimental condition clearly had difficulty recalling the omitted categories. If asked, they might feel as though they could not recall any more. Smith and Moynan (2008) showed that this was not true, however. After participants tried to recall the categories, they were given the category names, in turn, and asked to recall the examples. As can be seen in the bottom of

Figure 10.8, once the category names were given, the control and experimental participants recalled exactly the same number of items per category and recalled these at a very high rate. Thus, retention of the items was preserved, once the right cue appeared. Indeed, of the 10 death words experimental participants had encountered, they recalled nearly 60% (an amount identical to that recalled by the control group) when cued with the category, even though moments earlier, only 10% of the participants could even recall seeing death words on the list (compared to the 70% of the participants in the control condition). This illustrates that unpleasant experiences can sometimes be forgotten, given the right motivated biases in reminiscing about the event, and later recovered, given the right reminders.

But can cues really help recover memories that were intentionally forgotten? In one example, Goernert and Larson (1994) found that directed forgetting could be "released" by simply presenting a subset of the items participants studied on the first list as cues. Without any cues, participants showed a directed forgetting effect, with those people instructed to remember recalling 44% of the first list words, and those instructed to forget only recalling 21%. If participants received either four or eight cues, their first list recall increased to 29% and 31% respectively. Bäuml and Samenieh (2012a, 2012b) also observed these beneficial effects of cuing, but further found that if instead of providing cues, participants recalled the cue items on their own, the same benefits arose. Of course, cuing's potency is also shown when people receive to-be-forgotten items on a recognition test, in which directed forgetting effects are not usually observed (with the list-method). Seeing the item itself is a potent reminder, much like seeing a videotape of an experience we have tried to forget would prove an alarmingly effective cue.

Reinstating context can also help to recover memories that were intentionally forgotten. For example, Sahakyan and Kelley (2002) showed that reinstating mental context can undo the effects of instructions to forget in the list-method directed forgetting procedure. Participants were exposed to an unusual context just prior to encoding the first list of words: the presentation of the theme from the Star Wars® soundtrack. Later, on the final test, Sahakyan and Kelley asked participants to reinstate the mental context that they had been in upon entering the room, including anything that they could remember about how they felt or what they thought. Would reinstating the incidental context bring back intentionally forgotten material? When the context was not reinstated, participants showed a 22% deficit in the forget condition compared to the remember condition. The context-reinstatement group, however, showed only an 8% directed forgetting effect. These findings demonstrate that motivated forgetting processes often reduce the accessibility of unwanted memories, but do not alter their availability in storage. Often, these memories remain, awaiting a time when they are sought and when the right cues are available. One question that arises is whether experiences can reside in memory, untouched and inaccessible, and be reinstated after a long delay, given the right cues? Next, we consider an important societal issue on which our understanding of these processes bears and illustrate recovery in real life.

RECOVERED MEMORIES OF TRAUMA: INSTANCES OF MOTIVATED FORGETTING?

Most people have heard stories in which a person claims to have recovered a memory of a deeply unpleasant event, after years of being unaware of it. Sometimes famous cases receive media attention because they have led to legal charges of childhood sexual abuse against priests or parents. Other times, fictionalized cases appear on television or film, with a recovered memory as a plot device. Some people hear about recovered memories through friends or family who have had such experiences. As a memory instructor for many years, I have been approached by many students claiming to have recovered memories of abuse (several times a year). The idea that people can repress disturbing experiences is a central tenet of psychoanalytic theory.

Indeed, many therapists would say that they routinely see repression and recovery in their clients. Can an unpleasant experience be forgotten and then recovered years later?

There are good reasons to be cautious in interpreting such reports. Retrieval is imperfect. When people have difficulty remembering, they may engage in reconstruction and inference that adds things to memory that may not have taken place. Moreover, people sometimes confuse the sources of their memories, failing to distinguish things that they have imagined, heard about, read, dreamt, or seen in a film with things that truly happened. The risks of such possibilities grow when people participate in therapies that have the goal of uncovering repressed memories. Using hypnosis, guided imagery, and other suggestive techniques may create an environment in which discerning fact from fiction may prove difficult. The cost of a memory error might be the accusation of a family member of childhood abuse when none has occurred.

The possibility of false memories, and concern over their consequences does not, however, imply that recovered memories are untrue. One should place equal emphasis on the possibility that such experiences may reflect true events, and that failure to acknowledge this will have consequences for the victim and others who may suffer abuse at the hands of the perpetrator. In this section, we consider reports of recovered memories and the possible mechanisms by which such experiences might come about. We begin by describing several case reports in which the memory recovery experience came about in different ways.

Cases of recovered memories

The following are real recovered memory cases, although the names have been changed. In Case One, a person recovers a memory gradually, in suggestive therapy. Case Two recounts a woman who abruptly remembered an abuse memory, outside of therapy, when confronted with powerful reminders. Case Three is the story of a woman who recovered a series of deeply unpleasant events outside of therapy, and who, as a result, sought therapy.

Case One

As reported by Geraerts (2006), Elizabeth Janssen became very depressed. Her marriage was falling apart and she even quit her job for a while. Elizabeth and Carl went to a marriage counselor to solve their problems. After several sessions, the therapist referred them to a colleague because she could not figure out why they stopped caring for each other and why their sex life was unsatisfactory. Elizabeth and Carl then started individual therapy with this psychiatrist. Almost immediately, Elizabeth was diagnosed with a major depressive disorder. She was told that she had to uncover her repressed memories of early childhood abuse, as this was the underlying cause of her disorder.

At first, Elizabeth vehemently denied having been abused, and certainly not by her beloved father, like her psychiatrist insinuated. Her psychiatrist insisted that a childhood trauma must have happened to her; he had seen the same symptoms in so many patients. He started using guided imagery, instructing Elizabeth to imagine scenes of the supposed abuse even though Elizabeth continued to deny, although less fervently, that she had such memories. Because no abuse memories were surfacing, Elizabeth was given books about child abuse survivors to read; she was told that if something felt uncomfortable while reading these books, this would indicate that similar things happened to her. To help Elizabeth remember the abuse, hypnosis was used. After two months of intense therapy, Elizabeth gradually recovered vivid images of being abused. She said that she could see herself lying in bed as her father came into her room at night. While she was very anxious, he performed terrible and painful sexual acts on her. "Yes, even penetration." These traumatic events allegedly continued until she went to boarding school at age 12. Meanwhile, Elizabeth's husband Carl had been in therapy with the same psychiatrist. He was told that he also suffered from depression. After several weeks, Carl had recovered being sexually abused by several priests at boarding school.

When asked how she had felt after recovering these abuse memories, Elizabeth said that she had never felt such a relief. It turned out that not she, but her father was responsible for her depression. She broke off all contact with her parents. Contact with her sister and brother also became infrequent since they did not believe her story.

Case Two

Another report by Geraerts (2006) describes Mary de Vries, who had been working in the hospital as a pediatric nurse. She had a happy marriage and a three-year-old daughter. She had been very happy, that after several years of trying, she had finally become pregnant. However, the birth of her daughter Lynn elicited serious problems. When Mary came home with Lynn from the hospital, she felt uncomfortable when her husband was taking care of their baby. She almost never left him alone with their daughter; she always wanted to be there when he was washing her or changing her nappies. She really could not stand the thought of her husband doing something bad to Lynn. Her mistrust resulted in heavy arguments between the couple. Mary did not even know why she mistrusted him.

Almost at the same time, her mother fell ill. Her mother had been living alone on the coast since her second husband, Mary's stepfather, had left her. Mary reassured her mother and told her that she would come over for a couple of days with her baby and would help her with the housekeeping. While she was cleaning, she entered her former bedroom. Mary said that she suddenly had a complete recollective experience in which "a whole series of pictures were running through my head." The cascade of memories horrified, shocked, overwhelmed, surprised, and baffled her at the same time. Suddenly she remembered vulgar events that occurred in that room. She remembered that her stepfather had approached her several times while she was playing there. He had fondled her genitals several times. Mary just could not talk with her mother about these horrible memories. A few days later, when Mary got home, she called her sister. Mary told her what had happened at their mother's place. First, her sister said nothing. After a couple of minutes, she told Mary that she had always vividly remembered that she had been molested by their stepfather as well.

Case Three

Hermann and Schatzow (1987) report the following case, which subsequently appeared in *Science News* (Bower, 1993). After losing more than 100 pounds in a hospital weight-reduction program she had entered to battle severe obesity, Claudia experienced flashbacks of sexual abuse committed by her older brother. She joined a therapy group for incest survivors, and memories of abuse flooded back. Claudia told group members that from the time she was four years old to her brother's enlistment in the Army three years later, he had regularly handcuffed her, burned her with cigarettes, and forced her to submit to a variety of sexual acts. Claudia's brother had died in combat in Vietnam more than 15 years before her horrifying memories surfaced. Yet Claudia's parents had left his room and his belongings untouched since then. Returning home from the hospital, Claudia searched the room. Inside a closet she found a large pornography collection, handcuffs, and a diary in which her brother had extensively planned and recorded what he called sexual "experiments" with his sister.

What do we make of such cases?

The previous cases make several important points. First, memories can be recovered in many ways. In some cases, memories are recovered gradually, through active search and reconstruction, sometimes targeted at remembering abuse the person is not sure ever occurred. In other cases, the experience comes to mind spontaneously, without active search. Memories sometimes are recovered outside of therapy, triggered by a compelling need to explain some powerful reaction or feeling. Indeed, of the 634 cases of recovered memories reported by a sample of 108 British clinical psychologists in study by Andrews et al. (1999), 32% reported recovering their memories prior to therapy of any kind.

These cases also illustrate that corroboration is sometimes lacking. In Case One, no evidence was produced to prove that the abuse had occurred, other than the conviction of the therapist, and, eventually, of the patient. It is common for corroboration to be lacking, as the hypothetical event is usually thought to have taken place years earlier, outside the view of anyone other than the accuser, who, at the time of the event, is usually a child. In such cases, it is impossible to know whether corroboration is missing because the event is not real, or because care was taken to conceal it. Corroboration has often been possible, however, as illustrated in the latter cases. Indeed, there are many cases of individuals recovering memories that have been objectively corroborated (see the web resource, "Recovered Memory Archive," listed under "Recommended Readings" at the end of this chapter). These cases provide compelling proof of the phenomenon of recovery: it is possible to forget an emotionally significant event over many years and later recover it.

The cases also highlight a serious concern about some reports of recovered memories. Case One illustrates that some reports come through therapeutic techniques that are overly suggestive. Elizabeth Janssen had no predisposition to believe that her father had abused her, but her therapist was very insistent. In fact, the therapist appears eager to apply repression of abuse as a diagnosis. Despite her protests, Janssen was asked to repeatedly imagine and try to remember abuse she did not believe occurred, in some cases under hypnosis. Only then did Janssen come to believe in the event. Although repeated retrievals might have revealed real memories, as suggested by work on hypermnesia, it also seems possible that Janssen could no longer distinguish her previous imaginings from true memories, as suggested by the Henkel (2004) work discussed earlier. When a therapist has a conviction in a memory's reality, and a client starts to feel as though they are remembering (even if the remembering is of previous imaginings), it may grow difficult to discount the possibility that the memory is real. Thus, some cases of memory recovery may be false memories unwittingly encouraged by therapists who intend to help the patient.

Differing origins of recovered memory experiences

The preceding discussion suggests that recovered memories may be produced by different processes. On the one hand, memories recovered through suggestive therapy may reflect suggestions by the therapist rather than true recovery. On the other hand, memories recovered spontaneously, outside of therapy or in therapy, without suggestion, may be genuine. These memories could have been forgotten by any of the mechanisms outlined in this chapter. If so, corroboration should be more likely for memories recovered spontaneously than for memories recovered through suggestive therapy.

Geraerts and colleagues (2007) sought to corroborate abuse memories of people who have always remembered their abuse, and people who have recovered their memories. After filling out a questionnaire about their memory of the abuse, participants were queried about sources of corroboration. Independent raters, blind to the group in which a participant fell, used this information to seek evidence that would corroborate the event. A memory was considered corroborated if either (a) another individual reported learning about the abuse within a week after it happened, (b) another individual reported having been abused by the same perpetrator, or (c) the perpetrator admitted to committing the abuse. Strikingly, memories recovered spontaneously, outside of therapy, were corroborated at a rate (37%) that was comparable to that observed for people with continuously accessible memories (45%). Memories recovered through suggestive therapy, however, could never be corroborated (0%). Although the lack of corroboration does not imply that those recovered memories are false, the lack of evidence does not permit confidence in their reality and recommends caution in interpretation. More generally, these findings suggest that discontinuous memory does not make an experience any less real than something a person has always remembered.

The foregoing findings suggest that recovered memories may originate in different ways for people who recollect the abuse spontaneously, and for those wzho recall it through suggestive therapy. Geraerts and colleagues hypothesized that memories recalled through suggestive therapy may be more likely to be false, a possibility consistent with the lack of corroboration. People recall-

ing memories spontaneously, by contrast, may have genuinely forgotten the experience, and later remembered it. Alternatively, the spontaneously recovered group may have recalled the event, but may have forgotten that they have recalled it before. The latter possibility is suggested by a case reported by Jonathan Schooler (Schooler, Ambadar, & Bendiksen, 1997), in which a woman "recovered" a memory of childhood abuse for "the first time," only to be informed by her spouse that they had discussed the event at length years earlier. Might people who have spontaneous recovery experiences simply be forgetting having thought about it?

To explore these possibilities, Geraerts et al. (2006) first investigated whether people reporting recovered memories had a tendency to underestimate prior remembering. They invited people with recovered or continuous memories to write down a memory from their childhood for each of 25 titles. The titles described common things that happen to children like BEING HOME ALONE or GOING TO THE DENTIST. For some of these titles, participants were asked to concentrate on emotionally negative aspects of the event (e.g., for BEING HOME ALONE this might be the feeling of being frightened), but for others, the positive aspects (e.g., for the home alone title, this might be getting to do whatever you want). Everyone returned two months later and generated the same memories, yet again. There was one switch, however: sometimes people retrieved the events in the same emotional frame as before, but for other titles, they were asked to retrieve the event in the opposite emotional frame. So, for example, if they had recalled BEING HOME ALONE in a positive light during the first visit, they recalled the same event again, but focused on the negative aspects. When this second visit was complete, people returned to the lab for a third and final time two months later. They recalled all of the events yet again, but this time they recalled each one in the same emotional frame in which they had recalled it during the first visit. Critically, after recalling each memory, people were asked to remember whether they had recalled that same memory during the second (i.e., middle) visit. Interestingly, when the emotional framing on the final visit differed from the one on the second visit, people were quite likely to forget having remembered the event during that second visit, compared to when the emotional framing remained the same. Thus, shifting the way that people thought about the same memory (whether positively or negatively) from one occasion to the next made them forget thinking about the memory before. Importantly, this tendency was greater for people reporting recovered memories than it was for people reporting continuous memories, or people without any history of abuse.

So it seems that one reason why people may have a recovered memory experience is that they simply forget having remembered the event before. They may forget prior cases of remembering if, for example, the mental context present when they are having their recovery experience differs from the mental context on prior occasions in which they thought of the event. By this view, it's not that people have forgotten the event all those years, it's that they simply can't remember having remembered, perhaps due to context-dependent memory.

The discussion thus far does not explain why some people might show greater susceptibility to forgetting prior remembering. One possibility is that people with authentic abuse experiences may engage some of the motivated forgetting processes discussed in this chapter in order to limit intrusive remindings

of the unwanted experience. So, for example, they might learn to engage inhibitory control to suppress intrusive thoughts. If so, perhaps the reason why these people cannot remember their prior incidences of remembering is that these memories have been disrupted by the same processes at work in retrieval-induced forgetting or the think/no-think procedure discussed earlier. Thus people may learn to habitually suppress remindings of those events, causing them to forget their prior thoughts.

If the thought suppression hypothesis is correct, does this present an alternative to the idea that memories can be repressed, and later recovered? It depends. On the one hand, if a memory must be consistently inaccessible over many years for it to count as repression, this research suggests a different mechanism. On the other hand, Freud emphasized the *return of the repressed* and the idea that repression needed to be actively maintained. If repression requires continual reinstatement, then suppressing intrusive remindings over the span of many years simply reflects reinstatement. Further work is required to establish the mental and biological mechanisms that account for these, and other cases of motivated forgetting. It is clear, however, that what we remember is not random, and aligns with our motivations, and goals of emotional regulation (Anderson & Hanslmayr, 2014; Anderson & Huddleston, 2012).

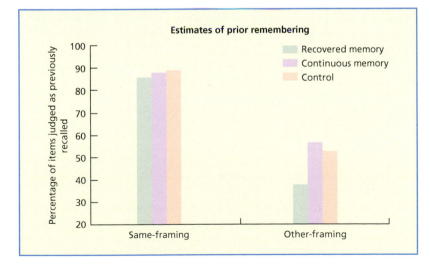

Figure 10.9 The ability to recall prior remembrances is diminished if the retrieval perspective differed between them (other-framing condition). Geraerts et al. (2006) found that this tendency is greatest in individuals who previously reported recovered memories of abuse, distinguishing them from abuse victims who reported continuous memories of their trauma and controls. Data from Geraerts et al. (2006).

SUMMARY

- People exhibit a pronounced positivity bias in their autobiographical memory, which may contribute to perceptions of life satisfaction.
- Having good memory for the past can sometimes be a problem.
- People are motivated to forget unpleasant events, to regulate their emotions, maintain a positive outlook, a positive self-image, or simply to concentrate.
- Motivation to forget can alter the way that memories are encoded or retrieved.
- Item-method directed forgetting research shows that people can limit encoding intentionally, both through selective rehearsal, and encoding suppression.
- List-method directed forgetting research shows that people can reduce access to encoded memories by intentionally suppressing access to a whole context of events.
- People will avoid reminders to an unwanted memory as a way to avoid retrieving experiences they'd rather not think about.
- When people cannot avoid reminders, they can stop retrieval of the unwanted memory with a process called retrieval suppression.
- Retrieval suppression may build on basic mechanisms of behavioral control that help us to stop actions, to stop retrieval.
- Retrieval suppression impairs memory for suppressed events, a phenomenon called suppression-induced forgetting.
- Retrieval suppression may contribute to "forgiving and forgetting" and also to managing fearful images of the future.
- Retrieval suppression can be accomplished by direct suppression, a process of shutting down the retrieval process, or thought substitution, a process of retrieving alternate distracting thoughts.
- Direct suppression is accomplished by down-regulating hippocampal activation, achieved by the right lateral prefrontal cortex. Thought substitution is achieved by retrieval processes supported by the left prefrontal cortex.
- Extreme emotional distress can induce dramatic loss of access to large chunks of one's personal past, and sometimes one's entire identity, a phenomenon known as psychogenic amnesia.
- Sometimes people wish to recover memories they had deliberately forgotten.
- A number of factors can contribute to the recovery of forgotten memories, including the passage of time, repeated retrieval efforts, provision of appropriate cues or physical context.
- Recovered memories of abuse have frequently been reported.
- Many documented cases of recovered memories have been demonstrated, with objective corroboration that the forgotten event had occurred, demonstrating the reality of the phenomenon.
- Concern has been raised about the reality of some recovered memories, and the possibility that overly suggestive therapeutic practices may be responsible for creating false memories of abuse.
- False memories constitute a significant hazard of overly suggestive therapeutic practices, because research has shown that people can be highly suggestible.
- Both true and false recovered memories are likely to exist.
- The mechanisms underlying cases of true recovered memories are unclear at present, though some of the mechanisms identified in laboratory studies of motivated forgetting, including retrieval suppression and changes in context, have been proposed.

POINTS FOR DISCUSSION

1 With the advent of affordable "life logging" wearable recording devices, one could, theoretically record photos or video of every moment of our lives. If you could do this, would you? Would remembering everything in your life make you happier? Why or why not? Can you think of cases in your life which you wished you could forget?

2 What are the main factors that predict when motivated forgetting will occur? Have you ever used any of the strategies or mechanisms described in this chapter to forget, or take your mind off something?

3 What has laboratory research shown about the conditions under which it might be possible to recover a memory that you have tried to forget?

FURTHER READING

Anderson, M. C., & Hanslmayr, S. (2014). Neural mechanisms of motivated forgetting. *Trends in Cognitive Sciences, 18*(6), 279–292.

Anderson, M. C., & Huddleston, E. (2012). Towards a cognitive and neurobiological model of motivated forgetting. In R. F. Belli (Ed.), *True and false recovered memories* (pp. 53–120). New York: Springer.

Anderson, M. C., & Levy, B. J. (2009). Suppressing unwanted memories. *Current Directions in Psychological Science, 17*, 441–447.

Bjork, R. A. (1989). Retrieval inhibition as an adaptive mechanism in human memory. In H. L. Roediger & F. I. Craik (Eds.), *Varieties of memory and consciousness: Essays in honour of Endel Tulving* (pp. 309–330). Hillsdale, NJ: Lawrence Erlbaum Associates.

Cheit, R. E. (Director). *Recovered memory archive*. Retrieved from www.RecoveredMemory.org.

Engen, H. G., & Anderson, M. C. (2018). Memory control: A fundamental mechanism of emotion regulation. *Trends in Cognitive Sciences, 22*(11), 982–995.

Erdelyi, M. H. (2006). The unified theory of repression. *Behavioral and Brain Sciences, 29*(5), 499–551.

Johnson, M. K., Raye, C. L., Mitchell, K. J., & Ankudowich, E. (2011). The cognitive neuroscience of true and false memories. In R. F. Belli (Ed.), *True and false recovered memories: Toward a reconciliation of the debate. Vol. 58: Nebraska Symposium on Motivation* (pp. 15–52). New York: Springer.

(Continued)

(Continued)

Loftus, E. F., & Davis, D. (2006). Recovered memories. *Annual Review of Clinical Psychology, 2*, 469–498.

Sahakyan, L., Delaney, P. F., Foster, N. L. & Abushana, B. (2013). List-method directed forgetting in cognitive and clinical research: A theoretical and methodological review. In B. H. Ross (Ed.), *Psychology of learning and motivation* (Vol. 59, pp. 131–189). New York: Elsevier.

REFERENCES

Abeles, M., & Schilder, P. (1935). Psychogenic loss of personal identity: Amnesia. *Archives of Neurology and Psychiatry, 34*, 587–604.

Anderson, M. C. (2003). Rethinking interference theory: Executive control and the mechanisms of forgetting. *Journal of Memory and Language, 49*(4), 415–445.

Anderson, M. C., & Green, C. (2001). Suppressing unwanted memories by executive control. *Nature, 410*(6826), 366–369.

Anderson, M. C., & Hanslmayr, S. (2014). Neural mechanisms of motivated forgetting. *Trends in Cognitive Sciences, 18*(6), 279–292.

Anderson, M. C., & Huddleston, E. (2012). Towards a cognitive and neurobiological model of motivated forgetting. In R. F. Belli (Ed.), *True and false recovered memories* (pp. 53–120). New York: Springer.

Anderson, M. C., & Levy, B. J. (2009). Suppressing unwanted memories. *Current Directions in Psychological Science, 17*, 441–447.

Anderson, M. C., Ochsner, K. N., Cooper, J., Robertson, E., Gabrieli, S. W., Glover, G. H., et al. (2004). Neural systems underlying the suppression of unwanted memories. *Science, 303*, 232–235.

Anderson, M. C., & Weaver, C. (2009). Inhibitory control over action and memory. In L. R. Squire (Ed.), *The new encyclopedia of neuroscience* (pp. 153–163). Oxford: Elsevier.

Andrews, B., Brewin, C. R., Ochera, J., Morton, J., Bekerian, D. A., Davies, G. M., et al. (1999). Characteristics, context and consequences of memory recovery among adults in therapy. *British Journal of Psychiatry, 175*, 141–146.

Aron, A. R., Robbins, T. W., & Poldrack, R. A. (2014). Inhibition and the right inferior frontal cortex: One decade on. *Trends in Cognitive Sciences, 18*(4), 177–185.

Arrigo, J. M., & Pezdek, K. (1997). Lessons from the study of psychogenic amnesia. *Current Directions in Psychological Science, 6*(5), 148–152.

Ballard, P. B. (1913). Oblivescence and reminiscence. *British Journal of Psychology Monograph Supplements, 1*, 1–82.

Barnier, A. J., Conway, M. A., Mayoh, L., & Speyer, J. (2007). Directed forgetting of recently recalled autobiographical memories. *Journal of Experimental Psychology: General, 136*(2), 301–322.

Basden, B. H., & Basden, D. R. (1996). Directed forgetting: Further comparisons of the item and list methods. *Memory, 4*(6), 633–653.

Basden, B. H., Basden, D. R., & Gargano, G. J. (1993). Directed forgetting in implicit and explicit memory tests: A comparison of methods. *Journal of Experimental Psychology: Learning, 19*(3), 603–616.

Bäuml, K. H. T., & Samenieh, A. (2012a). Influences of part-list cuing on different forms of episodic forgetting. *Journal of Experimental Psychology: Learning, Memory, and Cognition, 38*(2), 366–375.

Bäuml, K. H. T., & Samenieh, A. (2012b). Selective memory retrieval can impair and improve retrieval of other memories. *Journal of Experimental Psychology: Learning, Memory, and Cognition, 38*(2), 488–494.

Benoit, R. G., & Anderson, M. C. (2012). Opposing mechanisms support the voluntary forgetting of unwanted memories. *Neuron, 76*(2), 450–460.

Benoit, R. G., Davies, D. J., & Anderson, M. C. (2016). Reducing future fears by suppressing the brain mechanisms underlying episodic simulation. *Proceedings of the National Academy of Sciences of the USA, 113*(52), E8492–E8501.

Bergström, Z. M., de Fockert, J. W., & Richardson-Klavehn, A. (2009). ERP and behavioural evidence for direct suppression of unwanted memories. *NeuroImage, 48*(4), 726–737.

Bernsten, D. (1996). Involuntary autobiographical memories. *Applied Cognitive Psychology, 10*(5), 435–454.

Bjork, E. L., & Bjork, R. A. (2003). Intentional forgetting can increase, not decrease, residual influences of to-be-forgotten information. *Journal of Experimental Psychology: Learning, Memory, & Cognition, 29*(4), 524–531.

Bjork, R. A. (1970). Positive forgetting: The noninterference of items intentionally forgotten. *Journal of Verbal Learning and Verbal Behavior, 9*(3), 255–268.

Bjork, R. A. (1989). Retrieval inhibition as an adaptive mechanism in human memory. In H. L. Roediger & F. I. Craik (Eds.), *Varieties of memory and consciousness: Essays in honour of Endel Tulving* (pp. 309–330). Hillsdale, NJ: Lawrence Erlbaum Associates.

Bluck, S., Levine, L. J., & Laulhere, T. M. (1999). Autobiographical remembering and hypermnesia: A comparison of older and younger adults. *Psychology and Aging, 14*(4), 671–682.

Bornstein, B. H., Liebel, L. M., & Scarberry, N. C. (1998). Repeated testing in eyewitness memory: A means to improve recall of a negative emotional event. *Applied Cognitive Psychology, 12*(2), 119–131.

Bower, B. (1993). Sudden recall: Adult memories of child abuse spark a heated debate. Retrieved May 5, 2008, from www.thefreelibrary.com/ Sudden recall: adult memories of child abuse spark a heated debate.-a014458675

Brown, A. S. (1976). Spontaneous recovery in human learning. *Psychological Bulletin, 83*(2), 321–338.

Catarino, A., Küpper, C. S., Werner-Seidler, A., Dalgleish, T., & Anderson, M. C. (2015). Failing to forget: Inhibitory-control deficits compromise memory suppression in posttraumatic stress disorder. *Psychological Science, 26*(5), 604–616.

Charles, S. T., Mather, M., & Carstensen, L. L. (2003). Aging and emotional memory: The forgettable nature of negative images for older adults. *Journal of Experimental Psychology General, 132*(2), 310–324.

Depue, B. E., Banich, M. T., & Curran, T. (2006). Suppression of emotional and nonemotional content in memory. effects of repetition on cognitive control. *Psychological Science, 17*(5), 441–447.

Depue, B. E., Burgess, G. C., Willcutt, E. G., Ruzic, L., & Banich, M. T. (2010). Inhibitory control of memory retrieval and motor processing associated with the right lateral prefrontal cortex: Evidence from deficits in individuals with ADHD. *Neuropsychologia, 48*, 3909–3917. doi:10.1016/j. neuropsychologia.2010.09.013

Depue, B. E., Curran, T., & Banich, M. T. (2007). Prefrontal regions orchestrate suppression of emotional memories via a two-phase process. *Science, 317*, 215–219.

Diener, E., & Diener, C. (1996). Most people are happy. *Psychological Science, 7*(3), 181–185.

Engen, H. G., & Anderson, M. C. (2018). Memory control: A fundamental mechanism of emotion regulation. *Trends in Cognitive Sciences, 22*(11), 982–995.

Erdelyi, M. H. (2006). The unified theory of repression. *Behavioral and Brain Sciences, 29*(5), 499–551.

Erdelyi, M. H., & Kleinbard, J. (1978). Has Ebbinghaus decayed with time? The growth of recall (hypermnesia) over days. *Journal of Experimental Psychology: Human Learning and Memory, 4*(4), 275–289.

Fawcett, J. M., & Taylor, T. L. (2008). Forgetting is effortful: Evidence from reaction time probes in an item-method directed forgetting task. *Mem. Cognit., 36*, 1168–1181.

Freud, S. (1900). The interpretation of dreams. In J. Strachey (Ed.), *The standard edition of the complete psychological writings of Sigmund Freud*. London: Hogarth Press.

Freud, S. (1917). Repression. In J. Riviere (Ed.), *A general introduction to psychoanalysis* (p. 147). New York: Liveright.

Gagnepain, P., Hulbert, J., & Anderson, M. C. (2017). Parallel regulation of memory and emotion supports the suppression of intrusive memories. *Journal of Neuroscience, 37*(27), 6423–6441.

Geiselman, R. E., Bjork, R. A., & Fishman, D. L. (1983). Disrupted retrieval in directed forgetting: A link with posthypnotic amnesia. *Journal of Experimental Psychology General, 112*(1), 58–72.

Geraerts, E. (2006). *Remembrance of things past. The cognitive psychology of remembering and forgetting trauma*. Unpublished Ph.D. Thesis, Maastricht University, the Netherlands.

Geraerts, E., Arnold, M. M., Stephen Lindsay, D., Merckelbach, H., Jelicic, M., & Hauer, B. (2006). Forgetting of prior remembering in persons reporting recovered memories of childhood sexual abuse. *Psychological Science, 17*(11), 1002–1008.

Geraerts, E., Schooler, J. W., Merckelbach, H., Jelicic, M., Hauer, B. J., & Ambadar, Z. (2007). The reality of recovered memories: Corroborating continuous and discontinuous memories of childhood sexual abuse. *Psychological Science, 18*(7), 564–568.

Goernert, P. N. (2005). Source-monitoring accuracy across repeated tests following directed forgetting. *British Journal of Psychology, 96*(2), 231–247.

Goernert, P. N., & Larson, M. E. (1994). The initiation and release of retrieval inhibition. *The Journal of General Psychology, 121*(1), 61–66.

Goernert, P. N., & Wolfe, T. (1997). Is there hypermnesia and reminiscence for information intentionally forgotten?. *Canadian Journal of Experimental Psychology, 51*(3), 231–240.

Hanslmayr, S., Volberg, G., Wimber, M., Oehler, N., Staudigl, T., Hartmann, T., Raab, M., Greenlee, M. W., & Bäuml, K. H. T. (2012). Prefrontally driven downregulation of neural synchrony mediates goal-directed forgetting. *Journal of Neuroscience, 32*(42), 14742–14751.

Henkel, L. A. (2004). Erroneous memories arising from repeated attempts to remember. *Journal of Memory and Language, 50*(1), 26–46.

Hermon, J., & Schatzow, E. (1987). Recovery and verification of memories of childhood sexual trauma. *Psychoanalytic Psychology, 4*, 1–14.

Hertel, P., & McDaniel, L. (2010). The suppressive power of positive thinking: Aiding suppression-induced forgetting in repressive coping. *Cogn. Emot., 24*, 1239–1249.

Hotta, C., & Kawaguchi, J. (2009). Self-initiated use of thought substitution can lead to long term forgetting. *Psychologia, 52*, 41–49.

Hunter, I. M. L. (1968). *Memory.* Harmondsworth: Penguin Books.

Joslyn, S. L., & Oakes, M. A. (2005). Directed forgetting of autobiographical events. *Memory & Cognition, 33*(4), 577–587.

Kikuchi, H., Fujii, T., Abe, N., Suzuki, M., Takagi, M., Mugikura, S., et al. (2009). Memory repression: Brain mechanisms underlying dissociative amnesia. *Journal of Cognitive Neuroscience, 22*(3), 602–613.

Kopelman, M. D. (1995). The Korsakoff syndrome. *The British Journal of Psychiatry, 166*(2), 154–173.

Kopelman, M. D. (2002). Disorders of memory. *Brain, 125*(10), 2152–2190.

Kritchevsky, M., Chang, J., & Squire, L. R. (2004). Functional amnesia: Clinical description and neuropsychological profile of 10 cases. *Learning & Memory, 11*(2), 213–226.

Leigland, L. A., Schulz, L. E., & Janowsky, J. S. (2004). Age related changes in emotional memory. *Neurobiology of Aging, 25*(8), 1117–1124.

Levy, B. J., & Anderson, M. C. (2008). Individual differences in the suppression of

unwanted memories: The executive deficit hypothesis. *Acta Psychologica, 127*, 623–635.

Levy, B. J., & Anderson, M. C. (2012). Purging of memories from conscious awareness tracked in the human brain. *J. Neurosci., 32*, 16785–16794. doi:10.1523/JNEUROSCI.2640-12.2012

Lykken, D., & Tellegen, A. (1996). Happiness is a stochastic phenomenon. *Psychological Science, 7*(3), 186–189.

MacLeod, M. D., & Macrae, C. N. (2001). Gone but not forgotten: The transient nature of retrieval-induced forgetting. *Psychological Science, 12*(2), 148–152.

Manning, J. R., Hulbert, J. C., Williams, J., Piloto, L., Sahakyan, L., & Norman, K. A. (2016). A neural signature of contextually mediated intentional forgetting. *Psychonomic Bulletin & Review, 23*(5), 1534–1542.

Markowitsch, H. J., Kessler, J., Van Der Ven, C., Weber-Luxenburger, G., Albers, M., & Heiss, W. D. (1998). Psychic trauma causing grossly reduced brain metabolism and cognitive deterioration. *Neuropsychologia, 36*(1), 77–82.

Mather, M., & Carstensen, L. L. (2005). Aging and motivated cognition: The positivity effect in attention and memory. *Trends in Cognitive Sciences, 9*(10), 496–502.

Noreen, S., Bierman, R. N., & MacLeod, M. D. (2014). Forgiving you is hard, but forgetting seems easy: Can forgiveness facilitate forgetting?. *Psychological Science, 25*(7), 1295–1302.

Noreen, S., & MacLeod, M. D. (2013). It's all in the detail: Intentional forgetting of autobiographical memories using the autobiographical think/no-think task. *Journal of Experimental Psychology: Learning, Memory, and Cognition, 39*(2), 375–393.

Oehrn, C. R., Fell, J., Baumann, C., Rosburg, T., Ludowig, E., Kessler, H., Hanslmayr, S., & Axmacher, N. (2018). Direct electrophysiological evidence for prefrontal control of hippocampal processing during voluntary forgetting. *Current Biology, 28*(18), 3016–3022.

Pavlov, I. P. (1927). *Conditioned reflexes: An investigation of the physiological activity of the cerebral cortex.* (G. V. Anrep, Ed.). London: Oxford University Press.

Payne, D. G. (1987). Hypermnesia and reminiscence in recall: A historical and empirical review. *Psychological Bulletin, 101*(1), 5–27.

Postman, L., Stark, K., & Henschel, D. M. (1969). Conditions of recovery after unlearning. *Journal of Experimental Psychology, 82*(1, Pt. 2), 1–24.

Rescorla, R. A. (2004). Spontaneous recovery varies inversely with the training-extinction interval. *Learning & Behavior: A Psychonomic Society Publication, 32*(4), 401–408.

Rizio, A. A., & Dennis, N. A. (2013). The neural correlates of cognitive control: Successful remembering and intentional forgetting. *J. Cogn. Neurosci.*, *25*, 297–312.

Sahakyan, L., Delaney, P. F., Foster, N. L., & Abushana, B. (2013). List-method directed forgetting in cognitive and clinical research: A theoretical and methodological review. In B. H. Ross (Ed.), *Psychology of learning and motivation* (Vol. 59, pp. 131–189). New York: Elsevier.

Sahakyan, L., & Kelley, C. M. (2002). A contextual change account of the directed forgetting effect. *Journal of Experimental Psychology: Learning, Memory, & Cognition*, *28*(6), 1064–1072.

Sasaki, K., Gemba, H., & Tsujimoto, T. (1989). Suppression of visually initiated hand movement by stimulation of the prefrontal cortex in the monkey. *Brain Research*, *495*(1), 100–107.

Schacter, D. L., Wang, P. L., Tulving, E., & Freedman, M. (1982). Functional retrograde amnesia: A quantitative case study. *Neuropsychologia*, *20*(5), 523–532.

Schmitz, T. W., Correia, M. M., Ferreira, C. S., Prescot, A. P., & Anderson, M. C. (2017). Hippocampal GABA enables inhibitory control over unwanted thoughts. *Nature Communications*, *8*(1), 1311.

Schooler, J. W., Ambadar, Z., & Bendiksen, M. A. (1997). A cognitive corroborative case study approach for investigating discovered memories of sexual abuse. In J. D. Read & D. S. Lindsay (Eds.), *Recollections of trauma: Scientific evidence and clinical practice* (pp. 379–388). New York: Plenum.

Sedikides, C., & Green, J. D. (2000). On the self-protective nature of inconsistency/negativity management: Using the person memory paradigm to examine self-referent memory. *Journal of Personality and Social Psychology*, *79*, 906–922.

Sedikides, C., & Green, J. D. (2009). Memory as a self-protective mechanism. *Social and Personality Psychology Compass*, *3*, 1055–1068.

Sedikides, C., Green, J. D., Saunders, J., Skowronski, J. J., & Zengel, B. (2016). Mnemic neglect: Selective amnesia of one's faults. *European Review of Social Psychology*, *27*(1), 1–62.

Smith, S. M., & Moynan, S. C. (2008). Forgetting and recovering the unforgettable. *Psychological Science*, *19*(5), 462–468.

Squire, L. R. (1992). Memory and the hippocampus: A synthesis from findings with rats, monkeys, and humans. *Psychological Review*, *99*(2), 195–231.

Underwood, B. J. (1948). Retroactive and proactive inhibition after five and forty-eight hours. *Journal of Experimental Psychology*, *38*, 29–38.

Waldfogel, S. (1948). The frequency and affective character of childhood memories. *Psychological Monographs*, *62*(Whole No. 291).

Waldhauser, G. T., Dahl, M. J., Ruf-Leuschner, M., Müller-Bamouh, V., Schauer, M., Axmacher, N., … & Hanslmayr, S. (2018). The neural dynamics of deficient memory control in heavily traumatized refugees. *Scientific Reports*, *8*(1), 13132.

Wheeler, M. A. (1995). Improvement in recall over time without repeated testing: Spontaneous recovery revisited. *Journal of Experimental Psychology: Learning*, *21*(1), 173–184.

Wierzba, M., Riegel, M., Wypych, M., Jednoróg, K., Grabowska, A., & Marchewka, A. (2018). Cognitive control over memory–individual differences in memory performance for emotional and neutral material. *Scientific Reports*, *8*(1), 3808.

Contents

CHAPTER 11

AUTOBIOGRAPHICAL MEMORY

Michael C. Anderson

M y new significant other and I had finished cooking dinner and we had arranged the table, with candles and pleasant music. As we raised our wine glasses for a toast, my mobile phone rang. Reluctantly, I answered the call, which was from my Ph.D. student, Justin Hulbert. Justin said, "Are you almost here?" in a polite, if tense tone. Confused, I said "What do you mean? Where? I am just sitting down to eat." Awkward silence ensued. Finally, he said "Eh, you are supposed to be downtown with me in the cinema. Remember, you agreed to give an introductory lecture to the film *Eternal Sunshine of the Spotless Mind*, as part of the Memory Film Festival." The Memory Film Festival was the brainchild of Amy Milton, a professor of psychology, organized as part of the weeklong Cambridge Science Festival, a popular annual event at the University of Cambridge. Apparently, I had agreed to give this lecture because of my own research on forgetting, and I had, poetically, completely forgotten. Pressing ahead, Justin said "There are easily 200 people in the theater now, expecting the lecture in 15 minutes." This news elicited the feeling that one has during a dream, when one discovers oneself transported back to a busy high school hallway, without clothes. Shocked, I apologized to my significant other, immediately leaving her befuddled and alone at the table, as I sped to the theater. The organizers cleverly told the audience that they had decided the lecture would be better given after the film, as though it had been planned all along. Outside the theater, I frantically prepared my lecture for the next 60 minutes.

Now that I look back on this event years later, I can laugh at the irony of somebody who studies forgetting for a living, forgetting to give a lecture on a film about wanting to forget. In truth, I actually rather enjoy telling the story, as it fits a well-justified theme about me as an absent-minded professor. If I ever write an autobiography, I will surely try to fit this story in. We all have a collection of such personal memories that are special in that they are part of our life stories, and so seem more than just ordinary episodic memories. Autobiographical memory refers to the memories that we hold regarding ourselves and our interactions with the world around us, that help to define who we were at different times in the past, who we are currently, and who we hope to be in the future. It includes not only episodic memories that form part of our life stories, but also semantic autobiographical memory that includes historical facts, traits, and knowledge states that are not unique to any particular place or time.

Autobiographical memory is clearly important to each of us, as it helps to define

KEY TERM

Autobiographical memory: Memory across the lifespan for both specific events and self-related information.

our sense of ourselves as people. But is auto-biographical memory a separate kind of memory? On the one hand, it almost certainly depends on the episodic and semantic memory systems we have already discussed, and so may not be qualitatively different. Remembering facts about ourselves, such as our name, when we went to school, and where we live, is autobiographical but forms a personal aspect of semantic memory. Remembering what you had for breakfast today is also autobiographical but involves recollecting a specific episodic experience. The fact that autobiographical memory involves both of these suggests that it may be a complex blend of these other forms of memory. Nevertheless, as we will see later on in this chapter, evidence from neuroscience suggests that the idea that autobiographical memory is simply a mixture of episodic and semantic memory may not be entirely adequate, as it appears to involve qualitatively distinct brain mechanisms. Even without considering the mechanisms involved, it is worth distinguishing autobiographical memory simply because the role that it plays in our lives differs in interesting and important ways from other functions of memory.

We will begin by discussing the function of autobiographical memory and why it is important, leading on to the thorny question of how to study it. The problem here is that, unlike most of the research we have discussed so far, the experimenter typically has no control over the learning situation, which makes it difficult to analyze the processes involved in either the acquisition or forgetting of autobiographical memories.

WHY DO WE NEED AUTOBIOGRAPHICAL MEMORY?

Williams, Conway, and Cohen (2008) propose four functions of autobiographical memory. These include *directive* functions, for example what happened the last time you tried to change a car tire, and a more *social* function; sharing autobiographical memories can be a very pleasant and socially supportive activity (Neisser, 1988). In my own case, getting together with friends and reminiscing about our fun times is an example. Conversely, when autobiographical memory is disrupted by amnesia or dementia, this can be one factor that impairs relationships (Robinson & Swanson, 1990), leading to the feeling that "This is not the person I married." Autobiographical memories can also play an important role in creating and maintaining our *self-representation*, hence the value of reminiscence therapy (Woods, Spector, Jones, Orrell, & Davies, 2005), a process described in Chapter 16 whereby elderly patients with memory problems are encouraged to build up a set of reminders of their earlier life based on photographs and personal mementos—items that bring back memories of their younger days. Finally, autobiographical recollection can be used for emotion regulation, as when we need to cope with adversity, or build confidence. One of the problems of depression is that patients find it difficult to recollect positive life experiences when depressed, whereas negative recollections are more readily available, a retrieval effect known as *mood-congruent memory*, which is one form of context-dependent memory discussed in more detail in Chapter 8. Healthy individuals often engage in nostalgia about times past to maintain intimacy with friends, to teach others, and to enhance self-perceptions (Cheung, Wildschut, & Sedikides, 2018).

However, although these functions might be plausible, they are largely speculative. In an attempt to obtain empirical evidence on this matter, Hyman and Faries (1992) questioned people about memories they frequently talked about, and the situations in which they were discussed. They found very few reports of autobiographical memory being used directively to solve problems, with the sharing of experience and passing on of advice being more common. In a subsequent study, they used cue words to prompt memories, finding a distinction between memories that were used internally for self-related functions and those used in interacting with others, but again little evidence of directive use of autobiographical memory.

Bluck, Alea, Habermas, and Rubin (2005) devised the Thinking About Life Experiences (TALE) questionnaire, specifying particular situations and then categorizing the resulting reports as: directive, self-related, nurturing existing social relationships, or developing new social relationships. The factor analysis of the results found considerable overlap between the directive function, the self-related function, and those related to nurturing and developing relationships (e.g., *I enjoyed talking to John; so I think I'll accept his party invitation*). Hence, although it remains plausible that autobiographical memory has a number of different functions, it is unclear that they are clearly separable into different categories in actual practice.

One weakness with the research described so far is the problem of adequate methodology. The studies assume, for example, that participants are aware of the function of such memories and can remember their autobiographical memories and the situations that evoked them in sufficient detail to categorize them. In an area as complex as autobiographical memory, there is clearly a need for the development of a range of methods of study. I discuss this next.

METHODS OF STUDY

One method of tackling this problem is to use diaries in which participants record events, and subsequently try to remember them. This is a useful approach but one that places onerous and persistent demands on participants. A second approach is to probe memory, for example asking for a memory associated with a cue word such as *river*, then analyzing the nature of the responses. A third method is to ask for memories associated with either a specific time period, or a major public event such as the 9/11 attack on New York. Finally, as in the case of semantic and episodic memory, we can learn a good deal from individual differences in autobiographical memory as well as what happens when autobiographical memory breaks down, as the result either of brain damage or emotional stress. These approaches are discussed next.

Diary studies

A central problem in studying autobiographical memory is that of knowing what was initially experienced. Whereas laboratory studies can carefully control which stimuli participants are exposed to and also the encoding conditions, in autobiographical memory studies, every person's memories will differ, and experimenters have no way of knowing whether recall is accurate. One solution to this is to record events in a diary that allows later memories to be objectively checked. Linton (1975) used this method to study her own autobiographical memory. She kept a diary for over five years, recording two events per day, each being briefly described and written on an index card. She tested herself each month by randomly picking out two index cards and deciding whether she could remember the order in which incidents occurred and the date. Because she chose cards at random and then replaced them, she would sometimes test herself on the same incident on several occasions. As Figure 11.1 shows, she observed a powerful effect: The more often an event was probed, the better it was retained. This provided further evidence for the value of retrieval practice in long-term learning as discussed in Chapter 5.

A classic diary study was carried out by the Dutch psychologist Willem Wagenaar (1986), who kept a diary for over six years, on each day recording two events, together with four features or cues to that event. As shown in Figure 11.2, he recorded *who* was involved, *what* the event was, *where* it occurred, and *when*. He also rated the incident for its saliency and whether it was something that happened frequently or was rather unusual, in addition to recording the degree of emotional involvement and whether this was pleasant or unpleasant. He recorded a total of 2,400 incidents. He then tested his memory by selecting an incident at random and cuing himself with one, two, or three retrieval cues, randomizing the order in which the *who, what, where*, and *when* cues were presented. Figure 11.3 shows the mean percentage of questions answered correctly as a function of number of cues. As you can see in this figure, his recall improved as he added

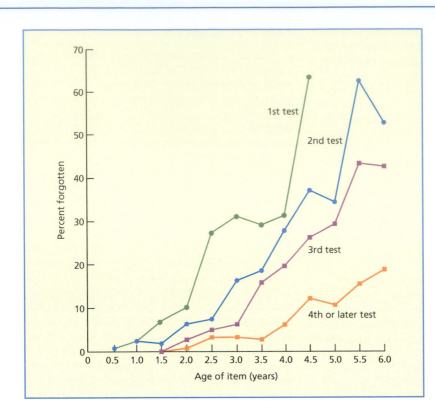

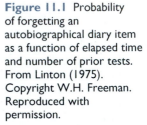

Figure 11.1 Probability of forgetting an autobiographical diary item as a function of elapsed time and number of prior tests. From Linton (1975). Copyright W.H. Freeman. Reproduced with permission.

more cues, an effect we discussed in Chapter 8 as a key determinant of retrieval success. Moreover, Wagenaar found that the *who, what,* and *where* cues tended to be equally good at evoking a memory, whereas the *when* cue, which simply provided the date, was much less efficient. This is perhaps not surprising. Can you remember where you were on July 19 last year? Neither can I, although as we shall see later, some people can.

Wagenaar reports that he found the task to be surprisingly difficult and unpleasant, but that given sufficient cues he could recollect most of the incidents eventually. In a number of cases, he could not remember anything, despite all his recorded cues. However, in those cases where another person was involved, they would typically be able to evoke a recollection, which could be verified by his providing additional information. Does that mean that we never forget anything? Almost certainly not. Wagenaar selected events that were most likely to be highly memorable; for example, going to see Leonardo da Vinci's painting of *The Last*

Supper, accompanied by scientific colleagues. The process of selecting the event would in itself involve retrieval, and in effect a rehearsal, while the process of deciding on his *who, where, what,* and *when* cues would involve a relatively deep level of processing (Craik & Lockhart, 1972). This degree of selection and implicit rehearsal is a problem for diary studies, because they result in memories that are atypically well encoded.

A somewhat more naturalistic approach to encoding of autobiographical memories is to use events reported in letters. One of the authors of this text, Alan Baddeley, has used this method, based on a series of letters sent to his widowed mother during a year in California some 40 years ago (Baddeley, 2012). Baddeley went through the letters, identifying anything that could be regarded as an integrated episode, then classifying each on the basis of the extent to which he could remember it. He distinguished three degrees of vividness of the recollection, together with episodes that "he knew" had happened but of which he had no recollective experience,

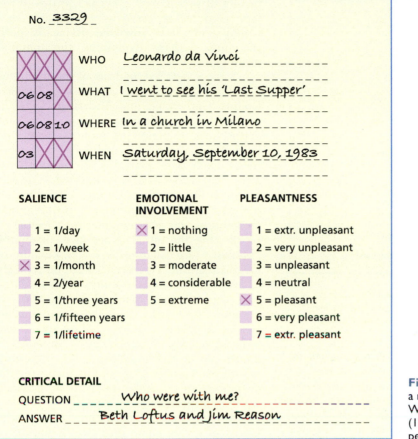

No. __3329__

⊠	⊠	⊠
06	08	⊠
06	08	10
03	⊠	⊠

WHO __Leonardo da Vinci__

WHAT __I went to see his 'Last Supper'__

WHERE __In a church in Milano__

WHEN __Saturday, September 10, 1983__

SALIENCE

 1 = 1/day
 2 = 1/week
⊠ 3 = 1/month
 4 = 2/year
 5 = 1/three years
 6 = 1/fifteen years
 7 = 1/lifetime

EMOTIONAL INVOLVEMENT

⊠ 1 = nothing
 2 = little
 3 = moderate
 4 = considerable
 5 = extreme

PLEASANTNESS

 1 = extr. unpleasant
 2 = very unpleasant
 3 = unpleasant
 4 = neutral
⊠ 5 = pleasant
 6 = very pleasant
 7 = extr. pleasant

CRITICAL DETAIL

QUESTION __Who were with me?__

ANSWER __Beth Loftus and Jim Reason__

Figure 11.2 An example of a recorded event from Wagenaar's diary study (1986). Reproduced with permission from Elsevier.

and those that were completely forgotten. Of 62 episodes identified in the letters, Baddeley judged that he could remember 23, about half of these vividly. One example that stood out for him involved losing his voice on a lecturing trip, then having a lively dinner with Endel Tulving, and the frustration of being unable to croak his own opinions with adequate vigor. The vivid memories were of nontrivial unique events that he remembered having told others about. Of the 62 total recorded episodes, Baddeley had forgotten 26 completely, nearly all trivial, with no recollection of retelling. Retelling of course is a form of rehearsal that, as Linton's (1975) diary indicated, has a major effect on subsequent recall.

The experience of rereading his letters changed Baddeley's view of his own autobiographical memory. Instead of seeing it as a landscape of potential memories extending into the distance with striking peaks of vivid memories and less clear valleys, the experience seemed to him much more analogous to perceiving a limited series of islands of memory in a sea of forgetting. Furthermore, the fact that the "islands" appear to depend on retelling over the years implies that they themselves may not be true memories, but rather memories of memories, a rather sobering thought! In fact, the tendency for our autobiographical recollections to be overly populated with memories about which we have frequently told stories illustrates how autobiographical memory may be different from episodic memory, as it is conventionally studied in the laboratory.

But perhaps this is only true of distant memories? Why should we want to remember relatively trivial events that happened 40

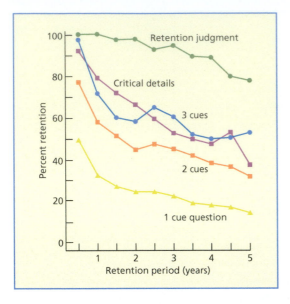

Figure 11.3 Recall of autobiographical incidents as a function of time, given one, two, or three retrieval cues. Reproduced with permission from Elsevier

years ago? And perhaps it is not surprising that surviving memories are rather special, or at least worth telling others about. Would nonselected relatively trivial memories survive over a much shorter period than those reported in diary studies? Brewer (1988) tried to avoid the biased selection of recorded memories in a study that sampled events at random. His 10 participants were each given a beeper and a tape recorder. The beeper went off at random intervals, at which point participants were to say what they were doing, where, what the significance of their activity was, its goal-directedness, and their emotional state. The incidents were tested at delays ranging from 0 to 46 days, using one or other of their ratings as a cue. A total of 414 events were recorded. When subsequently tested, 26% were correctly recalled, 28% were wrong, and 46% evoked a blank. It is likely that, given more cues, more would be recalled but it seems very unlikely that all of the 74% failed memories would be recollected. Indeed, if the study by Misra, Marconi, Peterson, & Kreiman (2018) discussed in Chapter 5 on learning is any guide, it is astonishing participants recalled any of the events at all. Note that in Brewer's study,

the act of providing the event features in the tape recorder to serve as subsequent cues would again have involved atypically deep encoding, perhaps explaining the minimal recall that did occur.

A more detailed analysis of the nature of the items recalled was made by Conway, Collins, Gathercole, and Anderson (1996) in a study involving two participants who kept diaries over a period of months, recording both "events" and "thoughts." These were then mixed with plausibly invented alternatives and recognition was required. This was followed by a categorization as to whether the item was "remembered," meaning that recognition was accompanied by a feeling of recollecting the initial experience, or simply "known" (see Chapter 8 for discussion of this distinction). True events were more likely to evoke a remember response than invented but plausible foils, with items classified as "events" being twice as likely to evoke recollection as entries that were "thoughts." The reduced feeling of remembering thoughts is interesting in that it points to an important role of perceptual experience in anchoring the experience of remembering, a topic to which we shall return later.

In conclusion, diary studies have been useful in giving some idea of the nature of autobiographical memory, and of the relative importance of different types of events and experiences. They do, however, suffer from problems of sampling bias in the events recorded, together with a tendency for the event reporting process itself to result in the enhanced learning of the events selected. Finally, the method requires considerable perseverance from the diarists, who are therefore likely to be a small and atypical sample of the general population.

The memory probe method

An alternative to the diary method is that of cued recall, a method first used by Galton (1879). It was subsequently revived by Crovitz and Shiffman (1974), who gave their participants a word and asked them to recollect an autobiographical memory associated with that word. For example, given the cue

Sir Francis Galton (1822–1911), a Victorian polymath, who in addition to his classic study of autobiographical memory, was a tropical explorer, geographer, meteorologist, anthropologist, and statistician.

word *horse*, this might evoke a memory of the first time you rode a horse. The method has also been adapted to probe for memories from a given time period such as childhood, or of a particular type of incident, for example a happy memory. Despite its simplicity and relative lack of control, this method has been used widely, and productively, including in many studies of brain imaging, as we will discuss later on.

A prominent feature of probed autobiographical memories is their distribution across the lifespan. When left free to recall memories from any period in their life, all healthy participants, whether young or old, tend to recall few autobiographical memories from the first five years of life, termed *infantile amnesia* (see Chapters 9 and 14 for further discussion). They also tend to produce plenty of memories from the most recent period. Those over the age of 40, however, also show a marked increase of memories from the period between the ages of 15 and 30, the so-called reminiscence bump (Rubin, Wetzler, & Nebes, 1986). A cross-cultural study illustrated in Figure 11.4 shows a similar pattern across participants from China, Japan, Bangladesh, England, and

KEY TERM

Reminiscence bump: A tendency in participants over 40 to show a high rate of recollecting personal experiences from their late teens and early twenties.

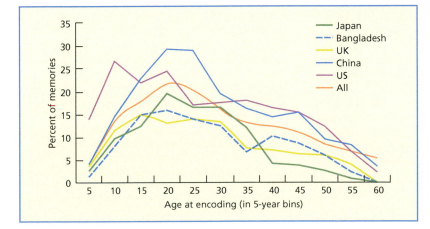

Figure 11.4 Lifespan retrieval curves for participants from five countries. From Conway et al. (2005). Copyright © 2005 Sage Publications. Reprinted by permission.

the US (Conway, Wang, Hanyu, & Haque, 2005). However, there are cultural differences in the average date for the first memory, which occurs at an average age of 3.8 for the US and 5.4 for Chinese participants (Wang, 2006a, 2006b). This might reflect differences in the way that mothers talk to their children, with the US interaction tending to be more elaborate, emotionally oriented, and focused on the past than occurs in Chinese culture (Leichtman, Wang, & Pillemer, 2003). This might also account for a tendency for US recollections of early memories to be longer, more elaborate, and more emotionally toned and self-focused than occurs with Chinese respondents, whose recollections tend to be briefer and to have a stronger collective than individual emphasis (Wang, 2001).

There have been a number of attempts to explain the pattern of autobiographical memories across the lifespan. It probably reflects both a recency effect (see Chapter 3, p. 50) and at least two other processes, one accounting for infantile amnesia (the lack of memories from the first one or two years of life) and the other concerned with the high rate of recalling episodes from the teens and twenties. Many interpretations of infantile amnesia have been proposed. Early theoretical proposals to explain this have included explanations based on Freudian repression and the late development of the hippocampus. More recently, however, a compelling account of infantile amnesia attributes this striking phenomenon to the rapid rate of increase in new neurons in the hippocampus, the introduction of which into the neural network makes it harder to reinstate memories prior to their inclusion. This phenomenon is known as neurogenesis-induced forgetting (see Chapter 9 for a discussion of this process). This account has the benefit that it explains infantile amnesia in many different species of nonhuman animals. However, given the powerful role of schemas in enhancing consolidation of long-term episodic memories, discussed in Chapter 6, the lack of early episodic memories may also be related to the absence, during infancy, of a coherent concept of *self*, a general set of schemas that would gradually be built up on

the basis of memories and experiences (see Chapters 9 and 14 for more on infantile amnesia).

Most interpretations of the reminiscence bump tend to focus on the fact that this is a period when many important things in our lives tend to happen. Berntsen and Rubin (2004) asked their participants to rate a number of important life events, finding that the average age for first falling in love was 16 years, college memories tended to be a rather later 22 years, marriage at an average age of 27, and children at 28. All fell within the period of the bump, making this an important period within what is sometimes known as the life narrative. This represents a coherent account that we create for ourselves as we progress through life—the story of who we are and how we got to this point in our life. Events that influence this are likely to be important to us, to be more likely to be retrieved, and to be more deeply encoded. Indeed, the attachment of salient events such as these to an organized narrative schema in long-term memory likely confers powerful benefits to both consolidation and memory search, as discussed in Chapter 6 on episodic memory. Furthermore, such events as beginning college, making new friends, and falling in love are all likely to be emotionally intense, a factor that increases the accessibility of memories (Dolcos, LaBar, & Cabeza, 2005), particularly when these are positive and occur in young adulthood (Berntsen & Rubin, 2002).

Glück and Bluck (2007) further elaborate the life narrative hypothesis. They collected a total of 3,541 life events from 659 participants aged between 50 and 90 years. Participants were asked to rate their memories on emotional *valence*, their *personal* importance,

> **KEY TERM**
>
> **Life narrative:** A coherent and integrated account of one's life that is claimed to form the basis of autobiographical memory retrieval. A life narrative provides an organized set of schemas with which key episodic events can be integrated, both increasing the chances of consolidation, and making memory retrieval efficient.

The reminiscence bump occurs in early adulthood and reflects memories from a period when many important life events, such as falling in love, getting married, and having children, tend to happen.

and the extent to which the rememberer felt that they had *control* over events. A reminiscence bump was found, but only for positive events over which participants felt that they had a high degree of control, a result that they interpret as consistent with the importance of autobiographical memory in creating a positive life narrative (Figure 11.5). In addition, as can be seen in Figure 11.5, the overall rate at which people recall positively memories overwhelmingly outstrips both negative and neutral memories, despite the fact that, in the weeks and months following initial encoding, negative events tend to be unusually memorable. This positivity bias is a widely reported phenomenon, as we will discuss later in this chapter. Both the positivity bias

and the absence of a reminiscence bump for negative autobiographical memories illustrate the role that motivation plays in shaping which memories remain accessible in long-term memory, a topic discussed in Chapter 10 on motivated forgetting.

An intriguing exception to the reminiscence bump in a person's early twenties occurs when memories are cued by smell. Despite an initial report by Rubin, Groth, and Goldsmith (1984), of equivalence across verbal, visual, and olfactory cues, Chu and Downes (2002) found that memories evoked by smell peaked at an earlier age (6–10 years) than the memories found in the typical verbally cued reminiscence bump. Willander and Larsson (2006) replicated this using a sample of 93 volunteers ranging in age from 65 to 80 years. They cued with items that could not only be represented as a word, but also as a picture or a smell (e.g., *violet, tobacco, soap, whiskey*). Like Chu and Downes, they found a distinct tendency for smells to evoke memories that are rated by their participants as earlier than visually or verbally cued events. How could we explain this? Are odor-induced memories more emotional? Both Herz (2004) and Willander and Larsson (2007) found that they were.

It is, of course, the case that the probe studies described all depend to some extent on the accuracy with which participants can date events. As we saw from Wagenaar's diary study, memory for dating of an incident was the weakest of all the cues. This also

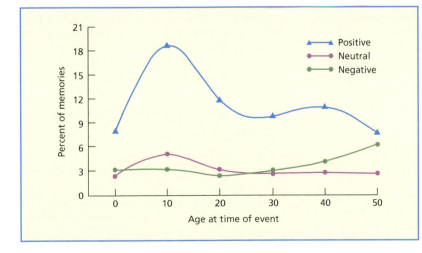

Figure 11.5 Distribution of involuntary memories for participants who were over 40 years old. Only positive memories show the reminiscence bump. From Glück and Bluck, (2007). Copyright © The Psychonomic Society. Reproduced with permission.

presents a problem for the many practically oriented survey studies that are retrospective in nature, requiring respondents to remember, for example, when they last went to the doctor, or how often they eat certain types of foods. A study by Means, Mingay, Nigam, and Zarrow (1988) asked patients who had made at least four medical visits in the last year to recall and report them, subsequently checking against the doctor's records. Performance was poor, particularly for visits that had clustered (25% correct versus 60% for more isolated occasions). People tend to date events indirectly, either by recollecting incidental features such as the weather or "the trees were bare," or by linking it to some other event that can itself be dated, such as a holiday in Paris or the eruption of Mount St. Helens (Baddeley, Lewis, & Nimmo-Smith, 1978; Loftus & Marburger, 1983). These, in turn, are likely to be located within the broader context of a life narrative.

THEORIES OF AUTOBIOGRAPHICAL MEMORY

The preceding discussion focuses on how autobiographical memory is measured, and some interesting generalizations discovered with those methods. But how does autobiographical memory work? What processes does it involve? One attempt to develop an overall theory of autobiographical memory is that proposed by Martin Conway (2005). Conway defines autobiographical memory as a system that retains knowledge concerning the *experienced self*, the "me." Autobiographical memory is always accessed by the cues about the content of the memory desired, but the results of memory search do not always produce recollective experience; hence you might know that you had a trip to Paris last year, but only recollect the episodic detail later, or indeed not at all. Such recollective experiences occur when autobiographical knowledge retains access to associated episodic memories with perceptual details, for example when the knowledge that you went to Paris connects with a specific

memory, such as seeing the Eiffel Tower in the rain. Thus, autobiographical memory includes both *generalized knowledge of events*, and specific episodes. Later in the chapter, we will discuss special cases of people who can recall the former type of knowledge, but who have severe deficits in the latter aspect of re-experiencing.

Such autobiographical recollections are transitory and are constructed dynamically on the basis of the autobiographical knowledge base. The knowledge base itself ranges from very broad-brush representations of lifetime periods to sensory–perceptual episodes, which are rapidly lost. Finally, the whole system depends on the interaction between the knowledge base and the *working self*. The working self is assumed to play a similar role in autobiographical memory to that played by working memory in cognition more generally (Conway & Pleydell-Pearce, 2000). These broad ideas were developed by Conway (2005) into a more detailed account of the way in which the self interacts with memory (Figure 11.6).

The working self comprises a complex set of active goals and self-images. For example, I have the active goal of describing Conway's ideas and am doing so while on a train en route to London's Kings Cross railway station. The goals active in the working self modulates access to long-term memory and is itself influenced by LTM. To write this, I need to access my knowledge of Martin Conway's views. The working self comprises both conceptual self-knowledge—my occupation, my family background, and my professional aims—which in turn are socially constructed on the basis of my family background, the influence of peers, school, myths, and other factors that make up the complex representation of myself.

KEY TERM

Autobiographical knowledge base: Facts about ourselves and our past that form the basis for autobiographical memory.

Working self: A concept proposed by Conway to account for the way in which autobiographical knowledge is accumulated and used.

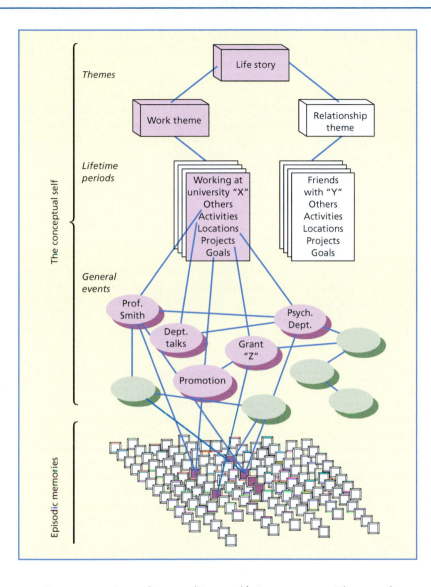

Figure 11.6 The knowledge structures within autobiographical memory, as proposed by Conway (2005). Copyright © Elsevier. Reproduced with permission.

To summarize, the working self is a complex knowledge structure that contributes to encoding information about *what is, what has been,* and *what can be.* To be effective, however, it needs to be both coherent and to correspond reasonably closely with outside reality. When this link is lost, problems occur, which might—in extreme cases—lead to confabulation or delusion (see Chapter 16). Conway and Tacchi (1996), for example, describe a patient suffering frontal-lobe damage following a road traffic accident who had comforting but totally false memories of the support provided by his family.

The *autobiographical knowledge base* is proposed to have a hierarchical structure, with an *overall life story* being linked to subsidiary themes; work and personal relationships, for example. These in turn split up into different time periods: for example, *When I was an undergraduate; My first job; My hopes for the future.* These comprise a number of general "events," which can include individuals and institutions as well as activities: for example, *The psychology department; Professor Smith; Departmental talks; Promotion.* These are still conceptualized at a relatively abstract level but can lead to specific episodic memories; for example, my interview with Professor Smith on applying for a job, or the last departmental research talk I heard. These in turn might have been stored at a more fundamental level containing more detailed sensory-perceptual information; for example, the room where the interview was held, the weather outside, or Professor Smith's tone of voice in offering me the job. In recollecting an event, it is this essentially arbitrary sensory detail that typically convinces us that we have a genuine memory rather than a confabulation (Johnson, Foley, Suengas, & Raye, 1988). Such detail is often visual in character, which is one reason why vivid visual flashbacks are so convincing and potentially so disturbing.

Following Tulving (1989), Conway refers to the process of recollecting such detail and re-experiencing it as being based on auto-noetic consciousness, the capacity to reflect on our thoughts. This ability to reflect on our memories is of course essential in deciding whether a recollection is an accurate record of our past or a confabulation. Accessing such detailed features tends to be relatively slow, typically taking several seconds, whereas access to semantic memory is often performed almost immediately (Haque & Conway, 2001). As we saw in Chapters 4 and 8, patients with frontal-lobe damage can have difficulty both in accessing autobiographical memories and also, once accessed, in evaluating them.

In a later account of the model, Conway and Jobson (2012) discuss the role in autobiographical memory of factors such as the parents' reminiscing style and subsequent discussion of memories with peers, as well as broader social factors such as the manner of thought in the local culture, local heroes and role models, myths, and general attitudes as to what is good and right. Such influences, in which the inner processes of autobiographical memory are shaped by the surrounding sociocultural world, are not depicted in Figure 11.6.

Conway and Jobson stress that the operation of autobiographical memory is goal-related, and that different goals tend to predominate in different cultures. There is, for example, considerable evidence for differences between individualistic cultures that tend to dominate in the West, and more communal and collective attitudes that are characteristic of many Asian cultures. Wang (2008) studied autobiographical memory in US participants who come from an Asian background, probing autobiographical memory related to their US or Asian identity and finding the latter generated more socially oriented memories in contrast to the greater self-focus for US-related memories. Marian and Kaushanskaya (2004) interviewed Russian-English bilingual participants in both languages. Regardless of the language of encoding of a specific autobiographical memory, recollections in Russian were more collectivist than those in English. At a more extended and integrated level, life schemas are also influenced by culture; hence a celebration such as a Bar Mitzvah is likely to tie participants into traditional Jewish culture and a first communion into a Catholic context (Berntsen & Rubin, 2004).

Conway's theory provides a useful framework that pulls together what we know about autobiographical memory, which in turn is likely to lead to further more theoretically oriented questions. For example, how might we test the assumption that the autobiographical database is divided in the way proposed by Conway (2005)?

EMOTION AND AUTOBIOGRAPHICAL MEMORY

So which memories from your life will you remember when you are 80? What factors determine which experiences "stick?" Naturally, one answer to this has to do with the role that memories play in our life narratives, and the corresponding integration this will

---

KEY TERM

Autonoetic consciousness: A term proposed by Tulving for self-awareness, allowing the remember to reflect on the contents of episodic memory.

cause with long-term memory schemata. Another factor concerns how often we recall and revisit a memory, as discussed earlier through the diary study reported by Marigold Linton. Apart from these factors, however, one must also consider the role of emotion in shaping what we remember. Are we destined to permanently remember anything that is highly emotional, regardless of whether it is pleasant or unpleasant? Does the emotion attached to a memory persist stubbornly over time, or does the punch that a memory has decline or event transform? Using some of the methods described at the outset, research on autobiographical memory has addressed these important questions, sometimes with surprising results. We discuss several key phenomena next.

Flashbulb memories are typically vivid, clear and persistent. What were you doing when you heard about the World Trade Center attacks on September 11th 2001?

Flashbulb memory

One might imagine that extraordinary and emotionally significant events could have a special privileged status in your autobiographical memory. Do you remember where you were when you first heard of the 9/11 attack on the World Trade Center? Unlike humdrum events such as routine visits to the doctor, certain occasions appear to give rise to remarkably clear detailed and persistent memories. Brown and Kulik (1977) asked people to recall how and when they had first heard of the assassination of President Kennedy. They found a degree of vividness and detail that was surprising, leading them to propose a new kind of memory system, which they termed flashbulb memory. They argued for a separate process that, given appropriate conditions, leads to a special mechanism resulting in a qualitatively different memory record. They termed this process the "now print" mechanism, whereby extreme emotion was assumed to lead to an almost photographic representation of the

event and its physical context. In subsequent years, this has proved to be an extremely popular area of study. It now seems that whenever a disaster occurs, a cognitive psychologist somewhere will be devising a questionnaire to establish whether flashbulb memories have occurred and trying to answer some of the questions raised by Brown and Kulik's claim.

There is no doubt that people do report very vivid recollections of the point at which they remember hearing about major disasters. It is also the case that the probability of report of a flashbulb memory depends on the degree to which the rememberer was likely to be affected by the event. African-Americans were more likely to have a flashbulb memory concerning the deaths of Martin Luther King and Malcolm X than were European American participants (McCloskey, Wible, & Cohen, 1988), and Danes who reported an involvement with the Danish resistance movement were more likely to have a flashbulb experience, and be able to report on the weather, time of day, and day of the week for the invasion and liberation of Denmark than did those who were less directly involved (Berntsen & Thomsen, 2005).

But do we need to assume a special mechanism to account for these results? The Brown and Kulik conclusions have been

KEY TERM

Flashbulb memory: Term applied to the detailed, vivid and apparently highly accurate memory of a dramatic experience.

scrutinized on two fronts. The first concerns the question of whether flashbulb memories are as accurate as they seem, and the second concerns whether one needs a special mechanism to explain them. In a study based on the Challenger space disaster, Neisser and Harsch (1992) compared the recall of the experience of learning about the event, testing people after one day and retesting after 2½ years, finding a substantial drop in accuracy. For example, after one day, 21% reported first hearing about the disaster on TV, whereas after 2½ years this had increased to 45%. Similarly, Schmoick, Buffalo, and Squire (2000) reported considerable forgetting of hearing the result of the OJ Simpson trial over a period of 32 months.

A further problem is the question of what should be the baseline against which one judges whether a memory is unusually accurate or vivid. Rubin and Kozin (1984) report that memories of high-school graduation or of an early emotional experience can be just as clear and vivid. Should one compare proposed flashbulb memories against distinctive, but nonlifethreatening events? Or against everyday events? Does the choice of control memories and how to measure them influence one's conclusion about whether flashbulb memories are unusually well retained and vivid?

To illustrate this issue, consider a study by Davidson, Cook, and Glisky (2006), who contrasted memory for the 9/11 World Trade Center attack with everyday memories, finding that after a year there was a correlation of 0.77 between the initial and subsequent recollection for the 9/11 incident, indicating very good retention, compared with a correlation of only 0.33 for more everyday memories. In contrast, however, Talarico and Rubin (2003) found the same degree of loss of detail of 9/11 memories and everyday memories. The crucial difference between these two studies appears to be that, whereas Talarico and Rubin's participants themselves produced and recorded their everyday events, (and hence generated their own retrieval cues) in the Davidson et al. study, the experimenters chose the events to be recalled by participants. Cuing an exceptional event (like 9/11) in an unambiguous

way is much easier for the experimenter than providing adequate cues for an everyday event in someone else's life. The latter study, therefore, might suggest that when a carefully crafted control memory is used, there is little difference in the rate with which flashbulb and everyday memories are forgotten over time. Nevertheless, Talarico and Rubin did find that, despite the comparable retention loss for details, participants reported higher ratings of conscious recollection, vividness, and other phenomenological aspects of the memories for flashbulb memories, consistent with superior retention. As we will discuss later on, the phenomenological experiences of remembering (perceived vividness and imagery) play a critical role in the function of autobiographical memory. Indeed, some individuals with severely impaired autobiographical memory, can remember the facts of an event whilst having no ability to re-experience it in their mind's eye. Talarico and Rubin's findings therefore suggest that the critical feature defining flashbulb memories may not be the extent or accuracy of factual detail, but the preservation of the sensory experiences of details that are remembered, and their capacity to evoke reliving.

Although flashbulb memories may not be as impressively accurate and persistent as suggested by Brown and Kulik, there is no doubt that people do have vivid autobiographical memories of flashbulb incidents. There are a number of reasons why this might be. First, such incidents are highly distinctive, with little danger of their being confused with other events, which is not the case for most everyday memories. Second, we tend to talk about such events and watch them repeatedly on TV; in effect, rehearsing them. Third, they tend to be important events that potentially change some aspect of our lives and surroundings; and fourth, they tend to give rise to heightened emotions. Given that all of these factors are likely to enhance memory in one way or another, do we need an additional quite separate theory? The debate on this point continues in the field (in our later discussion of PTSD, for example, we will return to this issue); indeed, despite initial skepticism about Brown and Kulik's proposal, considerable evidence is consistent with superior encoding (see, e.g., Conway, 2013 for a thorough discussion). One might ask whether it is worthwhile attempting to untangle these various contributions that operate under conditions that are by their very nature hard to control? But no doubt studies on this topic will continue, not only because the phenomenon is dramatic and intriguing, but also because the answers matters to victims of trauma, as we discuss later on. It is surely helpful, however, to attempt to understand the possible contributions independently, perhaps subsequently attempting to bring them to bear on the phenomenon of flashbulb memory.

Positivity bias

From the foregoing discussion, one might assume that emotional memories may, in general, enjoy a persisting advantage in long-term autobiographical memory, and be disproportionately represented, relative to more mundane and neutral events. On the whole, emotional events often are retained better. There is, however, a counterintuitive finding in research on autobiographical memory that suggests that negative memories, over time, do not fare nearly as well as do positive memories for most people. The disproportionate accessibility of positive, relative to negative autobiographical memories, over time is referred to as the *positivity bias*.

One of the first studies to examine this issue was reported over 70 years ago (Waldfogel, 1948). Waldfogel gave participants 85 minutes to write down all of the memories that they could remember from the first eight years of their childhood, and rate them as pleasant, unpleasant, or neutral. Waldfogel's participants rated 50% of their events as pleasant, 30% as unpleasant, and 20% as neutral. One explanation is that stimuli in their immediate environment biased participants in some manner to recall disproportionately more positive memories. This does not, however, appear to be correct. For example, Suedfeld and Eich (1995) did a surprising experiment in which they asked participants to float quietly in a sensory deprivation tank for a full hour, relaxing peacefully; after the

hour was up, he asked them to recall 12 memories while they were still floating, and rate each for pleasantness. Participants rated their recalled events as being pleasant (66%) more often than unpleasant (33%). This effect does not reflect a strategic bias in how people voluntarily recall their memories. For example, Berntsen (1996) asked participants to keep a diary of memories that involuntarily popped into mind, noting each memory as soon as it occurred. Such memories are generally triggered by stimuli in the immediate environment, and occur automatically, and so are unlikely to reflect voluntary memory search. Here too, Berntsen's participants were positively biased, reporting that 49% of the events were positive, 32% were neutral, and 19% were negative. Indeed, earlier in this chapter, we reported a vivid example of this positivity bias (see Figure 11.5) in the context of involuntary memory retrieval. In that example, the positivity bias seems to grow with the age of the memory, suggesting a process that gradually renders negative memories less accessible. Even when neutral probe cues are used (e.g., pool, medicine) and participants are explicitly asked to recall either a positive or a negative memory and given a full 25 seconds per cue, they are reliably less able to recall negative memories (35%) compared to positive memories (43%) (Storm & Jobe, 2012). This shows that the bias is not merely a tendency to favor reporting positive memories over negative ones, but instead reflects difficulty in accessing them.

What could account for this clear bias in accessibility? One possibility is that people are more motivated to selectively remember positive events in their lives, and to forget the negative events, which generate unpleasant feelings about themselves (see Chapter 10 on motivated forgetting). The previously mentioned study by Storm and Jobe provided interesting support for this possibility. In their study, they measured each participant's unique capacity to inhibit distracting memories via a simple laboratory version of the retrieval-induced forgetting procedure involving word lists (see Chapter 9 for a description of this method). They proposed that if people tend to inhibit unpleasant memories in daily life, then the better someone is at inhibition on a laboratory task (i.e., the more retrieval-induced forgetting they show), the harder it should be for that person to come up with negative autobiographical memories on an independent test. This is precisely what they found (see Figure 11.7). Interestingly, retrieval-induced forgetting did not predict the recall of positive autobiographical memories, which presumably would not have been targets of memory inhibition when they occurred in participants' lives.

But what evidence is there that people are disposed to forget negative memories out of emotional self-defence? Skoronski, Betz, Thompson, & Shannon (1991) asked participants to record a single distinctive event in a diary every day over several months. In addition, those same participants kept a diary recording events from a friend or relative. At the end of the experiment, participants were tested on their memory for their recorded incidents and also for those of their friend. Revealingly, participants showed a significant positivity bias for their own memories, but instead showed a significant negativity bias in memory for their friend's events, even when the perceived valence of the events was matched. This suggests that when unpleasant events are self-relevant, people are more

motivated to limit access to them in autobiographical memory (see Skowronski, 2011 for a discussion of the role of forgetting in self-enhancement).

Fading affect bias

Most people hope to lead a happy life. With advancing age, we hope to look back on wonderful memories that make us happy and have fewer that upset us. The positivity bias just described suggests one way we make these hopes come true. But what about those memories that do survive throughout our lives? Can we count on happy memories to retain their capacity to spark joy? What about negative memories? The psychology literature creates the impression that negative memories are especially powerful, and durable in their capacity to make us suffer. Indeed, Roy Baumeister proclaimed in the title of an influential paper, the generalization that in psychology, "Bad is Stronger than Good" (Baumeister, Bratslavsky, Finkenauer, & Vohs, 2001). Many people intuitively hold this view, envisioning that upsetting events will inescapably make us upset.

Fortunately for us, bad is not generally stronger than good, when it comes to

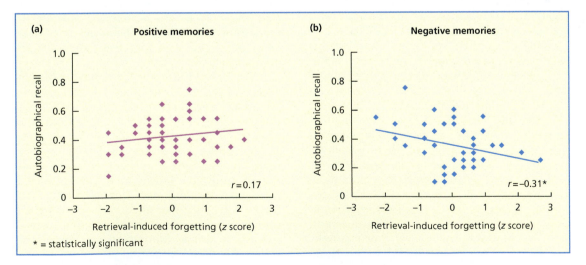

Figure 11.7 The relationship between retrieval-induced forgetting scores on a laboratory task and participants' success in retrieving negative or positive autobiographical memoires using the probe technique. People who are better at inhibiting memories generate fewer negative experiences overall (Storm & Jobe, 2012).

long-term memory. This is reflected in a highly counterintuitive and meticulously documented phenomenon known as the fading affect bias in autobiographical memory. Put simply, events that make us feel good when they happen to us tend to continue to feel good when they are later recalled, but events that lead us to feel bad when they happen tend to not sting nearly so much when they are later remembered. Thus, across time, negative affect for autobiographical memories fades more rapidly than does positive affect does for positive memories (Walker & Skowronski, 2009; Walker, Skowronski, & Thompson, 2003; see Skowronski, Walker, Henderson, & Bond, 2014 for an excellent review). In essence, in memory, *good can be stronger than bad*, in that the emotional kiss packed by good memories tends to outlast the emotional punch packed by bad memories.

Studies of the fading affect bias very often use the diary method (though some have used the probe method). For example, Walker, Vogl, and Thompson (1997) reported three studies in which participants kept a diary either for three months (study 1), two years (study 2), or nine months (study 3). In all three studies participants recorded a single autobiographical event on each day and rated it for its emotional valence and intensity on a seven-point scale ranging from −3 (extremely unpleasant) to +3 (extremely pleasant), with 0 representing neutral. At the end of the diary recording period, the diaries were collected, and the participants returned after an extended delay, which ranged from 3.5 months to 4.5 years. Upon return, participants were asked to use the same seven-point scale to rate how the event made them feel at the time of recall. In each study, they then compared the affect given at the time that the event was originally recorded in the diary, and the affect recorded on the final test by subtracting the latter from the former. The difference between these two scores provides an estimate of how much, in the subjects' eyes, the emotional response to the event changed over time. The results of these three studies can be seen in Figure 11.8. In every case, the intensity of the feeling changed more over time for unpleasant memories than for pleasant

ones, an effect that grew more pronounced as more time passed by since the event.

This pattern has been replicated extensively, under a range of conditions. For example, the fading affect bias occurs regardless of whether the event-related emotions are active (e.g., elated, angry) or passive (calm, sad). The effect begins to emerge as quickly as 24 hours after an event and can be seen for memories that are decades old. It occurs within different ethnicities in the United States (e.g., Caucasion, African-American, Native American, Latino), with differnet age groups (college aged to older adults), and in wide range of different countries internationally

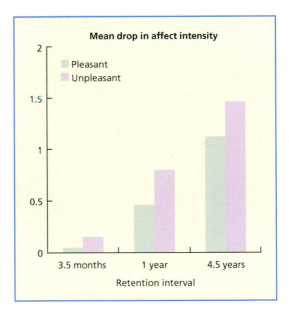

Figure 11.8 The average reduction in affect rating between the initial recording of an autobiographical memory in a diary and a delayed assessment of its affective intensity after 3.5 months, 1 year, or 4 years, separately for positive and negative autobiographical memories. In general, unpleasant memories are perceived as losing more affective intensity over time than positive ones (from Walker et al., 1997), which illustrates the fading affect bias.

(e.g., Europe, China, Ghana, New Zealand, and even Maori tribespeople). Most striking of all, it even occurs regardless of the beliefs of the participants in the experiment. For example, in one study (see Skowronski et al., 2014), students completed a survey that assessed their beliefs about memory, including a question that asked participants about what they believed happened to emotions in autobiographical memories. The options included: *Positive emotions fade more than negative emotions*; *Negative emotions fade more than positive emotions*; *Positive and negative emotions fade equally*, and *Positive and negative emotions get stronger*, or *Other*. Results showed that 49% of the participants believed that positive emotions fade more than negative emotions, whereas 26% believed that positive and negative emotions fade equally; a mere 22% endorsed the view that negative emotions fade more than positive emotions.

Interestingly, those same participants returned later in the day to complete a retrospective memory study in which they recalled three positive and three negative events. For each, they rated both the affect experienced when the event occurred and the affect they felt at the time of event recall. The findings of this test are plotted in Figure 11.9, sorted according to participants' prior beliefs (stated earlier in the day) about how different emotions fade over time.

This figure plots the difference in affect experienced currently and the experience at the time of the original event, separately for positive and negative events. As can be seen, negative events faded significantly more than positive events, which largely retained their positivity. This fading affect bias arose irrespective of participants' beliefs about emotion and memory. A similar finding was observed by Ritchie, Skowronski, Hartnett, Wells, and Walker (2009), except that participants were asked, when recording memories in a diary, to predict how the event will make them feel in two weeks. Upon returning two weeks later, participants exhibited the fading affect bias for negative memories, yet failed to correctly predict the fact that negative memories would fade more.

Thus, despite our fears about the lasting damage that negative emotional events may cause, we may take some comfort in the fact that the punch that negative memories pack fades more rapidly over time—much more so than for the events we feel are pleasant. There is truth in the adage that time heals all wounds, it seems. Unfortunately, however, for those suffering from depression or anxiety, the fading affect bias appears considerably less strong, and even, in some cases, absent (see Skowronski et al., 2014 for a review). What leads negative affect to fade more quickly than positive affect, and why might it be deficient in some populations? The answer, at present, is unknown. However, it seems likely to involve the ways in which people interact their memories when reminded of them, with positive memories likely to be welcomed and relived, and negative memories suppressed or even consciously reappraised to help us feel better about them. Such processes are known to be deficient in psychiatric disorders (see, e.g., Engen & Anderson, 2018). Indeed, when we seek meaning in our negative memories, the negative can at times transmute to positive feelings; indeed, how else could I cheerfully retell my story (related at the outset of this chapter) about how I forgot that I had to give a talk about forgetting. Clearly, it would be

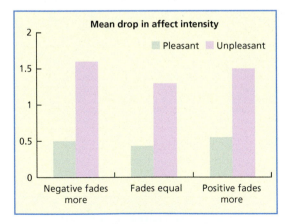

Figure 11.9 The fading affect bias (greater reduction in affect for negative memories over time) occurs, irrespective of participants' overall beliefs about how emotional intensity of experiences change over time. This suggests that the bias reflects a true change in affect for individual memories rather than a simple bias to match one's ratings to a general belief about memory and affect. Data from Skoronski et al., 2014.

helpful to examine the mechanisms underlying the fading affect bias, to better understand what it is that determines whether our pasts haunt us or helps us.

VARIATIONS IN AUTOBIOGRAPHICAL MEMORY FUNCTION

If you look back over your life, do you feel that you have rich memories that you can recall in detail, highlighting the best and most challenging moments of your life? Or, when you look back, does it feel vague and general? For example, perhaps you know many facts about your life, and when events happened, but it doesn't feel like you are "re-experiencing" whenever you remember things. Perhaps this whole idea of memory as "mental time travel" seems odd to you because it doesn't feel that way when you do it, at least for some of your memories. In fact, there is great variation in the extent, richness, and level of re-experiencing associated with autobiographical memories. These variations encompass not only ordinary individual differences in autobiographical memory functions, but also extraordinary cases in which people have either supernormal or highly deficient memory, despite being otherwise healthy. Variation in autobiographical memory also can arise from disease or stress. I describe a range of such cases next, considering the potential implications that this variation has for our understanding of autobiographical memory.

Highly superior autobiographical memory

Over the last decade, remarkable reports have emerged of people with exceptional autobiographical memory capacities. For example, one of the authors, Alan Baddeley, was contacted by a lady who claimed that her husband had a remarkable memory and wondered if he would like to test him. Baddeley was skeptical; people are, in general, not very

good at estimating the quality of their memory, but since they lived locally, he agreed to visit. He took along a few standard tests and an autobiographical inventory (AMI), which probes for information from different periods of life. Baddeley was welcomed by a sociable chap (RM) in his early forties, who worked in an administrative post in local government. RM's performance on standard episodic memory tests proved to be good but not outstanding, unlike his autobiographical memory, which seemed to be rich and quite detailed. However, as he pointed out, we had no way of knowing whether his recollections were accurate.

The next step therefore was to test him on verifiable information. One example was based on RM's support for Bradford City, a local soccer team with a long string of not very successful managers. He proved adept at recalling managers, together with dates, when they had been appointed and when sacked, sometimes coming up with further information as to where he first heard about the sacking. At this point Baddeley decided to enlist the help of Martin Conway, who is an expert in that field. Martin drew up a list of dates; on half of them some dramatic item of news had occurred, and on half this was not the case. Baddeley tested both RM and Martin on a sample of such dates. Below is a typical example:

AB: *"What happened on the 17th of January 1991?"*

Martin: *"Well I have to think to myself what was happening in life at the time. I was a young university lecturer in Lancaster and we would have been back at work after the Christmas break. I taught a course on consciousness. I do remember that (but not much else!)."*

RM: *"It was a Thursday and I do believe it was the first day of the Gulf War [correct]. I was working for the Department of*

Employment at the time and was involved in a training course at Hebden Bridge, I can't recall whether I was actually on the training course or whether I was contributing to the training, but I recall the day quite clearly."

AB: *"Can you remember hearing about the news?"*

RM: *"Yes I think I stayed up late to watch something on TV and I heard about it before I went to bed either later on the Wednesday night or the early hours of Thursday morning."*

RM was also good at generating the date on which events had happened, provided it was something within his interest. This included general elections, where he could provide the date of each British election together with the results in terms of which party had attained the majority of seats and how large the majority. He could reel off the last 34 UK prime ministers and the last 21 US presidents, mentioning that as a child he had carefully copied out and illustrated the many kings of England in chronological order.

He could not always remember particular days however, so given *19th December 2006* he responded:

It was a Tuesday and I have absolutely no idea what I was doing, but on the Monday I was offered a new job in the company where I was working at the time, I remember the guy ringing me and offering me a job. I remember on the Thursday we had a Christmas party and Friday we had friends around, then obviously into Christmas.

He was accurate in his dating of public events, pointing out that the date that a popular comedian had died of a heart attack on TV was not the date recorded in our book of notable events. Baddeley checked the date online, and he was correct.

When asked about his memory he remarked that for many years he had assumed it was just like everyone else's. He said that for him dates provided an important cue to memories and that this process depended on his capacity to work out the relevant day of the week. He reported that his memories typically involved visual imagery, mentally observing himself in a particular situation rather than re-experiencing the event from within. Finally, Baddeley asked him whether his remarkable memory was useful in any way. "Not very" he replied, "though it makes me a popular member of our pub quiz team!" Probably not much of an evolutionary advantage for homo sapiens!

I have described Baddeley's testing of RM in some detail to give a flavor of the way in which RM remembers. He is very different from AJ, that I described in Chapter 9. You may recall that AJ appears to remember every day in her life since her teens in intricate detail, experienced like a continuous movie that is full of emotion. Indeed, AJ describes memories flooding back to her continuously during her daily life, as though she was living with a "split screen" with real-life perception, on the one hand, and memories rolling by, on the other. None of this is true of RM whose memories seem very much like those you or I might have in recalling, for example, Wednesday of last week. The key exception appears to be that he can do this for specific days over many years.

How does he do it? Baddeley argues that RM's abilities rest on organizational structures in memory (Baddeley, 2012). Specifically, he argues that it relies on the difference between the two types of organizational structure. One is hierarchical, beginning with a general concept and systematically splitting it into subconcepts; the example I gave in Chapter 6 was minerals which were then split into metals and stones with the metals then dividing into precious versus nonprecious, etc. Broadbent, Cooper, and Broadbent (1978) contrasted this with an equally helpful matrix structure comprising a series of categories, each split into subcategories. An example might be a set of countries, with, for each, the capital city, a river, a mountain, and a language. For most of us, our autobiographical memory is likely, as Conway suggested, to be hierarchically organized, starting at a broad general level and moving to the more particular. In the above date-based example, Martin Conway began with a broad period of his life, followed by his job, followed by a course he was teaching, whereupon everything stopped because he could not map the course onto specific days. In contrast, RM uses a date-based calendar framework, encoding information on the basis of dates, rather as if he were able to consult his diary for that year. This, if successful, gives him a precise day, which if the information was of sufficient interest at encoding, gives a reasonable chance of retrieval. This only works of course if you are sufficiently interested in dates to use them in an encoding strategy, which RM certainly is, and apparently has been since childhood as indicated by his careful noting of the dates of the kings and queens of England. He mentioned also that in idle moments, such as when shaving, he notes the date and reflects on other things that have happened on that date in his life, a form of rehearsal not available to most of us.

At the same time as Baddeley was carrying out his investigation of RM's memory, the group in California who had discovered the remarkable autobiographical memory of AJ were conducting an extensive investigation into the generality of their earlier results (LePort et al., 2012). They advertised widely for people with what they described as Highly Superior Autobiographical Memory (referred to as HSAM) and were contacted by 150 adults who claimed this capacity. A series of telephone screening tests followed, using a public event quiz which led to a more demanding test based on dates; 31 contacts passed this test, of whom 11 were invited to their laboratory in Irvine,

California to take part in a range of further tests which were also performed by a matched control group.

So, were they like AJ, plagued by an uncontrollable stream of memories, or were they like RM, or were they different again? Their autobiographical memories were first tested by asking them to recall five personal events for which the answers could be verified for accuracy. These included the first day at university, at elementary school, an 18th birthday celebration, and so forth. They then had a series of more standard memory tests, including learning to associate names with faces, visual memory for unrelated objects, forward and backward digit span, recall of a prose passage, and paired associate learning. They were tested then for depression and for obsessionality, together with an interview and behavioral questionnaire about how they used their memory, their knowledge of calendar dates, etc. Finally, the 11 HSAM participants and controls were examined by MRI to look for possible anatomical differences in the structure of their brains.

So what were the results? First of all none of the HSAM group resembled JP in experiencing the stressful continuous stream of lifetime experiences. They were extremely good at recalling public events and dates; they had of course been selected on this basis. They were in addition very much better than controls in their autobiographical performance, both in terms of verified details and in terms of the richness of detail recalled. Like RM, their performance on standard laboratory tests of episodic memory was ordinary. They were slightly better than controls at remembering face–name associations and the array of visual stimuli, but did not differ from controls on backward or forward digit span, or memory for prose or paired associates. In short, their episodic LTM was unremarkable, in striking contrast to their autobiographical memories.

There were no clear personality differences. The HSAM group showed no evidence of depression, although there was a tendency for the group to be somewhat higher in obsessionality. Importantly, however, in a later detailed study of functional differences in brain activity during memory tasks,

---

KEY TERM

HSAM: An acronym for highly superior autobiographical memory cases in which people exhibit extraordinary memory for everyday autobiographical events over many years.

Santangelo et al. (2018) discovered that the superior memory of HSAM participants may owe, in part, to superior functional communication between the prefrontal cortex and the hippocampus, which we know to be important in general for successful retrieval. This suggests that the ability rests, in part, on amplified functionality of underlying networks that support successful memory retrieval in healthy individuals.

Nevertheless, this explanation in terms of brain networks may not be the whole story. Careful scrutiny of what the HSAM group did during retrieval revealed that nine out of 11 reported organizing their memories chronologically, sometimes retrieving events, on the basis of day, and date and year, with six reporting that they habitually recall their memories in this way as a means of passing time or going to sleep. LePort et al. conclude that:

Calendric ability is a unique and defining characteristic of the HSAM population. We speculate that this ability allows for application of a temporal order to their memory, an organisation that possibly facilitates the retrieval of details from their daily life.

(LePort et al., 2012, p. 86)

It is difficult to know how to interpret these findings. For example, did participants' superior functional communication between the prefrontal cortex and the hippocampus arise from intentionally recalling events in a calendrical manner? Perhaps they are rather like the participants who exhibited changes in underlying brain structure arising from extensive practice mentioned in our discussion of structural plasticity in Chapter 5? Alternatively, these participants may retrieve memories in a calendrical way precisely because they were good at it already (and already had the enhanced brain function), similar to participants who practice musical performance more because they have superior musical ability (see Chapter 5 for a discussion of genetic influences on superior performance). Whether calendrical organization

and retrieval are even conscious strategies in these individuals or simply a byproduct of their superior memory is not agreed, with some researchers arguing that intentional strategies cannot explain superior memory in all HSAM participants (Palombo, Sheldon, & Levine, 2018). These intriguing questions remain for future research.

Severely deficient autobiographical memory

In contrast to HSAM, some people have the opposite pattern in which they have severely deficient autobiographical memory, despite being otherwise healthy and high functioning. Several such cases were studied by Daniela Palombo, Claude Alain, Hedvig Söderlund, Wayne Khuu, and Brian Levine (2015), who introduced the term SDAM (severely deficient autobiographical memory) to describe the novel condition. One of the people that Palombo and colleagues studied is Professor Nicholas Watkins, a physicist at the University of Warwick, who has subsequently written eloquently about his personal experiences as somebody with this condition (Watkins, 2018, p. 44):

SDAM, meanwhile, is manifest in the way I experience the past and future. When I think about past events in my life I am aware that I was there, and frequently aware of details that are personal, and not told to me by others. I may also be aware of where people were sitting relative to me, and what color their clothes were. I saw the film Vertigo a few days ago, and still have a sense of the rich redness of the restaurant from the scene

KEY TERM

SDAM: An acronym for severely deficient autobiographical memory, referring to a neuropsychological condition in which otherwise high functioning individuals nevertheless are largely unable to remember autobiographical experiences or re-experience them.

where James Stewart first sees Kim Novak.
I have a feeling that I can form and store
some sort of unseen quasispatial memories.
What I don't have is the experience that
people describe of feeling that they are back
in another time and re-living it. This doesn't
mean that I am untroubled by the past or
future, quite the opposite, it just means that
the past really is "another country" to which
I have no passport. Like A E Housman I can
feel nostalgia for "the land of lost content ...
the happy highways where I went, and
cannot come again," but unlike him I don't
"see [the land] shining plain."
I do certainly feel I often have something in
memory that is at the same time stronger and
more personal than a semantic fact and
weaker than the full-blown episodic recall
experience. I certainly don't feel that I am
"living life in the third person," or "stuck
in time...."

Another one of the participants in the study, Susie McKinnon, described a more stark condition in which all remnants of episodic autobiographical memory appeared to be absent. In an interview with the *Star* newspaper (April 28, 2015), she reported that she only realized that her memory was different when she was 21 when helping out a friend on a class assignment in which they had to devise a quiz to detect early signs of dementia. Her friend noted that her responses to questions on the quiz were fairly unusual, which prompted her to ask others about their experiences of remembering past episodes. She was stunned by their replies.

" 'I just assumed everyone was making up
stories, because I certainly was,' she says,
adding she thought this was an accepted part
of social interaction. You just think up funny
little stories and just keep telling them over
and over again. And that makes them true
for you."

McKinnon said that because she couldn't replay "mental movies" of her past, she simply invented stories with lots of colorful details, some entirely wrong, or instead told stories she had overheard others tell. Sometimes she would base the stories on photos she'd seen. When asked if she remembers her high school prom, she said:

"If you ask me about prom, I know that
I didn't go to prom and I know that
I decorated for prom. But that's different
from remembering anything about it."

She apparently was able to commit these facts about herself to memory, upon being told them by others. Now that she realizes the ways in which she is different from others, she is happy to have a greater understanding of herself. But she is also untroubled about her memory deficit, though she occasionally feels sad when she hears her friends relating memories from their past.

Palombo and her colleagues conducted a wide range of cognitive and neuropsychological tests on the three participants, and also performed both EEG and fMRI. All three participants were in the normal range or higher on nearly all standardized tests. Indeed, they had high normal to superior intellectual abilities on both verbal and nonverbal IQ measures. Their language and working memory performance were perfectly normal. Intriguingly, their memory performance on standard *verbal* tests with stories or word lists was average to superior.

However, laboratory tests did reveal a pattern of memory deficits that help to better characterize the disorder. For example, when their visual memory was tested with the Rey Complex Figure Test (RCFT), in which they had to reproduce a complex visual figure after a 30-minute delay, they were severely impaired (see Figure 11.10). In contrast, when asked to simply copy the figures when they appeared directly in front of them, the SDAM group did perfectly fine, illustrating that there was not a problem with vision or dexterity. Second, when given humorous word-definition pairs (e.g., "A talkative featherbrain–parakeet") to study either

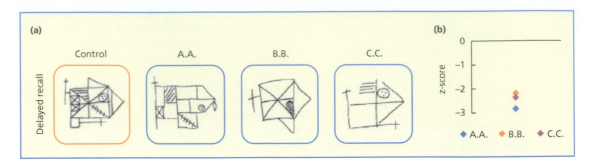

Figure 11.10 Examples of picture recall by three SDAM participants after a 30-minute delay, compared to recall of a typical control participant. Quantified recall scores are depicted in Panel B. All three participants showed marked deficits in visual recall success as reflected in the negative z-normalized scores, relative to age matched normative data. Data from Palombo et al., 2015.

auditorily or visually, they showed an interesting dissociation: after 30 minutes and also 24 hours, they showed largely intact recognition and cued recall of the words, when given the definitions. In contrast, when they were asked 24 hours later to choose whether they heard or saw the information, they were severely impaired, particularly when the item was one that they saw. Moreover, when a remember/know judgment was required (see Chapter 8 for more detail on this method), participants rarely claimed to consciously remember the event of being presented with the information. In tests of their autobiographical memory, participants could often recall facts about past memories, especially more recent ones, but their subjective ratings of the ability to visualize the memories were essentially at floor for all nearly all time periods examined. Taken together these findings suggest that participants' memory deficits related most strongly to visual perceptual information that would ordinarily form the basis of recollection (see also Greenberg & Knowlton, 2014).

What is it about these participants that makes it so hard for them to experience autobiographical remembering? Although much work remains to be done, Palombo's initial explorations with fMRI were revealing. When recalling autobiographical memories in the scanner, participants showed significant reductions in the core brain regions that have been associated with autobiographical memory retrieval, including the medial prefrontal cortex and posterior midline regions

including the precuneus. You may recall from Chapter 6 that the ventromedial prefrontal cortex is associated with the representation of schemas and in the consolidation of episodic experiences into long-term memory. The precuneus, in contrast, is associated with visual memory, which fits their condition very well. We will return to a discussion of these and other brain regions in our later section on neural mechanisms of autobiographical memory.

Perhaps the most intriguing feature of these participants is the extent to which their daily life was untroubled by the severity of their condition. Clearly, they had developed solutions, over the course of their development, that enabled them to cope very well with the demands of everyday life, and even to be somewhat unaware of how different they were. It bears emphasis that these participants are on one extreme of the spectrum of autobiographical memory function, and that a wide range of abilities surely exists in the general population (see Palombo et al., 2018, for a nice review on individual differences in autobiographical memory). Have you ever noticed whether anyone in your life doesn't remember things as well as you?

Psychogenic amnesia

In the preceding sections, we focused on extreme ends of the spectrum of autobiographical memory ability in individuals who are otherwise functioning well. There are, however, conditions in which access to auto-biographical memories can be severely disrupted, owing primarily to psychological distress. As described in Chapter 10 on motivated forgetting, emotion can have a marked effect on the capacity to remember events and experiences, and people often attempt to regulate the accessibility of memories that are distressing. In the extreme, emotional distress can lead to dramatic forgetting that can severely disrupt everyday life, as noted in the case of AMN discussed in Chapter 10. Here we discuss key varieties of *psychogenic amnesia*, or amnesia for autobiographical memories, the genesis of which is primarily psychological, rather than due to physical damage to the brain.

As you might imagine, cases of psychogenic amnesia are uncommon, making the phenomenon difficult to study scientifically. For these reasons, it is particularly remarkable that Michael Kopelman, a long-standing figure in research on this topic, reported an in-depth examination of 53 cases that he has identified over 18 years in his capacity as director of a memory disorders clinic in London (Harrison et al., 2017). In this work, he, Neil Harrison and colleagues identified four different syndromes within psychogenic amnesia, based on patterns in the memory deficits the different groups showed. Importantly, patients were excluded from this sample if they were accused of committing a crime, reducing the likelihood that any of the amnesic deficits reflect malingering for some ulterior motive. Sixteen of the patients underwent a fugue state in which they suffered a remarkable and profound loss of autobiographical memories that spanned the entire course of their lives, together with a total loss of personal identify (14 out of the 16 patients). This state was often accompanied by a period of wandering, often hundreds of miles from home, from which they emerged unsure of where they were or how they got there. For example, in one case, a 26-year-old male was reported missing and found by police six days later wandering around a London park. He had no idea where he was, why he was there, and what he was doing. When police took him home, he did not recognize his family. After a little under a

week in the hospital, he began to recall his autobiographical memories and his identity. In fact, most cases of fugue resolve quickly —in this sample, all within four weeks. This patient, like many, had become depressed and suffered anxiety about his finances and about caring for his sick mother. By his account, he said: "I had a breakdown. My brain decided to close down. I felt as if placed into a grown-up body without knowing the history of the body." In nearly all of the 16 cases of fugue identified in this sample, a neurological explanation could be ruled out.

In addition to fugue, Kopelman and colleagues distinguished three other groups, including fugue-to-focal retrograde amnesia (fugue-to-FRA), pure focal retrograde amnesia (i.e., the FRA group), and a final group they called "gaps in memory." The fugue-to-FRA group differed from the fugue group in two main ways. Like the fugue group, patients lost access to autobiographical memories and their personal identity, often with a period of wandering; but instead of rapidly recovering within four weeks, they continued to suffer

---

KEY TERM

Fugue state: A form of psychogenic amnesia in which a person abruptly loses access to all autobiographical memories from their life, and their personal identity, often resulting in a period of wandering without knowledge of how they got to a location or why. This condition often resolves quickly (within days or weeks).

Fugue-to-FRA: A distinct form of psychogenic amnesia which starts with fugue, but is followed by recovery or relearning of identity, but with persistent and long-lasting deficits in autobiographical memories, especially older ones.

Focal retrograde amnesia (FRA): A distinct form of psychogenic amnesia without fugue or significant loss of identity, but with an abrupt loss of autobiographical memories that can be extensive and persisting.

Gaps in memory: A distinct form of psychogenic amnesia without fugue or significant loss of personal identity, but with an abrupt loss of discrete periods of time, ranging from hours to months. Multiple gaps may be present.

persisting amnesia for their life history that spanned anywhere from six months to the entirety of their lives. Many of them reported "relearning" their identity. The 16 patients in the FRA group, in contrast, didn't generally lose their personal identity for long and didn't wander anywhere, but instead abruptly lost access to their autobiographical memories for much of their lives—a condition that persisted for the majority of the patients. Finally, the five patients in the gaps in memory group generally did not suffer a loss of personal identity and did not wander, and, in fact, retained most of their autobiographical memories. They are distinguished, however, in that they lost access to specific events or time periods, with the duration of the gap ranging from six hours to 90 days. Some patients had multiple gaps in their memories. A common theme in most of these patients, irrespective of group, was that the amnesia was typically preceded by (a) a severe crisis, (b) a past or current history of clinical depression and other disorders, and, in many cases (c) a prior history of head injury or other neurological symptoms, although this history could never be directly tied to the disorder, and in many cases, was entirely absent.

Kopelman and colleagues examined all patients in a variety of ways and found them not to differ substantially from control participants on IQ, executive function, or the ability to learn new things in standard memory tests, though there were modest deficits in visual recall. More importantly, all patients exhibited dramatic evidence of losing access to their personal semantics (general facts about themselves) and their autobiographical memories both during initial examination and, to varying degrees, on a delayed follow-up (see Figure 11.11). The fugue participants differed from the FRA groups in two important ways. First, as can be seen in the figure, whereas the fugue patients lost the entirety of their personal semantics and autobiographical memory across their whole life span, the FRA patient groups showed a temporally graded amnesia that was most severe for older memories, and less severe with memories closer in time to the onset of the amnesia. Kopelman and

colleagues refer to this as the reverse temporal gradient of retrograde amnesia, because it is precisely the opposite pattern that occurs for organic amnesic patients (as we will discuss further in Chapter 16 on memory disorders). Strikingly, however, upon a delayed follow-up, the fugue patients recovered almost fully their personal semantics and many of their autobiographical memories, whereas the FRA patients remained markedly impaired.

The previous findings paint a compelling portrait of the severity of these patients' deficit in autobiographical memory retrieval. They do not, however, give a good sense for what the condition feels like to the participants themselves. Interestingly, Kopelman and colleagues describe the types of personal experiences that some participants report about what it feels like to have their condition. He reports that participants often made remarks like "It's like a box locked away, and I don't really want to open it" and "I put things in boxes … I know the memories are there … but I cannot get access to them." These kinds of remarks suggest that the participants know that their memories are still there and can sense them, but that something has blocked access to them, presumably because they may be distressing. This is certainly consistent with the extreme emotional distress that typically elicits these conditions. Indeed, as discussed in Chapter 10 on motivated forgetting, there is evidence in such patients of the involuntary application of memory control mechanisms that may be responsible for limiting access to their past.

Several aspects of these conditions hold fascinating lessons for our understanding of autobiographical memory and its relationships to other forms of memory. First, although most of these participants lost access to their personal semantic knowledge,

---

KEY TERM

Reverse temporal gradient: The tendency, in focal retrograde amnesia, for the oldest autobiographical memories to be forgotten more than more recent ones, the opposite to what is shown in organic amnesia (see Chapter 16 on memory disorders).

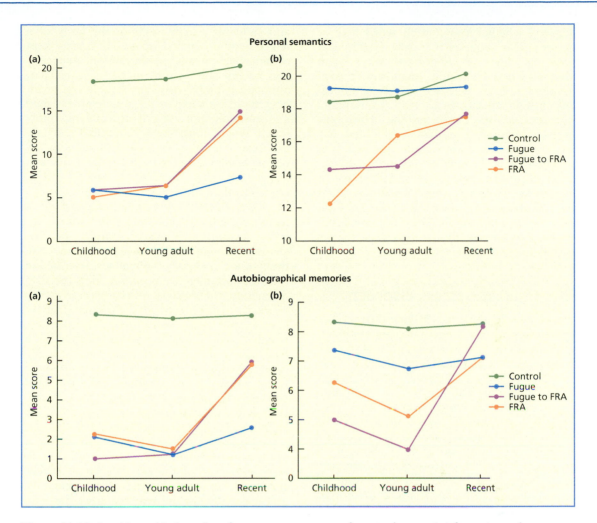

Figure 11.11 Autobiographical recall performance on measures of personal semantic information and autobiographical memory retrieval for memories of childhood, young adulthood, and recent time periods. The left column represents data collected from the initial assessment; the right column represents performance at a delayed follow-up test. Data from control participants, fugue, fugue-to-FRA, and FRA are plotted. Dramatic memory deficits are evident for both types of information at all time periods whereas the fugue patients recovered quickly (compare left panels vs right panels), especially for personal semantic information. The remaining patients exhibited an inverse temporal gradient, with more severe impairment for older memories, that persisted over sessions. Data from Harrison et al. (2017).

none of them lost the ability to talk or understand the objects or events in the world around them. In other words, they seemed to have intact semantic memory, with a selective impairment of the personal aspect of semantics. The fact that participants lost their personal semantics together with their autobiographical memories suggests that these forms of knowledge have something in common that distinguishes them from general semantic knowledge. This may provide support for the idea that autobiographical episodes and personal semantic knowledge are integrated in some manner, consistent with Conway's theory of autobiographical memory discussed earlier. Second, most patients showed preserved performance on standardized laboratory tests of episodic memory, whether tested with word lists or pictures. This suggests that autobiographical memories differ in important ways from laboratory-based episodic memories, raising questions about whether autobiographical and episodic memories as truly overlapping capacities, as one might assume. Third, the reverse temporal gradient exhibited by patients with focal retrograde amnesia suggests that it is the oldest and more consolidated memories that are most vulnerable to disruption. Together, these features suggest that psychogenic amnesia may be substantially tied to brain systems that represent consolidated memories, though this must remain speculative at present.

Post-traumatic stress disorder

In psychogenic amnesia, extreme distress triggers amnesia, but sometimes, the opposite outcome occurs: hyper-accessibility of the distressing autobiographical content. The term post-traumatic stress disorder (PTSD) applies to the symptoms that can follow from situations of extreme stress such as rape, near drowning, or a horrific traffic accident. PTSD involves "flashbacks," extremely vivid and involuntary memory intrusions of the scene of the initial terror. This is usually accompanied by nightmares and a more general state of anxiety (Foa, Rothbaum, Riggs, & Murdock, 1991). Whereas there is often a life-threatening aspect to the experience generating the flashback, this is not essential. As a student, one of the authors, Alan Baddeley, worked for a time as a hospital porter. He occasionally had to wheel bodies to the morgue, not something he found easy to adapt to, although the body was covered by a device known locally as the "tureen." Then, on one trip, he had to pass through the autopsy room

KEY TERM

Post-traumatic stress disorder (PTSD): Anxiety disorder whereby a dramatic and stressful event such as rape results in persistent anxiety, often accompanied by vivid flashback memories of the event.

and suddenly caught sight of the body of a naked woman ripped open. The image kept coming back at apparently random moments, and he can still "see it" over 50 years later, although happily with considerably less vividness. Baddeley's experience was relatively mild and certainly not directly threatening. How much worse must it be continually to re-experience a rape, or being surrounded by people being burned in a fire, or drowning in a shipping disaster (Cardena & Spiegel, 1993, Foa & Rothbaum, 1998)?

Do flashbacks represent a different kind of memory, perhaps something akin to the flash-bulb memories discussed earlier in this chapter? Brewin (2001) suggests that they do, though not in exactly the manner described in the flashbulb memory proposal. He suggests a distinction between *verbally accessible memory*, which links with the normal memory system, and *situationally accessible memory*, which is highly detailed when it occurs as a flashback but (diverging from the flashbulb memory concept) cannot be called to mind intentionally. It is certainly the case that considerable memory for detail can occur in the context of amnesia for other aspects of the situation. Harvey and Bryant (2000) describe a patient who was a passenger involved in a road traffic accident and who has vivid flash-back memories of the car they hit, its color, the floral hat worn by one of its occupants, and a soft toy in the rear window, but who could recall nothing after that point. He was a skilled professional driver and felt considerable guilt at not having called out to warn the driver. Eventually, it was demonstrated to him that his perception of the time available was illusory, and that he had absolutely no possibility of influencing the accident. He recovered from his PTSD, but never went back to driving as a professional.

The precise mechanism underlying memory disturbance in PTSD remains uncertain. One possibility is that it is based on classical conditioning, with the environmental stimuli associated with the horrific moment being powerfully associated with the feeling of terror (see Chapter 5 for detailed discussion of classical conditioning). As a result, incidental stimuli or thoughts can act as a conditioned stimulus that can trigger the emotional response, bringing back the associated memory. Indeed, some treatments of PTSD use this model, focusing on the extinction of the fear response. The response is cued by having the patient imagine the scene under safe conditions controlled by the therapist, leading gradually to the extinction of the fear response (Rothbaum & Davis, 2003). Sometimes, virtual reality is used; for example, having a pilot who has developed PTSD under combat conditions, fly a simulated helicopter sortie over "virtual Vietnam."

In many cases, such treatment leads to a reduction of the symptoms. However, this is not always the case. Furthermore, it is of course the case that, given an equivalent level of stress, a relatively small fraction of people develop PTSD, and those who do sometimes recover spontaneously. Figure 11.12 shows the approximate proportion of people responding in each of these ways following exposure to a traumatic event such as a terrorist attack or the death of a spouse (Bonanno, 2005). What makes the difference?

The answer to this question might lie in the response of the autonomic nervous system (ANS) to stress. In a threatening situation, the amygdala signals the ANS to release adrenalin and cortisol, stress hormones that alert the organism for flight or fight. When the danger passes, the brain normally signals the adrenal glands to stop producing stress hormones, gradually bringing the body back to normal. It is suggested that in PTSD patients, this corrective process is reduced, leading to a more prolonged period of stress. There is some evidence that treatment with propranolol, which aids this recovery process, might reduce the likelihood of PTSD (Pitman et al., 2002; Vaiva et al., 2003). This does not lead to forgetting of the traumatic event but it does reduce the emotional impact of the associated memories.

There is also some evidence that patients with PTSD might have a somewhat smaller hippocampal volume than those without. This raises the question of whether the stress has actively reduced the size of the hippocampus, or whether a small hippocampus has made the patient more vulnerable. Animal studies have suggested that prolonged stress can disrupt the operation of the hippocampus, possibly even leading to neuronal death (McEwen, 1999; Sapolsky, 1996). An ingenious study by Gilbertson et al. (2002) tackled this problem by studying Vietnam veterans who had developed PTSD, and who had a twin who had not experienced Vietnam. Both PTSD veterans and their unexposed twins had smaller hippocampi than veterans who had experienced stress in Vietnam without developing PTSD and their unexposed twins. It appears to be the case, therefore, that a reduced hippocampus makes one more vulnerable to PTSD, presumably because a smaller hippocampus is less able to recover from the huge surge in adrenalin associated with extreme stress.

Another factor that is likely to contribute to persisting intrusive memories in PTSD may have to do with the capacity of the person to voluntarily control the retrieval process. As discussed in Chapter 10 on motivated forgetting, people have the capacity, when confronted with reminders to unwanted memories, to suppress the episodic retrieval process, preventing the memory from coming to mind in response to the reminder. Under normal circumstances, in healthy individuals, suppressing retrieval in this manner makes

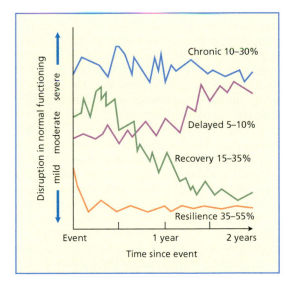

Figure 11.12 Patterns of recovery function following post-traumatic stress disorder (PTSD), with the approximate percentage of patients following each pattern. Data from Bonanno (2005).

people forget the suppressed content, resulting in a phenomenon known as suppression-induced forgetting (see Chapter 10 for review). One possibility is that this regulatory process may be deficient in the people who are most vulnerable to the development of PTSD, making it impossible for them to successfully suppress and eventually diminish accessibility of upsetting content.

Evidence for a deficit in memory inhibition in PTSD has now been reported in people with chronic PTSD (Catarino, Küpper, Werner-Seidler, Dalgleish, & Anderson, 2015; Waldhauser et al., 2018). For example, with Ana Catarino and colleagues, we tested whether repeatedly suppressing unpleasant scenes in response to highly related reminders led to suppression-induced forgetting in people diagnosed with PTSD and control participants who had undergone similar trauma, but who had not developed PTSD. Participants with PTSD showed significantly less suppression-induced forgetting than did control participants, exhibiting little ability to forget the distressing images (see Figure 11.13). Importantly, the deficit in suppression-induced forgetting shown by people with PTSD was related to the severity of their intrusive symptoms in everyday life, suggesting that the deficit in memory inhibition may contribute to their condition. In a related study, Markus Streb and colleagues found, in healthy individuals, an independent measure of suppression-induced forgetting predicted the vulnerability of their participants to developing memory intrusions in the week following exposure to a traumatic video (Streb, Mecklinger, Anderson, Lass-Hennemann, & Michael, 2016). Given these findings, the persisting nature of autobiographical memory intrusions may, in part, reflect a deficit in motivated forgetting.

NEURAL BASIS OF AUTOBIOGRAPHICAL MEMORY

When I sat down to write about how I forgot that I was supposed to give a lecture on forget-

ting, remembering the event felt like a combination of remembering a story and reliving an experience. I have told other people this story on many occasions, and so the story had a familiar structure and rhythm to it, along with a set of details I always choose to mention, and a slow and dramatic build-up of Justin's revelation of where I was supposed to be. At the same time, while I tell that story, I feel as though I can see the layout of the kitchen and hear Justin's voice on the phone; I can visualize where I was outside the cinema, how I felt while preparing the lecture, and what the cinema room looked like. In other words, the memory felt like a mixture of facts and episodic memory. Moreover, the ability to relive the sensory elements felt critical to the event being a real, true memory.

So, what was going on in my brain as I remembered that story? And do these processes of autobiographical memory retrieval differ from those involved in more simple laboratory memory tasks? Our discussion of different patients offers clues. For example, cases of severely deficient autobiographical memory (SDAM) confirm how imagery is key to reliving the past. For all SDAM participants, any task that rested on "seeing in the mind's eye," was extremely difficult; their memories had the character of factual knowledge, devoid of re-experiencing. Supporting this importance of imagery, Greenberg and Rubin (2003) note that neuropsychological patients with damage to the areas involved in visualization also have poor autobiographical memory. The psychogenic amnesia patients, in contrast, offer different lessons. They show that autobiographical memories and personal semantic knowledge about who you are can often be impaired together, even when general semantic knowledge about the world is spared. Importantly, both populations illustrate that it is possible to perform well on many laboratory tasks of episodic memory, while having profound impairment in retrieving autobiographical memories. So, are autobiographical and episodic memory related, or are they different?

Over the last two decades, a growing body of research has sought to address the brain mechanisms of autobiographical memory, including both imaging studies, and studies with neuropsychological patients.

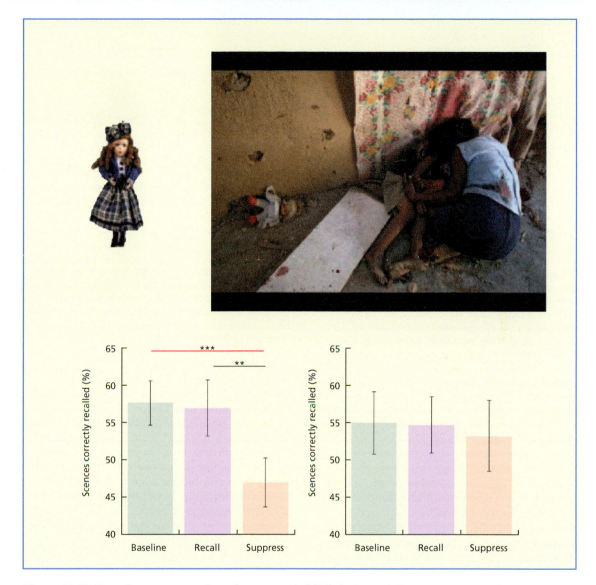

Figure 11.13 Typical cue-target pair from Catarino et al. (2015). Right panel illustrates participants' ability to recall the scene on the right, given the object on the left in the Baseline, Recall, and Suppression conditions, separately for the control participants (left) and participants with PTSD (right panel). Whereas suppression impaired participants' recall of scenes in the control group (relative to Baseline recall), this did not occur for people with PTSD, illustrating a deficit in the ability to forget unpleasant memories. Psychological Science, Failing to Forget: Inhibitory-Control Deficits Compromise Memory Suppression in Posttraumatic Stress Disorder, Vol. 26, Issue 5, 2015 © SAGE.

Some important general lessons are emerging from this work about what brain areas are important to remembering our personal past. Consider, for example, a recent meta-analysis of autobiographical memory studies using neuroimaging in healthy participants (Boccia, Teghil, & Guariglia, 2019). In this meta-analysis, they combined the data from 79 different fMRI experiments with over 1,400 participants, all of them instructed to retrieve their personal experiences using the probe method described earlier in this chapter. The results of this meta-analysis are illustrated in Figure 11.14. In general, when

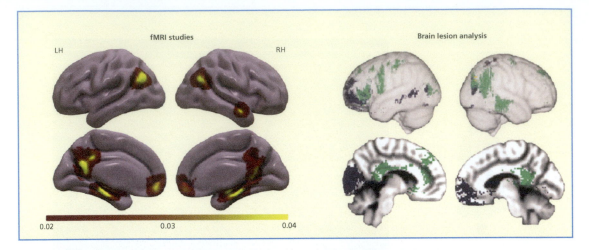

Figure 11.14 Left panel: Brain areas that are consistently activated during autobiographical memory retrieval tasks using the probe method (Boccia et al., 2019). Upper rows indicate activations on the left and right lateral surfaces of the brain; lower rows indicate activations in the left and right medial walls of the brain. Right panel: Brain areas that predict performance on retrieving personal semantic information (in black) and autobiographical events (in green) in neuropsychological patients. Green and black areas represent areas wherein lesions to the brain are significantly associated to test performance across a sample of 92 participants. Data from Phillipi et al., 2015 © OUP.

people retrieved autobiographical memories in response to cues, it activated a consistent set of brain regions, including both the left and right hippocampus and adjacent parahippocampal cortex, confirming an important role of this critical structure in retrieving older memories. You may recall from Chapter 6 in our discussion of episodic memory the critical role the hippocampus plays in memory, as vividly illustrated by the plight of Henry Molaison, who suffered from amnesia. Seeing the important role of the hippocampus in this analysis is consistent with the tendency for Henry and other amnesics to show retrograde amnesia, or to forget events from several years before their brain damage.

However, as the figure illustrates, the hippocampus was not the only region involved. Autobiographical retrieval also required activity in the posterior midline cortex (including posterior cingulate cortex, precuneus, and the parieto-occipital sulcus, visible in the left side of lower left panel of the fMRI plots). These regions have previously been found to be important for spatial imagery (e.g., Epstein, 2008), and contextually rich events, likely reflecting the retrieval

of detailed visuo-spatial features of personal memories. Consistent with this, Sheldon, Farb, Palombo, and Levine (2016) found that in healthy participants, individual differences in the ability to recall vivid sensory details of their autobiographical memories were related to how effectively this particular region interacted with the hippocampus. Perhaps unsuccessful interactions between the hippocampus and this region may be the basis for deficient re-experiencing of personal events in SDAM, a hypothesis worth testing.

Finally, as the lower two images in the fMRI panel illustrate, the ventromedial prefrontal cortex also appears to be critical in retrieving autobiographical memories. You may recall this region from Chapter 6, as playing a role in representing schematic

KEY TERM

Posterior midline cortex: An area adjacent to and including the posterior cingulate cortex, often including the precuneus and retrosplenial cortex, which appears to be critical for autobiographical memory retrieval, especially for the reinstatement of vivid visuo-spatial details.

knowledge, and in integrating new experiences with those schemas. Given that retrieving autobiographical memories relies on schemas, particularly schematic knowledge about oneself, the involvement of this region makes sense. Perhaps retrieving the "story" behind my memory of forgetting to give a talk, might have been driven by activity in this region, especially if my story became schematic over time. Indeed, the vmPFC appears to be more important for retrieving personal semantics than it is for retrieving the episodic and sensory elements of events, which rely more on the posterior midline areas just discussed. How do we know this? Carissa Phillipi, Daniel Tranel, Melissa Duff, and David Rudrauf (2015) studied 92 participants with damage to varying parts of the brain. They related these patients' performance on an autobiographical memory test to each voxel within the brain, to determine whether damage to each voxel predicted test performance. They found that memory for personal semantics relied heavily on vmPFC and other regions (seen in black in Figure 11.14 on the right side); in contrast, memory for episodic details of events relied on other regions, including the posterior midline area (shown in green in Figure 11.14).

Given that we have a clearly emerging picture of the brain areas involved in autobiographical memory, how can we explain why SDAM and psychogenic amnesia patients seem to have such problems with autobiographical memory, yet do fine on many simple tests of episodic memory done in the laboratory, with words, stories, and pictures? Work by Kathleen McDermott, Karl Szpunar, and Shawn Christ (2009) suggests one answer. These investigators conducted two meta-analyses over many different studies, one looking at areas of the brain involved in autobiographical retrieval (see Figure 11.15, in red), and the other looking at areas of the brain involved in conventional laboratory tests of episodic memory retrieval (see Figure 11.15, in blue). Intriguingly, the brain areas detected by these analyses suggest that autobiographical retrieval and standard episodic memory tasks involve quite different collections of processes, as the

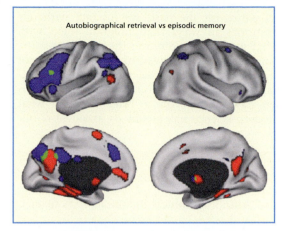

Figure 11.15 Brain areas that are consistently activated during memory retrieval in autobiographical retrieval tasks using the probe method (in red) and laboratory-based episodic retrieval tasks involving recognition of individual items (blue). Overlapping areas are in green. Data from McDermott et al., 2009. Reproduced with permission from Elsevier.

regions hardly overlapped (overlapping areas are colored in green in Figure 11.15). Much work is being done to try to pin down the precise processes that lead to these discrepancies. Is it that autobiographical memories are consolidated? More schematic? More richly visual? More dynamic? The origins of the differences remain unknown at present. At a minimum, these findings recommend caution in assuming that episodic memory and autobiographical memory are exactly the same. Perhaps this may explain why Nicholas Watkins and Susie McKinnon (people with SDAM) can remember the factual elements of their experiences but cannot re-experience them like the rest of us.

CONCLUDING REMARKS

Our past has the potential to bring joy or make us suffer. Whichever of these it does at any given time, our pasts always define who we are. Our memories are the remote horizons enabling us to see where we have been, and judge what we have done, and to rest comfortably, at long last, in advancing age, in the knowledge that we have had a life well lived.

As we revisit the past, we interact with our memories in ways that integrate them with what we know about and the world, creating a narrative for our lives, and with the aim of understanding ourselves, and making us feel happier and more meaningful. In this chapter, we have given you a brief tour of what modern science has taught us about how our personal autobiographies are formed, organized, and retrieved and have discussed whether this form of memory may be different than conventional episodic memory. Although there are very clearly relationships between the two constructs, it is also obvious that much remains to be understood about the human capacity for mental time travel.

SUMMARY

- Autobiographical memory refers to memories across the lifespan for both specific events and self-related knowledge.
- Autobiographical memory serves utilitarian, social, and emotional functions, including the construction of a representation of self.
- Autobiographical memory is difficult to study because we have no record from the time that the original memory was encoded, and so cannot easily judge people's accuracy.
- Diary studies ask people to record events in diaries as they occur, providing an objective record. However, the act of remembering one's day, choosing a memory, and recording it may modify the memory and strengthen it, making it unclear how well later memory for the events represents memory in daily life.
- Autobiographical memories are easier to recall if they have been retrieved a lot previously, and if more cues are available.
- Much research involves the probe method, whereby autobiographical memories are evoked either by presenting a cue word or by asking for memories from a specified life period.
- For people over the age of 40, the temporal distribution of recalled events typically shows a peak extending from the late teens to early thirties, the reminiscence bump, probably reflecting an important period in building up a life narrative.
- The reminiscence bump occurs for positive, but not negative memories.
- Conway proposed a theory of autobiographical memory composed of an autobiographical knowledge base and a working self. The autobiographical knowledge base is organized as a hierarchy with different life periods and themes, ultimately linking to specific episodic memories.
- Extraordinary and emotionally significant events often lead to superior autobiographical memories often referred to as flashbulb memories. Flashbulb memories are associated with a subjectively greater feeling of vividness and detail, although they are not necessarily more accurate or persistent than other memories.
- Most people's autobiographical memory exhibits a pronounced positivity bias, wherein positive memories enjoy greater accessibility than do unpleasant memories. This difference in accessibility may be linked to the manner in which they interact with their memories, upon being reminded of them, and their motivation to enhance positive experiences and minimize accessibility of unpleasantness.
- Over time, the emotion created by memories exhibits a phenomenon known as fading affect bias, in which the affective intensity of positive memories diminishes far less rapidly than the affective intensity of negative memories.

- Some people exhibit a phenomenon known as highly superior autobiographical memories in which they can recollect nearly every day of their lives, when simply given a random date. For some of these people, this may arise from adopting a unique calendrical organization to their memories, but for others, it appears less strategic and more involuntary. These patients show evidence of enhance prefrontal-hippocampal connectivity.
- Other people exhibit severely deficient autobiographical memories, in which they have little capacity to consciously recollect or re-experience the events of their lives. Often, such individuals can remember facts about the events in their lives, even when they lack a feeling of re-experiencing. This condition is often associated with deficits in mental imagery, and with reduced activity in brain structures relating to visuo-spatial processing.
- Neither people with superior nor deficient autobiographical memory show unusual performance on many standard laboratory tests of episodic memory, though SDAM participants do have difficulty in long-term visual memory tests.
- Psychogenic amnesia refers to profound deficits in autobiographical memory arising from purely psychological causes. There are different varieties, including fugue, focal retrograde amnesia, fugue-to-FRA, and gaps in memory.
- Psychogenic amnesia patients often perform perfectly fine on standard laboratory tests of episodic memory.
- Focal retrograde amnesia patients exhibit a reverse temporal gradient in their forgetting.
- Psychogenic amnesia doesn't just affect event memories, but also personal semantics, even though general semantic knowledge is intact.
- Post-traumatic stress disorder is a condition induced by a trauma that results in persisting flashbacks of the autobiographical experience. These flashbacks are extremely distressing and a central feature of the disorder.
- Many different factors may contribute to PTSD, including deficits in memory control processes discussed in Chapter 10.
- Autobiographical memory retrieval reliably engages the hippocampus, posterior midline cortex, ventromedial prefrontal cortex, and several other brain areas. Damage to the ventromedial prefrontal cortex is associated with deficits in personal semantic knowledge, whereas deficits in posterior midline cortex are associated with impaired autobiographical event retrieval and recall of sensory details.
- A direct comparison of the regions involved in autobiographical retrieval and episodic memory tasks reveals surprisingly distinct networks which may partially account for the many instances in which autobiographical memory can be disturbed without affecting performance on laboratory tasks. Researchers are still trying to understand what differences between these tasks lead to these differences in brain networks.
- Autobiographical memory and episodic memory are clearly related but may also be distinct in important ways.

POINTS FOR DISCUSSION

1 Would it matter if you lost access to your autobiographical memory? If so, in what way?
2 What are the relative strengths and weaknesses of diary studies and probe methods for studying autobiographical memory?
3 Upsetting events often lead to persisting thoughts about the unpleasant occurrence. Explain how it could be that, over time, positive memories enjoy greater lasting accessibility than negative memories.
4 If you had to describe the stages in your life to another person, and the sequence of major and minor events, what story would you tell? What does this reveal about the way you have your memories organized in your mind? Where are the biggest gaps in your autobiographical memories, and why do you think they occur?

FURTHER READING

Berntsen, D., & Rubin, D. (2012). *Understanding autobiographical memory: Theories and approaches*. Cambridge: Cambridge University Press.

Mace, J. (2019). *The organization and structure of autobiographical memory*. Oxford: Oxford University Press.

Watson, L. A. (2017). *Clinical perspectives on autobiographical memory*. Cambridge: Cambridge University Press.

REFERENCES

Baddeley, A. D. (2012). Reflections on autobiographical memory. In D. Berntsen & D. C. Rubin (Eds.), *Understanding autobiographical memory: Theories and approaches* (pp. 70–88). Cambridge: Cambridge University Press.

Baddeley, A. D., Lewis, V. J., & Nimmo-Smith, I. (1978). When did you last …? In M. M. Gruneberg, P. E. Morris, & R. N. Sykes (Eds.), *Practical aspects of memory* (pp. 77–83). London: Academic Press.

Baumeister, R. F., Bratslavsky, E., Finkenauer, C., & Vohs, K. D. (2001). Bad is stronger than good. *Review of General Psychology, 5*(4), 323–370.

Berntsen, D. (1996). Involuntary autobiographical memories. *Applied Cognitive Psychology, 10*(5), 435–454.

Berntsen, D., & Rubin, D. C. (2002). Emotionally charged autobiographical memories across the life span: The recall of happy, sad, traumatic and involuntary memories. *Psychology and Ageing, 17*, 636–652.

Berntsen, D., & Rubin, D. C. (2004). Cultural life scripts structure recall from autobiographical memory. *Memory and Cognition, 32*, 427–442.

Berntsen, D., & Thomsen, D. K. (2005). Personal memories for remote historical events: Accuracy and clarity of flashbulb memories related to World War II. *Journal of Experimental Psychology: General, 134*, 242–257.

Bluck, S., Alea, N., Habermas, T., & Rubin, D. C. (2005). A TALE of three functions: The self-reported uses of autobiographical memory. *Social Cognition, 23*, 91–117.

Boccia, M., Teghil, A., & Guariglia, C. (2019). Looking into recent and remote past: Meta-analytic evidence for cortical re-organization of episodic autobiographical memories. *Neuroscience & Biobehavioral Reviews, 107*, 84–95.

Bonanno, G. (2005). Resilience in face of potential trauma. *Current Directions in Psychological Science, 14*, 135–138.

Brewer, M. B. (1988). A dual process model of impression formation. In T. Srull & R. Wyer (Eds.), *Advances in social cognition* (Vol. 1, pp. 1–36). Hillsdale, NJ: Lawrence Erlbaum Associates.

Brewin, C. R. (2001). A cognitive neuroscience account of posttraumatic stress disorder and its treatment. *Behavior Research and Therapy, 39*, 373–393.

Broadbent, D. E., Cooper, P. J., & Broadbent, M. H. (1978). A comparison of hierarchical retrieval schemes in recall. *Journal of Experimental Psychology: Human Learning and Memory, 4*, 486–497.

Brown, R., & Kulik, J. (1977). Flashbulb memories. *Cognition, 5*, 73–99.

Cardena, E., & Spiegel, D. (1993). Dissociative reactions to the San Francisco Bay area earthquake of 1989. *American Journal of Psychiatry, 150*, 474–478.

Catarino, A., Küpper, C. S., Werner-Seidler, A., Dalgleish, T., & Anderson, M. C. (2015). Failing to forget: Inhibitory-control deficits compromise memory suppression in posttraumatic stress disorder. *Psychological Science, 26*(5), 604–616.

Cheung, W. Y., Wildschut, T., & Sedikides, C. (2018). Autobiographical memory functions of nostalgia in comparison to rumination and counterfactual thinking: Similarity and uniqueness. *Memory, 26*(2), 229–237.

Chu, S., & Downes, J. J. (2002). Proust nose best: Odors are better cues of autobiographical memory. *Memory and Cognition, 30*, 511–518.

Conway, M. A. (2005). Memory and the self. *Journal of Memory & Language, 53*, 594–628.

Conway, M. (2013). *Flashbulb memories*. New York: Psychology Press.

Conway, M. A., Collins, A. F., Gathercole, S. E., & Anderson, S. J. (1996). Recollection of true and false autobiographical memories. *Journal of Experimental Psychology: General, 125*, 69–95.

Conway, M. A., & Jobson, L. (2012). On the nature of autobiographical memory. In D. Berntsen & D. C. Rubin (Eds.), *Understanding autobiographical memory: Theories and approaches* (pp. 54–69). Cambridge: Cambridge University Press.

Conway, M. A., & Pleydell-Pearce, C. W. (2000). The construction of autobiographical memories in the self-memory system. *Psychological Review, 107*, 262–288.

Conway, M. A., & Tacchi, P. C. (1996). Motivated confabulation. *Neurocase, 2*, 325–338.

Conway, M. A., Wang, Q., Hanyu, K., & Haque, S. (2005). A cross-cultural investigation of autobiographical memory. *Journal of Cross-Cultural Psychology, 36*, 739–749.

Craik, F. I. M., & Lockhart, R. S. (1972). Levels of processing. A framework for memory research. *Journal of Verbal Learning and Verbal Behavior, 11*, 671–684.

Crovitz, H. F., & Shiffman, H. (1974). Frequency of episodic memories as a function of their age. *Bulletin of the Psychonomic Society, 4*, 517–518.

Davidson, P. S. R., Cook, S. P., & Glisky, E. L. (2006). Flashbulb memories for September 11th can be preserved in older adults. *Aging, Neuropsychology, and Cognition, 13*, 196–206.

Dolcos, F., LaBar, K. S., & Cabeza, R. (2005). Remembering one year later: Role of the amygdala and the medial temporal lobe memory system in retrieving emotional memories. *Proceedings of the National Academy of Sciences of the USA, 102*, 2626–2631.

Engen, H. G., & Anderson, M. C. (2018). Memory control: A fundamental mechanism of emotion regulation. *Trends in Cognitive Sciences, 22*(11), 982–995.

Epstein, R. A. (2008). Parahippocampal and retrosplenial contributions to human spatial navigation. *Trends Cogn. Sci., 12*, 388–396.

Foa, E. B., & Rothbaum, B. O. (1998). *Treating the trauma of rape: Cognitive behavioral therapy for PTSD*. New York: Guilford Press.

Foa, E. B., Rothbaum, B. O., Riggs, D. S., & Murdock, T. (1991). Treatment of posttraumatic stress disorder in rape victims: A comparison between cognitive behavioral procedures and counseling. *Journal of Consulting and Clinical Psychology, 59*, 715–723.

Galton, F. (1879). Psychometric experiments. *Brain: A Journal of Neurology, II*, 149–162.

Gilbertson, M., Shenton, M., Ciszewski, A., Kasai, K., Lasko, N., Orr, S., & Pitman, R. (2002). Small hippocampal volume predicts pathologic vulnerability to psychological trauma. *Nature Neuroscience, 5*, 1242–1247.

Glück, J., & Bluck, S. (2007). Looking back across the life span: A life story account of the reminiscence bump. *Memory and Cognition, 35*, 1928–1939.

Greenberg, D. L., & Knowlton, B. J. (2014). The role of visual imagery in autobiographical memory. *Memory & Cognition, 42*(6), 922–934.

Greenberg, D. L., & Rubin, D. C. (2003). The neuropsychology of autobiographical memory. *Cortex, 39*, 687–728.

Haque, S., & Conway, M. A. (2001). Sampling the process of autobiographical memory construction. *European Journal of Cognitive Psychology, 13*, 529–547.

Harrison, N. A., Johnston, K., Corno, F., Casey, S. J., Friedner, K., Humphreys, K., … & Kopelman, M. D. (2017). Psychogenic amnesia:

Syndromes, outcome, and patterns of retrograde amnesia. *Brain, 140*(9), 2498–2510.

Harvey, A. G., & Bryant, R. A. (2000). Memory for acute stress disorder symptoms: A two-year prospective study. *Journal of Nervous and Mental Disease, 188*, 602–607.

Herz, R. S. (2004). A naturalistic analysis of autobiographical memories triggered by olfactory, visual and auditory stimuli. *Chemical Senses, 29*, 217–224.

Hyman, I. E., Jr., & Faries, J. M. (1992). The functions of autobiographical memories. In M. A. Conway, D. C. Rubin, H. Spinnler, & W. A. Wagenaar (Eds.), *Theoretical perspectives on autobiographical memory* (pp. 207–221). Dordrecht, the Netherlands: Kluwer Academic Publishers.

Johnson, M. K., Foley, M. A., Suengas, A. G., & Raye, C. L. (1988). Phenomenal characteristics of memory for perceived and imagined autobiographical events. *Journal of Experimental Psychology: General, 117*, 371–376.

Leichtman, M., Wang, Q., & Pillemer, D. P. (2003). Cultural variations in interdependence and autobiographical memory: Lessons from Korea, China, India, and the United States. In R. Fivush & C. Haden (Eds.), *Autobiographical memory and the construction of a narrative self: Developmental and cultural perspectives* (pp. 73–98). Hillsdale, NJ: Lawrence Erlbaum Associates.

LePort, A. K., Mattfeld, A. T., Dickinson-Anson, H., Fallon, J. H., Stark, C. E., Kruggel, F., Cahill, L., & McGaugh, J. L. (2012). Behavioral and neuroanatomical investigation of Highly Superior Autobiographical Memory (HSAM). *Neurobiology of Learning and Memory, 98*, 78–92. doi:10.1016/j.nlm.2012.05.002

Linton, M. (1975). Memory for real-world events. In D. A. Norman & D. E. Rumelhart (Eds.), *Explorations in cognition* (pp. 376–404). San Francisco: Freeman.

Loftus, E. F., & Marburger, W. (1983). Since the eruption of Mount St. Helens, has anyone beaten you up? Improving the accuracy of retrospective reports with landmark event. *Memory and Cognition, 11*, 114–120.

Marian, V., & Kaushanskaya, M. (2004). Self-construal and emotion in bicultural bilinguals. *Journal of Memory and Language, 51*, 190–201.

McCloskey, C. G., Wible, C. G., & Cohen, N. J. (1988). Is there a special flashbulb-memory mechanism?. *Journal of Experimental Psychology: General, 117*, 171–181.

McDermott, K. B., Szpunar, K. K., & Christ, S. E. (2009). Laboratory-based and autobiographical retrieval tasks differ substantially in their neural substrates. *Neuropsychologia, 47*(11), 2290–2298.

McEwen, B. (1999). Stress and hippocampal plasticity. *Annual Review of Neuroscience, 22*, 105–122.

Means, B., Mingay, D. J., Nigam, A., & Zarrow, M. (1988). A cognitive approach to enhancing health survey reports of medical visits. In M. M. Gruneberg, P. E. Morris, & R. N. Sykes (Eds.), *Practical aspects of memory: Current research and issues* (pp. 537–542). Chichester, UK: John Wiley & Sons.

Misra, P., Marconi, A., Peterson, M., & Kreiman, G. (2018). Minimal memory for details in real life events. *Scientific Reports, 8*(1), 16701.

Neisser, U. (1988). Five kinds of self-knowledge. *Philosophical Psychology, 1*, 35–59.

Neisser, U., & Harsch, N. (1992). Phantom flashbulbs: False recollections of hearing the news about challenger. In E. Winograd & U. Neisser (Eds.), *Affect and accuracy in recall: Studies of 'flashbulb' memories* (pp. 9–31). New York: Cambridge University Press.

Palombo, D. J., Alain, C., Söderlund, H., Khuu, W., & Levine, B. (2015). Severely deficient autobiographical memory (SDAM) in healthy adults: A new mnemonic syndrome. *Neuropsychologia, 72*, 105–118.

Palombo, D. J., Sheldon, S., & Levine, B. (2018). Individual differences in autobiographical memory. *Trends in Cognitive Sciences, 22*(7), 583–597.

Philippi, C. L., Tranel, D., Duff, M., & Rudrauf, D. (2014). Damage to the default mode network disrupts autobiographical memory retrieval. *Social Cognitive and Affective Neuroscience, 10*(3), 318–326.

Pitman, R., Sanders, K., Zusman, R., Healy, A., Cheema, F., Lasko, N., Cahill, L., & Orr, S. (2002). Pilot study of secondary prevention of post traumatic stress disorder with propranolol. *Biological Psychiatry, 51*, 189–192.

Ritchie, T. D., Skowronski, J. J., Hartnett, J., Wells, B., & Walker, W. R. (2009). The fading affect bias in the context of emotion activation level, mood, and personal theories of emotion change. *Memory, 17*, 428–444. http://dx.doi.org/10.1080/09658210902791665

Robinson, J. A., & Swanson, K. L. (1990). Autobiographical memory: The next phase. *Applied Cognitive Psychology, 4*, 321–335.

Rothbaum, B. O., & Davis, M. (2003). Applying learning principles to the treatment of post-trauma reactions. *Annals of the New York Academy of Sciences, 1008*, 112–121.

Rubin, D. C., Groth, E., & Goldsmith, D. J. (1984). Olfactory cuing of autobiographical memory. *American Journal of Psychology, 97*, 493–507.

Rubin, D. C., & Kozin, M. (1984). Vivid memories. *Cognition, 16,* 81–95.

Rubin, D. C., Wetzler, S. E., & Nebes, R. D. (1986). Autobiographical memory across the adult lifespan. In D. C. Rubin (Ed.), *Autobiographical memory* (pp. 202–221). Cambridge: Cambridge University Press.

Santangelo, V., Cavallina, C., Colucci, P., Santori, A., Macrì, S., McGaugh, J. L., & Campolongo, P. (2018). Enhanced brain activity associated with memory access in highly superior autobiographical memory. *Proceedings of the National Academy of Sciences of the USA, 115*(30), 7795–7800.

Sapolsky, R. (1996). Why stress is bad for your brain. *Science, 273,* 749–750.

Schmoick, H., Buffalo, E. A., & Squire, L. R. (2000). Memory distortions develop over time: Recollections of the O. J. Simpson trial verdict after 15 and 32 months. *Psychological Science, 11,* 39–45.

Sheldon, S., Farb, N., Palombo, D. J., & Levine, B. (2016). Intrinsic medial temporal lobe connectivity relates to individual differences in episodic autobiographical remembering. *Cortex, 74,* 206–216.

Skowronski, J. J. (2011). The positivity bias and the fading affect bias in autobiographical memory: A self-motives perspective. In C. Sedikides & M. Alicke (Eds.), *The handbook of self-enhancement and self-protection* (pp. 211–231). New York: Guilford Press.

Skowronski, J. J., Betz, A. L., Thompson, C. P., & Shannon, L. (1991). Social memory in everyday life: Recall of self-events and other-events. *Journal of Personality and Social Psychology, 60*(6), 831–843.

Skowronski, J. J., Walker, W. R., Henderson, D. X., & Bond, G. D. (2014). The fading affect bias: Its history, its implications, and its future. In J. M. Olson & M. P. Zanna (Eds.), *Advances in experimental social psychology* (Vol. 49, pp. 163–218). San Diego, CA: Academic Press.

Storm, B. C., & Jobe, T. A. (2012). Retrieval-induced forgetting predicts failure to recall negative autobiographical memories. *Psychological Science, 23*(11), 1356–1363.

Streb, M., Mecklinger, A., Anderson, M. C., Lass-Hennemann, J., & Michael, T. (2016). Memory control ability modulates intrusive memories after analogue trauma. *Journal of Affective Disorders, 192,* 134–142.

Suedfeld, P., & Eich, E. (1995). Autobiographical memory and affect under conditions of reduced environmental stimulation. *Journal of Environmental Psychology, 15*(4), 321–326.

Talarico, J. M., & Rubin, D. C. (2003). Confidence, not consistency, characterizes flashbulb memories. *Psychological Science, 14,* 455–461.

Tulving, E. (1989). Memory: Performance, knowledge and experience. *European Journal of Cognitive Psychology, 1,* 3–26.

Vaiva, G., Ducrocq, F., Jezequel, K., Averland, B., Levestal, P., Brunet, A., & Marmar, C. (2003). Immediate treatment with propranolol decreases post traumatic stress two months after trauma. *Biological Psychiatry, 54,* 947–949.

Wagenaar, W. A. (1986). My memory: A study of autobiographical memory over six years. *Cognitive Psychology, 18,* 225–252.

Waldfogel, S. (1948). The frequency and affective character of childhood memories. *Psychological Monographs: General and Applied, 62*(4), i–39.

Waldhauser, G. T., Dahl, M. J., Ruf-Leuschner, M., Müller-Bamouh, V., Schauer, M., Axmacher, N., ... & Hanslmayr, S. (2018). The neural dynamics of deficient memory control in heavily traumatized refugees. *Scientific Reports, 8*(1), 13132.

Walker, W. R., & Skowronski, J. J. (2009). The fading affect bias: But what the hell is it for?. *Applied Cognitive Psychology: The Official Journal of the Society for Applied Research in Memory and Cognition, 23*(8), 1122–1136.

Walker, W. R., Skowronski, J. J., & Thompson, C. P. (2003). Life is pleasant—and memory helps to keep it that way!. *Review of General Psychology, 7,* 203–210.

Walker, W. R., Vogl, R. J., & Thompson, C. P. (1997). Autobiographical memory: Unpleasantness fades faster than pleasantness over time. *Applied Cognitive Psychology, 11,* 399–413.

Wang, Q. (2001). Cultural effects on adults' earliest childhood recollection and self-description: Implications for the relation between memory and the self. *Journal of Personality and Social Psychology, 81,* 220–233.

Wang, Q. (2006a). Relations of maternal style and child self-concept to autobiographical memories in Chinese, Chinese immigrant, and European American 3-year-olds. *Child Development, 77,* 1799–1814.

Wang, Q. (2006b). Earliest recollections of self and others in European American and Taiwanese young adults. *Psychological Science, 17,* 708–714.

Wang, Q. (2008). Emotion knowledge and autobiographical memory across the preschool years: A cross-cultural longitudinal investigation. *Cognition, 108,* 117–135.

Watkins, N. W. (2018). (A) phantasia and severely deficient autobiographical memory: Scientific and personal perspectives. *Cortex, 105,* 41–52.

Willander, J., & Larsson, M. (2006). Smell your way back to childhood: Autobiographical odour memory. *Psychonomic Bulletin and Review, 13,* 240–244.

Willander, J., & Larsson, M. (2007). Olfaction and emotion: The case of autobiographical memory. *Memory and Cognition, 35,* 1659–1663.

Williams, H. L., Conway, M. A., & Cohen, G. (2008). Autobiographical memory. In G. Cohen & M. A. Conway (Eds.), *Memory in the real world* (3rd edn., pp. 21–90). London: Psychology Press.

Woods, B., Spector, A., Jones, C., Orrell, M., & Davies, S. (2005). Reminiscence therapy for dementia. *Cochrane Database of Systematic Reviews.* doi:10.1002/14651858.CD001120.pub2

Contents

CHAPTER 12

EYEWITNESS TESTIMONY

Michael W. Eysenck

INTRODUCTION

You are a juror in a case involving serious assault. You find it very hard to decide whether the defendant is, indeed, the person who carried out the assault. This is because nearly all the evidence is indirect or circumstantial and so not very convincing. However, one piece of evidence seems very direct and revealing—the person who was assaulted identified the defendant as her assailant in a lineup. When you see this eyewitness questioned in court, you are impressed by her confidence that she has correctly identified her vicious attacker. As a result, you and your fellow jurors find the defendant guilty of serious assault and he is sentenced to several years in prison.

Is it safe for jurors to rely almost solely on eyewitness testimony? Simons and Chabris (2011) found that 37% of Americans believe the testimony of a single confident eyewitness is sufficient to convict a criminal defendant. However, the increased use of DNA testing in recent years has suggested that there are significant dangers associated with relying on eyewitness identification because more than 200 individuals convicted on the basis of mistaken eyewitness identification have been proved innocent by DNA tests.

Let's consider the case of Charles Chatman. He was 20 years old when a young woman who had been raped picked him out from a lineup. As a result of her eyewitness testimony, Chatman was sentenced to 99 years in prison in Dallas County, Texas. DNA testing led to Chatman being released after 26 years in prison. Chatman claimed that race was a factor: "I was convicted because a black man committed a crime against a white woman."

There have been several other cases in Dallas where guilty verdicts have been overturned on the basis of DNA evidence. This has happened because those involved in administering the law in Dallas are more likely than those in most other areas to store the original evidence. This raises the disturbing prospect that the lack of stored DNA evidence in many areas means that numerous innocent individuals languishing in prison have no chance of their guilty verdict being overturned. More generally, Smalarz and Wells (2012) estimated that in only approximately 5% of cases is DNA evidence potentially available that might show eyewitnesses have identified the wrong person.

Note, however, that DNA tests are not infallible. They can indicate that a given individual was present at the scene of the crime but not necessarily that he/she actually committed the crime.

IN THE REAL WORLD: SHOULD JURORS TRUST CONFIDENT EYEWITNESSES?

We have seen there are hundreds of cases where DNA evidence indicated that mistaken eyewitness identification had led to the conviction and imprisonment of innocent individuals. Garrett (2011) reviewed 161 such cases. What he discovered was that nearly all those eyewitnesses who had identified a totally innocent individual were nevertheless *certain* at trial that they had accurately identified the culprit. This suggests that eyewitnesses have extremely fallible memories and that the confidence they express in their identifications should be disregarded.

In fact, as we will see shortly, Garrett (2011) discovered that this conclusion is *not* warranted when he studied each case in detail. Consider, for example, Ronald Cotton. He was found guilty in 1985 of raping Jennifer Thompson based on her confident eyewitness identification of him as the culprit. However, he was exonerated by DNA evidence many years later having spent more than 10 years in prison. Garrett went back in the records to Jennifer Thompson's *initial* identification of Cotton from a photo lineup. On that occasion, she hesitated for nearly five minutes before eventually saying, "I think this is the guy." More generally, trial transcripts indicated that

eyewitnesses reported a lack of certainty about their earlier identifications in 57% of cases.

Why does eyewitness confidence often increase substantially from their initial identification of the person they believe is the culprit to their final courtroom identification? In the case of Jennifer Thompson, she became progressively more confident she had identified the culprit when she received positive feedback from the police following her initial identification. Steblay, Wells, and Douglass (2014) carried out a meta-analytic review based on approximately 7,000 participants of the effects of such feedback. There was a strong tendency for participants to remember mistakenly they had had been very confident of the accuracy of their identification *prior* to receiving the positive feedback. This is the post-identification feedback effect.

What conclusions can we draw? First, it appears we can trust eyewitnesses' confidence in their identifications provided we consider only their *initial* level of confidence. Further support for this conclusion comes from a real-life study of eyewitnesses' initial identifications (Wixted, Mickes, Dunn, Clark, & Wells, 2016). Only approximately 20% of eyewitness identifications of culprits were correct when their confidence was low. In contrast, the corresponding figure was 80% when their confidence was high.

Second, the disturbing findings we have discussed indicate the need for changes in the legal system. More specifically, as Steblay et al. (2014, p. 1) argued, "Testimony-relevant witness judgments should be collected and documented, preferably with videotape, before feedback can occur."

Knowledge about limitations of eyewitness memory

We might reasonably assume that most judges would be knowledgeable about potential problems with eyewitness testimony. Unfortunately, this assumption is incorrect. Wise and Safer (2004) found American judges substantially underestimated the importance of factors causing eyewitness testimony to be inaccurate. As a result, 77% of judges were willing to accept that a

Jennifer Thompson and Ronald Cotton. From Wixted and Wells (2017).

defendant should be convicted of a crime based solely on eyewitness testimony.

Wise and Safer (2010) found American judges' knowledge of factors influencing the accuracy of eyewitness testimony was comparable to that of undergraduate students. The findings strongly suggested that the number of wrongful convictions based on eyewitness testimony would be reduced if judges had greater relevant knowledge.

Desmarais and Read (2011) reviewed 23 studies where the knowledge of the impact of various factors on eyewitness accuracy was assessed by ordinary members of the public (from whom jurors are drawn). Their views agreed with an expert consensus on approximately two-thirds of the factors. However, it is of concern that lay knowledge differed from expert knowledge on the remaining one-third.

MAJOR FACTORS INFLUENCING EYEWITNESS ACCURACY

How reliable (or should it be unreliable?) is eyewitness testimony? That is the central issue we address in this chapter. We have already seen that DNA evidence indicates such testimony is sometimes seriously flawed. As we will see, several factors often cause eyewitness memory to be very unreliable. Some of these factors involve limitations in attention and/or perception at the time of the incident, whereas other factors depend more on memory distortions at the time of retrieval.

Change blindness

Our powers of observation are worse than we like to think. Striking evidence was reported in a well-known study by Simons and Chabris (1999). Their participants watched a video and some of them counted the number of times students dressed in white threw a ball to each other (see the video at www.simonslab.com/videos.html). At some point, a woman in a gorilla suit walks right

into camera shot, looks at the camera, thumps her chest, and then walks off (see Figure 12.1). Altogether she is on the screen for nine seconds.

Wouldn't you guess that virtually everyone would spot the "gorilla" taking several seconds to stroll across the scene? In fact, 50% of the observers failed to notice the "gorilla"! This failure to notice an unexpected object in a visual display is known as inattentional blindness.

Change blindness is a related phenomenon that also depends on attentional limitations. It involves a failure to detect changes in an object (e.g., it has been replaced; see Chapter 5). Change blindness is extremely common. You have undoubtedly experienced change blindness at the movies where there are unintended continuity mistakes when a scene has been re-shot. For example, in the movie *Skyfall*, James Bond is followed by a white car. Mysteriously, this car becomes black and then returns to being white! For more examples, type in "Movie continuity mistakes" into YouTube.

Figure 12.1 Frame showing a woman in a gorilla suit in the middle of a game of passing the ball. From Simons and Chabris (1999). Figure provided by Daniel Simons. dansimons.com.

KEY TERM

Inattentional blindness: The failure to perceive the appearance of an unexpected object in the visual environment.

Change blindness can cause problems when eyewitnesses try to remember an event (see later in the chapter). While it would appear that change blindness is an unfortunate defect, that is not necessarily the case. Fischer and Whitney (2014) argued that our visual world is typically relatively stable over short time periods. As a result, it is worthwhile for perceptual accuracy to be sacrificed occasionally (as in change blindness) so we have continuous, stable perception of our visual environment.

Change blindness blindness

Suppose we presented participants with videos previously used to show change blindness and asked them whether they would personally have detected the changes. Precisely this has been done in several studies (e.g., Jaeger, Levin, & Porter, 2017; Levin, Drivdahl, Momen, & Beck, 2002). It has been found consistently that participants massively overestimated their ability to detect changes. This phenomenon is known as change blindness blindness.

Clear-cut evidence we are often wildly optimistic about our own observational powers was reported by Levin et al. (2002). Participants saw videos of two people chatting in a restaurant. In one video, the plates on their table changed from red to white, and in another a scarf worn by one of them disappeared. A third video showed a man sitting in his office and then walking into the hall to answer the telephone. When the view switches from the office to the hall, the first person has been replaced by another man wearing different clothes.

The above videos had previously been used by the researchers, who found no participants detected any of the changes. Levin et al. (2002) asked their participants to indicate whether they thought they would have noticed the changes if they had not been forewarned. The percentages claiming they would have noticed the changes were as follows: 78% for the disappearing scarf; 59% for the changed man; and 46% for the change in color of the plates.

How can we explain change blindness blindness? When we look at the environment, we obtain only limited information from

peripheral vision. However, we often use top-down processes (e.g., expectations) to fill in the gaps in the information available to us. As a consequence, "We see far less than we think we see" (Cohen, Dennett, & Kanwisher, 2016, p. 324).

Expectations

Our memory for events is often influenced by our expectations, which can cause distortions in retrieval. This is notoriously the case with sporting contests—supporters of the two teams often have almost diametrically opposed memories of crucial moments in the game! Consider Hastorf and Cantril's (1954) classic study on a football game between two American universities (Princeton and Dartmouth). A film of the game was shown to Dartmouth and Princeton students instructed to detect rule infringements. Unsurprisingly, Princeton students detected more than twice as many rule infringements by Dartmouth players than did Dartmouth students.

Hastorf and Cantril's (1954) findings show confirmation bias—event memory is influenced and systematically distorted by the observer's expectations. More evidence of confirmation bias was reported by Lindholm and Christanson (1998). Swedish and immigrant students watched a videotaped simulated robbery where the perpetrator seriously wounded a cashier with a knife. The perpetrator was either Swedish (blond hair and light skin) or an immigrant (black hair and brown skin). The key finding was that both immigrant and Swedish eyewitnesses were twice as likely to identify as the culprit an innocent immigrant as an innocent Swede from color photographs. Immigrants are over-represented in Swedish crime statistics, and this influenced participants' expectations about the perpetrator's likely ethnicity.

> ### KEY TERM
>
> **Change blindness blindness:** Individuals' exaggerated belief that they can detect visual changes and so avoid *change blindness*.
>
> **Confirmation bias:** Distortions of memory caused by the influence of expectations concerning what is likely to have happened.

Bartlett (1932) explained why expectations color our memories. As discussed in Chapter 7, we possess numerous schemas or packets of knowledge stored in long-term memory. These schemas lead us to form certain expectations. For example, our bank-robbery schema includes the following information: robbers are male; they wear disguises; they wear dark clothes; they make demands for money; and they have a getaway car with a driver (Tuckey & Brewer, 2003a).

A major prediction from Bartlett's theory is that eyewitness memory should often be *distorted* to conform to the relevant schema. This prediction was tested by Tuckey and Brewer (2003b). Eyewitnesses were exposed to ambiguous information—for example, the robber's head was covered by a balaclava so their gender was ambiguous. As predicted, eyewitnesses generally interpreted the ambiguous information as being consistent with their crime schema (see Figure 12.2). Thus, for example, they tended to recall the robber whose head was covered by a balaclava as being male. This is a clear case of expectations distorting retrieval.

Shapiro (2009) studied the effects of gender schema on eyewitness memory. Some eyewitnesses saw a simulated crime involving a male criminal whose features, clothing, and behavior were "feminine." They often misremembered such gender-inconsistent information, using their male gender schema to infer that the criminal's features, clothing, and behavior were "masculine" rather than "feminine."

Expectations influence jurors as well as eyewitnesses. Pickel and Gentry (2017) considered a rape case where a woman was either assaulted by a stranger in a public place or by an acquaintance in a private home. They argued that jurors would expect the woman would develop post-traumatic stress disorder (PTSD) in the former case but only mild anxiety in the latter case. Pickel and Gentry predicted that jurors would be more likely to find the defendant guilty if the harm experienced by the rape victim was consistent with their expectations.

The findings were as predicted. When the woman was assaulted by a stranger, 82% of jurors judged the defendant guilty when she experienced PTSD compared to 68% when she experienced mild anxiety. In contrast, when the woman was assaulted by an acquaintance, 47% argued the defendant was guilty when she experienced PTSD compared to 65% when she experienced mild anxiety. Thus, jurors' rape schemas strongly influenced their decisions concerning the defendant's guilt.

Misinformation effect

Perhaps the most obvious explanation for the inaccurate memories of eyewitnesses is that they often fail to pay sufficient attention to the crime and the criminal(s). After all, the

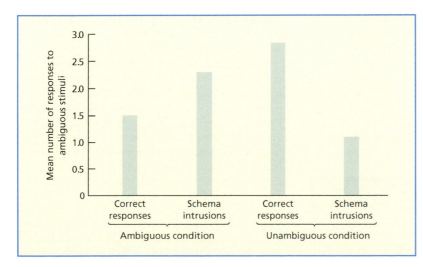

Figure 12.2 Mean correct responses and schema-consistent intrusions in the ambiguous and unambiguous conditions with cued recall. Data from Tuckey and Brewer (2003b).

crime they observe typically occurs suddenly and unpredictably. However, Loftus and Palmer (1974) argued that what matters is not only what happens at the time of the crime. According to them, eyewitness memories can surprisingly easily be distorted by what happens *after* observing the crime.

In a well-known study, Loftus and Palmer (1974) asked their participants to watch a film of a car accident. Afterwards, they described what had happened and then answered specific questions. Some participants were asked, "About how fast were the cars going when they hit each other?" Others were asked the same question but with the word *hit* replaced by *collided, bumped, contacted,* or *smashed into.*

What did Loftus and Palmer (1974) find? Speed estimates were highest (40.8 mph) when the word *smashed* was used, lower with *collided* (39.3), and lower still with *bumped* (38.1 mph), *hit* (34 mph), and *contacted* (31.8 mph). One week later, all participants were asked, "Did you see any broken glass?" There was no broken glass, but 32% of those previously asked about speed using the verb *smashed* said they had seen broken glass. In contrast, only 14% of the participants asked using *speed* using the verb hit claimed to have seen broken glass.

Thus, our memory for events is so fragile it can be systematically distorted by changing one word in one question! This exemplifies the misinformation effect—misleading information presented after an event causes distortions in memory for that event.

Loftus, Miller, and Burns (1978) obtained a misinformation effect triggered by more directly misleading information. Eyewitnesses saw several slides including one showing a red Datsun car stopping at a stop or yield sign. Afterwards they were asked, "Did another car pass the red Datsun while it was stopped at the stop sign?" or the word "stop" was replaced by "yield." In a third condition, the

KEY TERM

Misinformation effect: The distorting effect on eyewitness memory of misleading information presented after a crime or other event.

key question did not refer to a sign. Finally, the eyewitnesses decided which of two slides (car with a stop sign and car with a yield sign) they had seen previously. Eyewitnesses most often selected the wrong slide when the earlier question was misleading.

The findings discussed so far demonstrate retroactive interference (disruption of memory by the learning of other material during the retention interval between original learning and the memory test; see Chapter 9). Eyewitness memory can also be distorted by proactive interference (learning occurring *prior* to observing the critical event; see Chapter 9). Lindsay, Allen, Chan, and Dahl (2004) showed participants a video of a museum burglary. On the previous day, they had listened to a narrative thematically similar (a palace burglary) or thematically dissimilar (a school field-trip to a palace) to the video.

The participants made many more errors when recalling information when the narrative was thematically similar. This is potentially important. In the real world, eyewitnesses often have previous experiences of relevance to the questions they are asked about an event or crime and these experiences may distort their answers.

There is compelling evidence that the accuracy of long-term memory generally depends on various cognitive factors (e.g., intelligence; working memory capacity: Unsworth, 2019). Do individual differences in these cognitive factors also predict the misinformation effect? Evidence that the answer is yes was reported by Zhu et al. (2010a). Eyewitnesses with higher intelligence and greater working memory capacity were better at resisting misinformation.

Zhu et al. (2010b) found that ability to resist misinformation was associated with various personality characteristics such as being high in fear of negative evaluation and low in cooperativeness and reward dependence. Of interest, the effects of most personality characteristics were greater in those of lower intelligence (see Figure 12.3).

The misinformation effect has generally been found for *peripheral* or *minor* details (e.g., presence of broken glass in the study by Loftus and Palmer, 1974). Putnam, Sungkhasettee, and Roediger (2017) confirmed that the misinformation effect is much greater

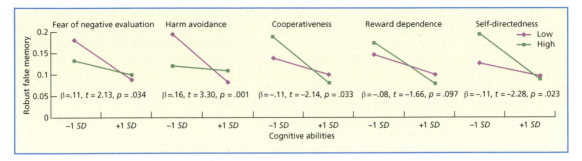

Figure 12.3 False memory as a function of cognitive abilities (low = −1 SD; high = +1 SD) and various personality characteristics. From Zhu et al. (2010b). Copyright © American Psychological Association. Reprinted with permission.

for relatively unmemorable than memorable details (see Figure 12.4).

Most textbook accounts claim the misinformation effect is nearly always found. However, Putnam et al. (2017) discovered that misinformation *enhanced* recognition memory for an event provided that participants detected (and remembered) *changes* between that event and the post-event misinformation. Why was that the case? Misinformation acted as a *cue* that facilitated retrieval of details from the actual event (see discussion of retrieval cues in Chapter 8).

Theoretical explanations

How does misleading information distort eyewitnesses' memory? Several factors are

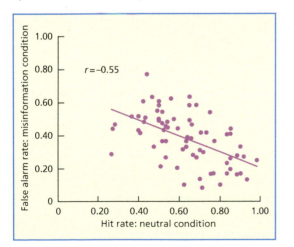

Figure 12.4 Size of the misinformation effect as a function of detail memorability in the neutral condition (i.e., absence of misleading information). From Putnam et al. (2017).

involved. One important factor is source misattribution (Johnson, Hashtroudi, & Lindsay, 1993). In essence, information about an event is remembered correctly but the source or context of that information is misremembered. Unsurprisingly, source misattribution is most likely to occur when the memories from one source closely resemble those from a second source. For example, Lindsay et al. (2004) presented participants with a narrative and a video. Source misattribution (intruding information from the narrative into their memory of the video) was much more common when the two events were similar.

Prull and Yockelson (2013) obtained evidence strongly suggesting the importance of source misattribution. Eyewitnesses who received a source-recognition test encouraging them to retrieve source information had a greatly reduced misinformation effect.

Rindal, Chrobak, Zaragoza, and Weihing (2017) explored an alternative explanation of the misinformation effect based on the explanatory role hypothesis. This hypothesis is based on the assumption that post-event misleading information is more likely to produce the misinformation effect when it provides a causal explanation for an outcome observed by an eyewitness. Rintal et al. obtained findings directly supporting this hypothesis. Also as predicted, they found the misinformation effect was reduced when the explanatory strength of misleading information was reduced by providing an alternative explanation that could also explain the same witnessed outcome.

A key theoretical issue is whether misinformation causes *permanent* alteration of memory traces from a witnessed event. Oeberst and Blank (2012) argued that misinformation typically does *not* permanently change memory traces. Instead, the misinformation effect occurs because eyewitnesses are instructed to recall the *single* correct account of an event. In their study, Oeberst and Blank told eyewitnesses they had received contradictory information and encouraged them to recall *everything* relating to the event and the misinformation. This manipulation had a dramatic effect—it totally eliminated the misinformation effect! This finding suggested that original memory traces were essentially intact.

Blank and Launay (2014) reviewed studies on the misinformation effect where eyewitnesses were warned of the presence of misinformation after viewing an event and being exposed to the misinformation. Such post-warning reduced the misinformation effect to between one-third and one-half its size when no warning was provided (see Figure 12.5). Higham, Blank, and Luna (2017) compared the effects of post-warnings that were *specific* (identifying event details for which misinformation had been presented earlier) and those that were *general* (indicating there had been misinformation). The misinformation effect was eliminated only with specific post-warnings.

The findings discussed so far imply that the misinformation effect is often due to *inaccessibility* of information about the original event rather than altered memory traces. However, some evidence supports the latter explanation. Edelson, Sharot, Dolan, and Dudai (2011) had eyewitnesses watch a crime scene in small groups and then recall the crime events three days later (Test 1). Four days after that, they were misinformed their fellow eyewitnesses remembered several events differently from them and then given a further test (Test 2). This caused many eyewitnesses to recall incorrect information corresponding to the alleged memories of their fellow eyewitnesses.

A week later, the eyewitnesses were told the answers allegedly given by their fellow eyewitnesses had been generated at random. Finally, they received another memory test (Test 3). What did Edelson et al. (2011) find? Some eyewitnesses continued to provide the same incorrect answers on Test 3 they had given on Test 2, suggesting their memories had genuinely changed.

Interventions

We have discussed a few ways in which the negative impact of misleading post-event information can be reduced. What else can be

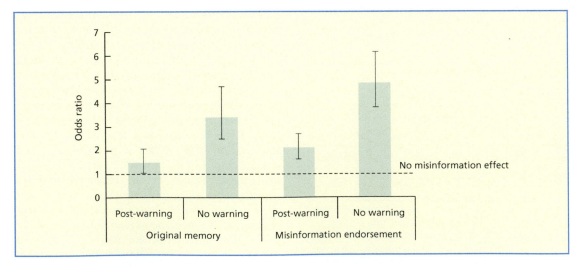

Figure 12.5 Extent of misinformation effects (expressed as an odds ratio) as a function of condition (post-warning vs. no warning) for the original memory and endorsement of the misinformation presented previously. From Blank and Launay (2014).

done? Gabbert, Hope, Fisher, and Jamieson (2012) argued that an early opportunity to recall the details of a witnessed crime would protect the relevant memory traces from distortion by misleading information. Eyewitnesses were shown the video of a bank robbery. After that, some of them then recalled all the details of the crime they could remember. One week later, all participants received misinformation followed by event recall. Those who had provided immediate recall were more resistant to this misinformation.

Szpitalak and Polczyk (2019) presented eyewitnesses with a four-minute video clip of a burglary followed by a post-event narrative containing misleading information. They then used what they called reinforced self-affirmation to reduce the subsequent misinformation effect. In essence, participants wrote down one of their greatest achievements in life, and then received positive feedback concerning their memory, perception, or independence of judgments. Reinforced self-affirmation reduced the misinformation effect because it increased participants' self-confidence and self-independence.

ANXIETY AND VIOLENCE

We have considered some of the main factors influencing the accuracy of eyewitness memory. An important factor concerns the extent to which eyewitnesses are exposed to potential or actual violence. For example, one of the authors (Alan Baddeley) was phoned one Sunday night by a caller announcing himself as a detective with the San Diego Police Department. He was investigating a multiple throat-slasher whose seventh victim had escaped. The woman claimed she would be able to identify her attacker. What, the detective asked, was the likely effect of extreme emotion on the reliability and accuracy of her testimony?

Experts' opinions on the answer to the above question differ dramatically. When 235 American lawyers were asked whether face recognition would be negatively affected by high levels of emotion, 82% of defense

lawyers argued that it would be impaired. In contrast, only 32% of prosecution lawyers believed high emotion impairs facial recognition.

Who is right? Does extreme emotion brand the experience indelibly on the victim's memory, or does it reduce their capacity for recollection? We will shortly turn to the relevant evidence. Bear in mind, however, that laboratory studies have for obvious reasons not exposed participants to extremely stressful conditions. For example, not even the most zealous experimenters try to convince their participants they are about to suffer serious injury.

Deffenbacher, Bornstein, Penrod, and McGorty (2004) combined the findings from numerous studies focusing on the effects of stress and anxiety on eyewitness memory. In their first analysis, face recognition was correct 54% of the time in low anxiety or stress conditions compared to 42% in high anxiety or stress conditions. Thus, heightened anxiety and stress have a negative effect impact on eyewitness identification accuracy.

In their second analysis, Deffenbacher et al. (2004) considered the effects of anxiety and stress on eyewitness recall of culprit details, crime scene details, and the central character's actions. The average correct recall of details was 64% in the low anxiety or stress conditions compared to 52% in the high anxiety or stress conditions.

Most of the research reviewed by Deffenbacher et al. (2004) was conducted under artificial laboratory conditions. In contrast, Dahl, Granér, Fransson, Bertilsson, and Fredriksson (2018) obtained eyewitness testimony from 13 eyewitnesses to a real-life, highly stressful incident in which the police killed a man with a knife. The accuracy of their testimony could be established because the incident was filmed on two cell (mobile) phones.

What did Dahl et al. (2018) find? Most eyewitnesses recalled the culprit's weapon, his direction of movement, and the number of shots fired reasonably accurately. However, they exhibited many distortions in their recollection of the order of events during the incident (see Figure 12.6). Of particular interest, most eyewitnesses showed very similar biases (e.g., underestimating the

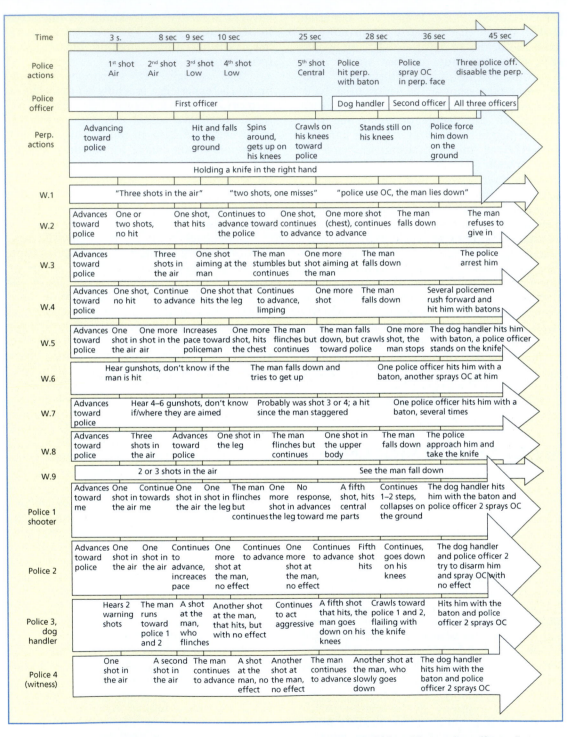

Figure 12.6 Timeline of a fatal incident as reported by nine eyewitnesses (W) and four police officers. From Dahl et al. (2018). © 2018 Dahl et al. This open access article is distributed under a Creative Commons Attribution (CC-BY) 4.0 license.

impact of the third and fourth shots on the culprit). A potential danger is that jurors might be unduly impressed by the similar (but inaccurate) reports of different eyewitnesses to the same incident.

Weapon focus

Much of the research on anxiety and eyewitness memory has investigated the weapon focus effect—the presence of a weapon causes eyewitnesses to attend to the criminal's weapon which in turn causes them to have reduced memory for details of the assailant and the environmental context. For example, Biggs, Brockmole, and Witt (2013) found that observers generally fixated weapons more than neutral objects. As a consequence, they fixated faces less often in the weapon condition.

Harada, Hakoda, Kuroki, and Mitsudo (2015) presented observers with pictures of weapons or neutral objects and then asked them to identify digits presented in peripheral vision when each picture was no longer visible. Their key finding was that observers' memory for the peripheral digits was less when a weapon had been presented. This finding is consistent with Easterbrook's (1959) hypothesis. According to this hypothesis, stress or anxiety causes a narrowing of attention to central or important stimuli which reduces people's ability to remember peripheral details. In other words, anxious or stressed individuals exhibit "tunnel vision," which makes sense when the situation is potentially threatening or dangerous.

Pickel (2009) pointed out that people often attend to stimuli that are *unexpected* in a situation, which impairs their memory for other stimuli. This led Pickel to argue that the weapon focus effect will be greater when the presence of a weapon is very unexpected. As predicted, there was a stronger weapon focus effect when a criminal carrying a folding knife was female, because it is more unexpected to see a woman with a knife. Also as predicted, the weapon focus effect was greater when a criminal with a knitting needle was male rather than female.

Fawcett, Russell, Peace, and Christie (2013) carried out a meta-analysis based on

> **KEY TERM**
>
> **Weapon focus:** The finding that eyewitnesses have poor memory for details of a crime event because they focus their attention on the culprit's weapon.

considered numerous studies on weapon focus. Overall, there was a moderate effect on eyewitness memory of weapon focus. Of importance, the size of this effect was similar regardless of whether the event occurred in the laboratory or in the real world.

Why does stress impair memory?

As we saw earlier, stress causes a narrowing of attention in which peripheral details receive little attention and are poorly remembered (Easterbrook, 1959; Harada et al., 2015). Yegiyan and Lang (2010) reported additional support in a study where they presented people with distressing pictures. As picture stressfulness increased, recognition memory for peripheral details decreased progressively whereas memory for central details was enhanced.

It is important to emphasize that the effects of stress on memory are relatively complex. For example, Quaedflieg and Schwabe (2018) discussed research showing that stress generally increases *rigidity* in learning and memory and reduces the involvement of episodic memory (see Chapter 6). Such rigidity reduces the extent to which contextual details are incorporated within the memory trace (as predicted by Easterbrook's hypothesis). However, stress also reduces the ability to modify existing memories in light of new information. As a consequence, stress can reduce the misinformation effect (discussed earlier) by "protecting" memories from updating by post-event misinformation (Schmidt, Rosga, Schatto, Breidenstein, & Schwabe, 2014).

In sum, it is an oversimplification to claim that stress and anxiety simply impair eyewitness memory. In reality, stress produces several effects on learning and memory, some of which are beneficial whereas others are not.

AGE AND EYEWITNESS ACCURACY

Another factor that can influence the accuracy of eyewitness testimony is their age. The accuracy of eyewitness testimony in children of different ages is discussed in Chapter 15. Here we will focus on comparisons between younger and older adults. Unsurprisingly, the eyewitness testimony of older adults is generally less accurate than that of younger ones. Fraundorf, Hourihan, Peters, and Benjamin (2019) reviewed 232 studies on recognition memory. Overall, the memory performance of older adults was inferior to that of younger ones. In addition, older adults were more likely to judge *old* items as *new*.

Healey and Kahane (2016) proposed a four-component model to explain age-related differences in long-term memory. First, older adults have reduced ability to sustain attention at the time of learning (or witnessing of an event). Second, they are less able to retrieve relevant contextual information to facilitate recall. Third, they find it harder to monitor their retrievals and reject incorrect items. Fourth, the retrieval process in older adults is less precise and more likely to produce "noise."

Older adults exhibit greater misinformation effects than younger ones. Jacoby, Bishara, Hessels, and Toth (2005) found the presentation of misleading information caused older adults to have a 43% chance of recalling false memories compared to only 4% for younger ones. Subsequent research indicated that this large difference occurred in part because older adults are less likely to monitor their own recall to reduce errors (Morcon, 2016).

Research has uncovered a complicating factor with respect to the effects of age on memory for faces. Wright and Stroud (2002) found that adults identifying culprits after viewing crime videos showed own-age bias—younger and older adults tend to show better facial recognition for individuals close to themselves in age. Martschuk and Sporer (2018) reviewed the evidence. Younger adults had generally better facial recognition memory than older ones. However, the difference was significantly less with old faces than young ones.

How can we explain own-age bias? It might be due to expertise—most of us have greater exposure to (and familiarity with) faces of individuals of our own age. Wiese, Wolff, Steffens, and Schweinberger (2013) reported supporting evidence. Young geriatric nurses had no own-age bias because they recognized old faces much better than did young controls because of their extensive experience with older people.

REMEMBERING FACES

The culprit's face is often easily the most important information eyewitnesses may or may not remember accurately. In what follows, we will consider in detail the processes involved in remembering faces and factors that can make it hard to do so.

"I never forget a face!" We sometimes hear people making such claims, but how justifiable are they? For many years, psychologists argued that most of us are experts in recognizing faces. However, as is discussed below, recent evidence has cast considerable doubt on that argument.

How well do we remember faces?

Young and Burton (2018) discussed whether or not we are face experts. In essence, they argued we are experts when recognizing *familiar* faces. However, we find it surprisingly hard to recognize *unfamiliar* faces. This is a finding of direct relevance when trying to understand the limitations of eyewitnesses' memory for the faces of culprits. However, it should be noted that eyewitnesses are often acquainted with the culprit with certain crimes (e.g., assault; rape).

KEY TERM

Own-age bias: The tendency for eyewitnesses to identify individuals of the same age as themselves more accurately than those much older or younger.

We are often surprisingly poor at recognizing unfamiliar faces even when we do not have to rely on our fallible memory. Bruce et al. (1999) focused on people's ability to identify someone on the basis of closed-circuit television (CCTV) cameras. Participants were presented with a target face taken from a CCTV video, together with an array of 10 high-quality photographs (see Figure 12.7). Their task was to select the matching face or to indicate that the target face was not present in the array.

Bruce et al. (1999) found performance was disappointingly poor. When the target face was present in the array, it was selected only 65% of the time. When it was NOT present, 35% of participants nevertheless claimed one face in the array matched the target face. Allowing participants to watch a 50-second video segment of the target person as well as a photograph of their face failed to improve identification performance.

Patterson and Baddeley (1977) discovered several factors that influence our ability to recognize unfamiliar faces. Participants were presented with photographs of individuals photographed undisguised or wearing a beard, wig, spectacles, or any combination thereof. The photographs were taken full face or in profile. The participants were familiarized with one photograph of each person in any one combination of disguised features. This was repeatedly presented until it was consistently recognized and the person's name given correctly. Their participants were then presented with photographs consisting of the target individuals in all possible combinations of disguise, either in full frontal view or in profile, together with a number of similarly disguised but unfamiliar people. Their task was to detect and name the target individuals.

What did Patterson and Baddeley (1977) find? There was a dramatic effect of disguise.

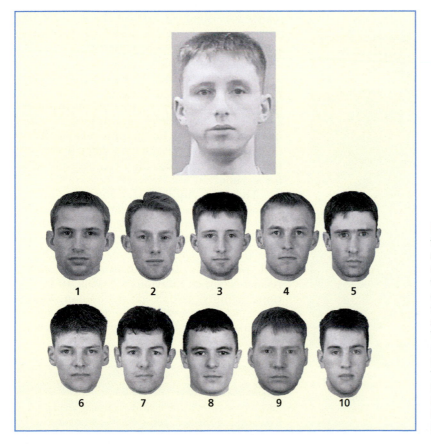

Figure 12.7 Example of full-face neutral target with an array used in the experiments. Readers might want to try the task of establishing whether the target is present in this array and which one it is. The studio and video images used are from the Home Office Police Information Technology Organisation. Bruce et al. (1999). Copyright © American Psychological Association. Reprinted with permission.

Every time an item of disguise was added or removed the probability of correct recognition decreased. Performance ranged from extremely good when the face was presented in its originally learned form to virtually guesswork when the maximum number of disguised features was changed. These findings suggest that criminals are well-advised to wear masks or other forms of disguise even if this makes them look very conspicuous!

Moniz, Righi, Peissig, and Tarr (2010) investigated the Clark Kent effect—the mysterious finding that Superman became unrecognizable as Clark Kent when he put on a pair of glasses. Moniz et al. demonstrated this effect—recognition memory for faces was reduced when glasses were added or removed after the initial learning.

Why do the apparently minor changes to facial appearance used by Patterson and Baddeley (1977) and Moniz et al. (2010) have large effects on face-recognition performance? Face recognition involves holistic processing meaning that information from several face regions is integrated (Richler, Cheung, & Gauthier, 2011). Thus, changes such as adding or removing a wig or glasses influence how other parts of the face are processed.

Dramatic evidence we have much greater problems with *unfamiliar* faces than *familiar* ones was reported by Jenkins, White, van Montfort, and Burton (2011). Participants were presented with 40 photographs (20 each of two Dutch celebrities unknown in the UK). Their task was to sort the photographs into separate piles for each person shown in the photographs. When this task was given to Dutch participants, the faces were familiar and their performance was almost perfect.

In another experiment by Jenkins et al. (2011), the same task was given to British participants for whom the faces were unfamiliar. On average, the participants thought 7½ different individuals were shown across the 40 photographs! This very poor performance was obtained without the need for the participants to remember the faces they were sorting—we would expect performance to be even worse if memory were involved.

The above findings mean that two photographs of the same person often look as if they come from two different individuals. The fact that a single photograph of an unfamiliar face conveys limited information helps to explain why eyewitnesses often have difficulties in identifying the person responsible for a crime.

There are individual differences in the ability to recognize unfamiliar faces. Robertson, Noyes, Dowsett, Jenkins, and Burton (2016) asked police officers to decide whether face pairs depicted the same person. Some had previously been identified as super-recognizers (i.e., individuals having an exceptional ability to recognize human faces). Mean accuracy was 96% for the super-recognizers compared to only 81% for police trainees.

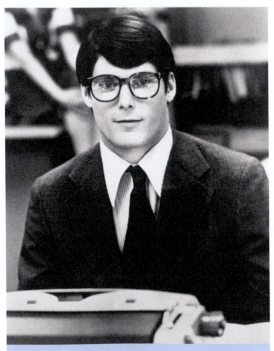

Moniz et al. (2010) investigated what they called the Clark Kent effect—the mystery that Superman became unrecognizable as Clark Kent when he put on a pair of glasses.

KEY TERM

Super-recognizers: Individuals having an outstanding ability to recognize human faces.

Unconscious transference

Eyewitnesses are sometimes better at remembering faces than at remembering the precise circumstances in which they previously saw a face. This can have serious consequences. For example, it can cause eyewitnesses to recognize correctly a face as having been seen before but to judge incorrectly that that person was guilty of committing a crime. This is unconscious transference.

A real-life case of unconscious transference involved the Australian psychologist Donald Thomson. He took part in a live television discussion on the unreliability of eyewitness testimony and was then picked up by the police some time later. At the police station, a very distraught woman identified him in a line-up and he was charged with rape. After a while, it became clear the rape had been committed while he was taking part in the television discussion. Donald Thomson said he had a perfectly good alibi, and numerous witnesses including an official of the Australian Civil Rights Committee and an Assistant Commissioner of Police. To this, the policeman taking his statement replied: "Yes, and I suppose you've got Jesus Christ and the Queen of England, too!" It turned out the woman had been raped while watching the program. For Thomson himself, it was an especially unpleasant way of discovering just how right he was to worry about eyewitness unreliability!

Davis, Loftus, Vanous, and Cucciare (2008) studied unconscious transference using a video of a simulated supermarket crime. There were two innocent bystanders. One walked down the liquor aisle and then passed behind a stack of boxes from which the criminal emerged and stole a bottle of liquor. The other bystander was shown in the produce aisle. Eyewitnesses subsequently inspected a lineup from which the criminal was absent. Worryingly, 23% of the eyewitnesses selected the innocent bystander who had passed behind the boxes and 29% selected the innocent bystander who had been in the produce aisle.

Fitzgerald, Oriet, and Price (2016) linked unconscious transference to change blindness (discussed earlier). Observers viewed a video in which an innocent person is seen walking through a building followed by another person committing a theft. Most viewers (64%) showed change blindness in that they did not realize the person had changed. Unsurprisingly, observers who showed change blindness were more likely than those who did not to misidentify the innocent person on a lineup in which the culprit was absent.

Verbal overshadowing

Suppose you are a police officer arriving at the scene of a crime that occurred only a few minutes ago. You find an eyewitness and must decide whether to ask them to provide a verbal description of the culprit's face. You would probably assume that doing so would improve the eyewitness's subsequent ability to identify the culprit. In fact, however, eyewitnesses' memory for faces is often *worse* if they have previously provided a verbal description! This effect is the verbal overshadowing effect—"the finding that describing a previously seen face can impair its subsequent recognition" (Schooler, 2014, p. 579).

Schooler and Engstler-Schooler (1990) provided the first demonstration of the verbal overshadowing effect. Eyewitnesses watched a film of a crime. After that, some eyewitnesses provided a detailed verbal report of the criminal's face, whereas others did an unrelated task. Those who had provided the detailed verbal report performed worse than the other eyewitnesses on a subsequent recognition-memory test. Subsequent research has produced somewhat mixed findings. However, Alogna et al. (2014) successfully replicated Schooler and Engstler-Schooler's (1990) findings.

KEY TERM

Unconscious transference: The tendency of eyewitnesses to misidentify a familiar (but innocent) face as belonging to the culprit.

Verbal overshadowing effect: The reduction in recognition memory for faces that often occurs when eyewitnesses provide verbal descriptions of those faces before the recognition-memory test.

Wilson, Seale-Carlisle, and Mickes (2018) clarified the conditions under which the verbal overshadowing effect is obtained. Observers provided verbal facial descriptions either immediately after viewing the target face or 20 minutes later (delayed descriptions). The delayed facial descriptions were much more general and less specifically relevant to the target face than those given immediately. Thus, much of the information contained in the delayed descriptions was relevant to non-target faces as well as the target face, and so was of little value in identifying the target face. As a consequence, there was a strong verbal overshadowing effect in the delayed condition but this effect disappeared in the immediate condition. The take-home message for the police is that eyewitnesses should provide verbal descriptions of the culprit's face as soon as possible after a crime has been committed.

Other-race effect

We will consider one final issue relating to eyewitnesses' ability to recognize faces. This is the other-race effect (sometimes known as the cross-race effect)—same-race faces are typically recognized more accurately than

other-race faces (see Young, Hugenberg, Bernstein, & Sacco, 2012, for a review). This effect depends on various factors. One such factor is expertise. Unsurprisingly, eyewitnesses having the most experience with members of another race have a smaller other-race effect than those with less experience (Hugenberg, Young, Bernstein, & Sacco, 2010).

For many years, it was assumed the other-race effect occurs because we find it hard to *remember* the faces of individuals of a different race. Megreya, White, and Burton (2011) showed this assumption is only partially correct because it also depends importantly on *perceptual* processes. British and Egyptian participants saw a target face and an array of 10 faces (see Figure 12.8) and decided whether the target face was in the array. If it was present, they identified which face it was. Of importance, this task imposed minimal demands on memory because all the photographs remained visible.

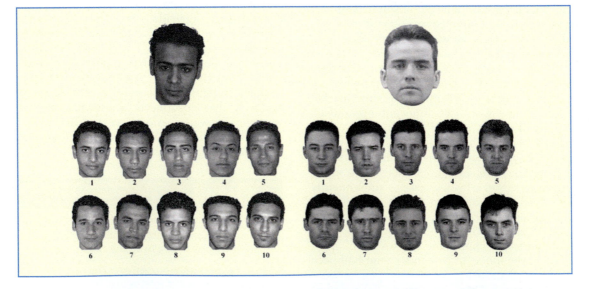

Figure 12.8 An example of Egyptian (left) and UK (right) face-matching arrays. The person shown at the top may or may not be one of the ten below. Subjects' task is to decide whether he is present, and, if so, which he is. From Megreya et al. (2011) Copyright © Experimental Psychology Society.

Even though perception rather than memory was involved, Megreya et al. (2011) obtained the other-face effect. When the target face was present, correct identification occurred on 70% of trials with same-race faces compared to 64% for other-race faces. When the target face was absent, a face in the array was mistakenly identified as the target on 34% of trials with same-race faces compared to 47% for other-race faces.

Megreya et al.'s (2011) findings suggest we have difficulty in encoding or processing the faces of individuals from other races when we see them. Support for this suggestion was reported by Brown, Uncapher, Chow, Eberhardt, and Wagner (2017) in a study where European American and African-American participants encoded (and then tried to remember) European American and African-American faces.

Brown et al. (2017) replicated the other-race effect. Of most theoretical importance, neuroimaging evidence indicated there was greater activation of fronto-parietal networks involved in top-down attention and cognitive control during encoding of same-race rather than other-race faces. These findings suggested that eyewitnesses may have problems in remembering other-race faces occur because such faces are encoded more superficially and using less attention than is the case with same-race faces.

How can face recognition be improved?

We saw earlier that most people are surprisingly poor at deciding whether photographs visible at the same time represent the same person. The take-home message of such research is that photographs of the same face often display considerable *variability* and this causes major problems in face recognition. These problems are much greater with unfamiliar faces than familiar ones and, of course, the culprits observed by eyewitnesses are typically (but not always) unfamiliar.

What is the relevance of all this to eyewitness identification? Eyewitnesses often find it hard to make a correct identification from a *single* photograph as they are frequently requested to do. However, their recognition-memory performance should be enhanced if information from multiple photographs of the same unfamiliar face were *combined* to create an average. Jones, Dwyer, and Lewis (2017) tested this prediction. Observers viewed a single front-view photograph of an individual (the target), seven photographs of that individual at different orientations, or seven computer-generated synthesized images of that individual at different orientations (see Figure 12.9). After that, the observers selected the target face from an array of five faces.

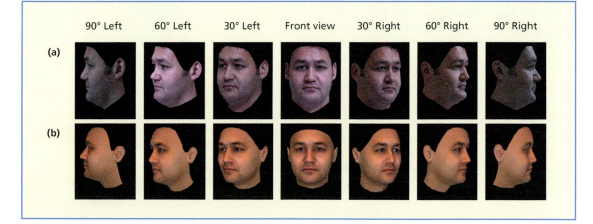

Figure 12.9 Panel (a): seven photographs of the same individual taken from different angles; panel (b): seven synthesized images of the same individual at different orientations. From Jones et al. (2017).

The findings reported by Jones et al. (2017) were as predicted. Face-recognition performance was worst following presentation of a single photograph and best following presentation of synthesized images. This is important because the police can use computer-based systems to generate such synthesized images from a single photograph.

POLICE PROCEDURES WITH EYEWITNESSES

The police obviously have no control over the circumstances at the time of the crime. Examples include the viewing conditions (e.g., lighting; duration of the event), the presence or absence of distracting stimuli (e.g., weapons; noises), and the eyewitness's internal state (e.g., attention; prejudice). These uncontrollable factors are sometimes described as estimator variables (Albright, 2017), and our focus up to this point has been on such variables.

However, there are also factors (system variables) that can be controlled by the criminal justice system. System variables include varying the way in which lineups are presented to eyewitnesses and the interview techniques used to question eyewitnesses. It should be noted that most research on system variables has been conducted in the United States and the United Kingdom. Thus, some of the findings to be reported may not be directly applicable to other countries where the police use different techniques to those employed in the United States and the United Kingdom.

Lineups

What happens with a lineup is that the suspect is present along with various non-suspects having broadly similar characteristics (e.g., age, race, height). The witness is asked if they recognize any member of the lineup as the culprit. It is very important that the suspect is not obviously different from the other members of the lineup if the evidence obtained is to be at all valid.

In days gone by, it was not unknown for this simple requirement to be ignored. Charman, Wells, and Joy (2011) had eyewitnesses observe a mock crime. This was followed by a lineup of two individuals resembling the culprit or a lineup consisting of the same two individuals plus four more individuals very dissimilar to the culprit (known as "duds"; see Figure 12.10). Note that the actual culprit was not present in either lineup.

When eyewitnesses made a mistaken identification, they were much more confident in the correctness of their choice when duds were present—this is the dud effect. This occurred because the presence of duds

Figure 12.10 Dud lineup and actual perpetrator from one of Charman et al.'s (2011) experiments. Copyright American Psychological Association. Reprinted with permission.

KEY TERM

Dud effect: An eyewitness's increased confidence in his/her mistakes when the lineup includes individuals very dissimilar to the culprit.

increased the perceived similarity of the other members of the lineup to the culprit.

There is considerable evidence indicating that eyewitnesses' performance is rather fallible when they attempt to select the culprit from a lineup. Valentine, Pickering, and Darling (2003) analyzed the findings from 640 eyewitnesses who tried to identify suspects in 314 real lineups organized by the Metropolitan Police in London. Only 40% of witnesses identified the suspect, 20% identified a non-suspect, and the remaining 40% failed to make an identification.

We will shortly discuss the merits of different ways of administering a lineup. Before doing so, however, we need to discuss the distinction between double-blind and single-blind administration. With double-blind administration, the lineup is conducted by administrators who do not know which lineup member is the suspect. With single-blind administration, in contrast, they have such knowledge.

Guilty suspects are identified more often using single-blind administration. However, there are compelling reasons for using double-blind administration (Kovera & Evelo, 2017). If administrators know beforehand which member of the lineup is the suspect, this may influence their behavior in such a way that it increases the probability that eyewitnesses select the suspect (even though the suspect may be innocent).

Lineups can be *simultaneous* (the eyewitness sees everyone at the same time) or *sequential* (the eyewitness sees only one person at a time). Wells, Steblay, and Dysart (2015) carried out a large-scale study involving eyewitnesses to actual crimes (rather than videoed or staged laboratory crimes). Their study was also more realistic than most others because eyewitnesses were allowed to say they were "not sure" (as happens in most real-life crime cases).

What did Wells et al. (2015) find? First, the suspect was identified 25% of the time with both simultaneous and sequential lineups. Second, there were more incorrect identifications of an innocent person with simultaneous than with sequential lineups (18% vs. 11%). Third, eyewitnesses used the "not sure" response more often with sequential lineups—they were unsure whether a subsequently viewed person might resemble the culprit more than the current one.

The above findings suggest sequential lineups are preferable. However, other findings complicate the picture. Wixted et al. (2016) also studied eyewitnesses to real crimes. Eyewitnesses identified 91% of suspects having independent evidence of guilt against them with simultaneous lineups compared to 76% with sequential lineups. When account was taken of eyewitnesses' confidence ratings, their overall performance was slightly better with simultaneous lineups.

What can we conclude? There is a greater probability of identifying the culprit with simultaneous than with sequential lineups. However, innocent individuals are generally more likely to be misidentified as the culprit with simultaneous lineups. What is of crucial importance is the precise magnitude of these two effects (which varies from study to study).

There is a final point. One might imagine that it is a simple matter for jurors to interpret an eyewitness's confidence in their identification of a suspect from a lineup. However, Grabman and Dodson (2019) found matters are more complicated. Participants told that an eyewitness had moderate confidence in their lineup identification interpreted their confidence as indicating a higher level of confidence when the identification matched the police's suspect than when it did not. Thus, contextual information can bias the interpretation of an eyewitness's identification confidence.

Cognitive interview

We have devoted much of this chapter to an examination of the many limitations of eyewitness memory. It is obviously important to recognize those limitations in order to minimize the probability of innocent individuals being wrongly convicted. However, it is also important for the police to make use of effective interviewing techniques so as to obtain as much accurate information as possible from eyewitnesses.

Historically, the police in most countries often used inadequate interviewing techniques.

For example, they would often ask closed-ended questions (e.g., "What color was the car?") which typically elicit very limited and specific information. A preferable approach is to ask open-ended questions (e.g., "What can you tell me about the car?"). Other problems with police questioning in the past was a tendency to interrupt eyewitnesses in the middle of saying something and to ask questions in a predetermined order taking no account of eyewitnesses' answers.

Over the past 30 years or so, the police have increasingly made use of various versions of the cognitive interview, which was originally devised by Geiselman, Fisher, MacKinnon, and Holland (1985). This approach is based on four general retrieval rules:

1   Mental reinstatement of the environment and any personal contact experienced during the crime.
2   Encouraging the reporting of every detail regardless of how peripheral it might seem to the main incident or crime.
3   Describing the incident in several different orders.
4   Reporting the incident from different viewpoints including those of other participants or witnesses.

Why might we expect the cognitive interview to be effective? In essence, it makes direct use of our knowledge how the human memory system works. The first two rules are based on the encoding specificity principle (Tulving, 1979). According to this principle, eyewitness memory will be greatest when there is maximal *overlap* or match between the context in which the crime was committed and the context in which the recall attempt is made.

The third and fourth rules are based on the assumption that memory traces are usually complex and contain various kinds of information (e.g., the person's mood at the time of learning). As a result, information about a crime can be retrieved using various routes, each of which may provide information about rather different aspects of the original experience.

Several modifications of the enhanced cognitive interview have been proposed over the years. For example, Paulo, Albuquerque, Vitorino, and Bull (2017) devised a revised cognitive interview differing from the traditional cognitive interview in two main ways. First, they omitted two of its rules (changing the order of reporting; changing perspective). Second, they introduced what category clustering recall. This involves instructing eyewitnesses to *organize* their memories of the crime into categories (e.g., culprit details, location details, action details, conversation details).

Findings

Memon, Meissner, and Fraser (2010) combined findings from numerous studies to compare the effectiveness of the cognitive interview against that of the standard police interview. Many more details were correctly recalled by eyewitnesses with the cognitive interview. This increase was comparable whether the crime or incident was viewed live or via videotape.

Memon, Meissner, and Fraser (2010) reported only one negative effect of the cognitive interview on eyewitness memory—there was a fairly small (but significant) increase in recall of incorrect details compared to the standard interview. They also found the adverse effects of misleading information on eyewitness memory were not reduced by using the cognitive interview.

Are *all* four components of the cognitive interview equally useful? No. Colomb and Ginet (2012) found mental or context reinstatement of the situation and reporting all the details both enhanced recall. In contrast, altering the eyewitness's perspective and changing the order of recall were ineffective. Dando, Ormerod, Wilcock, and Milne (2011) found that requiring eyewitnesses to recall information in a backward temporal order reduced correct recall and increased memory errors. These negative effects occurred because backward recall disrupted the temporal organization of eyewitness memory for the crime.

How can we increase eyewitness accuracy using the cognitive interview? Paulo, Albuquerque, and Bull (2016) found eyewitnesses' error rate was 6% when they seemed certain of what they were recalling but 23%

when they seemed uncertain. Thus, accuracy can be improved by taking account of eyewitnesses' confidence in their recall.

Finally, you will remember that Paulo et al. (2017) studied the effects of instructing eyewitnesses to organize their crime memories by using category clustering recall. This proved to be a very effective technique for maximizing eyewitness recall.

Evaluation

The cognitive interview has a well-established theoretical basis and has proved a very effective method for obtaining as much accurate information as possible from eyewitnesses. It is effective even when the incident was arousing and the eyewitness's memory is assessed only after a fairly long interval of time. The components most responsible for the effectiveness of the cognitive interview (e.g., mental or context reinstatement; reporting all details) have been identified. Finally, potentially important refinements of the cognitive interview have been proposed (e.g., Paolo et al., 2016, 2017).

What are the main limitations with the cognitive interview?

1   The small increase of incorrect information recalled by eyewitnesses can lead detectives to misinterpret the evidence.
2   It does not reduce the negative effects of misinformation (Memon, Zaragoza, Clifford, & Kidd, 2010).
3   Most versions of the cognitive interview do not require eyewitnesses to recall events with their eyes closed. However, Vredeveldt, Hitch, and Baddeley (2011) found this enhanced recall, and so it should be incorporated within cognitive interviews. Eye closure is beneficial because it reduces eyewitnesses' cognitive load and minimizes distraction.
4   The cognitive interview is less effective when the event was stressful. It is also less effective when there is a long delay between the event and the interview.

FROM LABORATORY TO COURTROOM

We have seen that psychologists have identified numerous reasons why jurors should be wary of accepting the validity of eyewitness testimony. These reasons include change blindness, witnesses' prior expectations, misleading pre- and post-event information, unconscious transference, verbal overshadowing, and weapon focus.

There is controversy concerning the extent to which psychologists' knowledge concerning the limitations of eyewitness testimony is sufficient to justify its extensive use in court cases. For example, Ebbesen and Konecni (1997, p. 2) argued, "The nature of what is known about humans memory is so complex that an honest presentation of this knowledge to a jury would only serve to confuse rather than improve their decision-making." In contrast, a recent report on psychological research on eyewitness misidentification by the National Academy of Sciences indicated there is "a long-overdue partnership between science and law" (Albright, 2017, p. 7763).

In light of these differing opinions, we must consider carefully what conclusions can validly be drawn from the available evidence. Two issues are of prime importance. First, there is ecological validity—whether laboratory findings *generalize* to real-life situations. If laboratory findings on eyewitness testimony lack ecological validity, it would clearly be inappropriate to provide jurors with such findings.

Second, even if laboratory research possesses ecological validity, it would not necessarily follow that eyewitness expert testimony should be presented to jurors. For example, such testimony might lead jurors to become so skeptical of the value of eyewitness evidence that they became excessively reluctant to find defendants guilty.

Laboratory findings are not relevant!

Those skeptical of the value of research findings on eyewitness testimony can point to several important differences between eyewitnesses' typical experiences in the laboratory and their experiences when observing a real-life crime. Below we identify some of the main ones. Many of these differences were identified by Flowe, Carline, and Karoğlu (2018), who compared characteristics of laboratory studies with those of actual criminal cases.

First, in the clear majority of laboratory studies, eyewitnesses of an incident or crime are bystanders rather than victims. In contrast, eyewitness evidence in real crimes is more likely to be provided by the victim than by bystanders. Flowe et al. (2018) found 56% of eyewitnesses to real crimes were victims compared to only 7% of eyewitnesses in laboratory studies.

Second, eyewitnesses in the laboratory are typically exposed to less stressful conditions than those in in real-life conditions. Flowe et al. (2018) found that practically no laboratory studies involved violence, whereas 59% of eyewitnesses to real crimes were exposed to violence. In addition, only 9% of laboratory eyewitnesses saw a weapon compared to 54% of eyewitnesses to real crimes.

Third, eyewitnesses in the laboratory generally observe the event from a *single* perspective in an essentially passive fashion. In contrast, eyewitnesses to a real-life crime are likely to move around and may be forced to interact with the individual(s) committing the crime.

Fourth, there are differences in the exposure time to the culprit(s). Flowe et al. (2018) found the median exposure time was eight minutes with real-life crimes compared to only one minute under laboratory conditions.

Fifth, Flowe et al. (2018) found that eyewitnesses to real-life crimes were acquainted with the suspect with 92% of assaults, 79% of rapes, and 21% of robberies. In contrast, none of the eyewitnesses in laboratory studies was acquainted with the culprit.

Sixth, there are differences in the culprit identification tasks used. Flowe et al. (2018) found that photo lineups (presenting eyewitnesses with photographs of several individuals) are more common under laboratory conditions than in real life (78% vs. 51%). In contrast, a live show-up (the eyewitness is presented with a single person) is far more common in real-life conditions than the laboratory (51% vs. <1%).

Seventh, the consequences if an eyewitness makes a mistaken identification in the laboratory are trivial (e.g., minor disappointment at their poor memory). In contrast, the consequences in an American court of law can literally be a matter of life or death.

In sum, there are many important differences between eyewitnesses' experiences in the laboratory and in real-life crimes, and these differences can systematically impact on their ability to identify the culprit or culprits. It is hard to say whether we should expect eyewitness memory to be better or worse in real-crime conditions than in the laboratory (discussed further below). Reasons why it might be better include the greater exposure time with real-life crimes and the higher probability that eyewitnesses are acquainted with the culprit. Reasons why it might be worse include the much higher likelihood of being a victim in real-life conditions and the greater probability of exposure to stress and violence.

What should we do? The most obvious requirement is for laboratory researchers to extend the range of conditions they use to reflect more accurately those prevalent with real-life crimes.

Findings

A key issue is whether the presentation of expert testimony improves the accuracy of jurors' decisions. Early evidence that it does not was reported by Leippe, Eisenstadt, Rauch, and Seib (2004). They considered the impact of expert testimony concerning eyewitness memory introduced towards the end of a murder-trial transcript. This was followed by a reminder about this testimony in the judge's final instructions.

The case used by Leippe et al. (2004) involved a holdup at night leading to a fatal stabbing. There were three versions of the case in which the evidence against the defendant was very strong, moderately strong, or weak. For example, in the very strong condition, DNA results indicated a 94% probability that a blood sample taken from the defendant's jacket was that of the victim. In addition, there was clear evidence the defendant had been in a struggle (e.g., swollen eye, scraped knuckles), and the victim's wallet was found in a trash can on the block where the defendant lived.

The presence of expert testimony produced a relatively large reduction in guilty verdicts regardless of the strength of the case. Even when the overall case was very strong, expert testimony reduced guilty verdicts from 74% to 59%. This suggests that exposing mock jurors to expert testimony made them focus too much on possible inaccuracies in the eyewitness's evidence at the expense of the otherwise strong evidence against the defendant. It is arguable that these findings were obtained because the expert testimony was somewhat biased. For example, the expert concluded his testimony by saying that, "A person attempting to judge whether an eyewitness had identified the criminal or an innocent suspect should avoid placing too much faith in the eyewitness's confidence" (Leippe et al., 2004, p. 530).

Martire and Kemp (2011) reviewed research on the effects of expert evidence on jurors' decision making. They emphasized the distinction between sensitivity and skepticism. *Sensitivity* is the ability to evaluate accurately the evidence provided by an eyewitness, whereas *skepticism* is the tendency to disbelieve an eyewitness regardless of the quality of their evidence. Martire and Kemp found expert evidence generally increases jurors' skepticism without increasing their sensitivity—the exact opposite of what is required.

Laboratory findings are relevant!

In the previous section, we identified major differences between eyewitnesses' experiences in the laboratory and real life. Of crucial importance is whether these differences have large and systematic effects on the accuracy of eyewitness memory. Lindsay and Harvie

(1988) had eyewitnesses watch an event shown in a slide show, a video film, or live staging. The accuracy of culprit identification differed only slightly across these three conditions, suggesting that artificial laboratory conditions do not necessarily lead to distortions in the findings obtained.

Ihlebaek, Løve, Eilertsen, and Magnussen (2003) staged a robbery involving two robbers armed with shotguns. In the live condition, the eyewitnesses were ordered repeatedly to "Stay down." In the video condition, a video recorded during the live condition was presented to eyewitnesses. Eyewitnesses in both conditions exaggerated the duration of the event and the patterns of memory performance (i.e., what was well and poorly remembered) were similar. However, eyewitnesses in the video condition recalled more information—they estimated the robbers' age, height, and weight more closely, and they also identified the robbers' weapons more accurately.

More support for the relevance of laboratory findings for the legal system was reported by Pozzulo, Crescini, and Panton (2008). Eyewitnesses observed a staged theft live or via video. Identification accuracy of the culprit was comparable in the two conditions. However, eyewitnesses in the live condition reported more stress and arousal.

Tollestrupp, Turtle, and Yuille (1994) analyzed police records of eyewitness identifications for crimes involving fraud and robbery. Factors important in laboratory studies (e.g., exposure duration, weapon focus, retention interval) were also important in real-life crimes. For example, identification accuracy was greater when eyewitnesses were exposed to the culprit for a relatively long time and when the time interval between the crime and the initial questioning was short.

We saw earlier (Martire & Kemp, 2011) that the introduction of expert evidence often leads jurors to become excessively skeptical of eyewitness testimony. However, that may occur mostly because experts called by the defense typically emphasize limitations with eyewitness testimony.

Early evidence that expert evidence can enhance jurors' decision making was reported by Cutler, Penrod, and Dexter (1989). Mock jurors viewed a realistic videotaped trial concerning an armed robbery of a liquor store. The witnessing and identification conditions were poor or good. In the poor condition, the robber was disguised, he brandished a handgun, the identification took place 14 days after the robbery, and the lineup instructions were suggestive (the officer in charge did not explicitly provide the witness with the option of not choosing anyone). In the good condition, the robber was not disguised, his handgun was hidden throughout the robbery, the identification took place two days after the robbery, and the lineup instructions were not suggestive.

Cutler et al. (1989) found jurors' judgments on the accuracy of the eyewitness's identification were influenced by the quality of the witnessing and identification conditions when they were presented with expert testimony. In contrast, the conditions had practically no effect on jurors' judgments when this expert testimony was not presented. In addition, the jurors' verdict (innocent or guilty) was much more influenced by the witnessing and identification conditions when expert testimony was presented.

Expert evidence is potentially valuable in part because jurors often exhibit systematic biases. They regard DNA evidence as no more indicative of guilt than less valid forms of physical evidence (e.g., fingerprinting), and they *overweight* crime seriousness (defendants are more likely to be perceived as guilty with serious crimes). However, they substantially *underweight* the relevance of a defendant's criminal history (Pearson et al., 2018).

Safer et al. (2016) argued that it is possible to provide information about the strengths and limitations of eyewitness testimony so jurors' judgments are consistently improved. More specifically, they used the Interview, Identification, Eyewitness Factors (I-I-Eye) method: this written aid instructs jurors to follow three steps with respect to eyewitness testimony:

1 Evaluate the adequacy of how law enforcement agencies carried out eyewitness interviews.
2 Evaluate how identification procedures (e.g., lineups) were conducted.
3 Evaluate the eyewitness factors present at the crime scene (e.g., lighting; distance between the eyewitness and the culprit).

Safer et al. (2016) carried out a study in which mock jurors read a trial transcript where the eyewitness evidence was strong or weak. Before reading this transcript, the jurors had been presented with the I-I-Eye aid or a basic jury duty (JD) aid.

The findings are shown in Figure 12.11. Use of the I-I-Eye aid increased sensitivity rather than skepticism. Jurors receiving the I-I-Eye aid were *less* likely than those receiving the JD aid to return a guilty verdict when the case was weak, but were *more* likely to return a guilty verdict when the case was strong. Strikingly, jurors receiving the JD aid showed no sensitivity at all in discriminating between the strong and weak cases.

Conclusions

It is reasonable to conclude that the main findings of eyewitness researchers are relevant to the legal process and should be

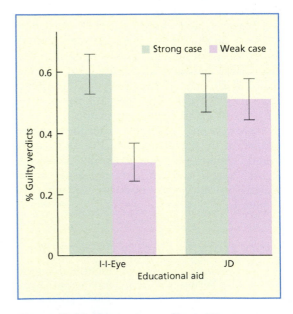

Figure 12.11 Mean percent guilty verdicts as a function of strength of the case (strong vs. weak) and type of aid (I-I-Eye vs. JD). From Safer et al., 2016.

made available to jurors. In spite of the many differences between eyewitnesses' experiences in the laboratory and in real-life crimes, findings in the two situations are generally in agreement. However, the presentation of this evidence to jurors should be done very carefully because expert evidence often increases their skepticism without enhancing their sensitivity (especially when experts have been called by the defense). However, it is very encouraging that the I-I-Eye method has proved successful in increasing jurors' sensitivity without increasing their skepticism. More generally, it is surely desirable that jurors are presented with factually accurate information concerning the strengths and limitations of eyewitnesses' memory.

SUMMARY

- There is convincing evidence (much involving the use of DNA) that many innocent individuals have been imprisoned primarily on the basis of eyewitness testimony.
- Jurors are impressed by eyewitnesses who express high confidence in their identification of the suspect even when this identification is incorrect. Such eyewitnesses often had low confidence in their identification initially but became increasingly confident when praised by the police for having identified the suspect.
- The beliefs of judges and jurors often differ from expert consensus concerning the factors influencing the accuracy of eyewitness testimony.
- What eyewitnesses claim to remember is influenced by their expectations concerning what is likely to have happened based on their crime-relevant schemas.
- Misleading information provided after (or before) an event can cause eyewitness memory for that event to be distorted. Such distortions are often due to inaccessibility of information about the original event rather than altered memory traces.
- The misinformation effect can be reduced by using techniques designed to increase an eyewitness's self-confidence and self-independence.
- Stress and anxiety typically reduce the ability of eyewitnesses to remember faces and other details of the situation.
- Eyewitnesses often attend so closely to the criminal's weapon that their memory for the criminal's features is impaired: this is the weapon focus effect. This effect occurs in part because of attentional narrowing of "tunnel vision."
- Older eyewitnesses have less accurate memory for events than younger adults. They often produce false memories and are strongly influenced by misleading suggestions.
- There is an own-age bias where eyewitnesses show more accurate identification when the culprit is of similar age to themselves. This bias depends mostly on greater experience of (and expertise with) own-age faces.
- Eyewitnesses are often poor at recognizing unfamiliar faces and even at deciding whether two photographs show the same person.
- Face-recognition memory is greatly reduced by disguise even when this involves apparently small changes (e.g., adding or removing sunglasses). This effect occurs because face processing is typically holistic (based on the overall arrangement of facial features).
- Eyewitnesses sometimes identify an innocent bystander as the culprit because their face seems familiar in a process of unconscious transference.

(Continued)

(Continued)

- Eyewitnesses' face recognition is often impaired when they have previously provided a verbal description of that person: the verbal overshadowing effect. This occurs because verbal descriptions are rather general and imprecise.
- Eyewitnesses are better at recognizing same-race than other-race faces: the cross-race effect. This occurs in part because eyewitnesses engage in more processing of own-race faces.
- Eyewitness recognition of unfamiliar faces can be improved if the police provide synthesized images (combining several photographs of an individual into one image) rather than a single photograph. This is because a single photograph of an individual is often unrepresentative of how that person typically looks.
- Lineups can be simultaneous or sequential. The former provide a greater probability of identifying the culprit but often make it more likely that an innocent individual will be misidentified as the culprit. What is of crucial importance is the precise magnitude of these two effects which varies depending on the precise conditions.
- More information is obtained from eyewitnesses using cognitive interviews than standard ones. The most useful components of the cognitive interview are the use of mental reinstatement of the crime scene and the requirement for eyewitnesses to recall every detail.
- The main disadvantage with the cognitive interview is that there is a small increase in the number of incorrect details recalled.
- There are many differences between eyewitnesses' experience in the laboratory and in real-life crimes. Laboratory conditions typically differ from real life in that the event is observed by bystanders rather than victims, there is little or no stress, and eyewitnesses have only a few seconds to study the culprit.
- When experts on eyewitness testimony provide evidence in court cases, this often has the negative effects of increasing jurors' skepticism without enhancing their sensitivity. This is the opposite of what is desirable. However, researchers have developed a new technique (the Interview, Identification, Eyewitness Factors [I-I-Eye] method that has shown to increase jurors' sensitivity to the strengths and limitations of eyewitness evidence without increasing their skepticism.

POINTS FOR DISCUSSION

1 What are the main factors causing eyewitness testimony to be inaccurate and/or distorted?
2 What are the effects of anxiety and stress on eyewitness memory?
3 Why is the eyewitness testimony of older adults generally inferior to that of younger adults?
4 Why do eyewitnesses often find it hard to remember faces? What can be done to enhance face recognition?
5 What are the characteristics of the most successful interviewing techniques used by the police with eyewitnesses?
6 How relevant is laboratory research on eyewitness testimony to the courtroom?

FURTHER READING

Blank, H., & Launay, C. (2014). How to protect eyewitness memory against the misinformation effect: A meta-analysis of post-warning studies. *Journal of Applied Research in Memory and Cognition, 3*, 77–88. Hartmut Blank and Céline Launay reported findings that clarify the processes involved in the misinformation effect.

Davis, D., & Loftus, E. F. (2018). Eyewitness science in the 21st century: What do we know and where do we go from here?. In E. A. Phelps & L. Davachi (Eds.), *Stevens' handbook of experimental psychology and cognitive neuroscience: Vol. 1: Learning and memory* (4th ed., pp. 529–566). New York: Wiley. Our current empirical and theoretical understanding of eyewitness testimony is discussed thoroughly by Davis and Loftus.

Fawcett, J. M., Peace, K. A., & Greve, A. (2016). Looking down the barrel of a gun: What do we know about the weapon focus effect?. *Journal of Applied Research in Memory and Cognition, 5*, 257–263. Jonathan Fawcett and colleagues summarize the ways in which eyewitness memory is influenced when the culprit has a weapon.

Geiselman, R. E., & Fisher, R. P. (2014). Interviewing witnesses and victims. In M. St-Yves (Ed.), *Investigative interviewing: Handbook of best practices* (pp. 29–63). Toronto, ON: Thomson Reuters. This chapter discusses effective ways for police to interview eyewitnesses with an emphasis on the cognitive interview.

Wixted, J. T., Mickes, L., & Fisher, R. P. (2018). Rethinking the reliability of eyewitness memory. *Perspectives on Psychological Science, 13*, 324–335. John Wixted and colleagues argue (backed by much relevant research) that eyewitness memory is reliable provided it is not contaminated by deficiencies in the processes used to assess it.

Young, A. W., & Burton, A. M. (2018). Are we face experts?. *Trends in Cognitive Sciences, 22*, 100–110. Andy Young and Mike Burton provide a useful overview of the reasons why we have only a rather limited ability to recognize unfamiliar faces.

REFERENCES

Albright, T. D. (2017). Why eyewitnesses fail. *Proceedings of the National Academy of Sciences of the USA, 114*, 7758–7764.

Alogna, V. K., Attaya, M. K., Aucoin, P., Bahník, Š., Birch, S., Birt, A. R., et al. (2014). Registered replication report: Schooler and Engstler-Schooler (1990). *Perspectives on Psychological Science, 9*, 556–578.

Bartlett, F. C. (1932). *Remembering*. Cambridge: Cambridge University Press.

Biggs, A. T., Brockmole, J. R., & Witt, J. K. (2013). Armed and attentive: Holding a weapon can bias attentional priorities in scene viewing. *Attention, Perception & Psychophysics, 75*, 1715–1724.

Blank, H., & Launay, C. (2014). How to protect eyewitness memory against the misinformation effect: A meta-analysis of post-warning studies. *Journal of Applied Research in Memory and Cognition, 3*, 77–88.

Brown, T. J., Uncapher, M. R., Chow, T. E., Eberhardt, J. L., & Wagner, A. D. (2017). Cognitive control, attention, and the other race effect in memory. *PLoS ONE, 12* (Article e0173579).

Bruce, V., Henderson, Z., Greenwood, K., Hancock, P., Burton, A. M., & Miller, P. (1999). Verification of face identities from images captured on video. *Journal of Experimental Psychology: Applied, 5,* 339–360.

Charman, S. D., Wells. G. L., & Joy, S. W. (2011). The dud effect: Adding highly dissimilar fillers increases confidence in lineup identifications. *Law and Human Behavior, 35,* 479–500.

Cohen, M. A., Dennett, D. C., & Kanwisher, N. (2016). What is the bandwidth of perceptual experience?. *Trends in Cognitive Sciences, 20,* 324–335.

Colomb, C., & Ginet, M. (2012). The cognitive interview for use with adults: An empirical test of an alternative mnemonic and of a partial protocol. *Applied Cognitive Psychology, 26,* 35–47.

Cutler, B. L., Penrod, S. D., & Dexter, H. R. (1989). The eyewitness, the expert psychologist, and the jury. *Law and Human Behavior, 13,* 311–332.

Dahl, M., Granér, S., Fransson, P.-A., Bertilsson, J., & Fredriksson, P. (2018). Analysis of eyewitness testimony in a police shooting with fatal outcome: Manifestations of spatial and temporal distortions. *Cogent Psychology, 5,* 1487271.

Dando, C. J., Ormerod, T. C., Wilcock, R., & Milne, R. (2011). When help becomes hindrance: Unexpected errors of omission and commission in eyewitness memory resulting from changes in temporal order at retrieval?. *Cognition, 121,* 416–421.

Davis, D., Loftus, E. F., Vanous, S., & Cucciare, M. (2008). 'Unconscious transference' can be an instance of 'change blindness'. *Applied Cognitive Psychology, 22,* 605–623.

Deffenbacher, K. A., Bornstein, B. H., Penrod, S. D., & McGorty, E. K. (2004). A meta-analytic review of the effects of high stress on eyewitness memory. *Law and Human Behavior, 28,* 687–706.

Desmarais, S. L., & Read, J. D. (2011). After 30 years, what do we know about what jurors know? A meta-analytic review of lay knowledge regarding eyewitness factors. *Law and Human Behavior, 35,* 200–210.

Easterbrook, J. A. (1959). The effect of emotion on cue utilization and the organization of behavior. *Psychological Review, 66,* 183–201.

Ebbesen, E. B., & Konecni, V. J. (1997). Eyewitness memory research: Probative vs. prejudicial value. *The International Digest of Human Behavior, Science, and the Law, 5,* 2–28.

Edelson, M., Sharot, T., Dolan, R. J., & Dudai, Y. (2011). Following the crowd: Brain substrates of long-term memory conformity. *Science, 333,* 108–111.

Fawcett, J. M., Russell, E. J., Peace, K. A., & Christie, J. (2013). Of guns and geese: A metaanalytic review of the "weapon focus" literature. *Psychology, Crime & Law, 19,* 35–66.

Fischer, J., & Whitney, D. (2014). Serial dependence in visual perception. *Nature Neuroscience, 17,* 738–746.

Fitzgerald, R. J., Oriet, C., & Price, H. L. (2016). Change blindness and eyewitness identification: Effects on accuracy and confidence. *Legal and Criminological Psychology, 21,* 189–201.

Flowe, H. D., Carline, A., & Karoğlu, N. (2018). Testing the reflection assumption: A comparison of eyewitness ecology in the laboratory and criminal cases. *International Journal of Evidence & Proof, 22,* 239–261.

Fraundorf, S. H., Hourihan, K. L., Peters, R. A., & Benjamin, A. S. (2019). Aging and recognition memory: A meta-analysis. *Psychological Bulletin, 145,* 339–371.

Gabbert, F., Hope, L., Fisher, R. P., & Jamieson, K. (2012). Protecting against misleading post-event information with a self-administered interview. *Applied Cognitive Psychology, 26,* 568–575.

Garrett, B. (2011). *Convicting the innocent: Where criminal prosecutions go wrong.* Cambridge, MA: Harvard University Press.

Geiselman, R. E., Fisher, R. P., MacKinnon, D. P., & Holland, H. L. (1985). Eyewitness memory enhancement in police interview: Cognitive retrieval mnemonics versus hypnosis. *Journal of Applied Psychology, 70,* 401–412.

Grabman, J. H., & Dodson, C. S. (2019). Prior knowledge influences interpretation of eyewitness confidence statements: 'The witness picked the suspect, they must be 100% sure'. *Psychology, Crime & Law, 25,* 50–68.

Harada, Y., Hakoda, Y., Kuroki, D., & Mitsudo, H. (2015). The presence of a weapon shrinks the functional field of view. *Applied Cognitive Psychology, 29,* 592–599.

Hastorf, A. A., & Cantril, H. (1954). They saw a game: A case study. *Journal of Abnormal and Social Psychology, 97,* 399–401.

Healey, M. K., & Kahane, M. J. (2016). A four-component model of age-related memory change. *Psychological Review, 123,* 23–69.

Higham, P. A., Blank, H., & Luna, K. (2017). Effects of post-warning specificity on memory performance and confidence in the eyewitness misinformation paradigm. *Journal of Experimental Psychology: Applied, 23,* 417–432.

Hugenberg, K., Young, S. G., Bernstein, M. J., & Sacco, D. F. (2010). The categorization individuation model: An integrative account of the other-race recognition deficit. *Psychological Review, 117,* 1168–1187.

Ihlebaek, C., Løve, T., Eilertsen, D. E., & Magnussen, S. (2003). Memory for a staged criminal event witnessed live and on video. *Memory, 11,* 310–327.

Jacoby, L. L., Bishara, A. J., Hessels, S., & Toth, J. P. (2005). Aging, subjective experience, and cognitive control: Dramatic false remembering by older adults. *Journal of Experimental Psychology: General, 134*, 131–148.

Jaeger, C. B., Levin, D. T., & Porter, E. (2017). Justice is (change) blind: Applying research on visual metacognition in legal settings. *Psychology, Public Policy, and Law, 23*, 259–279.

Jenkins, R., White, D., van Montfort, X., & Burton, A. M. (2011). Variability in photos of the same face. *Cognition, 121*, 313–323.

Johnson, M. K., Hashtroudi, S., & Lindsay, D. S. (1993). Source monitoring. *Psychological Bulletin, 114*, 3–28.

Jones, S. P., Dwyer, D. M., & Lewis, M. B. (2017). The utility of multiple synthesized views in the recognition of unfamiliar faces. *Quarterly Journal of Experimental Psychology, 70*, 906–918.

Kovera, M. B., & Evelo, A. J. (2017). The case for double-blind lineup administration. *Psychology, Public Policy and Law, 23*, 421–437.

Leippe, M. R., Eisenstadt, D., Rauch, S. M., & Seib, H. M. (2004). Timing of eyewitness expert testimony, jurors' need for cognition, and case strength as determinants of trial verdicts. *Journal of Applied Psychology, 89*, 524–541.

Levin, D. T., Drivdahl, S. B., Momen, N., & Beck, M. R. (2002). False predictions about the detectability of visual changes: The role of beliefs about attention, memory, and the continuity of attended objects in causing change blindness blindness. *Consciousness and Cognition, 11*, 507–527.

Lindholm, T., & Christianson, S.-A. (1998). Intergroup biases and eyewitness testimony. *Journal of Social Psychology, 138*, 710–723.

Lindsay, D. S., Allen, B. P., Chan, J. C. K., & Dahl, L. C. (2004). Eyewitness suggestibility and source similarity: Intrusions of details from one event into memory reports of another event. *Journal of Memory and Language, 50*, 96–111.

Lindsay, R. C. L., & Harvie, V. (1988). Hits, false alarms, correct and mistaken identifications: The effects of method of data collection on facial memory. In M. Gruneberg, P. Morris, & R. Sykes (Eds.), *Practical aspects of memory: Current research and issues, Vol. 1: Memory in everyday life* (pp. 47–52). Chichester, UK: Wiley.

Loftus, E. F., Miller, D. G., & Burns, H. J. (1978). Semantic integration of verbal information into a visual memory. *Journal of Experimental Psychology: Human Learning and Memory, 4*, 19–31.

Loftus, E. F., & Palmer, J. C. (1974). Reconstruction of automobile destruction: An example of the interaction between language and memory. *Journal of Verbal Learning and Verbal Behavior, 13*, 585–589.

Martire, K. A., & Kemp, R. I. (2011). Can experts help jurors to evaluate eyewitness evidence? A review of eyewitness expert effects. *Legal and Criminological Psychology, 16*, 24–36.

Martschuk, N., & Sporer, S. L. (2018). Memory for faces in old age: A meta-analysis. *Psychology and Aging, 33*, 904–923.

Megreya, A. M., White, D., & Burton, A. M. (2011). The other-race effect does not rely on memory: Evidence from a matching task. *Quarterly Journal of Experimental Psychology, 64*, 1473–1483.

Memon, A., Meissner, C. A., & Fraser, J. (2010). The cognitive interview: A meta-analytic review and study space analysis of the past 25 years. *Psychology, Public Policy and Law, 16*, 340–372.

Memon, A., Zaragoza, M., Clifford, B. R., & Kidd, L. (2010). Inoculation or antidote? The effects of cognitive interview timing on false memory for forcibly fabricated events. *Law and Human Behavior, 34*, 105–117.

Moniz, E., Righi, G., Peissig, J. J., & Tarr, M. J. (2010). The Clark Kent effect: What is the role of familiarity and eyeglasses in recognizing disguised faces?. *Journal of Vision, 10*(7) (Article 615).

Morcom, A. M. (2016). Mind over memory: Cuing the aging brain. *Current Directions in Psychological Science, 25*, 143–150.

Oeberst, A., & Blank, H. (2012). Undoing suggestive influence on memory: The reversibility of the eyewitness misinformation effect. *Cognition, 125*, 141–159.

Patterson, K. E., & Baddeley, A. D. (1977). When face recognition fails. *Journal of Experimental Psychology: Human Learning and Memory, 3*, 406–417.

Paulo, R. M., Albuquerque, P. B., & Bull, R. (2016). The enhanced cognitive interview: Expressions of uncertainty, motivation and its relation with report accuracy. *Psychology, Crime, & Law, 22*, 366–381.

Paulo, R. M., Albuquerque, P. B., Vitorino, F., & Bull, R. (2017). Enhancing the cognitive interview with an alternative procedure to witness-compatible questioning: Category clustering recall. *Psychology, Crime, & Law, 23*, 967–982.

Pearson, J. M., Law, J. R., Skene, J. A. G., Beskind, D. H., Vidmar, N., Ball, D. A., et al. (2018). Modelling the effects of crime type and evidence on judgments about guilt. *Nature Human Behaviour, 2*, 856–866.

Pickel, K. L. (2009). The weapon focus effect on memory for female versus male perpetrators. *Memory, 17*, 664–678.

Pickel, K. L., & Gentry, R. H. (2017). Mock jurors' expectations regarding the psychological harm experienced by rape victims as a function of rape prototypicality. *Psychology, Crime & Law*, 23, 254–273.

Pozzulo, J. D., Crescini, C., & Panton, T. (2008). Does methodology matter in eyewitness identification research? The effect of live versus video exposure on eyewitness identification of accuracy. *International Journal of Law and Psychiatry*, 31, 430–437.

Prull, M. W., & Yockelson, M. B. (2013). Adult age-related differences in the misinformation effect for context-consistent and context-inconsistent objects. *Applied Cognitive Psychology*, 27, 384–395.

Putnam, A. L., Sungkhasettee, V. W., & Roediger, H. L. (2017). When misinformation improves memory: The effects of recollecting change. *Psychological Science*, 28, 36–46.

Quaedflieg, C. W. E. M., & Schwabe, L. (2018). Memory dynamics under stress. *Memory*, 26, 364–376.

Richler, J. J., Cheung, O. S., & Gauthier, I. (2011). Holistic processing predicts face recognition. *Psychological Science*, 22, 464–471.

Rindal, E. J., Chrobak, Q. M., Zaragoza, M. S., & Weihing, C. A. (2017). Mechanisms of eyewitness suggestibility: Tests of the explanatory role hypothesis. *Psychonomic Bulletin & Review*, 24, 1413–1425.

Robertson, D. J., Noyes, E., Dowsett, A. J., Jenkins, R., & Burton, A. M. (2016). Face recognition by Metropolitan police super-recognizers. *PLoS ONE*, 11(2), e0150036.

Safer, M. A., Murphy, R. P., Wise, R. A., Bussey, L., Millett, C., & Holfeld, B. (2016). Educating jurors about eyewitness testimony in criminal cases with circumstantial and forensic evidence. *International Journal of Law and Psychiatry*, 47, 86–92.

Schmidt, P.-I., Rosga, K., Schatto, C., Breidenstein, A., & Schwabe, L. (2014). Stress the incorporation of misinformation into an established memory. *Learning & Memory*, 21, 744–747.

Schooler, J. W. (2014). Turning the lens of science on itself: Verbal overshadowing, replication, and metascience. *Perspectives on Psychological Science*, 9, 579–584.

Schooler, J. W., & Engstler-Schooler, T. Y. (1990). Verbal overshadowing of visual memories: Some things are better left unsaid. *Cognitive Psychology*, 22, 36–71.

Shapiro, L. R. (2009). Eyewitness testimony for a simulated juvenile crime by male and female criminals with consistent or inconsistent gender-role characteristics. *Journal of Applied Developmental Psychology*, 30, 649–666.

Simons, D. J., & Chabris, C. F. (1999). Gorillas in our midst: Sustained inattentional blindness for dynamic events. *Perception*, 28, 1059–1074.

Simons, D. J., & Chabris, C. F. (2011). What people believe about how memory works: A representative survey of the US population. *Public Library of Science One*, 6, e22757.

Smalarz, L., & Wells, G. L. (2012). Eyewitness-identification evidence: Scientific advances and the new burden on trial judges. *Court Review: The Journal of the American Judges Association*, Paper 385.

Steblay, N. K., Wells, G. L., & Douglass, A. B. (2014). The eyewitness post identification feedback effect 15 years later: Theoretical and policy implications. *Psychology, Public Policy and Law*, 20, 1–18.

Szpitalak, M., & Polczyk, R. (2019). Inducing resistance to the misinformation effect by means of reinforced self-affirmation: The importance of positive feedback. *PLoS ONE*, 14, e0210987.

Tollestrup, P. A., Turtle, J. W., & Yuille, J. C. (1994). Actual victims and witnesses to robbery and fraud: An archival analysis. In D. F. Ross, J. D. Read, & M. P. Toglia (Eds.), *Adult eyewitness testimony: Current trends and developments* (pp. 144–160). New York: Wiley.

Tuckey, M. R., & Brewer, N. (2003a). How schemas affect eyewitness memory over repeated retrieval attempts. *Applied Cognitive Psychology*, 7, 785–800.

Tuckey, M. R., & Brewer, N. (2003b). The influence of schemas, stimulus ambiguity, and interview schedule on eyewitness memory over time. *Journal of Experimental Psychology: Applied*, 9, 101–118.

Tulving, E. (1979). Relation between encoding specificity and levels of processing. In L. S. Cermak & F. I. M. Craik (Eds.), *Levels of processing in human memory* (pp. 405–428). Hillsdale, NJ: Lawrence Erlbaum Associates.

Unsworth, N. (2019). Individual differences in long-term memory. *Psychological Bulletin*, 145, 79–139.

Valentine, T., Pickering, A., & Darling, S. (2003). Characteristics of eyewitness identification that predict the outcome of real line-ups. *Applied Cognitive Psychology*, 17, 969–993.

Vredeveldt, A., Hitch, G. J., & Baddeley, A. D. (2011). Eyeclosure helps memory by reducing cognitive load and enhancing visualization. *Memory & Cognition*, 39, 1253–1263.

Wells, G. L., Steblay, N. K., & Dysart, J. E. (2015). Double-blind photo lineups using actual eyewitnesses: An experimental test of a sequential versus simultaneous lineup procedure. *Law and Human Behavior, 39*, 1–14.

Wiese, H., Wolff, N., Steffens, M. C., & Schweinberger, S. R. (2013). How experience shapes memory for faces: An event-related potential study on the own-age bias. *Biological Psychology, 94*, 369–379.

Wilson, B. M., Seale-Carlisle, T. M., & Mickes, L. (2018). The effects of verbal descriptions on performance in lineups and showups. *Journal of Experimental Psychology: General, 147*, 113–124.

Wise, R. A., & Safer, M. A. (2004). What US judges know and believe about eyewitness testimony. *Applied Cognitive Psychology, 18*, 427–443.

Wise, R. A., & Safer, M. A. (2010). A comparison of what US judges and students know and believe about eyewitness testimony. *Journal of Applied Social Psychology, 40*, 1400–1422.

Wixted, J. T., Mickes, L., Dunn, J. C., Clark, S. E., & Wells, S. (2016). Estimating the reliability of eyewitness identifications from police lineups. *Proceedings of the National Academy of Sciences of the USA, 113*, 304–309.

Wixted, J. T., & Wells, G. L. (2017). The relationship between eyewitness confidence and identification accuracy: A new synthesis. *Psychological Science in the Public Interest, 18*, 10–65.

Wright, D. B., & Stroud, J. N. (2002). Age differences in lineup identification accuracy: People are better with their own age. *Law and Human Behavior, 26*, 641–654.

Yegiyan, N. S., & Lang, A. (2010). Processing central and peripheral detail: How content arousal and emotional tone influence encoding. *Media Psychology, 13*, 77–99.

Young, A. W., & Burton, A. M. (2018). Are we face experts?. *Trends in Cognitive Sciences, 22*, 100–110.

Young, S. G., Hugenberg, K., Bernstein, M. J., & Sacco, D. F. (2012). Perception and motivation in face recognition: A critical review of theories of the cross-race effect. *Personality and Social Psychology Review, 16*, 116–142.

Zhu, B., Chen, C., Loftus, E. F., Lin, C., He, Q., Chen, C., et al. (2010a). Individual differences in false memory from misinformation: Cognitive factors. *Memory, 18*, 543–555.

Zhu, B., Chen, C., Loftus, E. F., Lin, C., He, Q., Chen, C., et al. (2010b). Individual differences in false memory from misinformation: Personality characteristics and their interactions with cognitive abilities. *Personality and Individual Differences, 48*, 889–894.

Contents

CHAPTER 13

PROSPECTIVE MEMORY

Michael W. Eysenck

INTRODUCTION

Has the following ever happened to you? You are introducing two people to each other but suddenly realize you have forgotten one of their names. If you have had that experience, you will know how acutely embarrassing it can be. Frustration is another emotion we can experience when forgetting occurs, as when a student sitting an examination goes blank and can't remember what they know about a topic. These are failures of retrospective memory, which involves remembering events, words, and so on from the past, generally (but not always) when deliberately trying to do so.

There is an important distinction between retrospective memory and prospective memory. The latter is a type of memory that involves remembering to carry out intended actions without being instructed to do so. Failures of prospective memory (absent-mindedness when action is required) can also be embarrassing as when you completely forget you had arranged to meet a friend at a coffee shop. Freud (1901, p. 157), in his usual over-the-top style, argued that the motive behind many of our forgotten appointments is, "an unusually large amount of unavowed contempt for other people."

Why is prospective memory important?

Most human behavior is *goal-directed*. It is often essential we perform actions intended to facilitate goal attainment at the appropriate time, which requires use of prospective memory. For example, if you set the goal of having a vacation during a given week, you must remember to book the flights, a hotel to stay in, and so on in good time.

Failures of prospective memory can have fatal consequences. For example, almost 40 children a year die of heatstroke in cars in the United States because of prospective-memory failures by parents forgetting to take their child out of the car. They are known as "hot car deaths." For example, consider what happened to one-year-old Ray Ray Reeves-Cavaliero on May 25, 2011. Her father (Brett) was late in driving her to the daycare center. As he drove through Austin, Texas, he arrived at a T-junction. He should have turned left to the daycare center, which was only 300 yards away. Instead, he turned right, which was on his route to work. Hours later, Ray Ray was discovered dying in the back seat of the car.

KEY TERM

Retrospective memory: Memory for people, words, and events experienced in the past.

Prospective memory: Remembering to carry out some intended action in the absence of any explicit reminder to do so; see retrospective memory.

Diamond (2019) has identified various reasons why such tragic events occur. First, there may be few environmental cues to remind the parent that their infant is in the car. In the above case, nearly all of Brett Reeves-Cavaliero's drive to work on that fateful morning was the one he would have taken if his infant daughter had *not* been in the car. In addition, a parent may forget the child is in the car because they are unusually quiet rather than interactive.

Second, there may have been a change in the usual routine. For example, a father may typically drive a given route to take his infant child to a daycare center before continuing to his place of work. If, for some reason, he takes a different route, he may absent-mindedly simply drive to work leaving his child asleep in the car.

Failures of prospective memory also play an important part in many aircraft accidents. In the mid-1990s, a DC-9 landed in Houston without the landing gear in place. The crew failed to notice the gear wasn't down because they hadn't switched the hydraulic pumps to high. Why did this failure in prospective memory occur? The crew had been concentrating on coping with a complicated approach to the landing strip—they prioritized this task over ensuring that the landing gear was in place. The role of prospective memory in fatal aircraft accidents is discussed more fully later in the chapter.

We conclude this section with an extremely common form of prospective-memory failure. In the United States and the United Kingdom, millions of individuals suffer from chronic health conditions requiring regular medication. Surprisingly, 50% of them show at least partial failure to adhere to their recommended schedule of medication.

There are numerous reasons for this non-adherence to medication schedules. However, deficient prospective memory is an important factor. Zogg, Woods, Sauceda, Wieber, and Simoni (2012) reviewed research showing the importance of prospective memory in the treatment of several conditions including HIV/AIDS, rheumatoid arthritis, and diabetes. For example, Woods et al. (2009) found among patients with HIV/AIDS that those making errors on a laboratory task involving prospective memory were nearly *six times* more likely to be nonadherent to their medication regime than those making no errors. Avci et al. (2018, p. 877) reviewed research on patients with HIV and concluded, "Overall, the literature provides consistent evidence for a significant relationship between performance-based PM [prospective memory] and medication adherence in HIV."

Prospective vs. retrospective memory

Prospective memory differs most obviously from retrospective memory in its emphasis on the *future* rather than the *past*. However, there are several other important differences. First, retrospective memory generally involves remembering *what* we know about something and is often high in informational content. In contrast, prospective memory generally focuses on *when* to do something and has relatively low informational content. Its low informational content means that nonperformance of the prospective-memory task is unlikely to be due to retrospective memory failure. Second, prospective memory (but not retrospective memory) relates to the plans or goals we form for our daily activities.

Third, more external cues are generally available with retrospective memory than with prospective memory. In everyday life, for example, we often assess someone's retrospective memory by asking them a question about the past.

Fourth, as Moscovitch (2008, p. 309) pointed out, "Research on prospective memory is about the only major enterprise in memory research in which the problem is not memory itself, but the uses to which memory is put."

Fifth, we interpret failures of prospective and retrospective memory in different ways. Failures of prospective memory involving promises to another person are interpreted as indicating poor motivation and reliability. In contrast, failures of retrospective memory are simply attributed to having a poor memory. As Graf (2012) argued, deficient prospective memory means "flaky person" whereas deficient retrospective memory means "faulty brain."

In spite of the above differences between prospective and retrospective memory, remembering and forgetting in our everyday lives often involve a mixture of the two. For example, two things need to happen if you are to carry out your intention of buying various goods at the local super-market for you and your friends. First, you must remember your intention to go to the supermarket (prospective memory). Second, you must remember precisely what you had agreed to buy (retrospective memory).

Uttl, White, Cnudde, and Grant (2018) discovered several similarities between pro-spective and retrospective memory. First, both forms of memory correlated moderately highly with intelligence. Second, both forms of memory correlated with processing speed and working memory (although the cor-relations were greater with retrospective memory). Third, prospective and retro-spective memory correlated significantly with each other.

Assessing prospective memory: Self-report measures

How good is your prospective and retro-spective memory? Answer that question by completing the questionnaire below taken from Crawford, Smith, Maylor, Della Sala, and Logie (2003).

In order to demonstrate that a question-naire is valid (i.e., it measures what it is claimed to measure), we need to show that what individuals *say* on the questionnaire corresponds to their actual *behavior*. Rel-evant evidence was reported by Zimprich, Kliegel, and Rast (2011). First, they con-firmed that the PRMQ contains separable (although highly correlated) factors of pro-spective and retrospective memory. Second, individuals reporting poor prospective memory on the PRMQ performed worse than those reporting good prospective memory on various prospective-memory tasks.

In spite of Zimprich et al.'s (2011) positive findings, the relationship they reported between self-reported prospective memory and prospective-memory perfor-

mance was fairly modest. Part of the explanation may lie in somewhat deficient metamemory, which refers to "people's awareness and understanding of their own memory and learning" (Susser & Mulligan, 2019, p. 43). Schnitzspahn, Zeintl, Jäger, and Kliegel (2011) found that participants' judgments of their future prospective-memory performance generally *underesti-mated* that performance.

Nature of prospective memory

Prospective memory involves several sepa-rate processes or stages. Zogg et al. (2012) provided a conceptual model of the com-ponent processes involved (see Figure 13.1). A major implication of this stage- or process-based approach is that there are several different ways prospective memory can fail. We will work through this model stage by stage:

1 *Intention formation*: At this stage, the individual forms or encodes the intention that is linked to a specific cue. This cue may be a specific event (e.g., "I will talk to my friend when I see him") or it may be time-related (e.g., "I will phone my friend at 8 o'clock").

2 *Retention interval*: There is typically a delay of between several minutes and weeks between intention formation and intention execution. During that time, there is typically some monitoring of the environment for task-relevant cues (i.e., event cues or time cues). This monitoring may involve automatic or strategic (resource-requiring) processes (see theoretical section later in the chapter).

3 *Cue detection and intention retrieval*: This stage requires the individual to detect and recognize the relevant cue (event or time), followed by the self-initiated retrieval of the appropriate intention. As Zogg et al. (2012) pointed out, this is the defining stage of prospective memory that most clearly distinguishes it from retrospective memory.

Box 13.1 The Prospective and Retrospective Memory Questionnaire (PRMQ)

1   Do you decide to do something in a few minutes' time and then forget to do it?
2   Do you fail to recognize a place you have visited before?
3   Do you fail to do something you were supposed to do a few minutes later even though it's there in front of you, like take a pill or turn off the kettle?
4   Do you forget something that you were told a few minutes before?
5   Do you forget appointments if you are not prompted by someone else or by a reminder such as a calendar or diary?
6   Do you fail to recognize a character in a radio or television show from scene to scene?
7   Do you fail to buy something you planned to buy, like a birthday card, even when you see the shop?
8   Do you fail to recall things that have happened to you in the last few days?
9   Do you repeat the same story to the same person on different occasions?
10 Do you intend to take something with you, before leaving a room or going out, but minutes later leave it behind, even though it's there in front of you?
11 Do you mislay something that you have just put down, like a magazine or glasses?
12 Do you fail to mention or give something to a visitor that you were asked to pass on?
13 Do you look at something without realizing you have seen it moments before?
14 If you tried to contact a friend or relative who was out, would you forget to try again later?
15 Do you forget what you watched on television the previous day?
16 Do you forget to tell something you had meant to mention a few minutes ago?

Retrospective memory items: 2, 4, 6, 8, 9, 11, 13, and 15
Prospective memory items: 1, 3, 5, 7, 10, 12, 14, and 16

On the basis of administering the PRMQ to 551 people, Crawford et al. (2003) reported the following statistics (approximately 68% of participants had scores within 1 standard deviation of the mean):

- Prospective memory: Mean = 20.18; standard deviation = 4.91
- Retrospective memory: Mean = 18.69; standard deviation = 4.98
- Total score: Mean = 38.88; standard deviation = 9.15

4   *Intention recall*: The individual successfully retrieves the intention from retrospective memory. There may be problems at this stage because of the complexity of the intention, its relationship to other stored intentions, or the presence of other competing intentions.
5   *Intention execution*: This is typically a fairly automatic and undemanding process.

PROSPECTIVE MEMORY IN EVERYDAY LIFE

How common are failures of prospective memory in everyday life? Marsh, Hicks, and Landau (1998) found people reported an average of 15 plans for the forthcoming week of which 25% were not completed. The main reasons for these noncompletions were rescheduling and reprioritization with only 3%

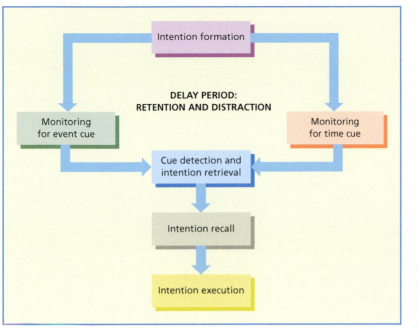

Figure 13.1 Conceptual model of the component processes of prospective memory. Reproduced from Zogg et al. (2012) with permission from Springer.

being forgetting. One reason why most individuals rarely forget future intentions is because they devote so much to thinking about prospective memory: Anderson and McDaniel (2019) found prospective memory occupied our thoughts approximately 13–15% of the time. Of these thoughts, 39% were *externally* cued (triggered by something in the environment) and 61% were *internally* cued.

In this section, we consider prospective memory in various groups of people. First, we consider individuals (e.g., pilots, air traffic controllers) for whom forgetting of intended actions can prove fatal. Second, we discuss individuals with obsessive-compulsive disorder, who are often regarded as having poor prospective memory.

Obsessive-compulsive disorder and checking behavior

It could be argued that individuals suffering from obsessive-compulsive disorder (OCD; an anxiety disorder involving obsessional and checking behavior) have especially poor memory. Many patients with this disorder have so little confidence in their memory (and such an inflated sense of personal responsibility) that

they check repeatedly that they have locked their front door, that the gas stove has been turned off, and so on. In spite of all this repeated checking, obsessive-compulsive patients (and healthy individuals with obsessive-compulsive symptoms) tend to be uncertain whether they have actually performed the actions they intended to perform.

How can we explain such checking behavior? One obvious explanation is that obsessional individuals have poor *retrospective* memory causing them to forget whether they have engaged in checking behavior. As a result, they feel the need to perform the checking behavior repeatedly. However, Cuttler and Graf (2009a) found in a review that compulsive checkers did *not* differ from controls in retrospective memory.

Perhaps checkers have poor *prospective* memory. Cuttler and Graf (2009b) found checkers had impaired performance on event-based and time-based prospective memory

Box 13.2 Plane crashes—pilots and air traffic controllers

Fatal accidents involving aircraft occur for many reasons, some of which are of relevance to psychology and some of which are not. Detailed information on the causes of 1,104 fatal aircraft accidents between 1960 and 2015 is contained in the PlaneCrashInfo.com.accident database, which you can access for an update. According to this database, 58% of these fatal accidents were due at least in part to human error. Of the remaining fatal accidents, 17% were due to mechanical failure and smaller percentages were due to adverse weather or sabotage. If you are nervous about flying, note that the chances of dying on a flight with one of the top 39 airlines is only 1 in 19.8 million—this is much less than the probability of being killed in a car accident on any given day.

Dismukes and Nowinski (2006) considered 75 reports of fatal accidents where memory failure by pilots or other crew was responsible. In 74 cases, there was a failure of prospective memory, with only *one* case involving retrospective memory!

What causes pilots to exhibit failures of prospective memory? Latorella (1998) identified an important reason—commercial pilots interrupted while flying a simulator made 53% more errors than those not interrupted. Such interruptions are relatively common in actual flying conditions. Gontar, Schneider, Schmidt-Molt, Bollin, and Bengler (2017) discovered pilots on average experienced eight interruptions per turnaround. Unsurprisingly, the adverse effects of interruptions on task performance are greater with longer interruptions (Altmann, Trafton, & Hambrick, 2017).

Interruptions increase performance errors because they impair prospective memory for intentions that could not be performed at the typical point in a sequence. We can provide a more detailed account with reference to Shelton and Scullin's (2017) dynamic multi-process framework (discussed later). According to this framework, we can remember to perform an intended action because of *bottom-up processes* (e.g., encountering a relevant cue). When pilots are not interrupted, each item in an action sequence cues the next action. However, such cuing is lacking if actions are performed out of sequence.

Shelton and Scullin (2017) argued that we can also remember to perform an intended action because of *top-down processes* (i.e., monitoring for cues and rehearsing the intention). However, it is effortful and demanding to use these processes when interrupted during task performance.

The errors made by air traffic controllers also often involve prospective-memory through failure to perform intended actions while monitoring a display. Loft and Remington (2010) found prospective-memory errors made by participants in a simulated air traffic control task occurred more often when interruptions caused them to deviate from well-practiced or strong routines rather than less practiced ones. Air traffic controllers (and pilots) devote much of their time to habitual tasks involving strong routines. Such tasks are carried out fairly "automatically" due to habit capture which can cause prospective-memory failures when something unexpected happens (Dismukes, 2012).

Wilson, Farrell, Visser, and Loft (2018) studied interruptions on a simulated air traffic control task. There were three conditions: (1) interruptions involving a blank screen; (2) interruptions involving a secondary air traffic control (ATC) task resembling the main one; and (3) a no-interruption control condition. Both interruption conditions increased the time taken to resume the main air traffic control task (see Figure 13.2) because participants had to reactivate information relevant to the main ATC task. There were most failures to resume the interrupted task following a secondary ATC task because the demands of the secondary task caused increased forgetting of the interrupted task.

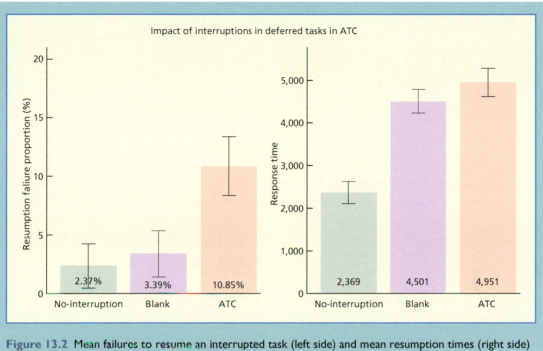

Figure 13.2 Mean failures to resume an interrupted task (left side) and mean resumption times (right side) for no-interruption, blank interruption, and air traffic control (ATC) task interruption conditions.

tasks. Palmer, Durkin, and Rhodes (2015) investigated the relationship between various measures of prospective memory and checking behavior. Their key finding was that individuals with the most checking behavior tended to have more prospective memory failures.

Other research has focused on patients with OCD. Such patients have impaired prospective-memory performance on time-based and event-based tasks (Bhat, Sharma, & Kumar, 2018; Yang et al., 2015).

It is possible that poor prospective memory leads obsessional individuals to engage in excessive checking. However, excessive checking may also lead to poor prospective memory because their numerous checks mean they find it hard to remember whether they have performed a check recently. Relevant evidence has been obtained using an experimental design originally proposed by van den Hout and Kindt (2004). They asked some participants to engage in repeated checking of a gas stove. On the final trial, these participants had less vivid and detailed

memories of what had happened than those who had not engaged in repeated checking.

Linkovski, Kalanthroff, Henik, and Anholt (2013) carried out a similar study. They also assessed participants' level of inhibitory control because obsessional patients have deficient inhibitory control leading to intrusive thoughts and memory problems. Repeated checking did not impair prospective-memory performance. However, it did reduce memory vividness and detail and also lowered participants' confidence in their memory. All these effects were much stronger in participants with poor inhibitory control (see Figure 13.3).

Van den Hout, van Dis, van Woudenberg, and van de Groep (2019) carried out a meta-analysis (see Glossary) of studies using versions of the repeated checking task introduced by van den Hout and Kindt (2004). Overall, repeated checking produced large decreases in memory confidence, vividness, and detail but only small or nonsignificant effects on prospective-memory accuracy.

What can we conclude from research on obsessive-compulsive disorder (and high levels

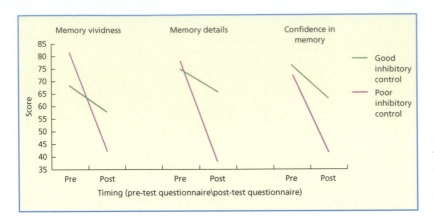

Figure 13.3 Meanscores for the pre-test and post-test repeated checking questionnaire for participants with good and poor inhibitory control.

of obsessionality in healthy individuals) and checking behavior? First, obsessional individuals generally have worse prospective memory than nonobsessional ones. Second, individuals with poor prospective memory are more likely than those with good prospective memory to engage in excessive checking behavior on the repeated checking task. Third, repeated checking impairs individuals' metamemory (see Glossary) by reducing their memory confidence, vividness, and detail without impairing their accuracy. This probably happens because repeated checking causes checking behavior to become "automatic" and so relatively inaccessible to conscious awareness (Toffolo, van den Hout, Radomsky, & Engelhard, 2016; van den Hout et al., 2019).

In sum, obsessional individuals are less confident that nonobsessional ones that they have carried out intended actions (e.g., checking behavior). The present state of knowledge was summarized by Toffolo et al. (2016, p. 60):

Even though it is still unknown what comes first (the tendency to use more checking behavior in general or OCD), ... when people who are vulnerable for OCD use more checking, this may [reduce] memory confidence. This may subsequently lead to the vicious cycle of increased checking behavior and memory distrust, eventually contributing to the development of new OC [obsessional compulsive] symptoms.

TYPES OF PROSPECTIVE MEMORY

There are several types of prospective memory. However, the most important distinction is between event-based and time-based prospective memory. Event-based prospective memory is assessed by tasks involving remembering to perform a given action in the appropriate *circumstances* (e.g., passing on a message when you see someone). In contrast, time-based prospective memory is assessed by tasks involving remembering to perform a given action at a given *time* (e.g., phone a friend at 8.00 p.m.). Unsurprisingly, performance on time-based tasks depends in part on the accuracy (or inaccuracy) of any given individual's time estimation (Waldum & McDaniel, 2016).

Prospective memory is typically better with event-based tasks than with time-based ones. Kim and Mayhorn (2008) compared the two types of prospective memory in naturalistic settings and the laboratory. Prospective-memory performance was superior to that on

KEY TERM

Event-based prospective memory: A form of prospective memory in which some event provides the cue to perform a given action.

Time-based prospective memory: A form of prospective memory in which time is the cue indicating that a given action should be performed.

time-based tasks (especially under laboratory conditions). Time-based tasks were performed better in naturalistic settings than in the laboratory for an obvious reason—participants often used alarm clocks or reminders from friends in the former setting.

Further evidence that event-based prospective memory is generally better than time-based prospective memory was reported by Conte and McBride (2018). In the time-based condition, participants were instructed to say, "Time's up," after one, three, or six minutes had elapsed. In the event-based condition, they said, "flower word," when the name of a flower was presented after one, three, or six minutes. Prospective-memory performance was better in the event-based condition than in the time-based condition at all time intervals: overall accuracy was 91% vs. 68%, respectively.

Why is performance generally better on event-based tasks than time-based ones? The main reason is that environmental cues to perform the appropriate action are more likely to be present on event-based tasks. In contrast, time-based tasks often require extensive self-initiated processing. As a result, event-based tasks are typically less demanding than time-based ones.

Hicks, Marsh, and Cook (2005) confirmed that the processing demands of event-based tasks are generally less than those of time-based ones. However, they also found both kinds of tasks were more demanding when the task was ill-specified (e.g., detect animal words) than when it was well-specified (e.g., detect the words *nice* and *hit*). A well-specified time-based task was no more demanding than an ill-specified event-based task.

How similar are the strategies used by individuals given event- and time-based prospective memory tasks? There is no single or simple answer to that question given the variety of both types of tasks. Kvavilashvili and Fisher (2007) compared the strategies used when participants made a phone call at a given time after an interval of one week (time-based task) or when they received a certain text message (event-based task) which arrived after one week. Participants averaged nine rehearsals over the week with the time-based task and seven with the event-based

task. About 50% of the rehearsals with both tasks occurred "automatically" (i.e., the task simply popped into the participant's head) and very few involved deliberate retrieval of the task. Performance was better on the event-based task than the time-based task (100% vs. 53% punctual phone calls) because the text message in the event-based task provided a useful external cue.

In spite of Kvavilashvili and Fisher's (2007) findings, the strategies used on time-based and event-based tasks often differ considerably. Cona, Arcara, Tarantino, and Bisiacchi (2015) argued that the occurrence of prospective-memory cues is typically more *predictable* on time-based than event-based tasks. As a result, individuals often engage in only sporadic monitoring of prospective-memory cues on time-based tasks with the extent of such monitoring increasing as the time at which an action should be performed approaches.

In contrast, as we will see, there is much more evidence of continuous monitoring on event-based tasks because of unpredictability concerning the cue's occurrence. Cona et al. (2015) showed the importance of predictability with event-based tasks: the pattern of monitoring resembled that typically found with time-based tasks when the occurrence of prospective-memory cues was predictable.

Cona, Arcara, Tarantino, and Bisiacchi (2012) reported clear-cut differences between event- and time-based prospective memory tasks. On the ongoing task, five letters were presented and participants decided whether the second and fourth letters were the same or different. At the same time, they performed an event-based task (detect the letter "B" in the second or fourth position) or a time-based task (respond every five minutes). Cona et al. assessed processing activities by using event-related potentials (ERPs), which reveal the electrophysiological reaction of the brain to specific stimuli over time.

What did Cona et al. (2012) discover? The effects of event-based and time-based tasks on event-related potentials are shown in Figure 13.4. Overall, the amplitude of the ERPs was greater in the event-based than the time-based condition. The increased amplitude between 130–180 ms after stimulus

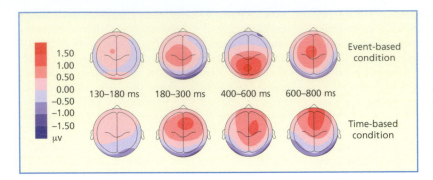

Figure 13.4 Scalp distribution of ERP differences in event-based and time-based prospective memory conditions. From Cona et al. (2012). Copyright G. Cona, G. Arcara, V. Tarantino, and P. S. Bisiacchi

onset in the event-based condition may reflect the greater use of attentional resources in that condition. In contrast, the greater amplitude between 400–600 ms in the event-based condition may be due to the greater frequency of target checking in the event-based condition.

Most research has focused on event-based rather than time-based prospective memory. Why is that the case? One reason is that factors influencing event-based prospective memory (e.g., environmental cues varying in the strength of their relationship to the intended action) are generally easier to manipulate than factors influencing time-based prospective memory.

THEORETICAL PERSPECTIVES

Since most research has focused on event-based prospective memory, it is unsurprising that most theories attempt to explain that form of prospective memory. Accordingly, we will mostly consider theories of event-based prospective memory in this section.

Multi-process framework

Einstein and McDaniel (2005) put forward their very influential multi-process framework. This framework was subsequently developed by McDaniel, Umanath, Einstein, and Waldum (2015) into the dual-pathways model. These theoretical approaches are so similar they will be considered jointly.

According to the multi-process framework, various cognitive processes (including attentional ones) are often used when performing prospective memory tasks. However, the detection of cues for response will typically be "*automatic*" (not involving attentional processes) when the following criteria (especially the first one) are fulfilled:

1   The ongoing task (a task performed at the same time as the prospective-memory task) is a focal task—one that "encourages processing of the target [on the prospective-memory task] and especially those features [of the target] that were processed at encoding" (McDaniel et al., 2015, p. 2). Here is an example: the ongoing task involves deciding whether each letter string is a word and the prospective-memory task involves responding to the word *sleep*.
2   The cue and the to-be-performed action are highly associated.
3   The cue is conspicuous or salient.
4   The intended action is simple.

McDaniel et al. (2015) distinguished between focal and nonfocal ongoing tasks.

A nonfocal task "does not encourage processing of those features … processed at encoding [of the prospective-memory target" (p. 2). For example, the ongoing task requires participants to decide whether each letter string is a word (thus making it a lexical decision task), whereas the prospective-memory task involves responding to any word starting with the letter *r*. Thus, there is much less *overlap* or similarity between the processing required on the prospective-memory and ongoing tasks when the latter is nonfocal.

It is assumed theoretically that the processes typically used with focal and nonfocal tasks differ substantially (see Figure 13.5). Strategic monitoring involves top-down attentional control processes to maintain the prospective-memory intention and to search for relevant cues on that task. It is used much more often with nonfocal than focal tasks. Since strategic monitoring (with its involvement of attentional control) requires processing resources, it is predicted that performance on the ongoing task will be more disrupted when the prospective-memory task is nonfocal rather than focal.

According to the dual-pathways model, retrieval on the prospective-memory task can occur in two ways: (1) spontaneous retrieval involves bottom-up processes triggered by the relevant stimulus and does not require prior

monitoring; (2) intentional retrieval is based more on top-down processes and requires prior monitoring. Nonfocal tasks involve *intentional* retrieval. In contrast, focal tasks generally involve *spontaneous* retrieval but can also involve intentional retrieval. Finally, the main brain areas associated with the cognitive processes involved in prospective memory are identified.

Dynamic multi-process framework

Shelton and Scullin (2017) proposed a dynamic multi-process framework that is mostly consistent with the multi-process theory (see Figure 13.8). According to this framework, two cognitive processes underlie successful prospective memory performance:

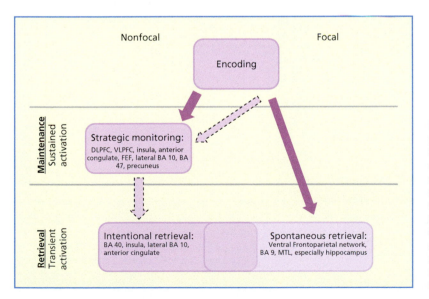

Figure 13.5 The dual-pathways model. The solid arrows indicate the sequence of processing stages; the dashed-line arrows indicate that strategic monitoring can be used even with focal tasks and that nonfocal tasks sometimes do not involve retrieval from long-term memory. From McDaniel et al. (2015).

Box 13.3 Key features of event-based prospective memory

How important is the above distinction between focal and nonfocal tasks in terms of its effects on prospective memory? Moyes, Sari-Sarraf, and Gilbert (2019) addressed this issue. The ongoing task was a lexical decision task (deciding whether letter strings form words). There were two prospective-memory tasks: (1) specific target words (e.g., *tower*); (2) category targets (e.g., *animal words*). In the former condition, the ongoing task is a focal task, because the processing involved in deciding whether a word has been presented overlaps substantially with that required on the prospective-memory task. In the latter condition, the ongoing task is a nonfocal task, because the processing required on the prospective-memory task is very different from that required on the ongoing task.

What did Moyes et al. (2019) find? First, as predicted, decision response times on the ongoing lexical decision task were longer when it was a nonfocal task than when it was a focal task (see Figure 13.6). This finding confirms that processing demands on the prospective-memory task were greater with nonfocal than focal tasks.

Moyes et al. (2019) pointed out that the additional processing with nonfocal tasks compared to focal ones might occur only during the presentation of stimuli on the ongoing task or it might also occur in the gaps between successive stimuli. They addressed this issue by measuring pupil size (the pupil increases in size when individuals engage in more demanding processing). The findings based on pupil size are shown in Figure 13.7. Participants engaged in more demanding processing (e.g., monitoring) in the nonfocal (category) condition throughout the experimental session. Thus, monitoring occurred even in the gap between trials.

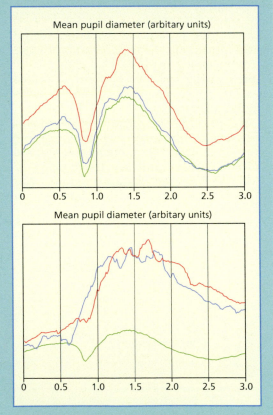

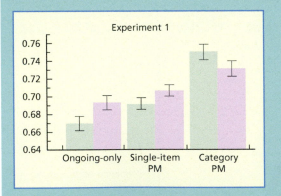

Figure 13.6 Mean lexical decision times on word (green columns) and nonword (purple columns) trials when the ongoing task was performed on its own, as a focal task (single-item PM), or a nonfocal task (category PM). PM = prospective memory. From Moyes et al. (2019).

Figure 13.7 Mean pupil diameter as a function of time after stimulus onset; red line = nonfocal (category) task; blue line = focal (single-item) task; green line = ongoing task only. From Moyes et al. (2019).

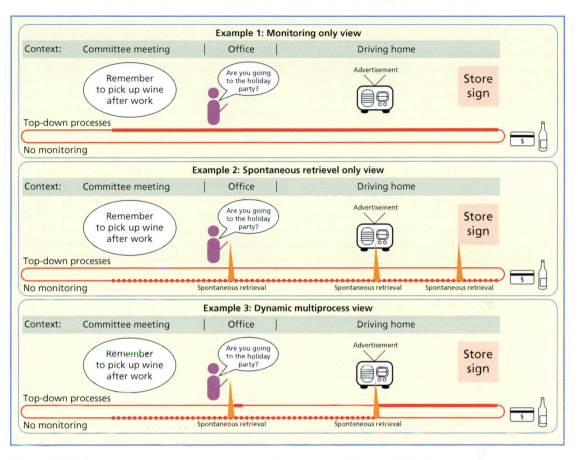

Figure 13.8 Top-down monitoring processes operating in isolation (Example 1); bottom-up spontaneous retrieval processes operating in isolation (Example 2); dual processes operating dynamically (Example 3). From Shelton and Scullin (2017). © SAGE.

1 *Monitoring*: this involves top-down attentional control to search for cues indicating the prospective-memory action should be performed.

2 *Spontaneous retrieval*: this involves bottom-up processing triggered by processing a cue.

What influences which process is used? First, monitoring is cognitively demanding and often impairs ongoing task performance because it competes for processing capacity. As a result, monitoring is used only rarely when the ongoing task is perceived as important (e.g., a committee meeting).

Second, monitoring is typically used when prospective memory cues are expected (e.g., when close to a wine shop if the prospective-memory task is to buy wine: see Figure 13.8).

Third, it is assumed within the dynamic multi-process framework that use of top-down monitoring or bottom-up spontaneous retrieval is *not* an either-or matter. Instead, these processes *interact* dynamically with each other. Of key importance, the use of monitoring depends on metamemory (knowledge and beliefs about one's own memory processes and performance). For example, if you believe the prospective memory task will be easy because of the presence of strong retrieval cues, you would probably rely on spontaneous retrieval. In contrast, if you believe the prospective memory task will be hard because retrieval cues will be weak or absent, you would probably rely on extensive monitoring.

In sum, the dynamic multi-process framework differs from previous theories because it is based on the assumption that the processing strategies used on prospective memory tasks are *flexibly* influenced by metamemory processes. The multi-process theory is less flexible —it assumes that processing on prospective memory tasks is predominantly determined by the nature of the task (focal vs. nonfocal).

Findings

According to the dynamic multi-process framework, successful performance on a prospective-memory task can sometimes be achieved via spontaneous retrieval (especially with focal tasks). Supporting evidence was reported by Scullin, McDaniel, Shelton, and Lee (2010). They almost eliminated monitoring for prospective-memory cues by presenting only a *single* prospective-memory target after over 500 trials and by emphasizing the importance of the ongoing task. This target was detected by 73% of participants with a focal task but only 18% on a nonfocal task. This is consistent with the theoretical assumption that spontaneous retrieval occurs much more often with focal tasks.

Since metamemory processes are emphasized within the dynamic multi-process framework, we will now consider their role in prospective memory. Lourenço, Hill, and Maylor (2015) required participants to perform two tasks at the same time: (1) an ongoing lexical decision task (deciding whether letter strings form words); and (2) a prospective-memory task that involved responding to animal words. For some participants, the target animal words during practice were typical animals (e.g., *dog*) but only atypical animal words (e.g., *raccoon*) were presented as targets on the subsequent experimental trials.

Lourenço et al. (2015) discovered that these participants showed very little monitoring during the initial experimental trials because they expected the prospective-memory task to be easy. However, they used monitoring much more when they realized the task was harder than expected. Thus, strategy use was *flexible*: our use of monitoring increases (or decreases) as a result of experience and expectation involving metacognition.

Imagine you were given an ongoing task requiring you to count the number of living objects presented on a screen containing about 20 objects. At the same, you had to perform the prospective-memory task of detecting a given target object (e.g., *apple*) presented in the screen's upper right corner. On some trials, an object semantically related to the target (e.g., *banana*) is presented and on other trials an object semantically unrelated to the target (e.g., duck) is presented.

The prediction from the dynamic multi-process framework is that fixating the semantically related object (e.g., *banana*) should often produce spontaneous retrieval of the intention on the prospective-memory task. This in turn should lead to monitoring (revealed by rapid fixation of the screen's upper right corner). The findings were precisely as predicted (see Figure 13.9).

Evidence that strategies on prospective-memory tasks can be flexible and variable was reported by Scullin et al. (2018). Participants performed an ongoing lexical decision task (deciding whether letter strings formed words). At the same time, they performed the prospective-memory task of responding to target words belonging to the category of *animals* for some participants and the category of *fruits* for others; this is a nonfocal task (see earlier discussion).

Scullin et al. (2018) were primarily interested in participants' self-reported

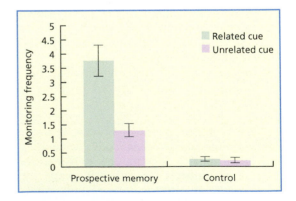

Figure 13.9 Frequency of cue-driven monitoring following presentation of semantically related or unrelated cues; there was no prospective-memory task in the control condition. From Shelton & Christopher (2016).

accounts of the strategy they adopted immediately following the instructions on the prospective-memory task. The findings were surprising—only 51% of participants did as instructed by thinking about the designated general category (e.g., *animals*; *fruits*)! Of the other participants, 26% thought about specific examples of animals or fruits (thus producing a focal task) and 23% engaged in mind wandering and hardly thought about the prospective-memory task.

Overall evaluation

Considerable progress has been made in understanding the underlying processes involved in prospective memory. The distinction between focal and nonfocal tasks has been shown to be of great importance, as is the distinction between monitoring and spontaneous retrieval. Recent evidence indicates that there is much flexibility in terms of the processing strategies used on prospective-memory tasks. This flexibility depends in large measure on metamemory.

What are the limitations of the theoretical approaches discussed in this section? First, there are concerns that laboratory-based findings on prospective memory lacks ecological validity (see Glossary), meaning that it may not be applicable to real-life conditions (Meier, 2019). For example, it is highly probable that monitoring is generally much less important in real life than in the laboratory—we can sustain effortful monitoring for several minutes in the laboratory but it would be incredibly inefficient to sustain it for hours or days in the real world.

Second, it is assumed within the dynamic multi-process framework that monitoring is rarely used if the ongoing task is perceived as important. This theoretical assumption could easily be tested by manipulating the perceived importance of the ongoing task but very few studies have done this.

ENHANCING PROSPECTIVE MEMORY

How can prospective memory be improved? One answer to that question was discussed earlier when we saw that failures of prospective memory often occur when we are interrupted while carrying out an action plan (Dodhia & Dismukes, 2009). This problem can largely be overcome if we form an explicit intention to resume the interrupted task as soon as possible.

Another practical measure is to place salient and distinctive reminder cues where they will be seen at the appropriate time (Dismukes, 2012). For example, if you intend to take a book into college tomorrow, you could leave it close to your keys. Another measure is to avoid performing several other tasks at the same time in order to minimize the extent to which attention is focused away from the prospective-memory task.

Motivation is also important. Cook, Rumel, and Dummel (2015) found prospective memory was enhanced by providing monetary reward for good performance. Bruening, Ludwig, Paschke, Walter, and Stelzel (2018) also found monetary reward enhanced prospective-memory performance. They investigated the brain mechanisms associated with this beneficial effect and discovered several parietal and prefrontal areas were more activated in the reward condition. Increased activation within the anterior prefrontal cortex in the reward condition was of most theoretical relevance because that area is associated with intention encoding. The neuroimaging data also suggested that reward led to sustained investment of additional effort to maximize the probability of detecting the cue signaling that the intention should be retrieved.

Implementation intentions

A simple (but effective) technique for enhancing prospective memory is based on the theorizing of Gollwitzer. He defined his key concept of implementation intentions as

KEY TERM

Implementation intentions: Plans spelling out in detail how individuals are going to achieve the goals they have set themselves.

follows: "'If situation Y is encountered, then I will perform the goal-directed response Z!' Thus, implementation intentions define exactly when, where, and how one wants to act toward realizing one's goals" (Gollwitzer, 2014, p. 306).

We can see what is involved in implementation intentions by considering an early study by Gollwitzer and Brandstätter (1997). They instructed participants to write a report on how they spent Christmas Eve within the two days following that day. The findings were dramatic: 75% of those forming implementation intentions achieved the intended goal of writing the report on time, compared to only 33% of those not forming such intentions. The large effect of implementation intentions on performance was probably due to enhanced prospective memory as well as increased motivation.

Findings

Chen et al. (2015) found in a meta-analysis that implementation intentions enhance prospective memory. There was a medium effect size of such intentions on improving prospective memory in young adults, and a somewhat larger effect size in older adults. The beneficial effects of implementation intentions were comparable regardless of whether the ongoing task was focal or nonfocal. Overall, implementation intentions had a more powerful effect when the intention was encoded using imagery and verbal information than when it involved only imagery or verbal information.

Why are implementation intentions effective? Scullin, Kurinec, and Nguyen (2017) addressed this issue by asking participants what they were thinking about shortly after they had received implementation-intention instructions. These instructions led participants to focus more closely on specific aspects of the prospective-memory task and they reduced mind wandering. Thus, implementation-intention instructions increased the amount of attention devoted to the task and reduced attention to task-irrelevant thoughts.

Gollwitzer (e.g., 2014) hypothesized that forming an implementation intention is like forming an "instant habit," meaning that an implementation intention permits the rapid and relatively "automatic" retrieval of intentions. Support for this hypothesis was reported by Rummel, Einstein, and Rampey (2012). They obtained two key findings. First, prospective-memory performance was enhanced by implementation intentions. Second, and of direct relevance to the hypothesis, participants continued to retrieve their intentions "automatically" on trials where they had been told *not* to respond to target words from the prospective-memory task.

Conclusions

Performance on prospective-memory tasks is generally improved by the use of implementation intentions by young and older adults. This happens in part because implementation intentions strengthen associations between cues and intentions and thus permit intentions to be retrieved "automatically." In addition, implementation intentions led to increased attention devoted to the task and reduced mind wandering.

Implementation intentions may sometimes be more effective under laboratory conditions than in real-life conditions. For example, implementation intentions tend to be less effective when individuals are simultaneously pursuing multiple goals than when pursuing only one goal (Dalton & Spiller, 2012). The simultaneous pursuit of several goals is more common in real life than in the laboratory.

KEY TERM

Meta-analysis: A form of statistical analysis based on combining the findings from numerous studies on a given research topic.

SUMMARY

- Prospective memory focuses on the future whereas retrospective memory focuses on the past. Another important difference between the two forms of memory is that only prospective memory is intimately related to our plans and goals.
- Remembering (and forgetting) in the real world typically involves a mixture of prospective and retrospective memory. The two forms of memory are moderately highly correlated suggesting they involve some common processes.
- Some failures of prospective memory can have serious or even fatal consequences (e.g., hot car deaths; airplane crashes; impaired health if medication is not taken).
- Our metamemory (knowledge of the effectiveness or otherwise of our own prospective memory) is limited.
- Pilot errors (and those of air traffic controllers) are due far more to failures of prospective than of retrospective memory. Such prospective memory errors are especially likely to occur when pilots or air traffic controllers are interrupted while carrying out a sequence of actions and are too busy to generate a new plan of action.
- Memory problems in compulsive checkers involve prospective memory and are due in part to low confidence in their memory ability. Poor prospective memory partly causes excessive checking and excessive checking partly causes poor prospective memory.
- Prospective memory involves several stages: intention formation; retention interval; cue detection and intention retrieval; intention recall; and intention execution.
- Prospective memory can be event-based (respond when some event occurs) or time-based (respond at a given time). Event-based prospective memory is generally better than time-based prospective memory because the former involves explicit environmental cues. However, performance differences between the two types of prospective memory depend in part on how well-specified the task is.
- Continuous monitoring is more common with event-based than time-based tasks because the occurrence of the cue for response is generally more predictable in the latter case.
- According to the multi-process theory, less monitoring is involved with focal ongoing tasks than nonfocal ones.
- According to the dynamic multi-process framework, processing on prospective-memory tasks is more flexible than assumed by previous theories. For example, monitoring is used less often on prospective-memory tasks when the ongoing task is important than when it is not. In addition, there is less monitoring on the prospective-memory task when it is perceived as easy than when it is perceived as hard.
- The use of implementation intentions typically enhances prospective memory with both focal and nonfocal ongoing tasks. This occurs because implementation intentions strengthen associations between cues and intentions and thus produce "automatic" retrieval of intentions. Another reason is that implementation intentions reduce mind wandering and increase attentional focus on the prospective-memory task.

POINTS FOR DISCUSSION

1 What are the main similarities (and differences) between retrospective memory and prospective memory?
2 Discuss some of the potential real-life consequences of failures of prospective memory and consider why these memory failures occur.
3 What are the main types of prospective memory? How do they differ?
4 Describe major theoretical approaches to prospective memory. What are the main factors influencing prospective memory identified within these theories?
5 What can be done to enhance our prospective memory?

FURTHER READING

Boag, R. J., Strickland, L., Heathcote, A., Neal, A., & Loft, S. (2019). Cognitive control and capacity for prospective memory in complex dynamic environments. *Journal of Experimental Psychology: General* (Epub 2019 April 22). Russell Boag and colleagues identify the complex attentional and control processes involved in performing an air traffic control task.

Shelton, J. T., & Scullin, M. K. (2017). The dynamic interplay between bottom-up and top-down processes supporting prospective remembering. *Current Directions in Psychological Science, 26*, 352–358. This article provides an excellent account of how findings in prospective memory can be explained within the dynamic multi-process framework.

Smith, R. E. (2017). Prospective memory in context. *Psychology of Learning and Motivation, 66*, 211–249. Rebekah Smith provides an up-to-date discussion of theory and research on prospective memory.

Uttl, B., White, C. A., Cnudde, K., & Grant, L. M. (2018). Prospective memory, retrospective memory, and individual differences in cognitive abilities, personality, and psychopathology. *PLoS ONE, 13*, e0193806. Bob Uttl and his colleagues compare prospective and retrospective memory with respect to several dimensions of individual differences.

REFERENCES

Altmann, E. M., Trafton, J. G., & Hambrick, D. Z. (2017). Effects of interruption length on procedural errors. *Journal of Experimental Psychology: Applied, 23*, 216–229.

Anderson, F. T., & McDaniel, M. A. (2019). Hey buddy, why don't we take it outside: An experience sampling study of prospective memory. *Memory & Cognition, 47*, 47–62.

Avci, G., Sheppard, D. P., Tierney, S. M., Kordovski, K. L., Sullivan, K. L., & Woods, S. P. (2018). A systematic review of prospective memory in HIV disease: From the laboratory to daily life. *The Clinical Neuropsychologist, 32*, 858–890.

Bhat, N. A., Sharma, V., & Kumar, D. (2018). Prospective memory in obsessive compulsive disorder. *Psychiatry Research, 261*, 124–131.

Bruening, J., Ludwig, V. U., Paschke, L. M., Walter, H., & Stelzel, C. (2018). Motivational effects on the processing of delayed intentions in the anterior prefrontal cortex. *NeuroImage, 172,* 517–526.

Chen, X.-J., Wang, Y., Li, L.-L., Cui, J.-F., Gan, M.-Y., Shum, D. H. K., & Chan, R. C. K. (2015). The effect of implementation intention on prospective memory: A systematic and meta-analytic review. *Psychiatry Research, 226,* 14–22.

Cona, G., Arcara, G., Tarantino, V., & Bisiacchi, P. S. (2012). Electrophysiological correlates of strategic monitoring in event-based and time-based prospective memory. *PLoS ONE, 7*(2), e31659. doi:10.1371/journal.pone.003 1659

Cona, G., Arcara, G., Tarantino, V., & Bisiacchi, P. S. (2015). Does predictability matter? Effects of cue predictability on neurocognitive mechanisms underlying prospective memory. *Frontiers in Human Neuroscience, 9*(188). doi:10.3389/fnhum.2015.00188

Conte, A. M., & McBride, D. M. (2018). Comparing time-based and event-based prospective memory over short delays. *Memory, 26,* 936–945.

Cook, G. I., Rummel, J., & Dummel, S. (2015). Toward an understanding of motivational influences on prospective memory using value-added intentions. *Frontiers in Human Neuroscience, 9* (Article 278).

Crawford, J. R., Smith, G., Maylor, E. A., Della Sala, S., & Logie, R. H. (2003). The Prospective and Retrospective Memory Questionnaire (PRMQ): Normative data and latent structure in a large non-clinical sample. *Memory, 11,* 261–275.

Cuttler, C., & Graf, P. (2009a). Checking-in on the memory deficit and meta-memory deficit theories of compulsive checking. *Clinical Psychology Review, 29,* 393–409.

Cuttler, C., & Graf, P. (2009b). Sub-clinical compulsive checkers show impaired performance on habitual, event- and time-cued episodic prospective memory tasks. *Journal of Anxiety Disorders, 23,* 813–823.

Dalton, A. N., & Spiller, S. A. (2012). Too much of a good thing: The benefits of implementation intentions depend on the number of goals. *Journal of Consumer Research, 39,* 600–614.

Diamond, D. M. (2019). When a child dies of heatstroke after a parent or caretaker unknowingly leaves the child in a car: How does it happen and is it a crime?. *Medicine, Science and the Law, 59,* 115–126.

Dismukes, R. K. (2012). Prospective memory in workplace and everyday situations. *Current Directions in Psychological Science, 21,* 215–220.

Dismukes, R. K., & Nowinski, J. L. (2006). Prospective memory, concurrent task management, and pilot error. In A. Kramer, D. Wiegmann, & A. Kirlik (Eds.), *Attention: From theory to practice* (pp. 225–236). Oxford: Oxford University Press.

Dodhia, R. M., & Dismukes, K. R. (2009). Interruptions create prospective memory tasks. *Applied Cognitive Psychology, 23,* 73–89.

Einstein, G. O., & McDaniel, M. A. (2005). Prospective memory: Multiple retrieval processes. *Current Directions in Psychological Science, 14,* 286–290.

Freud, S. (1901). *The psychopathology of everyday life.* New York: W. W. Norton.

Gollwitzer, P. (2014). Weakness of the will: Is a quick fix possible?. *Motivation and Emotion, 38,* 305–322.

Gollwitzer, P. M., & Brandstätter, V. (1997). Implementation intentions and effective goal pursuit. *Journal of Personality and Social Psychology, 73,* 186–199.

Gontar, P., Schneider, S. A. E., Schmidt-Molt, C., Bollin, C., & Bengler, K. (2017). Hate to interrupt you, but.... Analyzing turn-arounds from a cockpit perspective. *Cognitive Technology & Work, 19,* 837–853.

Graf, P. (2012). Prospective memory: Faulty brain, flaky person. *Canadian Psychology, 53,* 7–13.

Hicks, J. L., Marsh, R. L., & Cook, G. I. (2005). Task interference in time-based, event-based, and dual intention prospective memory conditions. *Journal of Memory and Language, 53,* 430–444.

Kim, P. Y., & Mayhorn, C. B. (2008). Exploring students' prospective memory inside and outside the lab. *American Journal of Psychology, 121,* 241–254.

Kvavilashvili, L., & Fisher, L. (2007). Is time-based prospective remembering mediated by self-initiated rehearsals? Role of incidental cues, ongoing activity, age, and motivation. *Journal of Experimental Psychology: General, 136,* 112–132.

Latorella, K. A. (1998). Effects of modality on interrupted flight deck performance: Implications for data link. *Proceedings of the Human Factors and Ergonomics Society 42nd. Annual Meeting, Vols. 1 and 2,* 87–91.

Linkovski, O., Kalanthroff, E., Henik, A., & Anholt, G. (2013). Did I turn off the stove? Good inhibitory control can protect from influences of repeated checking. *Journal of Behavior Therapy and Experimental Psychiatry, 44,* 30–36.

Loft, S., & Remington, R. W. (2010). Prospective memory and task interference in a continuous monitoring dynamic display task. *Journal of Experimental Psychology: Applied, 16,* 145–157.

Lourenço, J. S., Hill, J. H., & Maylor, E. A. (2015). Too easy? The influence of task demands conveyed tacitly on prospective memory. *Frontiers in Human Neuroscience, 9* (Article 242).

Marsh, R. L., Hicks, J. L., & Landau, J. D. (1998). An investigation of everyday prospective memory and executive control of working memory. *Journal of Experimental Psychology: Learning, Memory and Cognition, 24,* 336–349.

McDaniel, M. A., Umanath, S., Einstein, G. O., & Waldum, E. R. (2015). Dual pathways to prospective remembering. *Frontiers in Human Neuroscience, 3*(392) doi:10.3389/inhum.2015.00392

Meier, B. (2019). Toward an ecological approach to prospective memory? The impact of Neisser's seminal talk on prospective memory research. *Frontiers in Psychology, 10* (Article No. 1005).

Moscovitch, M. (2008). Commentary: A perspective on prospective memory. In M. Kliegel, M. A. McDaniel, & G. O. Einstein (Eds.), *Prospective memory: Cognitive, neuroscience, developmental, and applied perspectives* (pp. 309–320). New York: Lawrence Erlbaum Associates.

Moyes, J., Sari-Sarraf, N., & Gilbert, S. J. (2019). Characterizing monitoring processes in event-based prospective memory: Evidence from pupillometry. *Cognition, 184,* 83–95.

Palmer, L. E., Durkin, K., & Rhodes, S. M. (2015). Checking behaviors, prospective memory and executive functions. *Behaviour Change, 32,* 74–92.

Rummel, J., Einstein, G. O., & Rampey, H. (2012). Implementation-intention encoding in a prospective memory task enhances spontaneous retrieval of intentions. *Memory, 20,* 803–817.

Schnitzspahn, K. M., Zeintl, M., Jäger, T., & Kliegel, M. (2011). Metacognition in prospective memory: Are performance predictions accurate?. *Canadian Journal of Experimental Psychology, 65,* 19–26.

Scullin, M. K., Kurinec, C. A., & Nguyen, K. (2017). The effects of implementation intention strategies on prospective memory cue encoding. *Journal of Cognitive Psychology, 29,* 929–938.

Scullin, M. K., McDaniel, M. A., Dasse, M. N., Lee, J. H., Kurinec, C. A., Taml, C., et al. (2018). Thought probes during prospective memory encoding: Evidence for perfunctory processes. *PLoS ONE, 13* (Article e0198646).

Scullin, M. K., McDaniel, M. A., Shelton, J. T., and Lee, J. H. (2010). Focal/nonfocal cue effects in prospective memory: Monitoring difficulty or different retrieval processes?. *Journal of Experimental Psychology: Learning, Memory, and Cognition, 36,* 736–749.

Shelton, J. T., & Scullin, M. K. (2017). The dynamic interplay between bottom-up and top-down processes supporting prospective remembering. *Current Directions in Psychological Science, 26,* 352–358.

Susser, J. A., & Mulligan, N. W. (2019). Exploring the intrinsic-extrinsic distinction in prospective metamemory. *Journal of Memory and Language, 104,* 43–55.

Toffolo, M. B. J., van den Hout, M. A., Radomsky, A. S., & Engelhard, I. M. (2016). Check, check, double check: Investigating memory deterioration within multiple sessions of repeated checking. *Journal of Behavior Therapy and Experimental Psychiatry, 53,* 59–67.

Uttl, B., White, C. A., Cnudde, K., & Grant, L. M. (2018). Prospective memory, retrospective memory, and individual differences in cognitive abilities, personality, and psychopathology. *PLoS ONE, 13,* e0193806.

van den Hout, M., & Kindt, M. (2004). Obsessive-compulsive disorder and the paradoxical effects of perseverative behavior on experienced uncertainty. *Journal of Behavior Therapy and Experimental Psychiatry, 35,* 165–181.

van den Hout, M. A., van Dis, E. A. M., van Woudenberg, C., & van de Groep, I. H. (2019). OCD-like checking in the lab: A meta-analysis and improvement of an experimental paradigm. *Journal of Obsessive-Compulsive and Related Disorders, 20,* 39–49.

Waldum, E. R., & McDaniel, M. A. (2016). Why are you late? Investigating the role of time management in time-based prospective memory. *Journal of Experimental Psychology: General, 145,* 1049–1061.

Wilson, M. D., Farrell, S., Visser, T. A. W., & Loft, S. (2018). Remembering to execute deferred tasks in simulated air traffic control: The impact of interruptions. *Journal of Experimental Psychology: Applied, 24,* 360–379.

Woods, S. P., Dawson, M. S., Weber, E., Gibson, S., Grant, I., Atkinson, J. H., et al. (2009). Timing is everything: Antiretroviral nonadherence is associated with impairment in time-based prospective memory. *Journal of the International Neuropsychological Society, 15,* 42–52.

Yang, T.-X., Peng, Z. W., Wang, Y., Geng, F. L., Miao, G.-D., Shum, D. H. K., et al. (2015). The nature of prospective memory deficit in patients with obsessive-compulsive disorder. *Psychiatry Research, 230,* 479–486.

Zimprich, D., Kliegel, M., & Rast, P. (2011). The factorial structure and external validity of the prospective and Retrospective Memory Questionnaire in older adults. *European Journal of Ageing, 8*, 3–48.

Zogg, J. B., Woods, S. P., Sauceda, J. A., Wiebe, J. S., & Simoni, J. M. (2012). The role of prospective memory in medication adherence: A review of an emerging literature. *Journal of Behavioral Medicine, 35*, 47–62.

Contents

CHAPTER 14

MEMORY ACROSS THE LIFESPAN: GROWING UP

Alan Baddeley

nlike most creatures, we are born helpless, with a huge amount to learn and a brain that is far from mature. Our need to learn and remember continues throughout our lifespan with a capacity for new learning that gradually reduces and is increasingly threatened by disease and dementia. The next two chapters are concerned with attempts to understand this process of development and decline. The first of these chapters considers the processes involved in the development of the brain, going on to discuss learning and memory during infancy, involving ingenious new methods of investigation created to study the evolution of the various types of learning and memory. We then move on to the study of memory during childhood resulting in the creation of measures that reflect improvement of performance with age but can also be used to study differences among individuals at the same age. This has led to the area known as psychometrics or mental testing, leading to the creation of a multimillion dollar international industry. Finally, while the study of development is of interest in its own right, our own emphasis will be on the extent to which learning and memory development can throw light on our understanding of the field more generally. We conclude with two examples of the ways in which research on childhood memory has been applied, one in education and the other to the role of children in eyewitness testimony.

HOW THE BRAIN DEVELOPS

Development of the brain is a continuous process in which one stage then enables the next. For example, in order to be able to walk children need to learn hip balance and posture before first being able to stand alone and then take their first steps, typically at between 10 and 18 months of age. This pattern applies equally to hearing, vision, language, and attention, each dependent on a strict sequence of stages. These in turn depend on the gradual development of the nervous system particularly the brain together with appropriate environmental support and stimulation (Cypel, 2013).

Figure 14.1 shows the development of the brain which begins with the development of the neural tube a few weeks after conception. This gradually differentiates into the brain, the brain stem, and the spinal cord. The neurons, once formed, migrate to a specific location in one of the regions of the brain to form the "gray matter" which comprises the outermost layer of the brain. At this point the neurons begin to connect with each other, forming synapses, contacts between different neurons. Such connections are formed at an amazing 700 per second. Such connections are gradually coated with myelin forming a sheath, like the insulation typically used on electric wires, that helps to avoid losses during transmission of information. This process continues until adolescence at least.

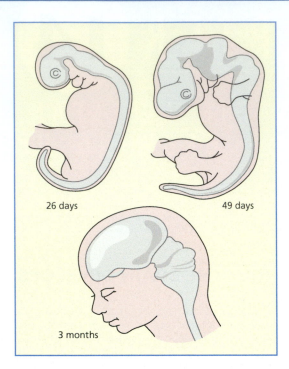

Figure 14.1 The early stages of development of the human brain.

During the early stages these are likely to depend mainly on carers whose provision of adequate stimulation and, importantly, emotional support, plays a crucial role in development. The child begins life with far more neurons than necessary, many of which are gradually eliminated if they are not actively used, a process known as "pruning" that extends up to adolescence. The development of synapses relevant to different psychological functions follows as the child begins to engage with the environment; regions concerned with hearing and vision peaking before those involved in language and speech followed later by the slower development of the prefrontal cortex responsible for a broad range of executive functions, as shown in Figure 14.2 (Cypel, 2013). In order to develop normally, however, the brain requires adequate nutrition during pregnancy and early infancy, together with appropriate environmental stimulation and emotional and social support. Unfortunately in many parts of world, these are by no means guaranteed, a situation that can have severe and long-term consequences.

While development before birth is largely determined genetically as is true for other organs such as the heart, once born, the environment becomes increasingly important as the child develops the capacity to perceive the world around, providing access to an increasingly rich environment as mobility develops. Language follows, providing an increasingly wide range of social and intellectual stimuli.

COGNITIVE DEVELOPMENT AND MALNUTRITION

While the world produces sufficient food for everyone, it is not distributed evenly across populations with malnutrition still relatively

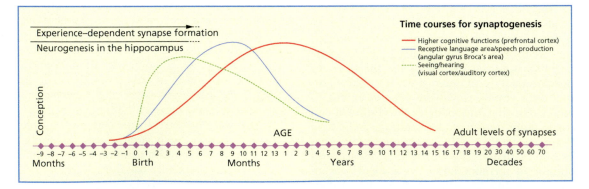

Figure 14.2 Subsequent development of the brain. Areas related to perception develop first, followed by those responsible for movement while those responsible for cognition develop somewhat later. Data from Cypel (2013).

widespread. The standard physical marker of deprivation is that of stunted growth where poor long-term nutrition or disease may lead to shorter stature with stunting being defined as two standard deviations or more below the World Health Organization's expected height for a child at that age. A more serious sign is "*wasting*" where the child is of seriously low weight even for its height. Wasting reflects more acute malnutrition and can be a strong predictor of mortality in the under five-year-olds. Although these are both physical measures they serve as indicators of more serious and general long-term consequences. Such markers of malnutrition have happily been reducing over the last two decades from a world estimate of 255 million stunted children in 1990 to 159 million in 2015. However, this remains a major problem as does the incidence of 50 million wasted children and 16 million severely wasted.

The consequences of stunting are severe and long-lasting. Black et al. (2013) summarized data from low- and middle-income countries providing extensive evidence that such signs of malnutrition at age two are associated with reduced adult height, a range of health problems, less schooling, and lower economic productivity. Effects on cognition are reviewed by Grantham-McGregor (1995) who finds stunting to be associated with lower IQ, poorer cognitive function, worse school achievement, and increased behavioral problems in stunted children as compared to matched controls and to a lesser extent to their nonstunted brothers and sisters. Happily, she also reports improvement following a change in environment resulting from targeted intervention or adoption. As she points out, however, such a correlation does not necessarily imply causation. Malnourished children are likely to have malnourished parents who lack energy and opportunity to provide appropriate stimulation or access to educational or employment opportunities. So can nutritional intervention and/or social and cognitive stimulation help?

Fortunately, it is possible to reverse such effects both on a short-term and a longer-term basis. Simeon and Grantham-McGregor (1989) compared three groups of Jamaican children: a stunted group, a wasted group, and a matched control group on a range of cognitive measures. The children were tested on successive weeks, on half the occasions having been provided before testing with breakfast or a non-nutritional cup of tea. A deficit was still found but was greatly reduced by having a pretest breakfast, a practise that is now followed by a number of schools worldwide who provide "breakfast clubs." McGregor's Jamaican group has been responsible for some of the most careful and extended research in the field. They conducted a trial involving 129 growth-retarded children aged between nine and 24 months involving nutritional supplementation and/or psychosocial stimulation. This involved weekly one-hour visits from a specially trained local care worker who would assist the mother in developing caring skills that importantly included play with the child.

By the end of the two-year programme, the stunted children had caught up with the physical and cognitive scores of the nonstunted control children. When retested at age 18, there remained an advantage to the treated group on 11 out of 12 tests although this was found to reflect the psychosocial rather than the nutritional treatment. When tested again at 22 years of age, although the overall performance of the stunted children remained somewhat lower than the matched controls, the weekly psychosocial stimulation led to higher educational achievement, better knowledge, higher IQ, and less depression and importantly less violent behavior (Walker, Chang, Vera-Hernández, & Grantham-McGregor, 2011). This is a remarkable study extending over 20 years by an outstanding group, raising the question as to whether the results can be generalized to a different situation run by a different group on a different population. This issue was addressed in a study focused on attempting to supplement the diet and/or to enrich the home environment of 1,489 low-income families in Pakistan. It showed a clear effect of stimulation on cognition when tested at two years of age that was sustained when children were retested at age four (Yousafzai, Rasheed, Rizvi, Armstrong, & Bhutta, 2014).

The studies described so far have typically involved children with mothers, who although they themselves may be malnourished and socially disadvantaged, are at least able to provide maternal care and support. This was not the case for a large number of children in Romania during the dictatorship of Ceauşescu who wanted to maximize the population of his country. He did so by encouraging large families and banning birth control and abortion. This led to a growing number of unwanted children, some handicapped others simply neglected who were housed in large state nurseries with poor food and minimal adult attention. When Ceauşescu was overthrown, the plight of these children became internationally recognized and many of them were subsequently adopted. Rutter et al. (2007) describe the outcome at age 11 of 144 children raised in institutions, who were adopted for placement with UK families before the age of 42 months. They were compared to a sample of 52 noninstitutionalized UK children adopted before the age of six months who were studied in the same way. Somewhat surprisingly, children adopted before the age of six months were relatively unaffected by the institutional experience. Beyond this age, however, the effect of institutional deprivation was clear. It was not strongly related to time in the institute before adoption, but the presence on arrival in the UK of even very minimal language skills such as imitation of speech sounds was linked to enhanced subsequent recovery. In general, these children showed very few negative cognitive effects of deprivation by age six although they and other groups tended to show problems of inattention and overactivity. When retested at age 11, children from the orphanages had significantly lower academic attainment than adoptees from within the UK but this did not vary with amount of time within the institution. The academic differences were associated with IQ and to a lesser extent to inattention/overactivity.

A parallel US-based study from the same institutional population did find a small effect of time in the orphanage. It used a potentially more sensitive design in which 136 orphans were randomly divided into two groups, one of which was fostered while the other remained in the orphanage (Nelson et al., 2007). Both

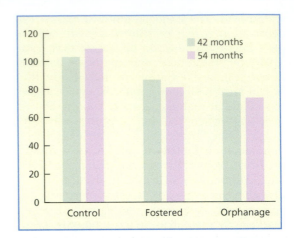

Figure 14.3 Mean IQ after 42 and 54 months of normally parented children, orphanage children who were fostered, and children who remained in the orphanage. Data from Nelson et al. (2007).

groups were compared with 80 parented children. The results are shown in Figure 14.3.

Both studies therefore find an advantage to adoption or fostering but with a remaining cost, except for children adopted within a few months of birth.

In conclusion it is clear that malnutrition during infancy can result in physical stunting, impairs cognition, and that both this and lack of social stimulation can lead to later behavioral problems. However, a combination of feeding together with provision of maternal stimulation during the early years can reduce these deficits. Most of the work discussed at this point has used a range of broadly cognitive tests rather than focusing specifically on memory which, as the next section shows, is far from easy to assess during the first few years of life.

LEARNING AND MEMORY IN INFANTS

With so much to learn, there is no time to lose and evidence suggests that some learning at least occurs even before we are born. The environment before birth is of course somewhat constrained; not much chance of learning to walk, for example. However, there is evidence from animal studies that adaptation to novel tastes and smells can occur, reaching the developing fetus either through injection into the amniotic fluid or through food consumption by the mother. An intriguing example of such adaptation in humans was shown by Schaal, Marlier, and Soussignan (2000) who took advantage of the fact that local cuisine in Alsace involves aniseed in a range of dishes favored by some but not all of the population. They divided pregnant mums into two groups, those who did and those who did not use aniseed in their cooking. They then exposed the newborn babies to an aniseed smell or a control smell and noted their reaction. Babies of aniseed-consuming mums showed positive head turning and facial reactions as evaluated by judges unaware of the test condition unlike control babies, when tested both immediately and four days after birth.

Hearing develops relatively early during gestation and a number of studies have shown that newborn babies show a preference for their mother's voice over the voice of another female (DeCasper & Fifer, 1980) and do indeed show evidence of learning something of their native language, behaving in a way that prolongs passages of speech in their native tongue compared with another language (Moon, Cooper, & Fifer, 1993). In another study, expectant mothers read one of two nursery rhymes aloud three times a day for four weeks starting at 33 weeks gestation. At 37 weeks the familiar nursery rhyme and an unfamiliar one was read aloud by another talker while fetal heartrate was measured. It declined significantly more to the familiar than the unfamiliar rhyme. All of these show evidence of some kind of learning, but it is important to note that testing typically occurs after a relatively short delay and that the extent and breadth of learning appears to be relatively limited. Hence, although there is evidence that newborns favor the theme tune of their mum's favorite soap opera, courses claiming that you can induce a love of classical music or facilitate the learning of a second language while awaiting the arrival of your offspring should be treated with considerable caution!

It is rather easier to test memory in babies once they have been born, but still very difficult. They cannot of course be given verbal instructions or provide verbal responses and their capacity for coherent responding is distinctly limited, while gaining and keeping their attention is far from easy. There have however been a number of ingenious studies, notably by Rovee-Collier and colleagues demonstrating both learning and retention in infants as young as two months. In a classic series of studies, Rovee-Collier, Sullivan, Enright, Lucas, and Fagen (1980) used a task in which a mobile suspended above the child's head was attached to a ribbon which was then attached to the child's foot with the result that kicking with that foot moved the mobile (see Figure 14.4). This increased the occurrence of kicking compared to a condition in which the ribbon was tied to the cot rail rather than the mobile. The association between the mobile and kicking appeared to be retained for up to two days then apparently forgotten. However, a reminder by the adult moving the mobile led to retention of delays of up to two weeks. The mobile task is less appropriate for older children, for whom Hartshorn (2003) devised a task in which children of ages ranging from seven to 18 months learned to press a lever to make a miniature train move around a track.

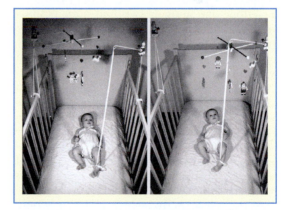

Figure 14.4 Testing a baby's capacity to learn and remember. When the ribbon is tied to a mobile, the baby learns to kick to move the mobile, an action that is retained even when the ribbon is disconnected. As the baby gets older, retention time increases. Rovee-Collier et al., 1980.

Given a reminder, older children showed some evidence of memory after 18 months, provided they had been given an appropriate reminder. It is clear therefore that babies can learn to make responses if they are suitably rewarded, and can retain information initially over a relatively short period but much longer if reminded.

A major influence on developmental psychology during the middle years of the last century was Jean Piaget whose careful observations and ingenious experimental methods led to an approach to cognitive development based on the assumption that it involves passing through a series of cognitive stages. While he was not principally concerned with memory he did develop the use of imitation as a way of investigating memory (Piaget, 1952) noting that infants have a tendency to imitate, copying action by the tester on an object such as a puppet. Using this approach, Barr, Rovee-Collier, and Campanella (2005) showed that six-month-olds were able to imitate a target action one day after its initial presentation and when the action was performed repeatedly, retain it for up to 10 weeks after learning. Babies have also been shown to learn to associate pairs of objects presented together, even though they were not rewarded for this. Giles and Rovee-Collier (2011) exposed children to two fluffy puppets—a yellow duck and a pink rabbit—for either one hour or two half-hour periods on successive days. During this time the tester performed an action on one of the furry animals. After a delay the child was presented with the other animal whereupon it imitated the action, showing memory lasting up to four weeks, with two short presentations being better than one long. Retention was actually better for the younger than the older children which Giles and Rovee-Collier interpret as suggesting an earlier phase of enhanced capacity to form associations between stimuli, although it seems possible that the more active older children would simply have experienced a wider range of events that could potentially interfere with memory during the delay period.

Another important method within this area is that of preferential looking. Given two stimuli, one of which has been presented repeatedly and one that is novel, babies prefer novelty. Quinn, Eimas, and Rosencrantz (1993) used this to demonstrate that babies were capable of distinguishing between two categories, for example cats and dogs, an early form of semantic memory. When presented with a series of pictures of different dogs they showed more looking responses when a cat was introduced. Using this technique, Eimas and Quinn (1994) showed that infants of 3–4 months distinguished between a series of varied pictures of horses and varied pictures of cats, zebras, or giraffes. When habituated to a sequence of cats, their behavior suggested that they treated these as different from horses or tigers, but not female lions; by 6–7 months however female lions were no longer treated as cats. In a later study, Quinn, Westerlund, and Nelson (2006) obtained similar results when, instead of preferential looking, they used an electrophysiological measure based on the pattern of evoked responses to detect the child's capacity to identify within category exemplars.

Similar methods have been used to detect evidence of memory for repetition of pictures within sequences of objects where differential responses to repetition of recently presented items implies some type of retention. One such study was based on the observation that the pupil of the eye dilates when a remembered item is presented. Hellmer, Söderlund, and Gredebäck (2016) presented 40 line drawings of objects for three seconds each to groups of adults, seven-month-old infants and four-month-olds. They found evidence for dilation to repeated items for the adults and the seven-month-olds but not for those of only four months, a result they attributed to the immaturity of the hippocampus at this younger age.

In conclusion, it is clear that a wide range of learning mechanisms and processes are active during the first months of life, a period in which the brain is developing rapidly. The link between brain development and performance during infancy seems likely to continue to be a very active area of research.

It is clear therefore that babies can show a relatively wide range of learning capacities, but can they remember? Do they have episodic memory? The demonstration that children respond differently to pictures that have previously been presented may be based on an automatic familiarity response rather than showing any clear evidence of recollection. Indeed, there might appear to be evidence against episodic memory in infants as represented by the phenomenon of *infantile amnesia*. This appears to have been first reported by Miles (1893) who asked people to report their earliest memories and attempt to date them, finding that first memories were typically dated at around three years of age, with very few earlier reports. Freud (1905/1953) created the term "infantile amnesia" and attributed it to the repression of memories of earlier infantile passions, the first and possibly least well-supported of a range of later interpretations, of which more later.

INFANTILE AMNESIA

What is your own earliest memory? How old were you at the time? How do you know? Does it mean you did not have episodic autobiographical memories before that time? Detecting episodic memory becomes more feasible with the development of language as illustrated by the case of Emily, who was observed at the age of 21 months to adopt a habit of chatting to herself before going to sleep (Nelson, 1989). Her soliloquies were unstructured and tended not to include important issues like the birth of a sibling or Christmas festivities, but were rather more likely to comment on issues such as the quarrel between two other children in the playgroup. They could however extend back as far as two months before. Around 24 months her comments became more generalized such as "can't go down basement with jamas on" or "when Emily go mormor [grandma] in the day time … that's what Amy do sometimes" or speculations about the future "maybe the doctor take my jamas off." At the age of 36 months Emily stopped soliloquizing and the study ended. It seems clear that Emily was remembering potentially verifiable experiences, although they were not organized in any obvious way, and did not seem to reflect the importance of any given event, quite unlike most adult autobiographical memory.

By the age of three, many children are sufficiently verbal to allow episodic memory to be probed systematically. Sheingold and Tenney (1982) questioned children about their memory for the birth of a sibling, finding no evidence for memory in children under three years old, gradually increasing to almost 100% by age nine. Bauer (2012) reports two studies showing the retention of events experienced at age three when tested at ages ranging from 4.5 to 8.5, finding that retention was excellent for up to 2½ years, then declines. In a related study, Morris, Baker-Ward, and Bauer (2010) varied the age of the children tested, holding the delay constant at one year. They found that five-year-olds retained 67%, six-year-olds 78%, and eight-year-olds 91% of the events. These two studies make it clear that retention over a matter of years is possible in three-year-olds but that younger children appear to forget faster.

So to return to the question of infantile amnesia, are infants indeed amnesic, do they lack episodic memory, and if not, why do we adults have so few memories from these early months of life? The evidence reviewed is consistent with some form of ongoing capacity to retain information over increasing delays from the early months of life although, until the development of language, it is hard to establish that this necessarily implies recollection. Once language develops, it is possible for the child to communicate either directly through questions or indirectly as in Emily's soliloquies, suggesting that some form of recollection does appear to be possible. It does however seem to be unstructured with little evidence of organization based on relative importance. As children develop, their capacity to remember autobiographical events improves, both in initial encoding and in durability.

But why should this produce the apparently dramatic absence of memories below the age of five years? A range of theories have been produced from Freud's initial proposal that the amnesia results from repression of threat-related thoughts regarding sexual feelings to one's parents, for which there is very little support, to a range of explanations based on changes that almost certainly *do* occur and probably do contribute to childhood amnesia. These include the maturation of the hippocampus, which continues to develop up to adolescence. The potential role of language is another probable factor: many studies rely on verbal report which will clearly be limited by language development. A study by Simcock and Hayne (2003) encouraged children between 24 and 48 months to play with a "magic shrinking machine" in which objects appeared to go in large and come out small. Memory was tested 24 hours later by verbal recall, picture recognition of objects used, or enactment, showing how the machine works. Verbal report was poorest, particularly for the younger group.

Yet another hypothesis links infantile amnesia to the development of a self concept. Howe and Courage (1997) for example propose that infants can only form autobiographical memories once they have begun to develop a sense of self to which events of personal significance can be related, a process they suggest begins around the age of two years. They measure its onset by surreptitiously applying a red spot to the infant's nose and then allowing the child to see itself in a mirror. Self-awareness is indicated by the child reaching to its own nose, a process that develops rapidly during the period around 21–24 months (Lewis & Brooks-Gunn, 1979). Howe, Courage, and Edison (2003), working with infants aged between 15 and 23 months, find self-recognizers have better memory for personal events while they found not a single child showing good performance on the memory task before reaching self-recognition. However, the observation that performance on two tasks is highly correlated does not of course necessarily imply that one causes the other. It is equally plausible to claim that both are the result of one or more of the many other rapid changes that are occurring at this point.

This is view taken by Fivush and Nelson (2004) who relate the development of autobiographical memory to cultural factors and in

When infants can recognize their own reflection, by reaching for their own nose rather than the one in the mirror, they are considered to have developed a sense of self-awareness.

particular to the interaction of the child with its parent, resulting in the development of a sense of self within the child. Mothers differ in their mode of interaction with their child both within and across different cultures. Nelson (1989) observed the interaction between mothers and children as they wandered around a US museum, categorizing the interactions as "practical" or "freely interacting." The practical mothers ask questions such as "What do you think this statue is made of?" while the freely interacting mothers tended to relate what was seen to previous experiences shared with the children. When tested a week later about the content of the museum, the children of freely interacting mothers were able to answer an average of 13 out of 30 questions compared to only four for the children of more practical mothers. Jack, McDonald, Reese, and Hayne (2009) provide the link between the reminiscing style of mothers and childhood amnesia by showing that 12-year-olds whose mothers had an elaborate reminiscent style had earlier first memories than children whose mothers had a more restrained style of interaction.

Further evidence for the influence of maternal interaction on the earliest memories reported comes from cross-cultural studies where Wang (2001, 2006) reports a clear difference in style of mother–child interaction between China and that typical of the US, where mothers were much more likely to interact with their child about the past, bringing in phrases such as "remember when we went to Vermont and saw cousin Bill?" Chinese mothers tended to be more pragmatic and direct. Wang found a clear difference between the average age of first memory of US participants (3.8 years) and that of Chinese participants (5.4 years). Thus both groups show clear evidence of childhood amnesia, but suggest that its extent will be influenced by cultural factors reflecting the richness and type of information that is initially encoded which in turn influences the likelihood of later recollection. It is not clear however that this reflects the development of self as suggested by Fivush and Nelson (2004) as it could simply be based on setting up a wider and richer range of potential retrieval cues which may or may not reflect a developing self concept.

In conclusion, while infantile amnesia is readily demonstrable and has given rise to a range of different interpretations, all tend to be linked to different but related aspects of development. The relevant factors are however likely to have their impact at different stages. One influential approach was proposed by Bauer (2006) who suggests an initial set of limitations that are due to slow maturation of brain areas responsible for both encoding and consolidating information. As these areas mature, memory becomes less dependent on encoding and consolidation and increasingly reflects improvement in the capacity to retrieve encoded memories which in turn is based on the richer range of cues available to the developing child. These increasingly allow the "what," "where," "when," and "how" of an experience to be encoded and linked into a developing self-reference system as an episodic memory. This leads to the next question of how episodic memory continues to develop throughout childhood.

DEVELOPMENTAL CHANGES IN MEMORY DURING CHILDHOOD

Working memory

Gathercole, Pickering, Ambridge, and Wearing (2004) used the multicomponent working memory framework to study boys and girls between the ages of four and 15 across a range of working memory tasks. Three tests focused on the phonological loop, three on the visuo-spatial sketchpad, and three on the central executive. The results are shown in Figure 14.5. An overall analysis of the data suggests that the structure of working memory, the way in which the components are linked, is consistent from an early age with that found in adults, a conclusion confirmed by Michalczyk, Malstädt, Worgt, Könen, and Hasselhorn (2013) in a study based on children aged between five and 12 years. They also found the same three components originally identified by Baddeley and Hitch and, like Gathercole et al. (2004), also found a stable relationship between the three components across that age range.

Thus, not only do the different components of working memory appear to improve steadily over the childhood years, but their relationship to each other also remains constant. However, while this might seem to simply reflect a steady development of the working memory system, closer examination suggests something rather more complex. First of all, it is important to note that the amount of variability within a given age is considerably greater than that between successive ages, reflecting the fact that children of the same age may differ markedly in their scores. Thus, some nine-year-olds will perform at the level of seven-year-olds on a given test while some may more closely resemble children aged 11. Furthermore, for individual children, the increase from one year to the next varies considerably, suggesting cognitive growth spurts and relative plateaux. This also makes it very difficult to provide an accurate and reliable measure of the effect of interventions such as attempts to increase WM capacity through training

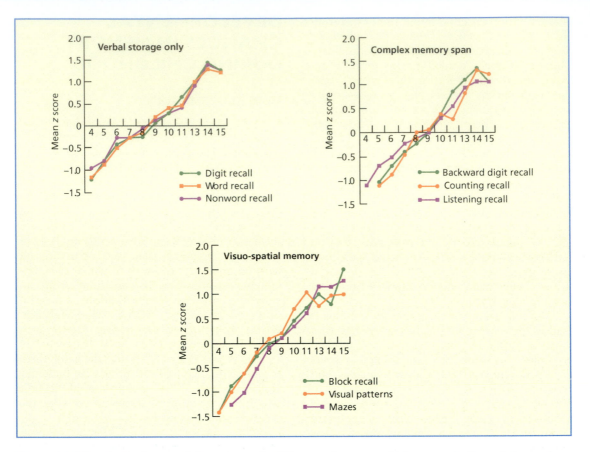

Figure 14.5 Standardized scores (adjusted to make different tasks comparable) across ages for verbal, complex executive, and visuo-spatial memory tests. Data from Gathercole, Pickering, Ambridge and Wearing (2004).

(see Chapter 4, p. 94), since a low-scoring child may be approaching a growth spurt while a high scorer might be at a temporary plateau at the point that training occurs.

In the case of the all-important central executive component, Case, Kurland, and Goldberg (1982) proposed that the pool of available attentional capacity remains the same during development, but is used more efficiently as skills such as articulation and semantic chunking develop. However, while there is little strong evidence that the pool of executive capacity remains constant, there is evidence that brain structure gradually changes between ages six and 16. Bathelt, Gathercole, Johnson, and Astle (2017) assessed a total of 153 children measuring cortical thickness at different parts of the brain and suggest an important role for development of the corpus callosum, linking the two hemispheres, and of the white matter associated with executive aspects of working memory, followed by the later development of a distributed system relying on more long-range connections within the cortex which they suggest reflects the development of the working memory subsystems. It seems unlikely therefore that the capacity of this complex and developing system remains constant, as Case et al. (1982) suggest.

In general, therefore, the development of working memory throughout childhood seems likely to reflect a range of potentially separable subsystems where the apparent simplicity of the developmental trend reflects the underlying complexity, both of the systems and their interaction, together with their varying rates of development both within and between individual children. It is probably fair to say that the multicomponent model is broadly compatible with the process of development; however, the pattern is a complex one that does not clearly favor one model of working memory over other current theories.

Long-term memory

We have so far focused our attention on autobiographical memory and potential explanations for infantile amnesia. However, Bauer's hypothesis of two stages should in principle be applicable to LTM more generally, resulting in an initial relatively rapid enhancement as the development of the neural basis allows enhanced memory consolidation, followed by the more gradual impact of ever richer encoding leading to more successful sequent retrieval.

One source of relevant information comes from standardized memory tests for children and in particular memory for prose. This forms a major component of most adult memory scales (e.g., Wechsler, 1992; Wilson, Cockburn, & Baddeley, 1985) and has been shown to be a good indicator of everyday memory performance (Sunderland, Harris, & Baddeley, 1983). Prose recall forms an important component of both the Children's Memory Scale (Cohen, 1997) and the children's version of the Rivermead Behavioural Memory Test (Wilson, Ivani-Chalian, & Aldrich, 1991) with both showing improved retention with increased age but with little evidence of further improvement beyond the age of 10 or 11. It is important to note however that the prose passages used in both cases change substantially in content across ages. In the Cohen (1997) test for example it changes from a simple story about a cat and kittens for the five-year-olds to a relatively complex paragraph for 16-year-olds about the interaction between native Americans, settlers, and the disappearance from the plains of the vast buffalo herds. By this age, performance is broadly equivalent to that of adults (Wilson et al., 1991). The need to change materials across ages however suggests that there are important differences across groups, if not in basic learning capacity, at least in capacity to comprehend the material with a probable knock-on effect on later recall.

Returning to Bauer's (2006) distinction between two major stages of memory development, one might see the earlier years as reflecting steady improvement based on the gradual development of the brain and of the capacity to encode and consolidate material. This is then followed by the proposed second stage, dependent on having a sufficient knowledge base to allow this basic capacity to be used most efficiently by encoding a richer and more coherent range of potential retrieval cues. The role of such relevant background knowledge is clearly demonstrated in the case of expertise such as that shown by children who are expert chess players. As shown in Figure 14.6, they remember chess positions considerably better than less expert adults who do however exceed the performance of children on nonspecialized material.

A more general case of the role of semantic memory comes through the increasing vocabulary acquired by children. Here, it is not simply knowledge of the meaning of individual words. The 5-year-olds in Cohen's (1997) test might well know the words buffalo, native American, and settler, but would be unlikely to have the background knowledge to appreciate the nature of the potential conflict. Examples of the development of this process of extending and testing semantic knowledge come from two of my own grandsons. One, on hearing that my

Memory for chess positions depends largely on expertise and hardly at all on age.

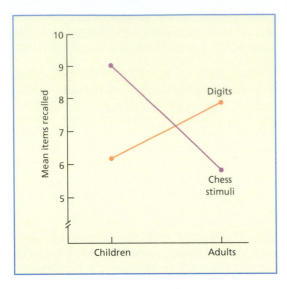

Figure 14.6 Immediate recall of chess positions and digits in children (mean age 10 years 6 months) with expert knowledge of chess and in adults with limited knowledge of chess. Adapted from Chi (1978).

brother, his uncle, had died asked "Was he struck by a meteorite?" presumably overgeneralizing what he had recently heard about the extinction of the dinosaurs. Another grandson asked my wife, "Granny, do you believe in owls?" presumably reflecting the fact that, like dragons, they appear frequently in books but, as a city-living child, had not actually been encountered. The importance of background knowledge was studied by O'Reilly, Wang, and Sabatini (2019) who tested 3,534 high school students on the impact of background knowledge of environmental issues on retention of information from a passage on ecology. They found an overall correlation between knowledge and performance. However, this was shown only for familiarity with relatively complex concepts such as "ecosystem" and "habitat"; degree of knowledge of more basic concepts did not correlate with performance.

The capacity to use available knowledge most effectively is of course also likely to depend on working memory, not only through its role in comprehension, but also from its active use in strategy. A clear example of the development of strategy across age groups comes from studies of memory for sequences of words and pictures. In a series of studies, Graham Hitch and colleagues required children of different ages to remember short lists of simple line drawings of objects that were readily nameable (Hitch, Woodin, & Baker, 1989). They showed that, older children, like adults, remembered sequences whose names rhymed such as *hat* and *cat* less well than those with dissimilar names. This variant of the phonological similarity effect in STM discussed in Chapter 3 suggested that the pictures were being stored in terms of their spoken names. This evidence of using a phonological code to store visually presented pictures was, however, not found with five-year-old children. Instead they showed poorer performance when the pictures were visually similar, for example a *fork* and a *toothbrush*, suggesting a reliance on visual rather than verbal coding. This reliance on visual coding begins to change around the age of six, when phonological coding tends to overtake visual coding. It is important to bear in mind however that like all strategy effects, its adoption is optional with different children switching from visual to verbal coding at somewhat different ages. Adoption of one strategy over another is likely in turn to depend on "metamemory," the child's increasing knowledge of the strengths and weaknesses of his or her own memory, something that gradually increases as a result of experience, allowing memory to be used more efficiently.

Procedural learning

As described in Chapter 5, implicit and procedural learning comes in many forms. In the case of motor skills, for example, it may develop automatically as in learning to walk, but be constrained by the need to acquire earlier skills such as balance. Later and more specialized skills such as swimming may require deliberate learning but may still depend on the development of earlier capacities such as breath control. Likewise, perceptual skills such as discriminating between letter shapes in the beginning reader may depend on earlier visual maturity while yet other phonological skills are likely to be involved in acquiring language fluency. You will therefore not be surprised to learn that different skills are likely to develop in different ways and at different rates as the child grows up.

So at this point you might be thinking "we already knew that working memory and long-term memory were made up of several interacting components. They all seem to improve until the teenage years and because they interact it is hard to separate one from the other. So why is it important to study the way memory develops in children?" As a parent, it does of course suddenly become fascinating to see your child develop, and to note that memory forms an important part of this process. There are however many situations in which knowledge of the development of learning and memory during childhood extends well beyond satisfying parental curiosity. We conclude by discussing in more detail two examples of ways in which an analytic cognitive approach to the study of memory in children has been applied to important practical problems.

APPLICATIONS

Working memory and education

A seminal moment in the history of psychology came following a request from the French government to the psychologist Alfred Binet to develop a method of identifying children whose limited cognitive abilities meant that they would need a special form of education. This led to the development of the intelligence test and subsequently to a multinational testing industry together with some of psychology's most virulent controversies. Binet's initial question remains and tests of intelligence still form an important part of the educational psychologist's tool kit with different patterns of performance associated with different educational problems (Rourke & Tsatsanis, 1995). As we saw in Chapter 4 (p. 88) working memory appears to offer a way of analyzing some of the components underpinning intelligence test performance and hence of providing the

educational psychologist and the teacher with more specific guidance in understanding school performance and the problems encountered by some children.

As mentioned in Chapter 4 there are several different approaches to working memory based on somewhat different assumptions. Most however have at their heart a concept of a limited capacity mental workspace that can be used to tackle a range of cognitive tasks. Case et al. (1982) explained the development of working memory in children in terms of a central pool of capacity which they refer to as M Space. This is assumed to remain constant over time but to be used increasingly effectively as the child develops more effective or speedier methods of using this capacity. Other approaches also emphasize some form of limited capacity workspace, but assume that capacity increases with age (e.g., Barouillet & Camos, 2014; Cowan, 1997, 2005; Engle, Cantor, & Carullo, 1992). Such approaches may however differ on their assumptions regarding the role, if any, of the verbal and visuo-spatial aspects of working memory that play an important role in the multicomponent model. We know from the previously mentioned studies of Gathercole et al. (2004) that on average, the relationship between the various components remains the same as children develop but is this true of all individuals or do some people show a different pattern of strengths and weaknesses across the components of WM? If so is this atypical pattern reflected in their academic performance that if detected can potentially help the teacher to find ways of capitalizing on strengths and minimizing weaknesses?

Evidence that individuals may show very different patterns of working memory capacities comes from the study of people with specific inherited learning disabilities. In most cases of learning disability the pattern is complex, and the potential genetic origin of the disability remains unclear, unsurprisingly perhaps given the very large number of genes that appear to contribute to performance on intelligence tests (Plomin, 2018). However, occasionally people show a very characteristic pattern that can be traced to specific genes, although even here it is important to note that large individual differences occur in both the severity and the precise nature of the deficit. The development of working memory in two such groups was studied by Wang and Bellugi (1994), and further developed by Jarrold and colleagues (Jarrold, Baddeley, & Hewes, 1999). People with Down syndrome form one of these groups. They typically show physical growth delays, mild to moderate intellectual disability, characteristic facial features, and tend to have a pleasant sunny temperament. The degree of learning disability varies substantially, but generally involves poor immediate verbal memory, relative to its spatial equivalent (see Figure 14.7).

A second group, people with Williams syndrome show a contrasting pattern. Their facial features are often described as "elfin," their verbal memory is good, with a surprisingly large vocabulary. They are very sociable, but tend to have difficulty making friends because the content of their conversation tends to be more limited than their fluency would suggest. They tend however to have impaired spatial span (see Figure 14.7) and poor spatial abilities.

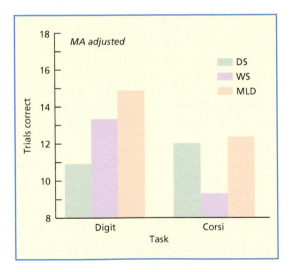

Figure 14.7 Performance of people with Down syndrome, Williams syndrome, and minimal learning disability on digit span (left) and spatial Corsi block spatial span (right), with scores adjusted to equate overall mental age. Note that Down syndrome leads to a particular deficit on digit span, whereas Corsi span is more reduced in Williams syndrome. Data from Jarrold et al. (1999).

However, although these such syndromes lend further support to the idea of separable verbal and visuo-spatial STM systems, they are highly atypical of children in general or of most children with learning difficulties, raising questions as to how useful it might be to apply the multicomponent model to children within the normal educational system. This issue was addressed by Susan Gathercole and colleagues (2004) who began by devising a battery of tests that aimed at separating visuo-spatial and verbal memory each tackled at two levels. One level comprised simple span in which the participant would reproduce a sequence of verbal or visual items, hence involving storage but not manipulation and assumed to depend mainly on the phonological loop and its visuo-spatial equivalent the sketchpad. The second level involves tests of "complex span," tests that are assumed to reflect the additional role of the central executive. These require simultaneously storing and processing information, as in the case of the widely used sentence span test (see Chapter 4) developed initially by Daneman and Carpenter (1980). These tasks were chosen so as to be understood and performed by children as young as seven years old, but to gradually increase in difficulty allowing level of performance to be measured across a wide age range. Gathercole and colleagues went on to test over 3,000 children, selected from schools representing the whole range of prosperity within the UK. This initial stage allowed them to measure the average level of performance on each of these tests for children of a given age. This stage was then followed by a number of studies aimed at testing the relationship between test performance and academic achievement.

In one study, they found that low working memory scores at age seven were correlated with poor performance on national academic tests of English and mathematics, with visuo-spatial and complex span measures being particularly sensitive. They observe for example an association between early arithmetic and visuo-spatial working memory, a link supported by later cross-cultural studies. Reeve, Reynolds, Paul, and Butterworth (2018) for example showed a similar pattern of association for both indigenous children from a remote region in Northern Australia in a culture that contained few counting words or practices and for nonindigenous children from an Australian city.

An overall reduction in WM performance is typically much more problematic than a more specific visual on verbal deficit. Gathercole and Pickering (2000) tested 83 seven-year-old children who were split into two groups on the basis of their academic performance on National Curriculum tests. Working memory scores across the two groups were clearly different with complex span scores being particularly clearly related to academic achievement. So having a low working memory span is clearly not good for academic achievement, but why? The important next step was to go into schools and observe children with low working memory span noting how they responded in the teaching situation.

Gathercole, Lamont, and Alloway (2006) describe David, a typical example of a child with low working span, as reserved, well-behaved, and reasonably well-liked by his classmates. His scores on the phonological loop tests were normal, but performance on complex span tests fell considerably below that to be expected by a child of his age. Academically he was placed in the lowest class for numeracy and slightly above for literacy. Extensive teacher ratings on low working memory span children suggested that they were typically described as being inattentive, distractible, and poor at monitoring the quality of their work and at generating new solutions. This led to a more extended careful observational study of a small number of children over several days. Another typical child, Joshua, performed normally on tests of phonological loop capacity and on nonverbal ability tests, but poorly on complex memory span. He was quiet, obedient in class, and well-liked but tended to respond slowly and often failed to follow general class instructions, requiring frequent reminders; his teacher describes him as being "in a world of his own." He was in the lowest ability groups for both numeracy and literacy, often showing overt signs of frustration, pulling faces and banging his head with his hands. Observation of the performance of such chil-dren in class suggested that they had great difficulty in following instructions. For example, when Joshua was handed his computer login cards and told to go and work on computer number 13, he failed to do this because he had forgotten which computer he had been told to use.

It rapidly became clear that the teaching situation often requires children both to hold and manipulate information at the same time, leading to memory lapses. This can become particularly acute when instructions are complex or when a complex strategy is involved, a strategy that might for example be expected to help the child perform an arithmetic task. In some cases, the child can become frustrated, potentially leading to behavioral problems. Quite often, however, they simply and passively underperform.

There appeared to be a clear link to the diagnosis of ADHD (Attention Disability Hyperactivity Disorder) where children become attentionally very distractible with excessive activity, often creating problem behaviors. Gathercole's results suggest the possibility however that rather than reflecting a unitary ADHD syndrome, it may reflect the *combination* of two separable problems, one a working memory-based attentional limitation and the other a separate problem of hyperactivity. Only when the two coincide will the child be reported as troublesome and be referred for further investigation, leaving low working memory children who are not hyperactive to struggle quietly without their problem being recognized. Gathercole and colleagues were able to produce a book aimed at teachers explaining how to identify children with poor working memory, to realize the situations that cause them difficulty and modify their teaching accordingly (Gathercole & Alloway, 2008).

CHILDREN AS WITNESSES

Our second example of applying research comes from the study of LTM and its relevance to the increasing number of legal cases in which the testimony of one or more children becomes critical. Suppose you yourself are asked to serve on a jury where the outcome depends on the testimony of one or more children, how skeptical should you be? The traditional view is that "children are highly unreliable witnesses—so unreliable that early researchers had claimed that children's evidence can only mislead jurors (Brainerd & Reyna, 2012, p. 225). A dramatic example of this was provided by the McMartin preschool trial in which members of the McMartin family who ran a preschool in Manhattan Beach California were charged with many acts of sexual abuse of children in their care. This led to trials and legal investigations which ran from 1984 to 1990, resulting in no convictions and all charges being dropped, by which time it had been the longest and more expensive trial in American history. It proved to be a tragic object lesson in how not to interview children, beginning with a form letter from the police to around 200 parents of children who had attended the school suggesting a whole series of potential criminal acts about which the parents should question their child. Several hundred children were interviewed with the claim that 360 had been abused of whom 41 testified to the subsequent Grand Jury and about a dozen in the actual trial, some making bizarre accusations of satanic abuse and flying through the air. It later became clear that the children had been subjected to improper, coercive cross-examination following a rigid script that was totally inappropriate for children, resulting in conclusions that were so biased as to be quite unusable (Garven, Wood, Malpass, & Shaw, 1998). It is clear from this that children can indeed be dramatically unreliable witnesses; it should be noted of course that this can also be applied to adults, as reflected in the controversy regarding recovered memories of childhood abuse reported in Chapter 10. So are children so unreliable as to make their testimony useless?

It is clear that children as young as five certainly *can* remember specific events, given suitable cues. Fivush, Hudson, and Nelson (1984) studied memories of a visit to a Jewish museum in New York which involved explaining archeological methods and the chance to dig in a sandbox to find buried artefacts. Although considerable forgetting occurred, when interviewed some six years later, the children successfully recalled 87% of the original information when given the appropriate cues. This raises the question of what is forgotten and what cues are appropriate? In one study (Candel, Merckelbach, Jelicic, Limpens, & Widdershoven, 2004), seven- and 10-year-old children listened to an emotional story and were later questioned about both the central events and the more peripheral information using suggestive questions about both. In a second study, 82 children watched an emotional video fragment and again were asked about central and peripheral details. Both studies found the younger children to be more suggestible to be influenced by misleading questions, an effect that was more pronounced for peripheral details.

The assumption that younger children are more suggestible was tested in a study by Ceci, Baker, and Bronfenbrenner (1988) who read a story to children aged between three and 10. The story involved Lauren who has eggs for breakfast on her first day at school. She develops a stomach ache but forgets about it when allowed to play with another child's toy. Misleading information was introduced, for example by asking "Do you remember the story about Lauren, who had a headache because she ate her cereal too fast? Then she got better when she got to play with her friend's game?" Two days later the children were tested individually by being shown pairs of pictures and asked to choose one. One for example involved Lauren eating eggs and other eating cereal. The results are shown in Figure 14.8. When wording was unbiased, recall was good for all groups, whereas the introduction of misleading information impaired performance, particularly for the younger groups. In a later review of the literature, Ceci and Bruck (1993) found that 83% of the studies reviewed found that suggestibility reduced as children became older.

Why should younger children be more susceptible? Ceci and Bruck suggest first of all that they are more likely to yield to social pressure, particularly in the absence of a clear memory. Such pressure need not necessarily be through introducing false information, but

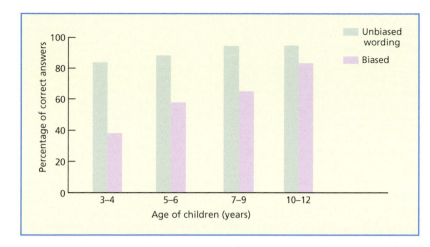

Figure 14.8 This graph shows the effects of misleading information on the memory of children of different ages. When unbiased wording is used, recall is more or less equally high across the age range, but under biased conditions younger children are more easily misled. (Ceci et al., 1988).

may be much subtler, for example by asking a question again if the desired answer was not given and using subtle cues of intonation or smiling to encourage the provision of wanted and discourage unwanted replies (Sparling, Wilder, Kondash, Boyle, & Compton, 2011). Thus, even without inserting misleading information, the interviewer can influence a child's response either intentionally or incidentally. This was shown by Zajac and Hayne (2005) who studied the effect of a challenging questioning style on recall of an earlier staged event in five- and six-year-olds (Zajac & Hayne, 2003), repeating this with children of 9–10 years (Zajac & Hayne, 2005). Both studies showed similar results although children of this age were more likely to change incorrect than correct memory responses when challenged. They did however change over 40% of their challenged correct responses showing a clear negative effect of aggressive questioning on overall accuracy.

The observation that detail is less well remembered than central events is unsurprising since it is typically less important. Hence if you were to see two people arguing, for example, the observation that one was clearly the aggressor would typically be more important than what they were wearing or the color of a passing car. As such it is unsurprising that such peripheral information is easier to modify during questioning. However, within the context of a trial, detail can often be of great importance and the

failure of a witness to remember it might be crucial. The effect of giving different answers on successive cross-examinations can also be particularly damaging to the credibility of the witness. This issue was tackled by O'Neil and Zajac (2013) who tested 5–6 year-old and 9–10 year-old children who took part in a surprise event after which they were then questioned. Either one week or six months later, the children were reinterviewed, half with the same questions and half using an analogue of cross-examination designed to challenge their earlier responses. All the children did worse on the second interview irrespective of age or length of delay, an effect that was more marked for younger children. For both groups the cross-examination method led to increased inconsistency between the two sessions even though no attempt was made to change the child's response. Repeated interviews are therefore a potential source of error.

What can be done?

One suggestion has been to use pretrial training in coping with the type of questioning involved in cross-examination (O'Neil & Zajac, 2013) or to attempt to improve the child's capacity to assess the source of their memories more accurately (Thierry & Spence, 2002). However, it is unclear how acceptable extensive training would be to a court which might regard it as unfair coaching of the young witness. It is however possible to include neutral practice questions that are unrelated to the content of the trial as part of the questioner's explanation of what is to follow, offering a sensible compromise. It is of course also sensible to incorporate methods that have proved helpful in helping adults to recall events, provided they have also been validated for children. A good example of this is the recent suggestion that children should close their eyes while trying to remember the relevant episode, a method that enhances memory for visual detail in both adults (Perfect et al., 2008; Vredeveldt, Hitch, & Baddeley, 2011), and children (Mastroberardino, Natali, & Candel, 2012). Another potentially valuable method is to attempt to reinstate the context within which the remembered event occurred. Priestley, Roberts, and Pipe (1999) required children between five and seven years of age to participate in an event that involved their dressing up as pirates, finding that a later recall was about 40% greater when the pirate props were provided.

One problem with recall in young children may be the lack of adequate language to express their memory. A possible aid to remembering therefore might be to encourage children to draw the events they are remembering. In one such study, Butler, Gross, and Hayne (1995) tested the memory of 5–6 year-olds after a visit to their local fire station. One day later, half were asked to draw what happened on the visit and half to tell. Memory was tested in three ways: free recall in which both sets of children were asked to tell what had happened, directed recall where the child was asked specific questions about the visit, and photo recall in which the child was asked to recognize a series of people or objects encountered during the visit. As shown in Figure 14.9, drawing was helpful in the directed questioning condition which also proved to be the most effective approach.

CONCLUSION

As Chapter 12 showed, obtaining reliable testimony is fraught with potential problems

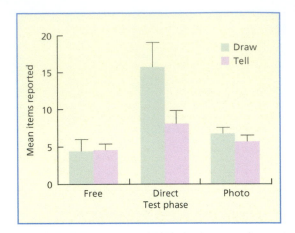

Figure 14.9 The effect of drawing on subsequent memory for people and objects encountered during an earlier visit, as a function of method of recall which involved either free recall, directed questioning, or recognition of a photograph. Directed questioning with drawing was clearly advantageous. Data from Butler et al., (1995).

even with healthy adult witnesses. The problems are even greater with children, but this does not mean that they cannot provide valuable information. Perhaps the major progress in this field has been through the gradual development of research-based evidence and its subsequent incorporation into a careful and detailed protocol, complete with clear guidelines as recommended by the US National Institute of Child Health and Development (Lamb, Orbach, Hershkowitz, Esplin, & Horowitz, 2007). It recommends a series of stages which begin by carefully building rapport with the child followed by the encouragement to recall some recent neutral event, a form of training. A series of nonsuggestive prompts then try to access the target events and, when this is achieved, broad free recall is encouraged: "Tell me everything," followed by more focused prompts (e.g., "Did it happen one time or more?" and "Then what happened?"). Only then is detail questioned such as "When did it happen?" Importantly, throughout the whole interview, suggestive utterances implying a specific response are strongly discouraged.

SUMMARY

- During pregnancy the brain develops from a neural tube a few weeks after conception to a spinal cord and a brain. During this period neurons migrate to specific locations and begin to form synapses coated with a myelin sheath. The brain develops to allow first perception then mobility and finally language and complex cognition.
- Synapses develop at an extremely rapid rate and subsequently need to be "pruned," a process finally completed during adolescence.
- Adequate nutrition is needed for optimal development. Without this the child may become stunted in height or even wasted, with potential impairment of subsequent cognitive development.
- Maternal care and emotional support are also important, together with adequate stimulation through play. Their absence can have long-term consequences for cognitive, emotional, and social development.
- Learning can begin in utero but becomes much more important following birth.
- A range of ingenious methods have succeeded in demonstrating learning with retention for up to two weeks in infants as young as two months, provided a reminder is given.
- Babies of six months are able to imitate a target action and retain for up to 10 weeks if performed repeatedly.
- Preferential looking can be used to detect the capacity to distinguish between two categories of pictures such as cats and dogs from the age of 3–4 months.
- Infantile amnesia refers to the fact that memory for events over the first 3–5 years of life when tested in later adults is very low.
- Once children are able to talk it becomes possible to investigate this in more detail, suggesting that episodic memory does occur but is not well organized.
- A range of explanations for infantile amnesia have been proposed including the development of the hippocampus, the role of language, and the gradual development of the sense of self.
- These are not mutually exclusive and may all contribute to infantile amnesia.
- The systematic study of individual differences in the cognitive development of children began with the work of Alfred Binet who observed that performance across a wide range of tasks increased systematically with age.
- This allowed him to express individual differences between children of a given age in terms of their mental age, the age at which their score is achieved by the average child.
- A similar pattern of gradual development is also found across a range of memory tasks and probably reflects several different factors.
- These include an increase in basic cognitive capacity, the development of a knowledge base, the acquisition of strategies and metamemory, together with the ability to select and use such strategies.
- Working memory in children shows a similar structure to that in adults, with verbal and visuo-spatial components being controlled by a limited capacity executive system.
- Although average development is gradual, individual children may develop at different rates with growth spurts and plateaux in performance.

(Continued)

(Continued)

- This is true of all aspects of memory. However, all may not develop to the same extent with Down syndrome showing a particular deficit in verbal working memory relative to its visuo-spatial equivalent, whereas Williams syndrome shows the opposite pattern.
- Long-term memory tends to increase gradually, reaching a peak during late teenage years.
- Applications of research on the development of memory include the analysis of deficits in working memory and their relevance for educational achievement with different aspects of working memory relevant at different points.
- Executive capacity is more generally important, with children who perform poorly on complex working memory tasks often showing problems in academic performance.
- This analysis has identified an important subgroup of children with poor working memory who have failed to cope academically but remain undetected because they are not troublesome. Ways of identifying and helping such children have been developed.
- An important practical question concerns the potential role of child witnesses who can be highly unreliable when questioned aggressively, potentially leading to major miscarriages of justice.
- They can potentially be relatively reliable witnesses but are more susceptible than adults to suggestion, following aggressive questioning and to social pressure more generally.
- Basic ground rules for questioning children have now been developed by the US National Institute of Child Health and Development in order to minimize these problems.

POINTS FOR DISCUSSION

1 Why is it difficult to study memory development in babies and what steps have been taken to circumvent these problems?
2 Describe the phenomenon of infantile amnesia and discuss *two* theoretical explanations of it.
3 What factors influence the development of working memory in children?
4 Why is it difficult to study long-term memory in children?
5 Discuss Bauer's two-stage hypothesis as applied to infantile amnesia and more generally to episodic memory.
6 How might the study of memory contribute to the work of an educational psychologist?
7 What can be done to maximize the accuracy with which child witnesses remember events?

FURTHER READING

Baddeley, A. D., & Hitch, G. (2000). Development of working memory: Should the Pascual-Leone and Baddeley and Hitch models be merged?. *Journal of Experimental Child Psychology, 77*, 128–137. A discussion of the relationship between the Baddeley and Hitch approach to working memory and an alternative based on the approach to psychology of the influential Swiss psychologist, Jean Piaget.

Camos, V., & Barrouillet, P. (2018). *Working memory in development.* Abingdon: Routledge. An excellent recent overview of the development of working memory in children.

Cowan, N. (2016). Working memory maturation: Can we get at the essence of cognitive growth?. *Perspectives on Psychological Science, 11*, 239–264. A recent account of the development of working memory from Cowan's embedded processes viewpoint.

REFERENCES

Barr, R., Rovee-Collier, C., & Campanella, J. (2005). Retrieval protracts deferred imitation by 6-month-olds. *Infancy, 7*, 263–283.

Barrouillet, P., & Camos, V. (2014). *Working memory: Loss and reconstruction.* Hove, UK: Psychology Press.

Bathelt, J., Gathercole, S. E., Johnson, A., & Astle, D. E. (2017). Differences in brain morphology and working memory capacity across childhood. *Developmental Science, 21*, e12579. doi:10.1111/desc.12579

Bauer, P. J. (2006). Constructing a past in infancy: A neuro-developmental account. *Trends in Cognitive Science, 10*, 175–181.

Bauer, P. J. (2012). The life I once remembered: The waxing and waning of early memories. In D. Berntsen & D. C. Rubin (Eds.), *Understanding autobiographical memory: Theories and approaches* (pp. 205–225). Cambridge, UK: Cambridge University Press.

Black, R. E., Victora, C. G., Walker, S. P., Bhutta, Z. A., Christian, P., de Onis, M., et al. (2013). Maternal and Child Nutrition Study Group. Maternal and child undernutrition and overweight in low-income and middle-income countries. *Lancet, 382*, 427–451.

Brainerd, C. J., & Reyna, V. F. (2012). Reliability of children's testimony in the era of developmental reversals. *Developmental Review, 32*, 224–267.

Butler, S., Gross, J., & Hayne, H. (1995). The effect of drawing on memory performance in young children. *Developmental Psychology, 3*, 597–608. doi:10.1037/0012-1649.31.4.597

Candel, I., Merckelbach, H., Jelicic, M., Limpens, M., & Widdershoven, K. (2004). Children's suggestibility for peripheral and central details. *Journal of Credibility Assessment and Witness Psychology, 5*, 9–18.

Case, R. D., Kurland, D. M., & Goldberg, J. (1982). Operational efficiency and the growth of short-term memory span. *Journal of Experimental Child Psychology, 33*, 386–404.

Ceci, S. J., Baker, J. G., & Bronfenbrenner, U. (1988). Prospective remembering and temporal calibration In M. M. Gruneberg, P. E. Morris, & R. N. Sykes (Eds.), *Practical aspects of memory: Current research and issues* (pp. 360–365). London: Wiley.

Ceci, S. J., & Bruck, M. (1993). The suggestibility of the child witness: A historical review and synthesis. *Psychological Bulletin, 113*, 403–439.

Cohen, M. J. (1997). *Children's memory scale.* San Antonio, TX: The Psychological Corporation.

Cowan, N. (1997). *The development of memory in childhood.* Hove, UK: Psychology Press.

Cowan, N. (2005). *Working memory capacity.* Hove, UK: Psychology Press.

Cypel, S. (2013). What happens in the brain as very young children learn. *Early Childhood Matters, Early Childhood Magazine*, 13–17.

Daneman, M., & Carpenter, P. A. (1980). Individual differences in working memory and reading. *Journal of Verbal Learning and Verbal Behaviour, 19*, 450–466.

DeCasper, A. J., & Fifer, W. P. (1980). Of human bonding: Newborns prefer their mothers' voices. *Science, 208*, 1174–1176.

Eimas, P. D., & Quinn, P. C. (1994). Studies on the formation of perceptually based basic-level categories in young infants. *Child Development, 65*, 903–917. doi:10.2307/1131427

Engle, R. W., Cantor, J., & Carullo, J. J. (1992). Individual differences in working memory and comprehension: A test of four hypotheses. *Journal of Experimental Psychology: Learning, Memory, and Cognition, 18*, 972–992.

Fivush, R., Hudson, J., & Nelson, K. (1984). Children's long-term memory for a novel event: An exploratory study. *Merrill-Palmer Quarterly, 30*, 303–316.

Fivush, R., & Nelson, K. (2004). Culture and language in the emergence of autobiographical memory. *Psychological Science, 15*, 573–577. doi:10.1111/j.0956-7976.2004.00722.x

Freud, S. (1905/1953). Childhood and concealing memories. In A. A. Brill (Ed.), *The basic writings of Sigmund Freud*. New York: The Modern Library.

Garven, S., Wood, J. M., Malpass, R. S., & Shaw, J. S. (1998). More than suggestion: The effect of interviewing techniques from McMartin preschool case. *Journal of Applied Psychology, 83*, 347–359.

Gathercole, S. E., & Alloway, T. P. (2008). *Working memory and learning: A practical guide for teachers*. London: Sage.

Gathercole, S. E., Lamont, E., & Alloway, T. P. (2006). Working memory in the classroom. In S. Pickering (Ed.), *Working memory and education* (pp. 220–241). London: Elsevier Press.

Gathercole, S. E., & Pickering, S. J. (2000). Working memory deficits in children with low achievements in the national curriculum at seven years of age. *British Journal of Educational Psychology, 70*, 177–194.

Gathercole, S. E., Pickering, S. J., Ambridge, B., & Wearing, H. (2004). The structure of working memory from 4 to 15 years of age. *Developmental Psychology, 40*, 177–190.

Giles, A., & Rovee-Collier, C. (2011). Infant long-term memory for associations formed during mere exposure. *Infant Behavior and Development, 34*, 327–338. doi:10.1016/j.infbeh.2011.02.004

Grantham-McGregor, S. (1995). A review of studies of the effect of severe malnutrition on mental development. *The Journal of Nutrition, 125*, 2233S–2238S. doi:10.1093/jn/125. suppl_8.2233S

Hartshorn, K. (2003). Reinstatement maintains a memory in human infants for 1½ years. *Developmental Psychobiology, 42*, 269–282. doi:10.1002/dev.10100

Hellmer, K., Söderlund, H., & Gredebäck, G. (2016). *Pupillometry as a measure of very young infants' recognition memory*. Paper presented at the ICIS 2016, New Orleans, US.

Hitch, G. J., Woodin, M., & Baker, S. L. (1989). Visual and phonological components of working memory in children. *Memory and Cognition, 17*, 175–185.

Howe, M. L., & Courage, M. L. (1997). The emergence and early development of autobiographical memory. *Psychological Review, 104*, 499–523.

Howe, M. L., Courage, M. L., & Edison, S. C. (2003). When autobiographical memory begins. *Developmental Review, 23*, 471–494. doi:0.1016/j.dr.2003.09.001

Jack, F., MacDonald, S., Reese, E., & Hayne, H. (2009). Maternal reminiscing style during early childhood predicts the age of adolescents' earliest memories. *Child Development, 80*, 496–505. doi:10.1111/j.1467-8624.2009.01274.x

Jarrold, C., Baddeley, A. D., & Hewes, A. K. (1999). Genetically dissociated components of working memory: Evidence from Down's and Williams syndrome. *Neuropsychologia, 37*, 637–651.

Lamb, M. E., Orbach, Y., Hershkowitz, I., Esplin, P. W., & Horowitz, D. (2007). Structured forensic interview protocols improve the quality and informativeness of investigative interviews with children: A review of research using the NICHD Investigative Interview Protocol. *Child Abuse & Neglect, 31*, 1201–1231. doi:10.1016/j.chiabu.2007.03.021

Lewis, M., & Brooks-Gunn, J. (1979). *Social cognition and the acquisition of self*. New York: Plenum Press.

Mastroberardino, S., Natali, V., & Candel, I. (2012). The effect of eye closure on children's eyewitness testimonies. *Psychology, Crime & Law, 18*, 245–257. doi:10.1080/10683161003801100

Michalczyk, K., Malstädt, N., Worgt, M., Könen, T. & Hasselhorn, M. (2013). Age differences and measurement invariance of working memory in 5- to 12-year-old children. *European Journal of Psychological Assessment, 29*, 220–229.

Miles, C. (1893). A study of individual psychology. *American Journal of Psychology, 6*, 534–558.

Moon, C., Cooper, R. P., & Fifer, W. P. (1993). Two-day-olds prefer their native language. *Infant Behavior and Development, 16*, 495–500.

Morris, G., Baker-Ward, L., & Bauer, P. J. (2010). What remains of that day: The survival of children's autobiographical memories across time.

Applied Cognitive Psychology, 24, 527–544. doi:10.1002/acp.1567

Nelson, C. A., Zeanah, C. H., Fox, N. A., Marshall, P. J., Smyke, A. T., & Guthrie, D. (2007). Cognitive recovery in socially deprived young children: The Bucharest early intervention project. *Science, 318,* 1937–1940.

Nelson, K. A. (1989). Remembering: A functional developmental perspective. In P. R. Solomon, G. R. Goethals, C. N. Kelley, & B. R. Stephens (Eds.), *Memory: Interdisciplinary approaches* (pp. 127–150). New York: Springer-Verlag.

O'Neil, S., & Zajac, R. (2013). The role of repeated interviewing in children's responses to cross-examination-style questioning. *British Journal of Psychology, 104,* 14–38. doi:10.1111/j.2044-8295.2011.02096.x

O'Reilly, T., Wang, Z., & Sabatini, J. (2019). How much knowledge is too little? When a lack of knowledge becomes a barrier to comprehension. *Psychological Science.* doi:10.1177/0956797619862276

Perfect, T. J., Wagstaff, G. F., Moore, D., Andrews, B., Cleveland, V., Newcombe, S., … Brown, L. A. (2008). How can we help witnesses to remember more? It's an (eyes) open and shut case. *Law and Human Behavior, 32,* 314–324. doi:10.1007/s10979-007-9109-5

Piaget, J. (1952). *The origins of intelligence in children.* New York: International Universities Press.

Plomin, R. (2018). *Blueprint: How DNA makes us who we are.* London: Allen Lane.

Priestley, G., Roberts, S., & Pipe, M.-E. (1999). Returning to the scene: Reminders and context reinstatement enhance children's recall. *Developmental Psychology, 35,* 1006–1019. doi:10.1037/0012-1649.35.4.1006

Quinn, P. C., Eimas, P. D., & Rosenkrantz, S. L. (1993). Evidence for representations of perceptually similar natural categories by 3-month-old and 4-month-old infants. *Perception, 22,* 463–475.

Quinn, P. C., Westerlund, A., & Nelson, C. A. (2006). Neural markers of categorization in 6-month-old infants. *Psychological Science, 17,* 59–66. doi:10.1111/j.1467-9280.2005.01665.x

Reeve, R. A., Reynolds, F., Paul, J., & Butterworth, B. L. (2018). Culture-independent prerequisites for early arithmetic. *Psychological Science, 29,* 1383–1392. doi:10.1177/0956797618769893

Rourke, B. P., & Tsatsanis, K. D. (1995). Memory disturbances of children with learning disabilities: A neuropsychological analysis of two academic achievement subtypes. In A. D. Baddeley, B. A. Wilson, & F. N. Watts (Eds.), *Handbook of memory disorders* (pp. 501–531). Chichester, UK: Wiley.

Rovee-Collier, C. K., Sullivan, M. W., Enright, M., Lucas, D., & Fagen, J. W. (1980). Reactivation of infant memory. *Science, 208,* 1159–1161.

Rutter, M., Beckett, C., Castle, J., & Colvert, E. (2007). Effects of profound early institutional deprivation: An overview of findings from a UK longitudinal study of Romanian adoptees. *European Journal of Developmental Psychology, 4,* 332–350. doi:10.1080/17405620701401846

Schaal, B., Marlier, L., & Soussignan, R. (2000). Human foetuses learn odours from their pregnant mother's diet. *Chemical Senses, 25,* 729–737.

Sheingold, K., & Tenney, Y. J. (1982). Memory for a salient childhood event. In U. Neisser (Ed.), *Memory in its natural context.* San Francisco: Freeman.

Simcock, G., & Hayes, H. (2003). Age-related changes in verbal and non-verbal memory during early childhood. *Developmental Psychology, 39,* 805–814.

Simeon, D., & Grantham-McGregor, S. (1989). Effects of missing breakfast on the cognitive functions of school children of differing nutritional status. *The American Journal of Clinical Nutrition, 49,* 646–653.

Sparling, J., Wilder, D. A., Kondash, J., Boyle, M., & Compton, M. (2011). Effects of interviewer behavior on accuracy of children's responses. *Journal of Applied Behavior Analysis, 44,* 587–592.

Sunderland, A., Harris, J. E., & Baddeley, A. D. (1983). Do laboratory tests predict everyday memory? A neuropsychological study. *Journal of Verbal Learning and Verbal Behavior, 22,* 341–357. doi:10.1016/S0022-5371(83)90229-3

Thierry, K. L., & Spence, M. J. (2002). Source-monitoring training facilitates preschoolers' eyewitness memory performance. *Developmental Psychology, 38,* 428–437. doi:10.1037/0012-1649.38.3.428

Vredeveldt, A., Hitch, G. J., & Baddeley, A. D. (2011). Eye closure helps memory by reducing cognitive load and enhancing visualisation. *Memory & Cognition, 39,* 1253–1063.

Walker, S. P., Chang, S. M., Vera-Hernández, M., & Grantham-McGregor, S. (2011). Early childhood stimulation benefits adult competence and reduces violent behavior. *Pediatrics, 127,* 849–857.

Wang, P. P., & Bellugi, U. (1994). Evidence from two genetic syndromes for a dissociation between verbal and visual-spatial short-term memory. *Journal of Clinical and Experimental Neuropsychology, 16,* 317–322.

Wang, Q. (2001). Cultural effects on adults' earliest childhood recollection and self-description: Implications for the relation between memory and the self. *Journal of Personality and Social Psychology, 81*, 220–233.

Wang, Q. (2006). Relations of maternal style and child self-concept to autobiographical memories in Chinese, Chinese immigrant, and European American 3-year-olds. *Child Development, 77*, 1799–1814.

Wechsler, D. (1992). *Weschler adult intelligence scale for children* (3rd ed.). London: Psychological Corporation.

Wilson, B., Cockburn, J., & Baddeley, A. D. (1985). *The Rivermead Behavioural Test.* Titchfield, UK: Thames Valley Test Company.

Wilson, B. A., Ivani-Chalian, R., & Aldrich, F. (1991). *The Rivermead Behavioural Memory Test for children.* Bury St Edmunds, UK: Thames Valley Test Company.

Yousafzai, A. K., Rasheed, M. A., Rizvi, A., Armstrong, R., & Bhutta, Z. A. (2014). Effect of integrated responsive stimulation and nutrition interventions in the Lady Health Worker programme in Pakistan on child development, growth, and health outcomes: A cluster-randomised factorial effectiveness trial. *The Lancet, 384*(9950), 1282–1293. doi:10.106/S0140-6736(14)60455-4

Zajac, R., & Hayne, H. (2003). I don't think that's what really happened: The effect of cross-examination on the accuracy of children's reports. *Journal of Experimental Psychology: Applied, 9* 187–195. doi:http://dx.doi.org/10.1037/1076-898X.9.3.187

Zajac, R., & Hayne, H. (2005). The negative effect of cross-examination style questioning on children's accuracy: Older children are not immune. *Applied Cognitive Psychology, 20*, 3–16. doi:10.1002/acp.1169

Contents

CHAPTER 15

MEMORY AND AGING

Alan Baddeley

We all complain about the fallibility of our memories and, as we get older, we complain more. This is what Patrick Stewart, most widely known for his role in *Star Trek*, says about learning his lines on returning to the stage in *Macbeth* and as Malvolio in *Twelfth Night* (Box 15.1).

Box 15.1 Patrick Stewart, *Observer*, 29 July 2007, p. 37

With every year that passes I am more and more puzzled—and dismayed—by the mental process of learning, absorbing, internalizing and finally speaking lines of dialogue. It has become the only labour in this marvellous job I love so much.

Learning lines used to be a breeze. In rep. I'd do the show, go to the pub, knock back a couple of pints, and then home and head down, into the script, knocking off an act or so before bedtime.

Not any more. Now, learning has to be planned, soberly, in advance of rehearsals and—for me—usually undertaken early in the morning.

APPROACHES TO THE STUDY OF AGING

It is difficult to compare one's own memory with that of others, and comparing it with the state of one's own memory years ago itself involves memory. There is also evidence that we become somewhat less good at reporting memory lapses as we get older (Sunderland, Watts, Baddeley, & Harris, 1986), and that complaints about memory in the elderly relate more closely to depression than to actual memory performance (Rabbitt & Abson, 1990). We clearly need better evidence than our subjective feelings of progressive memory failure, especially given that impaired memory is the earliest and most powerful predictor of the onset of Alzheimer's disease, an increasingly serious problem with the gradual aging of the Western population. So what can you expect if you remain healthy but get older, and how will it differ from the onset of Alzheimer's?

The longitudinal approach

The study of aging involves the study of change, as opposed to most of the adult research described so far, which assumes a system that is relatively stable, although of course one that can change as a result of learning or forgetting. There are two principal methods of studying aging, the *longitudinal* and the *cross-sectional*. In a

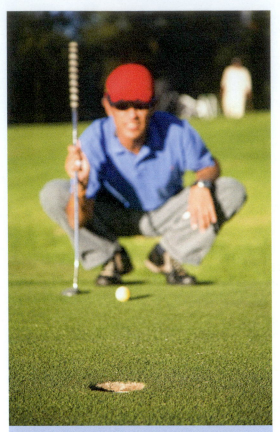

As we get older, it becomes harder at times of stress to shut out distractions, making it more likely that the older golfer will "choke" on the final putt that would have won the championship.

their genetic, physiological, and cognitive precursors.

Longitudinal designs do, however, have two major problems. The first stems from the fact that some participants will almost certainly drop out, because they move house or perhaps because they lose interest. Furthermore, people who drop out might be atypical of the rest of the sample, gradually making it less representative. There are statistical methods of attempting to correct for dropout, but this is inevitably a complex and potentially controversial issue. A second problem concerns measures of cognition in general, and memory in particular. Even though test sessions are separated by as much as five years, substantial learning occurs, not just because patients learn the particular items comprising the test but also because there are more general practice effects that can be sufficient to counteract any decrement due to aging.

The problem of practice effects is avoided if one uses a cross-sectional design in which different groups of people are sampled across the age range and their performance is measured on a single occasion. The drawbacks of this approach are that one cannot, of course, relate performance to the earlier data from that person, nor can one relate performance to the future development of the individual, without at least including a later test that will be influenced by practice effects from the first test session. A further problem with both of these designs is the so-called cohort effect, reflecting the very substantial changes in education, society, health, and nutrition that have occurred across decades, that might well have a major influence on performance. Average scores on the Raven's Matrices

longitudinal study, a sample of people, preferably selected so as to reflect the full range of the population, will be tested repeatedly, for example every five years, preferably over many decades (Rönnlund & Nilsson, 2006; Rönnlund, Nyberg, Bäckman, & Nilsson, 2005). The advantage of this approach is that the effects of age on the performance of each individual can be studied, subsequently allowing specified individuals, such as those developing Alzheimer's disease, to be singled out and their performance *before* the onset of the disease compared with that of more fortunate, healthy people. Such studies are expensive in time and funding but are already yielding crucial information about the development of a range of diseases and intelligence test have, for example, been increasing steadily since 1940 in many Western societies, known as the Flynn effect after its initial discoverer (Flynn, 1987). The health and longevity of the general population has also steadily increased in many parts of the world, again producing a Flynn effect. Comparing people currently in their twenties with current 80-year-olds thus involves more than a simple effect of aging.

A solution to these problems is to combine longitudinal and cross-sectional approaches by adding a new cohort of participants at each test age. In due course, comparison of these initial test groups across the years will provide a measure of any cohort effects, uninfluenced by earlier testing while comparing them with the relevant longitudinal group of that age will give a clear indication of any learning effects. This approach has been used by a number of studies including the Betula study carried out in Northern Sweden and named after the birch tree that predominates at those latitudes (Nilsson et al., 2004). The study emphasizes memory and is beginning to show some very interesting results. One of these is that both practice effects (Figure 15.1), and cohort effects (Figure 15.2) are very substantial with cognitive performance at a given age steadily increasing across successive cohorts (Rönnlund et al., 2005). Note also that there is a suggestion that the Flynn effect may be

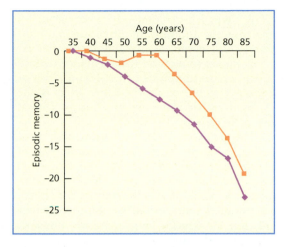

Figure 15.1 Decline in episodic memory performance between ages 35 and 85 as measured by a longitudinal (filled squares) or cross-sectional (diamonds) method. Based on Rönnlund et al. (2005).

leveling out in Sweden as in other relatively wealthy societies.

Using a correlational approach it is possible to identify some of the causes of enhanced performance in more recent cohorts. The Rönnlund et al. (2005) evidence suggests an important role for nutrition, as reflected in the gradual increase over the years in average height. Years of education also appear to be associated with memory performance, independent of age. Number of children in the

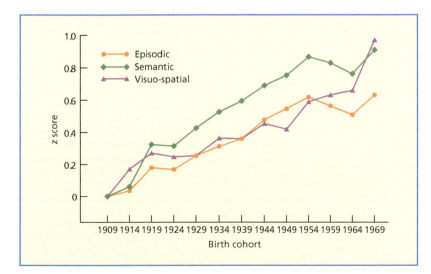

Figure 15.2 The Flynn effect for memory. Age-adjusted performance on tests of episodic memory, semantic memory, and visuo-spatial ability for individuals born at different times ranging from 1909 to 1969 show a steady increase. From Rönnlund & Nilsson, (2009). Copyright © Elsevier. Reproduced with permission.

family, which is tentatively interpreted as reflecting the amount of attention an individual child might receive within the family, is also linked to memory performance (Figure 15.3). A recent analysis of the Flynn effect in Norway concludes that the entire effect is due to social rather than genetic change (Bratsberg & Rogeberg, 2018).

The Betula study, in common with most similar studies, focuses on the specific part of the life span involved in aging. A longitudinal study extending over the whole lifespan would, of course, take a lifetime to complete. Even so, some studies that commence with pregnancy and test at regular intervals are ongoing, although they are—for the most part—not focused on cognition and have not yet been running for a lifetime. It was therefore with great excitement that Ian Deary, an Edinburgh psychologist with an interest in intelligence, discovered that well-validated IQ tests had been given to every child in Scotland who was 11 years old in 1932 ($N = 89,498$) and that these results were still available (Deary, Whiteman, Starr, Whalley, & Fox, 2004). Through local records and press advertising, they were able to contact 550 people in the Edinburgh area who had been born in 1921 and tested 11 years later. These volunteers were then retested by Deary and colleagues using the original IQ measure, together with a number of other psychological and physical measures.

People originally tested in 1932 were 80 at the time of retest and, by that point, many of the original sample had died. Deary et al. (2004) found that, for both men and women, the lowest IQ quartile had the lowest life expectancy; mortality differences between the remaining quartiles were small. A slight discrepancy in the general pattern occurred in the case of men during the 1940s and 1950s, which probably results from the effect of World War II, where certain dangerous operations such as aircrew tended to differentially select for a higher ability.

In terms of mental testing there proved to be a very high correlation between score at 11 and at age 80 ($r = 0.66$), although, as expected, level of performance at 80 was lower. In an attempt to identify factors that led to successful aging, IQ at 11 was correlated with a range of cognitive and physical fitness measures, namely grip strength, lung function, and time to walk to six meters (Deary, Whalley, Batty, & Starr, 2006). Physical fitness at 80 was predicted by IQ at 11 and was influenced by sex, social class, and the *APOE* gene, which Nilsson et al. (2004) had also found to be related to episodic and semantic memory performance in their elderly sample in the Betula study.

Cross-sectional studies

However, despite the growing importance of such large-scale longitudinal projects, much of the research in the field so far has relied on cross-sectional studies, typically involving the comparison of a young and an elderly

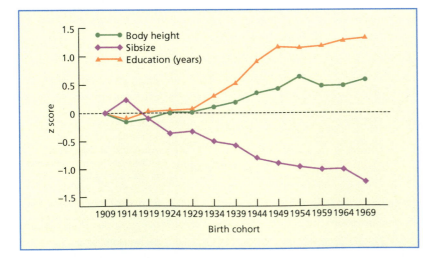

Figure 15.3 Age-adjusted height, family size, and years of education for Swedish people born between 1909 and 1969. People have become taller and better educated, while families have become smaller. From Rönnlund & Nilsson, (2008). Copyright © Elsevier. Reproduced with permission.

sample, approximately matched for educational and socioeconomic status. We will begin by viewing the results of such studies, looking in turn at the various components of memory, then moving on to theories of aging and attempts to optimize cognition in old age. We conclude by discussing what is known about the link between the structure and functioning of the brain and aging.

WORKING MEMORY AND AGING

Although both verbal and visual memory span tend to decline with age, the decline is far from dramatic, with mean digit span dropping from 6.6 items to 5.8 over the course of an adult life (Parkinson, Inman, & Dannenbaum, 1985) and spatial span using the Corsi block tapping task dropping from 5.1 to 4.7 blocks (Spinnler, Della Sala, Bandera, & Baddeley, 1988). Craik (1986) found a minimal drop in memory span for unrelated words in the elderly, a difference that increased substantially when the task was changed to one in which the words had to be recalled in alphabetic order (e.g., hear *pen dog zoo hat*, recall *dog hat pen zoo*). The crucial difference, of course, is the need to simultaneously hold and manipulate the material, in short, to use working memory.

There is broad general agreement that working memory is susceptible to the effects of age, although it is not always clear exactly which aspects are most vulnerable. Digit span is relatively resistant whereas sentence span in which participants must process a sequence of sentences and then recall the final word does tend to be sensitive to aging, the degree of decrement is however less marked than one might expect (Verhaeghen, Marcoen, & Gossens, 1993). Other complex working memory tasks however do seem more sensitive as in backward span in which items are recalled in reverse order and alphabet span as mentioned earlier. An extensive meta-analysis by Bopp and Verhaeghen (2005) of a wide range of tasks concludes that STM tasks involving simple storage are

less sensitive to aging than are working memory measures that combine storage with manipulation, with different manipulations being differentially sensitive. They go on to consider a range of possible explanations based on existing general theories of aging. Their analysis does however depend on the mapping of the various measures onto the relevant theories together with a complex form of analysis that is not without its critics.

A somewhat different approach was taken recently by Logie and colleagues as shown in Box 15.2. Rather than attempting to fit his results into a general theory of aging, he proposes that the different tasks draw on a range of different components of working memory that age at different rates. As Figure 15.4 shows, the effects of aging are

Box 15.2 Memory and aging

There is a saying that "you are as old as you feel." But how old is that? A study by Rubin and Berntsen (2006) suggests that, from their mid forties, people begin to feel younger than their age, with the perceived age being an average of 20% younger than their actual age. Why should this be? Is it a memory effect, or just that we view the world through rose-tinted spectacles?

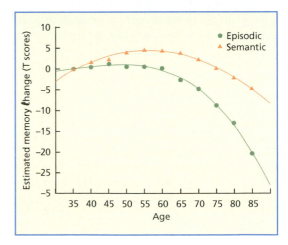

Figure 15.4 Estimated memory change across age (T scores) for the episodic and semantic factors on the basis of practice-adjusted longitudinal data.

not simply the reverse of childhood develop-ment where the various components of working memory develop in parallel and show a consistent pattern of relationship to each other across ages. In contrast, marked differences in rate of decline occur from the relatively robust verbal memory span to the rapid drop in performance on both visual feature binding in STM and visual pattern span. This is accompanied by a change in the relationship between the various measures which Logie, Horne, and Pettit (2015) suggest may reflect changing strategies in the attempt to cope with these different deficits. May, Hasher, and Kane (1999) suggest that the decline in sentence span could largely be the result of the buildup of interference from earlier sequences, reflecting a problem with inhibiting irrelevant material rather than one of combining storage and processing per se (May et al., 1999). This is consistent with the suggestion by Hasher and Zacks (1988; Hasher, Zacks, & May, 1999) that a major cognitive effect of aging is the reduced capa-city to inhibit irrelevant stimuli. You may recall that both Engle and Miyake propose models of working memory that assume a central role for the capacity to inhibit disrup-tion from irrelevant information.

An intriguing example of the decline of the capacity to inhibit irrelevant information with age comes from a study carried out by Bäckman and Molander (1986), who tested groups of competitive miniature golf players who were matched in skill under practice conditions. During competition however, the 50-year-old senior group showed a decline in performance in contrast to younger competi-tors. Under practice conditions, a heart-rate monitor indicated that both groups of players showed a slowing of the heart rate when making a shot, reflecting greater concentra-tion. During competition however slowing still occurred with the young golfers but was not seen in the older group. When subse-quently asked to describe specific shots, the older group showed a greater tendency to recall irrelevant information than the young, who appeared to be able to shut out potential distractions and concentrate on the stroke. Bäckman and Molander note, however, that very large individual differences do occur.

There tends to be a decline in performance with age in many skills that involve intense concentration, including those that do not involve physical strength, such as chess, where adapting to age appears to involve a gradual change in strategy. Charness (1985) studied the performance of chess players who differed in age but were matched for expertise. He found that the young players tended to scan a wide range of options, whereas the older players scanned fewer but in greater depth. This could reflect an increasing difficulty in keeping track of multiple sources of information.

There is considerable evidence to suggest that age impairs the capacity to divide atten-tion between two sources. There is no doubt that dual-task performance is often more affected by age than performance on the two components separately (see Riby, Perfect, & Stollery, 2004, for a review). The results of many such studies might, however, simply reflect the increased overall load rather than a specific deficit in the ability to coordinate two simultaneous tasks. If an elderly person has greater difficulty with each of the individual tasks, it is hardly surprising that they have even more difficulty in performing both at the same time.

Greenough, Black, and Wallace's (1987) study showed that rats who had lived in an enriched and interesting environment showed less cognitive decline than their counterparts who had lived in a more basic and less stimulating environment.

To demonstrate a deficit in task combination per se, it is necessary to ensure that level of performance on the individual tasks is equal for the young and old groups, if necessary by making the tasks easier for the elderly. In a series of studies to be described in the section on Alzheimer's disease (see Chapter 16, pp. 510–11), digit span and a visuo-spatial tracking task were combined (Baddeley, Baddeley, Bucks, & Wilcock, 2001a; Spinnler et al., 1988). When the level of performance on the individual tasks was equated, by using different memory loads and easier tracking for the older and the Alzheimer's groups, no reliable age decrement occurred. There was however a marked problem in combining two tasks in the Alzheimer's disease patients. This is discussed further in Chapter 16 (p. 506). Broadly speaking, however, it is probably wise to assume that working memory is progressively impaired as we grow older, particularly when it involves combining two or more tasks, as for example preparing a meal where several dishes must arrive at the same time as I myself can sadly confirm! Furthermore, tasks comprising either speed of processing or episodic long-term memory, which we consider next, are likely to be particularly vulnerable to the effects of aging.

AGING AND LONG-TERM MEMORY

Episodic memory

There is no doubt that performance on tasks involving episodic memory declines as we age. Although many studies have used relatively artificial material, such as the acquisition of pairs of unrelated words or the retention of geometric figures, the effects are by no means limited to such material. The Doors and People test (Baddeley, Emslie, & Nimmo-Smith, 1994) uses relatively realistic material, such as people's names and pictures of doors, and shows a decline for both recall and recognition of visual and verbal materials. A similar decline is shown in the Rivermead Behavioural Memory Test, which was designed to mirror everyday memory situations (Wilson, Cockburn, Baddeley, & Hiorns, 1989). Salthouse (1991) reviews over 40 real-world activities, from actors learning lines through recall of bridge hands to memory for conversations, all of which show a decline with age.

However, virtually all these results showing an apparent decrement from a relatively young age are based on cross-sectional studies. The Swedish Betula study has now reached a point at which it is possible to bring together their data, correcting the longitudinal data for practice effects and the cross-sectional data for differences in education (Rönnlund et al., 2005). When corrected, both approaches show a very similar pattern with semantic and episodic memory levels maintained until around the age of 60, after which both begin to decline (see Figure 15.4) It seems likely that this somewhat later onset of decline when measures are corrected in this way may also apply to working memory measures although I do not know of any equivalent analysis.

What, then, is the nature of the episodic memory decline with age? The magnitude of the decline varies depending on nature of the memory task and the method of testing retention. Fergus Craik and his collaborators propose three factors as crucial determinants of episodic memory performance in the elderly. The first of these is the overall decline in *episodic memory* per se. This is modulated by two other variables, one being the *processing capacity* of the learner and the other concerns the level of environmental support provided during retrieval (Craik, 2005).

Most learning experiments involve presenting material under time constraints, and given that age tends to slow processing, then the elderly may take longer to perceive and process the material, and may also be less likely to be able to develop and utilize complex learning strategies. Craik and colleagues have explored this aspect of learning by using a secondary task to reduce the available attention in younger participants, demonstrating that under some conditions at least, performance by the young then resembles that of the elderly (Craik & Byrd, 1982).

However, the fact that both age and an attentionally demanding task impair learning does not mean that they necessarily do so by influencing the same memory process. For example, it might be that the main source of impairment in the elderly is a basic memory deficit at the neurophysiological level, possibly reflecting poorer consolidation of the memory trace, whereas the deficit shown by the young when their attention is distracted might reflect a reduction of time spent on learning because of competition from the secondary task. This was tested in a series of experiments by Naveh-Benjamin (2000) in which young and older participants were presented with pairs of words that differed in whether they were semantically associated or not (e.g., *dog–bone* versus *cat–book*). Performance was then tested by recognition. There was found to be a substantial difference between the two age groups for the unrelated items, but not for associated pairs.

The initial interpretation of these results by Naveh-Benjamin (2000) was that their impaired attentional capacity meant that the elderly were less able to form associative links than the young. This was subsequently tested using young participants given an attentionally demanding concurrent task, with the prediction that the pattern of performance of the young would then resemble that of the elderly. This prediction was not supported by the subsequent experiments (Naveh-Benjamin, Guez, & Marom, 2003; Naveh-Benjamin, Hussain, Guez, & Bar-On, 2003). Unlike the age effect, the secondary task impaired both related and unrelated pairs to the same extent, suggesting that the difference between the young and old groups was attributable to basic learning capacity, rather than to attentional or strategic differences. Naveh-Benjamin refers to this as the associative deficit hypothesis, a problem in forming new associations between items or events as we get older.

A series of later studies has investigated the associative deficit hypothesis across a range of materials involving both words and pictures (Naveh-Benjamin, Guez, & Marom, 2003; Naveh-Benjamin, Hussain et al., 2003), in each case replicating the relative preservation of the capacity to recognize which items had been presented, together with a substantial deficit in the capacity to bind or associate unrelated word pairs. The fact that this deficit was not attributable to an attentional deficit was shown particularly clearly in a study by Naveh-Benjamin, Guez, and Shulman (2004) using face–name pairs. These were presented with or without a demanding concurrent task and tested by recognition or recall. As the first two sets of data in Figure 15.5 show, the recognition task showed little or no effect of age, but a clear effect of the concurrent task. The second memory test involved deciding which name went with which face. As this dataset shows, there was a substantial age effect, which was reliably greater than the effect of the demanding concurrent task. The fact that the age effect was not found for recognition but is clearly present in the name–face binding condition suggests an *associative* deficit that does not appear to be explicable in attentional terms.

Naveh-Benjamin's age-related associative binding hypothesis led to extensive further research. Old and Naveh-Benjamin (2008) conducted a meta-analysis of 90 studies involving 3,197 old and 3,192 young participants across a wide range of experimental paradigms, concluding that clear associative deficits are found under intentional learning but were less clear with incidental learning. However, such effects only occurred with recognition testing; with recall, both memory for associations and for the items to be associated showed an equivalent age effect.

KEY TERM

Associative deficit hypothesis: Proposal that the age deficit in memory comes from an impaired capacity to form associations between previously unrelated stimuli.

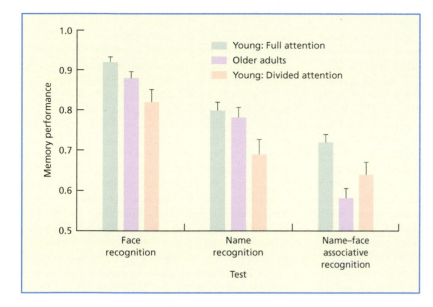

Figure 15.5 The effects of age or divided attention on recognition of individual faces or names, and recognizing a face–name association. From Naveh-Benjamin et al. (2004a). Copyright © American Psychological Association. Reprinted with permission.

This led Benjamin (no relation) to propose a simpler hypothesis, namely that older people remember less because of "a single mediating influence" (Benjamin, 2010). He suggests that recall demands memory for both the items and the association between them while for recognition memory, items are provided and only the association is required. My version of both this and the amnesic syndrome to be described in the next chapter is through the "mnemonic glue" hypothesis, a term meant to imply some form of trace consolidation that is less and less effective as we get older. Benjamin (2010) describes a similar though much more sophisticated computational approach to this issue in his DRYAD model. Both our approaches assume that recognition memory tasks differ in the extent to which they depend upon forming new associations as opposed to utilizing existing knowledge and that differences in susceptibility to the effects of aging will reflect the relative contribution of these two factors. In line with this distinction, an important feature of the studies by Naveh-Benjamin is the observation that the associative deficit shown by the elderly is much reduced when pairs of items are related (e.g., "dog–bone") rather than arbitrary ("cat–bone"). I assume that this is because strong associative links already exist for dog–bone hence demanding less additional "mnemonic glue."

Are there other ways in which the effects of aging on episodic memory may be minimized, perhaps for different reasons? This does occur in the case of the *self-performed task* effect. This might for example involve a subject attempting to remember a list of objects, each accompanied by an instruction, for instance "break the matchstick" and "shake the pen," each of which has to be either passively heard or performed. Performing the act leads to substantially better subsequent free recall than simply hearing the experimenter provide the action instructions, greatly reducing the age difference (Bäckman & Nilsson, 1984; Englekamp, 1998). The current view is that this procedure gains its advantage from providing an enriched level of coding involving auditory, visual, manual, and—perhaps importantly—self-related codes, with the multiple coding reducing reliance on any given feature or cue with the multiple cues making the memory trace more robust.

The third aspect of Craik's classification concerns the amount of environmental support provided at retrieval. It is in general the case that age effects show up most clearly in free recall, where there are no external cues; age decrements are somewhat less when retrieval cues are provided, and are least under recognition conditions (Craik, Byrd, & Swanson, 1987). However, although it is often the case that recognition memory can be relatively preserved in the elderly, in many such studies, as described above and demonstrated by Benjamin (2010), this might reflect the greater tendency of recall tests to involve an associative component, either explicitly, as in paired-associated learning, or implicitly, as in free recall, which is likely to depend on creating and retrieving associated chunks. As data from the Doors and People Test show, clear effects of age can be found using carefully matched recall and recognition measures (Baddeley et al., 1994). However, recognition tests typically *are* less demanding than recall, and tend to show less of a difference between younger and older groups, also consistent of course with Benjamin's DRYAD hypothesis. Both our approaches assume that recognition memory tasks differ in the extent to which they depend upon forming new associations as opposed to utilizing existing knowledge and that differences in susceptibility to the effects of aging will reflect the relative contribution of these two factors.

Remembering and knowing

An interesting feature of the effects of age on recognition memory is that older people appear to be much better at recognizing that an item has occurred than in remembering the context in which it occurred (Chalfonte & Johnson, 1996; Park & Puglisi, 1985). You might recall from Chapter 8 that recognition appears to be based on two separable processes: "remembering," in which the participant recollects the learning incident and its context (for example, remembering that the word *dog* reminded you of your childhood pet) and "knowing," in which a positive identification is based on a feeling of familiarity rather than a specific recollection. Parkin and Walter (1992) presented young, middle-aged, and elderly participants with a sequence of 36 words, each printed on a flash card. Next, participants were shown the 36 old items together with 36 new items for recognition. They were required to categorize any recognized items as members of the "remember" or "know" category. There was no difference between the young and old groups in the number of words correctly identified as "known" assumed to be based

on a feeling of familiarity. By contrast, however, correctly "remembered" words in which participants could recollect the experience of encoding that word, were greatest for the young and least for the elderly group.

Reviewing the literature on this issue, Light, Prull, LaVoie, and Healy (2000) conclude that there is strong evidence that the recollective process declines with age. Given that recollection is likely to depend on retrieving an association between an item and the context or experience of learning, this is consistent with the associative deficit hypothesis of aging and episodic long-term memory proposed by Naveh-Benjamin, Hussain, et al. (2003). Whether the familiarity mechanism is entirely free from any age effect is, however, more controversial. Conclusions depend on the assumptions made in computing the familiarity measure, and in particular on whether these two mechanisms are assumed to be independent or not.

The problem of linking a memory to the context in which it occurred is sometimes referred to as "source amnesia." As we will see in the next chapter it is characteristic of the amnesic syndrome, but as I myself can testify as I reach my mid-eighties, I am increasingly likely to encounter the question of "Have I have already told this to this person?" This is a particular problem with anecdotes about past events, which, I remind myself, is probably the origin of the phrase that someone is "in their dotage," an abbreviation I assume for "anecdotage."

To return from anecdotes to recognition memory: Is recognition entirely spared in the elderly? The answer would seem to depend on the precise nature of the recognition task. To the extent that recollection of the original experience contributes to the recognition decision, it clearly is not spared. However, if a general sense of familiarity is sufficient then recognition in the elderly is relatively well preserved.

Prospective memory

One of the most frustrating features of memory failure occurs when we plan or agree to do something and then forget to carry out that action, whether it is a relatively simple error, such as failing to pick up bread on the way home from work, or more serious, such as missing an important appointment. There is no doubt that as we get older we complain more about such everyday lapses, but are we in fact less reliable?

The easiest way to study prospective memory is in a constrained laboratory situation, such as that developed by Einstein and McDaniel (1990), in which participants perform an ongoing task and are instructed to respond either after a specified time or when a specific cue occurs (for further discussion, see Chapter 13). Their initial study (Einstein & McDaniel, 1990) found little evidence of age effects, whereas a later investigation (Einstein, McDaniel, Richardson, Guynn, & Cunfer, 1995) found a decrement for time-based but not for event-based tasks. However, later research suggests that both types of prospective memory tend to be impaired in the elderly.

One large-scale study involved 100 participants in each of 10 cohorts ranging from 35 to 80 years in age. The task was simply to remember to sign a form on completion of the test session. Whereas 61% of the younger 35–45 year-olds remembered, only 25% of 70–80 year-olds were successful (Mäntylä & Nilsson, 1997). Logie and Maylor (2009) included a prospective memory test in their Internet study involving 73,018 participants aged between 18 and 79 who were instructed to respond to a smiley face that was presented 20 minutes after the start of an extended set of memory tests. A clear age deficit occurred but this was reduced when a reminder was given involving presentation of the face immediately before testing began.

Major declines in prospective memory have also been reported by Cockburn and Smith (1991), while Maylor (1996) found that both time-based and event-based prospective memory declined with age. A meta-analysis of studies (Henry, MacLeod, Phillips, & Crawford, 2004) found broadly similar age decrements for both time- and event-based laboratory studies of prospective memory with the age decrement being greater when the prospective memory measure was embedded in more demanding activities.

However, older people performed *better* than young under naturalistic test conditions.

This discrepancy between everyday life and laboratory results is not uncommon and is often attributed to older people being aware of the limitations of their memory and using various strategies, such as diaries and reminders, to compensate, whereas the young tend to rely more on their still-fallible memory. Rendell and Craik (2000), however, explicitly instructed their subjects not to use external aids, and attribute the difference to the fact that their older participants lived more ordered and structured lives, making it easier to form a well-ordered plan. It could also be the case that a test of their memory was a more important feature of the lives of older than it was for the younger prospective rememberers. Motivation in the real world is probably a very important variable in prospective memory. I suspect most of us forget more dental appointments than parties, and to fail to get married because one forgot to turn up would not be regarded as a very plausible excuse. Indeed, one of the reasons why forgetting appointments might be so embarrassing is because of the suggestion that the event, and by implication the person involved, was not regarded as very important.

Direct evidence for the influence of importance on prospective memory comes from a study by Ihle, Schnitzpahn, Rendell, Luong, and Kliegel (2012) who suggested that even the studies requiring remembering outside the laboratory tend to be somewhat artificial in setting up a specific separate task such as sending a postcard at a particular time. In order to obtain a more realistic assessment of prospective memory, they used a diary-based approach where, over a sequence of five successive days, a younger and an older group were required to list their intentions for the following day and indicate their relative importance. On the day after, they were required to report whether the actions had in fact been completed, and if not, whether this was because they forgot or because they downgraded its importance. They were also asked to report their use of reminders. The results are shown in Figure 15.6 from which two main conclusions can be drawn. First of all, there is a clear

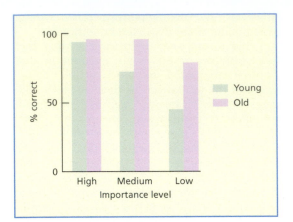

Figure 15.6 Results from Ihle et al., which suggest that the setting and regulation of goals may be something that develops with age and enhances prospective memory, despite declining episodic memory. Data from Ihle et al. (2012).

relationship between rated importance and probability of forgetting, with both groups being virtually perfect for items they regard as very important. Second, there is a clear advantage to the older group. There was no overall difference in number of reminders used, although the young reported a significantly higher stress level than the retired elderly. Ihle et al. suggest that the setting and regulation of goals may be something that develops with age and enhances prospective memory, despite declining episodic memory.

Semantic memory

Unlike the steady decline in episodic memory as we grow older, semantic memory is maintained, at least as measured by vocabulary knowledge, which even continues to grow slightly with age (Giambra, Arenberg, Zonderman, & Kawas, 1995). Knowledge of historical facts also increases as we get older (Perlmuter, Scharff, Karsh, & Monty, 1980), although speed of access declines (Burke, MacKay, Worthley, & Wade, 1991). Evidence of preserved semantic knowledge however typically depends on recognition rather than recall measures. In contrast, both the speed and the reliability of word finding declines as we get older with problems in remembering names being particularly common. The word

or name itself is not forgotten and can frustratingly be on the tip of your tongue, something that happens more for names than words becoming more frequent as we get older (Burke et al., 1991). Why should that be and why names in particular?

It seems likely that names are in general harder to retrieve and probably harder to learn and that aging simply exaggerates the vulnerability. Maylor (1997) points out that names tend to be less frequent than most commonly used words and when they are relatively more frequent such as the name Smith, they are likely to be attached to many different individuals, resulting in potential retrieval interference effects. Names are also specific to a particular individual and cannot readily be substituted whereas nouns and adjectives often can, for example replacing *house* with *home* or *cottage* or just *place* without the meaning of a sentence being grossly disturbed. In contrast if you are telling a friend of an event that happened, to a mutual acquaintance, and can't remember their name, the conversation tends to grind to an embarrassing halt. Finally, meaning, which offers us ways around using specific nouns or adjectives, is of little help in remembering names since any connection to an earlier occupation or hair color has long been lost. So John Brown may be blond and Margaret Thatcher had very little connection to roofing cottages. It seems likely therefore that my problem with learning the names of new students or indeed suddenly blocking on the name of a colleague of many years, simply reflects the more basic problem of my declining speed and reliability of access to information more generally.

Both the robustness of recognition measures of vocabulary to the effects of aging and the sensitivity of speed of access have been used to provide the basis for a clinical test of language competence, the Speed and Capacity of Language Processing (SCOLP) test (Baddeley, Emslie, & Nimmo-Smith, 1992). Semantic memory is probed via a vocabulary entitled Spot-the-Word in which the participant must choose between pairs of items, one a word and the other a pseudo word. These range from the very obvious, for example *rabbit–flotter* to more obscure pairs such as *lapidary–halitation*. Performance correlates highly with other measures of vocabulary and of verbal intelligence and is resistant to the effects of age, or indeed Alzheimer's disease (Baddeley et al., 2001; Baddeley & Crawford, 2012).

The second component of the SCOLP involves a task based on the original semantic memory studies of Collins and Quillian (1969), who you may recall from Chapter 7 required participants to verify simple statements about the world as rapidly as possible.

Sentences are either obviously true or obviously false, e.g., *snakes travel on their bellies* versus *beef steaks travel on their bellies*. Errors are uniformly low, indicating that the problem is not lack of knowledge but speed of access to that knowledge. This is highly sensitive to age (Baddeley et al., 1992) but has also proved applicable to a range of other variables from traumatic brain injury (Sunderland, Harris, & Baddeley, 1983) to cross-cultural cognition (Baddeley, Meeks Gardner, & Grantham-McGregor, 1995). Try it yourself (Box 15.3).

Box 15.3 Semantic processing test (otherwise known as the silly sentences test)

Decide as rapidly as possible whether each sentence is true ("Yes") or false ("No")

	Yes	No
Pork chops can be bought in shops		
Jamaica is edible		
Oranges drill teeth		
California is a state of America		
London is a place		
Potatoes move around searching for food		
Drills are scientists		
Aunts are relatives		
Spaghetti is a dish		
Corporals can be bought in shops		
Beer is a liquid		
Gin is sold by butchers		
Fish and chips are an alcoholic drink		
Peas are edible		
Antarctica tends the sick		
Beefsteaks are people		
Chairs are furniture		
Priests wear clothes		
Flies carry disease		
Mayors are elected representatives		
Asia has high mountains		
Paris is a living creature		
Rattlesnakes move around searching for food		
Bees treat the mentally ill		
Knives are manufactured goods		
Trout have fins		
Squirrels are fish		
Lions are four-legged animals		
Sharks have wheels		

Although vocabulary is well preserved, the use of language can be constrained by age in other more subtle ways. This was shown in an ingenious study by Kemper (1990), involving the analysis of diaries kept over a period of 70 years by pioneers settling the American Midwest. Because the diaries were written by the same individual over a long period of time, they provide a naturalistic longitudinal study of language.

The diaries tend to show an increase in ambiguity over the years through the use of indeterminate pronouns such as "he" as in "Cousins Robert and John visited us last week, despite the terrible weather. He was full of stories about the old days…" As they became older, diarists seemed to attempt to avoid this source of ambiguity by reducing the number of pronouns used. Later diaries also tended to avoid left-branching sentences such as "A roof over his head is the right of every man" which tend to place a heavier load on working memory than their right-branching equivalent "Every man has a right to a roof over his head." Despite the more constrained nature of the later diaries, independent judges tended to rate them as better written and more interesting (Kemper, Kynette, & Norman, 1992).

Implicit learning and memory

Given that implicit learning and memory involve a range of different processes, it is perhaps unsurprising that the effects of aging are not uniform. Reviewing the extensive literature, Light et al. (2000) conclude that, on balance, there is evidence for a clear but moderate age effect on priming tasks that involve response production, such as stem completion in which a list of words is presented and then tested by giving participants the first few letters of a word and asked to produce a possible completion. They contrast this with *identification* tasks, such as deciding whether an item is a real word or not, or identifying a fragmented picture as rapidly as possible, where age effects tend to be smaller or absent. This difference may however reflect a greater contribution of episodic memory to production than to identification

tasks. The substantial vulnerability of episodic memory to aging may also be responsible for a tendency for the elderly to be more open to being misled by subsequent false information (Cohen & Faulkner, 1989; Schacter, Koutsaal, & Norman, 1997), perhaps failing to remember either its questionable source or the earlier correct version.

The effect of age on the acquisition of motor skills is also complex. There is no doubt that motor *performance* tends to decline as we get older, reflecting a decline in the speed of both perception and movement (Welford, 1985). This can lead to a slower rate of learning time-based tasks such as pursuit tracking, which involves keeping a stylus in contact with a moving target (Wright & Payne, 1985). However, whereas skilled *performance* certainly can be impaired, it is less clear whether, given appropriate conditions, the rate of *learning* is necessarily slower. For example, the rate of learning a sequence of motor movements or a new stimulus–response mapping might not show an age difference (Wishart & Lee, 1997). Similarly, on a task involving responding serially to four separate stimuli under self-paced conditions, young and older adults showed a comparable rate of learning (Howard & Howard, 1989), while Willingham and Winter (1995) found that older adults, who had never used a computer mouse before, were as adept at learning to navigate a maze on a computer as were younger participants.

So can old dogs learn new tricks? It appears to depend on the tricks. As in the case of priming, it seems likely that in tasks in which the response is obvious, and performance is measured purely in terms of improved speed, the elderly will show slower initial performance with a preserved rate of subsequent learning, whereas tasks in which new and unobvious links must be learned are likely to create problems for the older adult. A good example of such a task was devised by Wilson, Cockburn, and Baddeley (1989), who required patients to learn how to enter the time and date into a small palm-computer. Rate of learning was extremely sensitive to episodic memory deficits. Although relatively few steps were involved, patients who had even relatively mild memory loss had great difficulty in acquiring them. Unfortunately, the rapid development of technology means that there is a constant need to learn such basic and ever-changing skills.

Use it or lose it?

There is no doubt that individual differences become more marked as people get older, probably for a number of different reasons. One factor is certainly differences in encountering declining health, which in turn is linked to both genetic and lifestyle differences. It appears to help if you are healthy, eat appropriately, take lots of exercise, and remain mentally active, in the sense that all of these tend to be correlated with comparative resistance to age-related impairment. However, a comparison of university professors and blue-collar workers in Sweden by Christensen, Henderson, Griffiths, and Levings (1997) found no difference in rate of memory decline. A study of university professors in their thirties, fifties, and sixties by Shimamura, Berry, Mangels, Rustings, and Jurica (1995) found clear evidence of a decline in reaction time and paired-associate learning, but no difference in prose recall, suggesting that meaningful material might allow the active learner to compensate for declining episodic memory. A review by Hertzog, Kramer, Wilson, and Lindenberger (2008) concludes that a reliable impact of lifestyle on aging has not, so far, been well established, with existing studies suffering from a number of problems of interpretation, including atypical samples of participants, unsatisfactory measures of cognition, and the problem of other correlated variables such as socioeconomic status, nutrition, and health.

This conclusion is consistent with an analysis of over 2,812 people (aged 65–101 years) who were questioned in detail about activities engaged in both currently and retrospectively, engaged in at around the age of 45. Performance in old age correlated positively with number of reported activities with the correlation being stronger for people of low educational level (Ihle et al., 2015). However, there was no clear association between the specific activities reported at 45

and later performance although this negative result could of course reflect unreliable reporting due to forgetting. In general therefore while many lifestyle factors correlate with preserved cognitive function, demonstrating clear and specific causal links is difficult.

A much more powerful way of demonstrating causation is, of course, to intervene by introducing training of each potentially relevant factor. This involves recruiting a sizable and representative sample of participants. One group then receives an intervention that is thought to be potentially helpful, while another group is provided with an intervention that is likely to be equally interesting, but unlikely to delay the normal aging process. Given the increasing size of the aging population and the cost, both financial and in terms of suffering imposed by Alzheimer's disease, there is considerable current interest in whether is it possible, by slowing the process of cognitive aging, to enhance levels of cognitive functioning and to reduce the likelihood of Alzheimer's disease.

There is indeed convincing evidence for a positive effect of *exercise* on maintaining cognitive function. In a typical study, Kramer et al. (1999) studied 124 sedentary but healthy older adults, randomizing them into two groups. One group received aerobic walking-based exercise, while the control group received toning and stretching exercises. The groups trained for about an hour a day for three days a week over a six-month period. Cognition was measured by a number of tests including task switching, attentional selection, and capacity to inhibit irrelevant information. They found a modest increase in aerobic fitness, together with a clear improvement in cognitive performance. A subsequent meta-analysis of a range of available studies by Colcombe and Kramer (2003) found clear evidence for a positive impact of aerobic exercise on a range of cognitive tasks, most notably those involving executive processing (see Figure 15.7).

While these studies made a strong case for the value of physical exercise in preserving cognition, they did not investigate the mechanism underlying this advantage. This issue was tackled by Monica Fabiano and

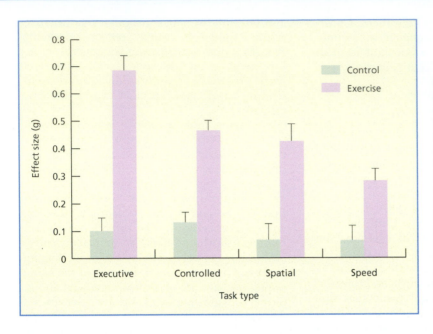

Figure 15.7 Effect sizes of mean differences in cognitive performance between older adults in aerobic fitness training (mauve bars) and those in a control condition (green bars) for different types of cognitive tasks. The greatest impact of training is on tasks involving executive processing. Adapted from Colcome and Kramer (2003). From Hertzog et al. (2009). Copyright © American Psychological Association. Reprinted with permission.

colleagues (Tan et al., 2017) who found that the elasticity of a person's arteries was positively linked to both cardio-respiratory fitness and brain structure with greater elasticity linked to preservation of both gray and white matter overall. Furthermore, elasticity of the left middle cerebral arteries that feed speech-related Broca's area was linked to greater verbal fluency, the capacity to rapidly generate items from a category such as animals, while elasticity of arteries feeding the frontal lobes was correlated with working memory span. It appears therefore that the clear effects of exercise on preserving cognition operate at least in part through improving blood flow to the brain.

A number of studies have addressed this point, a good example being that of Ball et al. (2002), who divided a total of 2,832 elderly participants into four groups, each of which underwent a training program of 5–6 weeks. One group received memory training involving the teaching of strategies, accompanied by extensive practice on remembering words and shopping lists. A second group received training on a range of verbal reasoning tasks. A third group received speed training on visual search and divided attention tasks. Finally, a fourth group served as controls and received no explicit training. All groups were subsequently tested on all three relevant areas and, in addition, an attempt was made to assess the impact of the training on everyday functioning. Each of the three groups improved on the skills trained, even though they were tested using a different format. No change occurred for the untrained skills, indicating that only the specific training had been effective. Unfortunately, however, there was no reliable evidence that any of the gains transferred to everyday functioning, although the authors speculate, somewhat optimistically, that the training might have a protective effect in slowing subsequent age-related decline. This result is broadly in line with attempts to train working memory in children described in Chapter 4 (p. 94) which found transfer of learning to similar tasks but no broad cognitive enhancement.

It is, of course, easier to do controlled intervention studies with animals, and here the evidence is clear in showing beneficial effects of both environmental enrichment and exercise (see van Praag, Kempermann, & Gage, 2000 for a review). Rats raised in an enriched cage environment show less decline in learning with age than rats that have spent their lives in comfortable but less interesting homes (Greenough et al., 1987). Animal studies have the further advantage that it is possible to look for the mechanism whereby enrichment or exercise influence subsequent performance. A study by Black, Isaacs, Anderson, Alcantara, and Greenough (1990) studied the effects on aging rats of both fitness training and motor skill learning. One group had access to activity wheels, resulting in aerobic training, while the other learned nonaerobic skills such as crossing rope bridges and climbing under and over obstacles. The motor skill group showed an increase in synapses in the cerebellum, an area that is important for motor behavior, whereas fitness training led to increased vascularization in other parts of the brain, potentially important in providing increased oxygen to such regions. Later studies reviewed by Kempermann (2008) present further evidence of neurotrophic factors that enhance cell and neuron growth and facilitate synaptic plasticity, particularly in the dentate gyrus of the hippocampus, helping maintain and promote learning and memory.

So where do we stand on the use-it-or-lose-it question? Does more activity result in better memory, or does declining memory cause people to be less active? On balance, I myself would tend to favor the use-it-or-lose-it

Henry Ford is said to have minimized the cost of his cars by carefully avoiding over-engineering any of the components, with the result that everything tended to wear out at the same time. Some claim that evolution took a similar approach to the process of aging, while others favor a weakest link view, claiming for example that the frontal lobes deteriorate faster than the rest of the brain.

hypothesis; even if it does not protect you from cognitive decline, using it is likely to lead to a rather less boring old age.

THEORIES OF AGING

In recent years, there have been a number of attempts to account for the effects of aging on cognition in terms of one or other single factor. Probably the most influential of these macro theories has been that proposal by Salthouse (1996) that the cognitive effects of aging can all be explained by the reduced speed of processing that is a marked feature of aging. This conclusion is based on a very extensive series of correlational studies, which do indeed tend to show that the best overall prediction of performance in the elderly is provided by measures that depend on speed of processing, rather than processing accuracy or memory performance. There does, however, seem to be evidence that memory decline might be separable from a more general decline in cognitive function with age (Salthouse & Becker, 1998). Nonetheless, as Salthouse (1992, 1996) shows, it is possible to account for much of the influence of age on cognition in terms of a general speed factor.

One problem with such a conclusion is that it is not meaningful to talk about speed independent of the task on which it is assessed. If one combines speed across a wide range of tasks, then one could argue that one is sampling many aspects of performance, not just one. In response to this, Salthouse focused on an individual task, the Digit Symbol Substitution Test (DSST) taken from the Wechsler Adult Intelligence Scale (WAIS). This is indeed a good predictor of the overall effects of age on performance but it is far from being a pure speed test. Good performance almost certainly involves strategy and working memory as well as perceptual speed. Given that it correlates highly with measures of both verbal and nonverbal intelligence, it should, according to Parkin and Java (2000), be regarded as a measure of working memory rather than simple perceptual speed. A test based on rate of number cancellation, which might be expected to provide a purer measure of perceptual speed, proved to be a poor predictor of age decrement in their study.

Another problem with using purely correlational methods is that many physical and intellectual capacities decline together as we age, making it difficult to assign a causal role to one over and above the remainder. The method used by Salthouse and many others in the field is to look for the most powerful and robust correlation, the measure that can account for most of the statistical variance in the results. However, this depends not only on the nature and purity of the measure as described above, but also on the reliability of the measure, which in turn depends on the number of observations on which it is based. Speed tests typically involve a large number of repetitions of a simple task leading to results that are consistent across trials, as in the case of reaction time studies. Executive measures such as tests of reasoning are more likely to depend on fewer but more difficult subtasks that may need to be changed between test trials to prevent learning, resulting in less reliability and hence to lower correlations with other measures. Finally, the best prediction of overall performance will depend crucially on the particular set of tasks chosen for inclusion, which will of course reflect the views of the investigator.

Whereas speed measures frequently do provide the highest correlations, this is not always the case. An extensive series of studies by Paul Baltes and his group in Berlin concentrated more attention on perceptual factors, finding initially that the best predictors were auditory and visual sensory thresholds, which depend on accuracy rather than speed (Baltes & Lindenberger, 1997). One might possibly argue that these would be influenced by such factors as neural transmission speed. However, Baltes and colleagues subsequently found that an even better predictor of the decline in cognition with age was grip strength, giving a whole new meaning to the term "losing one's grip"! As Lindenberger and Pötter (1998) point out, there is a danger of forgetting that correlation does not equal causation.

Perhaps the time has come to abandon the search for the single factor that underpins the decline of cognition as we get older, returning to the Ford car (or in its UK version, the Woolworths' bicycle pump) hypothesis: An optimally engineered product will aim to manufacture all its parts to the same quality, rather than waste money on over-engineering some components. The result of this is that the parts all tend to last for about the same length of time before failing. Perhaps evolution is equally parsimonious?

The correlational approach is certainly not the only method of developing theories of cognitive aging. For example, Craik and colleagues, using an experimental approach, have emphasized the impact of reduced processing resources on learning and memory in the elderly, often finding that their young participants perform in a similar way to their elderly group when an attentionally demanding concurrent task reduces their available processing capacity (e.g., Craik & Byrd, 1982; Craik & Jennings, 1992). There is no doubt that attentional capacity is an important variable but, as the previously described studies by Naveh-Benjamin and colleagues indicate (Naveh-Benjamin, Guez, et al., 2004; Naveh-Benjamin, Guez, & Marom, 2003; Naveh-Benjamin, Guez, & Shulman, 2004; Naveh-Benjamin, Hussain, et al., 2003), reducing the attention available to the young does not always result in performance resembling the elderly.

In the case of episodic memory, the aging deficit seems closer to a very mild amnesia than to a purely attentional limitation. Similarly, whereas there might be a tendency for the elderly to have difficulty in inhibiting irrelevant material, as suggested by Hasher et al. (1999), it is not clear why this should influence free recall, one of the most sensitive tests of aging. One might expect increased susceptibility to inhibition to influence short-term forgetting performance on the Peterson and Peterson (1959) task, where forgetting appears to be principally the result of proactive inhibition (Keppel & Underwood, 1962). However, provided initial level of performance is matched, there seems to be no difference in rate of forgetting as a function of delay, between young and old (Parkinson et al., 1985). Hence, although age can reduce our inhibitory capacity, it seems unlikely that it is the principal cause of episodic memory decline.

A popular hypothesis over recent years has been to interpret the effects of aging in terms of the declining functions of the frontal lobes. Evidence in favor of this view has principally come from studies showing an association between the size of the aging effect and performance on tasks assumed to depend on frontal lobe function. Such tasks are varied and numerous, typically involving the executive component of working memory, and possibly also the capacity for inhibition, together with a wide range of other executive functions that are themselves still poorly understood. It is not clear how useful a general frontal hypothesis would be, at this stage. The evidence supporting the frontal aging hypothesis was reviewed by Phillips and Henry (2005), who conclude that the direct evidence for a causal link between frontal-lobe atrophy and age-related cognitive decline is currently weak and that the present hypothesis relies on a simplistic interpretation of both the neuroanatomy and the neuropsychology of the frontal lobes. That does not, of course, rule out an important role for the frontal lobes in normal aging, but it does suggest that any theory that assigns a special role to the frontal lobes in aging will need to be grounded more firmly both neuropsychologically and neuroanatomically.

THE AGING BRAIN

As we grow older, our brain shrinks. This shows most clearly in the expansion of the ventricles, the channels in the brain filled by cerebrospinal fluid, which take up more space as the brain becomes smaller. While this is a good overall measure of brain size, it is not a very good measure of function, as functional change depends—crucially—on what part of the brain is shrinking. As mentioned earlier, this tends to be the frontal lobes, with the temporal and occipital lobes shrinking more slowly. The hippocampus, crucial for memory, loses 20–30% of its neurons by the age of 80 (Squire, 1987), reflecting an initial slow decline, which subsequently accelerates,

possibly as the result of disease (see Raz, 2000, for further discussion). The electrophysiological activity of the brain, as reflected in evoked response potential (ERP) measures (see Chapter 2, p. 29), slows steadily throughout the lifespan (Pelosi & Blumhardt, 1999), with the latency of the P300 component increasing at an average of two milliseconds per year, a rate of slowing that becomes more severe in dementia (Neshige, Barrett, & Shibasaki, 1988).

Studies of brain function using neuroimaging also tend to show age effects. Cabeza et al. (2004), studying working memory and visual attention, observed that older subjects tended to show activation in both cerebral hemispheres on tasks that activate a single hemisphere in young participants. A comparable result was observed by Maguire and Frith (2003) in a study of autobiographical memory, with the young showing predominantly left hippocampal involvement, while the involvement of the elderly was bilateral. Reuter-Lorenz (2002) and others have attributed the broader spread of activation to an attempt by the elderly to compensate for overload in one component of the brain by utilizing other brain structures. However, other interpretations have been proposed (Nyberg et al., 2010).

It is not always the case that greater activation is shown in the elderly, particularly on tasks where it may be helpful to involve relatively complex strategies. A study by Iidaka et al. (2001) required participants to remember pairs of related or unrelated pictures. Both young and old showed more left frontal activation for the unrelated pictures, but only the young showed additional occipito-temporal activation. This probably indicates the active use of visual imagery, as this was an area observed by Maguire, Valentine, Wilding, and Kapur (2003) to be activated when using the method of loci, a classic visual-imagery-based mnemonic strategy. This method is itself very demanding, and while consistently aiding the young, only 50% of the older subjects tested by Nyberg et al. (2003) were found to benefit from using the method of loci. It appears to be the case, therefore, that older participants will attempt to compensate for cognitive decline by using additional strategies, reflected in a wider range of brain activation. However, this might no longer be possible when the task is already complex, potentially inducing reliance on a simpler strategy.

The principal contribution of studies based on neuroimaging at this point has been to identify the anatomical localization associated with different cognitive processes. An exciting new development is based on the capacity to image the distribution and operation of the neurotransmitters that play a crucial role in the neural basis of cognition. One such study concerns the link between aging and the neurotransmitter, dopamine. Post-mortem studies have indicated that as we age, dopamine levels show a loss of 5–10% per decade. This finding has been confirmed by studies using positron emission tomography (PET) (see Chapter 2, p. 31), whereby the density of dopamine receptors is measured using the radioactive labeling of ligands, substances that selectively bind to specific types of dopamine receptor (Antonini et al., 1993). Further evidence for the importance of dopamine comes from Bäckman et al. (2011) in a study based on working memory training. While training does not typically generalize to academic or related activities (see Chapter 14) it does lead to a clear improvement of broadly similar executive tasks. Bäckman et al. gave five weeks of training on a memory updating task, finding transfer to a related n-back task and evidence that training was linked to enhanced dopamine release in brain regions specifically involved in updating.

It is known that dopamine is implicated in many cognitive functions, and that its depletion is associated with cognitive deficits in both Parkinson's disease (Brown & Marsden, 1990) and Huntington's disease (Bäckman et al., 1997). Pharmacological studies using healthy young participants confirm the importance of dopamine. Bromocriptine, which is known to facilitate dopamine function, is found to improve spatial working memory (Luciana & Collins, 1997), whereas haloperidol, which interferes with dopamine function, has the opposite effect (Luciana & Collins, 1997; Ramaekers et al., 1999).

Bäckman et al. (2000) used PET to measure dopamine binding in volunteers across the age range. They found a substantial correlation between dopamine levels in the brain and episodic memory that accounted for some 38% of the variance in performance on word recognition, and 48% in the case of face recognition. When the effect of dopamine level was removed statistically, age had only a minimal impact on memory performance, a result that has subsequently been replicated by Erixon-Lindroth et al. (2005, see Figure 15.8). Further studies summarized by Bäckman, Lindenberger, Li, and Nyberg (2010) indicate an important role for dopamine across ages on both episodic and working memory and that such differences are linked to age-related decline in performance.

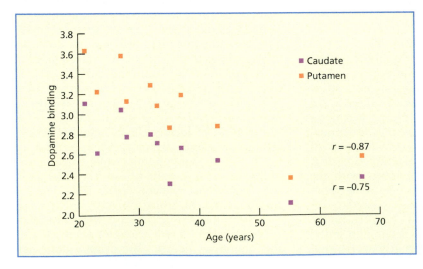

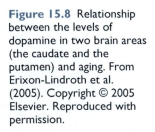

Figure 15.8 Relationship between the levels of dopamine in two brain areas (the caudate and the putamen) and aging. From Erixon-Lindroth et al. (2005). Copyright © 2005 Elsevier. Reproduced with permission.

Of course, dopamine is by no means the only aspect of the brain related to both aging and cognition. Figure 15.9(a) shows variability across individuals in hippocampal volume across ages. Note the variability, with a few 80-year-olds having the same volume as some 20-year-olds. A similar pattern is found for episodic memory (see Figure 15.9[b]). Figure 15.10 shows similar diversity in memory decline over a decade. In a group matched on initial performance many maintained their scores while others showed a clear decline, a pattern that was reflected in fMRI blood flow measures. This raised the question of

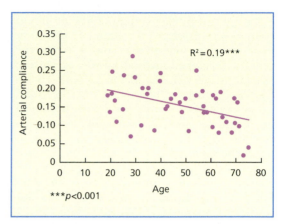

Figure 15.10 Arterial stiffness increases with age. Data from Tan et al. 2017.

what determines these substantial differences? Can they be predicted and perhaps avoided? Is there a secret to what has become known as successful aging?

There are in fact many features that are correlated with longevity, starting with genetic differences. The children of long-living parents tend to live longer lives. This is due in part to genetic factors, probably reflecting a small contribution from many genes with one gene, APOE, accounting for 1–2% of the variance in cognitive decline, an effect that principally emerges beyond the age of 60 (Papenberg, Lindenberger, & Bäckman, 2015). Health, education, and lifestyle also contribute, but these again are small effects, described by Corley, Cox, and Deary (2018) as "marginal gains not magic bullet." Does this mean that there is nothing to be done to encourage successful aging? Certainly not; it means that a correlational approach is a very limited way of investigating a situation in which many factors are present, are often highly intercorrelated and likely to interact with each other. Carefully designed intervention studies focusing on specific factors offer a much more powerful means of analysis and as discussed earlier are already showing clear effects in the case of exercise together with considerable promise in studies of social and cognitive interventions.

Why should exercise slow the process of cognitive aging? The most likely explanation is by maintaining the capacity and flexibility

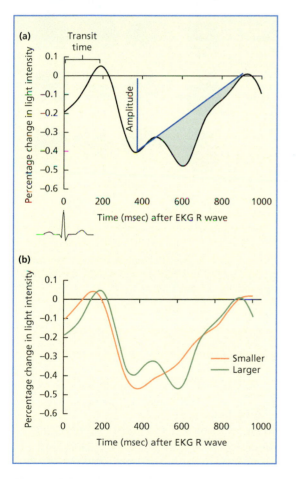

Figure 15.9 Measuring pulse amplitude and arterial elasticity. The green area in (a) represents elasticity and the difference between participants with high and low elasticity is shown in (b) where lower elasticity is shown by nonresponse to minor fluctuations. Based on Fabiani et al. 2014 Figure 2.

of the cardiovascular system, allowing blood to flow more freely to the brain. Evidence in favor of this hypothesis comes from the recently developed method known as Diffuse Optical Imagery (Fabiani et al., 2014). This is a method whereby blood flow to the brain can be detected, not through its disruption of the magnetic field, but optically, with each beat of the heart influencing the flow of blood showing up as an increase or decrease in light reflected. This allows a number of measures, including an indication of the flexibility of the blood vessels in that specific location (Fabiani et al., 2014).

In a later study, Tan et al. (2017) used diffuse optical imagery to study arterial health of participants aged between 55 and 87. They showed that arterial health decreases with age as does the thickness of the gray matter of the brain and degree of overall atrophy. As Figure 15.11 shows, however, people differ in the compliancy of their blood vessels with some older individuals showing equivalent compliance to some younger. Such variability in the onset of aging effects is of course also characteristic of cognitive performance measures. Overall arterial flexibility however is not the whole story. The working memory capacity of each member of the group was tested using operation span, a standard measure of working memory capacity. This was specifically linked to localized compliance in the frontotemporal region of the cortex, the area assumed to be most closely linked to executive processing while working memory performance was not correlated with compliance either across the brain as a whole or within the visual cortex. This does not of course necessarily imply that compliance in other specific parts of the brain might not be associated with deficits in performance on other tasks.

In conclusion, recent developments in neuroscience are increasingly throwing light on the psychology of aging and offering hints as to how we might achieve successful aging.

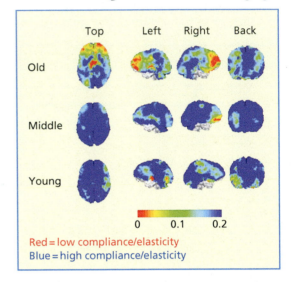

Figure 15.11 Reduced compliance across age. Note the tendency of the frontal regions to be particularly impaired. Data from Tang et al. (2017).

SUMMARY

- The study of aging is concerned with the study of change and can be pursued using two basic designs: longitudinal or cross-sectional.
- Longitudinal designs involve studying the same individuals across time.
- Cross-sectional involves testing of people of different ages at a single point in time.
- Studies are beginning to emerge that combine these to give a more accurate picture.
- Much current evidence on aging and memory comes from cross-sectional studies, which suggest the following:
  - STM is relatively preserved (working memory is less so).
  - Episodic memory certainly declines, but can benefit from environmental cues and support.

- However, apparent decline in cross-sectional studies is substantially greater than those in employing a longitudinal design.
- Individuals vary substantially in their rate of decline.
- In the case of working memory, some attempt to interpret design in terms of broad theories of aging, while others focus on the differential vulnerability of different aspects of the tests.
- The associative deficit hypothesis proposes that aging leads to a reduced capacity to form new associations.
- The associative deficit hypothesis can be attributed to an overall impairment in memory consolidation, with tasks involving new associations being particularly demanding.
- Prospective memory declines when tested under laboratory conditions, but in a real-world context older people can prove more reliable.
- Time- and event-based perspective memory tasks are both potentially vulnerable to aging within an experimental context.
- The content of semantic memory continues to accumulate, as reflected in increasing vocabulary, but speed and reliability of access declines.
- Implicit memory tends to hold up reasonably well but varies with task.
- A number of unitary theories of cognitive decline with age have been proposed, but the tendency for many different measures to decline at the same time makes strong conclusions questionable.
- The brain tends to shrink as we get older.
- Greater shrinkage in brain volume is associated with reduced blood flow to the brain which in turn is linked to arterial elasticity.
- Dopamine level declines with age and is correlated with cognition.
- It can be increased with brain training, although there is currently no strong evidence that training transfers to everyday performance.
- There is however well-established evidence for a positive effect of physical exercise.
- There is some evidence for the use-it-or-lose-it hypothesis whereby cognitive and a social activity are beneficial, although this is not as strong as that of exercise.
- Neuroimaging suggests that older people tend to show a wider spread of neural activation, possibly resulting from an attempt to compensate for a cognitive deficit.

POINTS FOR DISCUSSION

1 What are the relative strengths and weaknesses of longitudinal and cross-sectional approaches to the study of aging? How can they be tackled?
2 What impact on everyday life would you expect from the effects on memory of aging?
3 What are the effects of cognitive and physical training on memory and aging? How might these be linked to brain function?
4 Why do we become more forgetful as we become older?
5 What advice would you give to someone just about to retire?
6 What are the similarities and difference between the way in which memory develops during childhood and its decline as we age? Is one the mirror image of the other?

FURTHER READING

American Journal of Geriatric Psychiatry: Special Issue on "Successful aging" (2006) volume 14, issue 1. Focuses on the question of how we can best adapt to the inevitable process of aging.

Bäckman, L., Nyberg, L., Lindenberger, U., Li, S.-C., & Farde, L. (2006). The correlative triad among aging, dopamine, cognition: Current status and future prospects. *Neuroscience and Biobehavioral Reviews, 30*, 791–807. A review of some of the exciting developments in the neurobiology of aging. It suggests an important role for dopamine in determining the effects of age on cognition.

Hillman, C. H., Erickson, K. I., & Kramer, A. F. (2008). Be smart, exercise your heart: Exercise effects on brain and cognition. *Nature Reviews Neuroscience, 9*, 58–65. An overview of the positive effects of exercise on healthy aging.

Perfect, T. J., & Maylor, E. A. (2000). Rejecting the dull hypothesis: The relationship between method and theory in cognitive aging research. In T. J. Perfect & E. A. Maylor (Eds.), *Models of cognitive aging* (pp. 1–18). Oxford: Oxford University Press. A discussion and critical evaluation of attempts to provide a general theory of cognitive aging. An overview of the cognitive psychology of aging by someone who has worked extensively using both experimental and longitudinal designs.

Rabbitt, P. M. A. (2015). *The aging mind: An owner's manual*. London: Routledge. Based on a lifetime of scientific research on aging to provide an account of what it means to grow older, appropriately described by one reviewer as "witty, pithy and wise."

Salthouse, T. A. (1996). The processing-speed theory of adult age differences in cognition. *Psychological Review, 103*, 403–428. An influential attempt to provide a unitary theory of cognitive aging in terms of processing speed.

REFERENCES

Antonini, A., Leenders, K. L., Meier, D., Oertel, W. H., Boesiger, P., & Anliker, M. (1993). T2 relaxation time in patients with Parkinson's disease. *Neurology, 43*, 697–700.

Bäckman, L., Almkvist, O., Andersson, J., Nordberg, A., Winblad, B., Reineck, R., & Langstrom, B. (1997). Brain activation in young and older adults during implicit and explicit retrieval. *Journal of Cognitive Neuroscience, 9*, 378–391.

Bäckman, L., Ginovart, N., Dixon, R. A., Robins Wahlin, T. B., Wahlin, A., Halldin, C., & Farde, L. (2000). Age-related cognitive deficits mediated by changes in the striatal dopamine system. *American Journal of Psychiatry, 157*, 635–637.

Bäckman, L., Lindenberger, U., Li, S.-C., & Nyberg, L. (2010). Linking cognitive aging to alterations in dopamine neurotransmitter functioning: Recent data and future avenues. *Neuroscience and Biobehavioral Reviews, 34*, 670–677. doi:10.1016/j.neubiorev.2009.12.008

Bäckman, L., & Molander, B. (1986). Adult age differences in the ability to cope with situations of high arousal in a precision sport. *Psychology and Aging, 1*, 133–139.

Bäckman, L., & Nilsson, L.-G. (1984). Aging effect in free recall: An exception to the rule. *Human Learning, 3*, 53–69.

Bäckman, L., Nyberg, L., Soveri, A., Johansson, J., Andersson, M., Dahlin, E., ... Rinne, J. O. (2011). Effects of working-memory training on striatal dopamine release. *Science, 333*, 718. doi:10.1126/science.1204978

Baddeley, A. D., Baddeley, H., Bucks, R., & Wilcock, G. K. (2001). Attentional control in Alzheimer's disease. *Brain, 124*, 1492–1508.

Baddeley, A., & Crawford, J. (2012). *Spot the word* (2nd ed.). Topics in Cognitive Science. Oxford: Pearson.

Baddeley, A. D., Emslie, H., & Nimmo-Smith, I. (1992). *Speed and Capacity of Language Processing test (SCOLP)*. Bury St Edmunds, UK: Thames Valley Test Company.

Baddeley, A. D., Emslie, H., & Nimmo-Smith, I. (1994). *Doors and people: A test of visual and verbal recall and recognition*. Bury St Edmunds, UK: Thames Valley Test Company.

Baddeley, A., Meeks Gardner, J., & Grantham-McGregor, S. (1995). Developing tests for developing countries. *Applied Cognitive Psychology, 9*(7), S173–S195.

Ball, K., Berch, D. B., Helmers, K. F., Jobe, J. B., Leveck, M. D., Marsiske, M., ... Willis, S. L. (2002). Effects of cognitive training intervention with older adults: A randomised control trial. *Journal of the American Medical Association, 288*, 2271–2281.

Baltes, P. B., & Lindenberger, U. (1997). Emergence of a powerful connection between the sensory and cognitive functions across the adult lifespan: A new window to the study of cognitive ageing?. *Psychology and Ageing, 12*, 12–21.

Benjamin, A. S. (2010). Representational explanations of "process" dissociations in recognition: The DRYAD theory of aging and memory judgments. *Psychological Review, 117*, 1055–1079 doi:10.1037/a0020810

Black, J. E., Isaacs, K. R., Anderson, B. J., Alcantara, A. A., & Greenough, W. T. (1990). Learning causes synaptogenesis, whereas motor activity causes angiogenesis, in cerebellar cortex of adult rats. *Proceedings of the National Academy of Sciences of the USA, 87*, 5568–5572.

Bopp, K. L., & Verhaeghen, P. (2005). Ageing and verbal memory span: A meta analysis. *Journal of Gerontology, Series B, Psychological Sciences and Social Sciences, 60*, 223–233.

Bratsberg, B., & Rogeberg, O. (2018). Flynn effect and its reversal are both environmentally caused. *Proceedings of the National Academy of Sciences of the USA, 115*, 6674–6678. doi:10.1073/pnas.1718793115

Brown, R. G., & Marsden, C. D. (1990). Cognitive function in Parkinson's disease: From description to theory. *Trends in Cognitive Sciences, 13*, 21–29.

Burke, D. M., MacKay, D. G., Worthley, J. S., & Wade, E. (1991). On the tip of the tongue: What causes word finding failures in young and older adults. *Journal of Memory and Language, 30*, 542–579.

Cabeza, R., Prince, S. E., Daselaar, S. M., Greenberg, D. L., Budde, M., Dolcos, F., ... Rubin, D. C. (2004). Brain activity during episodic retrieval of autobiographical and laboratory events: An fMRI study using a novel photo paradigm. *Journal of Cognitive Neuroscience, 16*, 1583–1594.

Chalfonte, B. L., & Johnson, M. K. (1996). Feature memory and binding in young and older adults. *Memory & Cognition, 24*, 403–416.

Charness, N. (1985). Ageing and problem-solving performance. In N. Charness (Ed.), *Ageing and human performance* (pp. 225–260). Chichester, UK: John Wiley & Sons.

Christensen, H., Henderson, A. S., Griffiths, K., & Levings, C. (1997). Does ageing inevitably lead to declines in cognitive performance? A longitudinal study of elite academics. *Personality & Individual Differences, 23*, 67–78.

Cockburn, J., & Smith, P. T. (1991). The relative influence of intelligence and age on everyday memory. *Journal of Gerontology: Psychological Sciences, 46*, 31–36.

Cohen, G., & Faulkner, D. (1989). Age differences in source forgetting: Effects on reality monitoring and on eyewitness testimony. *Psychology and Aging, 4*, 10–17.

Colcombe, S., & Kramer, A. F. (2003). Fitness effects on the cognitive function of older adults: A meta-analytic study. *Psychological Science, 14*, 125–130.

Collins, A. M., & Quillian, M. R. (1969). Retrieval time from semantic memory. *Journal of Verbal Learning and Verbal Behavior, 8*, 432–438.

Corley, J., Cox, S. R., & Deary, I. J. (2018). Healthy cognitive ageing in the Lothian Birth Cohort studies: Marginal gains not magic bullet. *Psychological Medicine, 48*, 187–207. doi:10.1017/S003329171700148

Craik, F. I. M. (1986). A functional account of age differences in memory. In F. Klix & H. Hagendorf (Eds.), *Human memory and cognitive capabilities: Mechanisms and performances* (pp. 409–422). Amsterdam: Elsevier Science Publishers, North-Holland.

Craik, F. I. M. (2005). On reducing age-related declines in memory and executive control. In J. Duncan, L. Phillips, & P. McLeod (Eds.), *Measuring the mind: Speed, control and age* (pp. 273–290). New York: Oxford University Press.

Craik, F. I. M., & Byrd, M. (1982). Aging and cognitive deficits: The role of attentional resources. In F. I. M. Craik & S. Trehub (Eds.), *Aging and cognitive processes* (pp. 191–211). New York: Plenum.

Craik, F. I. M., Byrd, M., & Swanson, J. M. (1987). Patterns of memory loss in three elderly samples. *Psychology and Aging, 2,* 79–86.

Craik, F. I. M., & Jennings, J. M. (1992). Human memory. In F. I. M. Craik & T. A. Salthouse (Eds.), *Handbook of ageing and cognition* (pp. 51–100). Hillsdale, NJ: Erlbaum.

Deary, I. J., Whalley, L. J., Batty, G. D., & Starr, J. M. (2006). Physical fitness and lifetime cognitive change. *Neurology, 67,* 1195–1200.

Deary, I. J., Whiteman, M. C., Starr, J. M., Whalley, L. J., & Fox, H. C. (2004). The impact of childhood intelligence on later life: Following up the Scottish mental surveys of 1932 and 1947. *Journal of Personality and Social Psychology, 86,* 130–147.

Einstein, G. O., & McDaniel, M. A. (1990). Normal aging and prospective memory. *Journal of Experimental Psychology: Learning Memory & Cognition, 16,* 717–726.

Einstein, G. O., McDaniel, M. A., Richardson, S. L., Cunfer, A. R., & Guynn, M. J. (1995). Aging and prospective memory: Examining the influence of self-initiated retrieval processes. *Journal of Experimental Psychology: Learning Memory & Cognition, 21,* 996–1007.

Englekamp, J. (1998). *Memory for actions.* Hove, UK: Psychology Press.

Erixon-Lindroth, N., Farde, L., Robins Wahlin, T. B., Sovago, J., Halldin, C., & Bäckman, L. (2005). The role of the striatal dopamine transporter in cognitive aging. *Psychiatry Research: Neuroimaging, 138,* 1–12.

Fabiani, M., Low, K. A., Tan, C. H., Zimmerman, B., Fletcher, M. A., Schneider-Garces, N., … Gratton, G. (2014). Taking the pulse of aging: Mapping pulse pressure and elasticity in cerebral arteries with optical methods. *Psychophysiology, 51,* 1072–1088. doi:10.1111/psyp.12288

Flynn, J. R. (1987). Massive IQ gains in 14 nations: What IQ tests really measure. *Psychological Bulletin, 101,* 171–191.

Giambra, L. M., Arenberg, D., Zonderman, A. B., & Kawas, C. (1995). Adult life span changes in immediate visual memory and verbal intelligence. *Psychology and Aging, 10,* 123–139.

Greenough, W. T., Black, J. E., & Wallace, C. S. (1987). Experience and brain development. *Child Development, 58,* 539–559.

Hasher, L., & Zacks, R. T. (1988). Working memory, comprehension, and aging: A review and a new view. In G. H. Bower (Ed.), *The psychology of learning and motivation* (Vol. 22, pp. 193–225). San Diego, CA: Academic Press.

Hasher, L., Zacks, R. T., & May, C. P. (1999). Inhibitory control, circadian arousal, and age. In D. Gopher & A. Koriat (Eds.), *Attention and performance, XVII, Cognitive regulation of performance. Interaction of theory and application* (pp. 653–675). Cambridge, MA: MIT Press.

Henry, J. D., MacLeod, M. S., Phillips, L. H., & Crawford, J. R. (2004). A meta-analytic review of prospective memory and aging. *Psychology and Aging, 19,* 27–39. doi:10.1037/0882-7974. 19.1.27

Hertzog, C., Kramer, A. F., Wilson, R. S., & Lindenberger, U. (2008). Enrichment effects on adult cognitive development: Can the functional capacity of older adults be preserved and enhanced. *Psychological Science in the Public Interest, 9*(1), 1–65.

Howard, D. V., & Howard, J. H., Jr. (1989). Age differences in learning serial patterns: Direct versus indirect measures. *Psychology and Aging, 4,* 357–364.

Ihle, A., Oris, M., Fagot, D., Baeriswyl, M., Guichard, E., & Kleigel, M. (2015). The association of leisure activities in middle adulthood with cognitive performance in old age: The moderating role of educational level. *Gerontology, 61,* 543–550.

Ihle, A., Schnitzpahn, K., Rendell, P. G., Luong, C., & Kligel, M. (2012). Age benefits in everyday prospective memory: The influence of personal task importance, use of reminders and everyday stress. *Aging, Neuropsychology, and Cognition: A Journal on Normal and Dysfunctional Development, 19,* 84–101. doi:10.1080/13825585.2011.629288

Iidaka, T., Sadato, N., Yamada, H., Murata, T., Omori, M., & Yonekura, Y. (2001). An fMRI study of the functional neuroanatomy of picture encoding in young and older adults. *Cognitive Brain Research, 11,* 1–11.

Kemper, S. (1990). Adults' diaries: Changes made to written narratives across the life-span. *Discourse Processes, 13,* 207–223.

Kemper, S., Kynette, D., & Norman, S. (1992). Age differences in spoken language. In R. West & J. Sinnott (Eds.), *Everyday memory and aging: Current research and methodology* (pp. 138–152). New York: Springer-Verlag.

Kempermann, G. (2008). The neurogenic reserve hypothesis: What is adult hippocampal neurogenesis good for?. *Trends in Neuroscience, 31,* 163–169. doi:1016/j.tins.2008.01.002

Keppel, G., & Underwood, B. J. (1962). Proactive inhibition in short-term retention of single items. *Journal of Verbal Learning and Verbal Behavior, 1,* 153–161.

Kramer, A. F., Hahn, S., Cohen, N. J., Banich, M. T., McAuley, E., Harrison, C. R., ... Colcombe, A. (1999). Aging, fitness and neurocognitive function. *Nature, 400*, 418–419.

Light, L. L., Prull, M. W., La Voie, D., & Healy, M. R. (2000). Dual process theories of memory in older age. In T. J. Perfect & E. Maylor (Eds.), *Theoretical debate in cognitive aging* (pp. 238–300). Oxford: Oxford University Press.

Lindenberger, U., & Pötter, U. (1998). The complex nature of unique and shared effects in hierarchical linear regression: Implications for developmental psychology. *Psychological Methods, 3*, 218–230.

Logie, R. H., Horne, M. J., & Pettit, L. D. (2015). When cognitive performance does not decline across the life span. In R. H. Logie & R. Morris (Eds.), *Working memory and ageing* (pp. 21–47). Hove, UK: Psychology Press.

Logie, R. H., & Maylor, E. A. (2009). An internet study of prospective memory across adulthood. *Psychology and Aging, 24*, 767–774.

Luciana, M., & Collins, P. F. (1997). Dopaminergic modulation of working memory for spatial but not object cues in normal humans. *Journal of Cognitive Neuroscience, 9*, 330–367.

Maguire, E. A., & Frith, C. D. (2003). Lateral asymmetry in the hippocampal response to the remoteness of autobiographical memories. *Journal of Neuroscience, 23*, 5302–5307.

Maguire, E. A., Valentine, E. R., Wilding, J. M., & Kapur, N. (2003). Routes to remembering: The brains behind superior memory. *Nat, Neurosci., 6*, 90–95.

Mäntylä, T., & Nilsson, L.-G. (1997). Are my cues better than your cues? Recognition memory and recollective experience in Alzheimer's disease. *Memory, 5*, 657–672.

May, C. P., Hasher, L., & Kane, M. J. (1999). The role of interference in memory span. *Memory & Cognition, 27*, 759–767.

Maylor, E. A. (1996). Does prospective memory decline with age?. In M. Brandimonte, G. O. Einstein, M. A. McDaniel, & N. J. Mahwah (Eds.), *Prospective memory: Theory and applications* (pp. 173–198). Hove, UK: Lawrence Erlbaum Associates.

Maylor, E. A. (1997). Proper name retrieval in old age: Converging evidence against disproportionate impairment. *Aging, Neuropsychology, and Cognition, 4*, 211–226.

Naveh-Benjamin, M. (2000). Adult age differences in memory performance: Tests of an associative deficit hypothesis. *Journal of Experimental Psychology: Learning Memory & Cognition, 26*, 1170–1187.

Naveh-Benjamin, M., Guez, J., Kilb, A., & Reedy, S. (2004). The associative memory deficit of older adults: Further support using face-name associations. *Psychology and Ageing, 19*, 541–546.

Naveh-Benjamin, M., Guez, J., & Marom, M. (2003). The effects of divided attention at encoding on item and associative memory. *Memory and Cognition, 31*, 1021–1035.

Naveh-Benjamin, M., Guez, J., & Shulman, S. (2004). Older adults' associative deficit in episodic memory: Assessing the role of decline in attentional resources. *Psychonomic Bulletin and Review, 11*, 1067–1073.

Naveh-Benjamin, M., Hussain, Z., Guez, J., & Bar-On, M. (2003). Adult age differences in episodic memory: Further support for an associative deficit hypothesis. *Journal of Experimental Psychology: Learning Memory & Cognition, 29*, 826–837.

Neshige, R., Barrett, G., & Shibasaki, H. (1988). Auditory long latency event-related potentials in Alzheimer's disease and multi-infarct dementia. *J. Neurol. Neurosurg. Psychiat., 51*, 1120–1125.

Nilsson, L.-G., Adolfsson, R., Bäckman, L., de Frias, C., Molander, B., & Nyberg, L. (2004). Betula: A prospective cohort study on memory, health and aging. *Aging, Neuropsychology and Cognition, 11*, 134–148.

Nyberg, L., Salami, A., Andersson, M., Eriksson, J., Kalpouzos, G., Kauppi, K., ... Nisson, L.-G. (2010). Longitudinal evidence for diminished frontal cortex function in aging. *Proceedings of the National Academy of Sciences of the USA, 107*, 22682–22686. doi:10.1073/pnas.1012651108

Nyberg, L., Sandblom, J., Jones, S., Neely, A. S., Petersson, K. M., Ingvar, M., & Bäckman, L. (2003). Neural correlates of training-related memory improvement in adulthood and aging. *Proceedings of the National Academy of Sciences of the USA, 100*, 13728–13733.

Old, S. R., & Naveh-Benjamin, M. (2008). Differential effects of age on item and associative measures of memory: A meta-analysis. *Psychology and Aging, 23*, 104–118. doi:10.1037/0882-7974.23.1.104

Papenberg, G., Lindenberger, U., & Bäckman, L. (2015). Aging-related magnification of genetic effects on cognitive and brain integrity. *Trends in Cognitive Sciences, 19*, 506–514. doi:10.1016/j.tics.2015.06.008

Park, D. C., & Puglisi, J. T. (1985). Older adults' memory for the color of matched pictures and words. *Journal of Gerontology, 40*, 198–204.

Parkin, A. J., & Java, R. I. (2000). Determinants of age-related memory loss. In T. Perfect &

E. Maylor (Eds.), *Debates in cognitive aging* (pp. 188–203). Oxford: Oxford University Press.

Parkin, A. J., & Walter, B. M. (1992). Recollective experience, normal aging and frontal dysfunction. *Psychology and Aging, 7,* 290–298.

Parkinson, S. R., Inman, V. W., & Dannenbaum, S. E. (1985). Adult age differences in short-term forgetting. *Acta Psychologica, 60,* 83–101.

Pelosi, L., & Blumhardt, L. D. (1999). Effects of age on working memory: An event-related potential study. *Cognitive Brain Research, 7,* 321–334.

Perlmuter, L. C., Scharff, K., Karsh, R., & Monty, R. A. (1980). Perceived control: A generalized state of motivation. *Motivation and Emotion, 4,* 35–45.

Peterson, L. R., & Peterson, M. J. (1959). Short-term retention of individual verbal items. *Journal of Experimental Psychology, 58,* 193–198.

Phillips, L. H., & Henry, J. D. (2005). An evaluation of the frontal lobe theory of cognitive aging. In J. Duncan, L. Phillips, & P. MacLeod (Eds.), *Measuring the mind: Speed, control and age* (pp. 191–216). Oxford: Oxford University Press.

Rabbitt, P., & Abson, V. (1990). 'Lost and found': Some logical and methodological limitations of self-report questionnaires as tools to study cognitive aging. *British Journal of Psychology, 81,* 1–16.

Ramaekers, J. G., Louwerens, J. W., Muntjewerff, N. D., Milius, H., de Bie, A., Rosenzweig, P., ... O'Hanlon, J. F. (1999). Psychomotor, cognitive, extrapyramidal, and affective functions of healthy volunteers during treatment with an atypical (amisulspride) and a classic (haloperidol) antipsychotic. *Journal of Clinical Psycholopharmacology, 19,* 209–221.

Raz, N. (2000). Aging of the brain and its impact on cognitive performance: Integration of structural and functional findings. In F. I. M. Craik & T. A. Salthouse (Eds.), *The handbook of aging and cognition* (2nd ed., pp. 91–153). Mahwah, NJ: Erlbaum.

Rendell, P. G., & Craik, F. I. M. (2000). Virtual week and actual week: Age-related differences in prospective memory. *Applied Cognitive Psychology, 12,* S43–S62.

Reuter-Lorenz, P. A. (2002). New visions of the aging mind and brain. *Trends in Cognitive Sciences, 6,* 394–400.

Riby, L. M., Perfect, T. J., & Stollery, B. (2004). The effects of age and task domain on dual task performance: A meta-analysis. *European Journal of Cognitive Psychology, 16,* 863–891.

Rönnlund, M., & Nilsson, L.-G. (2006). Adult life-span patterns in WAIS block design performance: Cross sectional versus longitudinal age gradients and relations to demographic predictors. *Intelligence, 34,* 63–78.

Rönnlund, M., & Nilsson, L.-G. (2009). Flynn effects on sub-factors of episodic and semantic memory: Parallel gains over time and the same set of determining factors. *Neuropsychologia, 47,* 2174–2180.

Rönnlund, M., Nyberg, L., Bäckman, L., & Nilsson, L.-G. (2005). Stability, growth, and decline in adult life-span development of declarative memory: Cross-sectional and longitudinal data from a population-based study. *Psychology and Aging, 20,* 3–18.

Rubin, D. C., & Berntsen, D. (2006). People over forty feel 20% younger than their age: Subjective age across the lifespan. *Psychonomic Bulletin and Review, 13*(5), 776–780.

Salthouse, T. A. (1991). *Theoretical perspectives on cognitive aging.* Hillsdale, NJ: Erlbaum.

Salthouse, T. A. (1992). *Mechanisms of age-cognition relations in adulthood.* Hillsdale, NJ: Lawrence Erlbaum Associates.

Salthouse, T. A. (1996). The processing-speed theory of adult age differences in cognition. *Psychological Review, 103,* 403–428.

Salthouse, T. A., & Becker, J. T. (1998). Independent effects of Alzheimer's disease on neuropsychological functioning. *Neuropsychology, 12,* 242–252.

Schacter, D. L., Koutsaal, W., & Norman, K. A. (1997). False memories and aging. *Trends in Cognitive Sciences, 1,* 229–236.

Shimamura, A. P., Berry, J. M., Mangels, J. A., Rustings, C. L., & Jurica, P. J. (1995). Memory and cognitive abilities in academic professors: Evidence for successful aging. *Psychological Science, 6,* 271–277.

Spinnler, H., Della Sala, S., Bandera, R., & Baddeley, A. D. (1988). Dementia, ageing and the structure of human memory. *Cognitive Neuropsychology, 5,* 193–211.

Squire, L. R. (1987). *Memory and brain.* New York: Oxford University Press.

Sunderland, A., Harris, J. E., & Baddeley, A. D. (1983). Do laboratory tests predict everyday memory? A neuropsychological study?. *Journal of Verbal Learning and Verbal Behavior, 22,* 341–357. doi:10.1016/S0022-5371(83)90229-3

Sunderland, A., Watts, K., Baddeley, A. D., & Harris, J. E. (1986). Subjective memory assessment and test performance in the elderly. *Journal of Gerontology, 41,* 376–385.

Tan, C. H., Low, K. A., Kong, T., Fletcher, M. A., Zimmerman, B., Maclin, E. L., ... Fabiani, M. (2017). Mapping cerebral pulse pressure and arterial compliance over the adult lifespan with optical imaging. *PLoS ONE, 12.* doi:10.1371/journal.pone0171305

van Praag, H., Kempermann, G., & Gage, F. H. (2000). Neural consequences of environmental enrichment. *Nature Reviews Neuroscience, 1,* 191–198.

Verhaeghen, P., Marcoen, A., & Gossens, L. (1993). Facts and fiction about memory aging: A quantitative integration of research findings. *Journal of Gerontology: Psychological Sciences, 48,* 157–171.

Welford, A. T. (1985). Changes of performance with age: An overview. In N. Charness (Ed.), *Aging and human performance* (pp. 333–369). New York: Wiley.

Willingham, D. B., & Winter, E. (1995). Comparison of motor skill learning in elderly and young human subjects. *Society for Neuroscience Abstracts, 21,* 1440.

Wilson, B. A., Cockburn, J., & Baddeley, A. D. (1989). Assessment of everyday memory functioning following severe brain injury. In M. E. Miner & K. A. Wagner (Eds.), *Neurotrauma: Treatment, rehabilitation, and related issues* (pp. 83–99). Stoneham, MA: Butterworths.

Wilson, B. A., Cockburn, J., Baddeley, A. D., & Hiorns, R. (1989). The development and validation of a test battery for detecting and monitoring everyday memory problems. *Journal of Clinical and Experimental Neuropsychology, 11,* 855–870.

Wishart, L. R., & Lee, T. D. (1997). Effects of aging and reduced relative frequency of knowledge of results on learning a motor skill. *Perceptual and Motor Skills, 84,* 1107–1122.

Wright, B. M., & Payne, R. B. (1985). Effects of aging on sex differences in psychomotor reminiscence and tracking proficiency. *Journal of Gerontology, 40,* 179–184.

Contents

CHAPTER 16

WHEN MEMORY SYSTEMS FAIL

Alan Baddeley

We all have memory lapses, some more embarrassing than others. On one occasion, I agreed to talk about memory on a live radio phone-in program, the *Jimmy Mack Show* from Glasgow. As I lived in Cambridge at the time, it was agreed that I would participate from the local radio station. That morning I was reading the newspaper before checking my diary and setting off for work, when I glanced at the TV and radio section, prompting the awful realization that I should at that moment be telling the world about the wonders of memory. I leapt on my bike and arrived just before the end of the program, sheepishly muttering about the terrible traffic in Cambridge, to be asked by the host if I could give the listeners a few hints on how to improve their memory! On another occasion, I turned up to give an important lecture on amnesia, only to discover that I had forgotten my slides.

So we all have bad memories (though perhaps not as bad as mine), but what is it like to have a genuine memory problem—not the devastatingly dense amnesia experienced by Clive Wearing and described in Chapter 1, but the much more common level of memory deficit that accompanies many conditions including stroke, Alzheimer's disease, and traumatic brain injury? A very good account of the problems associated with memory deficit is given by Malcolm Meltzer, a clinical psychologist who experienced memory problems following a heart attack that led to anoxia (Meltzer, 1983). Having given you some idea as to what it is like to experience a serious memory problem, I will move onto a brief account as to the role that cognitive psychology can play in helping to deal with such problems. This will be followed by an account of two of the most frequent causes of memory disruption, Alzheimer's disease (AD), an increasing problem with aging population, and traumatic brain injury (TBI) such as might follow a road traffic accident or a sports injury often occurring in a young population and resulting in a lifetime of cognitive handicap of which memory is a prominent feature.

AMNESIA: THE PATIENT AND THE PSYCHOLOGIST

The patients' view

Meltzer's heart attack was followed by a period of coma lasting for six weeks before he finally recovered consciousness, knowing who he was and recognizing his family, but thinking he was 33 years old whereas in fact he was 44. On returning home, he could not remember where things were kept and, unlike a pure amnesic patient, also had problems in remembering skills such as how to set an alarm clock, when bills should be paid, where was a good place to go for a vacation, and how one might get there. He also had problems with his working memory:

Organization of thinking was hampered …
I had trouble keeping the facts in mind,
which made it difficult to organize them …
comparing things along a number of variables
is difficult to do when you cannot retain the
variables.
(Meltzer, 1983, p. 4)

Meltzer found it hard work to watch films or TV because of the difficulty in remembering the plot or, in the case of sports, which team was which and which was ahead. He tended to find spatial orientation difficult and even walks in a familiar neighborhood were liable to result in his getting lost. A particular problem was the impact of his amnesia on his capacity to interact with people:

Having conversations could become a trial.
Often in talking with people I was
acquainted with, I had trouble remembering
their names or whether they were married, or
what our relationship had been in the past.
I worried about asking where someone's wife
is and finding out that I had been at her
funeral two years before.
Often if I didn't have a chance to say
immediately what came to mind, it would be
forgotten and the conversation would move
to another topic. Then there was little for me
to talk about. I couldn't remember much
about current events or things I read in the
paper or saw on TV. Even juicy tit-bits of
gossip might be forgotten. So in order to have
something to say, I tended to talk about
myself and my "condition." My conversation
became rather boring.
(Meltzer, 1983, p. 5)

Eventually, with considerable perseverance, Meltzer recovered sufficiently to return to work, and of course to write a paper, pro-

viding for carers and therapists a very clear insight into the problems that result from memory deficit.

The view from psychology

Some years ago, I and a number of cognitive psychologists, interested in what memory deficits could tell us about normal memory, got together for a joint conference with a group of clinical neuropsychologists directly concerned with helping patients. I agreed to give the opening lecture, somewhat ambitiously attempting an overview of the whole of human memory in 55 minutes. The meeting was well attended and, to my relief, I managed my overview, without too many in

Box 16.1a Test your memory

First copy the figure below:

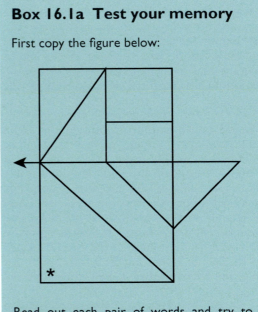

Read out each pair of words and try to remember which word goes with which.

head—hair
bread—crust
dog—cat
sheep—roof
house—sheep
fork—carpet

Now turn to p. 506, Box 16.1c

the audience going to sleep and indeed had time for questions. A chap at the back then stood up and asked "How does all this help me when I see my next patient on Monday morning?" A fair question? Perhaps not at that point in the conference, but a question I have continued to bear in mind and use to guide my continuing interest in applying cognitive psychology to clinical questions.

As I hope you will have noticed from previous chapters, the study of patients with memory problems has made a very substantial contribution of our understanding of how memory works. Patient HM convinced people of the need to separate long-term and short-term memory (see Chapter 2, p. 25). Patients with impaired STM such as PV have played a crucial role in the fractionation of working memory and of the usefulness of the concept of a phonological loop (see Chapter 4, p. 74), while clinical evidence has been crucial in understanding both semantic memory (see Chapter 7) and autobiographical memory (see Chapter 11). In my experience, patients are almost invariably generous in helping us understand the nature of their deficit, even though it is made clear to them that they themselves are unlikely to derive direct benefit. They typically report that if studying them can help others, then they are very happy to take part. But has cognitive psychology been clinically helpful? When and how has it been useful?

I want to try to answer this question by taking you through the various stages whereby a clinician might try to help a patient complaining of memory problems, highlighting the way in which the cognitive psychology of memory can contribute and at the same time telling you something about the disorders that the clinician might encounter. I will illustrate some of the clinical tests commonly used and encourage you to try brief versions, not of the tests themselves, since making them generally available would compromise their clinical value, but using material of a similar type. As you will see, there are often clear links between many such tests and earlier research by cognitive psychologists.

So if you were the clinician, seeing a patient next Monday morning, what would you need to do? You would be likely to begin

Box 16.1b Test your vocabulary

Each of these pairs contains a word and an invented nonword. Your task is to spot the word and mark it with a tick.

	a	b
1	porridge	brantle
2	implusion	estuary
3	venusial	osculate
4	fractious	jimble
5	ruminant	filliary
6	interpractic	episcopal
7	actuarial	strictive
8	exultist	trumpery
9	felucca	lapidism
10	autoplast	vacillating
11	imprecation	tuppler
12	asteroid	interfractive
13	phrenotide	trappist
14	interplosion	apparel
15	oboe	lentism
16	craster	vizier

Answers: 1a, 2b, 3b, 4a, 5a, 6b. 7a, 8b, 9a, 10b, 11a, 12a, 13b, 14b, 15a, 16b.

by assessing the patient allowing you to contribute to diagnosis. In doing so, you would probably identify the patient's principal problems, leading in due course to treatment and its subsequent evaluation. You would begin by talking to the patient and possibly an accompanying carer about their own views of the problem and what they hope to achieve, tactfully making it clear that a complete restitution of memory is very unlikely. The patient's account is important but not necessarily reliable; some patients are painfully aware of their difficulties while others are not. One of the first amnesic patients I tested responded to each failure to remember with the exclamation "How strange, I pride myself on my memory!"

Assessment is important in a number of ways. It contributes to the diagnosis of the clinical problem underlying the memory deficit, a process that will involve combining such test results with information from a number of other professionals and, if available, from neuroimaging techniques. Standardized test results will allow the patient's performance to be compared to healthy people using standardized norms, and to be related to the clinician's experience of others suffering from cognitive impairment. Such data are also important in communicating information about the patient to other professionals in a standardized way, and if the patient is to receive rehabilitation, then their pattern of strengths and weaknesses will be important in planning the treatment program. Finally, if the psychologist is conducting research, then specification of the patient is essential for any subsequent publication.

Assessment tests thus play an important role in treatment, and in addition provide a means whereby new discoveries can begin to influence clinical practice. Assessment is likely to depend ultimately on earlier research, much of it influenced by both concepts and methods that originated in the cognitive laboratory. This is also true of the methods devised to help the patient cope with memory problems. These will be discussed later, although it is important to bear in mind that rehabilitation will need to call on knowledge and expertise that goes well beyond the remit of cognitive psychology.

Unlike many of the patients described in earlier chapters because of their theoretical relevance a typical patient may have a range of perceptual, motor, cognitive, and potentially also emotional problems. All need to be assessed and taken into account in planning further treatment. For present purposes, however, we will focus on memory deficits, referring to other factors only in as far as they interact with problems of memory. We begin with two important and frequent sources of memory problems, Alzheimer's disease (AD), a problem of old age where memory is likely to deteriorate progressively over time while the other, traumatic brain injury (TBI), often occurs in young people who will probably experience their memory problems throughout a life of normal length. We will then look at what our knowledge of memory can tell us about such deficits, concluding with a discussion of how such patients can be helped to cope with the problem of living with a memory disorder.

ALZHEIMER'S DISEASE

In 1907, Dr Alois Alzheimer first described the disease that bears his name. It is a devastating disease of the elderly with symptoms that vary but always include an increasingly severe deficit in episodic memory. Alzheimer's disease (AD) is the most prominent but by no means the only cause of senile dementia (see Box 16.2). It does however comprise over 50% of dementia cases and occurs in about 10% of the population over the age of 65 with the rate increasing with age.

Diagnosis

Box 16.3 shows 10 potential signs of Alzheimer's disease described in a report by the US Academy of Neurology. Because of the varied range of symptoms, the early stages of AD can be difficult to diagnose; diagnosis requires that there is a memory impairment together with at least two other deficits, which can include problems of language, action control, perception, or executive

> **Box 16.1c Testing your memory**
>
> First, try to remember and draw the figure you copied.
>
> Now try to remember the words that were linked to each of the following:
>
> dog?
> fork?
> head?
> house?
> sheep?
> bread?
>
> Turn back to p. 504 and check your answers.

Box 16.2 The dementias

Dementia is an umbrella term describing symptoms that occur when the brain is affected by diseases. They are typically progressive and associated with aging, although earlier forms of dementia also occur. There is a range of types of which the following are more common.

Alzheimer's disease

The most common cause as discussed in the text.

Vascular dementia

Reduced oxygen supply to the brain may lead to cell death. This can occur either suddenly following a stroke, or more gradually through a series of strokes.

Dementia with Lewy bodies

Named from the small spherical structures that develop inside nerve cells leading to degeneration of the main tissue. Initial symptoms tend to be visual rather than memory problems. It is suggested it may be related to dementia that sometimes occurs with Parkinson's disease, for which motor symptoms are most common.

Fronto-temporal dementia

Involves deterioration of neurons in the frontal and/or temporal lobes resulting in changes in behavior and personality, and potentially leading to difficulties with language. Relatively rare.

Semantic dementia

Progressive loss of semantic memory involves failing comprehension of both words and pictures. Associated with atrophy of the temporal lobes, particularly in the left fronto-temporal region. Relatively rare but important theoretically because of its implication for understanding semantic memory (see Chapter 7).

function. The disease is progressive over time and, ultimately, diagnosis currently depends on a post-mortem examination of the brain tissue, revealing two cardinal signs of AD: amyloid plaques and neurofibrillary tangles. Plaques are created by faulty protein division. This results in the production of beta amyloid, which is toxic to neurons and leads to the formation of the clumps of amyloid that form the plaques. Neurofibrillary tangles occur within the neurons and are based on the microtubules that structure and nourish the cell. Abnormal proteins form, resulting in the twisting and collapse of the microtubules, and ultimately in cell death (St George-Hyslop, 2000).

However, while the amyloid hypothesis has dominated the field for many years, it has recently been increasingly questioned. Both plaques and tangles are often found in the normal aging brain, while cases of dementia have been found in the absence of plaques and tangles. A few hours after writing this sentence, it was announced that a major trial involving collaboration between three drug

Box 16.3 Warning signs of Alzheimer's disease

The American Academy of Neurology proposed the following guidelines (Petersen et al., 2001):

1 Memory loss that affects job skills
2 Difficulty performing familiar tasks
3 Problems with language
4 Disorientation to time and place (getting lost)
5 Poor or decreased judgment
6 Problems with abstract thinking
7 Misplacing things
8 Changes in mood or behavior
9 Changes in personality
10 Loss of initiative

It is suggested that people who show several of these should see their doctor for a thorough examination.

companies based on the amyloid approach had been discontinued, together with an announcement from the Alzheimer's Drug Discovery Foundation that future trials would focus on treatments other than those focused on the amyloid hypothesis. They report that of the 102 drugs currently being tested to treat Alzheimer's disease, 74% focused on targets other than amyloid (Neuro Central news bulletin, July 19, 2019).

The disease typically develops through a series of stages (Braak & Braak, 1991) beginning in the medial temporal lobes and hippocampus, creating the initial memory problems, and then progressing to the temporal and parietal lobes and to other brain regions. Consistent with this anatomical diversity, a close examination of an extensive sample of well-studied patients indicated a wide and varied pattern of neuropsychological deficits (Baddeley, Della Sala, & Spinnler, 1991). A further extensive analysis of data from 180 patients and over 1,000 normal elderly individuals suggests that despite the potential presence of a varied range of other cognitive deficits, AD is basically characterized by a single overall feature, namely that of defective episodic memory (Salthouse & Becker, 1998). It is important to note, however, that a memory deficit is necessary for diagnosis, so this is perhaps unsurprising.

At the level of the individual patient, the disease can develop from an initial tendency to absentmindedness and memory failure, progressing to increasingly severe and potentially varied cognitive symptoms. These were well illustrated in a case study of the Oxford philosopher and novelist Iris Murdoch, as described by Garrard, Malony, Hodges, and Patterson (2005). They compared the sentence content and structure of one of Murdoch's early novels, *Flight from the Enchanter*, with a middle novel, *The Sea, the Sea*, and her final novel, *Jackson's Dilemma*. They found that her last novel used considerably shorter sentences and more high-frequency words, suggesting that she was adapting to her growing language constraints. As the disease progressed, her linguistic problems increased, including word-finding difficulties, which she avoided

Iris Murdoch was a famous novelist who suffered from Alzheimer's disease and displayed many typical cognitive symptoms and linguistic constraints. Her life story was turned into the 2001 film *Iris* starring Kate Winslet and Judi Dench as the younger and older Iris respectively. It went on to win an Oscar, a Golden Globe, and a BAFTA, amongst many other awards.

by circumlocutions. She showed major problems in word definition, for example describing a bus as "something carried along." Her spelling deteriorated, with a word such as *cruise* being written as *crewes*, and her capacity to name pictures or to generate items from a given semantic category such as animals was increasingly impaired.

Although the decline in cognitive performance in dementia can be very worrying, social and emotional deterioration can be even more distressing, sometimes leading to the feeling of a spouse that "this is not the person I married." In the case of Iris Murdoch, she appeared to maintain a very amiable disposition (Bayley, 1998), but sadly this is by no means always the case. For present purposes, however, we will limit discussion to the effects of AD on memory.

Episodic memory

By the time AD has been reliably diagnosed, patients are likely to show a substantial deficit in episodic memory whether measured by recall or recognition, using verbal or visual material or based on measures of everyday memory (Greene, Hodges & Baddeley, 1995; Spinnler, Della Sala, Bandera, & Baddeley, 1988). As in the classic amnesic syndrome, the recency effect in free recall is relatively well preserved, although performance on earlier items is grossly impaired. There is evidence that as the disease progresses even recency tends to decline (Miller, 1971).

Forgetting

Despite the difficulty AD patients have in acquiring new information, once learned it appears to be forgotten no more rapidly than occurs in the normal elderly (Christensen, Kopelman, Stanhope, Lorentz, & Owen, 1998). Kopelman (1985) took advantage of the fact that people tend to be very good at picture recognition, taking care to vary the exposure time so as to equate the performance of normal, AD, and elderly participants when tested after five minutes. He then retested them after a 24-hour delay and found equivalent performance across the groups.

As noted in the case of Iris Murdoch, semantic memory declines as the disease progresses. Hodges and colleagues devised a battery for measuring semantic memory using a range of different tasks designed to ensure that any deficit observed is general, and not the result of perceptual or linguistic problems. A clear semantic deficit would be reflected in difficulties in naming pictures of objects or animals, in picking the appropriate picture given its name, in describing the characteristic of a named or pictured object, or in answering general questions such as whether an elephant has pricked up or floppy ears. In a series of studies, the Hodges group observed a steady decline in semantic memory in AD patients that was associated with degree of temporal lobe atrophy (Hodges & Patterson, 1995; Hodges, Patterson, & Tyler, 1994). The decline of semantic memory is even more precipitous in semantic dementia, a disease in which episodic memory is relatively well preserved, with atrophy occurring principally in the left temporal lobe rather than the more medial focus that tends to be found in AD (Snowden, Neary, & Mann, 1996).

Nuns from the Sisters of Notre Dame convent in Minnesota, who were participants in Snowden's (1997) longitudinal study of aging.

Implicit memory

Perhaps unsurprisingly, given that implicit learning and memory can reflect a number of different systems, the pattern of deficit in AD is somewhat complex. Heindel, Salmon, Shults, Walicke, and Butters (1989) tested patients with AD on the pursuit rotor, which you may recall is a task which requires keeping a stylus in contact with a moving target. The patients performed less well initially, but improved at the same rate as an elderly control group. Similarly, Moscovitch (1982) found little impairment in the rate at which AD patients learned to read mirror-reversed words.

Fleischman, Vaidya, Lange, and Gabrieli (1997) found normal priming in a lexical decision task involving the speed of deciding whether a sequence of letters comprised a real word or not. However, unlike the classic amnesic syndrome, implicit memory was not spared when tested by stem completion, in which patients were shown a word (*stamp*) and later ask to "guess" a word beginning with *st*. In general, patients with AD tend to show intact priming on relatively automatic tasks but reduced priming on more complex tasks, for example when recall is primed by presenting associatively related cue words (Salmon & Heindel, 1992; Salmon, Shimamura, Butters, & Smith, 1988).

Working memory in Alzheimer's disease

A working memory deficit occurs but is typically less marked than that of episodic memory, with modest but reliable deficits in both digit span and on the Corsi block tapping test of visuo-spatial memory (Spinnler et al., 1988). Patients are able to maintain small amounts of material over an unfilled delay but, when the delay is filled with articulatory suppression, patients with AD rapidly forget, whereas normal elderly participants show a decline only when the interpolated task is intellectually demanding, counting backwards in threes (Morris, 1986; Morris & Baddeley, 1988). This suggests that maintenance by simple articulation remains, but that more complex or attention-demanding forms of rehearsal are lost.

To test the executive capacity of patients with AD, Baddeley, Logie, Bressi, Della Sala, and Spinnler (1986) devised a series of tasks that combined auditory digit recall, like repeating a telephone number, with a concurrent nonverbal task. In one study, for example, number of digits was adjusted so that AD, elderly, and young participants all performed at the same level of single task accuracy. A similar matching occurred for a secondary tracking task in which participants had to keep a stylus in contact with a moving spot of light, with the difficulty modulated by varying the speed of movement of the spot. Having equated the two groups on the individual tasks, they were then required to perform the memory span and tracking tasks simultaneously. Young and normal elderly subjects both showed an equivalent small decrement under the combined condition, whereas the patients with AD showed a marked decline in performance, that became more marked as the disease progressed (Baddeley, Baddeley, Bucks, & Wilcock, 2001). The AD deficit in dual-task performance was not simply due to task difficulty, as young, older, and AD groups responded in a similar way to an increase in difficulty level on a single task, while AD patients but not controls continued to show a dual-task deficit even when each of the combined tasks were very easy (Logie, Cocchini, Della Sala, & Baddeley, 2004). The fact that AD patients but not healthy elderly have difficulty in combining tasks is potentially useful for diagnosis. Memory testing is crucial but can be harder to interpret since performance is also likely to be impaired by a range of other conditions, including of course normal aging (see Chapter 15).

More recently, measures of visual working memory have been studied in AD, yielding a very striking new effect, namely a clear impairment in the capacity to bind features such as color and shape into remembered objects (see Chapter 3, p. 57). A series of studies by Mario Parra of the Edinburgh neuropsychology group has not only demonstrated this (Parra et al., 2009) but has extended his work to a rare genetic form of familial AD found in Colombia in which any family member with the specific gene suffers early-onset AD, typically beginning in their forties. Parra was able to demonstrate the sensitivity of his binding measure to already diagnosed cases, but remarkably, was also able to detect which family members possessed the fatal gene at a time when they appeared to have no other current symptoms of AD (Parra et al., 2010). This task clearly also has the potential, given further development, to serve as an early detector of AD.

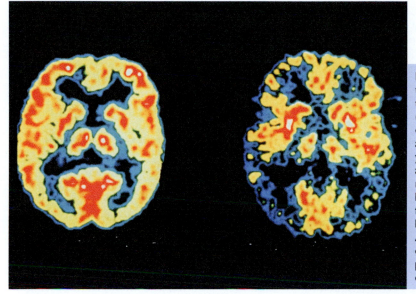

Positron emission tomography (PET) scans of the brain of a normal patient (left) versus an Alzheimer's disease patient. High brain activity displays as red and yellow; low activity as blue and black. The scan on the right shows reduction of both function and blood flow in both sides of the brain, a feature often seen in Alzheimer's. Alzheimer's disease is the most prominent cause of senile dementia.

Other aspects of attentional control have been less thoroughly studied, but the evidence available suggests that some at least are comparatively spared. For example, the capacity for sustained attention or vigilance does not appear to be particularly compromised (see Perry & Hodges, 1999, for a review).

As we learn more about AD, we are likely to become better at early diagnosis, but then what?

Treatment

In an extensive review of available treatments, Doody et al. (2001) discuss both pharmacological and behavioral attempts to alleviate AD. At that time, they identified three drugs that appeared to have some effect in slowing the course of the disease, namely *donepezil*, *rivastigmine*, and *galantamine*. These operate as inhibitors of cholinesterase, a substance that breaks down the neurotransmitter acetylcholine. Acetylcholine tends to be depleted in AD, hence the value of drugs that resist further depletion. There is a huge interest in this area within the pharmaceutical industry, given that AD is a disease that inflicts enormous cost on society at both a financial and human level. This cost is increasing as the age structure of the population changes from the historic pattern in which the young greatly outnumbered the old, to one in which more and more of the population survive into old age.

Over the past 25 years there has been an intense search for a drug that could arrest the progress of the disease, but currently, as described above, with little obvious progress.

In the meantime, there is growing interest in the need to provide emotional and social support to both the patients and carers in what is inevitably a highly stressful situation in which the magnitude of cognitive disruption may be less important than potential changes in personality—"this is not the person I married!", or in the potential breakdown of what was already a difficult relationship. This had led to an extensive studies of psychotherapeutic approaches with some limited evidence for their effectiveness (e.g., Benbow & Sharman, 2014; Cheston & Ivanecka, 2017) although whether improvements preserved are sufficient to make them cost effective in a financially limited medical service remains in doubt (Orgeta, Qazi, Spector, & Orrell, 2015; Søgaard et al., 2014).

In the meantime, there is considerable interest in behavioral approaches to individual patients and their carers. It is possible to use some of the methods described in the final section of this chapter to teach skills that will stand the patient in good stead as the disease advances (Clare et al., 2000). For example, patients can be taught to use simple memory aids, such as message boards or calendars, to avoid the need constantly to ask carers the same question, which is one of the most wearing features of supporting a densely amnesic patient. A related approach is to modify the environment in simple but useful ways. Moffat (1989), for example, describes the case of a patient who was constantly mislaying his spectacles and his pipe. His frustration level was reduced by a program training him always to return his spectacles and pipe to a bright orange bag (hopefully fire proof!). He would not remember where he left them, but could find them easily.

A number of programs have attempted to bring together techniques and skills aimed at helping the patient and the carer to cope as the disease progresses. Spector, Davies, Woods, and Orrell (2000) describe a program that improved performance on the specific areas trained, and tended to reduce levels of depression, although—as in the case of other programs of memory training for the elderly —this did not generalize to other aspects of performance.

As mentioned earlier, the purely cognitive aspects of AD are not typically the most distressing, and there is increasing interest in ways of helping patients and carers to cope with the social and emotional stresses imposed by AD. One disturbing feature of memory loss can be the problem of maintaining a sense of personal identity. This is particularly likely to be a problem for patients who need to move to a care home, and so are separated from their normal home environment and hence are surrounded by new and unfamiliar people. A number of approaches to this problem have been developed. One is reality orientation training (ROT), which involves helping patients maintain orientation in time and place, not necessarily a pleasant prospect given certain realities. An occupational therapist tells the story of an elderly man admitted to a hospital based in a rather grand Victorian building. He was densely amnesic and interpreted his situation as staying in a rather splendid hotel at the seaside. The overenthusiastic therapist carefully taught him to look at the calendar to say the date and to announce the name of the hospital where he was living, which he duly did, only to wink and say "But I know I am really at a grand hotel at the seaside!"

A rather more helpful approach is provided by a technique known as reminiscence therapy, which helps patients to maintain a sense of personal identity by recollecting their past (Woods & McKiernan, 2005). This can involve constructing a personal life story book, including photographs and other mementoes from earlier days. This not only has the advantage of reminding patients of their earlier life, but in a group context provides links with other patients who share experience of the past. It also provides things that they can tell the therapist, allowing a more natural interaction than might typically occur. However, although psychological approaches can be helpful, the best hopes

Reminiscence therapy helps patients to maintain a sense of personal identity by recollecting their past by constructing a personal life-story book including photographs and other mementoes.

KEY TERM

Reality orientation training (ROT): A method of treating patients in the latter stages of dementia who have lost their orientation in time and place.

Reminiscence therapy: A method of helping dementia patients cope with their growing amnesia by using photographs and other reminders of their past life.

for the future must lie with pharmacology, although progress has not been rapid.

In the meantime however there is a great deal that can be done to improve the quality of care of patients by providing adequate training of carers, institutional and in the home so as to understand the problems facing the patient, realizing for example that stimulation is not necessarily helpful and finding ways to avoid potential disruptive situations and irritating habits such as continually being asked the same question. Adequate input to carers by trained professionals at this level *is* likely to be cost effective (Clare, 2017).

TRAUMATIC BRAIN INJURY

A second common potential source of memory problems comes from traumatic brain injury (TBI) when the head perceives a sharp blow or is subject to a sudden acceleration on deceleration as in a car crash. The brain swirls around, resulting in damage from the bony protuberances within the skull, and from the twisting and shearing of fibers within the brain. The potential effects of TBI are extensive and can include social and emotional problems. However, for present purposes we will confine the discussion to cognitive deficits in attention and memory.

A few years ago I was waiting in a line of cars to leave a side road near a sea-coast resort when suddenly a blue figure arced in the air, to the horror and consternation of onlookers. It was a motorcyclist hit by a car turning into the side road, probably resulting in a serious head injury. Such injuries happen mainly to young men, and in the UK over 95% will survive with varying degrees of handicap. Other causes of TBI include falls, sports injuries, and, in the case of war veterans, blast, with an estimated 10–20% of returnees suffering from TBI. Overall, it was estimated that some 5.3 million Americans were currently living with some degree of TBI (Langlois, Rutland-Brown, & Wold, 2006).

So what sort of memory problems might our unfortunate motorcyclist expect? First of all, if the brain injury was severe, he might be expected to be in a coma, sometimes for many weeks. Indeed in the most serious cases, the patient may be left in what is known as a *persistent vegetative state* in which physical functions continue to perform but mental functions do not. This in turn leads to the terrible ethical problem as to how long one should artificially maintain life in such a case. Fortunately, in most cases there will be a gradual recovery, often so gradual that it can be missed by the medical support staff. To optimize this process of monitoring, Shiel, Wilson, McLellan, Horn, and Watson (2000) developed a scale entitled the Wessex Head Injury Matrix Scale (WHIM), which picks up the tiny changes that occur in behavior as the brain slowly recovers from major trauma.

Many of the most prevalent cognitive difficulties across a wide range of diseases result from impaired episodic memory. I will therefore begin by describing a pure case of impaired episodic memory as reflected in the classic amnesic syndrome, not because such a pure case is typical, but because it provides a very clear indication of types of problems that are likely to be encountered to a greater or lesser degree, by a wide range of patients.

EPISODIC MEMORY IMPAIRMENT

Anterograde amnesia

A crucial distinction is that between anterograde amnesia and retrograde amnesia. Anterograde amnesia refers to a problem in encoding, storing, or retrieving ongoing information that can be used in the *future*,

KEY TERM

Anterograde amnesia: A problem in encoding, storing, or retrieving information that can be used in the future.

Retrograde amnesia: A problem accessing events that happened in the past.

hence the prefix *antero*. By contrast, retrograde amnesia refers to loss of access to events that happened in the *past*, typically before the onset of the disease. The densely amnesic patient HM described in Chapter 1 is the classic case of anterograde amnesia because his capacity for new learning was greatly restricted while his ability to recall events from before his operation was relatively preserved. This is in contrast to Clive Wearing, also described in Chapter 1, who showed both dense anterograde amnesia together with retrograde amnesia reflected in his very patchy access to earlier memories. Hence, these two forms of amnesia will be discussed separately. The broad pattern of episodic memory deficit shown by HM has now been replicated many times although pure cases with no evidence of further cognitive impairment are relatively rare. As a reminder of the pattern to be expected, I will describe one case with a particularly clear episodic memory deficit before discussing current interpretations of this syndrome and its theoretical implications.

Keith was a company director who in his 59th year experienced a headache combined with vomiting which continued for several days followed by extreme drowsiness. He seemed disoriented, did not appear to recognize his wife, and could only manage a few words. He was diagnosed with a brain infection, recovering slowly. He began rehabilitation only to relapse some five months after his initial attack, with further evidence of brain infection, accompanied by seizures. His brain infection was brought under control and eventually he was admitted to Rivermead Rehabilitation Centre in Oxford where his cognitive functioning was assessed (Wilson & Baddeley, 1988).

Despite his complex and stormy medical history, Keith proved to have a very pure deficit in episodic memory. He was highly intelligent with an IQ of 134. His perceptual and motor skills were excellent and he showed no evidence of executive deficit when tested on standard tests such as the Wisconsin Card Sorting Test, a sorting task which involves switching categories, while his verbal fluency, generating as many words as possible beginning with S and V in 90 seconds, was

also excellent. His immediate memory span was good, seven digits forward and six backward without error while his Corsi spatial memory span was above average for his age group. Performance on the Peterson short-term forgetting task was also normal whether retaining trigrams or three-digit numbers.

In contrast his episodic memory performance was grossly impaired. He could recall a prose passage immediately, with an above-average score but failed to recall anything after an hour's delay. Similarly he could copy a complex figure and recall it immediately, but completely failed after 40 minutes and did not even recognize the figure. His verbal free recall showed the classic pattern (Baddeley & Warrington, 1970) of normal recency with grossly impaired retention of earlier items. Keith showed the classic pattern of preserved procedural learning with consistent improvement over trials on pursuit rotor performance indicating good motor learning (Brooks & Baddeley, 1976) together with improvement in reading mirror written script (Cohen & Squire, 1980) and preserved capacity for learning words when prompted by stem completion (Warrington & Weiskrantz, 1970).

In short, Keith showed the classic pattern of results to be expected in any dense but pure amnesic patient. He was functioning intellectually at a high level on all except memory tests, showing grossly impaired performance on tests of episodic memory but with preserved performance on STM tasks and on tests involving procedural learning. Importantly, in Keith's case, semantic memory for events occurring before his brain infection was also preserved as measured not only by performance on vocabulary tests or speed of sentence processing, but also autobiographical memory when tested by semantically oriented questions such as the names of his school teachers, or memory for specific episodes. He could for example recount episodes experienced during the war and when questioned was able to describe the color of the dresses of the bridesmaids at his wedding. In short, Keith had substantial anterograde but preserved retrograde amnesia for events before his illness.

There is general agreement that in its pure form, the amnesic syndrome involves

The 2001 film *Memento* chronicles the story of Leonard, an ex-insurance investigator who can no longer build new memories, as he attempts to find the perpetrator of a violent attack which caused his post-traumatic anterograde amnesia and left his wife dead. The attack is the last event he can recall.

grossly impaired episodic memory together with preserved working memory, semantic memory, implicit memory, and intelligence. In practice, however, although episodic memory deficits are relatively common, they will often be accompanied by other cognitive deficits that need to be taken into account in treating the patient. Nevertheless, the episodic memory deficit is often a central feature of the problems encountered by many patients, reflecting a wide range of diagnoses. Hence understanding its nature is important if the patient is to be helped. Attempts to explain the amnesic syndrome can operate at two separate but related levels. One of these concerns the psychological functions that are disturbed, while the other concerns their neurobiological underpinnings. We will begin with explanations of amnesia at the psychological level, moving on later to the role of neurobiology.

Early hypotheses included greater susceptibility to interference leading to a retrieval deficit (Warrington & Weiskrantz, 1970), faster forgetting (Huppert & Piercy, 1979) and an incapacity for deep processing (Cermak, Butters, & Moreines, 1974), although all of these subsequently ran into problems (see Baddeley, 1990, ch. 16 for a discussion). It is, however, too soon to reject the possibility that faster forgetting, and/or susceptibility to interference may play a part

in some patients, possibly reflecting further additional deficits. However, whatever the precise mechanism, it seems likely that amnesia disrupts the capacity to associate a *specific* event or episode with its *context*, its location in time and place and that this allows individual specific memories to be retrieved. In a study using rats, Winocur and Mills (1970) observed that animals with hippocampal lesions were particularly bad at making use of environmental context in a spatial learning task, suggesting to Winocur (1978) that a failure to associate memories with context may also apply to human amnesic patients. This was later related to the discovery of specific "place cells" in the hippocampus (O'Keefe, 1976) a discovery that formed the basis for the award of a Nobel prize to John O'Keefe, while others have identified cells that appear to be time-based (Eichenbaum, 2014) making the hippocampus a very appropriate system for encoding contextual cues that can later be used to identify and retrieve specific events distinguishing for example remembering what you did this morning from events happening on many other mornings. This can make it difficult to know what is the origin of a particular memory, a process known as "source memory." This was demonstrated by Schacter, Harbluk, and McLachlan (1984), using as their material the answers to trivial pursuit questions such as what was the favorite food of the comedian and film star Bob Hope, finding that although amnesic patients may be able to recall the "fact," they are bad at recalling that they had just been given this information.

You may recall from Chapter 6 (pp. 164, 192), Tulving's description of episodic memory as a system that allows "mental time travel." Amnesic patients clearly have problems in traveling to the recent past; what about the future? Amnesic patients may indeed have difficulty in imagining future activities, such as lying on a sandy tropical beach surrounded by palm trees. However, the patients *were* able to imagine the component experiences, but could not integrate them into a whole, a deficit that Hassabis, Kumaran, Vann, and Maguire (2007) attribute to the importance of the hippocampus for spatial processing as well as memory.

A simplified model

In an attempt to pull together the overall pattern of data on the amnesic syndrome, I proposed what I termed a modal model of amnesia, a simple interpretation of the amnesic syndrome that appeared to capture most if not all of the evidence (Baddeley, 1990). This accepted a deliberately unspecified consolidation hypothesis, whereby learning in episodic memory involves associating items with their context using some form of "mnemonic glue." This clearly nontechnical term was deliberately selected so as to indicate that it was *not* based on any sophisticated neurobiological evidence but simply accepted that a neurobiological interpretation of some form seemed necessary. This view is consistent with a contextual hypothesis, on the assumption that the essence of episodic memory is the capacity to "glue" experiences to a specific context, thus providing a contextual tag that allows individual experiences to be retrieved.

This simplified model of amnesia assumed that recall and recognition involve the same underlying storage processes, although they place different constraints on subsequent retrieval. It assumed that semantic memory represents the residue of many episodes. Over time, the capacity to retrieve individual

experiences might have been lost through forgetting, but it was assumed that semantic memory, based on those common features that accumulated over repeated episodes, could be retrieved through a separate mechanism based on long-term knowledge. Although this modal model seemed to give a plausible account of the classic amnesic syndrome, it was not clear how to test it and I myself ceased to work on amnesia.

Some years later, however, I was asked to talk about amnesia at a retirement symposium for the distinguished neuropsychologist Elizabeth Warrington. Because of our earlier work together, I agreed. I had not subsequently published anything on my speculative modal model of amnesia and thought it would be a good opportunity to obtain feedback from an expert audience. Despite absent-mindedly leaving my slides on the train en route, the talk seemed to go reasonably well. Then, shortly after the meeting, I was invited by Faraneh Vargha-Khadem, a neuropsychologist from the Institute of Child Health in London, to visit and test a patient, Jon. I accepted. Testing Jon rapidly convinced me that my modal model of amnesia was wrong. The reason was simple; if semantic memory is built up through an accumulation of episodes and Jon has had episodic memory deficits from an early age, then he should have grossly impaired semantic memory. He did not. Indeed Jon's amnesia differed from the classic pattern in a number of ways that challenge existing theory. Unlike most amnesic patients, despite having severely impaired recognition, Jon had well-preserved recall memory, again challenging an assumption of my simple modal model (see Figure 16.1).

A similar level of relatively preserved recognition performance together with marked recall deficit was found on a wide range of other tests by Vargha-Khadem, Gadian, and Mishkin (2001) and have subsequently been reported for a range of similar developmental cases (Bindschaedler, Peter-Favre, Maeder, Hirsbrunner, & Clarke, 2011; Brizzolara, Casalini, Montanaro, & Posteraro, 2003).

However, it was Jon's semantic memory that appeared to create the most crucial problem for my simple modal model. If it is

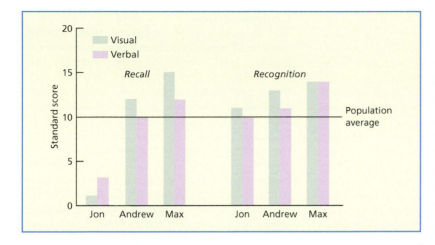

Figure 16.1 Performance on the Doors and People Test of visual and verbal recall by Jon, a developmental amnesic patient, and two controls. Jon is impaired on recall but not recognition. From Baddeley et al. (2001b). Copyright © 2001 MIT Press. Reproduced with permission.

based on the accumulation of episodic memories then Jon's semantic memory should be grossly impaired as should his level of education, vocabulary, and verbal IQ. In fact Jon had relatively high IQ, with good vocabulary, and while his scholastic achievements were less than might be expected given his IQ, they were respectable. Furthermore he could discuss UK politics and could tell you all about the novels of Terry Pratchett and the associated "Discworld." Subsequent research suggests, however, that although Jon's knowledge of the world is excellent, it might take him longer than controls to acquire new facts (Gardiner, Brandt, Baddeley, Vargha-Khadem, & Mishkin, 2008). Finally, if recall and recognition involve essentially the same storage process, why, in Jon's case, can recognition be so well preserved and recall so impaired?

A hint as to the answer to this question comes from the previously described distinction between *remembering* and "knowing" (see Chapter 8). You will recall that "remembering" is based on the capacity to recollect an episode, "to travel backwards in time" to re-experience it, in contrast to the capacity to *know* that one has previously encountered an item, in the absence of such recollective experience (see Chapter 8). We attempted to assess Jon's capacity to "remember," but had considerable difficulty teaching him the distinction between remembering and knowing. Eventually, he declared that he understood the distinction and we went ahead. Jon used

the remember-and-know categories about as often as controls. However, when control participants made a remember judgment they could describe their recollection, for example *The word "dog" reminded me of my granny's dachshund.* Jon did not. He reported that he tried to form a visual image of the cards on which the words had been presented, and if his image of the word was clear and bright then he categorized this as remembering. In short, he appeared to be using a strength rather than a recollective criterion, a suggestion that is further supported by questioning Jon about how he tried to perform the remember-know discrimination and by the different brain activity associated with these two mental states (Maguire, Vargha-Khadem, & Mishkin, 2001). This gives a possible explanation of Jon's relatively preserved recognition memory, but what about his excellent semantic memory?

A possible way of preserving the modal model's assumption of a common basis for semantic and episodic memory recently resulted from my writing a relatively personal account of my long and intellectually lively friendship with Endel Tulving (Baddeley, in press). Let us suppose that the hippocampus is not principally a structure necessary for learning per se, but is instead responsible for attaching time- and place-based retrieval cues to learning episodes that are created elsewhere within the medial temporal lobes, preserved in Jon but disrupted in most amnesic patients. Episodic retrieval would fail because of the lack of such crucial cues, while cuing using familiarity or pre-existing semantic associations will remain. The idea has survived for long enough to be included as an invited personal contribution to a respected neuropsychological journal, though whether it survives later critical examination remains to be seen.

There is no doubt that Jon is far from typical as an amnesic patient, most of whom are impaired on both recall and recognition tests. He is not however atypical of people with developmental amnesia. A recent study (Dzieciol et al., 2017) describes 18 patients who are compared both to matched controls and to populations norms. Their intelligence is well within the normal range as is their working memory, literacy, and numeracy, with above-average scores on both verbal and visually based measures of semantic memory. In contrast, their performance on a range of episodic memory tasks was grossly impaired when compared to the matched control group.

This pattern may however be limited to developmental amnesia. Squire and colleagues have presented data from groups of amnesic patients who appear to have lesions limited to the hippocampus, and who behave in the standard way, with no evidence of preserved recognition memory (Manns & Squire, 1999; Reed & Squire, 1997). Why the difference? One possibility is that Jon acquired his hippocampal damage at a very early age whereas most amnesic patients become amnesic as adults and that the preserved capacity to learn reflects the greater plasticity of the infant brain. Some adult onset cases have however been reported (Aggleton & Brown, 1999; Mayes, Holdstock, Isaac, Hunkin, & Roberts, 2002), but the adult evidence is much less well studied than the developmental group.

We have so far discussed the proposed focal deficit in amnesia, namely the binding of items to their context, and located this deficit principally in the hippocampus. We consider next the process that is necessary for the long-term learning of such bound information, consolidation of the memory trace.

Consolidation

The dominant explanation of both antero-grade and retrograde amnesia at a neurobiological level rests on the concept of consolidation, the hypothesis that memory traces are initially fragile and become more resistant to forgetting as time progresses, a view that is at least a century old (Müller & Pilzecker, 1900). This was initially applied to the amnesic syndrome by assuming that consolidation depends crucially on the hippocampus and related areas, and that disruption to this system interferes with the consolidation process. Evidence in favor of the role of consolidation in learning comes from research on sleep as described in Chapter 5. This shows that when learning is followed by a period of sleep, long-term retention is better than occurs when remaining awake during that time (e.g., Gaskell & Dumay, 2003; Stickgold, James, & Hobson, 2000).

Evidence consistent with effects of both consolidation and interference comes from a group directed by Sergio Della Sala in Edinburgh. They report a number of studies demonstrating that the retention of information by some amnesic patients was greatly enhanced if learning is immediately followed by removal of the patient to a quiet, dim, interference-free room. In one study, four densely amnesic patients and six controls attempted to remember a story an hour later. When the hour was spent in a darkened room, patients performed almost as well as controls. However, when the hour was filled with the sort of cognitive tasks that would normally constitute patient assessment, the patients remembered virtually nothing (Dewar, Cowan, & Della Sala, 2010). Another study tested patients suffering from mild cognitive impairment (MCI), a condition typically reflecting poor memory and potentially a forerunner of Alzheimer's disease. It showed a similar improvement in retention by the patients when learning was followed by removal to a quiet dark room, whereas this made little difference to the healthy control group. An obvious interpretation of these findings is to suggest that amnesic patients are particularly susceptible to the disruption of the process of consolidation, particularly during the early stages. This was tested directly by Dewar, Fernandez-Garcia, Cowan, and Della Sala (2009) in a study in which MCI patients and controls learned a list of words and were tested after a delay of nine minutes. As shown in Figure 16.2, they found that the patients were much more susceptible and that the earlier the disruption, the greater the forgetting. In addition to its obvious theoretical significance, this finding has considerable potential practical importance if it should prove widely applicable, and the learning observed reasonably robust. The process of hippocampal consolidation over this initial period is presumed to operate at the cellular and subcellular level probably based on the mechanism of long-term potentiation (LTP) described briefly in Chapter 2 (p. 33). However, analysis of the amnesic syndrome at the subcellular level does not yet appear to be well advanced.

Retrograde amnesia

Whereas anterograde amnesia refers to the failure to acquire new memories, retrograde amnesia refers to the impaired capacity to retrieve old memories. Patients often suffer from both; however, the severity of antero-

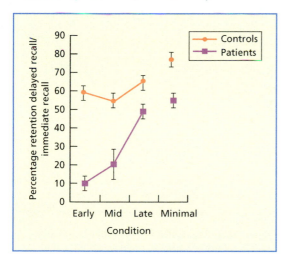

Figure 16.2 Dewar et al.'s (2009) study showed that amnesic patients are very susceptible to the disruption by later activity of the process of consolidation, particularly during its early stages. From Dewar et al. 2009. Copyright © American Psychological Association. Reprinted with permission.

grade is not highly correlated with degree of retrograde amnesia, suggesting different origins (Greene & Hodges, 1996; Shimamura & Squire, 1991). For example, two patients studied by Baddeley and Wilson (1986) both had dense but pure amnesias with high and well-preserved intelligence, but one (Keith, described earlier) appeared to have excellent retrograde memory and could, for example, talk in great detail about his wartime experiences, whereas the other had at best only a hazy memory of his past. He knew he had been in the Navy and gone to university but could not remember in what order; he knew he had previously broken his arm, but could not recall how.

Measuring the degree of retrograde amnesia presents one problem that is not shared with anterograde amnesia, namely that the tester typically does not have control over the learning of the material to be recalled, as learning might have occurred many years before. An early attempt to quantify degree of retrograde amnesia was made by Sanders and Warrington (1971), who presented their patients with photographs of people who were famous for a limited period at different points in time, finding that their amnesic patients typically performed more poorly on this task than controls. They also observed that earlier memories were better preserved, so-called *Ribot's law*. This asserts that older memories are more durable than those acquired more recently (Ribot, 1882).

A number of similar scales have subsequently been developed using a range of material, including news events, winners of classic horse races, and TV shows that aired for a single season (e.g., Squire, Haist, & Shimamura, 1989). This general method suffers from two practical problems. First, the degree of knowledge of news events or horse races is likely to vary substantially across patients; second, scales of this sort are, of course, continually aging, as the recent events become progressively more remote in time, hence requiring a continuous process of revising and revalidating.

An alternative method is to probe the patient's memory of their earlier life by requesting autobiographical recollections, which can then if necessary be checked through a spouse or carer (Zola-Morgan, Cohen, & Squire, 1983). Unfortunately, this is a somewhat laborious process; patients tend to produce large amounts of material, which must then be transcribed, checked, and evaluated, not a very practical method in a busy clinical context.

In an attempt to reduce these methodological problems, Kopelman, Wilson, and Baddeley (1990) developed the Autobiographical Memory Interview (AMI), which involved asking people to remember specific information selected from a range of time periods. Some were remote, for example the name of their first school, others intermediate, such as their first job, yet others probed more recent events, such as where the patient spent last Christmas. These were essentially factual questions that could be regarded as probing a form of personal semantic memory. In addition, for each life period, participants were asked to recollect a *specific* personal event. An example from childhood might be winning a race at school. These episodic recollections were then rated in terms of amount and specificity of information retrieved.

The test was validated using both healthy people and a range of patients and was found to be sensitive and reliable. Even patients with Korsakoff syndrome, who are commonly believed to be inclined to confabulate, produced either accurate recall, as validated by relatives, or simply said they could not remember (Kopelman et al., 1990). This and related scales have been used increasingly widely in line with the increased interest in autobiographical memory and its disorders (see Chapter 11). Retrograde amnesia generally leads to impairment in autobiographical memory on both the personal and the semantic scales. However, cases who show differential impairment do occur. De Renzi, Liotti, and Nichelli (1987) describe an Italian woman who could remember events of her personal life very well, but recalled virtually no public

events, neither the war which she had lived through, for example, nor the assassination of the Italian prime minister. The only public event that she seemed to remember was the wedding in England of Prince Charles to Lady Diana Spencer, who she described as a scheming girl just like the one that married her own son; a public event that she had personalized. Other studies have reported the opposite pattern. Dalla Barba, Cipolotti, and Denes (1990) describe a patient with alcoholic Korsakoff syndrome and a severe episodic memory deficit who was good at recalling famous people and events but could not remember aspects of personal autobiography.

It is important to distinguish between retrograde amnesia resulting from neurological damage and psychogenic amnesia that is typically a temporary state associated with emotional stress (see Chapter 10, pp. 318, 331). Figure 16.3 shows the pattern of retrograde amnesia as measured using the autobiographical episodes component of the Kopelman et al. (1990) test, given both during and after memory recovery (Harrison et al., 2017).

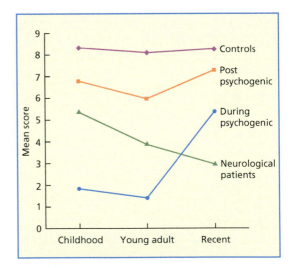

Figure 16.3 Recall of autobiographical events by patients suffering from psychogenic amnesia and neurological memory-disordered patients. The psychogenic group show particularly marked loss of memory from childhood and young adulthood during the amnesic episode, but show a much more normal pattern on recovery. Neurological patients remember earlier incidents better. Data from Harrison et al. (2017).

During the psychogenic amnesic phase more distant memories are less likely to be recalled, a pattern that disappears following recovery. The opposite pattern is shown by the neurological patients, a pattern that tends to persist over time.

Confabulation

Confabulation occurs when the reported autobiographical information is false but not intentionally misleading. A distinction can be made between spontaneous and provoked confabulation. Provoked confabulation can occur as a result of an amnesic patient's attempt to fill in a gap in knowledge, so as to avoid embarrassment. In one sense this is not too different from normal behavior, when we might produce a reasonably accurate account but include detail beyond what we can really remember, perhaps to make a better story. Spontaneous confabulation tends to be much more florid, is less common, and tends to be linked to frontal lobe damage.

Consider, for example, patient RR mentioned in Chapter 4, who had extensive bilateral damage to his frontal lobes following a driving accident (Baddeley & Wilson, 1988). When asked about the accident, he happily provided a detailed account that involved his getting out of his car and carrying out a polite but extremely repetitive conversation with the driver of the lorry that had hit him, with each apologizing to the other multiple times. He had in fact been unconscious for a lengthy period following the accident and could almost certainly not remember it. He was no longer capable of driving and gave a totally implausible account of how he had subsequently driven himself to the rehabilitation center, giving a lift to a fellow patient he rather ungallantly described as "a fat piece." Confabulation can also result in action. On one occasion, RR was found heading along the road outside the center pushing a fellow patient in a wheelchair to show his friend a sewage farm he was working on as an engineer. He had in fact worked on such a project, but it was many years ago and a good distance away.

Confabulation is typically found in patients with a dysexecutive syndrome, disruption to the operation of the central executive component of working memory (see Chapter 4, p. 82), resulting from damage, typically to both frontal lobes. This probably interferes with autobiographical memory in two ways. First, such patients have difficulty in setting up appropriate retrieval cues. The previously described patient RR, for example, was very poor at generating items from semantic categories. Given the category *animals*, for example, he produced *dog ... animals ... there must be thousands of them! ... Did I say dog?* However, given appropriate retrieval cues, *an Australian animal that hops*, for example, he readily came up with the right answer.

A second problem is that of evaluating the outcome of a memory search, with the result that information that would clearly be implausible to most normal or indeed most brain-damaged people is accepted and elaborated. RR responded in an autobiographical memory study to the cue word *letter*. He described sending a letter to an aunt recounting the death of his brother Martin. When he was reminded that Martin visited him regularly, he accepted this, claiming falsely that his mother had had a later son, also called Martin (Baddeley & Wilson, 1986).

Explaining retrograde amnesia

There have been fewer studies of retrograde than anterograde amnesia, and less extensive theoretical analysis. This has begun to change in recent years with a number of models proposed, often accompanied by computer simulations to check that they are indeed able to predict the results claimed. Three of these models—those of Alvarez and Squire (1994); McClelland, McNaughton, and O'Reilly (1995); and Murre (1996)—differ in detail, but all assume that the hippocampus and surrounding regions play a crucial role in memory consolidation. They typically assume two types of consolidation. The first, *hippocampal consolidation*, a relatively rapid process, operates at the cellular and subcellular level and involves the initial encoding of new information within the hippocampus. A second more long-term process termed *systems consolidation* is subsequently involved in gradually transferring information from the hippocampus to other brain regions for more long-term storage. These two types of consolidation are not, of course, mutually exclusive, although failure to consolidate at a cellular level will presumably interfere with any subsequent system consolidation.

The above three models differ in detail but all assume that the hippocampus and associated regions act as an intermediary, detecting and storing novel information at a relatively rapid rate, then holding it while it is gradually transferred to more cortical areas. Unlike hippocampal storage, which is relatively rapid but temporary, links within the cortex are assumed to take longer to set up, but are more durable. This consolidation process continues to progress within the neocortex after traces have been lost from the hippocampus, with the result that memory traces that have been in the brain for many years will be particularly robust, thus accounting for Ribot's law, the greater durability of early memory traces. The extent to which this process is consistent with my recent view of the hippocampus as a system for attaching retrieval cues rather than a basic learning system remains to be explored.

An alternative model is offered by the Multiple Trace Hypothesis, proposed by Nadel and Moscovitch (1997, 1998). They argue for the role of the hippocampus in *retrieval*, as well as encoding. They accept a version of the model just described, which they refer to as the "standard model," but assume that the process of long-term consolidation sets up recorded traces of experience within the hippocampal complex, leading to multiple replicas of earlier experiences. However, while this explains why retrieving memories is an effective method of learning as shown by Karpicke and Roediger (2008; see Chapter 5, p. 127), this does not explain why some densely amnesic patients have good long-term autobiographical memory while others do not (Baddeley & Wilson, 1988). The question of whether this or one of the more standard models gives the better account of retrograde amnesia remains an open question.

The study of relative "pure" memory disorders and their links to clearly specified areas of the brain has proved enormously useful in developing both our theories of memory and our knowledge of brain func-

tion. However, the typical clinician is likely to encounter many more patients for whom a serious memory deficit is only one of a range of symptoms, and where the association between the deficit and its anatomical localization is often unclear. From the patient's viewpoint, however, regardless of its origin, a memory deficit can be a crippling affliction. It is therefore important to study memory performance in diseases of this type, and to try to develop methods of helping patients to cope with the associated memory problems.

POST-TRAUMATIC AMNESIA AND CONSOLIDATION

On recovering consciousness, a patient with TBI from a severe fall, for example, is likely to move into a state of post-traumatic amnesia (PTA), in which attention can be disturbed and the capacity for new learning grossly impaired. Once again, it is important to be able to monitor this gradual recovery, and to do so a number of scales have been devised (Levin & Hanten, 2002). A study by High, Levin, and Gary (1990) monitored the progress through PTA of 84 patients whose brain injury was sufficient to lead to coma. They typically first recovered *personal knowledge*, who they were; followed by *place*, where they were; and finally *temporal orientation*. The estimated current date was typically displaced backwards, especially in more severe cases, where there could be an error of up to five years. As the patients recovered, the degree of error reduced, reflecting a shrinkage of their retrograde amnesia.

Length of time in PTA can vary considerably, and provides a rough, although not infallible, guide to level of probable recovery

(Levin, O'Donnell, & Grossman, 1979). Having recovered from PTA, the patient is likely to be left with a degree of retrograde amnesia. This might initially be quite extensive, but will shrink over time, as in the classic case described below.

A green-keeper, aged 22, was thrown from his motorcycle in August 1933. There was a bruise in the left frontal region and slight bleeding from the left ear but no fracture was seen on X-ray examination. A week after the accident he was able to converse sensibly and the nursing staff considered that he had fully recovered consciousness. When questioned, however, he said that the date was February 1922, and that he was a school boy. He had no recollection of 5 years spent in Australia and 2 years in the UK working on a golf course. Two weeks after the injury he remembered the 5 years spent in Australia and remembered returning to the UK; the past 2 years were, however, a complete blank as far as his memory was concerned. Three weeks after the injury, he returned to the village where he had been working for 2 years. Everything looked strange and he had no recollection of ever having been there before. He lost his way on more than one occasion. Still feeling a stranger to the district he returned to work; he was able to do his work satisfactorily but had difficulty in remembering what he had actually done during the day. About 10 weeks after the accident the events of the past 2 years were gradually recollected and finally he was able to remember everything up to within a few minutes of the accident.
(Russell, 1959, pp. 69–70)

The shrinkage in degree of retrograde amnesia is variable and typically less dramatic than that shown by our Australian green-keeper.

In Yarnell and Lynch's (1970) study of "dinged" American football players the player could generally recall the name of the play that had led to the collision immediately, but not when questioned later.

The dense period of continuing amnesia immediately preceding the TBI is, however, very characteristic. Is the problem one of registering the experience in the first place, or consolidation of the memory trace? Light is thrown on this issue by a study by Yarnell and Lynch (1970) of American football players who have been "dinged." As they were led off, the investigator asked the name of the play that had led to the collision (e.g., Pop 22). Typically, the player could remember it immediately, but not when questioned later. Although other interpretations are possible, this certainly is consistent with a lack of early neural consolidation of the memory trace.

There has, in recent years, been a growing interest in the long-term effects of playing high-contact games like American football. Gina Geffen, an Australian neuropsychologist, was asked to examine an Australian-rules football player who had sustained a head injury. To obtain a comparison group, she tested a number of his colleagues using a test of speed of semantic processing developed by Baddeley, Emslie, and Nimmo-Smith (1992). This involves the patient in reading a series of brief sentences that are either obviously true or obviously false. Typical positive sentences are *Nuns have religious beliefs* and *Shoes are sold in pairs*. Negative sentences are created by recombining positive instances, as in *Shoes have religious beliefs* and *Nuns are sold in pairs*. Go to Box 15.3 (p. 485) to try the test yourself.

Geffen found that not only her patient but also his team-mates in this extremely vigorous sport were somewhat slowed on this sensitive speed test of semantic processing (Hinton-Bayre, Geffen, & McFarland, 1997). Others have found similar results in other high-contact sports players, and regular testing has now become an important feature within American football and increasingly in other sports (Sahler & Greenwald, 2012). This residual deficit is of course much less severe than that found in PTA, and in American college football players typically appears to resolve within a few days (McCrea et al., 2003), although a too speedy return to playing can increase the chance of a further incident and lead to slower recovery particularly in the immature brain when it can prove fatal.

Cognition may typically recover from a mild head injury in 1–3 weeks, with a recovery rate of 1–3 months for a moderate to high TBI (Schretlen & Shapiro, 2003), although the effects tend to be cumulative meaning that players who suffer repeated head injuries should certainly retire.

An important reason for this is the association between TBI and later dementia where a recent study by Fann et al. (2018) using an extensive Danish population study found that people reporting TBI during their twenties were 63% more likely to suffer from AD during the next 30 years. As someone who has experienced a couple of instances of mild TBI playing rugby however I am glad to point out that the actual incidence of such early dementia is still quite low, 5.3% versus a baseline of 4.7% of this Danish sample population. However, a recent study of professional American football players by Randolph, Karantzoulis, and Guskiewicz (2013) involving 513 retired NFL players aged 50 or older, found preliminary evidence that some 35% showed signs of mild cognitive impairment (MCI) a condition that is predictive of progression to dementia. This is already giving rise to law suits in the US, and internationally to an increasing concern regarding sports-based concussive injuries, notably in Rugby Union where the laws of the game have been changed in an attempt to reduce contact with the head.

REHABILITATION OF PATIENTS WITH MEMORY PROBLEMS

As discussed earlier, attempting to enhance memory function in dementia is an uphill struggle, given the progressive nature of the disease and its tendency to impact on an increasingly wide range of cognitive, social, and emotional capacities. Fortunately, many memory problems are not progressive, and here, the psychologist can certainly help, not to restore memory function, but to enable the patient to make full use of remaining skills and capacities. Consider for example the biker I described in the TBI section. He would be expected to have a normal life expectancy accompanied by memory problems. How might a psychologist help him, and others suffering memory deficits from stroke or encephalitis or alcoholic Korsakoff syndrome? This will of course depend on the individual patient, their age, the severity of their memory deficit, and importantly what specific aspects of their life are most important to them. The therapist cannot bring back their memory but may be able to help them solve at least some of the everyday problems they face.

Let us begin with the biker mentioned earlier. Although there is likely to be some spontaneous recovery of cognitive function, full recovery of episodic memory after serious TBI is unlikely. Our own study of everyday memory in TBI found no difference in memory performance between patients tested a few months after injury and those whose injury had occurred several years before (Sunderland, Harris, & Baddeley, 1983). However, it is certainly possible to help the biker to make the most of his remaining memory capacity. An important aspect of any treatment is its evaluation, monitoring to check whether treatment is actually leading to an improvement over and above any recovery that might have spontaneously occurred over time. What treatments are possible and how could they be evaluated?

External aids

For most patients, the main way of supplementing their impaired memory is through external aids, changing the environment in a way that helps them remember. Typical strategies for severe deficits such as occur in Alzheimer's disease might, as discussed earlier, involve labeling cupboards, drawers, and doors, perhaps providing signposts from one room to the next. More generally, patients with severe memory problems benefit from building in a consistent routine, whereby objects are always kept in the same place, and everyday tasks always done in the same order. In all of these cases, of course, learning is necessary and the patient may well need considerable help from the psychologist, occupational therapist, and most importantly from a carer.

Fortunately, however, most patients subsequently develop at least some coping strategies independently or with the help of carers, although for patients with dense amnesia these are usually not enough to live independently, although there are occasional exceptions. One such case is that of JC, who was a first-year law student at Cambridge University when he experienced an epileptic seizure during a tutorial caused by a brain hemorrhage. This left him with a very pure but dense amnesia, but otherwise intellectually unimpaired. In due course he underwent rehabilitation, being taught to use external aids, mnemonics, and rehearsal strategies. He made very good use of both a diary and a notebook and in due course recovered sufficiently to help in his father's shop. This potentially caused problems when he had to leave the counter and fetch a particular article for the customer. He coped here by subvocally verbalizing the item and a brief description of the customer, for example, "blue tights for Mrs Pointy Nose."

He went on subsequently to develop what he described as "The Grand Plan" which involved a weekly sheet on his desk, a daily sheet with details from the weekly sheet and one of appointments from his diary, using a Filofax with different colored sheets for different activities and different individuals. He supplements this using a Dictaphone on which he records events as they occur, carefully transferring them every evening. This is an abbreviated account of an extremely carefully devised and complex system that JC followed rigorously and remarkably successfully. Using it he was able to live independently, and to take a course in furniture renovation that allows him to support himself (Wilson & Watson, 1996).

While the case of JC demonstrates that it is possible to live an independent and full life despite an extremely severe amnesia, he is clearly quite atypical in his intelligence, determination, and preparedness to organize his life in extreme detail. What about the rest of us?

Help has come from the increasingly sophisticated development of electronic devices such as pagers and mobile phones. While these are used widely, there is often little effort to assess their usefulness. A valuable exception to this came from a study of NeuroPage, a system developed by a neuropsychologist and an engineer who is the father of a young man who sustained a severe TBI (Hersh & Treadgold, 1994). Wilson, Evans, Emslie, and Malinek (1997) sought to evaluate the system in the United Kingdom, initially starting with 15 patients with memory/or planning problems. Each client selected a behavior they wanted to remember each day (e.g., "Take your tablets"; "Prepare your packed lunch"). Over a six-week baseline, relatives monitored whether or not the targets had been achieved. The patients were then provided with the reminder system NeuroPage for a period of 12 weeks. NeuroPage is a simple paging device that can be set up to ring or buzz at prespecified times, at which one press of a button will present a message. The pager increased target behaviors from an average of 37% correct at baseline to over 85% during treatment. A major advantage of this approach is that it is usable by a wide range of patients varying in their neurological problems and in their cognitive capacity. It is now of course possible to deliver a similar service by a mobile phone, although the simplicity of the original NeuroPage device is likely to make it easier to use for older patients.

So does this remove the need for the psychologist? Certainly not, since the NeuroPage experience showed that its effectiveness depended crucially on first of all establishing exactly *what* is important for the patient, programming it accordingly and ensuring that the patient actually uses the system, which is not as straightforward as it might seem. It is important to recognize that almost any system for improving a patient's everyday memory will require some degree of new learning. So how can this be achieved?

Internal aids

This term refers to ways in which a patient can be helped by acquiring new habits or strategies, a task that becomes more difficult the more severe the amnesia, and the more extensive the accompanying problems. However, in practice, almost all patients have some preservation of episodic memory with truly dense amnesia being rare, so it is important to make full use of any residual memory capacity. Learning is likely to be difficult, and hence it is important to focus it on specific problems that particularly concern the individual patient, trying to ensure that steady progress is made, and for motivational reasons, that this is visible to the learner. As different patients will have different priorities and different preserved capacities, group evaluation is often not practical. However, a series of single-case methods originally derived from Skinnerian approaches to learning have been fruitfully adapted for clinical use.

All single-case treatment methods involve beginning with a measure of *baseline performance* across a series of trials before treatment is introduced. This baseline is used to determine whether genuine progress has been made by noting if improvement begins or greatly accelerates *only* after treatment has begun. It may however be possible to treat several problems at the same time, in which case it is sensible to introduce the different treatments at different points, to ensure that the patients are not simply showing a period of spontaneous recovery in overall cognition.

One such study is described by Wilson (1987) who attempted to teach amnesic patient TB, a 43-year-old man with Korsakoff syndrome, three relevant activities. The first activity involved finding his way around the rehabilitation center. This improved spontaneously and hence needed no further treatment. The second, reading and remembering a news story, applied a system known as PQRST to reading and remembering, in this case using as an example a newspaper paragraph. PQRST is an acronym for *Preview, Question, Read, State,* and *Test.* Learning to apply this approach greatly improved performance. The third task of face–name learning was based on the use of imagery, for example remembering the name of a therapist called Stephanie might be remembered by imagining her sitting on a step and clutching her knee, a method which, in this case, proved highly effective. Not all strategies suit all patients, however; the use of imagery can be too demanding for some patients, while another patient who was entirely capable of using it rejected it on the grounds that it was "silly."

Visual imagery can however often be helpful for name learning, as shown in Figure 16.4. This uses another variant of single-case design, in this example by using the same imagery-based strategy but applying it to several patients, always establishing a flat baseline before subsequently introducing the imagery strategy. Note that in each case, improvement occurs only after the strategy is introduced, making clear its causal role in the improvement observed.

We have described two methods of enhancing learning, and in general, approaches that facilitate learning in healthy people such as those described in Chapters 11 and 17 are also likely to be potentially useful for patients, although progress is likely to be slower. There is however one important exception to this. The retrieval practice effect described in Chapter 5 (p. 126) which proves so powerful for healthy learners can create problems for amnesic patients. Repeated

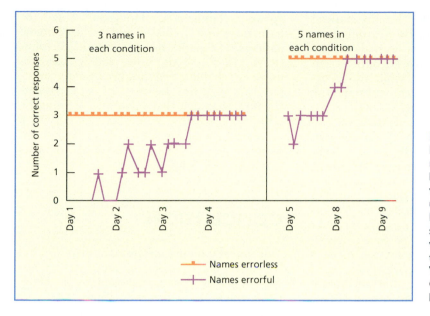

Figure 16.4 Rates of learning the names of rehabilitation staff members by ED, a young man with very severe head injury using errorful and errorless learning strategies over a series of days. He began with three names and this then increased to five. From Wilson et al. (1994). Copyright © Psychology Press.

attempts at retrieval may enhance learning in healthy young college students, but are not advisable for amnesic patients for whom errors made at retrieval can be particularly persistent and disruptive. This conclusion stems directly from the application of the results of basic research in cognitive psychology.

You will recall from Chapter 5 (p. 143) that a distinction can be made between explicit and implicit memory, with explicit episodic memory being impaired in amnesic patients, while a range of implicit learning tasks are preserved. We were tantalized by the question of whether these preserved capacities could be used to help the patient.

Reflecting on the characteristics of the preserved tasks, it seemed to us that many were either procedural tasks in which time rather than errors was the mark of success, or as in the case of classical conditioning in which the conditioned response is evoked automatically by the conditioned stimulus. In contrast, typical episodic memory tasks are measured in terms of error reduction. Could it be that the absence of episodic memory might make it particularly difficult for amnesic patients to remember their earlier performance and use this to avoid future errors? We decided to test this by contrasting a learning situation in which people were

encouraged to guess if uncertain, a strategy often encouraged by therapists, with one that minimized errors. Errorless learning had previously been shown in pigeons by Terrace (1963) and for a time was applied to assist learning-disabled people (Sidman & Stoddard, 1967). By this time however it appeared to have been abandoned clinically, or recommended as a final strategy only if normal learning had failed, by which time disruptive errors would of course already have become established.

Our own approach to errorless learning began with a task based on stem completion and involved presenting a series of five-letter words, cued by presenting the first two letters. Words were selected so that when given the first two letters there were several potential completions, for example *quote*, *quiet queen*, and *quite*. In the errorful condition participants were encouraged to guess the answer both initially and during learning. People in the errorless condition were told the answer each time, for example "I am thinking of a five-letter word beginning with QU and the word is QUOTE, please write it down."

We compared three groups, amnesic patients, elderly controls, and young controls. They were tested over nine trials with rest points in between each group of three trials

(Baddeley & Wilson, 1994). Results showed little difference between the two learning conditions for the young or normal elderly group, who seemed to have no difficulty in dealing with earlier guesses, while the errorless learning condition was substantially better for the amnesic patients.

It could of course be argued that we had used a very artificial task that might not generalize. We therefore moved on to a subsequent study using single-case treatment designs, in each case comparing errorless learning to the standard error correction approach, We studied a number of patients on several practically relevant learning tasks (Wilson, Baddeley, Evans, & Shiel, 1994). One task involved learning to use an electronic device; our amnesic patient succeeded using the errorless approach but failed completely to learn an equivalent task using an error-prone approach. Other patients showed a clear errorless advantage in tasks such as learning the names of staff, acquiring general knowledge, and orienting themselves in time and location. Barbara Wilson immediately changed her clinical practice which had previously been to encourage patients to guess if unsure.

The method has subsequently been widely used, not only with amnesic patients (Kessels & de Haan, 2003) but also with aphasic (Fillingham, Hodgson, Sage, & Lambon-Ralph, 2003) and schizophrenic patients (O'Carroll, Russell, Lawrie, & Johnstone, 1999). It is now widely used in memory rehabilitation, not because it guarantees learning but because it is a patient-friendly approach that facilitates learning by optimizing the use of implicit memory and minimizing a major source of difficulty and frustration in memory-impaired patients (Middleton & Schwartz, 2012).

CONCLUSION

Our understanding of human memory has benefitted greatly from the study of patients with memory deficits, particularly in those cases where the deficit was limited to a specific memory system. This knowledge has fed back into the memory clinic, helping in the assessment, diagnosis, understanding, and in the treatment of the patient's memory problems. As such the cognitive study of memory provides one component of the array of clinical knowledge and skills available to the clinical neuropsychologist. Unfortunately, these will not "cure" the memory deficit, but they can maximize the capacity of patients to cope with their affliction.

SUMMARY

- Many kinds of disruption of normal brain function result in problems of learning and memory.
- These can be very severe and tend not to be reversible.
- Memory problems are a principal feature of Alzheimer's disease.
- The disease is progressive with increasing disruption of other aspects of cognition.
- With an aging population, dementia is a growing problem.
- Alzheimer's disease is its most common form involving a memory deficit of increasing severity.
- Traumatic brain injury (TBI) is nonprogressive and may occur at a young age and persist over a lifetime.
- Episodic memory is particularly vulnerable and disabling across a wide range of causes of memory disorders.
- It is found in its purest form in the amnesic syndrome.

- Its principal feature is anterograde amnesia, failure to lay down new episodic memories.
- Implicit learning and memory are typically preserved.
- Anterograde amnesia is thought to result from failure to associate experiences with their context or location in time and space.
- This in turn is commonly thought to result from impaired consolidation of the episodic memory trace.
- Retrograde amnesia involves failure to access earlier memories including those acquired before the onset of amnesia.
- There is typically a gradient with items acquired earlier in life being better preserved.
- Traumatic brain injury occurs when a blow or sudden deceleration cause damage to the white matter through sheering or twisting.
- In severe cases, a period of coma may be followed by post-traumatic amnesia during which attention and new learning is disturbed.
- Both retrograde and anterograde amnesia will typically follow but become less severe over time.
- While organic memory deficits cannot be reversed, patients can be helped to cope.
- External aids such as diaries, reminders, and pagers offer the most extensive help.
- Patients still need to be trained to use these and to acquire other information; methods of achieving this are discussed.

POINTS FOR DISCUSSION

1 Why is amnesia so disruptive of everyday life?
2 What are the central cognitive problems for patients with Alzheimer's disease?
3 How can they be helped?
4 How might the practical memory problems for a young person with TBI differ from those of an older AD patient?
5 What are the similarities and differences between anterograde and retrograde amnesia?
6 How might the autobiographical memory profile differ between a patient with a pure amnesia and one with an emotionally based functional amnesia?
7 How might this influence their personal life?
8 What are the strengths and weaknesses of single-case treatment designs?

FURTHER READING

Baddeley, A. D., Kopelman, M. D., & Wilson, B. A. (Eds.) (2002). *The handbook of memory disorders* (2nd edn.). Chichester, UK: Wiley. A good source of evidence on specific types of memory disorder. It contains chapters on various types of memory deficit, and on ways of helping patients cope with memory problems.

(Continued)

(Continued)

Baxendale, S. (2004). Memories aren't made of this: Amnesia at the movies. *British Medical Journal, 329*, 1480–1483. An amusing analysis of the way in which amnesia is portrayed in movies, and a discussion of the implications of this for the public perception of memory and its deficits.

Clark, I. A., & Maguire, E. A. (2016). Remembering preservation in hippocampal amnesia. *Annual Review of Psychology, 67*, 51–82. A review of aspects of learning and memory that are preserved despite bilateral impairment of the hippocampus, as in the case of patient Jon.

Heyworth, N. C., & Squire, L. R. (2019). The nature of recollection across months and years and after medial temporal lobe damage. *Proceedings of the National Academy of Sciences of the USA*. doi:10.1073/pnas.1820765116. An interesting account of recollection of a walk with staged incidents by amnesic patients and controls after delays of up to 2.6 years. Healthy participants typically recall events in order whereas amnesic patients do not. Implications for how people remember past events are discussed.

Julien, J., Joubert, S., Ferland, M. C., Frenette, L. C., Boudreau-Duhiame, M. M., Malo-Véronneau, L., & de Guise, E. (2017). Association of traumatic brain injury and Alzheimer disease onset: A systematic review. *Annals of Physical and Rehabilitation Medicine, 60*, 347–356. doi:10.1016/j.rehab.2017.03.009. Combines evidence from 18 well-designed studies.

Kopelman, M. D. (2019). Anomalies of autobiographical memory. *Journal of the International Neuropsychological Society*, 1–15. doi:10.1017/S135561771900081X. A useful overview of three disorders of autobiographical memory. One a neurologically based retrograde amnesia, a second involving spontaneous confabulation while a third concerns psychogenic amnesia. Provides an excellent review of phenomena and current theories.

Parkin, A. J. (Ed.). (1997). *Case studies in the neuropsychology of memory*. Hove, UK: Psychology Press. Accounts of individual patients that give a feeling for the way in which different forms of memory disorder influence the lives of patients.

Wearing, D. (2005). *Forever today*. New York: Doubleday. Deborah's Wearing's account of the devastating amnesia suffered by her husband, Clive, casting light on the human cost of severe memory disorder.

REFERENCES

Aggleton, J. P., & Brown, M. W. (1999). Episodic memory, amnesia, and the hippocampal-anterior thalamic axis. *Behavioral and Brain Sciences, 22,* 425–489.

Alvarez, P., & Squire, L. R. (1994). Memory consolidation and the medial temporal lobe: A simple network model. *Proceedings of the National Academy of Sciences of the USA, 91,* 7041–7045.

Baddeley, A. D. (1990). *Human memory: Theory and practice.* Hove, UK: Psychology Press.

Baddeley, A. D. (in press). On trying to prove Endel wrong: A revised modal model of amnesia. *Neuropsychologia.*

Baddeley, A. D., Baddeley, H., Bucks, R., & Wilcock, G. K. (2001). Attentional control in Alzheimer's disease. *Brain, 124,* 1492–1508.

Baddeley, A. D., Della Sala, S., & Spinnler, H. (1991). The two-component hypothesis of memory deficit in Alzheimer's disease. *Journal of Clinical and Experimental Neuropsychology, 13*(2), 372–380.

Baddeley, A. D., Emslie, H., & Nimmo-Smith, I. (1992). *Speed and Capacity of Language Processing test (SCOLP).* Bury St Edmunds, UK: Thames Valley Test Company.

Baddeley, A. D., Logie, R., Bressi, S., Della Sala, S., & Spinnler, H. (1986). Dementia and working memory. *Quarterly Journal of Experimental Psychology, 38A,* 603–618.

Baddeley, A. D., & Warrington, E. K. (1970). Amnesia and the distinction between long- and short-term memory. *Journal of Verbal Learning and Verbal Behavior, 9,* 176–189.

Baddeley, A. D., & Wilson, B. (1986). Amnesia, autobiographical memory and confabulation. In D. Rubin (Ed.), *Autobiographical memory* (pp. 225–252). Cambridge: Cambridge University Press.

Baddeley, A. D., & Wilson, B. (1988). Frontal amnesia and the dysexecutive syndrome. *Brain & Cognition, 7*(2), 212–230.

Baddeley, A. D., & Wilson, B. A. (1994). When implicit learning fails: Amnesia and the problem of error elimination. *Neuropsychologia, 32,* 53–68.

Bayley, J. (1998). *Iris: A memoir of Iris Murdoch.* London: Duckworth.

Benbow, S., & Sharman, V. (2014). Review of family therapy and dementia: Twenty-five years on. *International Psychogeriatrics, 26,* 2037–2050. doi:10.1017/S1041610214001343

Bindschaedler, C., Peter-Favre, C., Maeder, P., Hirsbrunner, T., & Clarke, S. (2011). Growing up with bilateral hippocampal atrophy: From childhood to teenage. *Cortex, 47,* 931–944. doi:10.1016/j.cortex.2010.09.005

Braak, H., & Braak, E. (1991). Neuropathological stageing of Alzheimer-related changes. *Acta Neuropathologica, 82,* 239–259. doi:10.1007/BF00308809

Brizzolara, D., Casalini, C., Montanaro, D., & Posteraro, F. (2003). A case of amnesia at an early age. *Cortex, 39,* 605–625.

Brooks, D. N. & Baddeley, A. D. (1976). What can amnesic patients learn?. *Neuropsychologia, 14,* 111–122.

Cermak, L. S., Butters, N., & Moreines, J. (1974). Some analyses of the verbal encoding deficit of alcoholic Korsakoff patients. *Brain and Language, 1,* 141–150.

Cheston, R., & Ivanecka, A. (2017). Individual and group psychotherapy with people diagnosed with dementia: A systematic review of the literature. *International Journal of Geriatric Psychiatry, 32,* 3–31.

Christensen, H., Kopelman, M. D., Stanhope, N., Lorentz, L., & Owen, P. (1998). Rates of forgetting in Alzheimer dementia. *Neuropsychologia, 36,* 547–557.

Clare, L. (2017). Rehabilitation for people living with dementia: A practical framework of positive support. *PLoS Med, 14*(3), e1002245. doi:10.1371/journal.pmed.1002245

Clare, L., Wilson, B. A., Carter, G., Breen, K., Gosses, A., & Hodges, J. R. (2000). Intervening with everyday memory problems in dementia of Alzheimer type: An errorless learning approach. *Journal of Clinical and Experimental Neuropsychology, 22,* 132–146.

Cohen, N. J., & Squire, L. R. (1980). Preserved learning and retention of pattern-analyzing skill in amnesia: Dissociation of knowing how and knowing that. *Science, 210,* 207–210.

Dalla Barba, G., Cipolotti, L., & Denes, G. (1990). Autobiographical memory loss and confabulation in Korsakoff's syndrome: A case report. *Cortex, 26,* 525–534.

De Renzi, E., Liotti, M., & Nichelli, P. (1987). Semantic amnesic with preservation of autobiographical memory: A case report. *Cortex, 23,* 575–597.

Dewar, M., Cowan, N., & Della Sala, S. (2010). Forgetting due to retroactive interference in amnesia: Findings and implications. In S. Della Sala (Ed.), *Forgetting* (pp. 185–209). Hove, UK: Psychology Press.

Dewar, M., Fernandez Garcia, Y., Cowan, N., & Della Sala, S. (2009). Delaying interference enhances memory consolidation in amnesic patients. *Neuropsychology, 23,* 627–634.

Doody, R. S., Stevens, J. C., Beck, C., Dublinsky, R. M., Kaye, J. A., Gwyther, L., ... Cummings, J. L. (2001). Practice parameter: Management of dementia (an evidence-based review): Report of the Quality Standards Sub-Committee of the American Academy of Neurology. *Neurology, 56,* 1154–1166.

Dzieciol, A. M., Bachevalier, J., Saleem, K. S., Gadian, D. G., Saunders, R., Chong, W. K. K., ... Vargha-Khadem, F. (2017). Hippocampal and diencephalic pathology in developmental amnesia. *Cortex, 86,* 33–44. doi:10.1016/j.cortex.2016.09.016

Eichenbaum, H. (2014). Time cells in the hippocampus: A new dimension for mapping memories. *Nature Reviews Neuroscience, 15,* 732–744. doi:10.1038/nrn3827

Fann, J. R., Ribe, A. R., Pedersen, H. S., Fenger-Grøn, M., Christensen, J., Benros, M. E., & Vestergaard, M. (2018). Long-term risk of dementia among people with traumatic brain injury in Denmark: A population-based observational cohort study. *The Lancet Psychiatry, 5,* 424–431. doi:10.1016/S2215-0366(18)30065-8

Fillingham, J. K., Hodgson, C., Sage, K., & Lambon Ralph, M. A. (2003). The application of errorless learning to aphasic disorders: A review of theory and practice. *Neuropsychological Rehabilitation, 13,* 337–363.

Fleischman, D. A., Vaidya, C. J., Lange, K. L., & Gabrieli, J. D. E. (1997). A dissociation between visuoperceptual explicit and implicit memory processes. *Brain and Cognition, 35,* 42–57.

Gardiner, J. M., Brandt, K. R., Baddeley, A. D., Vargha-Khadem, F., & Mishkin, M. (2008). Charting the acquisition of semantic knowledge in the case of developmental amnesia. *Neuropsychologia, 46,* 2865–2868.

Garrard, P., Malony, L. M., Hodges, J. R., & Patterson, K. (2005). The effects of very early Alzheimer's disease on the characteristics of writing by a renowned author. *Brain, 128,* 250–260.

Gaskell, M. G., & Dumay, N. (2003). Lexical competition and the acquisition of novel words. *Cognition, 89,* 105–132.

Greene, J. D. W., & Hodges, J. R. (1996). The fractionation of remote memory-evidence from a longitudinal study of dementia of Alzheimer type. *Brain, 119,* 129–142.

Greene, J. D. W., Hodges, J. R., & Baddeley, A. D. (1995). Autobiographical memory and executive function in early dementia of Alzheimer type. *Neuropsychologia, 33*(12), 1647–1670.

Harrison, N. A., Johnston, K., Corno, F., Casey, S. J., Friedner, K., Humphreys, K., ... Kopelman, M. D. (2017). Psychogenic amnesia: Syndromes, outcome and patterns of retrograde amnesia. *Brain, 140,* 2498–2510.

Hassabis, D., Kumaran, D., Vann, S. D., & Maguire, E. A. (2007). Patients with hippocampal amnesia cannot imagine new experiences. *Proceedings of the National Academy of Sciences of the USA, 104,* 1726–1731.

Heindel, W. C., Salmon, D. P., Shults, C. W., Walicke, P. A., & Butters, N. (1989). Neuropsychological evidence for multiple implicit systems: A comparison of Alzheimer's, Huntington's and Parkinson's disease patients. *Journal of Neuroscience, 9,* 582–587.

Hersh, N., & Treadgold, L. (1994). Rehabilitation of memory dysfunction by prosthetic memory & cueing. *Neurorehabilitation, 4,* 187–197.

High, W. M., Levin, H. S., & Gary, H. E. (1990). Recovery of orientation and memory following closed-head injury. *Journal of Clinical and Experimental Neuropsychology, 12,* 703–714.

Hinton-Bayre, A. D., Geffen, G., & McFarland, K. (1997). Mild head injury and speed of information processing: A prospective study of professional rugby league players. *Journal of Clinical and Experimental Neuropsychology, 19,* 275–289.

Hodges, J. R., & Patterson, K. (1995). Is semantic memory consistently impaired early in the course of Alzheimer's disease? Neuroanatomical and diagnostic implications. *Neuropsychologia, 33,* 441–459.

Hodges, J. R., Patterson, K., & Tyler, L. (1994). Loss of semantic memory: Implications for the modularity of mind. *Cognitive Neuropsychology, 11,* 505–542.

Huppert, F. A., & Piercy, M. (1979). Normal and abnormal forgetting in amnesia: Effect of locus of lesion. *Cortex, 15,* 385–390.

Karpicke, J. D., & Roediger III, H. L. (2008). The critical importance of retrieval for learning. *Science, 319,* 966–968.

Kessels, R. P. C., & de Haan, E. H. F. (2003). Implicit learning in memory rehabilitation: A meta-analysis on errorless learning and vanishing cues methods. *Journal of Clinical and Experimental Neuropsychology, 25,* 805–814.

Kopelman, M. D. (1985). Rates of forgetting in Alzheimer-type dementia and Korsakoff's syndrome. *Neuropsychologia, 23,* 623–638.

Kopelman, M., Wilson, B. A., & Baddeley, A. D. (1990). *Autobiographical memory interview.* Bury St Edmunds, UK: Thames Valley Test Company.

Langlois, J. A., Rutland-Brown, W., & Wald, M. M. (2006). The epidemiology and impact of traumatic brain injury: A brief overview. *Journal of Head Trauma Rehabilitation, 21,* 375–378.

Levin, H. S., & Hanten, G. (2002). Post traumatic amnesia and residual memory deficit after closed head injury. In A. D. Baddeley, M. D. Kopelman, & B. A. Wilson (Eds.), *Handbook of memory disorders* (2nd ed., pp. 381–412). Chichester, UK: Wiley.

Levin, H. S., O'Donnell, V. M., & Grossman, R. G. (1979). The Galveston Orientation and Amnesia Test: A practical scale to assess cognition after a head injury. *Journal of Nervous and Mental Disease, 167,* 675–684.

Logie, R. H., Cocchini, G., Della Sala, S., & Baddeley, A. (2004). Is there a specific capacity for dual task co-ordination? Evidence from Alzheimer's disease. *Neuropsychology, 18*(3), 504–513.

Maguire, E. A., Vargha-Khadem, F., & Mishkin, M. (2001). The effects of bilateral hippocampal damage on fMRI regional activations and interactions during memory retrieval. *Brain, 124,* 1156–1170.

Manns, J. R., & Squire, L. R. (1999). Impaired recognition memory on the Doors and People Test after damage limited to the hippocampal region. *Hippocampus, 9,* 495–499.

Mayes, A. R., Holdstock, J. S., Isaac, C. L., Hunkin, N. M., & Roberts, N. (2002). Relative sparing of item recognition memory in a patient with adult-onset damage limited to the hippocampus. *Hippocampus, 12,* 325–340.

McClelland, J. L., McNaughton, B. L., & O'Reilly, R. C. (1995). Why there are complementary learning systems in the hippocampus and neocortex: Insights from the successes and failures of connectionist models of learning and memory. *Psychological Review, 102,* 419–457.

McCrea, M., Guskiewicz, K. M., Marshall, S. W., Barr, W., Randolph, C., Cantu, R. C., … Kelly, J. P. (2003). Acute effects and recovery time following concussion in collegiate football players: The NCAA concussion study. *Journal of the American Medical Association, 290,* 2556–2563.

Meltzer, M. L. (1983). Poor memory: A case report. *Journal of Clinical Psychology, 39,* 3–10.

Middleton, E. L., & Schwartz, M. F. (2012). Errorless learning in cognitive rehabilitation: A critical review. *Neuropsychological Rehabilitation, 22,* 138–168.

Miller, N. E. (1971). Extending the domain of learning. In M. E. Meyer & F. H. Hite (Eds.), *The application of learning principles to classroom instruction* (pp. 46–62). Bellingham, WA: Western Washington State College.

Moffat, N. (1989). Home-based cognitive rehabilitation with the elderly. In L. Poon, D. Rubin, & B. A. Wilson (Eds.), *Everyday cognition in adult and later life* (pp. 659–680). Cambridge: Cambridge University Press.

Morris, R. G. (1986). Short-term forgetting in senile dementia of the Alzheimer's type. *Cognitive Neuropsychology, 3,* 77–97.

Morris, R. G., & Baddeley, A. D. (1988). Primary and working memory functioning in Alzheimer-type dementia. *Journal of Clinical and Experimental Neuropsychology, 10,* 279–296.

Moscovitch, M. (1982). A neuropsychological approach to perception and memory in normal and pathological aging. In F. I. M. Craik & S. Trehub (Eds.), *Aging and cognitive processes* (pp. 55–78). New York: Plenum Press.

Müller, G. E., & Pilzecker, A. E. (1900). Experimentelle Beiträge zur Lehre vom Gedächtniss (Experimental contributions to the science of memory). *Zeitschrift für Psychologie. Ergänzungsband, 1,* 1–300.

Murre, J. M. J. (1996). TraceLink: A model of amnesia and consolidation of memory. *Hippocampus, 6,* 675–684.

Nadel, L., & Moscovitch, M. (1997). Memory consolidation, retrograde amnesia and the hippocampal complex. *Current Opinion in Neurobiology, 7,* 217–227.

Nadel, L., & Moscovitch, M. (1998). Hippocampal contributions to cortical plasticity. *Neuropharmacology, 37,* 431–439.

Neuro Central news bulletin. (July 19, 2019). www.neuro-central.com/news/

O'Carroll, R. E., Russell, H. H., Lawie, S. M., & Johnstone, E. C. (1999). Errorless learning and the cognitive rehabilitation on memory-impaired schizophrenic patients. *Psychological Medicine, 29,* 105–112.

O'Keefe, J. (1976). Place cells in the hippocampus of the freely moving rat. *Experimental Neurology, 51,* 78–109.

Orgeta, V., Qazi, A., Spector, A., & Orrell, M. (2015). Psychological treatments for depression and anxiety in dementia and mild cognitive impairment: Systematic review and meta-analysis. *British Journal of Psychiatry, 207,* 293–298.

Parra, M. A., Abrahams, S., Fabi, K., Logie, R., Luzzi, S., & Della Sala, S. (2009). Short-term memory binding deficits in Alzheimer's disease. *Brain, 132,* 1057–1066.

Parra, M. A., Abrahams, S., Logie, R. H., Mendez, L. G., Lopera, F., & Della Sala, S. (2010). Visual short-term memory binding deficits in familial Alzheimer's disease. *Brain, 133,* 2702–2713. doi:0.1093/brain/awq148

Perry, R. J., & Hodges, J. R. (1999). Attention and executive deficits in Alzheimer's disease: A critical review. *Brain, 122,* 383–404.

Petersen, R. C., Stevens, J. C., Ganguli, M., Tangalos, E. G., Cummings, J. L., & DeKosky, S. T. (2001). Practice parameter: Early detection of dementia: Mild cognitive impairment (an evidence based review). Report of the Quality Standards Subcommittee of the American Academy of Neurology. *Neurology, 56,* 1133–1142.

Randolph, C., Karantzoulis, S., & Guskiewicz, K. (2013). Prevalence and characterization of mild cognitive impairment in retired national football league players. *Journal of the International Neuropsychological Society, 19,* 873–880. doi:10.1017/s1355617713000805

Reed, J. M., & Squire, L. R. (1997). Impaired recognition memory in patients with lesions limited to the hippocampal formation. *Behavioral Neuroscience, 111,* 667–675.

Ribot, T. (1882). *Diseases of the memory: An essay in the positive psychology.* New York: D. Appleton and Company.

Russell, W. R. (1959). *Brain, memory, learning: A neurologists view.* London: Oxford University Press.

Sahler, C. S., & Greenwald, B. D. (2012). Traumatic brain injury in sports: A review. *Rehabilitation Research and Practice,* 1–10. http://dx.doi.org/10.1155/2012/659652

Salmon, D. P., & Heindel, W. C. (1992). Impaired priming in Alzheimer's disease: Neuropsychological implications. In L. R. Squire & N. Butters (Eds.), *Neuropsychology of memory* (2nd ed., pp. 179–187). New York: Guilford.

Salmon, D. P., Shimamura, A. P., Butters, N., & Smith, S. (1988). Lexical and semantic priming deficits in patients with Alzheimer's disease. *Journal of Clinical and Experimental Neuropsychology, 10,* 477–494.

Salthouse, T. A., & Becker, J. T. (1998). Independent effects of Alzheimer's disease on neuropsychological functioning. *Neuropsychology, 12,* 242–252.

Sanders, H. I., & Warrington, E. K. (1971). Memory for remote events in amnesic patients. *Brain, 94,* 661–668.

Schacter, D. L., Harbluk, J. L., & McLachlan, D. R. (1984). Retrieval without recollection: An experiment analysis of source amnesia. *Journal of Verbal Learning and Verbal Behavior, 23,* 593–611.

Schretlen, D. J., & Shapiro, A. M. (2003). A quantitative review of the effects of traumatic brain injury on cognitive functioning. *International Review of Psychiatry, 15,* 341–349. doi:10.1080/09540260310001606728

Shiel, A., Wilson, B. A., McLellan, L., Horn, S., & Watson, M. (2000). *The Wessex Head Injury Matrix (WHIM).* Bury St Edmunds, UK: Thames Valley Test Company.

Shimamura, A. P., & Squire, L. R. (1991). The relationship between fact and source memory: Findings with amnesic patients and normal subjects. *Psychobiology, 19,* 1–10.

Sidman, M., & Stoddard, L. T. (1967). The effectiveness of fading in programming a simultaneous form discrimination for retarded children. *Journal of Experimental Analysis Behavior, 10,* 3–15.

Snowden, J. S., Neary, D., & Mann, D. M. A. (1996). *Frontotemporal lobar degeneration: Frontotemporal dementia, progressive aphasia, semantic dementia.* New York: Churchill Livingstone.

Søgaard, R., Sørensen, J., Waldorff, F. B., Eckermann, A., Buss, D. V., Phung, K. T., & Waldemar, G. (2014). Early psychosocial intervention in Alzheimer's disease: Cost utility evaluation alongside the Danish Alzheimer's Intervention Study (DAISY). *British Medical Journal Open, 4,* e004105. doi:10.1136/bmjopen-2013-004105

Spector, A., Davies, S., Woods, B., & Orrell, M. (2000). Reality orientation for dementia: A systematic review of the evidence of effectiveness from randomized controlled trials. *The Gerontologist, 40,* 206–212.

Spinnler, H., Della Sala, S., Bandera, R., & Baddeley, A. D. (1988). Dementia, ageing and the structure of human memory. *Cognitive Neuropsychology, 5,* 193–211.

Squire, L. R., Haist, F., & Shimamura, A. P. (1989). The neurology of memory: Quantitative assessment of retrograde amnesia in two types of amnesic patient. *Journal of Neuroscience, 9,* 828–839.

St George-Hyslop, P. H. (2000). Piecing together Alzheimer's. *Scientific American, 283,* 76–83.

Stickgold, R., James, L., & Hobson, J. A. (2000). Visual discrimination learning requires sleep after training. *Nature Neuroscience, 3,* 1237–1238.

Sunderland, A., Harris, J. E., & Baddeley, A. D. (1983). Do laboratory tests predict everyday memory? A neuropsychological study?. *Journal of Verbal Learning and Verbal Behavior, 22,* 341–357. doi:10.1016/S0022-5371(83)90229-3

Terrace, H. S. (1963). Discrimination learning with and without "errors." *Journal of the Experimental Analysis of Behavior, 6,* 1–27.

Vargha-Khadem, F., Gadian, D. G., & Mishkin, M. (2001). Dissociations in cognitive memory: The syndrome of developmental amnesia. *Philosophical Transactions of the Royal Society: Series B, 356,* 1435–1440.

Warrington, E., K,, & Weiskrantz, L. (1970). Amnesic syndrome: Consolidation or retrieval?. *Nature, 226,* 628–630.

Wilson, B. A. (1987). Single-case experimental designs in neuropsychological rehabilitation. *Journal of Clinical and Experimental Neuropsychology, 9,* 527–544.

Wilson, B. A., & Baddeley, A. D. (1988). Semantic, episodic and autobiographical memory in a post-meningitic amnesic patient. *Brain & Cognition, 8,* 31–46.

Wilson, B. A., Baddeley, A. D., Evans, J., & Shiel, A. (1994). Errorless learning in the rehabilitation of memory-impaired people. *Neuropsychological Rehabilitation, 4,* 307–326.

Wilson, B. A., Evans, J. J., Emslie, H., & Malinek, V. (1997). Evaluation of NeuroPage: A new memory aid. *Journal of Neurology, Neurosurgery and Psychiatry, 63,* 113–115.

Wilson, B. A., & Watson, P. C. (1996). A practical framework for understanding compensatory behaviour in people with organic memory impairment. *Memory, 4,* 465–486.

Winocur, G. (1978). Effects of interference on discrimination and learning and recall by rats with hippocampal lesions. *Physiology and Behavior, 22,* 339–345.

Winocur, G., & Mills, J. A. (1970). Transfer between related and unrelated problems following hippocampal lesions in rats. *Journal of Comparative & Physiological Psychology, 73,* 162–169.

Woods, B., & McKiernan, F. (2005). Evaluating the impact of reminiscence on older people with dementia. In J. D. Webster & B. K. Haight (Eds.), *The art and science of reminiscing: Theory, research, methods, and applications* (pp. 233–242). Washington DC: Taylor & Francis.

Yarnell, P. R., & Lynch, S. (1970). Retrograde memory immediately after concussion. *Lancet, 1,* 863–865.

Zola-Morgan, S., Cohen, N. J., & Squire, L. R. (1983). Recall of remote episodic memory in amnesia. *Neuropsychologia, 21,* 487–500.

Contents

CHAPTER 17

IMPROVING YOUR MEMORY

Michael W. Eysenck

INTRODUCTION

Many (or even most) people complain about their memory. In spite of the power and elegance of the human memory system, it is by no means infallible and we have to learn to live with that fallibility. Interestingly, it is regarded as much more acceptable to blame a social lapse on "a terrible memory" rather than to attribute it to stupidity or insensitivity.

How much do we actually know about our own memory? Obviously, we need to remember our memory lapses in order to know just how bad our memories are! One of the most amnesic patients ever tested by one of us (Alan Baddeley) was a woman suffering from Korsakoff's syndrome, which severely impaired long-term memory following chronic alcoholism. The test involved presenting her with lists of words. After each list, she commented with surprise on her ability to recall the words, saying, "I pride myself on my memory!" In fact, she performed very poorly on the recall test compared to other people. She seemed to have forgotten just how bad her memory was.

Evidence that many of us have poor memories for important information comes from the study of passwords. Brown, Bracken, Zoccoli, and Douglas (2004) found 31% of their sample of American students admitted to having forgotten at least one password. This was the case even though 45% of the students used their own name in password construction. Unsurprisingly, the number of different passwords an individual has makes a difference. Pilar, Jaeger, Gomes, and Stein (2012) found 84% of individuals with between seven and nine different passwords had experienced memory problems with their passwords. This figure dropped to 53% among those with between one and three passwords.

While this chapter is devoted to ways of improving your memory, it is important to note that we should not assume that forgetting is always a bad thing. Nørby (2015) identified three useful functions of forgetting:

1 It can increase psychological well-being by reducing access to painful memories.
2 When remembering what we have read or heard, it is generally useful to remember the overall gist and forget the specific details.
3 Most importantly, it is useful to forget outdated information (e.g., where your friends used to live) so it does not interfere with current information (e.g., where your friends now live). In similar fashion, Richards and Frankland (2017) argued that a major purpose of memory is to improve decision making. This purpose is facilitated when we forget outdated information.

DISTINCTIVE PROCESSING

Suppose you were presented with a list of 20 words to learn. All the words are printed in black except for the 10th word which is printed in bright red. Most people would guess the word printed in red would be well remembered because it is distinctive or different from all the other words in the list. Von Restorff (1933) carried out experiments along those lines. She confirmed that the distinctive word was more likely to be recalled than nondistinctive ones. For obvious reasons, this became known as the von Restorff effect: "When one item is isolated, or made distinctive from other items in a list, memory for the isolated item is improved" (Chee & Goh, 2018, p. 49).

Von Restorff (1933) studied the effects of distinctiveness by manipulating the *visual* properties of stimuli which presumably influenced *internal* processing. Eysenck and Eysenck (1980) manipulated internal processing more directly. They used nouns having irregular pronunciations (e.g., *comb* has a silent "b"). In one condition, participants said these nouns distinctively (e.g., pronouncing the "b" in *comb*). In another condition, they simply pronounced the same nouns normally (nondistinctive processing). Long-term memory was much better for words processed distinctively. Hunt (2013) concluded in a review that learning material associated with distinctive processing is reliably better remembered than learning material not associated with such processing.

It is tempting to regard distinctiveness as simply meaning that processing of one or a few items differs from the processing of other items. However, Hunt (2013, p. 10) argued distinctive processing should be defined as, "the processing of difference in the context of similarity." Empirical support for this view of distinctiveness is discussed in Box 17.1.

KEY TERM

von Restorff effect: The finding that a to-be-remembered item that is distinctively different from other items is especially likely to be remembered.

Box 17.1 Demonstration of the effects of distinctiveness on long-term memory

Below is a list of 45 words with five words belonging to each of nine categories:

CHAIR	CAT	TANK
PIANO	ELEPHANT	KNIFE
CLOCK	GIRAFFE	POISON
TELEPHONE	MOUSE	WHIP
CUSHION	TIGER	SCREWDRIVER
APPLE	BICYCLE	DRESS
GRAPEFRUIT	TRACTOR	MITTENS
COCONUT	TRAIN	SWEATER
PEACH	CART	SHOES
BLUEBERRY	SLED	PYJAMAS
CARROTS	MICHAEL	DONNA
LETTUCE	DANIEL	PAULA
ASPARAGUS	JOHN	BETH
ONION	RICHARD	SUSAN
POTATO	GEORGE	ANNE

Ask a friend to consider the list words category by category. Their task is to write down one thing common to all five words within a category (Condition 1). After they have finished, present them with everything they have written down and ask them to recall as many list words as possible.

Ask another friend to consider the list words category by category. Within each category, they should write beside each word one thing they know about that word that is *not* true of any other word presented in that category (Condition 2). After that, present them with what they have written down, and ask them to recall as many words as possible.

This task is based closely on an experiment reported by Hunt and Smith (1996). They found recall was far higher in Condition 2 than Condition 1 (97% correct vs. 59%). The reason is that the instructions in Condition 2 led to much more distinctive or unique memory traces than those in Condition 1 because each word was processed differently from the others.

Distinctiveness is important in everyday life. For example, we frequently have to learn to associate names with faces. Watier and Collin (2012) found names were more likely to be accurately recognized or recalled when paired with a distinctive rather than a typical face. Similarly, faces were more likely to be recognized when paired with a distinctive name.

The effects of distinctiveness on memory performance have been studied using the Deese-Roediger-McDermott paradigm. In this paradigm, all the list words are associatively related to a word that is NOT presented. Thus, for example, the list might contain the words *nurse*, *sick*, *hospital*, and *patient* but not the word *doctor*. The typical finding with this paradigm is that the word not presented (e.g., *doctor*) is often falsely recognized because it is hard to discriminate between studied and nonstudied items. However, there is less false recognition when participants engage in distinctive encoding during study (e.g., Bodner, Huff, Lamontagne, & Azad, 2017).

Theoretical considerations

How can we explain the effectiveness of distinctiveness in enhancing long-term memory? Eysenck (1979) argued that an important factor is the extent to which the information available at the time of retrieval allows us to *discriminate* between the correct memory trace and incorrect ones. Such discrimination is greatest when the retrieval cue is *uniquely* associated with a single distinctive item.

Important theoretically relevant research was reported by Chee and Goh (2018). They distinguished two potential explanations for the beneficial effects of distinctiveness as represented by the von Restorff effect. First, distinctive items may attract additional attention and processing at the time of study. Second, distinctive items may be well remembered because of effects occurring at retrieval. Suppose the distinctive item is printed in red whereas all other items are printed in black. In this case, the retrieval cue (recall the red item) uniquely specifies one item and so facilitates retrieval as suggested by Eysenck (1979).

Chee and Goh (2018) contrasted the two above explanations. In one experiment, they presented a list containing 18 words referring to species of birds and also the word *kiwi*. Of importance, *kiwi* is a homonym (a word having one spelling but two different meanings): it can mean a species of bird but is also a type of fruit. The key manipulation was a hint provided before study (encoding condition) or after the study phase (retrieval condition): "One of the words will be/was a type of fruit." Thus, the word *kiwi* was made distinctively different from the other list words either *before* study or *after* study but before retrieval.

Chee and Goh's (2018) findings are shown in Figure 17.1. The key finding was that the von Restorff effect was found in the retrieval condition in the *absence* of distinctive processing at study. The implication is that the von Restorff effect is entirely due to distinctiveness at the time of retrieval.

Chee and Goh's (2018) conclusion is perhaps too extreme. Eysenck (1972) argued that one reason why distinctive items are remembered better than nondistinctive ones is because they attract more attention at encoding. Berlyne, Craw, Salapatek, and Lewis (1963) had previously discovered that novel, surprising, or incongruous stimuli were attended to more than stimuli lacking those characteristics. Eysenck obtained evidence of the von Restorff effect when one of the presented stimuli was novel, surprising, or incongruous. These findings suggest that processes occurring at encoding can influence the effects of distinctiveness on memory.

TECHNIQUES TO IMPROVE MEMORY: VISUAL IMAGERY

In this section, I will focus on some of the numerous techniques that can be used to improve your memory. As you probably know, every self-help book designed to improve your memory provides many examples of effective mnemonic techniques (e.g., Foer, 2011). Indeed, there are more

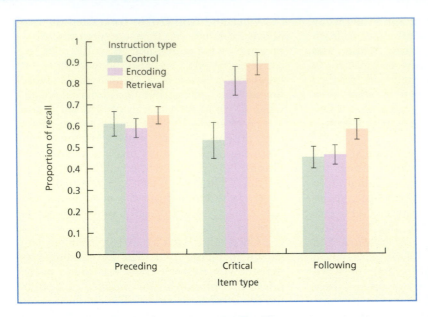

Figure 17.1 Percentage recall of the critical item (i.e., kiwi) in the encoding, retrieval, and control conditions; also shown is percentage recall of preceding and following items in the three conditions. From Chee and Goh (2018).

such techniques than you can shake a stick at. Here we will consider a few of the most important mnemonic techniques including an assessment of their strengths and limitations.

In this section, we consider primarily mnemonics relying on visual imagery whereas the next section focuses on word-based mnemonics. However, the distinction is only relative—many mnemonics techniques involve a combination of words and images.

In this section and the next, the emphasis is on describing the main mnemonics and assessing their effectiveness. The crucial issue of explaining *why* these techniques are effective is discussed in a concluding section. If you want to know the answer at any point, simply read that section (it starts on p. 545).

Method of loci

Mnemonics based on visual imagery have been common at least since classical times. According to Cicero, writing in the first century BC, the first such mnemonic was devised by the Greek poet Simonides in about 500 BC. A Greek who had won a wrestling victory at the Olympic Games gave a banquet at his house to celebrate. Simonides attended the banquet and gave a recitation in honor of the victor.

Shortly after completing his eulogy, Simonides was called away … fortunately for

him, because just after he left, the floor of the banqueting hall collapsed, killing and mutilating the guests. Many bodies were unrecognizable.

How could the victims' relatives identify them and give them a decent burial? Simonides found he could easily remember where most guests had been when he left, and so could identify the bodies. This set him thinking. If his visual memory was so good, couldn't he use it to help himself recall other material? He therefore devised a system in which he visualized a room in great detail and then imagined various items in special places in the room. Whenever he needed to remember those items, he would "look" at the appropriate location in his mind's eye and mentally recall.

The above system (the method of loci) remains popular to this day. As you will find if you give it a serious trial, it works very effectively and easily (see Box 17.2).

One of us (Alan Baddeley) has frequently used the method of loci in student laboratory

KEY TERM

Method of loci: A memory technique in which to-be-remembered items are associated with various locations well known to the learner.

Box 17.2 How the method of loci works

First of all, think of 10 locations in your home, choosing them so the sequence of moving from one to next is obvious—for example, front door to entrance hall to kitchen to bedroom, and so on. Check that you can imagine moving through your 10 locations in a consistent order without difficulty. Now think of 10 items and imagine them in those locations. If the first item is a *pipe*, you might imagine it poking out of the letterbox in your front door, and great clouds of smoke billowing into the street. If the second is a *cabbage*, you might imagine your hall obstructed by an enormous cabbage, and so on. When it comes to recall, all you need to do is to rewalk mentally the route around your house.

Now try to create similarly striking images associating your 10 chosen locations with the words below:

*shirt eagle paperclip rose camera
mushroom crocodile handkerchief
sausage mayor*

The same set of locations can be used repeatedly, as long as only the most recent item in a particular location is remembered. Earlier items in that location will suffer from the usual interference effects, unless of course you deliberately link them into a coherent chain.

Try to recall the 10 items listed two paragraphs ago. No, don't look! Rely on the images you created at various points around you.

It is certainly possible to create a system having more than 10 locations; this was true of classical mnemonic systems and of the complex and somewhat mystical systems developed during the Middle Ages. Ross and Lawrence (1968) discovered that people using the method of loci could recall more than 95% of a list of 40 or 50 items after a single study trial.

classes and it almost invariably works extremely well. It is very easy to use with concrete words (e.g., names of objects), but is still effective when remembering abstract words (e.g., *truth*, *hope*). The use of imagery can be prevented by introducing an interfering spatial task, so do not use this method while skiing down a mountain or driving a car!

Findings

The method of loci is typically very effective. Bower (1973) found learners using the method of loci recalled 72% of the items presented compared to only 28% for those not using that method. Maguire, Valentine, Wilding, and Kapur (2003) studied contestants at the World Memory Championships. Of those who reported using strategies to enhance their memory performance, 90% made use of the method of loci.

Which locations should you use to maximize the usefulness of the method of loci? Massen, Vaterrodt-Plünnecke, Krings, and Hilbig (2009) addressed this issue. They discovered the method of loci was more effective when people imagined a route to work than one inside their home. Why was that? It is better to use a route that is constant or unchanging (e.g., route to work) rather than one that is variable (e.g., moving around your home).

Suppose you use the same locations to learn several different word lists. It seems likely you would become somewhat confused by the time each location has been associated with several different objects. Think back to Chapter 9 where there is a discussion of proactive interference (the disruption of memory by previous learning). Proactive interference is especially great when the same stimulus is associated with several different responses, which is exactly the case here.

Massen and Vaterrodt-Plünnecke (2006) addressed the above issue. There was proactive interference with the method of loci (but not greater than with other learning strategies) when each learning lists consisted of words from the same category. However, there was minimal proactive interference when each list consisted of words drawn from different categories. Bass and Oswald (2014) confirmed that there is proactive interference with the method of loci when successive lists consist of words from the same category. However, there was less proactive interference than in a condition where participants were not instructed to use any particular learning strategy.

The method of loci possesses some limitations. First, it is hard to recall any given item without working your way through the list in sequence until you reach it. Second, it has often been argued that the method is artificial and of modest usefulness in the real world. However, De Beni, Moè, and Cornoldi (1997) found the method of loci was more effective than rehearsal with a lecture-style oral presentation at short and long retention intervals (see Figure 17.2). In contrast, it was ineffective when the text was in written form (a finding replicated by De Beni & Moè, 2003) because the visual nature of the presentation interfered with the use of visual imagery associated with the method of loci.

The above findings indicate that the method of loci does have real-world application. Further evidence was provided by Werner-Seidler and Dalgleish (2016) in a study on individuals in remission from chronic depression. These individuals used either the method of loci or rehearsal to facilitate access to positive self-affirming personal memories.

Those who used the method of loci had better recall of those memories and were more likely to access them to offset negative mood states.

Pegword method

The **pegword method** resembles the method of loci in that it relies on visual imagery and allows you to remember sequences of 10 unrelated items in the correct order. First of all, you memorize 10 pegwords. Since each pegword rhymes with a number from one to 10, this is fairly easy. Try it for yourself:

One = *bun*   Two = *shoe*   Three = *tree*
Four = *door*

Five = *hive*   Six = *sticks*   Seven = *heaven*
Eight = *gate*

Nine = *wine*   Ten = *hen*

> **KEY TERM**
>
> **Pegword method:** A memory technique in which to-be-remembered items are associated with pegwords, each of which rhymes with a different number between one and ten.

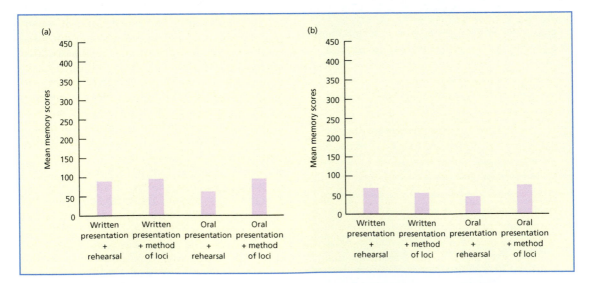

Figure 17.2 (a) Memory performance at a short retention interval as a function of type of presentation (written vs. oral) and learning strategy (rehearsal vs. method of loci). (b) Memory performance at a 1-week retention interval as a function of type of presentation and learning strategy. Data from De Beni et al. (1997).

Having mastered this, you are ready to memorize 10 unrelated words. Suppose these are as follows: *battleship, pig, chair, sheep, castle, rug, grass, beach, milkmaid, binoculars*. Take the first pegword (*bun* rhyming with one) and form an image of a bun interacting with *battleship*. You might, for example, imagine a battleship sailing into an enormous floating bun.

Now take the second pegword, *shoe*, and imagine it interacting with *pig*, perhaps a large shoe with a pig sitting in it. Pegword three is *tree*, and the third item is *chair*, so you might imagine a chair wedged in the branches of a tree. Work through the rest of the items, forming an appropriate interactive image in each case. We are reasonably confident that when you have completed the task, you will be able to recall all 10 items in the correct order even though you have never before tried to remember 10 unrelated items in a given order.

The pegword method closely resembles the method of loci. They both produce distinctive encodings via elaborative processing and serial organization of the to-be-learned material with the locations or pegwords provides a well-learned retrieval structure. All three authors of this book have tried the pegword method and were relieved to find it worked for us! Wang and Thomas (2000) found it was as effective as the method of loci. It might be thought that reusing the same pegwords over successive lists would cause interference. However, the limited available evidence suggests this is *not* the case (Carney & Levin, 2011).

Limitations

What are the limitations of the pegword method? First, it requires extensive training so learners have reliable and rapid access to the pegwords. Second, it is harder to use the method with abstract than with concrete material (Worthen & Hunt, 2011). Third, it has restricted applicability to real life because we rarely need to remember a sequence of several unrelated items.

Remembering names

Most people have problems remembering the names of people they have just met. You have undoubtedly experienced the embarrassment caused when you are introducing people to each other and suddenly realize you have forgotten someone's name! One solution is to remember people's names using a three-stage face–name mnemonic strategy (see Figure 17.3). First, a name clue resembling the individual's name is selected. Second, a prominent facial feature is selected. Third, an interactive image linking the name clue and the prominent feature is constructed.

In an early study, Morris, Jones, and Hampson (1978) found this visual imagery mnemonic increased recall of names to faces by almost 80%. Carney and Levin (2014) also found this technique was effective even with less distinctive/more abstract stimuli, but less so than with more distinctive/concrete stimuli.

The finding that the face–name mnemonic strategy works well in the peace and calm of the laboratory does not necessarily mean it will be effective in real-life social situations. In such situations, being involved in conversation may make it hard to find the time to construct good mnemonics. Morris, Fritz, Jackson, Nichol, and Roberts (2005)

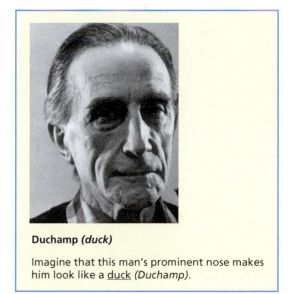

Duchamp *(duck)*

Imagine that this man's prominent nose makes him look like a <u>duck</u> *(Duchamp)*.

Figure 17.3 The man's name (Duchamp) suggests the concrete name clue duck; his nose is a prominent facial feature; imagine his nose makes him look like a duck. From Carney and Levin (2014).

invited first-year university students to a party having received instructions about learning the names of their fellow students. One group was instructed to use the face–name mnemonic strategy. A second group received the same instructions but was told to retrieve the names at increasing intervals after first hearing them (expanded retrieval practice). There was also a control group simply instructed to learn people's names.

A few days later, students wrote the names under the photographs of the students who had been at the party. Morris et al. found students in the expanded retrieval practice condition recalled 50% more names than those in the control condition. In contrast, those only told to use the face–name mnemonic remembered even fewer names than the controls. Thus, putting in the effort to use the face–name mnemonic with people you have just met can pay considerable dividends in terms of enhanced long-term memory except when you are under severe time pressure.

Helder and Shaughnessy (2011) also studied memory for names while participants carried out another cognitively demanding task at the same time. Their findings resembled those of Morris et al. (2005) in that repeated retrieval practice for names greatly increased name recall. The beneficial effects of retrieval practice were greater when the times at which retrieval practice occurred were *self-generated* rather than controlled by the experimenter. This probably occurred because participants could engage in self-generated retrieval practice when the demands of the other task were relatively low.

In sum, successful use of the face–name mnemonic depends on two factors discussed elsewhere in this chapter. First, there is an emphasis on distinctiveness of facial features. Second, the finding that name recall is greatly enhanced by retrieval practice exemplifies the testing effect (discussed later).

TECHNIQUES TO IMPROVE MEMORY: VERBAL MNEMONICS

The mnemonics devised 2,000 years ago relied mainly on visual imagery. However, this was less so in later times. For example, the Puritans favored verbal systems over those based on visual imagery. They did so for a rather curious reason—they regarded images as wicked and liable to give rise to "depraved carnal affections"!

Verbal mnemonics are useful and widely used in many situations. Suppose you want to remember the colors of the spectrum in order (red, orange, yellow, green, blue, indigo, and violet). You start with the first letters of the colors (ROYGBIV) and use those first letters to construct a sentence (e.g., Richard Of York Gave Battle In Vain).

One of the best-known anatomy mnemonics refers to the names of the cranial nerves: On Old Olympia's Towering Top A Finn And German Vault And Hop (olfactory, optic, oculomotor, trochlear, trigeminal, abducens, facial, auditory, glossopharyngeal, vague, accessory, and hypoglassal). Such mnemonics are effective if we assume medical students know the particular names but cannot reliably retrieve them in the correct order.

Story mnemonic

One of the most effective verbal learning strategies is the story mnemonic. This mnemonic is used to remember a series of unrelated words in the correct order by linking them together within a story. The story mnemonic is discussed here as an example of a verbal mnemonic, but note that it often also involves the use of visual imagery.

We will show this method at work with the 10 words used earlier to illustrate the

KEY TERM

Story mnemonic: A memory technique that involves constructing a story linking unrelated words together in the correct order.

pegword method (*battleship, pig, chair, sheep, castle, rug, grass, beach, milkmaid, binoculars*):

In the kitchen of the BATTLESHIP, there was a PIG that sat in a CHAIR. There was also a SHEEP that previously lived in a CASTLE. In port, the sailors took a RUG and sat on the GRASS close to the BEACH. While there, they saw a MILKMAID watching them through her BINOCULARS.

Bower and Clark (1969) discovered that the story mnemonic is extremely effective. Participants recalled 12 lists of 10 nouns each in the correct order when given the first words of each list as cues. Those who had constructed narrative stories recalled 93% of the words compared to only 13% for those who did not! Subsequent research has confirmed that the story mnemonic is generally very effective (Worthen & Hunt, 2011).

Hu, Ericsson, Yang, and Lu (2009) studied the mnemonist Chao Lu. In 2005, he became the World Champion at reciting *pi*: he did so to 67,890 digits without making any errors. Chao Lu studied 40 words and then recalled all of them in the correct order having spent only 9 or 10 seconds learning each word. His memory performance depended on the story mnemonic—he mentally arranged the words into eight groups of five, and constructed a vivid story at a given location for each group.

Evaluation

The story mnemonic has proved effective. It has the advantage over the method of loci and the pegword method that it does not require any prior learning (e.g., of pegwords). It also has the advantage that very different stories can be constructed for each list of words, thus reducing the likelihood of proactive interference from previous list learning.

What are the limitations of the story mnemonic? First, it requires fairly extensive training—I took a few minutes to construct the story given above! Second, you generally have to work your way through the list if you want to find a given item (e.g., the seventh

one). Third, it has restricted applicability to real-life situations. However, you could use it when trying to remember things you need to do when preparing for a holiday (Worthen & Hunt, 2011).

WHY ARE MNEMONIC TECHNIQUES EFFECTIVE?

The success of mnemonic techniques such as the method of loci, the pegword method, and the story method owes much to the fact that they allow us to make use of our pre-existing knowledge (e.g., the spatial layout of familiar environments; the sequence of numbers). However, that is only part of what is involved (see below).

Suppose we asked cab drivers and students to recall lists of streets in the city in which they live. We would expect the cab drivers (with their excellent knowledge of the spatial layout of the city's streets) to outperform the students. In fact, matters are more complex. Kalakoski and Saariluoma (2001) asked Helsinki taxi drivers and students to recall lists of 15 Helsinki street names in order. When the street names were presented in an order forming a spatially continuous route through the city, the taxi drivers had much higher recall than students (87% vs. 45%). In contrast, when nonadjacent street names taken from all over Helsinki were presented in a random order, the cab drivers and students had comparable recall.

How can we explain the above findings? The cab drivers obviously knew considerably more than the students about the spatial layout of Helsinki's streets. They used this knowledge effectively to facilitate learning and memory when all the streets were fairly close together within that spatial layout. However, this knowledge was of little or no use when the street names were distributed randomly around the city.

In spite of the research by Kalakoski and Saariluoma (2001), relevant knowledge is the key to understanding the effectiveness of most mnemonic techniques. As Gobet (2016, p. 40) pointed out, "Mnemonics work by using LTM [long-term memory] as a means to compensate for the limited capacity of STM [short-term memory] by creating what are known as *retrieval structures*."

Ericsson (1988) provided a detailed account of the three main requirements for achieving advanced memory skills:

1 *Meaningful encoding*: to-be-learned information should be processed meaningfully by relating it to pre-existing knowledge. Examples include using known locations (method of loci) or the number sequence (pegword method) or cab drivers using their knowledge of spatial layouts. This is the *encoding principle*.

2 *Retrieval structure*: cues should be stored with the information to aid subsequent retrieval. The connected series of locations or the number sequence both provide an immediately available retrieval structure, as does the knowledge of spatial layout possessed by taxi drivers. This is the *retrieval structure principle*.

3 *Speed-up principle*: extensive practice allows the processes involved in encoding and retrieval to be carried out increasingly rapidly. The importance of extensive practice can be seen in the generally superior memory for street names shown by taxi drivers compared to students in the study by Kalakoski and Saariluoma (2001). This is the *speed-up principle*.

Yoon, Ericsson, and Donatelli (2018) wondered whether someone who had acquired advanced memory skills by developing the appropriate retrieval structures would retain those structures over a long period of disuse. They studied Dario Donatelli, who in the mid-1980s used mnemonic techniques to increase his digit span from eight to 106 digits after 800 hours of training. When re-tested 30 years later, his initial span was only 10 digits. However, this increased to 19 digits after three days of testing. Thus, Donatelli had retained some aspects of his acquired retrieval structures over the 30-year period, although his performance was markedly worse than it had been 30 years earlier.

Ericsson and Kintsch (1995) developed the ideas of Ericsson (1988) discussed above. They introduced the notion of a long-term working memory used to store relevant information in long-term memory and access it through retrieval cues in working memory. Thus, stored information about retrieval structure is accessed to enhance memory performance. More specifically, the crucial notion is that, "fast ... transfer to LTM [long-term memory] becomes possible with expertise via knowledge structures, which enables LTM to be used during WM [working memory] tasks, thus giving the appearance of expanding individuals' WM capacity" (Guida, Gobet, & Nicolas, 2013).

A key prediction from Ericsson and Kintsch's (1995) theoretical approach is that experts can use their retrieval structures to memorize information rapidly and efficiently regardless of whether the information is presented in its natural order or a random order. Several findings are inconsistent with this prediction (Gobet, 2016). For example, Coughlin and Patel (1987) presented information concerning a clinical case of acute bacterial endocarditis in a natural or random order to highly trained doctors. Their memory for the details of the case was significantly worse when the information had been presented in a random order.

Evidence more supportive of Ericsson and Kintsch's (1995) approach was reported by Ericsson, Cheng, Pan, Ku, Ge, and Hu (2017). They studied Feng Wang, who won the World Memory Championship by recalling 300 digits presented at a rate of one digit per second. Ericsson et al. found Feng Wang had perfect recall of 200 digits presented at the same fast rate because he used retrieval structures incredibly efficiently. Feng Wang achieved this extraordinary performance by dividing the digits into four-digit clusters, with the clusters being associated with previously memorized lists of location or loci.

In sum, the main reason mnemonic techniques are effective is because they enable memorizers to use previously learned retrieval structures stored in long-term memory. These retrieval structures can be used very rapidly by individuals who have spent prolonged periods of time acquiring the requisite retrieval structures (e.g., Feng Wang). However, experts who have not explicitly devoted considerable time to developing retrieval structures (e.g., doctors) can have problems in using retrieval structures effectively when information is presented in a random order. Finally, it is probably unnecessary to hypothesize the existence of a brand new form of working memory given the imprecise nature of Ericsson and Kintsch's (1995) theory of long-term working memory (Foroughi, Werner, Barragán, & Boehm-Davis, 2016).

WORKING MEMORY TRAINING

As we have seen, most mnemonic techniques have limited applicability. We also have a limited theoretical understanding of the reasons why these techniques are effective. These limitations suggest it would be advantageous to focus on ways of improving memory based more directly on memory processes and/or structures known theoretically to be of general importance.

We saw in Chapter 4 that working memory is a crucially important part of the human memory system. Accordingly, a potentially important approach to improving memory would involve training designed to enhance the capacity and/or efficiency of the working memory system. It has often been assumed that this would lead to enhanced performance of a wide range of cognitive activities (many of which involve memory). This approach has led numerous companies to provide "brain-training" programs allegedly enhancing cognitive skills (including memory) (Simons et al., 2016). Note that

approaches focusing on training working memory are also discussed in Chapter 4.

Why might working memory training enhance long-term memory? First, it might increase the capacity of the various components of the working memory system (the central executive; episodic buffer; phonological loop; visuo-spatial sketchpad) (see Chapter 4).

Second, individuals with high working memory capacity have greater attentional control than those with low capacity. For example, Unsworth and McMillan (2013) found high-capacity individuals exhibited less mind wandering than low-capacity ones during a reading task. Enhanced attentional control during learning would undoubtedly increase long-term memory.

Shipstead, Redick, and Engle (2012) reviewed research on working memory training. Such training sometimes enhanced attentional and also led to increased long-term recall. However, the effects were small and often non-significant. Of most importance, any beneficial effects were typically found only on tasks very similar to those involved in training and were not observed on tasks dissimilar to the training tasks. In other words, there was some evidence of *transfer of training*—positive effects on performance caused by prior training. However, these beneficial effects were found only for near transfer (high similarity between current and training tasks) and not for far transfer (low similarity between current and training tasks).

Gathercole, Dunning, Holmes, and Norris (2019) provided an updated review of research on working memory training including many studies published after Shipstead et al.'s (2012) review. The positive effects of training were only small to moderate, and were greatest when the original and transfer tasks were the same or very similar. Positive transfer effects (enhanced performance on a task because of prior practice with a different task) were mostly found when the original training task was unfamiliar and required learning specific cognitive processes also required on the transfer task.

In sum, there are grounds for arguing that working memory training might have various beneficial effects including enhancing long-term memory. So far, however, it has proved elusive to demonstrate wide-ranging positive effects of such training. It remains possible that training programs teaching a broader range of skills and abilities would be more successful.

MEMORY EXPERTS

You have probably heard about the amazing memory feats performed by extremely gifted individuals. Some of these feats appear so remarkable that you may have suspected that the claims made are grossly exaggerated. There have undoubtedly been some charlatans. However, solid evidence of truly outstanding memory powers has been obtained from several individuals (Worthen & Hunt, 2011).

Naturals vs. strategists

Are individuals with exceptional memory "naturally gifted" or have they devoted substantial time and practice to developing effective mnemonic techniques? Wilding and Valentine (1994) considered this question. They assessed the memory performance of contestants at the World Memory Championships using two kinds of memory tasks:

1   Strategic tasks (e.g., associating names and faces) susceptible to the use of memory strategies.
2   Nonstrategic tasks (e.g., recognition of snow crystals).

KEY TERM

Synesthesia: The tendency for one sense modality to evoke another.

Box 17.3 Shereshevskii: The greatest mnemonist (memory expert) of all time?

The Russian Solomon Shereshevskii (often referred to as S) was possibly the most extraordinary of all the mnemonists (memory experts). This remarkable man was studied by the Russian psychologist Alexander Luria, who wrote a fascinating book about him, *The Mind of a Mnemonist* (Luria, 1968). His extraordinary memory abilities were discovered while he was working as a journalist: his editor noticed that S was able to repeat everything said to him word for word without taking any notes.

The editor sent him to Luria, who found S rapidly learned complex material (e.g., lists of over 100 digits). More dramatically, S could remember such material perfectly (even in reverse order) several years later. According to Luria (1968, p. 11), "There was no limit either to the *capacity* of S's memory or to the *durability of the traces he retained.*"

What was Shereshevskii's secret? He had exceptional imagery. Not only could he rapidly and easily create a wealth of visual images, he also had an amazing capacity for synesthesia (the capacity for a stimulus in one sense to evoke an image in another sense). For example, when presented with a tone having a pitch of 2,000 cycles per second, he said, "It looks something like fireworks tinged with a pink-red hue. The strip of color feels rough and unpleasant, and it has an ugly taste—rather like that of a briny pickle" (p. 23).

Do you envy S's memory powers? Ironically, his memory was so good it disrupted his everyday life. For example, this was his experience when trying to make sense of a prose passage: "Each word calls up images, they collide with one another, and the result is chaos" (p. 65). His mind came to resemble "a junk heap of impressions." His acute awareness of details meant he sometimes failed to recognize someone he knew if, for example, their facial coloring had altered because they had been on holiday. These limitations of his memory made it hard for him to live a normal life and he finished up in an asylum.

Wilding and Valentine (1994) classified their participants as strategists or naturals. Strategists reported frequent use of memory strategies. In contrast, naturals claimed naturally superior memory ability from childhood. As predicted, the strategists performed much better on strategic tasks than nonstrategic ones, whereas the naturals did well on both kinds of memory tasks (see Figure 17.4). The data are plotted in percentiles (50th percentile = average person's score). Easily the best memory performance (surpassing that of over 99% of the population) was obtained by strategists on strategic tasks. This should provide encouragement for us all—excellent memory can be developed through training.

Dresler et al. (2017) provided a more detailed account of brain functioning in individuals with exceptional memory. These individuals had greater functional connectivity than those with ordinary memory ability across various brain networks including the medial temporal lobes. This increased functional connectivity within the brain was especially strong in the dorsolateral prefrontal cortex, the medial prefrontal cortex, and the medial temporal lobe, areas known to be strongly associated with learning and memory processes. Dresler et al. also found that memory training in individuals with ordinary memory ability led to increased functional connectivity within the brain resembling that found in those with exceptional memory.

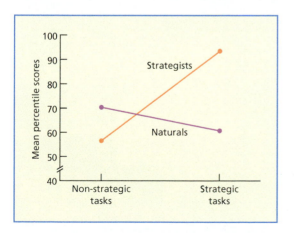

Figure 17.4 Memory performance strategists and naturals on strategic and nonstrategic tasks. Based on data in Wilding and Valentine (1994).

The evidence discussed above strongly suggests that exceptional memory depends on prolonged practice. If so, individuals with exceptional memory should show only average memory performance on tasks for which they have not developed specific strategies. This prediction was strikingly confirmed with Rajan Mahadevan, who for several years held the world record for memorizing the maximum number of digit of *pi* (31,811 digits). Ericsson, Delaney, Weaver, and Mahadevan (2004) assessed his symbol span using 10 symbols (e.g., ?, @, #, and *). His initial symbol span was only six symbols (the same as college students). He eventually increased his symbol span to nearly 30 items, but only by recoding each symbol into a different digit and then using his usual memory strategies to remember the resulting digit string.

Face recognition

Several studies have focused on individuals having exceptional face recognition ability. For example, Russell, Duchaine, and Nakayama (2009) identified four individuals claiming to have extremely good face-recognition ability. For example, one of them said, "It doesn't matter how many years pass, if I've seen a face before I will be able to recall it. It only happens with faces" (p. 253). All four individuals performed exceptionally well on tasks involving face recognition (e.g., identifying famous people from photographs of them when they were children). Russell et al. called these individuals "super-recognizers."

Genetic factors partly explain the existence of super-recognizers. Wilmer et al. (2010) studied face recognition in monozygotic (identical) twins (sharing 100% of their genes) and dizygotic (fraternal) twins (sharing only 50% of their genes). The face-recognition performance of identical twins was much more similar than that of fraternal twins, indicating that face-recognition ability is influenced by genetic factors. Face-recognition ability correlated very modestly with other forms of recognition (e.g., abstract art images) suggesting it is very specific. In similar fashion, Turano, Marzi, and Viggiano (2016) found good and poor face recognizers did not differ with respect to car-recognition ability.

Tardif et al. (2019) shed light on the processing strategies used by super-recognizers. Among individuals having average face-recognition ability, the most important regions for face recognition are the eyes and eyebrows followed by the mouth. An important reason why super-recognizers had outstanding face-recognition performance was that they were especially likely to focus on those face regions during a face-recognition task.

Learning strategies

Several individuals have exhibited outstanding memory ability to recite *pi* to thousands of decimal places. The current record holder is Suresh Kumar Sharma of India. On October 21, 2015, at the age of 21, he recited *pi* to 70,030 digits without making any errors over a grueling 17 hours and 14 minutes. He has not discussed in detail the precise strategies he used to achieve this stupendous feat. However, when asked how he trains other people to learn large amounts of complex information, he said: "I make them learn different techniques which helps them to link subject content with objects, location and peg. I push them to follow the old Vedic system of learning by connecting everything with an image."

One of the most studied individuals with outstanding ability to recite *pi* was PI, who recited *pi* to over 64,000 digits at the age of 22 (Raz et al., 2009). PI used a modified form of the method of loci to learn this enormous digit sequence, considering the digits two at a time. Sometimes he converted two-digit groups to words based on the similarity of their pronunciations. At other times, he generated images resembling the physical characteristics of the digits (e.g., 10 looks like a putter and a hole and led to the word *golf*). Then PI produced stories based on his earlier processing. Perhaps surprisingly, PI's visual memory for neutral faces and common events was very poor.

An important reason why PI was so successful at reciting *pi* is that his working memory abilities exceed those of 99% of the population. Raz et al. (2009) assessed PI's brain activity as he recited the first 540 digits of *pi*. Areas within the prefrontal cortex associated with working memory and attentional control were strongly activated.

In sum, PI is typical of those showing outstanding ability to recall thousands of digits of *pi* in that he adopts a three-stage approach. First, adjacent digits are formed into small groups or chunks. Second, a visual image or word represents each chunk. Third, language is used to combine and integrate the information from successive chunks. Their memory strategies resemble an elaborated version of the story method (discussed earlier).

If you could recite *pi* to thousands (or tens of thousands) of places, you could boast to your friends. Apart from that, it would have no value in your everyday life. It would be more useful to have excellent memory for the events of your own life (i.e., autobiographical memory; see Chapter 11). As we will see, researchers have discovered several individuals with exceptional memory for their own lives; unsurprisingly, they are said to have highly superior autobiographical memory (HSAM).

Jill Price is one of the best-known individuals with HSAM. She has an incredible ability to recall detailed information about almost every day of her life. While you may envy her phenomenal autobiographical memory, she regards it negatively: "I call it

Jill Price, a participant in LePort et al.'s (2012) study of highly superior autobiographical memory.

a burden. I run my entire life through my head every day and it drives me crazy!" Strangely, her memory generally (e.g., recalling word lists) is unimpressive. Her autobiographical memory is outstanding because she has obsessional tendencies. She also has poor inhibitory processes and so finds it very hard to switch off her personal memories. You can see Jill Price on YouTube: The woman who could not forget—Jill Price.

More recent research (e.g., LePort, Stark, McGaugh, & Stark, 2016; Santangelo et al., 2018) indicates that most individuals with HSAM possess similar obsessional characteristics to Jill Price. Indeed, they often have as many obsessional symptoms as patients with obsessive-compulsive disorder. They also resemble Jill Price in having only average performance on standard laboratory memory tasks.

LePort et al. (2016) found that individuals with HSAM had comparable autobiographical memory to controls one week after an event. However, they were dramatically better than controls thereafter. These findings suggest their advantage depends on processes occurring after autobiographical memory acquisition (e.g., frequent rehearsal).

Santangelo et al. (2018) found individuals with HSAM retrieved autobiographical memories (but not other memories) much faster than controls. During retrieval of autobiographical memories, twice as many brain areas were activated in HSAM individuals as controls and they had enhanced connectivity between brain areas important in memory retrieval.

PREPARING FOR EXAMINATIONS

Students use numerous techniques to assist their learning and increase their ability to perform successfully on examinations. Dunlosky, Rawson, Marsh, Nathan, and Willingham (2013) discussed 10 such learning techniques with reference to the available research evidence. Some techniques were rated as low in usefulness. These included

summarization (writing summaries of texts), imagery for text (forming mental images of text materials), and rereading (restudying text material after an initial reading).

Other techniques were rated as of moderate usefulness. These included elaborative interrogation (generating explanations for stated facts), self-explanation (explaining how new information is related to known information), and interleaved practice (studying different kinds of material within a single study session). Of course, what is of most interest to you (and also of most theoretical interest) is to focus on the technique rated the most useful. This technique (the testing effect) is discussed first followed by a consideration of the second most useful technique (distributed practice). We conclude this section with a discussion of concept maps.

Testing effect

Answer this question taken from research by Karpicke, Butler, and Roediger (2009). Imagine you are reading a textbook for an upcoming examination. After you have read the chapter once, would you rather:

A   Go back and restudy either the entire chapter or certain parts of the chapter?
B   Try to recall the material from the chapter (without the possibility of restudying the material)?
C   Use some other study technique?

Karpicke et al. (2009) found 57% of students gave answer A, 21% gave answer C, and only 18% gave answer B. This pattern of responses makes sense on the intuitively appealing assumptions that learning occurs only while we are studying and that testing provides only an opportunity to assess how much we have learned. In fact, however, the least frequent answer (B) is actually the correct one! The reasons why that is the case are discussed below.

The phenomenon investigated by Karpicke et al. (2009) is known as the *testing effect*: "Receiving tests on recently learned items often enhances long-term memory for those items relative to restudying them" (Cho, Neely, Crocco, & Vitrano, 2017, p. 1211).

Box 17.4 Testing effect (Roediger & Karpicke , 2006)

Roediger and Karpicke (2006) asked students to read a prose passage covering a general scientific topic and to memorize it in one of three conditions:

1   *Repeated study*: the passage was read four times and there was no test.
2   *Single test*: the passage was read three times and then students recalled as much as possible from it.
3   *Repeated test*: the passage was read once and then students recalled as much as possible on three occasions.

Finally, memory for the passage was tested after five minutes or one week.

The findings are shown in Figure 17.5. Repeated study was the most effective strategy when the final test was given five minutes after learning, and the repeated test condition was the least effective. However, there was a dramatic reversal when the final test occurred one week after learning (this is the testing effect), and these findings are of most relevance to students preparing for an examination. The size of the testing effect is striking: average recall was 50% higher in the repeated test condition than the repeated study condition. That difference could easily make the difference between doing very well on an examination and failing it!

Why do so many students prefer repeated studying to repeated testing when revising for an examination? There are three main reasons:

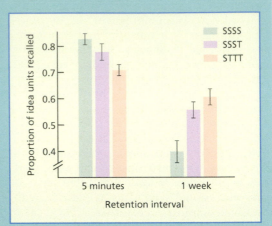

Figure 17.5 Memory performance as a function of learning conditions (S, study; T, test) and retention interval (five minutes vs. one week). From Roediger and Karpicke (2006). Copyright © Blackwell Publishing. Reproduced with permission.

1   Repeated studying produces short-term benefits (see Figure 17.5).
2   Roediger and Karpicke (2006) found students in the repeated study condition predicted they would recall more of the prose passage after one week than did those in the repeated test condition. This latter finding is a clear example of "lack of metacognitive awareness" (Roediger & Karpicke, 2018, p. 236), meaning the students had a poor understanding of their own cognitive abilities.
3   Studying is less effortful and demanding than testing, and this makes it more appealing to students.

Findings
The testing effect is surprisingly robust. Rowland (2014) carried out a meta-analysis: 81% of the findings were positive and overall the testing effect was moderately strong. A possible limitation of that meta-analysis is that it was based predominantly on laboratory studies. Accordingly, Schwieren, Barenberg, and Dutke (2017) reported a meta-analysis based solely on research conducted in the context of learning and teaching psychology. Reassuringly, the overall magnitude of the testing effect was comparable in such real-life contexts.

Theoretical accounts
Several theoretical explanations of the testing effect have been put forward over the years. However, most belong to one of two types of explanation (Rowland, 2014). First, one type

of theory emphasizes the importance of retrieval effort. The basic assumption is that the magnitude of the testing effect is greater when the difficulty or effort involved in retrieval during the learning period is high rather than low.

How does increased retrieval effort enhance the testing effect? Rickard and Pan (2018) provided an answer with their dual-memory theory (see Figure 17.6). In essence, restudy strengthens only the memory traces formed at initial study. When learners apply retrieval effort during testing, however, this strengthens the memory trace formed at initial study AND leads to the formation of a *second* memory trace. Thus, testing involving retrieval effort generally promotes superior memory to restudy because it promotes the acquisition of *two* memory traces rather than just *one*.

It is important to note that the above predictions apply *only* when feedback (provision of the correct answers) occurs during testing. If participants fail to supply the correct answers for any items during testing (and they receive no feedback), then no second memory trace will be formed for those items. Below we discuss a model that is applicable in those circumstances.

There is much support for the general approach taken by the dual-memory theory. Endres and Renkl (2015) asked learners to rate the mental effort they used during retrieval practice and restudy. They obtained a testing effect which disappeared when mental effort was controlled for statistically. More effortful or demanding retrieval tests (e.g., free recall) typically lead to a greater testing effect than easy retrieval tests (e.g., recognition memory) (Rowland, 2014).

Second, there is the bifurcation model (bifurcation means division into two) proposed by Kornell, Bjork, and Garcia (2011). According to this model, items successfully retrieved during retrieval practice are strengthened more than restudied items. However, the crucial assumption is that items *not* retrieved during testing practice (and also not receiving feedback) are not strengthened at all. As a consequence, such items are strengthened less than restudied items. This leads to the novel prediction that the testing effect can be reversed.

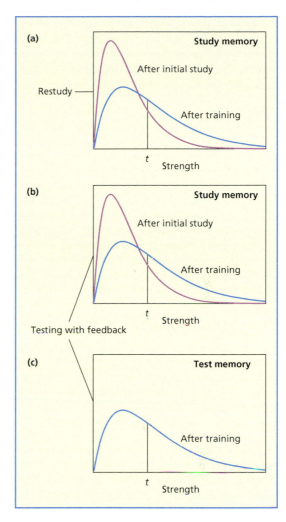

Figure 17.6 (a) Restudy causes strengthening of the memory trace formed after initial study; (b) testing with feedback causes strengthening of the memory trace; and (c) the formation of a second memory trace. t = the response threshold that must be exceeded for any given item to be retrieved on the final test. From Rickard & Pan (2018).

There is also support for the bifurcation model (Pastötter & Bäuml, 2016). Participants had retrieval (testing practice) or restudy practice for paired associates following a period of study. This was followed two days later by a memory test. Pastötter and Bäuml focused on those items not recalled on this memory test. According to the bifurcation model, nonrecalled items previously subject to retrieval practice should be weaker than those previously subject to restudy. This prediction was supported by findings from a further memory test occurring shortly after re-presentation of the word pairs.

Conclusions

The testing effect is generally strong and has been obtained almost regardless of the nature of the to-be-learned material. The dual-memory theory provides a plausible explanation of the testing effect. However, more research is required to identify the conditions in which testing leads to the formation of a second memory trace differing from the memory trace formed during initial study. The bifurcation model explains the reversed testing effect but does not clearly specify the underlying processes or mechanisms.

Distributed practice

As mentioned earlier, Dunlosky et al. (2013) found that distributed practice was the second most effective learning technique. More specifically, they discussed evidence supporting the *distributed-practice effect*— this refers to the finding that long-term learning is better when repeated study of material is distributed over time than when it occurs close together in time. Cepeda, Pashler, Vul, Wixted, and Rohrer (2006) reviewed 254 studies on distributed practice. Overall, there was clear support for the distributed-practice effect: students' recall was higher after distributed or spaced study (47%) than after massed study (37%).

Most of the studies considered by Cepeda et al. (2006) were limited because they were laboratory-based. Accordingly, Kim, Wong-Kee-You, Wiseheart, and Rosenbaum (2019) focused on learning during workplace training. They established that there is a large distributed-practice effect in real-world settings. Dunlosky et al. (2013) discussed research showing that the distributed-practice effect is typically found with most kinds of learning material and with participants ranging from young children to older adults.

In view of the magnitude of the distributed-practice effect, it may seem strange that many students engage in massed practice by cramming for tests and examinations. However, massed practice is reasonably effective when memory is tested at a short retention interval, and this may lead students to assume (incorrectly) that massed practice will also be effective with long retention intervals.

What is the optimal time period between successive learning episodes? The answer is perhaps more complex than you might imagine. Cepeda, Vul, Rohrer, Wixted, and Pashler (2008) investigated this issue and discovered that the optimal time depends on the retention interval (e.g., time before an important examination). More specifically, final memory performance was best when the time interval between successive study sessions was approximately 10–20% of the desired retention interval. Thus, for example, if you need to remember some material for a period of one week, you should ideally space your learning episodes about 12–24 hours apart.

How can we explain the distributed-practice effect? Several theoretical accounts have been proposed. However, there is probably most support for the notion that massed practice is less effective than distributed practice because of deficient processing (Gerbier & Koenig, 2015). In essence, when students re-study material shortly after studying it, they find it very easy to reread and so tend to process it only superficially. Conversely, they are likely to process to-be-learned material more thoroughly when they previously studied it longer ago.

There has been relatively little research designed explicitly to identify the precise factors responsible for the distributed-practice effect. However, in view of the magnitude of the effect, it seems likely that several factors are jointly involved in producing it (Dunlosky et al., 2013). More specifically, there may be important links between the distributed-practice effect and the testing effect (discussed above). The testing effect is typically strongest when considerable effort is required to retrieve the to-be-learned material, and this is most likely to be the case when a reasonable amount of time has elapsed since the to-be-learned material was studied. This suggests that the processes underlying the testing effect may also contribute to the distributed-practice effect.

Concept maps

There has been a substantial increase over the years in the use of concept maps. A concept map is "any node-link diagram in which each node represents a concept and each link identifies the relationship between the two concepts it connects" (Schroeder, Nesbit, Anguiano, & Adescope, 2018, p. 431). A concrete example is shown in Figure 17.7.

There are various reasons why concept maps might enhance learning and memory. First, students must be actively involved in the learning process to produce accurate concept maps. Second, most concepts are shown with several links or associations to each other. It is arguable this is more realistic (and easier to remember) than the linear

KEY TERM

Concept map: A diagram in which the links among general concepts (at the top of the diagram) and specific concepts (lower down) are shown.

presentation of information in texts. Third, concepts are typically reduced to one or two words within concept maps, extracting the essence of their meaning and ignoring trivial details.

Findings

Concept maps are undoubtedly useful in enhancing long-term memory. A thorough investigation of their effectiveness was reported

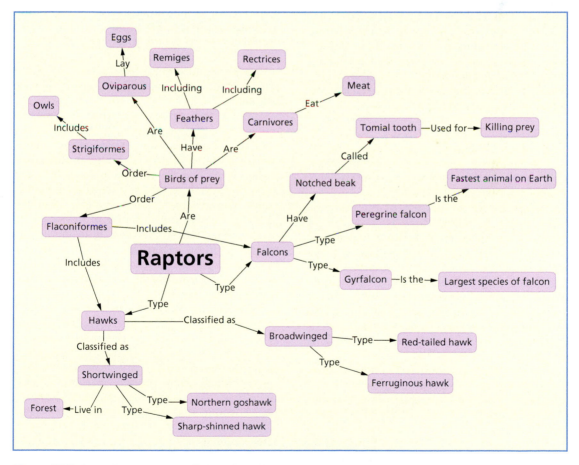

Figure 17.7 A simple concept map. Each node in the map represents a concept, and each link identifies the nature of the relationship between connected concepts. From Schroeder et al. (2018).

by Schroeder et al. (2018) in a meta-analysis (statistical analysis based on combining numerous findings). Overall, the use of concept maps enhanced learning and memory to a moderate extent.

Schroeder et al. (2018) carried out additional analyses and came up with two more conclusions. First, learning was much greater when students constructed their own concept maps than when they studied concept maps produced by someone else. Constructing maps required more elaborative cognitive processing than studying maps; such elaborative processing may have involved "self-questioning, reflection, and summarization" (p. 440).

Second, Schroeder et al. (2018) compared the effectiveness of concept maps with respect to STEM (science, technology, engineering, and mathematics) subjects with non-STEM subjects. The authors had hypothesized that concept maps would enhance learning more with STEM subjects because they depend more on integrated conceptual understanding. However, concept maps had comparably beneficial effects for both types of subjects, indicating their general applicability.

Evaluation

Learning and memory for academic information benefit from the use of concept maps. This is especially the case when students create their own concept maps.

What are the limitations of the concept-map approach? First, there is a dearth of theory-oriented research and so we have only a limited understanding of *why* concept maps are so effective. One common explanation is that concept maps foster meaningful learning. Another possible explanation is that concept maps reduce cognitive overload on verbal working memory because cognitive load is distributed between verbal and visual working memory.

Second, students sometimes find it hard to construct adequate concept maps when the to-be-learned material is complex. For example, Duarte, Loureiro, and Zukowsky-Tavares (2017) asked students to construct concept maps focusing on the interrelationships of concepts relating to immunology. They discovered that 31% of the propositions included in concept maps were inadequate.

Popular study strategies

In this chapter, we have discussed several strategies effective at enhancing learning and memory. However, as Miyatsu, Nguyen, and McDaniel (2018) pointed out, many students are reluctant to use these strategies because they have developed strong preferences for strategies or techniques they have used for many years. Accordingly, Miyatsu et al. argued it is important to consider the effectiveness of study strategies students actually use.

Miyatsu et al. (2018) identified five popular study strategies from a review of the relevant literature. The five were as follows (frequencies of use by students are shown in brackets): rereading (78%); flash cards to provide self-testing of what has been learned (55%); highlighting or underlining parts of texts (53%); note-taking during lectures and textbook reading (30%); and outlining focusing on the main points to be learned (23%). All of these study strategies often enhance students' memory. However, these strategies are generally not implemented optimally (see below).

As we saw earlier, rereading is typically much less effective than testing oneself following a single reading. How can we make rereading more effective? First, as discussed earlier, rereading should take place some time after the initial reading rather than immediately. The reason is that reading is more likely to involve only limited processing if it occurs immediately. Second, it is important when rereading to engage actively with the material (e.g., monitoring one's level of comprehension; paraphrasing the material; elaborating on the material).

How can using flash cards be made maximally effective? The main recommendation is for students to increase the amount of time they spend using flash cards. Students often drop any given flash card following one successful recall even though learning is still limited at that point. Vaughn and Rawson (2011) found that only 31% of items originally recalled once were also recalled 48 hours later compared to 71% of items originally recalled four or five times. Thus, learning (and memory) both increase when additional time is devoted to testing via flash cards.

Highlighting or underlining is potentially beneficial for two reasons: (1) selecting important information produces elaborative thinking; (2) it makes it easy to identify important information subsequently. How can these benefits be maximized? Training focused on text structure or organization has proved effective (Miyatsu et al., 2018). In addition, reading through the entire text *before* highlighting increases the probability that the sections selected for highlighting will actually be the most important ones.

Note-taking is ineffective when students copy lecture notes verbatim and then fail to review them subsequently. In contrast, note-taking is most effective when students engage in active processing of the material (e.g., summarizing or paraphrasing) because it increases the coherence and organization of the notes. In addition, there is evidence that the beneficial effects of reviewing notes is greater than the benefits associated with simply taking notes (Kobayashi, 2006).

Finally, we discuss outlining, which involves producing a hierarchical representation of the most important points in a text. Outlining is typically more effective when done *after* an entire section of text has been read because the text structure is likely to be clearer at that point than earlier.

Conclusions

One of the most important conclusions is that most people have deficient metamemory, which involves an understanding of one's own memory and how it functions. As Miyatsu et al. (2018, p. 400) pointed out, "Students are often unaware of the pitfalls associated with these strategies [the five strategies discussed above], including mistaking fluency for learning when rereading, highlighting too much, copying notes verbatim, and prematurely dropping flashcards from further study."

Another important conclusion is that the effectiveness of most study strategies can be greatly enhanced by making use of the knowledge of how human memory works accumulated by cognitive psychologists. For example, as Mandler (1967, p. 327) argued, "Organization is a necessary condition for memory … the organization of, and hence memory for, verbal material is hierarchical." In addition, what students remember of a lecture or a text depends strongly on their comprehension of it (including elaboration, identifying the key points, and paraphrasing). Finally, it is important that students test themselves frequently to maximize long-term memory.

SUMMARY

- Distinctive processing (the processing of difference in the context of similarity) is generally associated with enhanced long-term memory as is shown in the von Restorff effect.
- Distinctiveness enhances memory because it facilitates discrimination between the correct and incorrect responses at the time of retrieval. As a result, it reduces false memory as well as increasing correct memory.
- The von Restorff effect also occurs in part because distinctive items typically attract more attention (and processing) at encoding.
- Mnemonics based on visual imagery have been common since classical times. One of the most effective of such mnemonics is the method of loci. It can be used in lectures but is much harder to use with visually presented text. It has also been used to enhance mood states in depressed individuals.
- The pegword technique is similar to the method of loci and is also of proven effectiveness. However, it has limited applicability to real life because we rarely need to remember a sequence of unrelated items.

(Continued)

(Continued)

- Visual imagery can be effective when linking names to faces. Its effectiveness is greatly enhanced by retrieval practice, which often cannot be easily used in social situations.
- The story mnemonic can be extremely effective. However, it typically requires much time to construct stories to link together words. Thus, the method cannot be used effectively when to-be-remembered information must be processed rapidly.
- There are three ingredients in most successful mnemonic techniques: meaningful encoding (relating what is to be learned to pre-existing knowledge), retrieval structure (cues are stored to assist subsequent retrieval), and speed-up (extensive practice allows encoding and retrieval to occur faster).
- Information about retrieval structure is stored in long-term working memory from which it is easily accessed.
- Working memory training often has small or moderate beneficial effects on learning and memory. However, such beneficial effects are typically limited to situations where the same specific cognitive processes are required on the original training and transfer tasks.
- Most individuals with exceptional memory abilities make extensive use of learning strategies and prolonged practice. They generally combine information from two or more items into chunks and then use language to integrate information across chunks.
- Individuals with highly superior autobiographical memory typically have strong obsessional characteristics and enhanced connectivity between brain areas important in memory retrieval.
- Individual differences in face recognition depend in part on genetic factors specific to faces. In addition, individuals with excellent face recognition focus on the most important regions for face recognition (e.g., eyes; eyebrows).
- One of the most effective study techniques is based on the testing effect—the finding that retrieval practice enhances long-term memory much more than additional study or rereading. The main reason why the testing effect is so effective is probably because retrieval practice often leads to the formation of a second memory trace additional to the one formed at the time of original study.
- Concept maps enhance the organization and integration of information about concepts. This is especially the case when learners construct their own concept maps.
- Students often use study strategies such as rereading, use of flash cards, and highlighting parts of texts. These strategies are generally not used with maximal efficiency because students have deficient metamemory (understanding of their own memory).

POINTS FOR DISCUSSION

1. Why does distinctiveness enhance long-term memory?
2. Describe the main mnemonic techniques based on visual imagery. Why are these techniques effective? What are their limitations?
3. Describe training programs designed to enhance working memory. Discuss the effectiveness of these programs.
4. How can we account for the exceptional memories possessed by some individuals?

5 What is the testing effect? Why has it proved so effective?
6 Describe a few of students' most popular study strategies and discuss ways of maximizing their effectiveness.
7 How do actors manage to learn their roles verbatim?

FURTHER READING

Brown, P. C., Roediger, H. L., & McDaniel, M. A. (2014). *Making it stick: The science of successful learning.* Cambridge, MA: Belknap Press. This book (written by experts in the field) discusses effective ways in which you can enhance your learning and long-term memory.

Dunlosky, J., Rawson, K. A., Marsh, E. J., Nathan, M. J., & Willingham, D. T. (2013). Improving students' learning with effective learning techniques: Promising directions from cognitive and educational psychology. *Psychological Science in the Public Interest, 14,* 4–58. John Dunlosky and his colleagues discuss and assess the effectiveness of several techniques designed to enhance learning and memory.

Foer, J. (2011). *Moonwalking with Einstein: The art and science of remembering everything.* New York: Penguin Press. This self-help book on improving your memory is written by a man who transformed himself from a forgetful journalist into the United States Memory Champion.

Gathercole, S. E., Dunning, D. L., Holmes, J., & Norris, D. (2019). Working memory training involves learning new skills. *Journal of Memory and Language, 105,* 19–42. Sue Gathercole and colleagues review research showing that working memory training has some beneficial effects provided that the original and transfer tasks require the same specific cognitive processes.

Miyatsu, T., Nguyen, K., & McDaniel, M. A. (2018). Five popular study strategies: Their pitfalls and optimal implementations. *Perspectives on Psychological Science, 13,* 390–407. Toshiya Miyatsu and his colleagues evaluate the strengths and limitations of study strategies popular with students.

Pan, S. C., & Rickard, T. C. (2018). Transfer of test-enhanced learning: Meta-analytic review and synthesis. *Psychological Bulletin, 144,* 710–750. Steven Pan and Timothy Rickard discuss the important real-life issue of the factors determining whether the testing effect generalizes to situations other than those prevailing at the time of learning.

Rowland, C. A. (2014). The effect of testing versus restudy on retention: A meta-analytic review of the testing effect. *Psychological Bulletin, 140,* 1432–1463. Christopher Rowling discusses evidence concerning the main factors influencing the testing effect and evaluates theoretical accounts of that effect.

Tardif, J., Duchesne, X. M., Cohan, S., Royer, J., Blais, C., Piset, D., et al. (2019). Use of face information varies systematically from developmental prosopagnosics to super-recognizers. *Psychological Science, 30,* 300–308. Jessica Tardif and colleagues identify factors underlying individual differences in face recognition.

REFERENCES

Bass, W. S., & Oswald, K. M. (2014). Proactive control of proactive interference using the method of loci. *Advances in Cognitive Psychology, 10,* 49–58.

Berlyne, D. E., Craw, M. A., Salapatek, P. H., & Lewis, J. L. (1963). Novelty, complexity, incongruity, extrinsic motivation, and the GSR. *Journal of Experimental Psychology, 66,* 560–567.

Bodner, G. E., Huff, M. J., Lemontagne, R. W., & Azad, T. (2017). Getting at the source of distinctive encoding effects in the DRM paradigm: Evidence from signal-detection measures and source judgments. *Memory, 25,* 647–655.

Bower, G. H. (1973). How to … uh … remember!. *Psychology Today, 7,* 63–70.

Bower, G. H., & Clark, M. C. (1969). Narrative stories as mediators for serial learning. *Psychonomic Science, 14,* 181–182.

Brown, A. S., Bracken, E., Zoccoli, S., & Douglas, K. (2004). Generating and remembering passwords. *Applied Cognitive Psychology, 18,* 641–651.

Carney, R. N., & Levin, J. R. (2011). Delayed mnemonic benefits for a combined pegword-keyword strategy: Time after time, rhyme after rhyme. *Applied Cognitive Psychology, 25,* 204–211.

Carney, R. N., & Levin, J. R. (2014). Learning more about and with the face-name mnemonic strategy. *Applied Cognitive Psychology, 28,* 569–578.

Cepeda, N. J., Pashler, H., Vul, E., Wixted, J. T., & Rohrer, D. (2006). Distributed practice in verbal recall tasks: A review and quantitative synthesis. *Psychological Bulletin, 132,* 354–380.

Cepeda, N. J., Vul, E., Rohrer, D., Wixted, J. T., & Pashler, H. (2008). Spacing effects in learning: A temporal ridgeline of optimal retention. *Psychological Science, 19,* 1095–1102.

Chee, Q. W., & Goh, W. D. (2018). What explains the von Restorff effect? Contrasting distinctive processing and retrieval cue efficacy. *Journal of Memory and Language, 99,* 49–61.

Cho, K. W., Neely, J. H., Crocco, S., & Vitrano, D. (2017). Testing enhances both encoding and retrieval for both tested and untested items. *Quarterly Journal of Experimental Psychology, 70,* 1211–1235.

Coughlin, L. D., & Patel, V. L. (1987). Processing of critical information by physicians and medical students. *Journal of Medical Education, 62,* 818–828.

De Beni, R., & Moè, A. (2003). Imagery and rehearsal as study strategies for written or orally presented passages. *Psychonomic Bulletin & Review, 10,* 975–980.

De Beni, R., Moè, A., & Cornoldi, C. (1997). Learning from texts or lectures: Loci mnemonics can interfere with reading but not with listening. *Law and Human Behavior, 28,* 687–706.

Dresler, M., Shirer, W. R., Konrad, B. N., Müller, N. C. J., Wagner, I. C., Fernández, G., et al. (2017). Mnemonic training reshapes brain networks to support superior memory. *Neuron, 93,* 1227–1235.

Duarte, E. C., Loureiro, A. C., & Zukowsky-Tavares, C. (2017). Challenges and weaknesses in the use of concept maps as a learning strategy in undergraduate health programs. *Knowledge Management & E-Learning, 9,* 380–391.

Dunlosky, J., Rawson, K. A., Marsh, E. J., Nathan, M. J., & Willingham, D. T. (2013). Improving students' learning with effective learning techniques: Promising directions from cognitive and educational psychology. *Psychological Science in the Public Interest, 14,* 4–58.

Endres, T., & Renkl, A. (2015). Mechanisms behind the testing effect: An empirical investigation of retrieval practice in meaningful learning. *Frontiers in Psychology, 6* (Article 1054).

Ericsson, K. A. (1988). Analysis of memory performance in terms of memory skill. In R. J. Sternberg (Ed.), *Advances in the psychology of human intelligence* (Vol. 4, pp. 137–179). Hillsdale, NJ: Lawrence Erlbaum Associates.

Ericsson, K. A., Cheng, X., Pan, Y., Ku, Y., Ge, Y., & Hu, Y. (2017). Memory skills mediating superior memory in a world-class memorist. *Memory, 25,* 1294–1302.

Ericsson, K. A., Delaney, P. F., Weaver, G., & Mahadevan, R. (2004). Uncovering the structure of a mnemonist's superior "basic" memory capacity. *Cognitive Psychology, 49,* 191–237.

Ericsson, K. A., & Kintsch, W. (1995). Long-term working memory. *Psychological Review, 102,* 211–245.

Eysenck, M. W. (1972). *Conditions modifying memory: The von Restorff and 'release' effects.* Unpublished Ph.D. thesis, University of London.

Eysenck, M. W. (1979). Depth, elaboration, and distinctiveness. In L. S. Cermak & F. I. M. Craik (Eds.), *Levels of processing in human memory* (pp. 89–118). Hillsdale, NJ: Lawrence Erlbaum Associates Inc.

Eysenck, M. W., & Eysenck, M. C. (1980). Effects of processing depth, distinctiveness, and word frequency on retention. *British Journal of Psychology, 71,* 263–274.

Foer, J. (2011). *Moonwalking with Einstein: The art and science of remembering everything.* New York: Penguin Press.

Foroughi, C. K., Werner, N. E., Barragán, D., & Boehm-Davis, D. A. (2016). Multiple interpretations of long-term working memory theory: Reply to Delaney and Ericsson (2016). *Journal of Experimental Psychology: General, 145*, 1410–1411.

Gathercole, S. E., Dunning, D. L., Holmes, J., & Norris, D. (2019). Working memory training involves learning new skills. *Journal of Memory and Language, 105*, 19–42.

Gerbier, E., & Koenig, O. (2015). How do temporal intervals between repetitions of information influence its memorization? A theoretical review of the effects of distributed practice. *Année Psychologique, 115*, 435–462.

Gobet, F. (2016). *Understanding expertise: A multi-disciplinary approach*. London: Palgrave.

Guida, A., Gobet, F., & Nicolas, S. (2013). Functional cerebral reorganization: A signature of expertise? Re-examining Guida, Gobet, Tardieu, and Nicolas' (2012) two-stage framework. *Frontiers in Human Neuroscience, 7* (Article 590).

Helder, E., & Shaughnessy, J. J. (2011). Self-generated retrievals while multitasking improve memory for names. *Memory, 19*, 968–974.

Hu, Y., Ericsson, K. A., Yang, D., & Lu, C. (2009). Superior self-paced memorization of digits in spite of a normal digit span: The structure of a memorist's skill. *Journal of Experimental Psychology: Learning, Memory, and Cognition, 35*, 1426–1442.

Hunt, R. R. (2013). Precision in memory through distinctive processing. *Current Directions in Psychological Science, 22*, 10–15.

Hunt, R. R., & Smith, R. E. (1996). Accessing the particular from the general: The power of distinctiveness in the context of organization. *Memory & Cognition, 24*, 217–225.

Kalakoski, V., & Saariluoma, P. (2001). Taxi drivers' exceptional memory of street names. *Memory & Cognition, 29*, 634–638.

Karpicke, J. D., Butler, A. C., & Roediger, H. L. (2009). Metacognitive strategies in student learning: Do students practice retrieval when they study on their own?. *Memory, 17*, 471–479.

Kim, A. S. N., Wong-Kee-You, A. M. B., Wiseheart, M., & Rosenbaum, R. S. (2019). The spacing effect stands up to big data. *Behavior Research Methods, 51*, 1485–1497.

Kobayashi, K. (2006). Combined effects of note-taking/-reviewing on learning and the enhancement through interventions: A meta-analytic review. *Educational Psychology, 26*, 459–477.

Kornell, N., Bjork, R. A., & Garcia, M. A. (2011). Why tests appear to prevent forgetting: A distribution-based bifurcation model. *Journal of Memory and Language, 65*, 85–97.

LePort, A. K. R., Stark, S. M., McGaugh, J. L., & Stark, C. E. L. (2016). Highly superior autobiographical memory: Quality and quantity of retention over time. *Frontiers in Psychology, 6* (Article 2017).

Luria, A. R. (1968). *The mind of a mnemonist*. New York: Basic Books.

Maguire, E. A., Valentine, E. R., Wilding, J. M., & Kapur, N. (2003). Routes to remembering: The brains behind superior memory. *Nature Neuroscience, 6*, 90–95.

Mandler, G. (1967). Organization and memory. *Psychology of Learning and Motivation, 1*, 327–372.

Massen, C., & Vaterrodt-Plünnecke, B. (2006). The role of proactive interference in mnemonic techniques. *Memory, 14*, 189–196.

Massen, C., Vaterrodt-Plünnecke, B., Krings, L., & Hilbig, B. E. (2009). Effects of instruction on learners' ability to generate an effective pathway in the method of loci. *Memory, 17*, 724–731.

Miyatsu, T., Nguyen, K., & McDaniel, M. A. (2018). Five popular study strategies: Their pitfalls and optimal implementations. *Perspectives on Psychological Science, 13*, 390–407.

Morris, P. E., Fritz, C. O., Jackson, L., Nichol, E., & Roberts, E. (2005). Strategies for learning proper names: Expanding retrieval practice, meaning and imagery. *Applied Cognitive Psychology, 19*, 779–798.

Morris, P. E., Jones, S., & Hampson, P. (1978). An imagery mnemonic for the learning of people's names. *British Journal of Psychology, 69*, 335–336.

Nørby, S. (2015). Why forget? On the adaptive value of memory loss. *Perspectives on Psychological Science, 10*, 551–578.

Pastötter, B., & Bäuml, K.-H. T. (2016). Reversing the testing effect by feedback: Behavioral and electrophysiological evidence. *Cognitive and Affective Neuroscience, 16*, 473–488.

Pilar, D. R., Jaeger, A., Gomes, C. F. A., & Stein, L. M. (2012). Passwords usage and human memory limitations: A survey across age and educational background. *PLoS ONE, 7*(12).

Raz, A., Packard, M. G., Alexander, G. M., Gerianne, M., Buhle, J. T., Zhu, H. T., et al. (2009). A slice of pi: An exploratory neuroimaging study of digit encoding and retrieval in a superior memorist. *Neurocase, 15*, 361–372.

Richards, B. A., & Frankland, P. W. (2017). The persistence and transience of memory. *Neuron, 94*, 1071–1084.

Rickard, T. C., & Pan, S. C. (2018). A dual memory theory of the testing effect. *Psychonomic Bulletin & Review, 25*, 847–869.

Roediger, H. L., & Karpicke, J. D. (2006). Test-enhanced learning: Taking memory tests improves long-term retention. *Psychological Science, 17,* 249–255.

Roediger, H. L., & Karpicke, J. D. (2018). Reflections on the resurgence of interest in the testing effect. *Perspectives on Psychological Science, 13,* 236–241.

Ross, J., & Lawrence, K. A. (1968). Some observations on memory artifice. *Psychonomic Science, 13,* 107–108.

Rowland, C. A. (2014). The effect of testing versus restudy on retention: A meta-analytic review of the testing effect. *Psychological Bulletin, 140,* 1432–1463.

Russell, R., Duchaine, B., & Nakayama, K. (2009). Super-recognizers: People with extraordinary face recognition ability. *Psychonomic Bulletin & Review, 16,* 252–257.

Santangelo, V., Cavallina, C., Colucci, P., Santori, A., Macri, S., McGaugh, J. L., et al. (2018). Enhanced brain activity associated with memory access in highly superior autobiographical memory. *Proceedings of the National Academy of Sciences of the USA, 115,* 7795–7800.

Schroeder, N. L., Nesbit, J. C., Anguiano, C. J., & Adesope, O. O. (2018). Studying and constructing concept maps: A meta-analysis. *Educational Psychology Review, 30,* 431–455.

Schwieren, J., Barenberg, J., & Dutke, S. (2017). The testing effect in the psychology classroom: A meta-analytic perspective. *Psychology Learning and Teaching, 16,* 179–196.

Shipstead, Z., Redick, T. S., & Engle, R. W. (2012). Is working memory training effective?. *Psychological Bulletin, 138,* 628–654.

Simons, D. J., Boot, W. R., Charness, N., Gathercole, S. E., Chabris, C. F., Hambrick, D. Z., et al. (2016). Do "brain-training" programs work? *Psychological Science in the Public Interest, 17,* 103–186.

Tardif, J., Duchesne, X. M., Cohan, S., Royer, J., Blais, C., Piset, D., et al. (2019). Use of face information varies systematically from developmental prosopagnosics to super-recognizers. *Psychological Science, 30,* 300–308.

Turano, M. T., Marzi, T., & Viggiano, M. P. (2016). Individual differences in face processing captured by ERPs. *International Journal of Psychophysiology, 101,* 1–8.

Unsworth, N., & McMillan, B. D. (2013). Mind wandering and reading comprehension: Examining working memory capacity, interest, motivation, and topic experience. *Journal of Experimental Psychology: Learning, Memory, and Cognition, 39,* 832–842.

Vaughn, K. E., & Rawson, K. A. (2011). Diagnosing criterion-level effects on memory: What aspects of memory are enhanced by repeated retrieval?. *Psychological Science, 22,* 1127–1131.

von Restorff, H. (1933). Über die Wirkung von Brieichsbildungen im Spurenfeld. *Psychologische Forschung, 18,* 299–542.

Wang, A. Y., & Thomas, M. H. (2000). Looking for long-term mnemonic effects on serial recall: The legacy of Simonides. *American Journal of Psychology, 113,* 331–340.

Watier, N., & Collin, C. (2012). The effects of distinctiveness on memory and metamemory for face-name associations. *Memory, 20,* 73–88.

Werner-Seidler, A., & Dalgleish, T. (2016). The method of loci improves longer-term 8H retention of self-affirming memories and facilitates access to mood-repairing memories in recurrent depression. *Clinical Psychological Science, 4,* 1065–1072.

Wilding, J., & Valentine, E. (1994). Memory champions. *British Journal of Psychology, 85,* 231–244.

Wilmer, J. B., Germine, L., Chabris, C. F., Chatterjee, G., Williams, M., Loken, E., et al. (2010). Human face recognition ability is specific and highly heritable. *Proceedings of the National Academy of Sciences of the USA, 107,* 5238–5241.

Worthen, J. B., & Hunt, R. R. (2011). *Mnemonology: Mnemonics for the 21st century.* Hove, UK: Psychology Press.

Yoon, J.-S., Ericsson, K. A., & Donatelli, D. (2018). Effects of 30 years of disuse on exceptional memory performance. *Cognitive Science, 42,* 884–903.

GLOSSARY

Accessibility/availability distinction:
Accessibility refers to the ease with which a stored memory can be retrieved at a given point in time. Availability refers to the binary distinction indicating whether a trace is or is not stored in memory.

Activation level: The variable internal state of a memory trace that contributes to its accessibility at a given point.

Alcoholic Korsakoff syndrome: Patients have difficulty learning new information, although events from the past are recalled. There is a tendency to invent material to fill memory blanks. Most common cause is alcoholism, especially when this has resulted in a deficiency of vitamin B1.

Amygdala: An area of the brain close to the hippocampus that is involved in emotional processing.

Anterograde amnesia: A problem in encoding, storing, or retrieving information that can be used in the future.

Articulatory suppression: A technique for disrupting verbal rehearsal by requiring participants to continuously repeat a spoken item.

Associative blocking: A theoretical process hypothesized to explain interference effects during retrieval, according to which a cue fails to elicit a target trace because it repeatedly elicits a stronger

competitor, leading people to abandon efforts to retrieve the target.

Associative deficit hypothesis: Proposal that the age deficit in memory comes from an impaired capacity to form associations between previously unrelated stimuli.

Autobiographical knowledge base: Facts about ourselves and our past that form the basis for autobiographical memory.

Autobiographical memory: Memory across the lifespan for both specific events and self-related information.

Automaticity: When a skill is practiced to the extent that it no longer requires significant attentional monitoring to be performed and is less effortful.

Autonoetic consciousness: A term proposed by Tulving for self-awareness, allowing the rememberer to reflect on the contents of episodic memory.

Binding: Term used to refer to the linking of features into objects (e.g., color red, shape square, into a red square), or of events into coherent episodes.

Category-specific deficits: Disorders caused by brain damage in which semantic memory is disrupted for certain semantic categories (e.g., living things).

Cell assemblies: A concept proposed by Hebb to account for the physiological basis of long-term learning, which is assumed to involve the establishment of links between the cells forming the assembly.

Change blindness: The failure to detect that a visual object has moved, changed, or been replaced by another object.

Change blindness blindness: Individuals' exaggerated belief that they can detect visual changes and so avoid *change blindness*.

Chunking: The process of combining a number of items into a single chunk typically on the basis of long-term memory.

Classical conditioning: A learning procedure whereby a neutral stimulus (e.g., a bell) that is paired repeatedly with a response-evoking stimulus (e.g., meat powder), will come to evoke that response (salivation).

Cognitive control: The ability to flexibly control thoughts in accordance with our goals, including our ability to stop unwanted thoughts from rising to consciousness.

Cohort effect: The tendency for people born at different time periods to differ as a result of historic changes in diet, education, and other social factors.

Collaborative inhibition: A phenomenon in which a group of individuals remembers significantly less material collectively than does the combined performance of each group member individually when recalling alone.

Competition assumption: The theoretical proposition that the memories associated to a shared retrieval cue automatically impede one another's retrieval when the cue is presented.

Concept map: A diagram in which the links among general concepts (at the top of the diagram) and specific concepts (lower down) are shown.

Confabulation: Recollection of something that did not happen.

Confirmation bias: Distortions of memory caused by the influence of expectations concerning what is likely to have happened.

Consolidation: The time-dependent process by which a new trace is gradually woven into the fabric of memory and by which its components and their interconnections are cemented together.

Consolidation of memory: A process whereby the memory becomes more firmly established. It is commonly now divided into two processes, *synaptic consolidation*—a process that is assumed to involve the hippocampus and operate over a 24-hour timescale, and *systems consolidation*. This is assumed to operate over a much longer period, and to involve the transfer of information from the hippocampus to other parts of the neocortex (see Chapter 5, p. 140 for further discussion).

Context cues: Retrieval cues that specify aspects of the conditions under which a desired target was encoded, including (for example) the location and time of the event.

Context-dependent memory: The finding that memory benefits when the spatio-temporal, mood, physiological, or cognitive context at retrieval matches that present at encoding.

Context shift hypothesis: An alternative explanation for list-method directed forgetting, positing that forget instructions separate first-list items into a distinct context, which unless reinstated during the final test will make the later context a relatively ineffectual retrieval cue.

Contextual fluctuation: The gradual and persistent drift in incidental context over time, such that distant memories deviate from the current context more so than newer memories, thereby diminishing the former's potency as a retrieval cue for older memories.

Cortical reinstatement: The reactivation of sensory memory traces stored by neurons within individual cortical modulates, by virtue of back-projections from the hippocampus that activate the constituent parts of a memory, reinstating the original experience.

Corsi block tapping: Visuo-spatial counterpart to digit span involving an array of blocks that the tester taps in a sequence and the patient attempts to copy.

Cue-maintenance: When intentionally retrieving a target memory, the process of sustaining cues in working memory to guide search.

Cue-overload principle: The observed tendency for recall success to decrease as the number of to-be-remembered items associated to a cue increases.

Cue-specification: When intentionally retrieving a target memory, the control processes by which one specifies the nature of the target and any contextual features that may constrain retrieval, and establishes these as cues to guide search.

Deliberate practice: The engagement (with full concentration) in a training activity that is designed to improve a particular aspect of performance, including immediate feedback, opportunities for graduate refinement over repetitions, and problem solving.

Depth of processing: The proposal by Craik and Lockhart that, the more deeply an item is processed, the better will be its retention.

Digit span: Maximum number of sequentially presented digits that can reliably be recalled in the correct order.

Direct/explicit memory tests: Any of a variety of memory assessments that overtly prompt participants to retrieve past events.

Directed forgetting: The tendency for an instruction to forget recently experienced items to induce memory impairment for those items.

Distributed practice: Breaking practice up into a number of shorter sessions; in contrast to massed practice, which comprises fewer, long, learning sessions.

Double dissociation: A term particularly used in neuropsychology when two patient groups show opposite patterns of deficit, e.g., normal STM and impaired LTM, versus normal LTM and impaired STM.

Dual-coding hypothesis: Highly imageable words are easy to learn because they can be encoded both visually and verbally.

Dual-process theories of recognition: A class of recognition models that assumes that recognition memory judgments can be based on two independent forms of retrieval process: recollection and familiarity.

Dud effect: An eyewitness's increased confidence in his/her mistakes when the lineup includes individuals very dissimilar to the culprit.

Echoic memory: A term sometimes applied to auditory sensory memory.

Ecological validity: The extent to which research findings (especially laboratory ones) can be generalized to everyday life.

Elaborative rehearsal: Process whereby items are not simply kept in mind, but are processed either more deeply or more elaborately.

Electro-encephalography (EEG): A system for recording the electrical potentials of the brain through a series of electrodes placed on the scalp.

Emotion regulation: Goal-driven monitoring, evaluating, altering, and gating one's emotional reactions and memories about emotional experiences.

Encoding specificity principle: The more similar the cues available at retrieval are to the conditions present at encoding, the more effective the cues will be.

Environmental support: Characteristics of a retention test that support retrieval.

Episodic buffer: A component of the Baddeley and Hitch model of working memory model that assumes a multidimensional code, allowing the various subcomponents of working memory to interact with long-term memory.

Episodic memory: A system that is assumed to underpin the capacity to remember specific events.

Episodic sequence learning: The ability to represent the temporal sequence of occurrences within a larger event.

Evaluative conditioning: The tendency to one's liking of a stimulus to be influenced by how frequently it is followed by pleasant or unpleasant stimuli unrelated to it, with positive stimuli enhancing liking, and negative stimulus decreasing liking.

Event-based prospective memory: A form of prospective memory in which some event provides the cue to perform a given action.

Event-related potentials (ERPs): The pattern of electroencephalograph (EEG) activity obtained by averaging the brain responses to the same stimulus (or similar stimuli) presented repeatedly.

Everyday memory: Term applied to a movement within memory to extend the study of memory from the confines of the laboratory to the world outside.

Explicit/declarative memory: Memory that is open to intentional retrieval, whether based on recollecting personal events (episodic memory) or facts (semantic memory).

Fading affect bias: The consistent tendency for negative memories, over time, to lose affective intensity at a higher rate than positive memories.

Familiarity-based recognition: A fast, automatic recognition process based on the perception of a memory's strength. Proponents of dual-process models consider familiarity to be independent of the contextual information characteristic of recollection.

Features: Elementary components from which a complex memory can be assembled, including perceptual aspects such as color and object shapes, as well as higher level conceptual elements.

Flashbulb memory: Term applied to the detailed and apparently highly accurate memory of a dramatic experience.

Focal retrograde amnesia (FRA): A distinct form of psychogenic amnesia without fugue or significant loss of identity, but with an abrupt loss of autobiographical memories that can be extensive and persisting.

Focal task: An ongoing task that involves similar processing to that involved in encoding the target on a prospective-memory task performed at the same time.

Forgetting curve/retention function: The logarithmic decline in memory retention as a function of time elapsed, first described by Ebbinghaus.

Frames: A type of schema in which information about objects and their properties is stored.

Free recall: A method whereby participants are presented with a sequence of items which they are subsequently required to recall in any order they wish.

Fugue state: A form of psychogenic amnesia in which a person abruptly loses access to all autobiographical memories from their life, and their personal identity, often resulting in a period of wandering without knowledge of how they got to a location or why. This condition often resolves quickly (within days or weeks).

Fugue-to-FRA: A distinct form of psychogenic amnesia which starts with fugue, but is followed by recovery or relearning of identity, but with persistent and long-lasting deficits in autobiographical memories, especially older ones.

Gaps in memory: A distinct form of psychogenic amnesia without fugue or significant loss of personal identity, but with an abrupt loss of discrete periods of time, ranging from hours to months. Multiple gaps may be present.

Gestalt psychology: An approach to psychology that was strong in Germany in the 1930s and that attempted to use perceptual principles to understand memory and reasoning.

Habit learning: Gradually learning a tendency to perform certain actions, given a particular stimulus or context, based on a history of reward. Instrumental conditioning is a form of habit learning.

Highly superior autobiographical memory (HSAM): A newer term for hyperthymestic syndrome, which refers to individuals who have exceptional memory for life events, often showing little apparent forgetting of even trivial occurrences many years later, and an uncanny ability to retrieve memories by their precise date.

Hippocampus: Brain structure in the medial temporal lobe that is important for long-term memory formation.

HSAM: An acronym for highly superior autobiographical memory cases in which people exhibit extraordinary memory for everyday autobiographical events over many years.

Hypermnesia: The improvement in recall performance arising from repeated testing sessions on the same material.

Iconic memory: A term applied to the brief storage of visual information.

Immersion method: A strategy for foreign language teaching whereby the learner is placed in an environment where only the foreign language is used.

Implementation intentions: Plans spelling out in detail how individuals are going to achieve the goals they have set themselves.

Implicit/nondeclarative memory: Retrieval of information from long-term memory through performance rather than explicit conscious recall or recognition.

Inattentional blindness: The failure to perceive the appearance of an unexpected object in the visual environment.

Incidental forgetting: Memory failures occurring without the intention to forget.

Incidental learning: Learning situation in which the learner is unaware that a test will occur.

Infantile amnesia: Tendency for people to have few autobiographical memories from below the age of 5.

Inhibition: A general term applied to mechanisms that suppress other activities. The term can be applied to a precise physiological mechanism or to a more general phenomenon, as in proactive and retroactive interference. The level of activation associated with a trace is actively reduced to diminish its accessibility.

Integration: The process of linking new information to pre-existing knowledge structures, such as prior schemas, concepts, and events.

Intentional learning: Learning when the learner knows that there will be a test of retention.

Interference: The phenomenon in which the retrieval of a memory can be disrupted by the presence of related traces in memory.

Interference resolution processes: When trying to recall a particular target memory, control processes that help to resolve interference from competing memories coactivated by the cues guiding retrieval.

Irrelevant sound effect: A tendency for verbal STM to be disrupted by concurrent fluctuating sounds, including both speech and music.

Latent inhibition: Classical conditioning phenomenon whereby multiple prior presentations of a neutral stimulus will interfere with its involvement in subsequent conditioning.

Levels of processing: The theory proposed by Craik and Lockhart that asserts that items that are more deeply processed will be better remembered.

Lexical decision task: Participants presented with a string of letters must decide rapidly whether the string forms a word.

Life narrative: A coherent and integrated account of one's life that is claimed to form the basis of autobiographical memory retrieval. A life narrative provides an organized set of schemas with which key episodic events can be integrated, both increasing the chances of consolidation, and making memory retrieval efficient.

Longitudinal design: Method of studying development or aging whereby the same participants are successively tested at different ages.

Long-term memory: A system or systems assumed to underpin the capacity to store information over long periods of time.

Long-term potentiation (LTP): A process whereby synaptic transmission becomes more effective following a cell's recent activation.

Long-term recency: A tendency for the last few items to be well recalled under conditions of long-term memory.

Long-term working memory: Concept proposed by Ericsson and Kintsch to account for the way in which long-term memory can be used as a working memory to maintain complex cognitive activity.

Magnetic resonance imaging (MRI): A method of brain imaging that relies on detecting changes induced by a powerful magnetic field.

Magneto-encephalography (MEG): A system whereby the activity of neurons within the brain is detected through the tiny magnetic fields that their activity generates.

Maintenance rehearsal: A process of rehearsal whereby items are "kept in mind" but not processed more deeply.

Masking: A process by which the perception and/ or storage of a stimulus is influenced by events occurring immediately before presentation (forward masking) or more commonly after (backward masking).

Mental time travel: A term coined by Tulving to emphasize the way in which episodic memory allows us to relive the past and use this information to imagine the future.

Meta-analysis: A form of statistical analysis based on combining the findings from numerous studies on a given research topic.

Metamemory: Knowledge about one's own memory and an ability to regulate its functioning.

Method of loci: A memory technique in which to-be-remembered items are associated with various locations well known to the learner.

Misinformation effect: The distorting effect on eyewitness memory of misleading information presented after a crime or other event.

Modal model: A term applied to the model of memory developed by Atkinson and Shiffrin (1968).

Model: A method of expressing a theory more precisely, allowing predictions to be made and tested.

Mood-congruent memory: Bias in the recall of memories such that negative mood makes negative memories more readily available than positive, and vice versa. Unlike mood dependency, it does not affect the recall of neutral memories.

Mood-dependent memory: A form of context-dependent effect whereby what is learnt in a given mood, whether positive, negative, or neutral, is best recalled in that mood.

Motivated forgetting: A broad term encompassing intentional forgetting as well as forgetting triggered by motivations, but lacking conscious intention.

Multimodal representation: A representation that draws together inputs from many different sensory modalities, such as vision, hearing, touch, taste, and smell. A multimodal representation can also include conceptual and emotional features.

Nonfocal task: An ongoing task that involves different processes to those required when encoding the target on a prospective-memory task performed at the same time.

Nonsense syllables: Pronounceable but meaningless consonant-vowel-consonant items designed to study learning without the complicating factor of meaning.

Nonword repetition test: A test whereby participants hear and attempt to repeat back nonwords that gradually increase in length.

Object memory: System that temporarily retains information concerning visual features such as color and shape.

Obsessive-compulsive disorder: An anxiety disorder characterized by obsessional thoughts and by excessive checking behavior.

Offline processing: A process whereby the hippocampus, either during sleep, or in periods of quiet rest, periodically reinstates recent memories and knowledge in cortex, putatively by a process of hippocampal replay that drives neocortical activation of the elements of an event. Offline processing is assumed to be incidental and not goal directed.

Ongoing task: A task performed at the same time as a prospective memory task in studies on prospective memory.

Other-race effect: The finding that recognition memory for same-race faces is generally more accurate than for other-race faces.

Own-age bias: The tendency for eyewitnesses to identify individuals of the same age as themselves more accurately than those much older or younger.

Part-set cuing impairment: When presenting part of a set of items (e.g., a category, a mental list of movies you want to rent) hinders your ability to recall the remaining items in the set.

Pattern completion: The process whereby presenting a subset of features that represent a memory spreads activation to the remaining feature units representing that memory, completing the pattern of activity necessary to retrieve it.

Pegword method: A memory technique in which to-be-remembered items are associated with pegwords, each of which rhymes with a different number between one and ten.

Personal semantic memory: Factual knowledge about one's own past.

Personal semantics: Aspects of one's own personal or autobiographical memory combining elements of episodic memory and semantic memory.

Phonological loop: Term applied by Baddeley and Hitch to the component of their model responsible for the temporary storage of speech-like information.

Phonological similarity effect: A tendency for immediate serial recall of verbal material to be reduced, when the items are similar in sound.

Place cells: Neurons in the hippocampus that respond whenever an animal or person is in a particular location in a particular environment, the collective activity of which is believed to be a critical ingredient in representing particular spatial environments, either perceived or remembered.

Positivity bias: The tendency, increasing over the lifespan, to recall more pleasant memories than either neutral or unpleasant ones.

Positron emission tomography (PET): A method whereby radioactively labeled substances are introduced into the bloodstream and subsequently monitored to measure physiological activation.

Posterior midline cortex: An area adjacent to and including the posterior cingulate cortex, often including the precuneus and retrosplenial cortex, which appears to be critical for autobiographical memory retrieval, especially for the reinstatement of vivid visuo-spatial details.

Post-retrieval monitoring: During intentional retrieval, the processes by which one evaluates the products of memory search, to determine whether the retrieved trace is what we seek.

Post-traumatic amnesia (PTA): Patients have difficulty forming new memories. Often follows a severe concussive head injury and tends to improve with time.

Post-traumatic stress disorder (PTSD): Anxiety disorder whereby a dramatic and stressful event such as rape results in persistent anxiety, often accompanied by vivid flashback memories of the event.

Primacy effect: A tendency for the first few items in a sequence to be better recalled than most of the following items.

Priming: The process whereby presentation of an item influences the processing of a subsequent item, either making it easier to process (positive priming) or more difficult (negative priming).

Proactive interference: The tendency for earlier memories to disrupt the retrievability of more recent memories.

Process dissociation procedure (PDP): A technique for parceling out the contributions of recollection and familiarity within a recognition task.

Prospective memory: Remembering to carry out some intended action in the absence of any explicit reminder to do so; see retrospective memory.

Psychogenic amnesia: Profound and surprising episodes of forgetting the events of one's life, arising from psychological factors, rather than biological damage or dysfunction.

Psychogenic fugue: A form of psychogenic amnesia typically lasting a few hours or days following a severe trauma, in which afflicted individuals forget their entire life history, including who they are.

Rationalization: A term introduced by Bartlett to refer to the tendency in story recall to produce errors conforming to the rememberer's cultural expectations.

Reality monitoring: Using source monitoring processes to decide whether a piece of information in memory referred to a real event or instead to something imagined.

Reality orientation training (ROT): A method of treating patients in the latter stages of dementia who have lost their orientation in time and place.

Recency effect: A tendency for the last few items in a list to be well recalled.

Recognition memory: A person's ability to correctly decide whether they have encountered a stimulus previously in a particular context.

Recollection: The slower, more attention-demanding component of recognition memory in dual-process models, which involves retrieval of contextual information about the memory.

Reconsolidation: The process by which a consolidated memory restabilizes again after being reactivated by reminders. During the reconsolidation window, a memory is vulnerable to disruption.

Reconstructive memory: An active and inferential process of retrieval whereby gaps in memory are filled in based on prior experience, logic, and goals.

Reductionism: The view that all scientific explanations should aim to be based on a lower level of analysis: psychology in terms of physiology, physiology in terms of chemistry, and chemistry in terms of physics.

Remember/know procedure: A procedure used on recognition memory tests to separate the influences of familiarity and recollection on recognition performance. For each test item, participants report whether it is recognized because the person can recollect contextual details of seeing the item (classified as a "remember" response) or because the item seems familiar, in the absence of specific recollections (classified as "know" response).

Reminiscence: The remembering again of the forgotten, without learning or a gradual process of improvement in the capacity to revive past experiences.

Reminiscence bump: A tendency in participants over 40 to show a high rate of recollecting personal experiences from their late teens and twenties.

Reminiscence therapy: A method of helping dementia patients cope with their growing amnesia by using photographs and other reminders of their past life.

Repetition priming: Enhanced processing of a stimulus arising from recent encounters with that stimulus, a form of implicit memory.

Repetition suppression: Reduced activity in a brain area responsible for processing a stimulus when that stimulus is repeated, compared to when it is encountered for the first time.

Repression: In psychoanalytic theory, a psychological defense mechanism that banishes unwanted memories, ideas, and feelings into the unconscious in an effort to reduce conflict and psychic pain. Theoretically, repression can either be conscious or nonconscious. Often, the term *suppression* is used to refer to the conscious variety

Resource sharing: Use of limited attentional capacity to maintain two or more simultaneous activities.

Retrieval: The process of recovering a target memory based on one or more cues, subsequently bringing that target into awareness.

Retrieval-induced forgetting (RIF): The tendency for the retrieval of some target items from long-term memory to impair the later ability to recall other items related to those targets.

Retrieval inhibition hypothesis: A proposed mechanism underlying list-method directed forgetting suggesting that first-list items are temporarily inhibited in response to the instruction to forget and can be reactivated by subsequent presentations of the to-be-forgotten items.

Retrieval mode: The cognitive set, or frame of mind, that orients a person towards the act of retrieval, ensuring that stimuli are interpreted as retrieval cues.

Retrieval practice paradigm: A procedure used to study retrieval-induced forgetting.

Retroactive interference: The tendency for more recently acquired information to impede retrieval of similar older memories.

Retrograde amnesia: A problem accessing events that happened in the past.

Retrospective memory: Memory for people, words, and events experienced in the past.

Reverse temporal gradient: The tendency, in focal retrograde amnesia, for the oldest autobiographical memories to be forgotten more than more recent ones, the opposite to what is shown in organic amnesia (see Chapter 16 on memory disorders).

Reward-based enhancement of memory encoding: The tendency for offering rewards for successful memory to improve long-term retention of studied material.

Schema: Proposed by Bartlett to explain how our knowledge of the world is structured and influences the way in which new information is stored and subsequently recalled.

Scripts: A type of schema relating to the typical sequences of events in various common situations (e.g., having a meal in a restaurant).

SDAM: An acronym for severely deficient autobiographical memory, referring to a neuropsychological condition in which otherwise high functioning individuals nevertheless are largely unable to remember autobiographical experiences or re-experience them.

Semantic coding: Processing an item in terms of its meaning, hence relating it to other information in long-term memory.

Semantic dementia: A progressive neurodegenerative disorder characterized by gradual deterioration of semantic memory.

Semantic memory: A system that is assumed to store accumulative knowledge of the world.

Semantic priming: The finding that word processing is facilitated by the prior presentation of a semantically related word.

Semanticization: The phenomenon of episodic memories changing into semantic memories over time.

Sensory memory: A term applied to the brief storage of information within a specific modality.

Short-term memory (STM): A term applied to the retention of small amounts of material over periods of a few seconds.

Signal detection theory: A model of recognition memory that posits that memory targets (signals) and lures (noise) on a recognition test possess an attribute known as strength or familiarity, which occurs in a graded fashion, with previously encountered items generally possessing more strength than novel items. The process of recognition involves ascertaining a given test item's strength and then deciding whether it exceeds a criterion level of strength, above which items are considered to be previously encountered. Signal detection theory provides analytic tools that separate true memory from judgment biases in recognition.

Skill learning: A practiced induced change on a task that allows a person to perform it better faster and or accurately than before. Skill learning encompasses both cognitive and motor skills.

Sleep-dependent replay: The observation that during sleep, material learned prior to sleep is often reactivated or "replayed" in the hippocampus, which is thought to facilitate the consolidation of that content into long-term memory.

Sleep dependent triage: The finding that sleep improves memory for content learned before sleep in a selective way, favoring salient material (due to emotion or perceived importance) and facilitating the forgetting of less important material.

Source misattribution error: When deciding the source of information in memory, sometimes people make errors and misattribute their recollection from one source to another.

Source monitoring: The process of examining the contextual origins of a memory in order to determine whether it was encoded from a particular source.

Spatial working memory: System involved in temporarily retaining information regarding spatial location.

Spatio-temporal context: The particular place and time of an event, with spatial information about an environment contributing to specifying where something happened, and temporal information contributing to encoding when it happened.

Spontaneous recovery: The term arising from the classical conditioning literature given to the re-emergence of a previously extinguished conditioned response after a delay; similarly; forgotten declarative memories have been observed to recover over time.

Stem completion: A task whereby retention of a word is tested by presenting the first few letters.

Stereotypes: Schemas incorporating oversimplified generalizations (often negative) about certain groups.

Story mnemonic: A memory technique that involves constructing a story linking unrelated words together in the correct order.

Structural plasticity: The ability of the brain to undergo structural changes in response to altered environmental demands.

Subjective organization: A strategy whereby a learner attempts to organize unstructured material so as to enhance learning.

Super-recognizers: Individuals having an outstanding ability to recognize human faces.

Supervisory attentional system (SAS): A component of the model proposed by Norman and Shallice to account for the attentional control of action.

Suppression-induced forgetting: The impaired memory for a target item that often results when a person intentionally stops or suppresses the episodic retrieval of that target item triggered by a reminder cue.

Synesthesia: The tendency for one sense modality to evoke another.

Systems consolidation: Process of gradual reorganization of the regions of the brain that support memory. Information is consolidated within the brain by a process of transfer from one anatomically based system to another.

Task switching: A process whereby a limited capacity system maintains activity on two or more tasks by switching between them.

Test-enhanced learning: The tendency for a period of study to promote much greater learning when that study follows a retrieval test of the studied material.

Testing effect: The finding that long-term memory is enhanced when much of the learning period is devoted to retrieving the to-be-remembered information.

Think/no-think paradigm: A procedure designed to study the ability to volitionally suppress retrieval of a memory when confronted with reminders.

Time-based prospective memory: A form of prospective memory in which time is the cue indicating that a given action should be performed.

Time cells: Neurons in the hippocampus that code for particular moments in time in a temporal sequence, independent of any particular external stimuli, the activity of which may contribute to representing time in episodic memories.

Total time hypothesis: The proposal that amount learned is a simple function of the amount of time spent on the learning task.

Trace decay: The gradual weakening of memories resulting from the mere passage of time.

Transcranial direct current stimulation (tDCS): A technique in which a very weak electrical current is passed through an area of the brain; anodal tDCS often enhances performance.

Transcranial magnetic stimulation (TMS): A technique in which magnetic pulses briefly disrupt the functioning of a given brain area; administration of several pulses in rapid succession is known as repetitive transcranial stimulation (rTMS).

Transfer-appropriate processing (TAP): Proposal that retention is best when the mode of encoding and mode of retrieval are the same.

Traumatic brain injury (TBI): Caused by a blow or jolt to the head, or by a penetrating head injury. Normal brain function is disrupted. Severity ranges from "mild" (brief change in mental status or consciousness) to "severe" (extended period of unconsciousness or amnesia after the injury).

Typicality effect: The finding that the time taken to decide a category member belongs to a category is less for typical than atypical members.

Unconscious transference: The tendency of eyewitnesses to misidentify a familiar (but innocent) face as belonging to the culprit.

Unlearning: The proposition that the associative bond linking a stimulus to a memory trace will be weakened when the trace is retrieved in error when a different trace is sought.

Ventromedial prefrontal cortex: A portion of the prefrontal cortex located along the midline of the brain (i.e., in the middle), lower in the prefrontal cortex, thought to play an instrumental role in the integration of recent episodic experiences with well-consolidated background knowledge and schemas. The vmPFC (also referred to as medial prefrontal cortex in rodents) also plays a role in hastening the consolidation of schematically related episodic memories.

Verbal learning: A term applied to an approach to memory that relies principally on the learning of lists of words and nonsense syllables.

Verbal overshadowing effect: The reduction in recognition memory for faces that often occurs when eyewitnesses provide verbal descriptions of those faces before the recognition-memory test.

Visuo-spatial sketchpad: A component of the Baddeley and Hitch model that is assumed to be responsible for the temporary maintenance of visual and spatial information.

Visuo-spatial STM: Retention of visual and/or spatial information over brief periods of time.

von Restorff effect: The finding that a to-be-remembered item that is distinctively different from other items is especially likely to be remembered.

Weapon focus: The finding that eyewitnesses have poor memory for details of a crime event because they focus their attention on the culprit's weapon.

Word fragment completion test: A technique whereby memory for a word is tested by deleting alternate letters and asking participants to produce the word.

Word length effect: A tendency for verbal memory span to decrease when longer words are used.

Working memory: A memory system that underpins our capacity to "keep things in mind" when performing complex tasks.

Working memory capacity: An assessment of how much information can be processed and stored at the same time.

Working memory span: Term applied to a range of complex memory span tasks in which simultaneous storage and processing is required.

Working self: A concept proposed by Conway to account for the way in which autobiographical knowledge is accumulated and used.

PHOTO CREDITS

AUTHOR INDEX

SUBJECT INDEX

Y